PIMLICO

557

THE CHAMELEON POET

Robert Fraser has lectured at the universities of Leeds and London, and at Trinity College, Cambridge, where he was Director of Studies in English. His books include studies of Proust, Sir James Frazer and Victorian quest romance. *God's Good Englishman*, his bicentennial drama about Dr Johnson, toured through Britain, as did his plays on Byron and the composer-murderer Carlo Gesualdo. In 1987, at the poet's request, he compiled Barker's *Collected Poems*; in 1995 he edited the *Selected Poems*. He lives in South London with his wife and son and a 'cello.

THE CHAMELEON POET

A Life of George Barker

———

ROBERT FRASER

PIMLICO

Published by Pimlico 2002

2 4 6 8 10 9 7 5 3 1

Copyright © Robert Fraser 2001

Robert Fraser has asserted his right under the Copyright, Designs and Patents Act 1988 to be identified as the author of this work

This book is sold subject to the condition that it shall not, by way of trade or otherwise, be lent, resold, hired out, or otherwise circulated without the publisher's prior consent in any form of binding or cover other than that in which it is published and without a similar condition including this condition being imposed on the subsequent purchaser

First published in Great Britain by Jonathan Cape 2001
Pimlico edition 2002

Pimlico
Random House, 20 Vauxhall Bridge Road,
London SW1V 2SA

Random House Australia (Pty) Limited
20 Alfred Street, Milsons Point, Sydney,
New South Wales 2061, Australia

Random House New Zealand Limited
18 Poland Road, Glenfield,
Auckland 10, New Zealand

Random House (Pty) Limited
Endulini, 5A Jubilee Road, Parktown 2193, South Africa

The Random House Group Limited Reg. No. 954009
www.randomhouse.co.uk

A CIP catalogue record for this book is available from the British Library

ISBN 0-7126-9171-5

Papers used by Random House UK Limited are natural, recyclable products made from wood grown in sustainable forests; the manufacturing processes conform to the environmental regulations of the country of origin

Printed and bound in Great Britain by
Biddles Ltd, Guildford & Kings Lynn

CONTENTS

Preface: 'The Chameleon Poet' — vii

PART ONE: 1913–39

Chapter 1	A Street Ballad	3
Chapter 2	An Aboriginal Calamity	11
Chapter 3	'Balthus! Pure Balthus!'	22
Chapter 4	'Hand me that hammer'	40
Chapter 5	'Mellifluous smooth tongue'	51
Chapter 6	'Whispering Sibilant Fields'	58
Chapter 7	Tears in a Bottle	69
Chapter 8	Bitter Apples	77
Chapter 9	'The mass of roses face'	88
Chapter 10	'Sick of love'	97
Chapter 11	'The least qualified applicant in England'	104
Chapter 12	'There's someone here from Japan'	111

PART TWO: 1940–46

Chapter 13	'Swept overboard'	123
Chapter 14	'Oh begging rescue'	133
Chapter 15	'Angel Empress'	142
Chapter 16	'The lips of the possible'	150
Chapter 17	An American Ode	159
Chapter 18	'Five jaws of love'	168
Chapter 19	'Dying for you, Canada'	179
Chapter 20	'Yours in parallel'	186
Chapter 21	'The Geography of the Body'	196

Chapter 22	Sinner and saint	206
Chapter 23	'My tall dead wives'	213
Chapter 24	'Equating the paradox'	222
Chapter 25	'A bohemian motorist'	232
Chapter 26	'I won't make a fuss'	243

PART THREE: 1947–63

Chapter 27	Cassiopeia	255
Chapter 28	'This temperate October'	265
Chapter 29	A School for Poets	275
Chapter 30	'Happy, silly, a bit mellow'	282
Chapter 31	'Bear the day to me'	294
Chapter 32	'Rigor Leavis'	302
Chapter 33	'Art crap! Poetry crap!'	310
Chapter 34	'That boy has a tiger in his loins'	319
Chapter 35	'So you write verse too, baby?'	328
Chapter 36	'Give Biddy a shove, me dear'	336
Chapter 37	'A horse struck by lightning'	346
Chapter 38	'A divine fiat'	357
Chapter 39	'Transfiguring everywhere'	366
Chapter 40	'Love is what you do'	378

PART FOUR: 1964–91

Chapter 41	'Such peace upon the conscience'	391
Chapter 42	'Unscrew me, my dear'	401
Chapter 43	Bintry House	412
Chapter 44	'The day forgives'	422
Chapter 45	'Friends and oddfellows'	433
Chapter 46	'Your poacher is a pincher'	443
Chapter 47	'Dying upward like a hope'	450
Chapter 48	'The poem and the fountain'	459
Chapter 49	'We'll to the woods no more'	465
Chapter 50	'Ceremonies of memory'	472
Chapter 51	'At a time of bankers'	480
Chapter 52	'Abstain! Abstain! Abstain!'	491
Chapter 53	'We're looking for Hendrick van Loon, my dears'	498
Chapter 54	'Entering into the kingdom'	508
Chapter 55	A sprig of honesty	518

Acknowledgements	523
References	527
Index	561

PREFACE

'THE CHAMELEON POET'

Late one winter afternoon, in the Department of Manuscripts at the old British Library in Great Russell Street, I came across an appeal by the adolescent George Barker in the form of a journal entry dated 1930 and apparently addressed to his future biographer. It read, 'If after my death, which in the gloom of this interminable evening feels to be fearfully immanent [sic] and close, anyone should – to provide himself with a hobby or the public (!) with news – research into these rag tails and be stuffed with the odours of women and words and (all hope is vain, all effort null) ambition, I want to request him to be kind to me, and use his discrimination and selective decency in the job of counterpoising my rampant mind and poor repressed eructating sensuality.'

To read those words in the enforced hush of a library during an evening of my own 'research' into Barker's life was a disquieting, as well as an exhilarating, experience. It was all the odder and more heart-warming because in the unconfident musings of this passionate seventeen-year-old I quickly discerned the inflections of the much older man whom I had once known. In my imagination I could hear him speak those lines with their mixture of assurance and modesty. I could recognise the characteristic half-pun on the adjectives 'immanent' and 'imminent', could sense the slight pause of exclamation after the word 'public', the debunking self-parody in the phrases 'all hope is vain, all effort null'. True, I had never exactly associated Barker's sensuality with repression. But I had already, in the course of my work, had cause to 'counterpoise' his women and his words, had carefully observed the workings of this same rampant mind, had assiduously filled several bookshelves with the cast-offs or 'rag tails' of which he wrote. Should I, in view of this posthumous petition, prove my subject's ally by diligently exercising the 'selective decency' for which he had asked? Where, I wondered in the light of my discoveries, did the balance lie between his sensuality and his mind? How, in the face of the bewildering and contradictory evidence that I had gathered, could I best honour this uncannily voiced seventy-year-old request?

George Barker was a poet of outstanding gifts, an enchanter of souls, a verbal magician with a pot of gold beneath his tongue. When I first met him, he was sixty-eight and had lived more flamboyantly, had taken more risks, than any person whom I, at half his age, had ever known. He was also a forthright man, who prized emotional honesty above everything.

He knew, however, that privacy is a condition without which a poet's calling is impossible. During the ten years of our acquaintance he only ever made one remark concerning the then hypothetical possibility of anybody writing his biography. Whoever took on the task – and he did not believe that anyone would ever have the gall – would, he assured me, rapidly find that it could not be done. He had, he swore, laid far too many false trails.

Teasing had been a condition of his friendship. Often, when he talked or wrote about the past, he laid over it a bright veneer of fancy. Once you had learnt to understand it, however, this veneer turned out not merely to be more interesting than the bleak facts might have been, but to possess its own kind of truth. On such occasions he did not so much mislead as encode. The circumstances of his history were all present in his reminiscences and in clear outline. Sometimes, however, they tended to be precisely the wrong way round, or at forty-five degrees to the real. He evidently rejoiced in such fabrication. He might say north when he meant south, boy when he meant girl, dead when he meant alive. Similar tricks appeared in his poetry, where details derived from his own day-to-day existence were frequently transposed. He had the skills of a master of disguises, of a professional impersonator in either the criminal or the theatrical senses, even those of a casuist. I was reminded of that ubiquitous prankster in Barker's verses for children, Dibby Dubby Dhu, of whom the poet asks:

> Who is Old Dibby Dubby Dhu?
> Be careful for he might easily be
>   the person who's talking to you.
>
> (Myself, I think Dibby's an actor
>   who loves nothing so much as surprises,
>   and for this reason, in and out of season
>   he adopts multitudes of disguises.)

Such elusiveness survives death, playing havoc with records, journal entries and dates. The fact of its persistence threatened to make the task of writing Barker's life a long, frustrating and, ultimately, perhaps a fruitless exercise.

PREFACE

Fortunately, as I soon found out, his mischief had possessed a double twist. When, several years after Barker's death in 1991, I began work on this book, I immediately discovered that for somebody who wished to remain hidden he had behaved bizarrely. Playing back tape recordings made during his lifetime, I found disclosures lurking in the pauses between words, in revealing distortions and in dexterously dropped hints. At Bintry House in Norfolk, his home for the last twenty-four years of his life, a cache of plastic bags soon came to light. Out of them fell not merely helpful documents but just those ephemeral papers required to solve the most brain-fagging conundrums. Had he gathered them here himself, I asked myself, in careful if seemingly nonchalant disorder? The clues hidden in this trove then led to enquiries in out-of-the-way places, not all of which he had visited: in Canada and Tokyo, in various bars and the precincts of Lambeth Palace. I spoke at length to Barker's relations, his friends, his children and other members of his family, most of whom seemed to be as baffled and fascinated by the enigma of his life and personality as I was. At various points their recollections inevitably conflicted. Gradually, however, a picture began to emerge. The remainder of my task consisted of plain induction, sometimes at two in the morning, with a stub of pencil and a rough notepad and, always, the watchful eye of the decoder: serendipity and a little science.

Among the problems Barker had set me was the strange history of his reputation. Here was a writer whom in the 1930s W.B. Yeats had believed to be the finest poet of his generation, and to whose 'genius' his publisher and mentor T.S. Eliot had once referred. These assessments were made when Barker was in his mid-twenties, but his was evidently not a case of promise unfulfilled. Four years before his death I had edited his second and last *Collected Poems*; I was also engaged in choosing his *Selected Poems* (1995). Because of this, I was well aware that he had written more deftly, with increasing versatility and control, as the decades had passed. Despite this technical development, after the mid-1950s his reputation had gone into a steep decline. The reasons for his relative obscurity – relative, for example, to his more short-lived contemporary Dylan Thomas – had nothing to do with personal reserve. Barker had conducted his life with more bravura than many a poet whose celebrity is founded upon scandal. The extremity of his behaviour should have delighted the public: instead they had forgotten him. Some of his finest work appeared in the last twenty years of his life; it coincided with the sinking of his star to virtual oblivion. Despite a flicker of media attention towards the end, that is how matters stood at his death.

There were possible explanations for this state of affairs. Barker had never, for example, submitted to convenient historical classification. Admittedly, several attempts had been made to co-opt him retrospectively into various poetic 'schools': The Parton Street Poets, The Oakley Street Poets, The New Apocalypse (to which he had definitely never belonged), or the so-called New Romantic Movement. None of these rough-and-ready descriptions had ever really fitted him; nor had he slipped neatly into any of the 'generations' of whom academic critics of British poetry are so fond of talking. Though he had first been published in the 1930s and had flourished in the 1940s and 1950s, his best poetry had been written when he was already well past middle age. According to one widely accepted but mistaken stereotype, poets generally write their most characteristic work when young, and then diversify into other modes or decline into silence. After experimenting with a number of styles early on, Barker had advanced towards his authentic artistic selfhood bit by bit, coming into his own when the eyes of the public were no longer on him. From the point of view of the quality of his work, this approach had yielded impressive dividends. It had, however, simply puzzled the journalists and reviewers, who so often make, or else destroy, writers' reputations.

Socially, too, Barker had always been extremely difficult to pigeonhole. He had not, like Stephen Spender for example, possessed the cachet of an *haut bourgeois*; nor, despite his humble origins, had he ever adopted the stance of a proletarian. He was also averse to the striking of political attitudes. An upper-middle-class poet such as Dame Edith Sitwell occasionally appeals to the snobbery in the English reading public; a provincial roaring boy like Dylan Thomas recommends himself to its inverted snobbery. Since Barker's social position for the most part had been a matter of indifference to him, he had provoked neither of these automatic responses. The difficulty of typifying him had sometimes led those writing histories of the period simply to leave him aside. Careless of fame, he had expressed little but relief at this oversight.

Again, it is often customary for commentators on the literary scene to place writers in groups who happen to have been educated together at the same schools or colleges, such as the Bloomsbury Group with their strong Cambridge connections, or the Auden Generation, many of whom studied at Oxford. Barker had never belonged to these old boys' clubs, since he left school at the age of fifteen and never seems to have regretted his decision. The ageing man with whom I discussed literature, theology and science had been an accomplished autodidact and impressively well read. It was hard for me to think of a poet in the twentieth century who had educated himself so effectively and with so little help from tutors. To the last he had maintained towards the academic world an attitude less of hostility than of amused incomprehension, and had disseminated this attitude amongst his associates. Such indifference had not, however, enhanced his profile in circles where a respect for degree certificates prevails.

Barker had decided to be a poet at the age of nine; when he died, aged seventy-eight, he was still writing verse. For sixty-nine years he had adhered religiously to his vocation, allowing nothing to distract him. Apart from a few brief periods of teaching, he had earned his living by no other means. Such single-mindedness is practicable when there is a private income to support it, but Barker had enjoyed nothing of the sort. The annual royalty returns from his publishers, many of which he had kept, amounted at the most to a very few pounds. He had fifteen children. A consideration of his career would, I hoped, teach me something about that neglected subject: the relationship between poetry and economics. In 1987, at the age of seventy-four, he had summed up his destiny in a television documentary made about his life and work. 'I have had almost everything out of my life,' he told the viewers, 'everything including the flattery of people whom I respected. But I never had any Goddamned money!'

Lastly, and most crucially for a biographer, there was the riddle of his personality. Sometimes the individual I had met, in life or on record, possessed an unforgettable amiability, being charming, amenable and attentive: he was, for example, an inspired raconteur and among the funniest people I have ever known. At the next encounter, one could meet a wall of protective silence. I had witnessed him in contemplative moods, especially when work was in hand; I had been privy to moments of serenity and peace. On other occasions, the fury of Zeus might descend and one saw a man crucified by the intensity of his own rages. He was quite as varied as his work. There was the philanderer and the husband; the sensualist and in later life the most inventive father it would be possible to provide for a child. As this book will make clear, he had both revered and resented women. Even in his seventies he could on rare occasions speak or act like a bludgeoning sexual chauvinist, confusing or alienating many who did not know him well. Those who were familiar with his life, however, were well aware that he also possessed a certain amount of the feminine in his own nature. This ambiguity had at various times fed into his poetry; it had also enabled him to straddle the sexual divide, to understand the tension between men and women as neither the sensualist nor the romantic, in their separate delusions, properly can. John Keats once likened himself to a 'chameleon poet'; like Keats, Barker was a chameleon man.

Which of these visionaries, confidence tricksters or saints, a biographer could not help but ask, represented the authentic George Barker? My role was plain: once the dust had settled over his life, once the myths had been stripped away, I had simply to put down what had happened. After all, there were accounts in the safe and even a ledger of sorts. As to the wider implications of this tale, the reader must decide.

Whatever their verdict, few after reading this biography would deny the description of Barker given long ago by Eliot to another character who features in the book, and who herself lies at the bottom of one of its more superficial mysteries. It was a judgement delivered, I believe, in affection, concern and some admiration, and with a due sense of the ambiguity inherent in certain adjectives: Barker, Eliot remarked, was 'a *very* peculiar fellow'. But few either would contradict a judgement once delivered by Barker himself. Asked by me in his late seventies how he had managed to lead so active and variegated a life, he replied after a momentary pause, and through all the grating roughness of emphysema: 'It's *mi chawm*, my dear Robert, just *mi chawm*.'

As to the poetical Character itself, (I mean that sort of which, if I am any thing, I am a Member; that sort distinguished from the wordsworthian or egotistical sublime; which is a thing per se and stands alone) it is not itself – it has no self – it is every thing and nothing – It has no character – it enjoys light and shade; it lives in gusto, be it foul or fair, high or low, rich or poor, mean or elevated – It has as much delight in conceiving an Iago as an Imogen. What shocks the virtuous philosop[h]er, delights the camelion Poet.

John Keats to Richard Woodhouse, 27 October 1818

PART ONE

1913–39

All biographies, therefore,
– No matter what else they evince –
Open, like prisons, with adore.

The True Confession of George Barker (1950)

CHAPTER I

A STREET BALLAD

In 1930, when he was seventeen, George Barker wrote a summary of his ancestry in his journal. The account was meant principally for himself, though there is a hint of an attentive girl for whose benefit he is unravelling 'this queerly, queerly convoluted I':

> I am drawn entirely from my mother, except my face, which is an exact replica of my father's. Nor am I an Englishman, although I was born in Essex and my father in Lincolnshire. I am from my mother, Irish.[1]

The attentive girl was his sister Monica, who two years later typed the journal out and sent it to John Middleton Murry, the critic and editor of the influential magazine the *Adelphi*. Her initiative led to Barker's introduction to literary life and the beginning of his career. The following year he converted the journal into his first published book, a semi-autobiographical novel called *Alanna Autumnal*, in which the sister, the 'queerly, queerly convoluted I' and the lopsided view of ancestry all recur. So the work of George Barker may be said to have its germ in this unambiguous declaration of nationality, of paternal and maternal origins. In neither journal nor novel, however, does he mention the unpalatable fact that the name of the father from whom he is so keen to distance himself was also George Barker. In other words, he was called after the person in the world whose features most closely resembled his own, but with whose straight-backed Englishness he was so reluctant to identify.

In the journal he asks why his affinity with his mother should be so strong. The enquiry ends in a paradox, all the more powerful because it is applied both to the woman who bore him and to his manner of depicting her:

> I feel that I should project an anatomy of my mother's character and

3

temperament, and point out the mutualities which we share, she and I. But I will instead inform you that she conforms precisely to the popular conception of an Irishwoman. It is impossible for me to say anything clearer or less comprehensible. And that is how she is, and will remain I am certain to everyone who knows her, clear and incomprehensible.

The paradox, and Barker's reliance on a 'popular conception' of the Irish character, owed something to the fact that, though his mother had returned to Ireland several times during his childhood, not once had she taken him with her. When Marion Frances Taaffe Barker went back to see her family in the village of Mornington, nine miles downstream from Drogheda on the Boyne estuary, only George's younger brother, Kit went with her. The year before the journal entry, however, George's interest in his Irishness had been stimulated when his maternal grandmother came to live with his parents in London. With her she had brought the Marine Pilot's Certificate of her deceased husband John. Dated 1895, it stated that John Taaffe, forty-seven years old and a master mariner, had attained the position of pilot in the Port of Drogheda – 'First Class, entitled to pilot all vessels'. The certificate was framed and hung on the kitchen wall and Grandma Taaffe would sit before it in her black widow's weeds, sewing and staring at her needlework through horn-rimmed spectacles which hung round her neck on a string. She slept in the back bedroom, where she kept a bottle of whiskey in a holy-water stoup above the bedstead. She used it to anoint the teething gums of her great-grandchildren, George's nephews and nieces, whom she lulled to sleep with the Gaelic endearments of *acushla* (dearest) and *alanna* (child).

Eventually Grandma Taaffe grew muddled and took to wandering the streets around Holland Park, where she was forever being picked up by personable mounted policemen who would deliver her back to the Barker household. The family felt that the purpose of this repeated exercise was the policemen. Her vision of heaven was a plateau exclusively inhabited by 'young men on white horses who would escort her through valleys to a shore where mermen sung ballads that she knew'.[2] Long afterwards George's nephew John remembered her thus: the Celtic spirit of the house. To George she embodied that enigma of ancestry which, in 1937, he would explore in 'Poem on Ireland':

> My mother reminds me that my birth line,
> Accompanying undersea cables, carries
> From London back to a Drogheda origin.
> Being born in England, like miscarriages
> In tubes and taxis, means nothing, for my home
> Is there by the Boyne, where never I

> Have bathed with my cousins in summertime,
> Rowed in my grandfather's coracle, or ever
> Slept with my head on the afternoon arm
> Of Mourne. Not, not once have I made
> The pilgrimage along the Drogheda Road
> Where, crossed with stone, stands the martyrdom
> Of James O'Hanlon, who died at the hand
> Of the Black and Sin, the Blood and Tan.[3]

Both Barker's grandmother and his mother inhabited a predominantly oral culture. Word of mouth was paramount in the Taaffe family and from it George had been able to reconstruct the history of his mother's people, so that his connection with them seemed to stretch all the way from Mornington like an umbilical cord beneath the Irish Sea. For generations the menfolk had been sailors, John Taaffe's father among them. He was so vain about his appearance, Grandma Taaffe claimed, that he used to iron his shoelaces.[4] The family coracle was often talked of because two of George's cousins had drowned while rowing it across the estuary. 'The Black and Sin, the Blood and Tan' was Grandma Taaffe's way of describing the Black and Tans, local police reinforcements recruited by the British government during the Anglo-Irish war of 1919–21. They featured in the Taaffe demonology as traitors who had sold out to the British cause. At their hands, some said, had died James O'Hanlon, a Republican from the same neighbourhood, about whom in 1937 Barker was to attempt to write a play. O'Hanlon had been an activist in the local branch of the Irish Volunteers. The circumstances of his death, as recounted among the Taaffes, varied. According to one version he had perished in August 1914 while leading a detachment of the Meath Volunteers in an ill-timed insurrection, assisted by certain Taaffe relatives. According to another, the Black and Tans had shot him in 1920. The important point, however, was that he was a political martyr, killed by the British or their agents. For generations the Taaffes had been ardent Republicans and Barker's father, they were quick to observe, was not merely English, but for fifteen years had been a British soldier.

For three hundred years the Taaffes had been associated with Catholicism and rebellion. When the Irish chiefs rose against Elizabeth I at the Battle of Kinsale in 1601, the Taaffes had mustered in support. In the subsequent rout, many of them had fled to Catholic Europe, where several found employment in the Austrian Empire.[5] In 1649, when Cromwell overran Drogheda, putting all resistance to the sword, he also razed the churches to the ground. 'I believe', wrote Thomas Carlyle, 'that all of their friars were knocked on the head, promiscuously but two; the one of which was Father Peter Taaff, brother of the Lord Taaff, whom the soldiers took the next day and made an end of.'[6] In 1822 a John Taaffe had appeared in Byron's circle at Pisa, where he was insulted in the street by a passing imperial dragoon. Byron wished to lodge an official complaint on his behalf, but at the last moment Taaffe, 'the original cause of the Scene', 'whose head is apparently more Irish than his heart', lost his nerve. 'He came home with a Cock and a Bull story, about going to see the man's officer making peace.'[7] Taaffe – 'a very good man,' according to Byron, 'with a great desire to see h[imself] in print' – lived to publish a commentary on Dante's *Divina Commedia*, part of which he also translated.[8]

The fervent political beliefs, the volubility, the unswerving Roman Catholicism, were clan traditions. When George's mother, the youngest of Grandma Taaffe's three children, was born in Mornington in 1881, she joined a community whose historic loyalties were as unyielding as its faith. At her first communion she was received into the Children of Mary, a Catholic women's organisation widespread throughout Ireland and the diaspora. In London she kept the society's medallion in a drawer, eventually passing it on to one of her Catholic granddaughters.[9] From girlhood onwards she had close friends in the Republican movement and, while never active in politics, she supported the nationalist cause to the end of her life. Her marriage to a non-Catholic husband and home in London were anomalies which produced a tense and vibrant dynamic in her son George which would trouble and toughen his work as a poet.

When, in 1901, Marion Frances arrived in England aged twenty, the supposition among the Taaffes was that she would make some money and then rapidly return to Drogheda. She took a job as resident housemaid in a large house off the King's Road in Chelsea. She had moved on to a similar position with a family in Kensington when, strolling through Hyde Park one Sunday afternoon in the summer of 1904, she saw a soldier from the Coldstream Guards: George Barker. The story of their meeting was to enrich the family's oral culture. Maurice Carpenter, a habitué of the Barker household in the 1930s, later recalled the poet's version, in which two strongly contrasted personalities are as salient as the setting:

> One Sunday, she was walking in Hyde Park, up by Hyde Park Corner, where there were flowerbeds, a very splendid display. A soldier came strutting along in all his finery, his Sunday uniform which was a red jacket and a small pillbox hat and those dark blue trousers with a very broad strip down them. It was my father. She noticed that a suspender was hanging down his leg, and [he] being such a fine upstanding man it was ridiculous. She burst out laughing. My father apparently walked by, but stopped, offended by the insult of my mother's laughter. He turned

round to her and said, 'What are you laughing at?' Of course, she didn't tell him. He sat down. They began to talk.[10]

The couple were married in the Roman Catholic Church of Our Lady of Victories, Kensington High Street, on Sunday, 12 February 1905. He described himself as an 'Officer's Servant, Coldstream Guards'. The Taaffes did not attend the wedding.

At the time of his marriage, George Barker senior was twenty-five and had been a professional soldier for eleven years. He was a farm manager's son from Swaby in Lincolnshire, where he was born in 1880. His family were devout Methodists and the childhood home had been a tied cottage with an earth floor for livestock, from which a plain wooden ladder led to the living quarters above.[11] His father, Walter Barker, a keen amateur boxer, was so given to rages that he was rumoured to wrestle with his cattle. He also had a reputation for absenteeism and would sometimes disappear for months on end without explanation, leaving his diminutive wife Eliza to care for their six children, of whom George was the third.[12] For the boys, it was a cramped and limited existence, from which three of them escaped by joining the armed forces. George had been intended for the Methodist ministry,[13] but at fourteen he had taken the Queen's Shilling at the farm gate, attracted by the blandishments of a recruiting sergeant.[14]

The Royal Lincolnshire had been his first regiment. With them he had fought in the Sudan, helping to quell the forces of Al-Mahdi at the Battle of Omdurman in September 1898. During the long march along the banks of the Blue Nile preceding the battle, he had been one of a team of infantrymen detailed to carry Kitchener's grand piano across the burning sands. Ever afterwards he kept a shred of tapestry, in Sudanese herringbone stitching, which he proudly showed to visitors; he also possessed a cape, in black fabric embossed with gold, which he referred to as 'The Mahdi's Coat'. During the Boer War he had served with a battalion of mounted infantry and fought at Magersfontein. In 1902, however, he moved to the Coldstream Guards, where as a batman his duties were largely domestic. He distinguished himself by boxing as a middleweight. He possessed the upright bearing of a soldier and retained to the end of his days a passion for order and hierarchy not always in harmony with the tendencies of those around him, least of all those of his wife.

The couple could scarcely have been more different. She was a practising Roman Catholic and he a lapsed Nonconformist. She supported Sinn Fein, he the Tories. She became a passionate Londoner, while he remained a country boy whose green fingers were always itching to work in the garden. Temperamentally she was a nomad, while he longed to settle. What they had in common was a love of tall stories and of song. His songs, however, were all about military campaigns and hers about Ireland. Gradually they reached a truce. She went to Mass on Sundays, taking the children with her, while he remained at home. Politics were discussed exclusively in the kitchen, a room he seldom entered. For most of their life they lived in London at a succession of addresses around Chelsea, Battersea, Fulham and Kensington. By this means, Marion could satisfy her craving for movement, while convincing her husband that essentially they were staying put. At intervals he might persuade her to leave London and move to the suburbs, but after a few months they invariably returned to central London. Wherever they lived, there was an unofficial demarcation between the kitchen, where she entertained her visitors, and the living room, where he sat and smoked. So invariable was this arrangement that, though peripatetic, their household appeared to be constant. To later visitors, like the poet David Wright, the Barkers seemed a London miniature of the Irish problem: father cherishing his medals and his memories of the Sudan; mother sipping gin and voicing Dublin folk songs.

After their wedding, the couple set themselves up at 22 Coulson Street in Chelsea, a Regency-fronted house owned by the regiment and convenient for the barracks. It was there that their two oldest children were born: Olga Annette in 1905 and Eileen Cecilia in 1906. The girls called their mother Big Mumma; their father they referred to as Pa. Two years after Eileen's birth Pa left the Guards and found a position as butler to two wealthy American sisters living in Paddington. He was still in domestic service when Monica Adelaide Ursula, their third daughter, was born on 17 October 1910. By the time she was three the American sisters had died, bequeathing Pa £5,000, which he then lost through an unwise investment in an antiques business.

Having prevailed upon his wife to leave London for Loughton near Epping Forest, he took a house with a garden and became a temporary police constable. It was a role to which Pa was well suited with his erect bearing and assertive air. His father's professional connection with law enforcement would come as something of a shock to young George when he eventually discovered it on his birth certificate. Would his more bohemian friends, he wondered in the first book of his autobiographical work *The True Confession of George Barker* (1950), tolerate his filial relationship with the constabulary, should they come to hear of it? By then, however, the poet could perceive the potential for revolt in this 'ill-fitted paternity':

> So I, the son of an administer
> Of the facts of civil laws,
> Delight in uncivil and even sinister
> Violations. Thus my cause

>   Is simply, friend, to hell with yours.
>   In misdemeanors I was nourished –
>   Learnt, like altruists in Westminster,
>   By what duplicities one flourished.[15]

George was born at 116 Forest Road, Loughton on Wednesday, 26 February 1913 in the astrological 'Mansion of the Virgin'. The month of his birth was always to exercise a spell over his imagination: February, known to the Ancient Greeks as 'the Month of the Dead'. He was given his father's Christian name, to which Big Mumma added the second name of Granville. Ever afterwards the combination of Granville and Barker would lead strangers to suppose that he had been named after the actor-impresario Harley Granville-Barker, who at the time of his birth was directing *Twelfth Night* at the Savoy Theatre in the West End. In fact, 'Granville' came from the Granville Cinema, which Big Mumma used to visit in Loughton. In the early months of young George's life she pushed him in a perambulator through the 'dilapidated glades' of Epping Forest 'where the deer and girls / Mope like lost ones looking for Love's gaols', among 'the deer in the rain near the trees, the leaf-hidden shit, / The Sunday papers, and the foliage's falling world'.[16]

Much later Barker learned to refer to Essex with a rueful, downbeat pride, but at the time Big Mumma was having none of it. When her son was six months old the family left for 52 Juer Street, on the western fringes of Battersea Park, 'the Park railings and the gardens' evergreens', as he would later describe them, beyond which 'the barges on the Thames / [Lay] like leviathans in the fog'.[17] One of Barker's earliest memories was of contracting tonsillitis during infancy. His father wheeled him on his bicycle across Battersea Bridge to a hospital in Chelsea, which advertised a revolutionary cure. The cure involved sniffing pepper and then sneezing.[18] George sneezed, but the tonsils remained, as did the tonsillitis which afflicted him for decades.

It was in Juer Street that the Barkers' last child, a boy, was born on Sunday, 6 February 1916. He was to have been baptised Christopher Francis, but, a few days before the christening, Pa was informed of the death of his younger brother, nineteen-year-old Albert, on the Somme. At the last minute the baby's names were changed to Albert Gordon.[19] He was very small, and the fluffy white hair standing all over his head earned him the nickname 'Kitten'. When they were grown men, George would continue to call him this; to all others he was 'Kit'.

Now the family was complete and it was Big Mumma who kept them together as Pa was drawn back into the army. At thirty-six he volunteered once more for the Guards. In the two years he served on the Western Front he earned a field commission with the rank of major. (The family affectionately promoted him, bestowing on him the honorary rank of colonel.) Meanwhile, as the Zeppelins droned above, Big Mumma moved with the children to smaller quarters in Ethelburga Street, a short crescent off Battersea Bridge Road. When the sirens sounded, Kit was placed in a copper for safety, while the other children gathered for comfort round the cooking range. The searchlights, as they threaded the night sky, reminded Kit of the shuttle on Big Mumma's sewing machine darting back and forth on its unremitting task of making children's clothes.[20]

At the Armistice in November 1918 Pa found himself without a job and with a large family to feed. For eight years – the years of George's childhood – he struggled. Pa had never taken an examination and his skills, though well defined, were disparate.[21] He took the family north of the river to Fulham, where they found the cheapest accommodation available. In 1915 the philanthropist Samuel Lewis had established a trust to house poor, mainly Jewish, families. The resulting estate, the Samuel Lewis Trust Dwellings, was a row of five-storey, two-bay blocks, running along the north side of Ixworth Place to the south of Fulham Road. It shared the short street with a scrap-metal dealer, a French polisher and a cat's food seller, composing for George a childhood landscape he would never forget:

> And in the yard of the tenement
> – The Samuel Lewis Trust – I played
> While my father, for the rent
> (Ten bob a week and seldom paid),
> Trudged London for a job.[22]

The Trust had a policy of employing former members of the armed forces as wardens of each block. So Pa squeezed his family into a three-room flat and earned a small honorarium as caretaker while he searched London for full-time work and young George and tinier Kit scoured the bins for scraps. Evening after evening their father returned home with 'a twist of / drawn exhaustion in his face'.[23] George came to believe that the only thing that saved his father's self-respect at the period was the Colt 45 which he had kept after the war, and which he hid beneath his pillow. When money was especially tight, Big Mumma would pawn her wedding ring – every Wednesday as the poet remembered it. 'Hocking' small valuables to 'Uncle' became a way of life.[24] Kit was too young to recall these episodes in later life, but they coloured George's attitudes for ever.

He was hounded by a particular memory from this time. One day he and Kit found a snake in the dust and, filling a jam jar with water, they drowned it. Long afterwards, its writhings haunted him.[25]

CHAPTER 2

AN ABORIGINAL CALAMITY

For Big Mumma, the Samuel Lewis Trust Dwellings possessed the one indubitable advantage of lying within the ambit of the London Oratory on the Brompton Road. Soon after the construction of the Ixworth estate in 1915, the Oratory had appointed a Visitor to oversee the spiritual welfare of the Roman Catholic families living there and the Oratory's elementary school was at the bottom of Ixworth Place. At their marriage Pa had given an undertaking that the children would be educated as Catholics. So it was to the Oratory School that the girls were sent. In 1918, at the age of five, George went there too. On 18 December he wrote a Christmas letter for his parents: 'We are going to have a nice Xmas tree', he wrote, 'and a tea party at school.'[1] But in 1920, when George turned seven, Pa put his foot down. Big Mumma had had her way with the girls; she should not have *carte blanche* with their elder son, who was to be sent up the road to the council school on Sloane Avenue.

The Marlborough Street School was a three-storey building in red and brown brick, with the date AD 1902 above the lintel. There were 1200 pupils, two entrances and two playgrounds, one for boys and one for girls. It was a rough and bustling environment. In the boys' playground, George learned 'that contraceptives, / Blown up like balloons, could fly'[2]; he also 'memorized the Golden Rule: / Lie, lie, lie'. In order to survive he developed a triple front: as reluctant scholar, playground pugilist, and under-the-desk-top bibliophile.

Poetry was taught by Miss Christie, a Scot whom Barker remembered as 'the first person who told me that there were nice things in life as well as nasty things'.[3] She read the children the Scottish ballads, and made them memorise such anthology favourites as 'Big Steamers', 'The Camel's Hump' and 'The Yarn of the *Nancy Bell*'. They also learnt 'the shorter pieces from Shakespeare', 'the prettier pieces of Wordsworth' and a 'miscellaneous collection of oddments such as "Into Battle", "The Slave's Dream" and "Excelsior"'. If the learning was not done, or if discipline broke down, the miscreants were rapped over the head with a ruler. This was excellent training, Barker later thought.

The headmaster was George Sampson, man of letters, later Secretary of the English Association and editor of *The Shorter Cambridge History of English Literature*. George detested him, which was a pity since their backgrounds were not as dissimilar as he might have thought. Sampson had studied at home and entered teachers' training college at a late age. Throughout his life he regarded himself as an outsider. He hid his sense of insecurity behind a monocle and layers of Edwardian flourish. His office door was closed to most comers, particularly to members of staff who could not equal his precarious literary accomplishments. Sampson had, above all, ideas about poetry without being a poet himself, a limitation which, as soon as he became conscious of literature as an autonomous art, Barker knew to be fatal. 'We are not all poets,' Sampson wrote in his essay 'A Boy and His Books'; 'we are not even all dreamers'.[4] Later in life, on learning that Barker had been published by Faber & Faber, he wrote to him expressing disbelief that someone so unpromising, so seemingly feckless, rough hewn and absurd, should publish anything at all.[5]

When Barker looked back at his childhood from his teens, he could discern little except a series of physical sensations unconnected by any degree of self-reflection. He recalled, by way of illustration, 'spraining my ankle when leaping from a gate, a bath in water several degrees too hot', followed by 'the immediate withdrawal of my body from the bath, the immediate grasping of my ankle'. Two events stood out, however: his first juvenile sexual experiment, and the writing of his first poem. The experiment took place in the yard behind Ixworth Place. The consciousness with which he later described it owed a little to the teachings of the Oratory and lot more to hindsight:

> I can recall, with something of the maudlin sensuality perverts derive from titillating children, standing, as a boy of about nine, over the ten year old girl who had splayed herself out on the steps behind the tenement in which we lived. And I can see the terrified and delighted blue eyeballs gazing upward in bright crime as she wormed her hips out of her knickers: and I can feel the sensation of having solved all the enigmas which ever came over me as I stood and looked down at the place we go home into so long as the grave is too big. And with that knowledge of handling all our origins I felt the death of Beethoven, the death of Samson, the abdication of Edward VIII and the origin of the established church of England all together in my hand as it closed over the sex of vice, the nub of the womb, the bullseye, the x.[6]

One afternoon the same year George sat in the front room of the Barkers' tiny flat, mesmerised by the play of shadows on the window. As he looked, they transformed themselves into caparisoned knights tilting across the broad field of the Venetian blind. He spent the next few hours composing a ten-page 'monstrosity' entitled 'The Tournament' in the stanza of *The Faerie Queene*.[7] At nine Barker had discovered Edmund Spenser, in whose work he had been delighted by 'the elaboration and complication of the rhythm'.[8] He had also discovered his vocation:

> The sulking and son-loving Muse
>   Grabbed me when I was nine. She saw
> It was a question of self-abuse
>   Or verses. I tossed off reams before
> I cared to recognize their purpose.
>   While other urchins were blowing up toads
> With pipes of straw stuck in their arse,
>   So was I, but I also wrote odes.[9]

Even the blowing up of toads with a straw had a literary precedent: it is an instance of infantile cruelty referred to in Pope's 'Epistle to Dr Arbuthnot'.[10] In private Barker had already decided to be a poet; in public he preferred to be viewed as an effective young bruiser. The double act worked perfectly until during one lunch break he was caught reading a book. Mercifully for his playground reputation, this was not *The Faerie Queene* but Sir James Morier's picaresque story *The Adventures of Hajji Baba of Ispahan* (1824), in the World's Classics series. He was let off with mild derision and the bestowal of 'the highly distinguished moniker of "Hadji"'.[11]

Pa had been working for the waste-paper dealers, Phillips Mills and had moved on to become an insurance agent when he opened his ledger one morning to discover the front page covered by 'an over-large crypto-Renaissance catafalque inscribed "Georgius Barca, 1913–26"'. He was not pleased. For encouragement in his calling George had to look to Big Mumma, who once more pawned her wedding ring to buy him a second-hand typewriter from Selfridge's. The machine fulfilled a double purpose, since George wanted to be a writer and Monica a typist. She perfected her office skills by typing out his work.

Big Mumma had her own reading enthusiasms, the works of Addison among them. In Ireland she had learnt that poetry was an oral art, better recited than read. According to Barker, she recited poems 'by the thousand'.[12] She also communicated to her son the view that literature was a matter of personal taste, to which established canons and prescribed reading lists were irrelevant.

The books and poems that you knew were the books and poems that you loved. She believed the best of modern Irish poets, and the best of all war poets, to be Francis Ledwidge, a self-educated peasant who had grown up in Slane, twenty miles up the Boyne from Drogheda. Ledwidge, who was killed on the Western Front in 1917, had been a protégé of Yeats's friend Joseph Plunkett, Lord Dunsany. In 1919 Dunsany had collected and edited Ledwidge's *Complete Poems*, including war pieces like 'At Currabwe':

> Louder than the cricket's wing
> All night long their hammer's glee
> Times the merry song they sing
> Of Ireland glorious and free.
> So I heard Joseph Plunkett say,
> You know I heard them but last May.
>
> And when the night is very cold
> They warm their hands against the light
> Of stars that make the waters gold
> Where they are labouring all the night.
> So Pearse said, and he knew the truth,
> Among the stars he spent his youth.[13]

Before he left Marlborough Road School George had sent Dunsany 'a poem of laudation' on rescuing these poems. Big Mumma liked them because Patrick Pearse and the other leaders of the 1916 Easter Rising were an important element in her sense of nationhood. As a girl she had befriended another eventual participant in the rising, Countess Constance Markiewicz, author of *A Call to the Women of Ireland*.[14] Shortly after the rising Constance converted to Roman Catholicism. During the 1920s she visited Mumma several times in London; much later, Kit would remember her as his mother's 'great friend'. Big Mumma kept more or less open house. Her way of being Irish, which combined caresses and inflammatory talk of gunpowder in equal measure, was as warm as it was definite. She spoke English in a way distinctively her own, sometimes missing out parts of speech such as the indefinite article: 'The days pass like whirlwind'. In his twenties Barker would make this habit a feature of his poetic style. Her vocabulary, too, was completely unlike anyone else's. Pubs were 'churches'; bar tops 'prayer books'; beer pumps 'purse handles'. To Barker, she seemed to possess a positive genius for conviviality. Her doors were never open wider than at Christmas, when the kitchen was packed with relatives and friends for days on end. By the time he left school, George could look back on a whole succession of such festivities:

> Christmas again is come, and the night is alight with coloured bulbs and purse handles. Christmas for me has always brought hilarity and happiness in far excess of any other season. At home my mother received upward of twenty guests each year, every one a sincerely intimate friend, and did her best (which is a superlative best) to make their hearts dance and their minds laugh.[15]

Barker saw his father as trapped in history. His mother he regarded as timeless: presiding over a well-scrubbed table, brewing endless pots of tea, stubbornly prevaricating over the lesser task of making food. Sooner or later a flaky steak-and-kidney pie would be produced, while Mumma carried on talking, reproving her sons, encouraging newcomers, instilling Dutch courage into the less forthcoming by discreetly pouring nips of gin into their cups. The routine was modified on Sundays, when she set out on the half-mile walk to the Oratory. Having arrived opposite the double pillars of the church's west front, she would install the non-communicating members of the family at the public house opposite while, possibly with Kit, she went across to hear Mass. Afterwards, she would collect the others on her way home, or sit and drink until lunchtime.

For George, the Oratory was second home. Standing in its courtyard as a child, he stared up at the statue of John Henry Newman, who had founded the first English Oratory in Birmingham in 1849. Barker loved the late-nineteenth-century rococo architecture of the church's nave and, between its pilasters, the statues of the twelve apostles by Giuseppe Mazzuoli which had once lined the nave of Siena cathedral. He knew the Latin inscription, over the West door, to Father Frederick Willam Faber, who at Newman's bidding had established the London Oratory in 1854. He knew St Wilfred's Chapel in the north-east corner, and within it the shrine of St Cecilia with its marble effigy of the saint's incorruptible body. The effigy was an exact copy of Stefano Maderna's statue in the Church of Santa Cecilia in the Trastevere in Rome. Beneath her altar the patron saint of music lay, her head turned away, her hair sweeping down and off her severed neck: voluptuous in agony, an epitome of deference to the divine will, and of woman as victim. Hers was a potent image, as powerful as the music that played about her form when, every 22 November – her feast day – the Brothers of the Little Oratory performed an oratorio in her honour.

When Mumma did not go to the Oratory, the Oratory came to Mumma. Throughout George's childhood and youth, she would entertain its priests at home, among them the official Visitor to the Samuel Lewis Trust Dwellings, Father Kenneth Dale-Roberts. George was thirteen and had already received his first communion when Big Mumma showed Dale-Roberts some of his verses. His response was to suggest that George attend Oratory House between four and six o' clock every Tuesday and Thursday afternoon, to receive further instruction in Catholic history and the essentials of the faith.[16]

For decades, ever since the rapid growth in conversions during the late-Victorian period, the Roman Catholic Church in England had been wrestling with the problem of forming its own distinctive personality. It so happened that in 1926, when Barker began a course of theological instruction, he fell under the influence of the two Oratory fathers who represented the permissible extremes of doctrine and practice. Significantly, he remembered both of them as Irish, which they were not, and as cradle Catholics, when both were converts.[17] Be that as it may, they combined to produce what became his own complicated view of the Church, which would remain constant to the end of his life.

The first was Dale-Roberts himself, a Welshman and a Victorian high Catholic.[18] The son of a canon of Birmingham Cathedral, he had begun his own ministry as an Anglo-Catholic priest after graduating from Keble College, Oxford in 1903. Converted to Catholicism in his mid-twenties, Dale-Roberts worked for many years as a parish priest before, in 1918, persuading the bishop to let him join the Oratory, where he remained for the rest of his life. The city of Rome – its churches and history – was his passion. He was devoted to the more ornate cults of Catholicism: the Sacred Heart; the Precious Blood. Within the congregation of the Oratory his special province was spiritual instruction and pastoral care. For forty-eight years he directed the Children of Mary, of whom Big Mumma was a member. He was also Catechist at the Oratory Girls' School, which the Barker daughters attended. Ecclesiastically he was a reactionary. He had inherited from his father a fiery temper which, when provoked, he would let fly. When frustrated, he would stamp his foot or, more dramatically, pummel his white hair with both fists. In old age he refused a telephone, long after the other brothers had them, and he persisted in saying the Mass in Latin.

In Barker, Dale-Roberts instilled a lasting love of speculation, a theological conservatism and an enduring infatuation with Italy. The theology consisted of Father Kenneth's special loves: the *Confessions* of St Augustine; the *Fioretti* of St Francis; Thomas à Kempis's *Imitation of Christ*; the writings of St Francis de Sales and Cardinal Newman. His method of instruction corresponded to a catechistic variety of practical criticism. He would set before the student a passage of systematic theology and ask him to comment on it. One of Barker's most vivid youthful memories, which he recounted frequently, was of the moment when Father Kenneth laid before him the great peroration to Newman's *Apologia pro Vita Sua*:

To consider the world in its length and breadth, its various history, the many races of man, their starts, their fortunes, their mutual alienation, their conflicts; and then their ways, habits, governments, forms of worship; their enterprises, their aimless courses; their random achievements and acquirements, the impotent conclusion of long-standing facts, the tokens so faint and broken of a superintending design, the blind evolution of what turn out to be great powers or truths, the progress of things, as if from unreasoning elements, not towards final causes, the greatness and littleness of man, his far-reaching aims, his short duration, the curtain hung over his futurity, the disappointments of life, the defeat of good, the success of evil, physical pain, mental anguish, the prevalence and intensity of sin, the pervading idolatries, the corruptions, the dreary hopeless irreligion, that condition of the whole race so fearfully and exactly described in the Apostle's words, 'having no hope and without God in the world' – all this is a vision to dizzy and appal; and inflicts upon the mind the sense of a profound mystery, which is absolutely beyond human solution.

What shall be said to this heart-piercing, reason-bewildering fact? I can only answer, that either there is no Creator, or this living society of men is in a true sense discarded from his presence. Did I see a boy of good make and mind, with the tokens on him of a refined nature, cast upon the world without provision, unable to say whence he came, his birth-place or his family connexions, I should conclude that there was some mystery connected with his history, and that he was one, of whom, from one cause or other, his parents were ashamed. Thus only should I be able to account for the contrast between the promise and the condition of his being. And so I argue about the world; – *if* there is a God, *since* there is a God, the human race is implicated in some terrible aboriginal calamity. It is out of joint with the purposes of its Creator. This is a fact, a fact as true as the fact of its existence; and thus the doctrine of what is theologically called original sin becomes to me almost as certain as that the world exists, and as the existence of God.[19]

Barker knew the last three sentences by heart. To the end of his life he would recite them, laying emphasis on the clauses '*if* there is a God' and '*since* there is a God'. It was as if this passage distilled everything that the Catholic religion had taught him about pessimism: the mismatch between human potential and achievement, the inevitability of corruption, the cul-de-sac to which all rational enquiry leads, the sheer incapacity of unaided human nature to fend for itself. The pessimism bit deep, permanently affecting his vision of life. 'Ultimately', he later said, 'it is only a question of the degree of melancholia that you are going to allow yourself to suffer from. Where is there a categorical vision of spiritual responsibility that is really absolutely joyful? I am sure there is one somewhere, but I don't know about it.'[20] The doctrine of original sin penetrated his temperament; it invaded his humour; it laced his most intimate emotions with guilt. Politically it ensured his detachment from panaceas and programmes based on the premise of human perfectibility. Never would he be able to believe in utopias or in sanguine notions of progress.

A sense of sin was one insight to be derived from a reading of that passage in Newman, but there were others. There was, for example, the apparent ambivalence of Newman's way of believing. The force of '*since* there is a God' was to plunge the reader at once into tragedy, from which, mercifully, from the orthodox viewpoint, there was a redemptive release. The sense of '*if* there is a God' was quite different, since it opened up the possibility that there was not. From that vantage point, the aboriginal calamity was merely grotesque. The reader was left with the disquieting proposition that human beings are out of kilter with the non-existent purposes of their creation. This predicament might be viewed as funny, or sad; whatever the case, it could only disturb. Forty years later, in the second book of *The True Confession of George Barker* (1964), the poet was to describe his state of mind as sometimes, on his way to his twice-weekly instruction, he used to pause before the statue of Cardinal Newman in the Oratory courtyard. As this remembered self stares up into the cardinal's sombre marble face, he senses the belief at the heart of doubt. He also senses the doubt at the heart of belief:

> For, Father, once, I, a child, alone,
>   Stood looking up with reverence at you
> Where, near gardens, your stone statue
>   (How could you have a heart of stone?)
> Smiling as though the smile would christen
>   Cogitates by the Oratory.
> So, Prince Spiritual, not to me
>   But to a child lean down and listen.
>
> It is not, truly, out of despair
>   The guilty cry, nor is it their
> Intemperate desire to hear
>   What they most wish were so:
> No, father. It is truly, when
>   We believe, like Tertullian,
> What seems impossible. O then,
>   Then we cry to know.[21]

Before long, however, the duty of instructing the young Barker came to be shared by another priest. Father Philip Francis Oddy was a vast, dishevelled man, who had joined the Oratory in 1909.[22] Witty and incisive, he was regarded with awe by the other fathers for his swift, uncompromising tongue, his acid squibs and practical jokes. There were some who believed he had a touch of genius, an expansiveness characteristic of St Philip Neri, founder of the first Oratory in Rome. To others, he was a mere nuisance, a thorn in the flesh. Oddy was an anarchist and a debunker – more especially of reaction, which he reviled in all its forms. He was also a very different kind of Catholic from Dale-Roberts, who profoundly distrusted him. Merriment was his gift, and with it he drew in the young. In his photographs, he lolls, surrounded by young devotees and rocking with raillery and good humour. In Barker's mind this sacred fool, 'most uncommonly fat', coalesced with that creation of another humorous clergyman, Lewis Carroll's Father William:

> There was a priest, a priest,
>   A Reverend of the Oratory,
> Who taught me history. At least
>   He taught me the best part of his story.
> Fat Father William, have you ceased
>   To lead boys up the narrow path
> Through the doors of the Turkish Bath?
>   I hope you're warm in Purgatory.[23]

But if, like a character in *Alice in Wonderland*, Oddy sometimes stood logic on its head, he was far from old: thirty-seven, against Father Kenneth's forty-four and George's fourteen. He saw himself as a breath of fresh air in the stagnating atmosphere of Oratory House. Father Kenneth's more sentimental excesses – his devotion to *romanitá*, his fussing over the Sacred Heart – were his aversion, and towards them his levity was unsparing. The situation was not to last. In 1933, three years after Barker finished instruction, Oddy went on holiday to Rome. Unable to stand his ribaldry for a week longer, Father Kenneth used his absence to get him voted out of the Congregation. Oddy returned to be informed that his services were no longer required. He departed under a cloud to spend the rest of his days ministering to the Catholics of the Isle of Dogs.

It was seven years before Oddy's abrupt exit that he, Dale-Roberts and George sat down in the parlour of Oratory House and read the classics of Catholic literature. Physically, there could not have been a greater contrast between the two priests: Dale-Roberts, aquiline but gentle, his ascetic face occasionally breaking into the sweetest of smiles; Oddy, sardonic and huge, rippling with mirth and subversiveness. To Barker, 'a boy of good make and mind', they were the serious and comic masks of the faith.

An 'Augustinian Anarchist' was the oxymoronic way in which Barker was to describe himself in the second part of his *True Confession*. Dale-Roberts contributed the influence of Augustine, conveying in the process a fundamental reverence, while Oddy inculcated an irreverence that was to become inseparable from it. In his early notebooks, as the young Barker considers the received pieties of doctrine, the balancing irreverence is already present:

> When I asked J. to tell me why God made man, he said 'So he could worship him'. I don't know if this is theologically correct, as I don't know why I should believe in a God, but it seems a singularly hateful idea to me. Successful corpulent God, unaware of a circle of worshippers hidden by his immense and corpulent stomach; thoroughly satiated and satisfied with the knowledge that we must be worshipping him. Beastly old man, how much obscener than Mammon, with no one to worship him.[24]

Eventually, Barker's Catholicism became a highly personal blend of the orthodox and the heterodox: orthodox because he was a rebel who needed fixed points against which to react; heterodox because he needed the intellectual licence with which to spur his revolt. 'I am on a religious tether,' he admitted late in life.[25] The essence of a tether, of course, is that it is attached to something unmoving.

Catholic theology thus became the means by which Barker defined his sense of wrongdoing. It caught him up in a moral drama, intensifying his sense of sin. In time he would develop an almost Manichaean vision in which good and evil were locked in mortal conflict. The introspection of his meditative works, the transgressive wit of his humorous poems, would both feed on a sensation of guilt that needed strict parameters within which to work. It would have been of no help to him to possess shifting moral categories. The vigour of his expression was to depend on a marked sense of violation. He needed to know precisely where, and against what, the violation had occurred.

For most of his adult life he was to live in the paradoxical mood of T.S. Eliot's celebrated judgement on Baudelaire: 'Genuine blasphemy, genuine in spirit and not purely verbal, is the product of partial belief, and is as impossible to the complete atheist as to the perfect Christian. It is a way of affirming belief.' Barker would always practise that sort of perverse, partial affirmation. His poetry would become a means by which he could express both his sense of religious awe and the urgency of his revolt. 'It is absolutely impossible for anyone to write without having a particular philosophical point of view,' he remarked at the age of sixty-nine. 'And I know, because I have done some writing, that it has been written from a particular philosophical and theological point of view. That, I think, of a Catholic who has found it impossible to retain an absolutely total love of the Church. In other words, a renegade.'[26]

Yet long after he ceased to attend Mass with any regularity, and long after blasphemy had become a habit, Barker's Catholicism remained a vital ingredient in his self-definition. From the beginning it had been a means by which he associated himself with the underprivileged Irish rather than with the dominant English: that is, with his mother's culture rather than with his father's. Since he had been instructed while the family was poor, since the Oratory saw its mission as lying among the slum-dwellers of the district, Roman Catholicism became in his mind the religion of the oppressed. To that extent his identification with it was always a political act. Beyond that, it would form his paradoxical vision of human life in a way that nothing else did. By doing so, it nurtured and sustained his voice.

CHAPTER 3

'BALTHUS! PURE BALTHUS!'

One by one, the Barker sisters left school and took jobs in the offices of the West End. Even so times continued to be hard. In the bitterly cold winter of 1925 George and Kit improvised games under the table top, recreating ancient sea battles with miniature triremes, with the carpet for the Aegean and footstools for rocks. Afterwards they sat looking out at Ixworth Place, where the road was being relaid. They stared at the 'old man', or night watchman, as he huddled for warmth in his box-like shelter.[1] He was standing guard over tar blocks of wood, which were to be laid on the road and covered over with layers of bitumen and fine gravel before being levelled with a heavy roller.

On bitter nights the boys sneaked out to filch these blocks, which, placed in the grate, burned fiercely, exploding if they got too hot and shooting fiery stone chips into the room. One of the blocks served as the axle for George's first vehicle, a hand-made bicycle known as a 'ball-bearing scooter'.[2] It was made from the tar block, two spars of wood, two ball-bearings from a car and a meat skewer. On it, in the early spring of 1926, he rode off to the Imperial Exhibition in the new stadium at Wembley.

By 1926 Pa and the three girls were all in employment. With gradually increasing affluence, the Barkers were able to move into a furnished two-floor flat at the top of a four-storey early Victorian house at 174a Ladbroke Grove. The flat was above the rooms of a Commander Smiley, the smell of whose kippers drifted up the stairwell every morning. Outside, along the kerb, stood tall plane trees, while inside the rooms were high-ceilinged and light. On the top floor they had a 'blue room', with dark-blue grained wallpaper, white woodwork and a picture rail. On the floor below was a white room, in which stood an elegant Louis Seize chaise-longue with eight legs and 'sublime watered silk embroidery'. Years afterwards Kit would dream of the white room, which was 'cool and silvery in colour and not much used except for those who wanted to be quiet and read in the afternoon'. The light there, as he remembered it, was 'Balthus – pure Balthus'. During the General Strike that May the boys watched from the windows as city gentlemen rollerskated southwards down Ladbroke Grove on their way to the office.[3] In the road discontented crowds milled about, 'carelessly militant'. Even at the age of ten Kit could sense 'the air of disintegration, the feeling of almost elemental hatred seething beneath the surface'. When summer arrived the girls took to walking to and from work through Hyde Park, picking flowers on the way back to decorate the flat. On Sunday evenings they were swept off in sports cars, carrying picnic baskets, towards Cookham or Maidenhead. Returning on the Monday morning, they would dash out for work almost at once, just before George and Kit left for school.

In the spring of 1927, the year of his letter to Lord Dunsany, Barker left Marlborough Road. He moved to the secondary school attached to the Regent Street Polytechnic, which had been founded by Quintin Hogg in 1881 to spread humane and practical learning among the socially deprived. The following summer, after four terms, he 'decided to remove' himself. He was devoted to books, but he did not want others – with the possible exception of priests – to interpret them for him. His decision also expressed a deep distrust of systems. He had just started to keep a journal, in which he wrote that year, 'I respect neither my country nor myself nor any ethical regulation I ever investigated.' At school 'literature' meant criticism and analysis, for which he knew he was not cut out:

> I am certain that my mind is made if anything for self contained imaginative work: critical activity of any kind is alien to me, alien and dissonant. The values structuring a critical work must be either impersonal or strange; the individuality of the critic, except emotionally, is to be nullified. Such nullification I cannot affect. Either I am without an important analytical intelligence, or my imagination is monstrously oversize.[4]

He would do his reading at home and be the better for it.

It was the end of Barker's formal education. When asked later in life where he had been educated, he would reply 'at the Oratory'. Of one thing he was certain: though the play of the intellect fascinated him and words were his preoccupation, he would never be an academic: 'consecutive thinking, syllogism, or any concatenation of logically inter-dependent parts is one of the ornaments I shall never wear'.[5] His dilemma was that he had already decided to become a poet at a time when poets wore their learning on their sleeves. When he considered his situation from this angle, inadequacy consumed him:

'In my life I have never left England. Once I was for two weeks acquainted with an Italian. My German consists of the conjugation of *ich bin*; my French I have none; ditto Italiano. Graves speaks of the increasing cosmopolitanism of literature. Eliot has about seventeen languages, including Sanskrit. Deduce my mood.'[6]

It was 1928 and Barker was fifteen. He had straight dark-brown hair parted in the middle. Behind his spectacles, his eyes, like Big Mumma's, were piercing, intelligent and a brilliant blue. His only unfortunate feature was his nose, which was too large for his taste. His forehead sloped downwards towards a slight ridge of bone running above the eyebrows, as is sometimes seen in portraits of Michelangelo. In Tennyson's *In Memoriam*, which he was reading, this feature is attributed to the poet's friend Arthur Henry Hallam: 'And over those ethereal eyes / The bar of Michael Angelo.'[7] In Barker's journal there is a passage in which he sits before the mirror trying to persuade Monica that he, too, has this feature, which is characteristic of poets. She is not persuaded: 'You will not even make out the small effeminacy of my mouth or be nauseated by my vulgarly oversized nose. You will never see that I do possess that rare curio, the bar of Michelangelo, but faintly even in the hardest light. Forgive me, fairest, no one can see.'[8] As his confidence in his poetic abilities grew, the feature seemed to him to grow more prominent. In *Alanna Autumnal* diffidence has changed to conviction: 'she marvels at the rosy effeminacy of my mouth . . . she notes that I do in fact possess that rare curio, the bar of Michelangelo'.[9]

In the journal he asks, 'Am I a poet?' In the novel this has become 'I am a poet.' Barker was hovering between the two views of himself when, one afternoon in 1927, Monica brought back to Ladbroke Grove two beautiful, and almost inseparable, sisters, who had been fellow pupils of hers at the Oratory School. Kit and Jessie Woodward were from Parson's Green, where their father was a builder. From their mother Catherine, who was from Cork, they had derived their dark and delicate looks, as well as an astringent and puritanical Catholicism.[10] George was especially drawn to the younger, Jessie Winifred Theresa. She was nineteen, four years his elder. By turns lively and withdrawn, she had long, dark hair framing a pale face with high cheekbones and great Madonna-like eyes. Her apparent composure attracted him. 'Mona Lisa,' he called her, 'mia Mona Lisa'.[11]

Jessie enters Barker's journal at this point. At times, it is as if he were addressing her; at times, as if he were talking to Monica, or to both young women. And at times, they seem interchangeable. To secure Jessie's affections he bought her a puppy: 'Have just been taught the way to a woman's heart: buy her a puppy-dog, a white fluffy one, stumbley, enervated. Price about thirty-five shillings.'[12] He stuffed the puppy under his overcoat, knocked on the door of the Woodwards' home in Parson's Green and presented the creature to her. In the first flush of love he was given to such impulses. The strength of his feelings daunted him. His dilemma was that the more urgently he felt, the less able he seemed to put his feelings into words. 'Love:' he wrote in the journal, 'painfully inexpressible. And then I erase this seeing that the loveliness of love in this lies, that it cannot be expressed, and remaining within, causes weird pain, something like the pain of existing negatively or creatively being blotted out in death.'[13]

Emotional commitment, it seemed to Barker, had something in common with poetry. While insincerity in either was only too readily and facilely expressed, profundity was more likely to render one inarticulate. This was never truer than when attempting to express sentiment physically through sex, which, like literary style, appeared to be subject to a law of diminishing returns: 'Things expressible', he wrote, 'are invariably minor, sometimes wearing about them, though, the colouration of inexpressibles ... Into the kiss we strain to infuse the inexpressible: what is actually infused is not the love but the minor animular sexual evaluation, but tinged with the frictional pain of inexpressible love which knows it is inexpressible.' Even as he and Jessie strove to infuse mutual passion into their kissing, they found themselves distracted by the mere performance of the kiss.

From the adolescent standpoint an age gap of four years is considerable. In the early months of their acquaintance Jessie had an authority over the fifteen-year-old George which she shared with Monica. As he grew in inches and confidence, however, her authority declined, while his strengthened. To begin with the two of them moved about in a group with Monica and Jessie's sister Kit. Imperceptibly, as their relationship intensified, they detached themselves to form a couple. Progressively it became obvious to George that Jessie's surface placidity hid insecurity, even neurosis. The recognition provoked concern and then guilt. His notion of femininity had been partially based on what he knew of his sisters Olga and Eileen, both of whom were markedly self-sufficient. Jessie, by contrast, was inclined at moments of temperamental weakness to flaunt her vulnerability; she was prone to bouts of almost hysterical recrimination. The display incited in George a precocious and unwelcome sensation of responsibility. His compassion was stirred and, along with it, his conscience. He was disposed to feel contrite even when he had done no wrong.

Yet, even as he struggled with these unwelcome aspects of their relationship, George knew that Jessie completed him. 'The hand of God', he soon wrote, 'has descended upon me and drawn me from the roots of my youth. Of these roots there are five tentacles: my mother and my friend, my divine mistress, poetry and security. From the third issue paroxymal spasms of pain, and red blood. I am reborn, with indelible memories impressed upon my renewed body.'[14] As the initial blaze of mutual feeling softened to familiarity and affection, Jessie learned to call George 'Gran', an abbreviation of his middle name, while he converted 'Jessie' into the mellifluous 'Jessica'.

Above all, Jessica was serious. She had firm, upright handwriting and firm, upright principles. Her lean composure hid both nervous tension and taut self-control. Her piety, too, was a foil to George's habitual irreverence. Jessica's upbringing had inculcated in her a severe and disciplined view of the faith. The Woodwards had a strong respect for days of obligation, fixed habits of prayer and devotion and a literal and unyielding adherence to doctrine, although they also had fun occasionally. They owned a parrot, brought back by a family friend from East Africa. Because the bird was eloquent and would sometimes speak out of turn they named it 'George'. But such levity had its limits in a house where respectable and provident attitudes went hand in hand with devoutness of a kind scarcely known among the Barkers. The Woodwards were keen on duty and Jessica would always honour hers. She would tolerate and perhaps reclaim – even pray for – those among her acquaintance who were more relaxed or accommodating of weakness, including dedicated young poets. She regarded George's poetry as a vocation to be adhered to with the intensity of faith. 'Don't', she wrote to him, 'let a thought escape.'[15]

Because he had three older sisters who doted on him, George had learned to take female affection for granted. Because he had a younger brother who had always looked up to him, he learned to protect men. When not with Jessica, George was with his brother Kit, with whom he shared an enthusiasm for motor racing. During the autumn and winter of 1928 the boys spent their Saturday afternoons at the famous Brooklands circuit near Weybridge in Surrey, where they would hang around the pits. On one occasion, after a race, George persuaded the pit hands to let him take to the wheel. Many years later, in a mood of characteristic hyperbole, he would claim to have beaten the current track record. Whether this was true or not, both brothers became seriously obsessed with cars. Soon the innards of the internal combustion engine were as well known to them as the contents of the missal. To George the complicated workings of cars became sources of fascination similar to the complicated workings of poems. He was at Brooklands when Sir Henry Burton, driving for the Bentley team, was burnt on the arm from his car's exhaust, later dying when complications set in. He scoured the newspapers for details of foreign races, noting, for example, that on Sunday, 9 September, Louis Chiron won the Gran Premio d'Italia in three hours, forty-five minutes, driving a Bugatti T35C. Both brothers followed the fortunes of individual drivers keenly.

On Tuesday, 26 February 1929 George was sixteen. The Barker family gathered in Ladbroke Grove to celebrate: Kit, Mo, Eileen and the now-married Olga. George's pride was his present from Pa, a 300cc Zenith motorcycle, gleaming with chrome. After the party he drove it up Ladbroke Grove to the crossroads at Notting Hill Gate. At the junction a lorry was turning left. George drove the Zenith straight underneath its back axle. He was brought home with blood streaming down him and laid in the largest bed in the flat, a four-poster with curtains. Fifty years later Kit recalled his brother's screams: 'pure unspeakable agony' for George, he wrote, 'and for us'.

In the novella *Alanna Autumnal*, the accident appears in an altered form with the poet-protagonist as pure victim. As he is crossing the road, a motorcycle knocks him down and into an oncoming lorry. He opens his eyes in hospital to find himself surrounded by a policeman, a doctor and a tall girl. The girl is called Rose Elliot, but she strongly resembles Jessica. She loves the stricken pedestrian, but tells him that he is not nearly optimistic enough. 'Optimistic about what?' he enquires. Her looks are 'Botticellian' and draw him irresistibly. She suspects him of being homosexual. 'You use your hands so much', she remarks, 'like a girl.'[16]

The Barker family physician, Dr Abrahams, lived opposite at 170 Ladbroke Grove. He prescribed 'the bluestone remedy', an agonising procedure which involved bathing George's wounds in a solution of copper sulphate to cleanse them from tar, which had infiltrated from the still wet tar blocks. The treatment was followed by several months in bed. Big Mumma nursed him as he spent his days reading, sketching and improving his handwriting. The reading led him outwards from the core of interests which Father Dale-Roberts had laid down: through Italian history, to theology, art history and modern poetry. The sketching was mainly in pen and ink, a medium in which he developed a flowing linear style. The handwriting was italic. Hitherto, George had written a bold, copperplate hand; now he borrowed a book on Renaissance calligraphy from the library and painstakingly copied the characters.

After he had recovered, he went to the Victoria and Albert Museum's library: 'Draughts from the windows. Opposite me two female ginks copying photographs in watercolours. Of course, as they have thousands of times before, the attendants collaborate to disregard me. I have sat sketching here from half past two (it is now ten minutes to four) waiting for Van Gogh's Letters.'[17]

Grandma Taaffe arrived from Drogheda at this point. George spent his days in the library and when he got home there she would be 'sewing through her string-fixed spectacles'. In the silence he sat at the dark mahogany table, filling in the journal entry for the day with 'this pen, my new fountain'. In the kitchen Kit surreptitiously noted down their grandmother's oddities of speech: 'You do have a queer lot of walking to do, Be Dad'; 'A fiddler is that what I am?'; 'You take a long time to be sure with your breakfast.'[18] The flat was now too small for them all, so Pa moved the family out to West Ealing, where he would have a garden again.

The following February, on his seventeenth birthday, George sat in the branches of a tree reading his present from Monica: Edith Sitwell's critical study *Alexander Pope*, which had just appeared. He decided he liked neither Sitwell nor Pope, whom he compared to a lady and gentleman sitting down to tea. Besides, Pope misused the caesura. The antipathy George felt focused his mind on the kind of poetry he did like: 'I like poetry to be dirty with earthly mould, finger marks on it, and its napkin (if I may say so) not quite deodorised.'[19] Pope and Sitwell, in their different ways, proved too delicate for him. He preferred Paul Verlaine (read, presumably, in translation) who seemed to possess by contrast all the gusto of 'a healthy aromatic belch after a garish dinner'. He was increasingly convinced that, if he was to be a poet, he would belong to no defined school. Pope's neoclassicism was suspect, but so too was Shelley's Romanticism, and Barker knew by now that he wanted his own writing to be neither. 'Unless you're very careful you step straight out onto that elaborate dangerous road marked Romantic: along which may go only young men with Plato in their pockets, and Rome at the road end. Avoid this as you would chocolate, it makes the teeth ache.'

Since Kit had now also left school, the brothers spent a lot of time together. They developed complementary interests. George was practising odes, to write which was 'like handling stout clay. Press and turn and erect and erase and produce', while Kit was painting. Now Kit started to write poetry and George to paint and to draw. One morning, in a little over a quarter of an hour, he painted Salome: 'oval motif, her arms rotating, and the abstract idea of dancing as a background'.[20] The brothers set up a pottery in the garden shed. Both had recently discovered the novels of D.H. Lawrence and they devised a logo of a stylised phoenix rising from some equally stylised flames, which they stamped on the base of their pots. They called the enterprise the Phoenix Pottery.[21]

For all his inventiveness and intelligence, there was something inhibited and cautious about Kit. He was also painfully dependent, as younger brothers often are, on the approbation of his older sibling. The dependence brought out in George a solicitude and gentleness which eventually became a matter of habit in his demeanour towards younger men, especially those not gifted with his own looks and confidence. At fourteen, Kit went down with diphtheria and lay at death's door for three months while Big Mumma again nursed, hovering anxiously over him. The bout weakened his eyesight, obliging him to wear glasses permanently. When he recovered Mumma took him to Ireland. Kit was pious, with a literalness that he later shook off and, when not in the company of the far brasher George, he could be cripplingly timid. He was, for instance, too self-conscious to be able to enter a shop alone. Because of the family's frequent moves, as well as his own intermittent bouts of illness, his formal education was even more backward than George's. George guided his reading, steering him in directions which were constructive and useful to them both.

Even in its more boisterous moments, their relationship was one of protectiveness on the one hand, and loyalty on the other. In *Alanna Autumnal* George draws on Kit to create a composite character called Charles:

> He, my only friend, is overgrown with gentleness and kindness, speaks quietly with reticence. He is too dubious about himself, unsure whether he can legally be of enough account to breathe the air like other men. I feel half responsible for him because physically he looks as unprepossessing as a scarecrow, lanky, badly dressed; hurtfully self-conscious, mentally as callous as a pig; undeveloped, stunted emotionally from hanging on his mother.[22]

By day George supported himself with a series of menial jobs. One was with a firm in the Clerkenwell Road designing wallpaper. For a company in Holborn he put his technical knowhow to good use by testing radio transformers. Then, for months, he worked in a garage. Finally, he was taken on by the Janus Press, whose office was in the basement at 44 Great Russell Street, opposite the main entrance to the British Museum.[23] The press had recently been established by Desmond Harmsworth as an outlet for the works of Percy Wyndham Lewis, whose design of a Janus head appeared at the top of its notepaper. Harmsworth came and went, speaking, according to Barker, 'with so aristocratic an enunciation that I cannot easily follow his meaning. He trails behind him an atrophied and dirty poodle.' Barker was both 'office boy and char lady' and delivered books that he would have preferred to have written himself. Otherwise, 'we drink cups of tea, swear, and ignorantly discuss Mr Wyndham Lewis, whose genius presides over the establishment, as ubiquitously as our trade mark, by him drawn, stands at the head of all our stationery'.[24]

It was the sort of job that might have suited him, but like the others it did not last. Too often the buses carrying him to his places of employment passed the Corinthian portico of the National Gallery; rather than continuing, he would hop off to inspect Tintoretto's *The Birth of the Milky Way*, Holbein's portrait of Christina of Denmark, or – more usually – stand entranced before the Demidoff Altarpiece by the mannerist Venetian painter Carlo Crivelli (c. 1457–93), whose visions of heavenly grace, with their veined marble columns and swags of fruit, delicately observed brocades and attention to line, delighted him. He adopted Crivelli as his special master, buying Monica a reproduction of *Virgin Enthroned with Child and Saints* (1491), in which the Madonna sits beatified between the figures of Sts Francis and Sebastian.

George's enthusiasms in art and sport were proving complementary. When, in 1932, Tazio Nuvolari won the Targio Florio in an Alfa Romeo Tipo B 'P3', George and Kit took to sketching Alfa Romeos in the margins of their notebooks. Appropriately, both favoured schools of modern art in which symmetry of form was combined with intimations of physical impetus and power. Having inherited from Pa an appreciation of boxing and athletics, George in particular was drawn to styles of representation in which stasis was wrested from the kinesis of mechanical or human movement. He developed a passion for the compact, muscled torsos of the contemporary Serbian sculptor Ivan Mestrović. His eye was also caught by *Boxers*, a sculpture by the Ukranian Alexander Archipenko, in which the boxers' movements were rendered in cubic and ovoid shapes. Archipenko's geometric, almost robotic forms became part of a private aesthetic programme, rigorously pursued. In his own drawing, George developed a style of portraiture in which face and body, often elongated, were simplified into a precise and elegant confluence of lines, almost in the manner of the vorticist, Wyndham Lewis.

George's career prospects were not helped by his style of dress at the time, which was like a burlesque of Lewis himself. He became a proletarian dandy, wearing an outlandish black cape over his shoulders and a Spanish hat with a monstrously large brim over his eyes. He resembled, as he later remembered, a cross between Don Quixote and the silhouette on Sandeman port advertisements. When he wore this outfit to work he was summoned into the office and brusquely informed that the firm had no intention of continuing to employ someone who looked like an out-of-work violinist.[25] He was sacked.

In between jobs, he spent the days gloomily in Ealing. 'First and foremost,' he wrote, 'I pretend to be a writer, to be capable of putting a sentence together so that it translates a similar sentence inside me from feeling into words: and yet most of the days unravel doing odd jobs about the house, painting bad pictures, reading, generally avoiding any contact with pen or typewriter and diving out of sight of any considerable thought.' To focus his mind, he opened a new notebook with suggestions for poetic method. 'The definite and concrete is better than the indefinite and abstract,' he wrote. 'There are no such things as sentences in a poem; the poem is one, and cannot be subdivided into parts.' He noted the phonetic qualities of consonants and copied out sentences from Robert Graves's and Laura Riding's *A Survey of Modernist Verse*. Ominously he added, 'A long word is really always more musical and has usually such sweet changes of sounds in it (which all run into one another). For this I prefer it.'[26] In his diary he was more brutal: 'I must contract elephantiasis, or swelling of the word glands.' Then doubt assailed him. 'I am', he wrote, 'a Saxophone made by Stradivarius.'[27]

The days were diverted by a series of practical jokes devised by Mumma at Pa's expense. Pa adored sago puddings and, when especially irked, she would bake him one, hiding Olga's pearls in it so that he choked. Once, when he was out, she placed one of his stuffed crocodiles from the Sudan upright in the lavatory with a light bulb stuck in its head. When he switched on the light, he got the shock she felt he deserved. Pa withdrew into hauteur.

At night George went for walks and brooded: 'The night clouds are frigid and brittle in the sky and the winds snap like hounds. I've walked down the road to purchase cigarettes, an apple in each pocket to get me there. One for going and the other for the return. Cold cold my girl. To eat them was like biting balls of ice or taking the curved quarter of this Janus moon . . .' A few years before he had written in his diary, 'Death is the perianth of the seventy year stem.' Now, coming up to his eighteenth birthday, he recorded 'a tired attempt at suicide. God knows why. Even so, it was unspirited [sic] and very clumsy. I came up spluttering like a babe in a tub.'[28] It was the first of several desultory attempts, motivated less by misery than by morbidity. He was torn between a literary fascination with the theme of death and excitement at the possibilities of life. His sister Eileen had now married the photographic journalist Phillip Fletcher Jackson, whose second love was cricket but who spent much of the time abroad. When, in 1930, their son John, the Barkers' first grandchild, was born, they brought the baby to West Ealing, where George found himself deeply moved by his nephew's cries. 'Most harrowing thing in the world', he jotted in his notebook, 'to hear a healthy baby awaken.'[29]

Monica, meanwhile, had grown into a slender brunette with large eyes and full lips perpetually parted. She wore her hair short, with a slight fringe across her forehead and a curl at the cheek. George sketched her in profile, in pen and ink and then in words: 'Alanna has a somnolent mouth, the lips always separated, the muscles surrounding them slack.'[30] Alone among the girls, she possessed something of Kit's insecurity. Alone, too, she seemed to look to her men not simply to adore, but to protect her. George sheltered her, while she helped with his work, typing his poems, suggesting outlets of publication. It was Mo who, in the early days, kept George's belief in himself going, managing his career. She sent his poems to Gollancz, who promptly returned them. They sat dejectedly side by side in a café on the evening of that 'brumally dreary day'.

Then, at nineteen, Barker lost his religion. He sat outside the Oratory and, counting seventy female worshippers to every male, 'informally seceded from the Roman Catholic faith'.[31] With more seriousness, he noted in his diary, 'For three hours today burned my mind trying to resolve some kind of a belief in an infallible overhead divinity such as I was educated to believe in. Hopeless, hopeless it would be for me to repeat here all the uncertainties and incredulities that in those three hours seared across me. You may possibly obtain some idea if I say that when I was clear again I found I was in Kensington, from where we moved our home some six months ago.'[32]

As George's belief in religion dwindled, his interest in politics grew. He had already read Wyndham Lewis's defence of autocracy, *The Art of Being Ruled*. In February 1931, when it appeared, he borrowed from the library Lewis's apologia for German Socialism, *Hitler*. It was a culpably naïve book that portrayed the leader of the Nazis as a man of peace. 'The idea, in short, of Germany being a military menace can be entirely dismissed from the most apprehensive mind,' Lewis had written. Hitler was 'a truly socialist prophet – an armed socialist prophet – his originality lies in that'. Lewis had not seen the danger in Hitler's anti-Semitism, which he presented as a 'red herring'. He had, however, been persuaded of the cohesive potential of race, as opposed to class, consciousness. 'What I think it is safe to confirm', he concluded, 'is that Race, used as a propagandist engine, must tend to simplify and to concentrate. It promises political unity, at all events. It would, if followed out, draw people together.'[33] Barker saw the instability of Lewis's case; he was, for all that, more taken with Lewis's arguments than with those of the international socialists. 'Wyndham Lewis's Hitler:' he opened a paragraph in his journal. 'His convictions – for how long convictions? – suit me better than Mr Bronowski's or any of the bellicose constituents who rave their various ravings about Cosmopolitan Socialism and such like ramps. A nation is a nation, as homogenous and impossible of coalescence as a world. Foreign, I hope, will be valid coin for a number of years to come.'[34] This preference was phrased ambivalently and did not last. Two years later, with the burning of the Reichstag and Hitler's election as chancellor, Barker came to his senses. In 1983 he recalled his moment of political confusion, though he put back the whole experience by three years: 'I remember when I was fifteen reading a book on National Socialism and thinking, this is exactly what Europe needs, and then at seventeen realizing that I had only just missed something that would give one the heeby-jeebies.'[35]

By 1931 Barker was tiring of London, where he had lived for as long as he could remember. When his jobs would let him, he got out. There were expeditions to Richmond Park, where he and Jessica walked among the deer, or lolled on the grass, reading and talking. Because Jessica was older, because her piety endowed everything with a sense of moral responsibility, in retrospect these outings came to seem innocent. They were not. It was in Richmond Park that George took Jessica's virginity: 'I remember the gradual breaching of the hymeneal barrier, the edges coarse like an ice hole with its red board saying Danger, which was the blood that first baptized me in Adam's Sin.'[36] The doctrine of original sin dictates, too, the tone of his account in 'The True Confession':

> O long-haired virgin by my tree
>   Among whose forks hung enraged
> A sexual passion not assuaged
>   By you, its victim – knee to knee,
> Locked sweating in the muscled dark
>   Lovers, as new as we were, spill
> The child on grass in Richmond Park,
>   The cemetery of Richmond Hill.[37]

During summer months there were longer expeditions upriver. In *Alanna Autumnal* the narrator goes down to Shiplake, near Henley, to stay with Charles and his parents. In reality Shiplake was Sonning, where Pa had the use of a boat, a splendid skiff as Kit remembered it, named *Ivy*.[38] At weekends hampers were packed with cuts of chicken, veal in aspic and white wine. The family drove down to Surrey in two cars, Kit at the wheel of 'a very elegant Fiat saloon car with pale grey velvet upholstery'. From the boat George's sisters dived into the Thames, 'clumsy in bathing costumes'.[39] Later, in the darkest moments of the Second World War, George would recall these weekends as one long, enchanted idyll, untainted by political foreboding. As the girls had kissed their menfolk, he would fancifully imagine, 'History guffawed in a rosebush. O what a warning – If only we had known, if only we had known!' It was here that Monica met her husband-to-be, William Henry Humble, whom she called Bill. He worked as an accountant in the Ministry of Food and had two brothers who were to migrate to Canada and found Humble Oil. As a partner for Monica, he seemed solid enough, if uninspiring. In *Alanna Autumnal* brother and sister linger over their photograph album:

'There's me,' she says, showing me a snapshot of herself in a dark bathing costume, taken about two years ago near a swimming pool along the river. She walked up laughing straight into the face of the camera, her arms extended in front of her as if to upset the perspective of the picture or the attention of the photographer. But she failed, the snapshot showed her laughing head, the tiny beads of water clinging to her hair, the paraseteline texture of her skin. 'That's me at that place on the Thames, you remember the place on the Thames, Edward.' 'Yes, I remember. We never went swimming together, Alanna, did we. No, we never went swimming together. We shall have to go together one day, Alanna, shan't we.' But she does not hear me, she looks casually at the snapshots of the family. They might be a blank for all the expression she evinces.[40]

At Sonning, abandoning the girls to their men, George and Kit rowed downstream to the island, or up tempting tributaries. In *Alanna Autumnal* their counterparts frighten idling trout by holding large stones menacingly over the swiftly moving current. Then they tether the boat and loll on the bank for hours, reading.

Their reading remained voracious. George's taste for traditional verse had reconciled itself with modernity when, shortly after its first appearance in 1930, he had discovered T.S. Eliot's 'Ash Wednesday' with its image of a 'Lady of silences / Calm and distressed / Torn and most whole'. It was, then, possible to be religious and contemporary. Foremost in Barker's mind at that period, however, was Blake. 'Blake finds my weakness every time. The man not only wrote like an angel; he was an angel.' On Sunday, 12 April 1931, Barker himself noted a visitation, much like an archangel painted by Carlo Crivelli, looming over the river bank:

> Today I lay on a bank of Thames at Sonning oh the sun was shining too goldenly and I so lay that I could see only milkancreamy clouds which were tiny and puffing, companion to the sun, was revealed the vision of an angel with a countenance which considered me sweetly; and he was of such marvellous size, as he came down like water pouring from a vase, that he could gather the biggest trees into his hands like flowers and touch me as I would touch the biggest bird of paradise.[41]

This surrealist hyperbole catches the excitement felt by many, not just the Barker brothers, on Blake's recent re-emergence as a figure of literary importance. Though Blake's verse had memorably been edited at the beginning of the century by William Rossetti and W.B. Yeats, it was still not familiar to the reading public at large. Not until 1927, with Geoffrey Keynes's Nonesuch edition, did his more hermetic and suggestive work become known, even to scholars. In 1931 George and Kit were bowled over by the mysterious poem 'The Mental Traveller' with its vision of the corrosive and self-renewing force of love:

> And if the Babe is born a Boy
> He's given to a Woman Old,
> Who nails him down upon a rock,
> Catches his shrieks in cups of gold . . .

> Till he becomes a bleeding youth,
> And she becomes a Virgin bright;
> Then he rends up his Manacles
> And binds her down to his delight.[42]

Blake was far from being George and Kit's only literary enthusiasm that summer. In 1931 *Son of Woman*, John Middleton Murry's pioneering biographical study of D.H. Lawrence, was published. Reading Murry, the Barker brothers were directed less to Lawrence the novelist than to Lawrence the essayist. All summer they were obsessed with the ethical-cum-sexual sermon *Fantasia of the Unconscious*, which Murry thought Lawrence's greatest book. Barker could only read a chapter at a time: 'terrible, dark stunning inspissated genius'.[43] What was it that spoke to him? Was it Lawrence's sexual mysticism or his anti-academic attitude ('Let all schools be closed down at once')? Was it his conviction that by temperament and biology the two sexes are poles apart ('Every bit, every cell in a boy is male, every cell is female in a woman')?

Perhaps it was all these elements. And yet Barker's temporary adherence to Lawrence's dogmatic philosophy only really makes sense if you recognise that he came to his work after reading Murry first. Murry had known Lawrence, who had once attempted to convert him to his utopian outlook and sexual philosophy. Murry had resisted and *Son of Woman*, an act both of homage and atonement, is a testimony both to the friendship and to the failure. It portrays a man impaled on the cross of his own sexuality. In 1916 Murry and Katherine Mansfield had spent a few difficult months attempting to live as neighbours of Lawrence and his German wife Frieda at Zennor in north Corwall. The Lawrence they came to know there colours the whole of Murry's study: a tormented individual, hounded by feelings of personal inadequacy and a dread of official persecution by authorities suspicious of Frieda's nationality. The frustration vented itself in rages:

> Katherine and I were completely ignorant of the nature of the struggle which was devouring him like a disease. We saw, and felt on our pulses, only the incredible mingling of love and hatred that was in him. He seemed to us like a man possessed now by an angel, now by a devil. Both were beyond our comprehension. But to the angel we responded; the devil tortured us beyond endurance. It was painful to see him so transformed and transfigured by the paroxysms of murderous hatred of his wife, of us, of all mankind, that sweep over him. They would leave him white, bowed and shuddering.[44]

For Barker, Murry's writing evidently hit a nerve. In the early 1930s Murry was at the height of his influence as a leading Marxist critic and editor of the leading review, the *Adelphi*. Two years later, in *Alanna Autumnal,* George was to transform him into a literary panjandrum called Mr Levison, '("England's premier critic of pure literature" – Daily Press)'. Levision is 'a man invigorated with a splendid catholic philosophy, a philosophy which hit me like a sexual projectile. I mean that against it I could raise no barricades, because, somehow, I knew that to experience it – as distinct from experiencing the philosophies of other men – must be terrifically to my betterment as a unit in contemporary literature.'[45] As soon as George had finished reading *Son of Woman*, he entered a reminder to himself in his journal: 'I intend to write to M. It's simply silly to fling a fandango in the extremities of West Ealing, pathetically desolate and isolate.'

So, once Monica had typed out extracts from the journal, he sent them off to Murry at his country house, the Old Rectory at Larling in Suffolk. The protagonist of *Alanna Autumnal* risks a similar overture, suffering in the process an agony of anticipation: 'I expect him any day to tell me I am a presumptuous fool.' Mr Levison, however, is merciful and invites him down to stay with him near Diss in Norfolk, whither he is to travel 'on the 2.34 from Liverpool Street'.

In the novella Mr Levison develops a cough and the visit is postponed. In life the arrangements proceeded more smoothly. Murry invited Barker to tea with Sir Richard Rees, proprietor of the *Adelphi*, at four o'clock on Saturday, 19 March 1932, at the magazine's offices in Bloomsbury Street.[46] Murry was evidently courteous, though the contrast between the 'sexual projectile' George had been expecting and the cerebral figure whom he encountered that afternoon seems to have been very painful. Was this the man, Barker later wondered, who had wrestled with Lawrence on the clifftop at Zennor? Was this the visionary who had founded the *Adelphi* (meaning 'brothers') to spread Lawrence's ideals of fraternity and honesty among all men? Asked, fifty years later, what Murry had been like, the septuagenarian Barker would growl back, 'Nothing between his legs!'

But if the man was a disappointment, the tea was more palatable. It included bread, butter and blackcurrant jam, which strayed on to a copy of Michael Roberts's anthology of modern verse, *New Signatures*, which Murry handed to his young guest, commissioning a review.[47] In the review he was asked to combine Roberts's book with F.R Leavis's recent critical study *New Bearings in English Poetry*. Both books represented turning points in modern verse: one in its dissemination, the other in its academic reception. Roberts's anthology, in particular, had raised a banner for the most innovative of recent poetry, including that of Eliot, W.H. Auden and William Empson. When Barker's piece appeared in the June issue, however, it carried a rider from Murry: 'Mr

Barker is almost as much younger than the authors of *New Signatures* as I am older than they. Therefore I speak my word.' The reason was that Barker had gratuitously insulted Eliot, who, he said, 'was not a contemporary. He is concerned with problems which have mistakenly entered this century rather than oblivion.' He had just as emphatically written off the major part of Roberts's contributors, their work being described as 'half afraid of itself outside Empson's half-a-dozen pages'.[48]

That summer Barker decided his own poetry should read like modernised Blake. Shortly after meeting Murry he wrote 'Octalogue of Emotions', dedicated to Murry and to Jessica, and typed out by Monica. It bore the one-off imprint of the February Press, another alias for George himself and Kit and deriving from the month in which each had his birthday. It began with an evocation of the desolation after the First World War and its imagery drew on motor racing. In lines 13–23 the 'sweetheart' described could be either a car or its driver. In either case he resembled one of Archipenko's figures, half-man and half-machine:

>After all the tears that fell
>into patriotic mud;
>The Historical patrimonial tears,
>And the first tears of God –
>
>It appears
>That the years
>must be two thousand of God's tears for us –
>All that you have to do (must do, will do)
>Will expedite your tears, for which,
>Encasing the earth, observe
>Our bright cosmic and cosmetic handkerchief
>Bespread over all.
>
>   ii
>
>Chipping automobile gears
>my sweetheart expedites the years,
>Wearing beneath his overalls
>an handkerchief of rod and balls.
>
>   With which he can:
>Erase spiritual blemishes, incited upon
>His immobile body by the spinning gearteeth
>which

> Grip into him, tearing
> off divine shining skin,
> (have a banana).[49]

The 'Octologue' negotiated through various changes of gear towards a vision of the future, before looping back in a Blakeian cycle. An act of robotic mating, similar to that which concluded *R.U.R.*, the famous Futurist play of 1923 by the brothers Čapek, was then described. At the end of the sequence the poet's mind, 'Mental Traveller'-like, re-entered itself.

After Barker's review had appeared, Murry decided that Barker and Roberts must meet. He sent a letter of introduction to Roberts, who told Barker to call on him. Poet, mountaineer, editor, physicist, Roberts was an almost iconic figure to the new generation of the 1930s, an embodiment of what Auden was to call 'The Truly Strong Man'. After graduating in maths from Cambridge, he had taught science in Newcastle, while building up a steady reputation as a propagandist for all that was most virile in contemporary politics and art. Recently he had moved to London, where he was senior mathematics master at the Mercers School in Barnard's Inn, off Holborn (he was later to be sacked for his unorthodox religious opinions). The two men were to meet in a starkly furnished room above Fitzroy Square. Barker arrived first. A quarter of a century later, he would recall his nervousness as he waited:

> I sat for a long while. Then I got up, looked over the banisters, and saw a sweatered mountaineer ascending the staircase. This immensely impressive figure carried alpenstocks and spears and snowshoes and a whole paraphernalia of rods and instruments. When he entered the empty – or almost empty – room, I gave him a little note and he kindly gave me a bowl of macaroons. 'Just sit and eat those macaroons and listen to these', he said, and handed me some records. They were the quartets of Beethoven. (I tried to write a poem about this occasion)... 'I'm going to change,' he said. When he reappeared he was disguised as a literary physicist. 'Now let's talk', he began, and proceeded to do so for hours and I sat so bemused that I could neither speak nor hear a word. I was rendered invisible, inaudible and delighted by a bespectacled magician with a snake in his mouth. For I have never before and have not often since witnessed the glacial machine of transfigurations, the masculine intelligence, in its most brilliant operations. And in spite of or because of the fact that I have never been able to recall one word or idea that he uttered, I know that his act of intellectual callisthenics left me with one very clear recollection: this was the ease and grace with which he forgave me for being there.[50]

'BALTHUS! PURE BALTHUS!'

The Roberts depicted in this passage seems be a spiritual guide reminiscent of Father Dale-Roberts of the Oratory. Prophetically for Barker's later attitudes, one notices that the human intelligence at its most agile is defined as male. Roberts is a secular guide who leaves the young Barker spellbound, unable to reply, much as the middle-aged Barker was to leave others. The late Beethoven quartets were the musical equivalent, in their clarity and economy, of the poetry that Roberts most admired. Barker was not yet equal to the monologue on politics, physics and the state of poetry with which he was confronted. When his own volume, *Thirty Preliminary Poems*, appeared the following year, it contained a poem entitled 'On First Hearing Beethoven'. The theme was not original; Stephen Spender's *Poems* of that same year had included one called 'Beethoven's Death Mask'.[51] Barker's, however, said as much about Roberts as about Beethoven, or rather about his listening to Roberts while pretending to listen to Beethoven's music:

> I hear, in dense silence founded,
> By supernal sound, the immense harmonics like mountains
> Intensely imbedded in man.[52]

For all that, Roberts was sufficiently impressed with Barker to give him a valuable introduction. If it was politics and literature he was after, he had better investigate a radical bookshop which had just been established round the corner in Bloomsbury by a young man called David Archer. Barker took down the address, and wrote a letter introducing himself. He received a reply inviting him to call any afternoon at 4 Parton Street.

CHAPTER 4

'HAND ME THAT HAMMER'

In 1932 Parton Street was a narrow road connecting Southampton Row with Red Lion Square. The houses had peeling Georgian façades and the atmosphere was bohemian and subversive. On the south side Number 1 housed the Arts Café, otherwise known as Meg's Café, where young and penniless writers gathered to share the latest literary and political gossip. Diagonally opposite and adjoining Red Lion Square was Number 2 where, at the offices of the publishing firm John Wishart, the 35-year-old Marxist Edgell Rickword, former editor of the influential *Calendar of Modern Letters*, published a radical list which that year featured amongst other books Nancy Cunard's revolutionary anthology of black writing, *Negro*. Next door, Number 4 was shared. On the top floor were the headquarters of the Promethean Society, founded in 1930 after an appeal entitled 'The Revolt of Youth' in the magazine *Everyman* had elicited an encouraging response from those interested in combating 'the humbug and hypocrisy, the muddle and inertia that everywhere surround us today'.[1] The society had since dedicated itself to spreading the stolen fire of international socialism, sexual well-being and the works of D.H. Lawrence. Its discussion groups covered political and economic affairs, peace and sexology. 'So long as sex is regarded as, at best, a necessary evil,' ran the manifesto of the sexology group, 'we are concerned that the work of rationalizing sex is only beginning, and that it is our very urgent duty to take part in that work.' Barker found the Protheans humourless: 'There was a certain way of talking and dressing', he said later, 'that informed one instantly that one was in the company of somebody who believed that the moon was made of green cheese and that we were all allowed to fuck one another with impunity.'[2] Every month the society published the magazine *The Twentieth Century*, price one shilling, between arresting blood-red covers. Edited by Jon Randell Evans with Hugh Gordon Porteus as literary editor, it interspersed discussions of political affairs with literature, and was distributed on the ground floor in Archer's bookshop.

The Parton Street Bookshop was Barker's port of entry into literary London, and twenty-three years later, in the pages of John Lehmann's *London Magazine*, he paid it tribute.[3] The only son of a retired general from Castle Eaton in Wiltshire, David Archer was twenty-five and had come down from Cambridge three years earlier. He was pallid, slender and invariably dressed in a suit. As the result of a riding accident suffered by his mother when pregnant, he had a withered left arm, but he bore this disability stoically, carrying piles of books with the arm to offset its effect. His practical idealism permeated the shop. On the pavement outside, next to a packing case full of second-hand books, stood racks displaying the *Daily Worker*, *Soviet Weekly* and various radical publications of the New Left Book Club in yellow dust jackets. Around the walls hung official Soviet posters depicting workers in fields of ripe wheat. A large central table was devoted to volumes specially recommended for their political content. The back of the premises acted as a lending library, to which subscribers paid five shillings a year. There was a large room upstairs where Archer sometimes held parties, after which hungover guests would sleep in the bedrooms on the second floor, which were furnished with mattresses and packing cases. Here also Archer would provide free accommodation for short periods to homeless artists and writers. Among the short-term residents was the runaway schoolboy Esmond Romilly, who briefly made the shop notorious by editing from its address the subversive news-sheet *Out of Bounds*, aimed at other runaways. According to Barker, the temporary guests came and went 'like a furious rotation of tiger-moths'. Generosity was Archer's gift, but he possessed no commercial sense whatever and had only the vaguest idea about stocktaking or book-keeping. When money ran out, he would apply for refunding to his father in Wiltshire. In reality Archer much preferred to give away books than to sell them. He had little interest in profit, choosing rather to preside over an establishment which, like Sylvia Beach's 'Shakespeare and Company' in Paris, functioned as a combined arts centre and press. More importantly, Archer's shop was a meeting ground and home-from-home for ambitious young writers, many of them were younger than himself.

The most promising of these writers, David Gascoyne, was only sixteen. He was tall, slender and intense and bristled with suppressed nervous power. Barker was immediately drawn to him by the sort of magnetism that connects older with younger brothers, or the naturally extrovert with the congenitally and hopelessly introvert. The son of a former bank manager from Teddington, Gascoyne had been educated at Salisbury Cathedral School, where he had learned to love the music of the Renaissance; he had also studied at the Regent Street Polytechnic, which he attended intermittently from 1930, two years after Barker had left it. He had been reading modern French poets voraciously in the original for a couple of years and his informed enthusiasm for contemporary writers like Paul Eluard, Tristan Tzara and Louis Aragon supplemented his delicate and precise grasp of Rimbaud and the symbolists. Gascoyne was working on a systematic study of surrealism, and had already published at his own expense a volume of poems entitled *Roman Balcony*, as well as the autobiographical novel *Opening Day*. His recent poetry, heavily influenced by the surrealists, was to be published by Archer in 1936. Its deliberately disconnected title, drawn at random from a printer's worksheet, would be *Man's Life Is This Meat*.[4]

One year older than Gascoyne was John Cornford, son of the classicist Francis Cornford and his wife Frances, poet and granddaughter of Charles Darwin. Barker remembered him as 'filthy and consumed with a ferocity of nervous energy', and always wearing sandals heavily caked in mud. In London for a few months before going up to Trinity College, Cambridge, Cornford had taken lodgings at 1 Parton Street, from where he would emerge to spend afternoons either fingering through books in the library or bowling desultory googlies at a slender actor called Alec Guinness.[5] He was already groping his way towards the Young Communist League and service to a cause which, in common with so many of his generation, he strove to reconcile with poetry. He had by this time published several poems of his own, under a Welsh pseudonym, in the *Listener*.

Charles Madge was three years older than Cornford. After a childhood spent in South Africa, Madge had studied English at Magdalene College, Cambridge, under I.A. Richards, whose view of literary criticism as a form of social experimentation had profoundly influenced him. Eventually he would become a professor of sociology; already he possessed that interest in the close monitoring of social reality which would later lead him, with Gascoyne's brief collaboration, to the foundation of the social-science unit Mass Observation in 1936. It was an emphasis and an outlook in part shared by the 28-year-old Geoffrey Grigson, newly appointed literary editor of the *Morning Post*, who had just founded the poetry magazine *New Verse* in his spare time. In it Grigson hoped to encourage a group of writers whose conception of modernism reached beyond his own impressionistic observation of daily ephemera:

> The hours of the public place.
> In the morning how the old
> Man with his nurse meets
> The child with her nurse, between
>
> The rosebed and the violas.[6]

Into the bookshop, in 1934, wandered a thin, pale youth of twenty, with a scarf round his neck and the face of a hirsute cherub. Just up from Swansea, where his father was a schoolmaster and where he himself had not much appreciated working as a cub reporter on the *South Wales Evening Post*, Dylan Thomas had already written some of his best verse and was looking for a publisher. Archer, who by that time had already published Barker, was to bring out Thomas's first volume *Eighteen Poems*, priced at three shillings and sixpence.

The talents on offer in Archer's emporium encompassed more than literature. Albert Lancaster Lloyd was a rumbustious sheep-farmer from New South Wales who, after a career aboard whaling ships, had settled in London as a freelance author and folk-singer. Desmond Hawkins was an ironmonger's son from Surrey, a keen ornithologist and a member of the Prometheans, for whom he helped to edit the literary pages of the *Twentieth Century*. The connection with the journal made Hawkins a valuable contact for Barker, who recollected him as perpetually fiddling with a pipe whilst 'explaining how he could never finish his novel because when he reached the last page the first one revolted him'. The novel was eventually to see the light of day, in 1939, as *Hawk Among the Sparrows*.

Many of Parton Street's habitués were torn between poetry and politics. Maurice Carpenter, for example, was a serious-minded youth who had escaped from the *petit-bourgeois* respectability of Caterham, in Surrey, into the arms of the communist cause. He divided his attention between urgent political organisation and – by his own account – unsuccessful attempts to find someone to go to bed with.[7] Randall Swingler, author of *Poems* (1932) and *Reconstruction* (1933), was endeavouring to consolidate a reputation as a poet while being drawn towards Marxism. To Swingler's alarm, communism threatened to throttle the poetry out of him.[8] Not all of the habitués, however, were left wing. Among the revolutionaries and radicals the diffident figure of T.E. Lawrence would sometimes slip in, ignored by the others because of his supposed fascism.

The orchestrator of this intellectual symphony was David Archer himself. As Barker was later to recall, it was Archer's insight into contemporary verse that 'helped to form the poetic opinion of a generation'. Barker cherished a memory of him as forever up a ladder, fixing shelves. When not engaged in such practical tasks, he would spend much of his time attempting to reconcile differences between his customers. Troubles of his own, however, were later to engulf him with terrible finality. From the outset Archer seemed to Barker to be doomed: an almost sacrificial figure. He would on occasions seek relief by exaggerating his own helplessness, to the extent that others sometimes suspected him of parodying his own habit of self-deprecation. No writer himself, though a perceptive reader of verse, tongue-tied and at the mercy of younger men who seldom returned his amorous devotion, Archer would vent his frustrations in a stream of upper-class euphemisms.[9] When tired after a long day's work, he would be 'vaguely ebbing'; he could also be 'vaguely wilted', or, when the going got really tough, 'vaguely shattered', or even 'vaguely squiffy'. One of the few things that rendered him 'vaguely cheerful' was his trick of hiding pound notes in boxes of matches which he would then hand out to needy young writers. As often as not, the writers regarded the boxes with courteous puzzlement, and then threw them away ignorant of their contents. Archer bore such reverses with the self-denying good humour of one whose temperament vacillated between the melancholic and the phlegmatic: 'Silly me!' He reminded Barker of a cross between Marcel Proust's Robert de Saint-Loup and P.G. Wodehouse's Bertie Wooster, though he had neither Wooster's capacity for turning bad luck into good, nor a Jeeves to help him pick up the pieces.

On a bright September morning, when Archer was feeling 'vaguely squiffy', Barker called round at Number 4, to find him up a ladder fixing a shelf. Volumes were piled up everywhere as, 'with a look of desperation and relief', Archer swivelled and said, 'Be an angel; hand me that hammer.' As he turned, Barker caught an impression of him as a man held in a perpetual posture of crucifixion. Archer drove in the nail, then took Barker across the road to Meg's Café, where he proceeded to serve coffee from behind the counter. 'There was', Barker later recalled, 'an atmosphere of industrious conspiracy and illegal enthusiasms. Mr Grigson, like a feline mandarin in the shadows, was preparing his first or second issue of new blood. A dark horse was pointed out to me as the bright hope of new poetry; he had a sad ingratiating expression and bore his responsibility with deliberation. This was Charles Madge, most gracious of poets. Somewhere else an elongated Blue Boy was preparing to live down his recently published first novel. I can never remember whether David Gascoyne really spoke only French at this time, or whether he merely happened to give this impression.'[10]

It was the end of Barker's artistic isolation. For the first time he had the company of sympathetic individuals and access to fashionable publications. In their different ways both *New Verse* and *Twentieth Century* were symptoms of an ideological restlessness which he found refreshing. Barker could not, however, wholeheartedly subscribe to the ideologies of either. As a result, the poems which he was soon contributing to both magazines were implicitly sceptical of the very value of commitment. He submitted 'Tuition to Recruits' to Desmond Hawkins, who handed it on to Hugh Gordon Porteus at the *Twentieth Century* with the comment that he found it 'very remarkable'.[11] It was a burlesque of a marching song, the rhythms of which were compared to those of a typewriter.[12] To Grigson at *New*

Verse he gave 'Coward's Song', which could well be read as a paeon to passivity:

> Tone down the soul
> Plane away the storm ploughing mountain summits
> The sum and the whole,
> The total sorrow,
> Because your soul my man is not a sphere.[13]

Even if he was ideologically chary, however, Barker was susceptible to the artistic mood. Grigson's magazine was full of a sense of urgency, of things happening, of the need for a new kind of poetry. The first phase of high Modernism associated with Eliot and Pound now seemed elitist and otiose. A new tone was required, alert to everyday reality, astringent and condensed, a demand that was not being met by the poetry establishment. The death that year of Harold Monro, who had sought to keep the Georgian candle alight in his shop at 28 Great Russell Street, several blocks to the west of the British Museum, reinforced the feeling that an era was ending. Auden's *Poems* of 1930 and Roberts's anthology had shown the way. The first issue of *New Verse* had carried a poem by Louis MacNeice, and Auden's parody of upper-middle-class self-congratulation 'I have a handsome profile / I've been to public school'. With their tricks of language, their syntactical abbreviations and air of fervent immediacy – what MacNeice five years later was to call their 'telegraphese' – Auden, Spender and their school beckoned where the Prometheans and Grigson sought to follow.

Barker's response was to follow in his own distinctive way. In September he published an article in *Twentieth Century* entitled 'Poetry and Contemporary Inertia', which played the game of radical politics very much on its own terms. Its theory was that radicalism was a substitute religion. In society a pervasive sloth was evident which might be 'very mildly religious'. In answer, poetry might act as an instrument of political conversion, in the same way in which, for previous ages, it had served as a vehicle for mystical longing:

> By the phrase contemporary inertia I designate the condition which society today is lying in, the inability to originate a decisive movement into the future. What D.H. Lawrence called a purposive step ... It seems to me that this decisive movement ... could more concordantly be accomplished if accompanied by the passionate exhortation of poetry. This can in no degree of movement mean that the obviation of social and economic troubles consists in expatiating verses concerning the

superperfection of national or international ambitions. But if it were
possible that a majority of individuals in each country could be purely
educated in the national or international ideals, and efforts which must
be expended to attain these ideals, by the consequential unanimity
of concentration, the movement into the future could be practically
accelerated ... The education of this majority entails a readjustment of
the precepts at present underlying our serious poetry. It also means that
poetry shall become a passionate and profound instrument of national
and international propaganda.[14]

Yet, for all his declared solidarity with the enthusiasms of a generation just a few years older than his own, Barker was not entirely in step. The individuality of his stance, his detachment from the mainstream of political dissent, was due in part to a feeling of social exclusion. Much as he approved of the Auden revolution, he could not fail to recognise that its exponents were mostly products of the public school and university system. Between them and him there existed a social gulf of which he was instantly conscious. Politically and artistically Auden and Spender seemed to belong to a new world; personally and socially they came from the world of the Twenties' aesthetes. It was an identification of which Auden and his friends were themselves soon to become aware. 'We were', Auden later wrote in 'Letters from Iceland',

> the tail, a sort of poor relation
> To that debauched, eccentric generation
> That grew up with their fathers at the War
> And made new glosses on the noun Amor.[15]

'My parents kept me from children who were rough,' ran the opening line of one of Spender's *Poems* of 1933. Barker was rough. Sixty-two years later, a few months before his death in 1995, Spender stressed this element of incompatibility. Auden and their friends, he then confessed, had in reality been middle-class neo-aesthetes. Auden, for example, had the personal habits of a bourgeois who always paid his bills on time. As for Barker and Thomas, 'we patronized them, but we were afraid, really, of dirty boots on the carpet'.[16] With his sensitive social antennae, Barker promptly sensed this rejection. In 1933, when asked to review Spender's *Poems* for *Twentieth Century*, he was quick to stress the unacceptability of such exclusivity. Spender's poetry was fine. His self-congratulatory, elitist clannishness was not:

We need a new mature poetry divested of smarmy verbal beauty – oh beaauuutiful [sic] young comrades – of technical knacks to seduce the peruser, of striving after expression of contemporary impurities, for example Communism, which is nowhere near its maturity today ... We need a new mature poetry, one that is born straight out of the head in its maturity, in stark nude simplicity.[17]

Such remarks expressed a growing confidence; and there was certainly a new bounce and uplift to the prose that suggested its author's improving circumstances. Barker now had the company of stimulating and energetic companions. His reputation was beginning to spread among his peers. At home, too, Pa's fortunes had taken a decisive turn for the better. Benefiting from his experience as a batman with the Coldstream Guards, Pa had been appointed butler to Gray's Inn, responsible for the dining arrangements in the college's ancient hall. On the strength of the new position, Pa and Big Mumma were moving to a large two-floor flat with basement at 19a Upper Addison Gardens in Holland Park, where there would be ample room for Grandma Taaffe. Instead of joining them, George took an attic room of his own not far away in Westbourne Terrace, meeting the rent from his salary at the Janus Press, where his hours were flexible enough for him to devote more time to his writing. He was now reviewing regularly for *Twentieth Century*. In Murry's *Adelphi* he reviewed Eliot's poetic drama *Sweeney Agonistes*, perceptively remarking that it was written 'with the coccyx of that spine, fear', and going on to remark that 'in *Sweeney Agonistes* we observe poetry dissolving into a condition of exquisite, and perfectly lucid, decay'.[18] Uniquely among the contributors to these periodicals, Barker was known invariably to deliver his copy by hand, to save the cost of postage.[19] The reviews and poems brought in little money, but their acceptance did much to encourage him.

In March 1933 George took out the manuscript of his journal, including the extracts he had already sent to Murry. It had been gathering dust under his bed, but he now sat down and edited it. He then called in at Wishart's offices, next door to Archer's shop, and offered it for publication to Edgell Rickword and his co-director Douglas Garman.[20] Both were keen, but found the text too personal. They suggested that Barker convert it into a work of fiction and provide a novelistic title. During Passion Week Archer invited George to stay with his parents down at Castle Eaton. The holiday would not only provide George with a much-needed break from the hot-house atmosphere of Parton Street, but it would also enable him to work systematically on the book. So, gratefully missing a meeting of the Prometheans at Meg's Café convened to discuss the 'future activities of the sexology group', Barker drove down to Wiltshire with Archer. The weather was fine; on the way down, he noted 'The attentive line of my own face', which 'was at intervals caught / From the sunlight in outline – the chin's framed curve, / Lips, jaw's asseveration –

on the windscreen'. The same image appeared that month in another poem called 'Narcissus'.[21]

In the garden at Castle Eaton on Palm Sunday Barker put the finishing touches to *Alanna Autumnal*. On his return to London he carried it once more to Wishart's, taking Maurice Carpenter along with him for moral support. Carpenter stood in the road outside and watched through the lattice window as Barker and Garman gesticulated wildly inside, arguing about the advance, whilst Rickword stood apart. Eventually Barker came outside to report that they had at first offered him two pounds, which he had argued up to four.[22] The book appeared in October, between light-green boards, with George's pen sketch of Monica in profile reproduced in red on the front cover. Years later Gascoyne, among others, would recall the impact both of the book's appearance and of its gaudy, euphuistic prose.[23]

Alanna Autumnal begins as a study of the self-involved temperament of its author: 'this queerly, queerly convoluted I'. The self sits in a garden (a garden like Pa's) reading Edith Sitwell's recently published study of Pope. He has poetic ambitions, is called Edward, and has a sister, Alanna, who looks at him through the window. The sister seems to be a compound of Eileen and Monica; she has Mo's solicitousness, but, like Eileen, a husband who is often absent. Alanna was one of Grandma Taaffe's Irish endearments; it also sounds a little like Eileen, while being etymologically distinct from it. It was Mo, whose birthday fell on 17 October, who was 'Autumnal'. The dates, however, are wrong for naïve autobiographical interpretation: Alanna is nineteen when the book opens, while Edward is a year older. In reality, at the time when the book is set, George was eighteen and Monica twenty-one. What the printed text gives us is a version of the truth that is less a disguise than an adjustment to the requirements of fictionalisation. Other recognisable people appear – Kit as Charles, Murry as Levison – but neither plays quite the role in the story which his prototype did in life. Levison and Edward, for instance, never meet; nor are the demands that Charles makes on Edward of quite the same order as those that Kit made on George. That is as far as autobiography goes. The book is not a record of events. It is a close observation of the ebb and flow of two temperaments, the brother's and the sister's, who address the reader in turn.

Of these voices, the sister's is the more powerful. The book has its narcissistic passages, but they are more than compensated for by this evocation of the feminine mind *in extremis*. Alanna is pregnant by her elusive husband, with a boy child they have already named Francis Edward. Confused in her abandonment, she longs for the comfort of her husband, whose reluctance to return to her is intensified by her need of him. She goes to the doctor, requesting an implement with which to perform an abortion. She acquires the whirling syringe, but does not use it. Instead, she goes to a dance hall and flirts with an attentive stranger whom she refuses to see again, regarding him as no more than a diversion from her main problem. Gradually she is driven back on an older love for Edward, who alone might comfort her. Edward, however, is apprehensive of the incest taboo, of what are termed here 'gregarious ethics'. For all that, both brother and sister are aware of one another's needs and tempted to supply them. In her fits of distraction – intensified by her dread of childbirth – husband and brother merge in the sister's mind:

> Two years ago Mother took me for a month's holiday in the hunting country, to a village named Amney Crucis, in Wiltshire. I often saw the hunt in galloping pursuit: and once was shown a worn-out crochety mare, kept in a stall at the bottom of the field: she was with foal, her stomach dropping almost to the ground. 'She won't fall for a month,' the farmer said, 'and when she do she aint going to like it.' The mare lifted her nervous head and shoved her nozzle into his hand: he fondled it. They are queer people, those who care for horses. Where is there a man's hand to fondle me, Edward, where! I only ask for the trick all men have, of making danger look safe, I know that not even he who is gone, could, now he is needed, save me: nor Edward: neither of them, I know: but the secure illusion of their protection, of their proximity, this I do need, they are both tsetse flies, sycophants, cowards. Premonitions are visual fear but I see that I must be maimed unless Edward – And I will not die[24]

As for Edward himself, he is so splintered that the narrative divides him into an ego who vacillates between the need to protect and a dread of infringing taboos, and a super-ego who moralises stoically from the side lines. The super-ego adopts the style of a preacher whose congregation consists partly of the less inhibited aspects of Edward and partly of the reader, who is also, it is assumed, in thrall to 'gregarious ethics'. It is the super-ego who wins, holding Edward back from the decisive intervention that alone might save his sister. In the event the resulting incest occurs only in the sister's mind.

The book's achievement is to make this impulse seem as natural as breathing. Throughout, the carefully plotted alternation between expressions of tenderness and acts of mutual evasion and avoidance amounts to a choreography of embarrassment. The density of feeling permeates the style. The prose is flushed and allusive, with folk songs and prayers among the material blended in, but it is not overwritten. Incest – the daring theme – is not so much committed as interrogated. In Alanna's mind, permitted love dallies with illicit:

> REVISIT ME, incidents of my childhood. Remember the morning many years ago when Edward passionate boy first kissed me, closed his eyes, he was a much stranger youth then, and I so young. A later evening, when first I closed my eyes, that was not Edward's kiss.[25]

The graduation from familial to erotic feeling is subtly rendered. A Lawrentian version of Freudian psychology is at work somewhere, but the incest theme, which is implied rather than spelled out, is not where we find it. If the book is at all indebted to *Fantasia of the Unconscious*, it is in the too easy separating out of the psychology of gender. That said, it is Alanna who is the strong one, and Alanna who alone seems to recognise her drives, even to the extent of knowing that in the end she must die. As she contemplates the possibilities of such a death, the passages from Barker's journal concerning suicide are inserted, here ascribed to her. When in the closing pages she dies in childbirth, there is no sense in which the male sexual will can be said to have killed her, because the male sexual will is seen throughout to be feeble and feckless. It is Alanna who recognises the tenacity of her desires and their hopelessness. In her articulate stirring towards fulfilment – even the half-fulfilment of death – she recalls certain facets of Lawrence, but not his male-chauvinism. This is not a male-chauvinist book.

If the novel has a conspicuous fault, it is that the end comes too quickly and too summarily. Alanna's death – the child's fate is left uncertain – seems in the event contrived and excessive, much as she herself desires it to be. Fundamentally, the book mistakes its strengths. In one respect, it is typical of first novels by writers who are not natural novelists in that it strives too hard to convince us of the pressures of plot, providing a melodramatic nemesis where none was needed. *Alanna Autumnal* works perfectly well as a composition of interleaved monologues. It would have been ideally suited to the radio, since Barker already possessed the skill with speaking voices he was later to exploit for the Third Programme. It also looks forward to his later novels, *Janus* and *The Dead Seagull*. Its virtues, however, are less those of the later prose works than of the cycles of love poems of the early 1940s. Like them, it evokes both the pathology of sexual love and its intensity.

In purely literary terms, *Alanna Autumnal* is unprecedented. It is hard to think of another work of fiction which it resembles. There are moments when the density of its atmosphere recalls the early novels of Lawrence Durrell, which are almost its contemporaries. But it does not have the cynicism of Durrell's *The Black Book*, and satire is absent. If this early novella is couched in a manner which Barker would gradually abandon, undoubtedly only he could have written it.

CHAPTER 5

'MELLIFLUOUS SMOOTH TONGUE'

That, at least, was what the reviewers felt. Even in acerbic Cambridge, F.R. Leavis, who had probably noticed the single sympathetic sentence about him in Barker's review of his own book *New Bearings*, commissioned a piece for the academically orientated journal *Scrutiny*. This was written by Hugh Gordon Porteus, who knew Barker's circumstances well. Porteus began by raising the issues of class and auto-didacticism: Barker, he said, was 'an uneducated and sophisticated prodigy' and he praised him for his possession of 'all of the qualities that really matter'. In the end, however, Porteus did not know whether to adopt a London or a Cambridge stance. In his attempt to be indulgent but knowing, he finished by sounding arch: 'His malady is an ingrowing soul: his virtue, that he has diagnosed it. His prescription is – Excess: he will rage himself out.'

Barker would not have paid much attention to a university-based journal like *Scrutiny*. But in the *Listener Alanna Autumnal* was reviewed on 8 November by the Scottish poet Edwin Muir, who devoted the better part of a page to the book. Muir had left school at fifteen himself. He knew of Barker's circumstances, having learnt of them from the *Listener*'s literary editor, Janet Adam Smith, who was engaged to his friend Michael Roberts. After noting Barker's youth and relative immaturity, he set these facts aside and focused on the issue of sincerity in modern literature. Muir argued that there were two types of sincerity: the sincerity of the social realists and the sincerity of those writers who faced up to the less acceptable parts of themselves. Barker achieved the second feat and he did so in prose of great power:

The first kind of sincerity is a social virtue and often a high one; the other is both that and something else which it is difficult and perhaps impossible to define; but it is in any case a literary virtue. It implies both sincerity towards the outer world and knowledge of the nature of one's individual response to it; and that combination, it seems to me, is one of the marks of an original writer. The first book on this list . . . has this unmistakable and rare virtue . . . The quality of such a book can be shown only by quotation; here are a few passages: 'And then one day we had no money . . . and the little room in which we lived contracted and grew dark; and the bed sagged repulsively; and the water pipes which ran around the kitchen circled so fast we lost our senses.' 'When the handle of the door turned, I knew who it was: who turned that circle of guilt and desperation.' The book is written throughout in this vital and living style, which is poetic in the sense that it invents new equivalents for the things it describes, instead of accepting the approved counters of ordinary prose. The author's originality can be felt in every phrase that he uses; it is not a matter of occasional flashes, but of the whole texture of his style and thought; and this actually makes a first reading of the book somewhat difficult. *Alanna Autumnal* will not appeal, it is certain, to a wide public; it will irritate many people on first reading; but on the other hand it is one of the few books that should be read more than once, and it is, as I have found in my experience, even better on a second than on a first reading. It is certainly the work of a writer of great talent.

Here was a talent that Muir was anxious to draw out. When Barker telephoned to thank him for his accolade, Muir invited him to spend the evening with him and his wife Willa in Hampstead. The Muirs lived at 7 Downshire Hill in a rambling neo-Gothic house with many bedrooms, where they sometimes invited struggling artists to stay. On a wet November night Barker called, to be confronted by one of the more remarkable couples in modern literature: Edwin small and Orcadian; Willa ample, maternal and learned in many languages. Muir was a man of deep religious susceptibility with a profound resistance to the merely fashionable. He was, as Barker remembered, 'a silent clock that showed not the time but the condition, not the hour but the alternative'. In Muir he 'met for the first time a phenomenon I hope never to forget: the extraordinary gentleness that prevails in the presence of many men who are truly poets'.[1]

The Muirs invited Barker back for other evening sessions, at which they discussed the principles of poetry. Was verse embedded within language, they would ask, or could it fly free of it? Could poetry, as Eliot had stated, communicate before it was understood? Willa, who had translated Kafka, thought on the whole that Eliot was mistaken in this opinion. To put the point to the test, she moved across the elegant drawing room, pulled her copy of Homer's *Iliad* off the bookshelf and returned to the sofa. Then she read out the lines from the first book in which heart-broken Chryses trails along the foreshore, the harsh admonishments of Agamemnon dinning in his ears: 'Forth he went in silence along the shore of the loud-resounding sea':

Βῆ δ' ακέων παρὰ θῖνα πολυφλοίσβοιο θαλάσσης[2]

His discussions with the Muirs concentrated Barker's mind on the principle that, in whatever language it was written, the music of poetry lay in its vowels, a view already implicit in his own writing. On a clear day that spring, sitting in Meg's Café with David Archer and Maurice Carpenter, he had picked up the menu and scrawled across it the opening lines of 'Ode':

> O to us speak
> Bleak snow
> With your mellifluous smooth tongue[3]

The point of those verses resided in the patterning of 'o' and 'e' vowels in the first two lines, and in the synaesthesia of the third. Barker's other poetry was growing increasingly adventurous. He was experimenting with syntax and inversion in the style of W.H. Auden; but whereas Auden practised a highly individual form of ellipsis, cutting out inessential or merely connective words, Barker was seeking to balance this device with its opposite. As he explained in his notebook, he now sometimes preferred 'to place greater stress than others do on prepositions, conjunctions, and other parts of speech that are generally either ignored or stuffed in to make the necessary syllables'.[4] The conjunction of these two opposed techniques had thematic consequences. The Audenesque contraction of some of Barker's lines conveyed a political urgency, while in other lines a succession of minor words drew the sentences out to suggest lethargy or contemplative passivity. 'No feeble dream is as good as to act / Vigorously across pellucid air', began one poem of these months, issuing a highly topical call to political commitment. Barker's more individual manner, however, alternated such hortatory outbursts with images evocative of meditation, even of self-mortification. In some poems, the two manners co-existed within the same sentence, as in the fourth of Barker's 'Sequence of Ten Sonnets':

> (Father why hast thou forsaken us)
> We cannot interrogate, there is no time,
> Immediate work's to be done, and done by us,
> (We cannot spare the time for this one tune-up):
> Crisscross of cables this wicker electric chair
> He sits, staring at the telephone pole like a cross.[5]

In the last line, the futurist emblem of the telephone pole yields, by way of simile, to the Christian icon of the cross. The fusion is prepared for in the preceding lines, where the Christ-like cry of abandonment, 'Father why hast thou forsaken us', runs into the urgency of 'Immediate work's to be done'. The result is archaic and modern, intriguing and macabre.

Macabre sentiments were characteristic of Barker at this time. He was, as friends like Carpenter remembered him, not infrequently consumed with melancholia. When asked why, he cited Newman and his aboriginal calamity – a verdict all the more ominous now that his own faith had apparently collapsed and, along with it, any possibility of redemption. His weariness was exacerbated by the fact that he was working on several ambitious schemes at once: a novel provisionally entitled *The Mortals* in which all the characters were to die; an impassioned diatribe against life, under the title *Indigo Purple*. He declared himself to be in love 'with the heroic torsos of Mestrović, with Kevin Barry, with Alexander Archipenko, with the *Fantasia of the Unconscious*, with all Middle English Poetry, with the idea of Italy, and with myself'.[6] His apparent obsession and self-absorption concerned Carpenter, who, after briefly staying at Parton Street, had now moved in to share Barker's attic. Back at the bookshop, Carpenter mentioned his friend's morbidity to Archer, confiding that he feared George might attempt suicide. According to Carpenter's later account, Archer's reaction was to guffaw indulgently.[7] Even so, he too was anxious about Barker.

Archer's more helpful response was practical encouragement, for he had decided to publish Barker's poems. With *Alanna* now safely published, George concentrated over the summer on what he hoped would be a showcase for his verse. The title that he chose, *Thirty Preliminary Poems*, suggests something provisional and not quite ready: he was using this opportunity to demonstrate the skills he had mastered so far. There was, in the variety of styles, the blending of the personal with the up-to-date, a strong sense of alternative strengths being prepared for later use. Throughout collective politics were subsumed in the politics of the self. 'Coward's Song' had already posited a turning aside from garish social action; now he put topical issues to a subliminal and utterly personal use, as in 'Ode to a Dead Aeronaut':

> Of whom one, of whom one, is gone.
> All prosperous soil it seems was once
> A volatile body which on bright wings
> Within the minds bright winds sped
> Skirting the barren expanses, over the earth;
> Avid with danger, they lie waiting,
> There they lie awaiting

> The fall of the soaring soul, falling
> From the clouds, and higher than the
> Clouds.[8]

The ode describes the suicidal flight over Rome of the Italian aeronaut Lauro da Bossis in October 1931. The incident had recently inspired both Auden's 'Journal of an Airman', from *The Orators* of 1932, and Spender's poem 'Airman'. Barker's poem, however, was completely unlike either. Instead of examining the political iconography of the pilot, it used syntax to suggest an interrupted sensation of falling. In 'Poem on a Dream' (later retitled 'Narcissus'), the poet attends a political meeting. He is less interested in its programme of action than in the faces in the crowd, 'the features of every unrecognising face' which drift towards him, detaching themselves as art objects and projections of the self.[9]

By the time *Thirty Preliminary Poems* was ready for the printer, the alliance of convenience between Barker and the radicals who frequented Archer's shop was already coming to an end. In later years critics were to speak of him as constituting, along with Gascoyne and Thomas, a group called the 'Parton Street Poets'. Barker never accepted this label. Such typecasting of poets was, he believed, suggested by coincidences of generation, social status and education, rather than by their work. He felt no loyalty to the Auden school; nor did he belong to any alternative grouping, much though commentators or reviewers might attempt to construct one. He was his own man.

This independence was apparent to all who knew him. To Gascoyne, in 1933, Barker seemed civil, pleasant, but difficult to get to know well.[10] To Desmond Hawkins he appeared the least gregarious of his contemporaries. Unlike the slightly younger Thomas, Barker was neither loud nor assertive. He resisted being tied down to clique or occasion, preferring to meet in Meg's or at the bookshop rather than in pubs, where as yet he drank rarely and then only in the company of friends like Carpenter. To Hawkins, he seemed private, conspiratorial, shadowed.[11] When wishing to talk on matters to do with *Twentieth Century,* he would draw Hawkins aside behind one of Archer's bookshelves and speak softly, apparently relishing the feeling of confidentiality and exclusiveness thus created. Often he would suggest a walk together in Hyde Park, where conversations could not be overheard. Though a Londoner, he appeared to resent the town, telling Hawkins that he would escape to the country as soon as he was securely established.

The privacy, the politeness, the minding of p's and q's, were aspects of a carapace designed to protect Barker's subjectivity. To his peers he came across as a courteous colleague; to patrons as an assiduous worker. He cultivated orderly habits, getting up early each morning, refilling his pens, replying to every letter by return of post, drafting his answer in a fair italic hand, before typing it out immaculately. Behind all this, however, rebellion lurked. When asking for review work from Michael Roberts, he was deferential; afterwards, he would explode into his notebook: 'God blast you, Mr Roberts. I'm a book writer and not a literary arse for the careful excrementation of tasteful critical articles. Or nothing. Literary people are bloody, shallow, non committal, shrewdly constipated, contemptible ...'[12] He enjoyed the cross-currents of friendship and rivalry in Archer's shop, only later, in the privacy of his notebook, bursting out, 'Damn if I care. A year ago I wondered where shall I go and I must be nice. So many people are about to watch me. O bloody well damn if I care. I do as I wish in one place at least, upon the pages of my writing paper.'

Of all the English poets, he identified most strongly with Thomas Chatterton, the 'marvellous boy' from Bristol, who came to London in 1770 and took his own life with arsenic before his succession of literary aliases was exposed. Like Chatterton, Barker felt himself to be an outsider who had arrived from nowhere to surprise the world. The effect created, to the eye of a sympathetic observer like Edwin Muir, was of genuine need combined with what Muir continued to call patent sincerity. By the autumn Muir was worried enough to write soliciting the help of Walter de la Mare, to whom he described the twenty-year-old Barker as 'an extremely frank, sincere and clear-sighted youth – also very likeable'.[13] Nor was he, Muir wrote later, 'one of those silly people who think they have a claim on every chance comer because of their gifts'.[14] Barker painted and drew, Muir told de la Mare, as well as writing poems.

Financial problems, and the difficulties of adapting to a heavily politicised clique, were proving an emotional strain. To create a slight stir and then to withdraw was, anyway, Barker's natural instinct. To Hawkins he wrote that he wished as soon as feasible to move to the country, where one could deal with the literary world on one's own terms without the fear of others breathing down one's neck or expecting one to conform to type.[15]

There were other pressing reasons why a move had become advisable. In October Jessica discovered that she was pregnant. Her parents were strict and unyielding in their Catholicism. Her own faith was perhaps more gentle than theirs, but an abortion was unthinkable both to her and to George. The two of them were still very much in love. She had been a little slow to discover her pregnancy, so if they were to be married it had to be done quickly. They chose to marry at Jessica's local church in Parson's Green: Holy Cross, Ashington Road. They would then leave London, citing as a pretext George's need for seclusion to write. By this ruse the child could be born out of the way of censorious eyes – principally, as George later stated, those of the Woodward parents.[16] The nuptial mass was celebrated on Saturday, 18

November, and George borrowed a serge suit for the occasion. The register was signed by Archer. George was careful to discourage his other Parton Street acquaintances from attending, telling them that he was getting married out of necessity (which was about half true), that the whole thing was a bourgeois sellout, and that there would be – to them – offensive draperies and music in evidence. Then he spread the word, through Carpenter, that the service was to be held at the Oratory, so that if the habitués of Parton Street did turn up they would find themselves at the wrong church.[17]

To Muir he explained that Jessica had been working in an office from eight in the morning until seven at night. She had, he said, been unwell for two years until he had forced her to go to the doctor, who had diagnosed consumption and told her that she must live in the country. It was, Muir told de la Mare, a sad story and did Barker credit.[18] That he should have shielded Muir from the truth suggests just how uneasy the whole business made Barker. In 'The True Confession', looking back at that woefully embarrassed twenty-year-old bridegroom on the arm of his 24-year-old, two-months-pregnant bride, he pities their common defencelessness:

> But bright that nuptials to me now
>   As when, the smiling foetus carried
> Rose-decked today instead of tomorrow,
>   Like country cousins we were married
> By the pretty bullying embryo
>   And you, my friend: I will not borrow,
> Again, the serge suit that I carried
>   Through honey of moon to sup of sorrow.[19]

Among the writers who visited Archer's shop was Rosalind Wade, who was about to publish a novel, *Pity the Child!*, describing the unwanted pregnancy of one of her school friends; its appearance in January 1934 was to cause a scandal when author and publisher were sued by the headmistress for bringing the school in question into disrepute.[20] Wade told Barker that her mother Kathleen and her Aunt Phoebe owned a bungalow close to the sea on the Isle of Purbeck. As the bungalow was vacant during the winter months, George and Jessica might have it until April. Leaving Archer to see *Thirty Preliminary Poems* through the press, and having arranged for Kit to come down and spend part of the time with them, the young couple set off for Worth Matravers in Dorset.

CHAPTER 6

'WHISPERING SIBILANT FIELDS'

The village of Worth Matravers occupies a cleft to the extreme south of the Isle of Purbeck, between two humps of land known as the West and East Man. A mile-long path twists down from the village centre towards the sea, before opening out to form a low platform of granite, below which, on the shingle-covered ledge known as Winspit, the waves rage at all seasons. To the back of the platform the cliffs are honeycombed with caves. To its right two stones lean together to form a throne, where Barker would perch, gazing at the breakers. To the east, round Seacombe Cliff, lies Swanage; to the west coastal paths hug the clifftop towards the peaked promontory of St Aldhelm's Head and, beyond it, Chapman's Pool with its fringe of old quarry workings.

The village ascends from Winspit bottom by terraced degrees. Its limestone buildings include the parish church of St Nicholas of Myra, with its distinctive Saxon nave lined by grinning gargoyles. The focus of social life, then and now, is the Square and Compass pub, which is so cramped that it has no space for a bar: beer is sold through a narrow hatch. Barker had to stoop to enter, and the rooms are like snuggeries. It is in one of these rooms that the protagonist of his later novel *The Dead Seagull* squats, planning his future. Around the pub cluster cottages, blending with the landscape from which their stones have been hewn. Compass Cottage stands in sharp contrast: a pebble-dash bungalow put up a few years before the Barkers' arrival and set, together with a straggle of recent houses, among old railway carriages that had been converted into makeshift dwellings on the eastern edge of the village. Here, in summer, Kathleen Wade and her sister Phoebe stayed, Phoebe painting and Kathleen writing history books, which she published under the name of Eric Bentfield, a local quarryman.[1] From here, too, a few years before, Kathleen had directed the first-ever British production of Frank Wedekind's play about adolescent sexuality, *Spring Awakening*, causing consternation in the neighbourhood when it was staged in nearby Swanage.[2] From the outside the cottage seems dingy, but the view was magnificent, right across East and West Man, their slopes scored by the parallel lines of 'strip lynchets', ancient farming terraces which look from a distance like the trenches of wartime Belgium. Barker thought they might be recent, but a neighbour disabused him: the scene was 'mooch the zame as it ever were'. A large expanse of sky is also visible, providing a backdrop for the clouds, which Barker could watch out of the broad front window as he worked, vainly attempting to ignore the openness of the vista and the level edge of the sea.

Apart from writing and watching, there was little else for him to do. When the Barkers arrived in the third week of November, the summer visitors had departed, abandoning the village to its sheep, its quarry workers and its over-attentive rector, whose welcoming visit they dreaded. Barker was to become an inveterate country dweller, but in 1933 the contrast with grimy, congested London was extreme. In his novella 'The Bacchant', written at the time, he describes the protagonist standing in the tiny front room, staring out at the strip lynchets and the dead horizon of the sea, and wondering how to spend the winter: '"Today," I repeated to myself, "I shall receive a visit from the vicar, or give birth to twins or die."'

Other self-projections occur in the text. 'The premonition of an extreme occurrence is active within me like the urgency of the womb,' Barker wrote, a fairly obvious reference to Jessica's pregnancy. However, the birth was a long time off, in early summer. For the present Jessica sat and sewed, while George read, thought and planned projects. The landscape seemed fertile with poems, while the critical reception accorded to *Alanna Autumnal* had given him fresh confidence in his prose. He became, in that coupled seclusion, uncannily productive. Free of the social demands of the capital, he developed a routine more suited to his new, quieter circumstances: writing in the morning, reading and walking in the afternoon. In December an advance copy of *Thirty Preliminary Poems* arrived. It was followed by a sprinkling of reviews which, while not as encouraging as those for *Alanna*, spoke well of his way with rhythms. In *New Verse* Stephen Spender noted the book's modest title together with its immaturity, but went on to say: 'it becomes obvious that Mr Barker is a writer at present rather oppressed by his sensibility, but who should soon write with freedom and power'.[3] The encouragement was very welcome to George since he and Jessica were living on little more than hope. When so much seemed uncertain, this was just the sort of incentive he needed.

Their isolation did not last long. In January Carpenter and Kit arrived and, with them, the snow. One afternoon, in the teeth of a bitter wind, the three men struggled down to Winspit and then along the cliff path towards the neighbouring village of Langton Matravers.[4] Then they battled against the weather as far as St Aldhelm's Head, from which the drop was sheer: 350 feet to the rocks below. In the snow the cliff seemed sinister and still. On the headland they found a rectangular, eleventh-century chapel built on the spot where a father had stood watching as the ship carrying his newly-wed daughter and her husband to Normandy was sucked to its destruction. Back at the cottage, the following morning it was so cold that the water froze in the basin. Washing was too much effort.

Sequestered from the outside world, encased in winter cold, the whole peninsula seemed magical. It suggested to Barker a new way of looking at things, whereby cliffs, earthworks and coves were turned into symbols for his marriage – 'The land is you, forever must be us' – while the coast around Chapman's Pool became one stupendous metaphor for the body:

> I am that land, surrounding sea
> And sky; the structure of my hand
> Spreads promontories, and the mountains of knees
> Penetrate the great clouds of your desire . . .[5]

The prose and poetry which Barker wrote in the early weeks of 1934 were to find their way into the books *Janus* and *Poems*, both published the following year. The two projects were complementary, the preoccupations of the poems emerging in the prose and prose descriptions in the poetry. At no other time had this been the case: *Alanna* and the poems of 1933 had been quite distinct. But, cut off as Barker now was from most other influences, he seems to have been overtaken by the atmosphere around him. Images from the prose writing penetrate his verses, fertilising them, while the prose has a poetic quality quite unlike anything he had written before. In London he had needed willpower to stay outside politics, apart from relationships of various kinds and the stylistic influence of his peers. In Dorset he could concentrate without distractions, and the concentration bore fruit.

When the winds blew the visitors back to London, there was nothing for Barker to do but work. In twelve days, between 10 and 22 January, he sat down and wrote the 30,000 words of 'The Bacchant'. It took the peninsula as its setting with the cottage for its centre, but Jessica is blanked out. The protagonist is supported by his uncle while he compiles a work on art history; and there is a local girl called Ruth, big-boned and healthy, whose earthiness appeals to the protagonist's city-bred appetites. If the protagonist is Barker, then the disguise is heavier than in *Alanna Autumnal*. What is most clearly recognisable is the local seascape:

> Sometimes the hills which dominate the scene from my window appear

overnight to have altered, assumed more formidable and frightening guises. This morning, glancing at them as I passed from my room, it appeared that they had become prodigious amphibian monsters, distending their figures towards the sea; whilst the flutings or corrugations of ground which I have noted resembled fearfully the muscling or gathering of hide over their huge ribs. And the great headland St. Aldhelm, which leans over the edge of the land like a thirsting beast, had become the head of those heaving bodies, and might have been sucking up the sea for their foul relish.[6]

The narrator is both like and utterly unlike Barker. To distinguish him, he is provided with a history: a Scottish mother whose influence upon him has been predominant, and an absent father who, when he had been present, was a bully. The narrator harbours a nagging anxiety as to whether he is an artist or merely a commentator. In one respect he does seem to draw on the experience of the author, whose journal in 1931 had recorded a moment of disturbance in which 'a terrifying visitation of effeminacy slit open the brain and swerved in suddenly, as I lay upon the bed thinking about the future. So swerved that my thoughts were severed, and she only. No, fool: nothing amorous, nothing amorous but that I encountered a complete fusion of myself with things linear as distinct from the masculinity of things having mass . . . Never take such moments seriously. They lead into the bosom of the hated thing.'[7] Two years later, however, happily married and precariously secure, Barker seems to have wanted to go further. In 'The Bacchant' the unnamed protagonist also has a visitation of effeminacy, by which he is less terrified than fascinated. He stands before the mirror in a sort of Narcissus-like swoon, contemplating his own dandified loveliness:

Leaning on one side, I accentuate the long contour of the cheek and chin, which does not so much delimit as frame the formation of my face. The small, rounded, and crimson mounds of my lips purse themselves like the mouth of a child, and, with a sudden flirtatious coquetry, smile. Retreating from the mirror, my figure fills it, as, like a boyish Florentine nobleman, I stand, a hand on a hip, head to one side, concernedly scrutinizing; or adjust my attitude to one of more grace, as, with an easy movement, I advance my left foot and slightly erect my head. See, this body has the grace and elasticity of a girl, the hips slide with the seductive elasticity of an actress, and, touching my throat gently with my hand, the slenderness and equipoise of a courtesan. Enchanted, I remove my jacket, loosen my shirt at my throat, displaying the flesh, like a flawless triangular brooch, of my chest, free, perfectly, of hair; and of an almost colourless pallor. I remove my shoes, and my socks, showing my feet, which are untouched by deformations. I stand, clad only in my shirt, my trousers, and the tie, loosely hanging, an adornment.[8]

Correspondingly, in desiring Ruth, it is the masculine or hermaphrodite in her that attracts the protagonist. He is drawn to this he/she and, in so responding, is driven to define himself. But the act of love, imperfectly consummated, is like the inverted congress of sexual identities that have crossed: the she-man embracing the he-woman. It is this transient merging of genders that 'The Bacchant' seems to want to explore. Ruth appears robust, but is already suffering from the heart complaint that will kill her, while the narrator experiences recurrent bouts of neurasthenia. They fall ill alternately and when, on the eve of their wedding, Ruth dies, the narrator is impelled towards the clifftop – evidently St Aldhelm's Head – off which he hurls himself (according to Maurice Carpenter, many of the protagonists in George's unpublished stories died similarly).[9] He expires in a stylistic flourish quite as dandified as that which characterised his narcissism.

Throughout the story, the prose unfurls in long, polysyllabic sentences in which choice epithets are carefully set. The writing has a density and imagistic abundance that reminds one of the seventeenth century, and simultaneously of the nineteenth-century *fin de siècle*, as if a late Victorian stylistic varnish had been laid over an original penned by Sir Thomas Browne. The diction is polysyllabic and yet daring; as in the verse of *Thirty Preliminary Poems*, it is both archaic and arrestingly modern. On Monday, 22 January Barker put the manuscript in his drawer, deciding that this was his second novel.

The writing of the story had unforeseen consequences for his poetical career. In the third week of January, while contemplating the conclusion, Barker strode back up to St Aldhelm's Head to savour the atmosphere, and stood on the edge while the sea seethed and boiled below. Looking down, he had the idea of combining three strands: death by drowning, the myth of Icarus and the opening cadences of the airman poem just published in *Thirty Preliminary Poems*. These ideas came together in a longish poem in five sections called 'Daedalus', which begins:

> Like the enormous liner of his limbs
> and fell.
>   Remain behind, look on
> What's left of what was once in blighted remains.
> That imponderable body
>   Smote my desire, now smitten
> Mortally.

> I lift his head, his death dampens
> The moist palm of my hand like handled fear
> Like fear cramping my hand
> and stand.
>   Remain behind, entertain posthumous fear.
> I entertained.[10]

Barker typed the poem out and sent it to Edwin Muir in Hampstead. Muir liked it and forwarded it to Walter de la Mare, whose son Richard worked for the publishers Faber & Faber. De la Mare wrote to Barker that the piece was clearly accomplished, though not quite to his taste. Should Barker not now send a copy directly to Faber's poetry editor, T.S. Eliot? Barker did try Eliot, who wrote back immediately accepting the poem for the magazine of which he was also editor, the *Criterion*. Buoyed up by this encouragement, on his twenty-first birthday in February Barker wrote a lament for all his past selves, 'the figures of precedented I'. Calling the new poem 'Phoenix', a title which on second thoughts he changed to 'Elegy Anticipating Death', he sent this piece to Faber as well. In March Eliot replied that the poem was not as distinctive as 'Daedalus' ('the rhythms are not nearly as interesting'); it was, however, good enough for inclusion in a volume of verse. If Barker thought of putting together such a book, Eliot promised to consider it. He should call at Faber's offices at 24 Russell Square the next time that he was in London.[11] The following month, Eliot wrote reiterating his confidence: 'I will say again that I like your poetry very much.'[12]

It is not difficult to see what Eliot appreciated in 'Daedalus'. Like *The Waste Land*, the poem is based on an ancient myth, which it brings forward into a startling modern setting. In it, as in Eliot's poem, the speaker is ambiguous. As Daedalus, designer of the Minoan labyrinth and the wings with which he and Icarus have attempted to fly, turns over the 'blighted remains' of his dead son, is it he who addresses the reader, or the reader who addresses him? Barker's highly unusual use of pronouns intensifies the suggestiveness. In the first sentence, the subject pronoun and several other grammatical components are omitted. There follows an unusual form of the imperative in which the one who enjoins (Daedalus? the reader? the spectre of Icarus?) seems to change places with he who is enjoined. By the second section the speaking voice has broadened to become one of a conscience, haunting history – one which, like that of Tiresias in *The Waste Land*, has foresuffered all.

The versification is similarly imaginative, its fragmented line lengths mimetic of Icarus's broken body. Throughout the poem Barker uses the sort of controlled free verse with slight echoes of earlier poets that Eliot himself favoured. Here was a specimen of *vers libre* plainly written by someone already deeply read in more traditional forms. Above all, as remarks in Eliot's letters show, he had responded to Barker's rhythms.

Barker was detained in Dorset. In March, however, he sent another batch of poems to Russell Square, following them up with 'The Bacchant', which Eliot decided to hold over until more of Barker's verse was in print. Two weeks after 'Daedalus' had appeared in the April issue of the *Criterion*, Barker at last called on Eliot in person, taking several more poems with him. Barker has left us some of the most vivid descriptions ever written of calling on Eliot, who by 1934 was already considered the pontiff of modern letters.[13] It was both a privilege and an ordeal to meet the man whose religious poem 'Ash Wednesday' had won Barker's excited allegiance four years before, who was editor of a literary magazine of international importance and in charge of the most respected poetry list in England – published by the firm whose founder Geoffrey Faber happened to be the great-nephew of Father Faber, originator of the London Oratory. Barker went up in the lift and entered a tiny room, almost an eyrie, on the top floor. Here, glancing occasionally out of a window overlooking Woburn Square to the north, sat Eliot, weary and indulgent. What he had to suggest was that 'Daedalus' be regarded as a piece in a volume that Faber would commit themselves to publishing as soon as it was ready.[14]

Eliot's offer needs to be placed in context. Seven years before, when the twenty-year-old W.H. Auden, who had been to public school and Oxford, had sent him a selection of his work for consideration, Eliot had told him to go away and develop a little more.[15] Other educationally advantaged poets had received a similar response. Yet here was Barker at much the same age, with nothing behind him but elementary formal education, with his own style yet to be achieved, wary in the presence of authority – and Eliot was prepared to take a chance on him.

Anne Ridler, then Anne Bradley, who worked as Eliot's assistant in the late 1930s, remembers Eliot making two remarks about Barker at the time: the first that he was a 'genius', and the second that he should learn to consult the dictionary more often.[16] He repeated the second comment to Barker, whose vocabulary in 1934, despite its marked originality, was occasionally high-falutin' and sometimes inaccurate. Yet Eliot's good opinion of Barker's writing was manifestly accompanied both by personal warmth and some sense of private affinity. With him, for the April meeting, Barker had brought another poem called 'Narcissus', based on the myth which the young Eliot had once exploited in his own poem 'The Death of Saint Narcissus'. In addition, Barker was a lapsed Roman Catholic, while Eliot had been an Anglo-Catholic since 1926. They had similar spiritual concerns and shared a respect for tradition. Both men relished jokes, including puns. Barker's circumstances also appealed to the generosity that was never far from the surface in Eliot, who evidently felt this particular young poet required encouragement above all else; criticism could wait. In June he undertook to support Barker in applying for a grant from the Royal Literary Fund.[17] According to Virginia Woolf, Eliot was soon carrying Barker's poems around London in the inside pocket of his jacket and showing them to friends. Barker was, he wrote two years later, 'one of the very small number of younger poets whose work I consider important'.[18]

Whilst he was in London, Barker visited friends. Carpenter was now living in Camden Town in a house owned by a Glaswegian fitter. He was still looking for somebody to go to bed with and had identified a likely partner in a girl whom in his memoirs he simply calls 'B'. As Barker was in town, Carpenter invited him along to impress her. The mother insisted that the girl's sister go along as chaperone: 'He's immoral your friend; I know he's immoral.' The four young people picnicked behind the house. What poetry did the girls like, Barker enquired. The sisters – very pretty, very English – thought that they liked Rupert Brooke. 'How can you make love to a dinner plate?' Barker replied. They should read some decent poems, like Francis Thompson's 'The Hound of Heaven' – 'a poem of sexual pursuit and rape if ever there was one'. The girls' mother was outraged by the reported conversation, but the girls were delighted.[19] Barker went back to Dorset while Carpenter wrote to 'B', 'formally proposing sexual intercourse'. She refused. Barker was not asked to help again.

With Eliot's encouragement, Barker now set about creating a body of work that would respectably fill a volume. In poems like 'Fistral Bay' he again took soundings from the landscape. Reverting to a theme he shared with Eliot, he wrote two more Narcissus poems, the first of which was a meditation on Benvenuto Cellini. As the weather in Dorset grew milder, swimming became possible, and Barker turned this to advantage in a prose piece called 'The Swimmers', which was published in the *Listener* on 2 May and drew admiring glances, even from Cambridge. After 'Daedalus' had appeared in the April issue of the *Criterion, Scrutiny* noted the new materiality of the style: 'Mr Barker's work has what Eliot has often described as "intensity"; it has something else that might be described as "substance" and which I should define as a physical (almost tactile, as opposed to cerebral) apprehension of the word.'[20]

But spring had now arrived and Kathleen and Phoebe wanted the use of their cottage. So the Barkers packed their few belongings and drove to Geldeston in Suffolk, where they had rented a cottage called Danegelts for the summer. Geldeston was a small and pretty village and around it lay all of East Anglia to explore. For the first time Barker visited Norwich, which he found 'a city of memorials and church towers and gardens and large florid public buildings; obscure and angular little alleys with names like Unicorn Way and Swan's Way, Tudor courtyards with fountains dry for years and enormous, meaningless rectangles of shadow and stone where boots or ironmongery or beds are manufactured: it is a city of small private houses with dark windows and flower boxes, solicitors' and architects' offices and a luxury of public lavatories.'[21] In the Geldeston cottage he and Jessica awaited the birth of their child, while George worked to get together sufficient poems for his new volume, provisionally entitled *Daedalus and Narcissus*.[22] Perhaps because of the imminence of the birth, premonitions seem to have haunted him. On Tuesday, 22 May he was visited by a frightening vision of female power, which he recorded in a poem called 'The Amazons':

> Pallid the mirages, the palaces
> Appearing brilliant on the mountain tops, pale
> The whispering sibilant fields and pale
> The phantasmal countenances female
> Haunting our progress: in all climactic places
> Appear the brilliant the distraught and pallid faces . . .
>
> Queen Masters! Lying easy under the hills
> Of my home, concealed beneath the sun,
> – Gold man, king – I sense like one
> Lost in an alien land how your presence fills
> Whole atmospheres like thunders, and on
> My shoulders your compulsion falls.[23]

There passed an anxious time. Because he was now based out of London, it had become more difficult for Barker to obtain casual reviewing work. He was racked with worry about the family finances. To Eliot he wrote asking whether Faber might allow him a small advance on royalties for the forthcoming volume within the next six weeks: 'I have a hospital bill of my wife's to meet then. Please excuse me for saying this. The point is we simply have no money.'[24] The request was unprecedented – in the 1930s Faber never gave advances on first volumes – but, under the circumstances, Eliot persuaded the Board to allow Barker an advance of £25, £15 of which were sent straight away.[25]

On Saturday, 2 June a daughter was born. She was called Clare, after St Francis's spiritual sister, St Clare, and Barker registered her birth at Loddon on the 7th. To help with the household chores, the Barkers hired the services of a thirteen-year-old local girl, who came in daily.[26] In the early days, Jessica breastfed the baby, a sight George found poignantly reminiscent of the Renaissance madonnas he so loved. On Thursday, 21 June, as Jessica fed the baby by the side of a stream, he serenaded her as 'Mary of the quiet rivulets', beseeching her to 'Spread about me the embalming waters / Of your arms, and like the swallow / Set me free in the streams of air, that I may follow / Forever your love's tides and know no later tiring.'[27]

But if George had been apprehensive of his 'Amazons', Jessica was in terror of her mother. It was late June, so the baby would have been conceived in September and the marriage had not been solemnised until November. Though born within wedlock, the baby would have been regarded by Jessica's parents as illegitimate. At least, this is what Jessica seems to have feared. She wanted the baby to be adopted, an unsatisfactory solution so far as George was concerned, and psychologically disastrous for her. Without a doubt, both of them were motivated by fear of disapproval from the Woodwards and by the general stigma still attaching in the mid-1930s to any suggestion of illegitimacy. Through a local priest, Father John Owen of Gillingham Hall near Beccles, they arranged for Clare to be baptised. She was then confidentially adopted through a Catholic Adoption Society. She grew up a judge's daughter, not learning the secret of her birth until 1986.[28]

In poem after poem, Barker would regret her going. The 'Holy Poems' of 1939 are dedicated to Clare's memory, as is one of the most heartfelt of the 'Supplementary Personal Sonnets' of 1941, where she has pride of place beside his mother and Kit.[29] In the sonnet, written in far-off America, Barker imagines her a victim of the London Blitz: the devastating power of the air-raid which may have killed her seems, however, less overwhelming to her father than his own guilt, the 'love that whips me with your smile / Nine-tailed with tears that cut me to the quick'. These poems are all elegies: even in the immediate aftermath of Clare's loss, Barker seems to have regarded her as metaphorically dead. Late that September he remembered Carlo Crivelli; remembered, too, the upwardly drifting cherubs of Tintoretto's 'The Birth of the Milky Way'. He turned Clare into a putto, and wrote a valediction which came out in the *Listener* on 26 June, reappearing the following year in the volume which he had been preparing for Eliot. It was entitled 'Luctus in Morte Infantis', 'Mourning at the Death of a Child':

> O that adept evader
> Of the bubble or bomb
> Who from the immediate womb
> Leaped cloudward, to border
>
> The budded throne! He, though scarce
> Earth breathing once
> Intuitively analysed the air
> Contagious of fatal and sour

Ill, so sprang
Immaculate with his spring
Upon the skies' steps
Laughing with his leaps.[30]

CHAPTER 7

TEARS IN A BOTTLE

In October the Barkers' lease at Geldeston expired. They returned to Dorset, where they found another tiny cottage called Gaulter, in the village of Kimmeridge close to Corfe Castle. When Kit came down from London to join them, the brothers explored the castle's ruins. In 1646 its Royalist owner Lord Banks had, they learnt, resisted Cromwell's armies, whereupon, Kit noted in his journal, 'it was besieged a second time by Cromwell, who obtained possession through the treachery of Colonel Pitman, an officer of the garrison'.[1] Set on a mound, like the worn teeth of an enormous jaw, the ruins dominated the Purbeck peninsula. The arches of the chapel, of 'leprous white stone', lay open to the elements. At the foot of one of the walls the brothers dug into the rubble, unearthing 160 pieces of coarse green glass. On his return to London, Kit took them to Sotheby's, where they were identified as fragments of a Carolingian jordan bottle.[2] Such vessels, he observed, 'were probably intended to contain relics, or holy water, or, in some cases, possibly water from the river Jordan'. George preferred the idea that they had been receptacles for women's tears. Had Lady Banks, he wondered, wept into her jordan bottle while awaiting the descent of the Roundheads?

Throughout the winter of 1934–5 the brothers pursued interests in late medieval, Elizabethan and Stuart history. From the London Library Kit brought Hamilton Thompson's *Military Architecture in the Middle Ages*, Michaud's *Histoire des Croisades* and H.E. Rolling's *Old English Ballads*. In E.K. Chambers's and F. Sidgwick's anthology *Early English Lyrics* George discovered an attractively morbid dirge, 'Erthe out of erthe is wondirily wroghte', from the Thornton Manuscript in Lincoln cathedral, which he was to use as the epigraph for his next prose work. The mania for things medieval was soon shaping his writing. In the October issue of the *Criterion*, he published a mock-medieval dialogue, allegorical in mode, called 'The Hawk and the Dove'. In it the hawk speaks for the rapacious forces of death and the dove for the assertive power of love. Meanwhile Kit embarked on a saga of the crusades called 'The Griffin and the Lily', drafting it in George's journal.[3]

The most significant of these discoveries was to have an even deeper effect on George's development. That spring, in the published proceedings of the Harleian Society, the brothers found a fourteenth-century lyric of great sensuous power, called 'Quia Amore Langueo'. It was in two parts: 'The Appeal of the Blessed Virgin Mary to Man', and 'The Appeal of Christ to Mankind'. To their dismay, they learned that Arthur Quiller-Couch, when editing *The Oxford Book of English Verse* in 1925, had excised the first, and more erotically suggestive, of these sections. They determined at some future date to put this omission right.

Barker was now in a hurry. He was planning one book a year, and did not welcome distraction. When Geoffrey Grigson sent out a questionnaire soliciting the opinion of leading poets of the day on various topical issues for the October issue of *New Verse*, Barker delayed before replying in terms that made his distance from the metropolitan Marxists perfectly plain. Poetry, he stated, was only useful 'insofar as it may accord with the process of spiritual unravelling'; the origin of a poem was 'purely verbal'. To the question, 'Do you take your stand with any political or politico-economic party or creed?' he gave the emphatic answer, 'I do not.'[4]

At Geldeston he had made a firm note: 'I refuse to write a third novel.' On 10 October, however, he took out a manuscript of a work which he had announced prematurely the previous year under the title 'The Mortals'. Now he renamed it 'The Documents of a Death', structuring it around a batch of papers supposedly left behind by a young man after his suicide. That this new focus had its origins in 'The Hawk and the Dove' is strongly suggested by the prologue, in which the competing forces of love and death are imaged as twin birds, perching on the narrator's outstretched hands and singing antiphonally. In the tale that ensues the possibilities of love are represented by a sketchily described homosexual love affair, begun in Capri and unsatisfactorily concluded in the English countryside. The loved one remains a shadowy figure, epicene rather than male. The vision of his face glimpsed between the branches of a tree 'burns still more gold than fire, more fiery than gold'. In describing the two men's night of consummation, Barker draws on his journals where, three years previously, he had written, 'Does not every man suffer moments when the whole world, the prize of all effort, lies darkly between two female loins, within two female hands, under a soft belly?'[5] In the story this is rephrased to heighten both directness and sexual ambiguity: 'Surely all creatures suffer moments when the assuagement of all pain, the sating of all hate, lies darkly fixed between convex or concave loins! But upon me, as from a foul oil gusher, defacement and shame sprang out, and I, previously virgin of love, recoiled back and soiled and irredeemably befouled. That night of love!'[6] The guilty pursuit of such pleasures, however, is merely a displacement of the narrator's overwhelming desire to merge with the more potent forces of death. In early youth, he tells us, he attempted suicide by drowning; he was saved by his anxious mother, whom he now addresses. In the story's most arresting episode, he dives off a high rock into the river, where he encounters mortality as a skeletal figure shimmering just beneath the surface. This figure, which beckons silently, is imaginatively related to the languid projections of the self in Barker's Narcissus poems. The narrator is once more rescued, this time by his male lover, who draws him back towards the flickering flame of life. Yet life cannot triumph for ever. In the philosophical tug-of-war with which the story concludes death proves the stronger. Throughout the tone is set by the poem 'Erthe out of erthe is wondirily wroghte', which is set out at the beginning as an epigraph. This medieval death-vision is worked into the very fabric of the narrative, where strands of erotic desire and death-longing are inseparably intertwined. Ultimately death itself becomes the object of passion, the narrator's monologue a vehicle for his preoccupation with mortality as a culminating libidinous condition.

A fascination with sexual ambiguity seems to have stayed with Barker for some time. Twelve days after finishing 'The Documents of a Death', he published a poem called 'The Multiple Figure' in the *Listener*. Its subject was a hermaphrodite lover, or perhaps another projection of the self:

> That figure, multiple of common beauty,
> Enumerating the many of joy's myriads
> In a least touch, inhabits me like dryads
> Roaming and charming dark forests of the city.
>
> Hovering like gold eaglets whose breasts reveal gold
> the hands encircle slowly the confronting
> And invisible gilded air; it quick eyes' pointing
> Hither, promotes me subject, and am held
>
> In crystal concentration, a prisoner,
> Caught in glass bonds.[7]

This was to be the first of a number of such poems, written over the space of a year, portraying androgynously ambivalent love objects.

Barker sent 'The Documents of a Death' to Eliot, who immediately accepted it and suggested bringing it out in a volume with 'The Bacchant'[8] in about a year's time, after the book of verse, now retitled *Poems*. The plan was that the stories would boost the poems and vice versa. The prose book, however, needed a title; Eliot advised that it should be distinct from those attached to the individual stories. So Barker remembered his last job humping stock at the Janus Press and called the new book *Janus*. As well as indicating a two-way stance – towards the exuberance of 'The Bacchant' and the meditative seriousness of 'The Documents of a Death' – this suggested the ambivalent sexuality of both protagonists. The treatment of such themes in both stories was courageously candid, as Eliot was to stress in his blurb:

Here are two narratives of Love and Death. They are told in the form of a prose which Mr. Barker has invented, unprecedented. They will give pleasure to readers who are civilized enough to be primitive and honest enough to recognize their own feelings.

What exactly were those feelings that Eliot was inviting Barker's readers to be 'primitive and honest enough to recognize'? Obviously, there was the narcissism of one story, the homosexuality and death-fixation of the other. But these are only their most flagrant aspects and, for Eliot at least, probably the least interesting. In 'The Documents of a Death', which he seems to have preferred, there are also profounder glimpses of a dark night of the soul, akin to that which afflicted Eliot himself. At one point, Barker refers to the clause '*if* there is a God' in the passage from Newman's *Apologia pro Vita Sua* which, as a boy, he had studied with Father Dale-Roberts. He responds, 'And to the question, can God be or not, I return my answer that, demonstrated by the fact of death, there exists and can exist no God.' In effect, his rejoinder turns mortality, Newman's aboriginal calamity, into a demonstration of atheism. He also cites a well-known passage in the *Pensées*, in which the seventeenth-century mathematician and philosopher Pascal expresses his dread of cosmic emptiness: 'The eternal silence of those infinite spaces frightens me' ('Le silence éternel de ces espaces infinis m'effraie').[9] Barker relates Pascal's fear of the void to the Buddhist concept of Nirvana. The allusion is consistent with Eliot's own evocation of Pascal's 'vacant interstellar spaces', four years later, in 'East Coker': 'O dark dark dark. They all go into the dark.'

At one other point 'The Documents of a Death' anticipates the second of Eliot's *Four Quartets,* only to reprove it in advance. Late in the text the narrator envisages himself, like the evening sky in Eliot's 'The Love Song of J. Alfred Prufrock', as a patient etherised upon a table: 'Time now appears as a vivisection room containing only one subject, that being my being, my body extended upon the operating table, cut sickeningly open, heart, nerves, brain, loins, glands and reflexes exposed for all or any onlooker to examine. But the room stands empty, unvisited by any save my dissecting self.'[10] The surgeon to whom Barker implicitly compares the absent deity in this passage is reminiscent of the 'wounded surgeon' to whom Eliot would compare Christ in his own poem. The difference is that, deprived of this physician's expert care, Barker's narrator is obliged to operate upon himself. The contexts are too divergent to suggest borrowing, but the similarity of imagery seems to derive from a nightmare of pure negation which Eliot and Barker had endured in common. In the younger poet's work, troubled and anarchic though it was, Eliot may well have been discovering facets of his own nocturnal self.

For this and other reasons, Eliot was deeply interested in Barker's case. Faber & Faber never expected to make money from their poets, and yet Eliot clearly believed that this particular young writer was promising enough to be worth supporting at the firm's expense. Barker's circumstances evidently worried him. He was also concerned about Jessica, whom he had never met, but whose pregnancy Barker had disguised for his benefit as a debilitating, neurasthenic disease. Such was his concern that Eliot went further. In the autumn of 1934 he took the unprecedented step of writing to several wealthy friends, asking them if they would help support Barker for a year. On 5 December he was able to tell Barker that 'Four persons, who wish to remain anonymous, and who are interested enough in your work to want to support you through your present difficulties, have asked me to act as treasurer. The money collected or promised will amount to twenty-five shillings a week for a year. This is not very much, but it should help to ease the situation a little. I am to receive, and to pay out, the money quarterly.'[11] Soon afterwards the first cheque arrived.

The organisation of this fund was an enormous act of kindness from this busiest of men. Barker was never to forget the relief that it brought, nor the gratitude that he felt. The gifts, however, were anonymous, and he was never told the identity of his benefactors. In fact, the four subscribers to the fund were Lady Ottoline Morrell, Victor Rothschild, Bryan Guinness and Lady Dorothy Wellesley.[12] Eliot was always magnanimous towards impecunious young authors, but never before had he gone to such lengths. Did he perhaps remember another young poet with an occasionally depressive wife, a poet who in the year of *The Waste Land* had reached a not dissimilar low? In February 1922 it had been Ezra Pound who had asked thirty donors each to pledge £10 a year to free Eliot from the drudgery of his job at Lloyds Bank.[13] Pound's scheme had been called the 'Bel Esprit'. Though family pride and New England rectitude had caused him to refuse Pound's offer, Eliot had not forgotten the kindness. In effect, he was passing the bounty on.

In early December Maurice Carpenter came down to Kimmeridge, full of talk about the communist cause and acts of practical kindness by senior writers in London. He told Barker that he had recently organised a 'Poets' Brains Trust' at the Unity Theatre. Hugh MacDiarmid and David Gascoyne, amongst others, had read from the platform. When Gascoyne rose to his feet, he announced that he had no intention of reading anything of his own, but would instead read the audience some of the work of the Scottish poet, Edwin Muir. According to Carpenter, the gesture had been a calculated snub to MacDiarmid, who for several minutes had been snoring, none too quietly, in his chair.[14] Walter de la Mare had also sought Carpenter out at a writers' conference and had sent his regards to Dorset. For several weeks in the early autumn Muir had housed Carpenter in Hampstead. Now he was homeless again, struggling to reconcile his communism with his poetic vocation and an enthusiasm for medieval literature which he had contracted from Kit.

At Kimmeridge the Barkers did what they could to boost Carpenter's confidence as he stared out of the window at the sleet, or composed letters to his father back in Caterham. When Kit joined them from London, George was once more in the embrace of a male coterie. Kit and Carpenter shared an interest in music, which in Kit's case had blended with an absorption in English history. He was now much taken with Elizabethan song, which he performed in his light, fluting tenor voice. He and Carpenter practised the 'Ayres' of Thomas Campion, while George sat apart, reading the novels of Alexandre Dumas. Once, as the three men set out for the pub, George remarked that they resembled the three musketeers. They took to staging mock fights in the unlit streets of the village, fencing with their walking sticks.

Since both Kit and Carpenter seemed to be in the doldrums, George encouraged them with projects. Carpenter was writing political verse and Kit mock-medieval poems. As the February Press, under whose name the brothers had once published 'Octologue of the Emotions' was now defunct, George proposed another publishing venture, this time with the use of professional equipment. He had been studying classic Italian typefaces and had decided that the best font for printing verse was Bodoni. A printing press would give him the chance to demonstrate his increasingly definite ideas about book production, while enabling Kit and Carpenter to publish their own work. When Kit went back to Upper Addison Gardens, he bought a second-hand Adana press for six pounds from the market in the Portobello Road. Taking its name from the Phoenix Pottery that the brothers had inaugurated in their teens, the Phoenix Press would go into production as soon as circumstances permitted.

Just before Christmas George and Jessica joined the Barker family in Holland Park. For the first time Jessica experienced a Barker Christmas *en famille*. Big Mumma was effusive: 'How's every bit?' She entertained in the kitchen, while Grandma Taaffe nodded in the corner and Pa sat in his snuggery. When Carpenter called on Pa, he was regaled with stories of triumphs in the boxing ring which grew ever more lavish as the evening progressed. His own father, Pa boasted, had stood on a clifftop in Norfolk to hail a passing steamer, which had taken him all the way to Sydney, Australia, to see the black American heavyweight Jack Johnson fight. But what was this he heard about his elder son being some sort of a poet? He'd believe that when he produced something as stirring as Edward Fitzgerald's translation of Omar Khayyam.

The winter cold caused Barker to long for the Mediterranean, where a part of 'The Documents of a Death' was set. At the beginning of 1935, leaving Jessica in the care of his parents, he sailed for Capri in the company of a male friend, whom his diary does not identify. The ostensible purpose of the visit was to flesh out the geographical detail of the Capri sequence in the story. However, as his correspondence with Eliot makes clear, the final draft had already been submitted. Despite this, Barker obtained extra finance to cover the expedition, probably from Benjamin Astbury of the Royal Literary Fund.

It was the first time that Barker had been outside England and his real motive for leaving was, as his notebook confirms, the possibility of sexual adventure. 'Living so long in England, as I have,' he wrote on shipboard, 'having never so much as trod the Welsh removal or seen the Scilly scene, I know this of the location of love: it must be otherwise than here at home be looked for.' On setting out, he observed 'the ship straining away like a great female thought, hardly perceptible, without consternation, but leaving behind a slight atmosphere of sadness'. The boat crossed the Golfe de Lyon to Toulon, where 'the slim masculine seaplanes flit about in the silent harbour like beautiful gnats interminably purring'. Approaching Naples, Barker 'saw porpoises and mountains, and the façades of the huge Neapolitan hotels like museums and naval aeroplanes and the stars heaving over the deep sea; and heard the maddening ceaseless booming of the siren through the mists, and the regular hesitation of the engines, their conversation of love'.

Something about this brief trip made Barker uneasy. In March he wrote to Eliot mentioning the visit, the financial provisions for which he feared might have infringed the conditions of the collective fund. Eliot wrote back, 'As for your excursion to Capri, I quite understand the circumstances under which it was made.'[15] Despite Eliot's understanding, however, the Barkers were soon again beset by troubles. Two days after George had received Eliot's letter, the lease on the cottage in Kimmeridge expired. The couple found temporary accommodation for eleven days just outside London, at Nine Mile Ride, Finchampstead in Berkshire. From there on the following Saturday Barker wrote to Michael Roberts. Roberts was now teaching in Newcastle and editing the anthology that was to become *The Faber Book of Modern Verse*, to which he had invited Barker to contribute. With the disruptions and upheavals of the last few months, Barker had, he confessed in reply, been able to write only a few short poems, certainly nothing that could decently appear in the Faber book.[16] He promised to keep Roberts posted. In the meantime, he got on with reviewing Pound's *A Draft of XXX Cantos*, which Eliot had asked him to cover for the *Criterion*.[17]

On 1 April George and Jessica moved back to stay with Pa and Big Mumma in Upper Addison Gardens. George, Kit and Carpenter decided that it was now time for the Phoenix Press, which they had been planning since December, to be inaugurated. They acquired a full fount of Bodoni type, erected the press in the garden shed and started work on the first three books: one by Kit, one by Carpenter and one by an Indian writer called Iqbal Singh whom Carpenter had met in London. They decided to set Kit's poems, with their challenging mock-medieval spellings – in lines such as 'Mye trew love walkynge' – first.

When these had been printed, the amateur typesetters turned to Carpenter's new collection, *IX Poems*. Carpenter had already written a preface, which began with the prescient words: 'Between the initial impress and the final completion of a poem any number of accidents may intervene.' Working together, the three men set the text, letter by letter. After completing four poems, they went indoors for a break, passing through the kitchen, where Big Mumma was cooking. They opened the connecting door that led down by a short flight of steps to the basement. A fencing foil was leaning against the wall, next to one of Pa's walking sticks.[18]

George took the stick and Kit the unprotected foil. Neither brother was wearing a mask. They made a few preparatory passes, then began fencing in earnest. George manoeuvred Kit round to the foot of the steps. As Carpenter watched them, he could hear Big Mumma behind the door, busy with her pans. Kit mounted the steps backwards, keeping George at bay with the foil as he advanced slowly towards him. Then George shouted 'Ah!' and thrust the walking stick upwards. As he did so, Kit leaned forward.

The end of George's stick went through the right lens of Kit's spectacles, shattering the glass and grinding it into the eye-socket. When George looked up again, he saw Kit – 'my only friend' – crouching on the steps. He was holding his eye-socket with his right hand, while his left clutched the banister. His right eyeball and optic nerve were resting on his cheek, which was covered with lachrymal fluid and blood. From the kitchen, Big Mumma called, 'What is it?' The foil clattered down the steps. Big Mumma opened the door and stood framed at the head of the stairs, staring at her sons.

CHAPTER 8

BITTER APPLES

Big Mumma went first to reassure George; then she went to Kit and held him. Carpenter ran upstairs to phone for an ambulance, but his hand was trembling so violently that he could barely hold the receiver. In the ambulance he and George sat beside Kit, who told them that he was experiencing a vivid impression of the jagged outline of Corfe Castle in the empty eye-socket.[1] When they reached Hammersmith Hospital, they were told that there was no point in attempting to save the eye. The shattered glass from Kit's spectacles, embedded in the raw socket, put that out of the question. So George and Carpenter waited in an anteroom while the eyeball was surgically removed under local anaesthetic. Later Kit told them that he had felt nothing. But the manipulation of the nerves must have sent messages to his brain: during the operation he had seen an immense blue tulip swaying backwards and forwards gently, until severed at the stem.

It was a surrealist image, an image fit for an artist, which was what Kit wanted, above all else, to be. Now, however, he had been deprived of half of a painter's birthright. The doctors advised him to stay in hospital overnight. Carpenter returned to the house, while George took to the roads in his Morris Cowley, driving round the back streets of west London until morning broke over Holland Park.[2] He would never be able to make reparation. In a poem written as late as 1973 he was to describe the moment of the accident as 'an enormous natural calamity'. It was thus that he gradually came to see it: Newman's aboriginal calamity brought home; Adam's sin and Cain's.

All that he could do was to remember and re-create until mitigating distortions crept in. In Barker's own subsequent accounts, crucial details tended to alter. The walking stick metamorphosed into a foil;[3] more significantly, the incident came to be placed as far back as 1932, when George would have been nineteen and Kit sixteen. The circumstantial details provided by Barker himself and by others, however, make that impossible. At the time of the accident, Kit was nineteen and George twenty-two. Readjustment of the chronology had the effect of lending the incident a degree of innocence, as if they had been mere children playing. That Barker did not feel innocent at the time can nonetheless be inferred from a poem that he wrote eighteen months later: the dedicatory sonnet to his semi-narrative poem *Calamitteror*, the final line of which employed Kit's own image of surgical severing:

> The April horror grows over my September.
> I see my hand glittering with blood and tears
> Hanging at the bend of my arm like a leech member,
> Fatal, inspired to violence, sowing scars;
> Elevating itself in the anaconda stance
> Evolving devastation. I see my hand
> Passing over the palace of his face,
> Leaves it pale, bloody gap, blinded blanched;
> Leaving a wake of pain and leaving a loss
> Not to be rehabilitated by
> The perfect prize, the penny, or the cause,
> The blue tulip, the forget-me-not, or the sky.[4]

After Kit had been released from hospital, the three men carried on setting the Phoenix booklets. When these appeared simultaneously in May, an anonymous reviewer in the *Times Literary Supplement* praised Kit for 'a certain haunting music', and for an archaic language which caused the reader to linger over words. By contrast, Carpenter, who wanted to be a poet, was damned for being 'obsessed with words and images'.

The critical response to the Phoenix volumes was, however, overshadowed by that given to Barker's own *Poems*. Constructive as ever, Edwin Muir wrote in the *Listener* that Barker's work would recommend modern verse to a cautious poetry-reading public. To some more academically inclined reviewers, however, the notion of such an animal as the 'poetry-reading public' was anathema, and, in any case, Barker was not in any meaningful sense in the literary vanguard. *Scrutiny*'s reviewer subjected the line 'ironically echoing down the colonnade' from the poem 'Amazons' to a close reading. The adverb 'ironically', he concluded, suggested that 'our poet is determined to be modern in spite, one might say, of himself'.

It was in *New Verse* that the most damning notice appeared. Geoffrey Grigson, whose bile was up, wrote that in bringing out these poems Eliot had taken leave of his senses: 'Why has anyone published, does anyone praise, does anyone read, the verse of Mr George Barker?' Then he quoted several lines from the poem 'Have travelled that vernal avenue' to show that Barker 'has no knowledge of rhythmic form'. Finally, his exasperation rose to *fortissimo*: 'I have never attempted, I am certain, to review more nauseating poems, and I have never read more inept juvenilia. It may be excellent that Mr Barker should be healing himself in prose-poems, but he should do it by himself on the other side of the house.'[5]

In private some were grudging in their assessment of the book, others downright dismissive. When the critic and novelist Rayner Heppenstall sought to praise the volume to Dylan Thomas, Thomas conceded gloomily that it displayed 'a kind of muddy promise'.[6] On the other hand, the fastidious Norman Cameron – a contributor to *New Verse* whose general manner even the abrasive Grigson considered 'contemptuous' – believed that Barker's work gave experimentation a bad name. According to the poet John Pudney, who may have acquired the anecdote from Thomas, Cameron scoured the London bookshops for as many copies of *Poems* as he could buy, and burnt them all.

While *Janus* was awaited from the press, George and Jessica applied themselves to the frustrating business of house hunting. With Kit back from hospital and Grandma Taaffe still in occupation, there was little room now at Upper Addison Gardens. Besides, the couple were both missing Dorset. In August Jessica answered an advertisement in *The Lady* for a cottage in Plush, in the Piddle Valley, nine miles outside Dorchester.[7] The house was, according to the owner, unfurnished and in other respects a little basic. There was neither gas nor electricity. Nor was there a fireplace in any of the three bedrooms and the lavatory was an Elsan can in the shed. However, the situation promised to be quiet for writing; it was an old brick-built cottage rather than a modern bungalow, and would be theirs for £30 a year, plus an annual rate of £4. It also had an appealingly quaint address: The Butts, Plush, Folly, Mappowder, Piddletrenthide, Dorset.

One day in late August the Barkers piled the Morris high with all their belongings – tables, bed, crockery – and set out unsteadily westwards from London. George and Jessica sat in front, Kit and Carpenter behind. Every so often, the car stopped and Carpenter, a non-driver, would clamber out and crank up the stertorous old engine.[8] The Morris had no horn and so Carpenter's other job was to send blasts out of the back window with a trumpet that he had brought along for the purpose. The travellers stuttered down the Dorset lanes, watching pedestrians leap out of the way and bracing themselves against the inevitable moment when the big end would give. Through village after village – Piddleton, Tolpuddle, Piddlehinton, Byron's Piddle – they proceeded, until at Piddletrenthide the engine died on them once more. Carpenter got out and swung the handle. The engine sprang back into life and the others cheered. They continued westwards out of the village until, turning right, they started the long haul up the one-in-six gradient towards Plush.

Halfway up there was an ominous clattering and again the motor died. This time cranking was no use. So George took his foot off the brake to let the vehicle freewheel back down the hill to Piddletrenthide, where at Abbot's Garage Arthur, the proprietor, peered beneath the bonnet, pushed his cap to the back of his head and declared, 'Ah well. 'Er be a dead un, 'er be!' There was nothing for it but to complete the journey on foot. At Plush village they collected a flagon of cider from the Plush Arms and at length reached The Butts, which was set off the road behind the village, just beneath the brow of a hill and facing west. When they entered it, it smelt damp and sooty, so they lit a large fire in the twelve-by-twenty living-room and sat drinking the cider and discussing plans.

Autumn settled in and, once Carpenter had returned to London, the Barkers' seclusion deepened. Occasional ripples reached them from the wider world. *Poems* was still creating a little stir. In Dublin that September W.B. Yeats was compiling *The Oxford Book of Modern Verse*. He wrote to Lady Dorothy Wellesley, enclosing an introduction that he had drafted for one of her books and adding:

> I am tired, I have spent the day reading Ezra Pound for the Anthology – a single, strained attitude instead of passion, the sexless American professor for all his violence. I delight in a young poet called George Barker (Faber & Faber), a lovely subtle mind and a rhythmic invention comparable to Gerard Hopkins.[9]

Soon, forwarded from Russell Square, a letter arrived at The Butts headed by the blue 'Dominus Illuminatio Mea' motto of the Oxford University Press, asking permission to include four poems in the anthology: 'The Wraith-Friend', 'He comes among', 'The Leaping Laughters' and 'The Crystal'. At the bottom of the page Yeats had added a note, 'I have taken much from your work. I like you better than I like anybody else in the new generation.' The second sentence was a snub to Auden and his school, whose politics Yeats could not abide. As his letter to Lady Wellesley shows, Yeats was particularly taken with Barker's rhythms. In the preface to *The Oxford Book of Modern Verse*, which was published the following year, Yeats repeated the distinction: 'I would, if I could, have dealt at some length with George Barker who like MacNeice, Auden, Day-Lewis, handled the traditional metres with a new freedom – vers libre lost much of its vogue some five years ago – but has not their social passion, their sense of suffering.'[10] Elsewhere in his preface Yeats left his readers in little doubt that, so far as he was concerned, metrical dexterity was preferable to any amount of political engagement.

Left-wing commitment was more to the liking of Michael Roberts, to whom nonetheless Barker had sent the utterly apolitical 'Summer Idyll' as a contribution to *The Faber Book of Modern Verse*. It was in the lyrical, rhythmically syncopated style which had proved so attractive to Yeats. 'I hope', Barker wrote to Roberts, 'that Grigson does explode – to the smithereens and smithereens.'[11] When the *Faber Book* appeared, it also included 'Daedalus', 'Verses from a Nursery Wall' and 'The Chemistry of Love'. In reviewing the anthology, *New Verse* contented itself with the observation that Roberts had 'ventured prematurely into the Born 1914 class'. The indictment included Dylan Thomas, whose poems had appeared next to Barker's.

When *Janus* was published in October, Barker wrote to Roberts to ask if he liked it. 'I know that "The Bacchant" is bad,' he confessed, 'but feel that "The Documents of a Death" is very good.' He was in need of reassurance as the critics, by and large, had seen it the other way around. In *Scrutiny* Cambridge again delivered a severe judgement. Mr Barker was 'too much divorced from social realities', ergo worthless. His protagonist was a 'sexual pervert, mentally unbalanced, and somewhat of a masochist'. The much-vaunted, 'unprecedented' prose was 'a farrago of influences ranging from the Oscar Wilde of *Salomé* to some blundering imitations of Mr Empson being ambiguous'. This time there was no Edwin Muir to ride to the rescue. The *Times Literary Supplement* sounded the one redeeming note. *Janus*, it commented, had raged even further away from conventional story than had *Alanna Autumnal*. There was a kind of fuzzing of, or maybe flight from, narrative definition, as in Kafka. Yet the writing had great power: 'the slight but deliberate strangeness of the prose, the strange and vague somewhat self-cancelling metaphors and similes, the general lack of concreteness, and yet with all this an undeniable positive effectiveness of the bulk of the prose of both narratives' were undeniable and compelling.[12]

The generally lukewarm reception accorded to his new book did little to disturb the Barkers' domestic situation. With a lease at last taken out in their own names, and their finances established on a new – albeit impermanent – footing, the couple settled to a period of calm. The garden in front of the cottage covered two-thirds of an acre, run to seed until Jessica revived it. On one of Barker's visits to Faber Eliot told him how to plant potatoes. Groceries and meat were delivered to the door from a shop in Piddletrenthide. Jessica wore plain practical dresses and tied her hair back in a bun. They enjoyed bracing walks. Kit paid an early visit and Carpenter came too, on leave from his political activities. The four of them went 'scrumping'. Showing their city-bred ignorance, they assumed cider apples to be edible and bit into them, shrinking in disgust at the sourness. Soon the Barkers had acquired a black-and-white terrier called Sirrah. When next in London, George described the dog's frolicsome behaviour to Eliot, who preferred cats.

Barker's relationship with Eliot was deepening. Eliot encouraged him to write at length – a long poem, perhaps, or what about a book of criticism, examining the relationship between the poetic urge and the religious one, a subject on which they both knew more than a little? So directed, and feeling that Eliot and Yeats between them knew a little bit more about poetry than Grigson did, Barker began work on a long, semi-political poem provisionally entitled *Poem of Poverty and War*.

With his increasing recognition, Barker was again widening his social circle. No longer trapped in London, he was able to derive greater pleasure from his occasional visits there, from which he was at last learning how to create social ripples. He let more of his irreverence appear on the surface, using an outrageously subversive wit which could, he discovered, be both destructive and very exciting. In his journal he entered a note about the mixture of pleasure and misgiving that he felt during these 'felicitous periods when the mind clears of pros and cons and sees itself like a mirror held under water. I mean the gay feelings can mostly result from violating the world, as one does when one makes jokes, which is wrong and bad, and felicity is too often not the bright focus of the mind but the flash of narrow-mindedness.'[13] Much as he understood the dangerous potential of a witty tongue, he also knew just how much he and others enjoyed its free play.

Among the Londoners who appreciated this new spirit of levity was Sir Alexander Hoare, head of the international section of the Home Office and a noted patron of the arts. In October 1935, Hoare introduced Barker to his mistress and neighbour, the writer Emily Holmes Coleman. Daughter of a wealthy insurance executive from Connecticut, Coleman had once worked on the *Chicago Tribune* in Paris. With her teenaged son Johnny, she lived upstairs from Hoare at 7 Oakley Street in Chelsea. Coleman was thirty-seven years old and filled with a nervous, slightly unfocused energy. She had a forthrightness and a jaunty physical bearing which reminded her acquaintances of a boy. In 1924, after giving birth to Johnny, she had contracted puerperal fever, which led to a serious nervous collapse. Her subsequent incarceration in a mental hospital for several months had been the basis of her one novel, *The Shutter of Snow*, written in a lurid, disconnected, deeply self-immersed style akin in some respects to Barker's own recently published prose. She had a tendency to adopt people, especially younger men, whom she cultivated with such intensity that, sensing her dependency, in time they would break away and abandon her.

Though Emily was eleven years older than George, he soon discovered that they shared certain qualities: a mixture of intensity and irreverence.

She became half-patroness, half-friend. There was for all that, he quickly discovered, something offputting about her. Emily was forever stumbling over her enthusiasms, literary and amatory, forever explaining herself too much, going too far. David Gascoyne, for one, noted her affection for Barker, but thought him largely unaffected by it.[14] Although he responded to her liveliness, he was, as she recognised, careful to keep much of himself back. To her friend and compatriot Djuna Barnes, Coleman explained, 'He regards me as an American older woman who likes literature, who has gobs of money, travels the globe, knows the world, and hence has somewhat to be put up with.'[15]

Coleman's interest in Barker was partly the result of her dissatisfaction with Hoare, of whom she was fond, but who was, it seems, a reluctant lover. Late in October 1935 she wrote to her friend and near-neighbour Antonia White, telling her that she was determined to resolve this state of affairs by seducing Barker: 'I must get some little pleasure before I die. Barker will give me the calm necessary to stay with Alex.'[16] On Sunday, 22 March 1936, in her bedroom in Oakley Street, her plan was put into effect. After she and Barker had made love, he told her that he felt sick. When she asked him why, he said that he preferred men. He was, he insisted, bisexual and Jessica was a lesbian.[17] The comment, which Coleman duly copied down in her journal, was honest enough about himself; its claim concerning Jessica was preposterous. Essentially, it seems to have represented an attempt to discourage Emily, to whom Barker only seems to have made love out of compassion and politeness.

Throughout the spring and summer of 1936, Coleman's flat was the base for many of Barker's metropolitan activities. He started to lead a double life. Much of the week he spent in Dorset, writing. At weekends he was often in London, staying either at Upper Addison Gardens, from where he would go out to meet friends and acquaintances in pubs, or at Oakley Street. To friends who visited him in the country, he seemed frank and dedicated, even a model husband. In town he was more elusive. He would engage in passionate conversations of an elliptical sort, mostly *tête à tête*, and then suddenly disappear – perhaps back to the country, perhaps to some other London assignation.

In one respect he did much to encourage Coleman: in her mission to secure the publication by Faber of Djuna Barnes's novel *Nightwood*. Having taken upon herself the role of Barnes's unofficial agent, Coleman had already submitted the typescript six times to Eliot, who had invariably returned it. Undaunted, in April 1936, she called to see Eliot in Russell Square, where he proved 'very affable, and what's more, attractive. He has an odd face. He looks rather like a sea lion.' Coleman had anticipated a meeting of intense earnestness. Instead, to her surprise, the two of them spent an hour discussing

Barker amid whoops of appreciative laughter. He was, Eliot observed, 'a *very peculiar fellow*'.[18]

By now Eliot had clearly warmed to Coleman, to whom he gave the nickname 'Little Annie Oakley', partly in reference to her address and partly because of her resemblance to the resolute Wild West heroine. Over the spring and summer of 1936, he was gradually being drawn into Coleman's bohemian circle, where he was learning to adopt an informality seldom seen in the pages of his biographies. At that time in his life Eliot was evidently in a mood for taking social risks. As his commitment to a royalist high-Anglicanism hardened, he was, as it were in compensation, reaching out for personal and literary contacts which would allow him some relief from the austerity of his chosen stance. His probable attitude at the time is summed up in a passage from the preface he was to add to *Nightwood* when it appeared the following year:

> In the Puritan morality that I remember, it was tacitly assumed that if one was thrifty, enterprising, intelligent, practical and prudent in not violating social conventions, one ought to have a happy and 'successful' life. Failure was due to some weakness or perversity peculiar to the individual; but the decent man need have no nightmares. It is now rather more common to assume that all individual misery is the fault of 'society', and is remediable by alterations from without. Fundamentally the two philosophies, however different they may appear in operation, are the same. It seems to me that all of us, so far as we attach ourselves to created objects and surrender our wills to temporal ends, are eaten by the same worm.[19]

This is similar to the note which Eliot had struck in the blurb to *Janus*: an invitation, in all moral humility, to face the frailty of the flesh, especially in its less respectable manifestations. Eliot was, it should be remembered, currently living in conditions of near-monastic austerity in the Anglican presbytery at 9 Grenville Place, close to Gloucester Road station. On Sundays he served as churchwarden at nearby St Stephen's, and was active in various good works, including unpaid membership of the board of the *New English Weekly*, a high-minded periodical he had undertaken to prop up after the death of its leading spirit, Alfred Richard Orage. This, however, was the very same Eliot who in his Aristophanic drama *Sweeney Agonistes* had given Sweeney the lines:

> Any man might do a girl in.
> Any man has to, needs to, wants to
> Once in a lifetime, do a girl in

Barker had reviewed *Sweeney Agonistes* when it came out in book form in 1933. On one of Barker's routine visits to Faber, in January 1935, Eliot had told him to go and see the production then running at the Group Theatre in Great Newport Street.[20] In Barker and his associates, Eliot was to discover a worldliness that appealed to those aspects of his repressed self which he had expressed in the play. It was this quality of suppressed danger in Eliot, a slight menace beneath the surface civility, to which more anarchic spirits like Barker, Barnes and Coleman evidently responded. In their company Eliot could unbend a little. A clue to his paradoxical behaviour – so correct and yet so tolerant of laxity – is given in some words from St John of the Cross quoted both in his preface to *Nightwood* and the epigraph to *Sweeney Agonistes*: 'Hence the soul cannot be possessed of the divine union, until it has divested itself of the love of created beings.' In Coleman, Barnes, Barker and their circle, Eliot was meeting libertines, whose hedonism was apparent. To hold himself aloof would have been to make himself guilty of what, again in his preface to *Nightwood*, he was to call 'an inveterate sin of pride'. His Christianity compelled him to openness.

Barker himself was now being drawn further into this liberated social set dominated by female American expatriates. There was a brash quality, a casual emotional give and take among these women, which he found as exhilarating as it was occasionally disturbing. Barker clearly found their Americanness – which they shared with Eliot – refreshing. One afternoon that summer he emerged from the portico of the Victoria and Albert Museum to see Eliot, Emily Coleman and Djuna Barnes laughing their heads off in the back of a taxi. As the vehicle swept down the Brompton Road, Eliot leaned over, rolled down the window and gave him a cheery wave.

Through Coleman and Eliot, Barker now met Barnes, who told him that 'she believed her lesbianism to have been the consequence of her father raping her when she was a very young girl'.[21] Through Coleman, he also met her one-time employer, the heiress and gallery owner Peggy Guggenheim, who was soon taking a friendly interest in his development.

The third of Coleman's friends to whom he was introduced in 1936 was the novelist and cradle Catholic Antonia White, who asked for his address late that spring. After three disastrous marriages and two children, White was in an emotional limbo and much in need of the sort of stimulus an energetic young poet such as Barker might provide. Sensing that Barker was an up-and-coming young author, she obtained his two published works of fiction from Emily. Once she had read them, she wrote to him in Plush, expressing her admiration. On 21 May he replied:

I observe that in your letter you confess to have read both of my so-called novels and that you have not read my poems. Now this is a very suspicious sign, as both of my novels are supremely bad and my verses are supremely good. No, its hardly as simple as that. But I feel I must warn you off those novels. I think that, until you have read the critical and theoretical book on which I am now working you will not appreciate exactly *how* bad *Janus* and *Alanna* are. They seem to be – as indeed they are – fragmented relics of my fantastic youth; after all, they were written more than two years ago, I think. I will therefore confine myself to informing you that in the spring (next year, alas) Faber propose to issue both my critical work and a GIGANTIC poem on which I am working. So that we shall have no excuse for our absurd preference for prose novels – I visualize half London carrying heavy volumes under their arm on omnibuses and trains, and these volumes will contain the first four thousand cantos of my long poem.[22]

When they met, Barker found he had much in common with White, more perhaps than he had with Coleman, and certainly on a deeper level. Both had been raised as Catholics and both were at the time recusants. White's father was the schoolmaster Cecil Botting, co-author of the much-used Hillard and Botting Latin textbooks, who had brought to bear the full weight of a convert's determination on his daughter and had sent her to be educated at the Convent of the Sacred Heart, Roehampton. It was the resulting spiritual conflict that had in 1933 produced her novel *Frost in May*, in which her reactions to Catholicism were expressed with a sharpness and frankness equal to Barker's own.

Having recently broken with her third husband, Tom Hopkinson, White had moved into 105 Oakley Street, just up the road from Coleman, whom she outdid in emotional turmoil. Conscious that Antonia had caught an addiction to him from Coleman, Barker learnt to ration the time he spent in her company. Meeting her, he would pin her down with his great blue eyes, talking intensely for hours about the writer's art. Then he would suddenly and for no apparent reason stand up, nonchalantly wave, and leave the room, calling behind him, 'Bye bye! Must dash!'

Sensing a physical lukewarmness in Barker, White resolved to console herself with David Gascoyne. She invited him to her flat and told him the tormented story of her life while they sat in front of the gas fire, keeping this up until six in the morning. Gascoyne politely evaded her advances. The intimacy and the rebuff devastated her, while causing him to feel guilty and confused. 'But why,' he wrote in his journal, 'O why has all this come upon me?'[23]

Throughout the autumn of 1936 both Barker and Gascoyne were frequent visitors to Oakley Street, at Coleman's flat and at White's. The closeness of the two addresses was later to give rise to the misnomer, the 'Oakley Street Poets'.

As a categorisation of Barker and Gascoyne's work, this was as inaccurate as had been the earlier term, the 'Parton Street Poets'. Despite the lack of a shared artistic programme, however, the network of friendship persisted. Undeterred by their sexual rejection, White continued seeing both Barker and Gascoyne through that winter. Barker in the meantime had finished his affair with Coleman, who had since taken up with the film director Humphrey Jennings. By the spring of 1937 she was involved with Dylan Thomas, who was staying intermittently at 7 Oakley Street, as Barker had earlier been wont to do.

Barker seems to have wished to maintain his friendships with the opposite sex, even when reluctant to become emotionally involved. He continued to call at White's flat, while carefully confining their relationship to a professional and platonic level. Having identified in her an underlying depression – which to some extent mirrored his own – he arrived one evening to read her Coleridge's 'Dejection: An Ode', while she studied his face, which she found 'more various than any face I know. It can be quite blank – a mere neat arrangement of features – often quite mean and common – or quite remarkably beautiful . . . I find watching this face an endless fascination.' She clearly found him aesthetically pleasing, noting in her diary details that contradicted his own tentative misgivings over his appearance as expressed, for example, in his youthful journal: 'The nose is arched, small and pugnacious. The mouth very much curved over rather large teeth. A very characteristic look is with the eyelids dropped and the lips parted.' Barker was only twenty-three, but had already developed the authority and air of an older man, walking with a slight stoop at the knees. But, with all this, 'he has a boy's boastfulness, love of teasing, love of preposterous exaggeration, sudden unbounded contempt for "girls"'. In any case, he was well aware of the pull he exercised over others. He was, he told White romantically, born on the anniversary of Keats's funeral. Then, just as she was warming to him, he remembered an appointment and departed in his customary insouciant style, leaving her tantalised and ruminative, musing over her diary: 'I cannot write any more about Barker tonight though he is so much in my thoughts, and I have so much I want to record about him.'

CHAPTER 9

'THE MASS OF ROSES FACE'

There were quite a few places for Barker to dash off to. One was Taplow in Buckinghamshire, where in May 1936 he went to see Walter de la Mare. He sat under a fig tree in the garden reading his host one of his critical essays. In the middle of it, as if out of nowhere, came two claps of thunder. The first, which exploded close to the two men, was so violent that it caused Barker to duck. It was followed by another burst, next to a plum tree on the other side of the lawn.[1]

Two weeks later Barker was writing in the front room at Plush, when a large Bentley drew up outside, disgorging an elderly and dignified lady wearing a hat that resembled a nautical clipper. This apparition was the celebrated Bloomsbury hostess, patron of the arts and châtelaine of Garsington Manor, Lady Ottoline Morrell. She was, Ottoline informed Barker, holidaying at Studland Bay, and thought that she might drop in and see him.[2] She had asked for him in Swanage and Dorchester and got lost several times. Lady Ottoline presented him with two bone china cups and saucers and a copy of Aldous Huxley's novel *Eyeless in Gaza*. She was then driven back to the coast.

Meanwhile Barker had his long poem to write and, in between, his theoretical work, which he was calling *Essays on the Theory of Poetry*. Uncertain of his qualifications for this task, he sent it in instalments to Edwin Muir, who had escaped from the noise of London to a house outside St Andrews. There, Muir wrote, the happiness he shared with Willa was, if anything, more complete than what he heard of George and Jessica's in Dorset; yet The Butts must be doing Barker the world of good if the poetry was anything to go by. Muir wrote approvingly of the poem 'The Shades', which had just appeared in the *London Mercury*. It had a new confidence and charm: 'I think that the radiance and easy graceful movement of the latest poem give it a most lovely quality. You are developing as a poet should, a very rare thing to happen;

you're the white blackbird, the nonpareil. I'm the round peg in the square hole or, being an angular Scotsman, the square peg in the round hole . . .'[3]

In the spring of 1936 Jessica suffered a very early miscarriage, which caused her to feel exhausted, resentful and more regretful than ever that she had given up her daughter. Affected by her mood, Barker showed a new protectiveness when at her side. He also reshaped the long poem, making both the miscarriage and the accident with Kit's eye central to it. There are few signs here, or in much of Barker's writing of the time, of his other life in London. The images are mostly derived from his domestic circumstances and rural surroundings, and from his reading of the newspapers. If his social life had found a new fulcrum, his creative life was well and truly earthed at The Butts.

From Jessica's point of view, the marriage was closer than it had ever been. When in May, shortly after the miscarriage, David Gascoyne spent the weekend at Plush, he had the impression of a sacrosanct domestic felicity. On the Saturday evening he and the Barkers had talked and drunk around the fireplace in the living room before going to bed. Gascoyne could not sleep. In the early hours he wandered out into the garden, where he stood looking back on the little cottage huddled beneath the curve of the hill, the embers of the fire in the living room still sending a glow through the windows. Later he re-created the moment in his poem 'The Sacred Hearth', which was to possess something of the grave affability of Coleridge's conversation poems. With its images of a consecrated contentment, the poem reflects Jessica's view of the marriage more than George's:

> I wandered out across the briar-bound garden, spellbound.
> Most mysterious and unrecapturable moment, when I stood
> There staring back at the dark white nocturnal house,
> And saw gleam through the lattices a light more pure than gold
> Made sanguine with crushed roses, from the firelights that all night
> Stayed flickering about the sacred hearth. As long as dawn
> Hung fire behind the branch-hid sky, the strong
> Magic of rustic slumber held unbroken; yet a song
> Sprang wordless from inertia in my heart, to see how near
> A neighbour strangeness ever stands to home.[4]

Gascoyne's preoccupation with surrealism was proving increasingly absorbing. He had published the definitive *A Short History of Surrealism* the previous year and was now working with Roger Roughton and the English Surrealist Group on the preparation of a large exhibition devoted to the movement. It was to be held at the New Burlington Gardens Art Gallery in July. There were to be exhibits from Spain, France and England; André Breton, surrealism's founder and dogmatist, was to attend, as was Salvador Dalí, its most notorious proponent. To support the initiative, Roughton had launched a periodical entitled *Contemporary Poetry and Prose* from his lodgings above Meg's Café at 1 Parton Street, distributing it from Archer's bookshop opposite. The first number contained two poems by Dylan Thomas, together with his story 'The Burning Babe', about a Welsh minister who incinerates the fruit of his incestuous union with his daughter. There was also a poem by Gascoyne, who is described in the 'Notes on Contributors' as, 'at 19, England's only wholehearted Surrealist'.

The craze was proving contagious. Kit Barker, for one, was finding in surrealism something that gave shape to his aspirations as a painter. For a while it also rubbed off on George, who was looking for a way to organise his long and, currently, disconnected poem, envisaged as the first of a series of 'Cantos'. Suddenly disconnection was a virtue. George was grappling with images of childbirth and of blinding, while endeavouring to articulate his growing political unease. These were not easy concerns to bring together, but surrealism provided an artistic technique. After such images as the horrific slicing of an eye in Luis Buñuel's film *L'Age d'Or* (1930), which had recently been shown in London, Kit's half-blinding came to seem an archetypal artistic event. Barker could now hang discrete images next to one another and make their very inconsistency appear a virtue.

In July the Surrealist Exhibition opened, attracting publicity less by its declared programme than by the high jinks surrounding it. A figure appeared at the opening of the show with a face entirely smothered in roses, which Gascoyne had purchased from a street market.[5] Dylan Thomas came and, sensing that wilful oddness required a matching response, examined one of the sculptures before solemnly hanging a herring from it. Dalí attempted to deliver a speech in Catalan from inside a diver's suit, growing redder by the minute until Gascoyne, realising that his high colour stemmed not from eloquence but asphyxiation, let him out.

The exhibition closed after three weeks. Surrealism was never to put down secure roots in England, but it had influenced Kit's painting as well as, transiently, George's verse. Having briefly attended the exhibition during one of his flying visits from Dorset, he included the chief attractions in his 'Canto':

> I recall the rosetree that sprang from my breast.
> I recall the myriads of birds in the cage of my head,
> I recall my third finger the branch of myrtle,
> I recall the imprisoned women wailing in my bowels.
> I was the figure of the Surrealist Exhibition

> With the mass of roses face. I hung like the hawk
> Hungry over the running world, I hung
> Like sun that pulls the bright boys, like the spider.[6]

The poem was also influenced by the Spanish Civil War, which had broken out in May. On 22 October Gascoyne, weighed down with manuscripts and luggage, took the boat train from Victoria. In Paris he collected his visa from the bureau of the provisional Catalonian government and then flew to Barcelona, where he stayed at a flea-ridden *pension* off the Ramblas. Every morning for the next few weeks, he would journey by tram to his translating job at the Propaganda Ministry, from where at six in the evening he delivered a news bulletin in English to the city and to the world at large. Stephen Spender had also just arrived in Barcelona; hearing Gascoyne's familiar tones blasting from a roadside loudspeaker, he nearly jumped out of his skin. The broadcasts also caused some consternation in Teddington, where Gascoyne's parents could pick up transmissions on their wireless.[7]

Since the Spanish Church had given the fascist leader Franco their enthusiastic blessing, the war was a source of embarrassment to left-wing Catholics everywhere. Barker's personal response was to broaden the issues beyond their Iberian setting. He was one of those approached when Edgell Rickword's magazine *Left Review* confronted 121 writers with the blunt question 'Are you for, or against, the legal Government of the People of Republic Spain?' Though unimpeachably pro-Loyalist, his answer slipped nimbly between the unequivocal commitment to Spanish democracy enunciated by Spender and Gascoyne, and the measured neutrality of Eliot. He wrote, 'I AM FOR THE PEOPLE of Republic Spain, for the people of China, for the people of England, for the people of Germany, etc. I am against Fascism, Franco, Mussolini, Japanese generals, Hitler, Walter Chrystler, the Archbishop of Canterbury, etc.'[8] By cheekily placing the Anglican Primate among the fascists, Barker's remark implicitly aligned all English Catholics with the Republic. Meanwhile, back in Plush, he remembered the impact of the French Revolution on the young Blake. Drawing heavily on 'Visions of the Daughters of Albion', he converted his 'Canto' into an allegory of political awakening. The first ten stanzas were published in a special Picasso issue of *Contemporary Poetry and Prose* in September 1936: in them childbirth supplied a perfect image for the emergent political conscience. Now that Barker had a focus and a theme, the rest of the poem came easily. In December he wrote a conclusion which blended Blakeian echoes, surrealist juxtapositions and allusions to a thickening Spanish crisis:

> I remember again the three women weeping in Irun's ruins,
> Whose tears will wash the Rhone and the Rhine and whose grief
> Thrust up like crystal towers the architecture of Time.
> I see England
> With the underground mines run bleeding along like wounds
> I hear the great Lancastrian shafts delivering sounds
> Of sorrow and appeal, or watch the factory stacks
> Like hands for charity, or fallen, clenched.[9]

Then he sent the poem to Eliot, requesting that it be published either as *Cantos*, or else as *Poem of Love and War*. Eliot accepted the work, but disliked the suggested titles, especially the first (too academic-sounding and, anyway, already claimed by Ezra Pound). Then Barker proposed *Calamiterror*, which Eliot approved, explaining that in Latin 'calamus' meant a reed. Barker was less than jubilant about this contrivance, but if five directors of Faber & Faber thought it acceptable, who was he to argue?

On New Year's Day 1937 Barker trudged the lanes around Plush. They were covered in a snow which 'metamorphosed the place into a vision of crystal and pearl, rocks and capes of glory and the trees like aladdin's parasols'. When a forward spring arrived, he wandered towards the hamlet of Folly and gathered primroses from a ditch. One night he awoke in a panic to find on his body a rash compared in his journal to 'the syphilitic rose'. It was surely, he wrote, a false alarm – 'since I have neither had the Dean Street girls, nor been had by them'. In February he fell ill with flu – 'I had no idea the thing could wipe you out so completely.' He spent his twenty-fourth birthday in bed, as odours of stale fruit, bad breath, hidden urine and eau de cologne cavorted around the bedroom 'like *pagliacci*'.[10] He convalesced while watching the dancing of the ivy bush outside the window, 'like a spire suffering convulsions of ecstasy and agony'. Then he got up and corrected the proofs of *Calamiterror*.

When the weather broke, George and Jessica explored the nearby villages. At Cerne Abbas they stared up at its priapic chalk giant, contemplating the anomaly of pagan remnants amid the settled quietness. A few miles distant, at Minterne Magna, they discovered a large, ramshackle stately home with gardens by 'Capability' Brown. After they had stopped in the village for refreshments, Barker wrote a poem which indulges an old fancy of poetic visitation. His visitor this time is not Blake but 'Edmund my Spenser brooding about doom', whom he imagines squatting amid 'the adolescent Dorset downs' and receiving thank offerings from the local maidens.[11] This was a new kind of poem: an encounter with the ghost of a great English poet, which at the same time offers a reading of his work. Barker returned to the genre several times. The next encounter is set in Notting Hill, where the poet meets a compound phantom called 'Orpheus–Apollo'.[12] More successfully, in 'Resolution of Dependence', Barker describes running into an elderly Wordsworth among the crowds on Bournemouth promenade. The strength of the poem lies in its taunting of the latterday, reactionary Wordsworth with the ideals of his revolutionary youth. It also allowed Barker an opportunity to place the collectivist panacaeas of the 1930s in a wider historical perspective:

> 'Not you and not me, but all of them.
> It is the conspiracy of five hundred million
> To keep alive and kick. This is the resolution,
> To keep us alive and kicking with strength and joy.
> The past's absolution is the present's resolution.
> The equation is the interdependence of parts.'[13]

In 'The Allegory of the Adolescent and the Adult' Barker recorded a moment of personal revelation in which a young man, filled with daydreams of a wonderful future as he walks the Hampshire downs, suddenly recognises that far greater marvels lie around him in wind, grass and hill.[14] It was the natural and everyday that reached out to him in Plush. An uncomplicated delight in ordinary things is visible too in photographs of life at The Butts: they show Big Mumma with Pa and Kit outside a barn; Pa relaxed in his shirt-sleeves; Mumma sitting big-hipped in a generous gingham dress, peering beatifically down as Jessica sews and Kit strokes Sirrah. In another snapshot, taken behind the cottage, Pa has his legs outstretched in a wicker easy chair and is pretending to read, while Mumma jokily tests the temperature of his bald head. These were happy days, halcyon days, as Jessica would remember them long after they were gone.

Throughout his life Barker had a talent for intimacy combined with a generosity which extended benevolently outwards, sometimes in extravagant ways. His instinct was to reach out to chance acquaintances and gather them to him in a spirit of conviviality and trust. One way to achieve this was to turn poetry into a vehicle for intimate communication. More than a century before Coleridge had done this in his poems to Charles Lamb. Could the Romantic convention of the conversation poem be revived?

In April 1937 Barker wrote to Dylan Thomas, who was then in Glamorgan, suggesting an exchange of letters in verse. Such pieces might be about anything, and might include references to friends, to social events, to grudges, to flushes of literary enthusiasm, even to politics if the writer were so inclined. That Barker should have chosen Thomas as his correspondent was unremarkable in itself, since the two poets were already associated in the public mind. This was partly the result of biographical accident and partly of a superficial similarity of style. Born in unglamorous circumstances within a year of one another, they had appeared side by side, since 1934, in successive issues of *The Year's Poetry*, edited for the Hogarth Press by John Lehmann, as well as in Roberts's *Faber Book of Modern Verse*. Since both at the time wrote in what could be called a torrential vein, they had already been classified by undiscriminating readers as poets of much the same school.

In this light, the fact that the two men were dissimilar in temperament and upbringing – that the one was lapsed Catholic Irish, the other lapsed Protestant Welsh – seems not to have been noticed. As it happens, far from being allies, they had not yet even met. Once they had exchanged a desultory wave across a room in Bloomsbury. They had also rubbed shoulders at one of the parties in Archer's upper room. By April, furthermore, they must forever have been missing one another by seconds at Emily Coleman's flat in Oakley Street, where Thomas had seen living on and off since January.

Since the beginning of their relationship, Thomas had gone to some lengths to persuade Coleman of the inferiority of Barker's verse. Unbeknown to Barker, Thomas already distrusted him with a tenacity springing partly from literary suspicion and partly from private envy. The two men were rivals in more than one sense. While stories about their social behaviour echoed one another, it is arguable that in this respect it was Thomas who imitated Barker's exploits. Thomas was, for instance, rumoured to get down on all-fours under the table and bark like a dog: a piece of social exhibitionism which made more sense when indulged in by the eponymous Barker, of whom the anecdote is also told.[15] Thomas was also sometimes seen cornering a girl with a mixture of swagger, hyperbole and insult. But this was Barker's characteristic manner of address, and for him it worked rather better, as Thomas might well have been aware from his dealings with Coleman. And so far as public recognition went, Barker was at this stage apparently the more successful poet, since he appeared on Faber's list.

Yet Thomas was not one to erect barriers. On 4 April he replied, accepting the idea about verse letters with an odd mixture of warmth and defensiveness.[16] He was, he wrote disingenuously, something of a recluse who knew very few poets: 'I know the one who looks as if he had an unfortunate sexual experience under the sea; and the one with little red pig eyes and a private income.' Those that he knew, he was not keen on; but by all means let them chatter away in verse, as long as in advance they fix a metre, a common mode of exchange: 'Who'll start?'

Barker did. The following month he published in *New Verse* an 'Epistle to D.T.' which stressed, not their differences, but a shared alienation, and undistinguished social beginnings. There was also a hint at their common exclusion from Auden's circle, to which Thomas had alluded obliquely in his letter. Their real link, however, was poverty:

> Now I know what was wanting in my youth,
> It was not water or a loving mouth.
> It was what makes the apple-tree grow big,
> The mountain fall, and the minnow die.
> It was hard cash I needed at my root.
> I now know that how I grew was due
> To echoing guts and the empty bag –
> My song was out of tune for a few notes.[17]

On one fact they might agree: the change in the climate of English poetry had as much to do with class as with style. When for the next issue of *New Verse* – an Auden double number – both poets were invited to contribute their respective 'Comments on Auden', the closeness of their remarks certainly suggested a shared perspective. Barker wrote, 'I like Auden's work because it exhilarates me in a way in which height, ozone, speed, drink, and violent exercise do not: I mean it has the singular effect of poetry on my senses. I dislike aspects of it because behind or through the poetry I discern a clumsy interrogatory finger questioning me about my matriculation certificate, my antecedents and my annual income.' Thomas wrote, 'I admire . . . the mature, religious and logical fighter, and deprecate the boy bushranger.'[18]

Thomas never replied to Barker's poem. In London they continued to just miss one another. Gascoyne was now back from Spain: on 13 April, over lunch in a Bloomsbury restaurant, Barker talked to him about literature for two hours, after which, Gascoyne's diary later remarked, 'I seem to have understood a lot more.' At three o'clock Barker walked his friend to Russell Square, where the two parted company in front of Faber's offices, arranging to meet at seven that evening outside a pub in Fitzrovia, where Antonia White and Emily Coleman would also be drinking. Gascoyne wandered off to Piccadilly Circus to look for a phone booth from where he could phone White to tell her about the arrangements. He had just found one when he spotted Dylan Thomas rolling through the crowds. Thomas was on his way to the cinema with an excitable young Irish girl, whom he introduced as Caitlin. Gascoyne agreed to accompany them part of the distance; halfway up Piccadilly Thomas felt a speck of dust in his eye and had to sit in a pharmacy while boracic acid was poured into the eye-socket: a most unpleasant sight, remarked Gascoyne, who was prone to moments of physical distaste. Thomas, he gathered, had just broken with Coleman. Tactfully, therefore, he forbore to mention the appointment with Barker and Coleman later in the evening. After that Dylan and Caitlin went on their way. The session in the pub turned out to be chaotic, anyway. The poet Ruthven Todd arrived after being roughed up by thugs. Nina Hamnet told drunken stories. A little after nine, resorting to his habitual disappearing act, Barker remembered his train to Dorchester and left.[19]

CHAPTER 10

'SICK OF LOVE'

Barker's visit to London that day had been motivated by a project he had been discussing with Eliot. For some time he had been attempting to interest the author of 'Ash Wednesday' in a scheme which had been dear to him since the months in Kimmeridge: the preparation of a proper edition of 'Quia Amore Langueo'. In 1925 Arthur Quiller-Couch had included the section headed 'The Appeal of Christ to Mankind' in his *Oxford Book of English Verse, 1250–1900*, but this was only half of what had come down from the late fourteenth century. Eight variant manuscripts of a complementary lyric, 'The Appeal of the Blessed Virgin Mary to Man', also existed which, ever since George and Kit had got to know it in the Harleian manuscripts, had seemed to them incomparably more lovely. Persuaded by Barker, Eliot commissioned H. S. Bennett, the medievalist and Fellow of Emmanuel College, Cambridge, to bring the two halves of the poem together in a slim volume illustrated with woodcuts by Eric Gill.[1] The restitution had the effect of re-investing the poem with the lingering sexual ambiguity to be found in 'The Song of Solomon', from which its refrain was derived: 'Stay me with flagons, comfort me with apples, for I am sick of love.' For Barker, it also had the advantage of setting the female voice of desire beside the male one, as he had done in *Alanna Autumnal*. The Virgin's restored lament possessed an erotic poise, enhanced by Gill's amorously spiritual illustrations:

> In a tabernacle of a toure,
> as I stode musying on the mone,
> a crowned quene, most of honoure,
> apered in gostly wyght ful sone.
> She made compleynt thus by hyr one,

for mannes soule was wrapped in wo:
'I may nat leue mankyndh allone,
    Quia amore langueo.

'I longed for loue of man my brother,
I am hys vokete to voyde hys vyce;
I am hys moder – I can no other –
why shuld I my dere chylde dispyce?
Yef he me wrathe in diuerse wyse,
through flesshes freelte fall me fro.
Yet must we rewe hym tyll he ryse,
    Quia amore langueo.'

In November 1937, when the book appeared in a limited edition of 400 copies, Eliot asked Barker to review it in the *Criterion*. 'If, after a half a dozen readings of the poem,' Barker wrote, 'the extraordinary merit of it is not plain to the neutral person, I give up. Without qualifications or conditions I merely insist that this is a great poem, and leave it at that.'

In the meantime, *Calamiterror* had appeared in April. Despite his undeniable and egregious mannerisms, Barker could not now be ignored. Some surprise was expressed at the book's political message. 'Perhaps', mused *Scrutiny*, 'the political Left will receive the new convert with rejoicing.' Though perhaps not, since the convert's passion was a little too eclectic: 'Mr Barker with his talent wants to be in everybody's swim.' A fairly recent publication, *Twentieth Century Verse*, edited from Croydon by a 25-year-old writer called Julian Symons, gave *Calamiterror* the most space. The reviewer was Desmond Hawkins, anxious that this niggling matter of Barker's reputation be settled once and for all. So far, Hawkins wrote, it had been 'based on promise and heavily mortgaged, with Gentle Geoffrey in the rôle of villain urging Mr Eliot to foreclose'. Might it not be most revealing to regard this still very young poet in the light of, say, the earliest Yeats, Yeats with his stilts on? 'Yeats has always been pretentious from the very nature of his character, in which a foreshadowing of what he ought to do preceded executive ability. So sometimes Barker's pretensions are targets made ready to be shot at tomorrow. The point is that these men make themselves into considerable poets by sheer pertinacity, by a slow and laborious transfiguration of youthful unchastities.'[2]

Friends were also forthcoming with admiration and counsel. Edwin Muir received *Calamiterror* as a fiftieth birthday present from Willa and sent a cheering letter.[3] In July Emily Coleman wrote from Skipton in Yorkshire, where she was recovering from her fall-out with Dylan Thomas. She had needed, she confessed to Barker, to overcome a prejudice against his work implanted during her months with Dylan. But *Calamiterror* now seemed to her incredibly beautiful. 'As I see it now it is a sort of recording of your breaking out from the skin of your self-love, emerging from the subjective chrysalis.'[4]

This was all well and good, but the Barkers' finances were in crisis. Eliot and the subscribers to his fund had now extended his allowance twice; to supplement it, Barker needed, he felt, to make his writing more lucrative. He was tempted by various kinds of hack work. For the *Shell Guides* he wrote an essay on Norwich, a city he had come to know and love from those months in Geldeston. The Castle Museum, he wrote, 'is a magnificent sham well worth seeing in eight minutes' fairly distant examination. From the city it has the appearance of a boy's fort left accidentally on a hill top, but seen closer it impresses a little better.'[5]

Taking a leaf out of Eliot's book, he also attempted verse drama. He sent to Russell Square a sprawling political fable entitled *Johannesburg Mask*, set in the mines of South Africa. Eliot returned it with the remark that it was 'overloaded with metaphor' (its implied theme was the Spanish crisis). Then Barker made Big Mumma's hero James O'Hanlon protagonist of a political tragedy, *Hanlon Omega*, about an abortive uprising in Drogheda on 4 October 1914.[6] In the play Hanlon jumps the political gun and organises a local rising without national support. When his wife dies in childbirth, he perceives the private consequences of public action and calls the uprising off. He is finally assassinated by his own brother for the greater good of the Republican movement. The play comes alive at only one point, when Hanlon undergoes his private change of heart. 'Burn this drivel!' Barker scrawled over the typescript and then decided to be a popular novelist.

With Kit he sketched out a commercial Book Society novel to be called *Nobby Arthur Rex*; it was followed by a lampoon travelogue, its title taken from the last line of George's favourite limerick: *The Smile on the Face of the Tiger*. This concerned an improvident young man by the name of Divine, who decides on a brisk trot round the continent in the company of his pet tiger, Timothy. The two of them reach Boulogne, where they become embroiled in the affairs of a joke fascist organisation, the 'Rexists'. At this point Divine's enthusiasm collapses, along with the text. Finally, reviving his earlier passion for the Crusades, Barker produced a historical saga written in a prose style resembling mock Walter Scott. It was called *Jerusalem* and in the late summer he sent that as well to Eliot.

Meanwhile, in Upper Addison Gardens, Grandma Taaffe had received a visit from her unmarried elder daughter, Margaret. The talk and the singing around the breakfast table revived Barker's interest in Ireland, inspiring two pieces of writing: his important 'Poem on Ireland', with its alternative version of the O'Hanlon legend and vision of a maternal land 'at its usual work: weeping among the seed potatoes'; and a shorter piece, 'By the Boyne', published in the *Listener* in July. Hearing the old songs, Barker was impelled to try his hand at a ballad, though one with an American refrain. It was a promise of things to come:

> So down I went to the Shenandoah river
> Floating along like a ship or a queen,
> I floated down past the world and then went
> Into the greatest place that I have ever been.[7]

While they waited to hear *Jerusalem*'s fate, George and Jessica looked for distraction. Recalling his visit to Capri three years earlier, Barker was keen to visit the mainland of Italy: a trip that would have been well beyond his means had it not been for the participation of Delano Ames, a successful detective-story writer from America, who was courting Jessica's older sister Kit and would later marry her. George, Jessica, Kit and Ames decided to explore the northern Italian lakes. In early August they packed the car – Ames's, rather than one of Barker's bangers – and set off across France and Switzerland, eager for their first sight of the Dolomites. At night, with Barker at the wheel, they roared across the Alps, descending at dawn to the 'broad Brescian march'. Passing through the ample valleys of the foothills, then skirting lakes Maggiore and Como, they found their hotel nestling by the side of the Lago d'Iseo. Here, on the sultry evenings that followed, Barker lay listening to girls splashing in the water beneath his balcony. The air was so still that the music of two mandolins could clearly be heard from the opposite shore. It was a perfect holiday, welcome after the stresses and strains of the last few months, and Barker would later remember it, in sorrow, as the apogee of his marriage. They stayed there for three weeks. After climbing Monte Cuola, George and Jessica were back in Dorset by 8 September.

While they were away, a 23-year-old Canadian writer called Elizabeth Smart had been in London on holiday. Smart belonged to an affluent Ottawa family, was the second of three sisters and had travelled in Europe, New Zealand and Australia. While in London, she studied the piano with the well-known recitalist Katharine Goodson, and harmony and composition with Goodson's husband Arthur Hinton; later, for a term, she attended lectures on literature at King's College. She had written poetry since her teens and her gift for prose was already evident in her journals. In August 1937 she was in search of an act of self-definition. One hot afternoon late that month, she had stood in the shade of Better Books, a bookshop on Charing Cross Road, and taken down from the shelf a copy of George Barker's *Poems*, with its light-blue cover and flattering blurb by

Eliot. Turning to the poem 'Daedalus', she had read: 'I lift his head, his death dampens / The moist palm of my hand, like handled fear / Like fear cramping my hand.' Impressed at once by the urgency of the language, she bought the book and decided to find out more about its young author.

By late September George and Jessica were back in Dorset at The Butts, listening to the hail wreck the last few stalks of the harvest; later, a thoroughgoing storm buffeted the apple trees out in the garden. There was bad news from Eliot, to whom the flurry of Barker's summertime projects had spelled desperation. Eliot was now uneasily conscious that by extending Barker's allowance he was merely helping him keep his head above water, while encouraging him to take on projects for which he had no talent. After reading *Jerusalem*, Eliot put it aside for several weeks and then wrote a letter. The novel, he acknowledged, had a haunting music not unlike the music of Barker's old love, Edmund Spenser: 'there is the same quaint, sharply defined dream imagery, in which one scene melts imperceptibly into another'. But there was too much of the old visceral symbolism. And now Barker was attempting to please a general public 'whose tastes, as the chairman and I both think, you are not equipped either to understand or to gratify'. To save himself from such excesses, it was essential that he now obtain some form of paid employment as far as possible from literature ('I had eight years in the bank myself'). This would see him through the fallow periods while making him independent both of charity and of the debilitating effects of Grub Street. But the allowance would cease. The gist of Eliot's message lay in these words:

> I believe in your genius, so far as one is ever justified in believing in genius except in retrospect, and I believe that it is genius if anything and not talent. If I am right, that is the best reason for not blunting your gifts on hackwork. Although it may be natural for you to write a great deal, I believe that yours is a concentrated kind of gift – you should scrap a good deal and publish little. I cannot believe that you are one of those – nearly always second-rate – persons who can expect to make a living out of writing. You ought to be in a position in which you could be indifferent to frequent publication and its immediate financial rewards, and cultivate an attitude which would enable you to observe the prosperous parade of more facile and accommodating talents. You should be prepared to be acclaimed late, if at all.[8]

The advice was an honest reflection of Eliot's belief in Barker's more experimental writing, in which from the beginning he had relished a sensation almost of free fall. It was only when the writing assumed borrowed properties, or, as in *Jerusalem*, strove to be popularist, that Eliot lost patience. He had cavilled at details of diction, but selectively, permitting any amount of linguistic bending so long as the object had been clearly in focus. 'Their eyes are mauves' had been fine; 'lair' as a verb, 'freezed' as a past participle, had not. When Barker had attempted set forms, Eliot had grown uneasy, reassured only when the results were sufficiently wayward. In a sense, he had been more taken with Barker's vices than with his virtues. His advice had often amounted to this: be adventurous, be bold.

Temperamentally, Eliot did not simply want, but needed, Barker to be that 'very peculiar fellow' he had described to Emily Coleman. His fear for him was that acceptance and popularity might blunt his peculiarity, his distinctiveness. For Eliot, Barker was only truly himself when he was courageously odd, as in 'Daedalus'. It may have seemed to Eliot, as he looked back on his own earlier life, that he had never been more courageous in his literary experiments than in the years he had spent working at Lloyds Bank. All the more reason to steer his protégé towards a congenial and safe occupation that would give him the security to take risks on paper.

The argument was sound in theory, but it had little chance of succeeding in practice. What Eliot failed to appreciate was that Barker held too conventional a view of the artist ever to live out the paradox of external decorum and inner rage that Eliot himself so convincingly embodied. Barker as banker was never feasible for reasons that had as much to do with background as with temperament. Born into the professional classes and with his Harvard education, Eliot had been able to turn himself into a city clerk with a certain ease and grace. A poet like Barker, whose formal education had stopped at elementary school, was more likely to feel that the system had conspired to crush him. Eliot had been able to assume his rôle of pinstriped aplomb because, ultimately, he had known that his choice was a free one. Barker, by contrast, needed to assert his freedom in all outward respects – not simply in his art, but in his life too.

Yet for months Barker fretted, while trying to do Eliot's bidding. Eliot had thought that he might be able to fix him up with a job in advertising, while Muir and Roberts both tried to get him teaching jobs, for which he was completely unqualified. On several occasions he put in for university posts, citing his published work in support. Without a matriculation certificate, let alone a degree, his case seemed hopeless. So he wrote self-pityingly to Emily Coleman, who was on an autumnal visit to America, funded by her insurance-executive father. Professional security, he complained, seemed as far off as ever; never having passed an examination in his life was an insuperable barrier to any kind of a job. In November, from 55th Street, New York, Coleman replied in terms which were salutary, affectionate, and profoundly revealing of their milieu:

I'm sure that any kind of a job, the way that you feel now, would be a relief to you. The way I regard life (I mean the way life has come to have any meaning for me) is that every one of us has some kind of a struggle. Yours seems to be the economic one – a particularly futile one, it seems to me; it can undermine one, and take away all of one's dearest, most bitterly-earned courage. Don't let it do that to you. Remember, Barker, I have had another struggle – a terrible one – and Tony [Antonia White] in her way has had a very bad one – against insanity, think of that, and Peggy [Guggenheim] has had another one, against her own nature, things that you do not know about – which has nearly done her in. And we can't begin to imagine the awful inner life, the barrenness, of Eliot. I'm saying this because I think that at times you tend to think of yourself as the most unfortunate of men – especially now you would be prone to feel that. But really, dear, every one of us, in some field, has a horrible time; and there are many who would give a great deal to be in your shoes (you won't believe it) – to have the peace that comes from your life with your wife – to have your growing talent – and, in a material way, the knowledge that whatever you write that is good Faber will print, and Eliot will appreciate. Not many people can look forward to that.[9]

CHAPTER 11

'THE LEAST QUALIFIED APPLICANT IN ENGLAND'

Coleman's letter made a great deal of sense. In November 1937 not many young writers could look forward to a brighter future than Barker, though many were more employable. His best option still seemed to be teaching. He was by now widely read and had, besides, eloquence and presence, and an enviable ability to make others trust him and to feel that what he said was of consequence. He also possessed clear and articulate opinions, even if these were not always phrased in the received language of critical discourse. These were all good qualifications for an academic appointment at a certain level. Eliot would have preferred him to take up a profession more distant from literature, but, if he wished to teach, was prepared to back him.[1] A reference from Eliot carried considerable weight in scholarly circles, but would be much enhanced if he was able to say that Barker had systematically applied himself to the production of criticism. With this in mind, Barker now set to work on his somewhat delayed *Essays on the Theory of Poetry*. Critical prose was not, he wrote to Muir, a task for which he felt himself ideally equipped. To assure himself of his fitness, and to test his speculations, he began to try the essays out on friends. One he sent to Muir in Scotland, others to Eliot, who in October 1937 published the most promising in the *Criterion*, under the title 'Poetry and Reality'.

The essay he showed Muir concerned poetry and religion as modes of assent. Both the poet and the believer, it argued, needed to make statements that were not true in a literal sense. This was most obviously the case when the poet was himself a believer, as in religious verse. Hopkins's state of mind when writing sonnets was analogous to that of St Ignatius Loyola performing spiritual exercises, or of St John of the Cross meditating. Barker then tried to extend this claim to secular poetry by annexing the terminology of the Cambridge critic I.A. Richards, who believed all poetry to consist of a series of 'pseudo-statements'. However, his attempt to marry Catholic theology to modern critical theory proved a little rich for the more conventionally religious Muir. When all was said and done, Muir protested, poetry and religion were very different activities: 'For poetry the actual Christ is not necessary; but for religion he is.'[2]

In the essay published in the *Criterion*, Barker compared literary theory and poetry to spiders spinning webs out of their vitals. Both were stable only when anchored in some corner of the real. But, if poetry was connected to reality, it should not be judged by the laws of verisimilitude. In the sixth book of his *Poetics* Aristotle had said that a plausible impossibility was preferable to a possible implausibility. By the same token, the poem should be judged by reference less to external truth than to its own internal consistency: 'the metaphor should not violate its own conditions'. Since poetry took its materials from the real world, a clash of principles would always be present: 'the exhilaration arising from the juxtaposition or clash of these two spheres supplies one of the major exhilarations of poetry'. Poetry was at its most effective when enabling the metaphor to filter downwards, transforming the everyday world into something unexpected. When, for example, in Tennyson's *The Princess*, the maid sang 'Tears, idle tears . . . Rise in the heart and gather to the eyes, / In looking on the happy Autumn fields, / And thinking of the days that are no more', the autumn fields became in the reader's mind something other than their physical counterparts in the everyday world: they became, in effect, manifestations of regret.[3]

By Christmas 1937 the rejection of so many recent projects and the withdrawal of Eliot's financial safety net had created a mood of deep gloom in Barker. Eliot believed him to be suffering from one of the dormant periods that had afflicted his own life. On 24 January 1938 he wrote:

Whether you stop writing for a time, or merely stop printing it, is a point on which no one can advise you; but I do feel that for the present you should stop publishing; except, of course, for 'trying things out' in periodicals. Poetry is either a matter of a brief outburst, or it is a matter of a lifetime's work: in either case it is a nuisance to be a poet. When it is a life's work, you are bound to find from time to time that your inspiration is exhausted, and that you either repeat yourself, or stop writing. These are painful, but necessary periods . . . There have been several such periods of considerable extent in my own life, when I have felt almost convinced that I should never be able to write again.[4]

Barker's depression was intensified by his recognition that the way of life Eliot seemed to be wishing on him was fundamentally impracticable. He had already applied for a lectureship at the University of Durham for which, he complained to Roberts, he had been 'the least qualified applicant in England'. Extra-mural teaching appeared the more promising avenue. In March Barker wrote offering his services to Mr Hardman, Secretary of the Board of Extra-Mural Studies at Cambridge.[5] The actual manner of applying seemed to amuse him hugely. He treated the interview like a cloak-and-dagger episode in a novel by Graham Greene, arranging to meet Hardman at noon on Tuesday, 5 April, in the Kardomah café by Piccadilly Circus; for the purpose of recognition each was to carry under his arm a volume in the bright-yellow covers of the Left Book Club. After their meeting, Barker was hired to give a course of twenty-four lectures on the history of English poetry from the Middle Ages to the late Victorians.

The appointment provided him with a reputable academic address. It also opened up to him a new way of presenting himself to the world, in academic guise, and the effort involved a certain amount of pleasurable hoodwinking. But ever afterwards 'playing the professor' was to be a byword for selling out. Even as Barker made these provisions for his and Jessica's upkeep, he seems to have regarded himself as being untrue to his vocation. Outwardly, he respected Eliot's counsel; inwardly, he seems to have protested against it. Only two weeks after his interview he was giving Antonia White precisely the opposite advice to that which Eliot had given him. She should, he insisted, relinquish her position as fashion editor on the *Sunday Pictorial* because it was interfering with the writing of her novels. White reported, 'he has a theory that I shall never get going until I am totally dependent on writing for my living'.[6] This creed, which flew in the face of everything that Eliot had told him, was to become a programme of action to which Barker was to adhere for much of his life and in which he encouraged others. Barker's associates often came to believe that poets did not take jobs.

White preferred Eliot's advice and kept her position in journalism. She was not unduly worried about Barker, who seemed always to land on his feet. Besides, Coleman had now thought of, not one, but two practical ways of helping him. A few years before her father had bought her a cottage near the Petworth estate in Sussex, which was convenient both for London and for visits to Peggy Guggenheim, who herself had a cottage twelve miles away, near Petersfield in Hampshire. Coleman, who was generally either in America or in London, or else staying with friends, had less and less use for this second home. She offered it to the Barkers for a peppercorn rent. At the same time, she persuaded Guggenheim to give Barker an allowance of £2 a week.

The Barkers were delighted. Dorset had been pretty and Jessica had been contented there. Plush, however, had been half a day's journey by train from London, where Barker's weekends had tended to stretch into weeks.

At the thought of moving to Sussex, he was, White confided to her diary, cock-a-hoop with joy.[7] He could see the two halves of his life coming together.

In the first week of May 1938 George and Jessica moved their few belongings to Sussex. Their cottage was named Boxholme after the box trees in the garden. Set back from the road, it was oak-beamed and exceptionally pretty. It was a mere stone's throw from the tiny hamlet of Ball's Cross, while further afield lay the Leconfield estate centred on Petworth House with its famous collection of Turners. Just across the Surrey border near Haslemere was Blackdown, where, in his later years, Tennyson – fleeing the tourists at Farringford – had built his retreat, Aldworth. For Barker, the location was highly convenient. If he caught the right train at Haslemere station, he could reach Soho in a couple of hours. He learned to treat Ball's Cross as a rural extension of London.

For Jessica there were both advantages and drawbacks to their new home. Though closer to London than The Butts, Boxholme itself was isolated. Ball's Cross consisted of nothing but a cluster of brick-built houses and a pub called the Stag Inn. The nearest Catholic church was several miles away in Haslemere; as a result, instead of regularly attending mass as she had been used to, she often performed her devotions privately at home. At Plush she had thrown herself enthusiastically into the pleasures of West Country living: rambling the lanes with George, entertaining guests from London, cultivating an extensive and well-stocked garden. At Boxholme the garden was smaller and the countryside less dramatic. On the other hand, she had the valued stimulus of friends. There was a constant stream of visitors, as well as new friends to be made in the neighbourhood. Ten minutes' walk away lived David Gill, a second cousin of the Catholic sculptor Eric Gill. He and his young wife Elizabeth, with their three-week-old son, had recently moved to Ball's Cross from Kent, where David had been a dairy farmer. Gill was tall, broadly built and gregarious: the kind of decent, open-handed, sanguine Englishman to whom Barker responded when in retreat from the more fractious company of Soho. When Barker was not immersed in his books, the two played boisterous games of ping-pong on the table in the Gills' front room, or, when the weather permitted, noisy bouts of badminton out on the lawn. When Kit came to stay at Boxholme, the three men would discuss art and politics at the Stag Inn. Gill was liberal in his beliefs, solid as a rock, knowledgeable about the weather, able to detect a shift in the wind with a lick of his finger, a giver to good causes such as the Sailors' Fund. He was the perfect antidote to artistic pretension and Barker loved him for it, accompanying him on walks northwards in the direction of Godalming, or south towards the South Downs and the coastal heathland beyond. On summer nights the Gills and the Barkers strolled back from the Stag Inn after closing time, singing Irish ballads – learned from Big

Mumma and still Barker's ruling passion – or current popular songs. When Elizabeth asked Barker for the words of 'Greensleeves', he wrote them out for her in his elegant, italic hand. A fondness grew up between the couples. Barker treated Gill with mocking affection, while Gill lengthened 'Gran', the abbreviation of his middle name by which Barker was still familiarly known, to the Italianate 'Granello'.

There had been a tradition in Ball's Cross of organising a fair on the feast day of St Iago da Compostela, 14 July. In 1938 George and Jessica helped the Gills to revive it. George's sister Eileen now had two sons: eight-year-old John and three-year-old Barry. She brought them down for the fair, where George and Kit paid for treats at the booths. 'Young John' stayed on at the cottage. When Barker needed to write, he would place his nephew at the living-room table and tell him to work at his sums. The garden lawn sloped a little, but it was level enough for cricket. In the summer evenings Barker coached young John as he practised drives and hooks among the box trees.[8] Afterwards, in the fading light, Barker would sit reading under the syringa, on an old rustic seat.

Barker's mood darkened after the Munich Agreement in September, and the consequent transfer of German-speaking Sudetenland from Czechoslovakia to Hitler's Reich. To politically astute friends such as David Gascoyne, war with Germany now seemed inevitable. Until then, Gill, who had given up farming, had been thinking of planting an orchard in the neighbourhood, but with affairs in Europe so unsettled, the investment did not seem worthwhile. Instead, Gill read the newspapers and toyed with the idea of introducing the French game of bar billiards into England.[9] Unobtrusively Barker laid aside two large projects – a continuation of *Calamiterror* and his book of essays – and concentrated on shorter poems and reviewing.

In October his course of extra-mural lectures began. The thoroughness with which he prepared these, typing out long synopses in advance, betrays his nervousness. After an introductory hour, he devoted the second lecture to 'Quia Amore Langueo'. The twenty-two classes which followed were given over to debunking the standard division between Classicism and Romanticism. In their place, Barker identified two tendencies in the history of English poetry, which he distinguished as, on the one hand, 'keeping your eye on the object', and, on the other, 'wearing rainbow spectacles'. The language he used to describe the first tendency owed something to cricket, but more to contemporary phenomena such as the sociological Mass Observation unit, about which Barker had been told by Gascoyne, one of its instigators. 'Keeping your eye on the ball' signified something broader than Classicism as it was narrowly defined. Its expression could also be found in Chaucer, Shakespeare and in early Wordsworth. Strict objectivity, however, was impossible for the poet. In the last lecture Barker proposed a solution whereby the two traditions could come together, so that one looked at things 'through a rainbow machine, which is the seven coloured pillar of blood that spins behind the eyeball'.[10]

'The seven coloured pillar of blood' was another way of conveying the procedure, already outlined in 'Poetry and Reality', by which metaphors filtered down to brighten the world. Already the implied method was revitalising Barker's own poetry, where he was learning to assemble social detail into a surreal bric-à-brac. The best of his writing from the end of 1938 was entirely composed of such kaleidoscopic effects. He had already tried out this new style in the torrid, tumbling 'Introductory Stanzas' to *Calamiterror*, set amid the milling crowds at Bournemouth. A more sustained example had been 'Five Stanzas on the Five-Pointed Star', published in the *Left Review* the previous year. Here, the ideological map had been projected in a panoramic vision set out like the points of a pentacle:

> West is where the wanderers go with double fear.
> First fear is failure in the American money gluts.
> Second is fear of the American Aphrodite, from
> The foam of the welter risen; she is no wife,
> She is like inverted volcano and swallows me whole,
> I fear to disappear in the glory hole.
>
> East is tundra and steppes echoing thunder from
> The terrible engines manufacturing the future like glass.
> East is two hundred million daubing the Shelley dome,
> East is militant for man and has guns of years,
> East is sunrise where the Russo-Japanese sun
> Toils in the double fury remaining one.[11]

The pentacle design meant so much to Barker that for years it would appear as a personal monogram at the bottom of his letters. The panoramic method also helped him to accommodate an idiosyncratic and personal vision within a received form. On 16 December Barker wrote 'Vision of England '38', in which the example of Shelley's 'Mask of Anarchy' served as the cue for a sweeping poetical survey of his native land, caught in the hush of dreadful apprehension. The poem had both gravitas and bite, its style enhanced by the rainbow dazzle of its metaphors and by its breathless syntax. Technically, it was one of his most accomplished pieces to date:

> From the Bay of Swanage as I came down to Dorset
> The shade of Alfred arose shaking a guilty hand;
> He pointed westward to Weymouth and with a hoarse voice
> Cried: 'See what a fatal gift I gave to England!'

> Manoeuvring over the broad water like gnats
> The naval seaplanes and the giant cruisers
> Spread their shadows over the boats and the bathers
> Who played in Weymouth Bay among the shadows.
>
> Then I saw that they floated in blood and blossoms,
> The blood of the bathers, the blossoms of the boughs
> That made the boats: under the dreadnought bosoms
> Crushed and bruised under the huge bows.
>
> Alfred arraigned. 'O my people, what have I done
> Unto thee, unto thee! O Arthur, Arthur!
> Go, boy, to Glastonbury and ask for Arthur,
> Ask there for Arthur. Say England needs a father.'[12]

In later stanzas the poet meets William Blake, who 'broke his mind on God' and, in Salisbury, William Longspée summoning 'the lost Gothic ache to heaven'. In Norwich he sees above the cathedral 'the angel of stone in the attitude of song'; and finally, on the open road, he witnesses the industrial north fleeing in the allegorical form of a vagrant mother. This was the last but one of Barker's encounter poems. In the New Year of 1939, for Keidrych Rhys's *Wales*, he wrote a final exercise in that mode, 'To Robert Owen', in which the poet meets the nineteenth-century philanthropist, socialist pioneer and owner of the New Lanark Mills, wandering 'under the winter tree'.[13] As ever, Barker is more impressed by the practical charity of men like Owen than by the ideologies of political parties. Two months later, in *Seven*, a newly founded magazine in Cambridge, he delivered 'A Sermon on May Day', extolling the virtues of Owen, 'a madly, a militantly simple man'.[14] Owen, he wrote, had achieved a system of social and economic reformation which had averted the worst evils of mass production, and of unquestioning obedience to religious or social conformity. This system, a genuine alternative, 'functioned without the expensive lubrication of the Orthodox Church, without the batched patchwork of private property, and most of all, without the sanctified single cylinder of normal marriage'. Owen had been *sui generis*. 'Some of you, no doubt,' Barker declared, 'have heard voices of seemingly divine language exhorting you to perform miracles in the Spring and your son has been born in the Autumn; but no such voices informed St Robert Owen how to make love to society.' Barker needed his own heroes: ones not provided, gift-wrapped, by the urban, left-wing intelligentsia. He was still his own sort of poet, and his own sort of radical.

CHAPTER 12

'THERE'S SOMEONE HERE FROM JAPAN'

Wales and *Seven* were part of a new wave of periodicals that came into being in the months immediately before the outbreak of war. By 1939 the world of small magazines was changing. Though Julian Symons's *Twentieth Century Verse* still survived precariously, Grigson's *New Verse* had ceased publication. Besieged by debts, David Archer had moved the Parton Press to Manchester, where the financial overheads promised to be less crushing. Roger Roughton's *Contemporary Poetry and Prose* had long since disappeared, as had *Left Review*. Eliot, moreover, was having doubts about the future of the *Criterion*. To take the place of the defunct magazines, several newcomers had sprung up. In addition to *Wales* and *Seven*, late 1938 witnessed the launch, with the arrival in London of the Ceylonese impresario James Meary Tambimuttu, of an audacious magazine called *Poetry London*.

Dylan Thomas, whose jealousy of Barker had by no means abated, saw an opportunity in this transformation of the literary scene. When Keidrych Rhys, editor of *Wales*, asked him to encourage Barker to contribute, Thomas wrote back sharply, 'I won't write to Barker asking for a poem. One of the outstanding things about *Wales* is that, so far, it has not printed one of Mr Barker's masturbatory monologues – as every other verse magazine of our time has done with disgusting frequency. And I think that *Wales*'s standards should be maintained.'[1] When *Poetry London* was announced, Thomas wrote to his fellow Welsh poet Vernon Watkins about a new paper edited by 'a man or woman called Tambimuttu'. There would, Thomas said, be no lack of submissions: 'Will you send in something? It may be honest; if so it shouldn't want to stuff its pages with the known stuff of the known boys; a new paper should surely give – say – Barker a rest. He must be very tired.'[2]

Thomas's low opinion of Barker's work was not shared universally. Robert Graves – soon to be forced by the international situation to flee his home on

Mallorca – was convinced of Barker's merits. Graves believed Barker to be a better poet than Auden and his associates; a more accomplished poet, too, than Watkins. If anyone was given to literary onanism, Graves was soon to tell his future biographer Martin Seymouth-Smith, it was surely Dylan Thomas.[3] Thomas's verdict, in any case, applied to a poetic self that Barker was fast putting behind him. The poems he had been writing in the last few months were very different from – and in Eliot's judgement a great improvement on – those that had gone before. It now seemed to Eliot prudent to steer Barker towards the publication of another volume, which would include his more politically responsive pieces. The dormant patch appeared to be over.

For all his creative abundance, Barker's financial woes continued. He and Jessica had considered themselves settled at Boxholme. To their dismay, they now received an apologetic letter from Emily Coleman in Connecticut, telling them that her father wanted to sell the cottage by the spring. To give the Barkers time to reorganise their affairs, would it, Coleman enquired, be reasonable to ask them to move out by April 1939? Barker was alarmed. The arrangement at Boxholme had been perfect; any change could only be for the worse. He and Jessica already owed money to the local tradesmen. The expense of moving goods and chattels yet again would be ruinous. To make matters worse, Peggy Guggenheim also wrote announcing that she would no longer be paying Barker his weekly allowance.

Barker was trapped in debt and accepting every small commission that came his way. Among these was a pioneering television broadcast to be transmitted from Alexandra Palace, in which he agreed to take part on 23 February. Dressed in a grey flannel suit, he was picked up by coach outside Broadcasting House at six-thirty in the evening in time for a camera rehearsal at seven. After a stand-up supper, he appeared in front of the primitive cameras for a discussion, broadcast live, on the state of the arts. Sir Kenneth Clark presided over two panels: one, of poets, included Barker and Spender; another, of painters, included Duncan Grant.[4]

Barker was busy assembling the poems for the new Faber volume when, in March, he noticed in the *News Chronicle* a photograph of a five-year-old boy killed during recent air-raids on Barcelona. The child had a rough number-tag around his neck, reading '4:21:35'. His left eye was closed as if blinded, his black tousled hair spread out against bald concrete; he would have been approximately the same age as Barker's daughter Clare. The damaged eye, the hair on the pavement, may also have set off in George a memory-impression of Kit. He scarcely responded to politics in the abstract: he needed a human face, benefactor or victim, to help him focus on the issues, as with his enthusiasm for Robert Owen.

With the capitulation of Madrid on 1 April, the Civil War in Spain was effectively over. In the space of two days Barker now wrote an 'Elegy on Spain', one of the most passionate and inward poems to be provoked by the Spanish crisis. The poem begins with the dead child. It then invokes the spirit of Spain as a bull brought down amid the dust of the ring. This image was possibly indebted to Federico García Lorca, whose elegy for a bullfighter, *Llanto por Ignacio Sanchez Mejias*, had been available in English translation for the previous two years. Spain, Barker's poem implied, had been a victim sacrificed for the ambitions of unscrupulous men and a scapegoat for non-interventionist Europe:

> This flower Freedom needs blood at its roots,
> Its shoots spring from your wounds, and the bomb
> Booming among the ruins of your houses, arouses
> Generation and generation from the grave
> To slave at your side for future liberation.
> Those who die with five stars in their hands
> Hand on their ghosts to guard a yard of land
> For the boot of the landlord and the band of war.[5]

'Elegy on Spain' was unusual among the many poems inspired by the Spanish crisis in that it portrayed the war in terms of a superb, blood-red, hieratic rite. Despite its distinctiveness, Barker was not eager to be identified as the author. He dispatched the poem to Manchester, where Archer had opened another of his makeshift emporia, with instructions that it be issued without his name on the title page. In May Archer published it between blood-red covers which bore the imprint of the 'Manchester Contemporary Bookshop'; the proceeds were to go to charity. Speculation as to who had written the poem was rife. On 12 July Julian Symons wrote asking Barker if hints as to its authorship might be dropped in *Twentieth Century Verse*.[6] Two days later Barker replied that he would have no fixed objection; the secret would be out, anyway, when his new book of poems appeared 'in the Autumn'. But in the meantime he preferred the cloak of anonymity: 'I merely wanted, and still as far as possible continue to want, the poem to be read more as a poetic orphan than a prize child.'[7] So Symons kept quiet and, for the time being, an orphan the elegy remained.

In 1939 elegies were increasingly relevant to the darkening public mood. There was, for example a vogue for the elegies of the Austrian poet Rainer Maria Rilke, written in exile during the First World War, poems that offered a model as to how a modern writer might address a public crisis. That spring the Hogarth Press issued a translation by Stephen Spender and J.B. Leishman of Rilke's *Duino Elegies*. Symons asked Barker to review it for *Twentieth Century Verse* – a timely suggestion since the book had been his bedside reading for weeks. When Barker sent Edwin Muir his Spanish elegy, he enclosed a covering letter about Rilke, to which Muir replied, 'I've been reading Rilke too.' For the *New Statesman and Nation*, Barker then produced a lyric entitled 'Rilke', in which he confessed his own indebtedness to the German poet. Rilke, it declared, had been a poet who could write, blatantly, about angels; whose 'X-ray' gaze saw beneath the hour to the condition. Like himself, Rilke had been an erstwhile Catholic who had found himself impelled to invent a secular theology; 'So he, doctor to whom the world was glass, / Saw God as matter.' Barker and he, the poem implied, were in much the same predicament.[8]

Finally, in May, in the columns of the *New English Weekly*, where Desmond Hawkins was now literary editor, Barker wrote an essay which was a virtual manifesto for the relevance of elegies. 'Therefore All Poems Are Elegies' identified and celebrated a form of writing that Barker would practise to perfect for the next fifty years. The piece began:

> To be so closely caught up in the teeth of things that they kill you, no matter how infinitesimally kill you, is, truly, to be a poet: and to be a poet in fact it is additionally necessary that you should possess the tongues and instruments with which to record this series of infinitesimal deaths. And, if on top of this, you also possess the architectural intellect with which to erect a philosophy upon these experiences then you may recognize that to be alive means for the poet merely this process of dying: so that at the last death, the one on a bed, only the finality of it will seem strange, and not the mechanics of it. This is the theology of poetry, the spiral of septenary death, each of whose circles creates the beatitude of the poem.[9]

In this piece Barker brought together the temporal and sexual senses of death, combining them for his own purposes with a Rilkean intimation of dying into being. He was to reprint the essay several times.

Financial embarrassment deepened his pessimism in these months, since tradesmen were still knocking at the door of Boxholme demanding settlement. All Barker could do, yet again, was to apply to friends for help. In early April he dashed up to town and across to 30 Cork Street, where the year before Peggy Guggenheim had opened an art gallery, Guggenheim Jeune.[10] Barker burst into a foyer convulsed in preparation for an Yves Tanguy exhibition which was scheduled to open the following day. He found Peggy centre-stage, directing operations. Barker began to harangue her, imploring, explaining his precarious finances yet again. Guggenheim tried to brush him off by suggesting that he apply to Djuna Barnes. The door then swung open to admit Barnes herself on the arm of Phyllis Jones, an American writer well used to extricating Guggenheim from difficult situations. Barker walked over to them, reiterating his case. It was not the ideal moment, but the women patiently heard him out. Barnes suggested that he talk to Peter Dawson, an art teacher and Surrealist, with whom Guggenheim sometimes stayed in London. Barker went to see Dawson, who advised him, first, that he should stay put at Boxholme and, second, that he should explain his predicament fully to Coleman in a letter.

Barker took Dawson's advice on 18 May, confessing to Coleman that, though her April deadline was already past, he saw no prospect of making alternative arrangements for his and Jessica's accommodation. To placate her, he enclosed another of his verse epistles, 'Epistle II', acknowledging their spiritual kinship, despite past emotional ups and downs and the physical distance that now separated them. The 'Epistle' was full of nullity and blasted hopes. The last section began with the words 'Day is dead, it is dark, I am near/ The elbow of a stream leaning over,/ Reflecting on my page, like me. It is – / It is that Life standing at my shoulder/ Silently protesting that I have not done it justice.'[11] The letter, with its enclosure, constitutes his sorriest communication at a difficult time.

After Barker had posted the letter, he hurried up to London once again, attempting to dodge his creditors. In so doing he missed a phone call from Lawrence Durrell. For the time being Durrell, who was over from his home in Corfu and keen to meet Barker, had to make do with a discussion on the relative merits of Thomas's and Barker's poetry with Eliot's secretary, Anne Ridler. Connecting the poets of the new generation with the landscapes evoked in their poems, they agreed that, while Dylan Thomas, a son of Swansea, was 'built out of the suffocating coal from a Welsh mine', Barker, a London-bred ruralist with marked medieval affinities, was 'made out of a town boy's school primer – *Piers Plowman*, say, where medieval England is green enough to make one weep for landscape'.[12] Durrell and Ridler were clearly thinking of the 'Vision of England '38', which alluded to Langland's poem, and which had appeared in the last issue of *Twentieth Century Verse*.

The following Tuesday Durrell received a letter from Barker protesting that, despite appearances, he was not avoiding him. In mitigation of his apparent elusiveness, he pleaded various troubles, adding, 'Anyhow, here we are down in the ditches and the dykes, observing the geometry of spring. It's delightful and suicidal, like a beautifully wall papered room with no windows.' Barker invited Durrell and his wife Nancy to stay at Boxholme, where for once he had a car, borrowed for three weeks from Pa's brother Charles, in which to ferry them about the countryside.[13]

The following week Durrell visited Boxholme, where he heard the full extent of the Barkers' woes. Since Jessica, who had not enjoyed the winter, was inclined to be weak and chesty, Durrell suggested that they move to the kinder climate of Corfu. True to his word, on his return to Greece, Durrell began making preparations to receive the Barkers there, imparting this plan amongst others to Henry Miller, who shared the news with Anaïs Nin in Paris.[14]

In many respects Durrell's rescue plan would have been a feasible solution to the Barkers' difficulties. At this juncture, however, fate intervened in the unlikely person of a barrel-shaped Englishman called Ernest Pickering – Unitarian minister, former MP for Leicester West, and currently lecturing in English at the University of Tokyo. He had been re-directed from Alaida Monro's Poetry Bookshop in Great Russell Street to Faber's offices in Russell Square. He was on a mission, having been entrusted by the English Literary Society of Japan with a delicate piece of recruitment for the Imperial Tohoku University at Sendai in the far north of the country. For nearly fifteen years the university had employed the British poet Ralph Hodgson as a lecturer in English poetry. Hodgson was about to retire, taking with him the Insignia of the Rising Sun as a token of the nation's esteem. The English Society of Japan wished to know if anybody could suggest a substitute, a bona fide poet for preference?

Eliot knew Hodgson and had once written a whimsical stanza about him beginning: 'How delightful to meet Mr Hodgson! / (Everyone wants to know him) / With his musical sound / And his Baskerville hound . . .'. Under the circumstances, he was the obvious person to consult. Eliot first suggested Spender, who was apparently tempted by the appointment; he had, however, recently married, and felt he must refuse. Pickering once again applied to Eliot, who recommended Barker.

Barker received a letter on 12 August from Leicester, where Pickering was visiting his former constituency, suggesting that they meet the following morning at Pickering's club, the National Liberal in Whitehall Place. They could then discuss possibilities:

> I regret to say that, owing to my absence abroad, I am not as well acquainted with your work and qualifications as I ought to be; but a common friend has spoken of you highly to me: if you are interested in this matter, then we ought to meet and go into detail on both sides. I am not, of course, empowered to make you any definite offer forthwith and in any case, I have to make good my lack of knowledge regarding your work. But I should like to see you.[15]

The letter arrived too late for Barker to be able to make the appointment it suggested. Pickering then disappeared to the Isle of Wight for two weeks: weeks during which Britain moved inexorably towards war. When Pickering and Barker eventually met, they discussed contractual terms, which Barker found reasonable. He decided to accept.

Some light on his decision is shed by a magazine article which Barker wrote that week. 'Elegy on Spain' had served to concentrate his mind, both on the ethics of war and on the poetry of García Lorca. On 19 August he marked the third anniversary of the Spanish poet's death in a prose piece, 'Funeral Eulogy', published in *Life and Letters Today*. 'Many of us', Barker stated, 'may choose to regard [Lorca] as a hero who died for the Republican cause, but I would rather regard him as a martyr who died because he had no cause; who, moving across the no-man's land inhabited mainly by poets and cowards and angels, took a bullet from the side that had the most guns and the most murderers.' The 'Eulogy' then shifted its angle to redefine Lorca as a martyr to the cause of poetry. 'The murder of Lorca, with the death of Byron, the heroic end of Rainer Maria Rilke refusing an anodyne in his agony, the sudden death of the atheist Shelley by an act of God, the retributory metamorphosis of Wordsworth into a pillar of salt, the mad assassination of Christopher Marlowe – all these tragedies cease to be tragedies and stand, like symbolic statues, adorning the principality of the poet, asserting, in the face of the world, that the poet has also a country for which he will die.'[16] Beginning as a defence of artistic neutrality, the article concluded by typifying poetry itself as a third force. The essay elucidates Barker's view of the poet as a man inevitably caught in the middle of contesting forces, endeavouring to defend his own precious and imperilled domain. It also elucidates his reasons for accepting the Japanese appointment. For Barker, art was the one cause that he felt impelled to honour. Residence in Japan, away from the main theatre of any prospective war, might help him to preserve that commitment, as well as constituting an attractive adventure, and a resolution of his housing and financial difficulties.

On 1 September, the day Germany invaded Poland, Barker travelled down to Teddington to visit David Gascoyne. At Hampton Court, a short bus ride away from Gascoyne's home, the two men sat close to the fountains in the South Garden, discussing the growing seriousness of public events. Politically the more astute of the two, Gascoyne was insistent that a continental conflagration was now only a few days away. The atmosphere of that meeting, affectionate and momentous, is caught in a poem that Barker wrote the following week, entitled simply 'To David Gascoyne':

> The marble Caesar who weeps his face away
> There, in the royal gardens by the royal river
> Where in the summer

> We talking walked the mazes of small dreams –
> This Caesar now steps down into our day,
> Striped like a sabre-tooth with blood and anger,
> Warsaw a fig in his claw, death as his drummer,
> Messerschmitts on his lips and in the dark
> Buoy of his eye the knowledge of his crimes
> Beating a seabell.[17]

Many years afterwards, in the 1970s, Barker was to write about this meeting again, in a poem called 'Kew Gardens'. Its title puzzled Gascoyne, who could distinguish Hampton Court from Kew, even if Barker could not;[18] no doubt the location had been less important than the mood.

On the morning of 3 September, George was back at Boxholme, playing cricket on the lawn with Kit and Young John. At eleven-fifteen Jessica called from the front room. George put down his bat and walked inside the cottage. Standing over the wireless set, he listened as the prime minister, Neville Chamberlain, announced the declaration of war.[19] In later years Barker would present this as the moment that clinched everything. A passage in *The True Confession* alters chronology, setting and mood, and adds a comic note of bathos:

> I sat one morning on the can
>   That served us for a lavatory
> Composing some laudatory
>   Verses on the state of man:
> My wife called from the kitchen dresser:
> 'There's someone here from Japan.
> He wants you out there. As Professor.
>   Oh, yes. The War just began.'[20]

Even then Barker's plans nearly came unstuck. On the evening of 24 September, he journeyed up to London to dine with Stephen Spender, to whom he confided his decision to accept the lectureship at Sendai.[21] The news placed his host in a considerable quandary. Spender's marriage had recently broken up; partly as a result of this, he had decided to accept the same job, which had earlier been offered to him, and had written to Pickering to this effect. The letter, Spender told Barker, was in the inside pocket of his jacket. After a few seconds of mutual embarrassment, Spender took the letter out. Recognising Barker's greater material and personal need, he carefully tore it up.[22]

But, *pis aller* or not, there was nothing for Barker to do but to press on. To Antonia White he wrote that the Japanese job seemed preferable to military conscription, which might well 'disturb my communication with Parnassus'. Then, after congratulating her on the recent Penguin edition of *Frost in May*, he touched her for a loan.[23] In early October he visited Eliot in Russell Square to discuss the forthcoming volume, now entitled *Lament and Triumph*. He found Eliot at his desk, watching the dusk descend over Bloomsbury. As Barker entered his office, Eliot made a remark which might have referred either to their appointment, or to the likely consequences of war: 'We have so very little time.'[24]

The news of Barker's job soon spread amongst his associates: despite his lack of formal qualifications, he had acquired a prestigious full-time academic position. The general surprise was compounded by the fact that, in announcing his appointment, Barker translated the Japanese term for 'lecturer' as 'professor', a title which Hodgson had never awarded himself. 'Barker's dying to get out of England,' commented the acerbic John Hayward. Others were more generous. The Poet Laureate, John Masefield, sent a congratulatory telegram.[25] From St Andrews, Muir conveyed his felicitations. From Taplow, Walter de la Mare wished the Barkers well, but added perceptively, 'the appointment in itself just now, in view of what are called international relations, is itself an interesting fact'.[26]

How many of these well-intentioned friends recognised the danger into which Barker was being sent? All eyes, of course, were now turned to Europe, from which vantage point Japan seemed distant. Yet Auden and Isherwood had recently published their *Journey to a War*, describing the Sino-Japanese conflict in Manchuria. Manifestly, Asia was not at peace. Despite this warning, the implications of the war in China, and of Japan's increasingly cordial relations with the fascist powers, seem to have registered only faintly.

Barker was needed at Sendai by the beginning of the following Japanese academic year, which started in March 1940. If he and Jessica left in November by the slow sea route westwards, they would then be able to visit America on the way. The British Council booked them on the SS *Fushimi Maru*, sailing from Tilbury on 18 November.[27] With England in the grip of the 'Phoney War', the Barkers started to pack. In accordance with government regulations, Jessica sewed makeshift blackout curtains for the windows at Boxholme. One evening in early November the Barkers were relaxing in their small front room with the Gills, when an air-raid warden knocked on the door to say that a pencil line of light was visible at the bottom of their door.[28] The Barkers were officially warned, but there would no opportunity for a further mistake.

Big Mumma and Kit came down to Boxholme for a few days to see them off and tidy the cottage after their departure. Big Mumma was later to say that she was convinced George would never return. Early on the morning of

18 November George and Jessica left the cottage, promising to phone before boarding the ship. They took an early train to Waterloo and then humped their bags across London to St Pancras, from where the ten-twenty boat train took them out to the docks. At the last moment, standing on the quay at Tilbury, Barker experienced a vivid pang of regret. It did not seem to him likely that he and Jessica would see the family, or their war-enmeshed country, for several years. At noon he sent a cable to Boxholme:[29]

> Forgive me for not telephoning: but truly there was no time. I write this in the ten minutes before the boat goes and it takes you our love and our hopes that you will be happy in the cottage and remain there as long as you want to: but mainly it takes our love.
>
> George and Jessica

Then the Barkers went on board and found their cabin as the *Fushimi Maru* manoeuvred out into the broad estuary of the Thames. When George and Jessica re-emerged on deck, it was to see Walter de la Mare's England fading fast to stern.

PART TWO

1940–46

There was a young lady of Riga,
Who smiled as she rode on a tiger:
    They returned from the ride
    With the lady inside,
And the smile on the face of the tiger.

                  Cosmo Monkhouse

CHAPTER 13

'SWEPT OVERBOARD'

As the *Fushimi Maru* steamed over the cold waters of the Atlantic, the Barkers got to know their fellow passengers, most of whom were Americans bound for New York. Among them was a wealthy twenty-year-old, originally from Indianapolis, called John Cooper Fitch 'a tall Jack with the sun on his wrist', as George would later describe him, 'And a sky stuffed up his sleeve'.[1] The Fitch family had made a fortune out of manufacturing shampoo, and John was currently enjoying himself on the proceeds.[2] After several weeks exploring Europe, he was returning to his racing cars, his apartment in Riverdale and a private yacht called *The Banshee*. He would be forthcoming about these baubles and then suddenly shut up; according to Barker, John's silences invariably resounded like statements. Soon they fell into a warm if lopsided friendship: older intellectual and younger playboy. Fitch possessed a bland assertiveness bred of his inherited wealth, but he was in temporary full-scale reaction against the tight-fistedness of the Midwest. The two men discussed the peculiarities of the internal combustion engine and Fitch promised to shepherd the Barkers around Manhattan as soon as they docked. Meanwhile, Barker sat on deck adding three to a series of elegies that he had written in Sussex. He retitled the sequence 'Seven Munich Elegies', and dedicated it 'To John Cooper Fitch'.[3] The sixth poem read 'Be gay, be gay, John o'London, for paradise nevertheless / Lies low on the horizon, not so far as the Hesperides / But glimmers and glows a gunshot to the west / Among the Hesperides.'

Back at Boxholme Big Mumma had had enough of the solitude, the blackouts, the muddy unkempt lanes. Having made up her mind to return to London, she set off boldly for Ball's Cross with Kit in tow and Sirrah under one arm. Learning that no transport was available to take them to Haslemere station, she peremptorily hired the village hearse.[4]

As the Barkers travelled westwards, Elizabeth Smart, whose devotion to

Barker's poetry had been constant since first discovering it in a London bookshop in 1937, was living in Mexico. After periods of residence in France and New York, Smart was staying with the artist Wolfgang Paalen and his poet wife Alice at Los Cedors y Begonias near San Angel, where she continued to pore over Barker's *Poems* and *Janus*. 'George Barker', she wrote in her journal on 14 December, 'grows into a long dangerous image and is woven among the undertones.'[5] She was immersed in *Undine*, Baron de la Motte's novel about a water nymph in love with a mortal. She was herself in love with her host Alice Paalen, whom she evoked in her journals, culling images from *Undine* and from Barker's 'Narcissus' poems. Alice, she wrote, 'leans over me as into a pool, tender, her hair falling'.[6] One evening she stood on a clifftop near Acapulco, thinking about the closing moments of *The Bacchant* in which the protagonist hurls himself into the waves: 'I think of George Barker leaping to his death . . . falling, falling . . .'[7] She had already obtained from London the typescript of 'Oh Who will speak from a Womb or a Cloud?' for twenty-five dollars. Pursuing her enthusiasm further, she wrote to Lawrence Durrell in Corfu, asking him if he could inform her where Barker now was.[8]

'In Japan,' replied Durrell. The answer should have been New York, where, with the *Fushimi Maru* in harbour for a few days, the Barkers were staying with Fitch at his apartment in Riverdale. Fitch introduced them to his fiancée Telte, a slender, highly strung girl from White Plains. The Barkers toured the landmarks of Manhattan with John and Telte as guides, exploring the bars, museums and stores. From their present position war was at most distant thunder, and they could appreciate the informality and social ease of America all the more: such a contrast to the British class system and what Durrell liked to call 'the English death'.

But by early December Barker and Jessica were obliged to re-embark for the next leg of the journey, which would take them through the Panama Canal to Los Angeles. At the taxi ranks in Panama City, Barker observed the cabbies in large sun hats nodding over week-old copies of the *New York Times*, awaiting the millionaire passenger who never came. The cabbies, he wrote, had 'umbrellas stuck where the whip should be – always open; for, when the sun goes in, a mad tropical shower invariably falls, so the old negros merely continue to sit under their huge umbrellas in the cab rank . . . It charmed me completely.'[9] He invested a little of his newfound affluence in a black notebook and an alligator belt bought for the equivalent of six shillings. On 22 December, having by now elicited his forwarding address from Faber, Smart dispatched an exploratory letter to Sendai. But Barker was sailing right past her. Shortly after Christmas, the *Fushimi Maru* called in at the Californian port of San Pedro, enabling the Barkers to enjoy some sightseeing in mild weather. On the west coast of America, George confided wistfully to the new notebook, 'one could live happily and healthily'.[10] In Los Angeles the war was even further away. Here the Californian abundance lay displayed – cosmetics, electric irons, pinewood furnishings and fresh fruit – tantalising to Jessica, since they were so soon to leave. 'And in California', he added, 'one is no more than a few hours ride from the Mexican border.'

At six o'clock on the morning of New Year's Day 1940, they stood on the aft deck and watched the Californian shoreline disappear in the distance, five thousand miles of Pacific emptiness and an uncertain future before them. Barker sat on deck, ruefully reading books about Japan, and attempting to gather some kind of mental picture of their destination from a passenger called Mikai. On 6 January the breeze stiffened and the sky darkened as a full-scale cyclone blew across from the Philippines. At midday Barker stood with Mikai in the deck door, watching the sea surge and tumble past. The *Fushimi Maru* 'rose up to an enormous wall of wave, tilted on the top like a scenic railway car and then, as she went shuddering down the gulf, with the green flat seas hissing over her deck as the stern ploughed under, we saw two forms struggling in the water no more than a couple of yards from the hull'. It was some time before Barker and Mikai realised that what they had seen were two junior ratings tossed overboard, holding hands in their terror.[11] 'But in less than an instant', wrote Barker, 'they were swept away in the wake and wave.' Then down went the ship again before climbing the face of another hugely mounting wave. As the stern plunged once more, sea water washed over Barker's shoes. Barker and Mikai joined a frantic huddle of passengers at the stern rail, throwing out life belts and boards in a desperate attempt at rescue. The last glimpse they caught of the sailors was of a lone arm lifted briefly above the foam, and then 'nothing but sea'. Barker was to describe the incident in 'Three Memorial Sonnets', the first of which begins:

> The seagull spreadeagled, splayed on the wind,
> Span backwards shrieking, belly facing upward,
> Fled backward with a gimlet at its heart
> To see the two youths swimming hand in hand
> Through green eternity. O swept overboard
> Nor could the thirty foot jaws them part
> Or the flouncing skirts that swept them over
> Separate what death had pronounced was love.[12]

Having dropped a board to mark the place, the *Fushimi Maru* sailed on. By eight o'clock that evening the storm had subsided. The ship turned in her tracks and steamed back towards the position at which the sailors had disappeared, reaching it at noon on Sunday the 7th. 'The ship's crew and the passengers',

Barker noted, 'spent more than three hours searching the seas with binoculars. Two sailors kept watch from the crow's nest, and the navigation officer from the near bridge.' Occasionally a foaming white horse would be mistaken for a lost sailor and a forlorn commotion of hope would swell and die among those on deck. The vain task was kept up until a little after three in the afternoon, when the captain ordered the ship to resume her journey towards Yokohama.[13]

To alleviate the boredom of the rest of the voyage, Barker sat alone in the ship's bar, sipping whisky and water. Never before had he drunk with such wretched persistence. After three weeks of relentless water, the *Fushimi Maru* docked at Yokohama on Wednesday, 24 January. Barker was at his usual post. Outside in the corridor there was a burst of activity and through the hubbub he detected a contortion of his name being called out in shrill, repeated monosyllables.[14] A young man entered the saloon briskly and handed him a scrap of paper. The note explained that he was the son of Professor Takeshi Saito of the English Department of the Imperial University of Tokyo, to whose house Barker was requested to report immediately. Master Saito then grabbed him by the arm and rushed him off the ship, as Barker shouted to Jessica over his shoulder that he would join her at the Imperial Hotel later that evening. He was taken by taxi to the district of Ushigome. There – among the cabins of the laundrymen, the sake vendors, the fishmongers, charcoal-dealers and clog-menders – was an estate of Western-style brick houses. To Barker's eyes, it resembled Golders Green set down in the Orient. In one of of the houses – 57 Minami Enoki-cho – the Executive Council of the English Literary Society of Japan solemnly awaited his appearance.

Barker was to discover that he had arrived in Japan at a peculiarly unfortunate time. Ever since the Manchuria Incident of 1931, the country had been in conflict with China. For several years the government had effectively been in the hands of the army. As a result Japan had turned in on itself, blocking the openness towards the West that had developed during the late nineteenth century. Increasingly isolated from the liberal democracies, the Japanese were now cultivating alliances with the fascist powers in Europe. Since 1936 separate treaties had been signed with Germany and Italy, to be co-ordinated in a Tripartite Pact on 27 September 1940. Barker was quick to sense in his hosts an inner embarrassment masked by a studied and compensatory show of hospitality. Their behaviour betrayed a fact of which all were aware: that the receptivity of the universities towards Western ideas was quite untypical of the country as a whole, where Westerners were now not merely suspect, but frequently subjected to active police surveillance. In railway carriages and public meeting places posters had begun to appear discouraging fraternisation with all foreigners, who were regarded by the authorities as potential, if not practising, spies.

The intelligentsia for their part clung to an increasingly naïve dream of an *entente cordiale* with Western culture, derived from the outdated liberalism of the Meiji period in the late nineteenth century, during which contacts with Europe had been encouraged. In the English departments of the country's universities the expectations placed on an expatriate lecturer in literature were founded principally on the singular and exemplary case of Lafcadio Hearn. A British citizen, Hearn had grown up in Corfu. In 1890, after a career as a journalist in Cincinnati, he had migrated to Japan, where a year later he had married Setsuko Koizumi, a woman of the *samurai* caste. Tiny, with a slight cast in one eye, sexually thwarted in America, Hearn had discovered among the Japanese a contentment and a professional advancement denied him elsewhere, serving as Professor of English Literature at the Imperial University of Tokyo from 1894 to 1899. Thereafter, he had settled happily into the role of cultural intermediary between Japan and the West. Hearn's books – *In Ghostly Japan*; *Shadowings*; *Japanese Miscellany* – had been masterpieces of tact and social interpretation, steeped in genuine ethnographic curiosity and a natural self-effacement. On his death in 1904 he had left an indelible impression of what an engaged and liberal mind could achieve in the face of inscrutable facts. But Hearn's Japan had long since disappeared. Barker, as his hosts were nervously conscious, had arrived at the peak of the new militarism. However extravagant their hospitality, nothing would disguise the new mood.

So when, on that Wednesday afternoon in January 1940, Barker was led up the ornamental garden path into Professor Saito's little hallway, there ensued a comedy of cultural and political incompatibility.[15] Saito was fifty-five and the doyen of English literary studies in Japan. A protégé of the English poet Edmund Blunden, whose Chair at the Imperial University he now held, he was a scrupulous bibliophile and president of the society that had invited Barker to Japan. He had translated Coleridge's 'The Rime of the Ancient Mariner' and Francis Thompson's 'The Hound of Heaven' into Japanese. He was also the author of an elegant and sympathetic study of Keats, published in London with an introduction by Blunden. Of Keats he had written, 'His was an original mind that formed a view of life out of his own experiences (which is knowledge) and with little help from a given theory.'[16] These were qualities which Saito might discern in Barker, if only Barker had let him.

In the hallway evidence of cultural assimilation was clearly on display. A bevelled mirror was hanging above an umbrella stand and a potted plant. Saito's son carefully removed his shoes. Following his example, Barker started to unlace his. He was politely informed by Professor Saito that he had come to a Western household and might remain shod. Saito then led him through a curtain into a drawing room where, on high-backed chairs arranged in a semi-circle, sat seven grave and shoeless gentlemen. Four of them wore black morning suits, the others crumpled lounge suits. As they were introduced one by one, their names merged into a blur. Their actual names were Professors Hidaka, Hori, Ichikawa, Ishida, Ishihata, Jodai and Katta.[17] In recounting this episode Barker twisted them into barbarisms; he even distorted Saito's name to Mukai, a fairly obvious transference from his shipboard companion, Mikai.[18] Saito delivered a formal speech of welcome and sat down. Pickering had warned Barker that a silence would probably follow. The silence, which was impenetrable, lasted several minutes.

Barker devoted the interval to studying Professor Ichikawa's socks. Eventually, thinking the pause prolonged, he prepared to address Professor Jodai. He was forestalled by Professor Hidaka, who observed civilly, 'Mr Barker, you will be the *third* Lafcadio Hearn.' Barker replied that, on the face of it, this seemed unlikely, seeing as there had never been a second. Hidaka explained that Professor Saito was the second. How could this be, enquired Barker, since Saito was Japanese? But Saito, Professor Hidaka explained carefully, had written about Keats and the English tradition. By this means, just as Hearn had interpreted Japan for the West, Saito had interpreted the West for Japan. The logic was impeccable, but Barker could not follow it. His hosts were paying him the ultimate compliment of regarding him as a potential cultural intermediary. But for Barker, who as yet knew very little about Hearn, this prospective role was a complete irrelevance. Barker had no intention of turning himself into a mere middleman. Besides, as he was already dimly aware, Hearn had not written a single line of verse.

Saito took Barker through to his study, where the shelves were lined with first editions of English classics, including *Paradise Lost* and *Lyrical Ballads*. He presented him with an inscribed copy of his *Keats's View of Poetry* with its preface by Blunden, and informed him that Professor Fukuhara had invited him to deliver an address that Saturday at Bunrika University, recounting his initial impressions of Japan.

After this formal welcome Barker joined Jessica at the Imperial Hotel and spent two days reading MacNeice's *Autumn Journal* and Spender's *Still Centre*, and sightseeing. Fifteen years previously, on his own arrival in the Japanese capital, Hodgson had written, 'Tokyo is exciting, strange, quaint, wonderfully old and new.'[19] In contrast, Barker seems principally to have noticed the sewage carts. On 27 January he stood before an audience at Bunrika University reminiscing nostalgically about November in Ball's Cross, which 'Autumn had aggrandized into an empire'. He spoke more of poetry than of Japan. The object of poetry was admiration 'of all things from automobiles to the dynamics of planets'. The poem was nothing less than 'the apotheosis of common things'.[20]

Two days later he and Jessica took an express train two hundred miles north to Sendai. Outside the station a second reception committee awaited them. It consisted of two students, and Dean Kochi Doi of the Faculty of Letters and Jurisprudence, shivering in eight inches of snow. Dean Doi carried an umbrella in one hand, and a packet of Cherry cigarettes in the other. His shoes appeared to be three sizes too big for him. This, the Barkers soon learned, was no disgrace in a university town where most students wore wooden platforms called *geta*. As soon as George and Jessica appeared, Doi presented Barker with the cigarettes. One of the students stepped forward briskly. He said, 'Welcome to Japan,' and stepped back smartly. The Barkers were driven in a battered Buick to the Imperial Hotel in the centre of the city. In the lobby a group of local journalists sat round a charcoal burner. The journalists plied the Barkers with yet more questions, while sifting through the ashes with frost-bitten fingers. That evening Professor and Mrs Doi entertained the Barkers to dinner at the hotel. And 'in this morgue', wrote Barker in his diary, 'the four of us sat freezing between grey walls saying nothing and ignoring the so called food placed before us. To bed with the drums of the mad Buddhists booming through the streets – Ah, bloody nightmare!'[21]

If Edinburgh is the Athens of the north, Saito had once written, then Sendai is the Edinburgh of Japan. This was not Barker's initial impression. Instead, he was consumed by a vision of squalor. Wherever he and Jessica walked crowds of ragged children followed them. In his journal he was candid: 'Oh, the poverty and the insuperable filth of the side streets and the manginess of the dogs and the utterly threadbare clothes of the people in the streets, and the exquisite coiffures of the geishas,' and the next day, 'but, oh my god, the poverty!' Culture shock brought to the fore odd aspects of his psyche. That Wednesday, 31 January, he and Jessica lunched at a restaurant specialising in European cuisine. They found themselves sitting opposite a woman who was feeding her baby through the open top of her dress, tilting the child's head slightly in an attempt to conceal her breast. The sight stirred in George a mixture of awe, squeamishness and misogyny. He was, he confessed in his diary, 'fascinated and extraordinarily elated at this spectacle. And not a little appalled.'[22]

On Friday morning, after breakfasting at the hotel, they were taken to the staff house that had been allocated to them. It was a two-storey stucco building, surrounded by a wooden fence six feet in height. Its façade was flawed by a conspicuous crack, the result of earthquake movement. This building, they gathered, had recently been moved and reassembled on site. Its present location was the middle of the home straight of the university's athletics track. This proved less convenient for the house's occupants than for the athletes, who obligingly ran to either side of it. The house possessed a hall, on each side of which were two multi-purpose rooms. Barker claimed one of these, decorated in what seemed to him a ghastly brown, for his study. The knobs on all internal doors were fixed so close to the doorframes that, whenever they entered or left a room, George and Jessica scuffed their knuckles. The lavatory could only be locked from the outside. There was a resident maidservant called Akeko-san with whom Jessica could not communicate. She was incompetent and plainly in the pay of the secret service. Every evening a flustered official would scuttle past the window of the study. As Barker pressed his face against the window pane to watch, this man would surreptitiously scratch at the kitchen door. Akeko-san then addressed him for several minutes in a confidential undertone. The official would copy her observations down in his notebook. Then he would thank her and leave beneath Barker's amused gaze. As he passed the window, he smiled up wanly.[23]

The day after they moved in, Barker had an appointment to sign his contract[24] with the university's president, Kotaro Honda. He called to find him standing in the middle of his immense office, surrounded by metal screens. Honda was a highly distinguished metallurgist and a member of the family who had founded the famous motorcar company. Had Barker known this fact, an interesting conversation might have been possible. But neither man spoke the other's language. After a courteous ceremony of signing, Honda took him across to the metal screens. He proceeded, smiling, to remove a number of small birds from his pockets and to position them at various places on the surface. The interpreter intoned, 'The President of the University is a famous metallurgist. He has invented magnetised birds that permit the design of the screen to be varied at will. Do you like these birds?' 'Of course,' said Barker, nodding politely. He then returned to his flimsy house on the athletics field and typed a desperate appeal to Elizabeth Smart, whose letter from Mexico had just reached him. 'I'm going absolutely nuts here,' he wrote, 'and unless I can succeed in getting back across the Pacific in a matter of months at the most, it's flowers and curtains for the Chrysostom birds inside me.' If she could arrange this, he could promise her the manuscript of *Alanna*, which Archer had in safe keeping. If not, he would reach Los Angeles 'on skis and a couple of handkerchiefs'.[25] To his diary he explained 'for I recognize only too plainly that a long or even prolonged stay here will crush me with the immense brutalities and grind me under the innumerable absurdities'.[26]

There were reasons for this despair, outer and inner. The outer are more easily explained. The University of Sendai resembled nothing so much as a training ground for the Chinese slaughter. Founded in 1907, it occupied approximately twenty-five buildings scattered over three square miles of the suburb of Aoba-ku. The buildings were constructed in a variety of styles ranging from the drably functional to the neo-oriental. The most distinctive was a half-built pagoda housing the university sports hall, from which emanated the sound of students playing ping-pong and mah-jong. Within earshot the college cadet force prepared for war. In full view of the house its members performed exercises employing wooden poles for guns and strutted past a rostrum on which a bantam-sized officer took the salute. Their band brayed out-of-date German military tunes and weirdly distorted Sousa marches. Against this cacophony Barker attempted to concentrate at his desk, his hand poised above a large glass ashtray in the form of a dice, bought by Jessica to catch the Cherry cigarette ash which, in their agitation and bewilderment, they had both been dropping all over the linoleum. Every few seconds, as he smoked and watched, a pair of plimsolls appeared in the window frame as if from nowhere. They belonged to a lone sportsman pole vaulting on the other side of the fence.

His teaching duties, Barker soon discovered, were minimal. Seventy-seven students were registered in the Faculty of Letters, but only a few read English with any competence. The schedule of lectures for the academic session of 1940 lists three courses as having been taught by 'G. Barker': 'Lecture on English Literature', 'Modern English Literature' and 'History of English Literature'.[27] These titles sound suspiciously vague and repetitive. At any rate, on the first morning, only two students appeared. Their names were Hiraku and Takiushi and to them, in an arctic hall, Barker attempted half-heartedly to teach the poetry of A.E. Housman. He gave them the *Last Poems* in the blue covers of the 1922 Grant Richards edition and asked them to read from page 24:

> The chestnut casts his flambeaux, and the flowers
>   Stream from the hawthorn on the wind away.
> The doors clap to, the pane is blind with showers.
>   Pass me the can, lad; there's an end of May.

Barker glossed some of the more demanding vocabulary, such as the noun 'flambeaux'. There was then total silence for several minutes. At length Hiraku rose to his feet and observed, 'Mr Barker. The first line is meaningless. You say that flambeaux are torches. Chestnut trees cannot throw torches away. They do not possess torches.' Barker explained that the figure was a metaphor, but Hiraku shook his head and replied, 'Mr Barker. Either the chestnut tree has torches, or it does not have torches. Which is it?'[28]

Barker concluded that, however deft their employment of conventional symbolism, the Japanese possessed no feeling for the arbitrariness of metaphor. But Hiraku and Takiushi both showed an insatiable appetite for the private lives of Auden and Isherwood, about whom they had heard so much. So Barker reconciled himself to sitting in the echoing hall for hour after hour recounting the unholy loves of the Auden circle. Perhaps his teaching methods left something to be desired. He regarded himself not as a poet-teacher, but as a poet who, in order to pay the rent, had elected to teach. Nine years previously, at an earlier stage of the Manchurian War, another British poet, William Empson, had likewise taught Housman to his class at the Tokyo University of Literature and Science. Far from demonstrating a resistance to Housman, Empson's students had responded to the fatalism of *A Shropshire Lad*, if anything, a little too readily.[29]

Baffled by his students, Barker shrank within himself, failing to respond even to the cultural stimulus on offer. Moreover, he felt his colleagues to be a disappointment. The only other Englishman was Edward Gatenby, 'a tall bird of a schoolmaster, an atheistic heron who has spent eighteen years here feathering his English nest'. Gatenby lectured on Swinburne and English prose; more usefully, from Barker's point of view, he recommended a reputable bank in Tokyo. Then there was gentle, self-effacing Doi, who enjoyed a high reputation amongst Japanese scholars of English. In the 1920s Blunden had credited Doi with 'exact knowledge of and full-toned expression upon the best in English thought and fancy'.[30] According to Saito, he was 'a philosophically trained critic in the manner of Walter Pater'.[31] Recently, he had turned his attention to the infant science of stylistics. In the early months of 1940 he was preparing an article about the punctuation in Blake's *Songs of Innocence and Experience*. He also invariably wore his flies undone. One evening Doi visited the Barkers in their little house to see if they were happy. He handed his article on Blake to George, asking him if he would kindly read it through and comment.[32] The article proved to be a jot-and-tittle account of the punctuation devices in Blake's 'Songs' in which Doi had, for example, discovered twenty-nine exclamation marks.[33]

The next time he met the dean, Barker asked him, 'Dean Doi, do you propose to establish a theory of Blake's use of punctuation, or do you make these assessments merely for mathematical amusement?' Dean Doi folded his hands and said, 'Yes.'

CHAPTER 14

'OH BEGGING RESCUE'

Kochi Doi might have been of more use to Barker, had Barker paid more attention to him. Twenty years before Doi had translated with Amy Lowell a set of diaries written by courtesans of old Japan. These had included the adulterous journal of the eleventh-century poetess Izumi Shikebu, whose poetry Doi had found 'evanescent and half-expressed, vague as the mountain scenery of her country, with no pronouns at all, and without verb inflections.'[1] Barker found Doi himself less evanescent than inscrutable. Just as, in his schooldays, he had put down Headmaster Sampson as a literary poseur, he was now prepared to dismiss Dean Doi as at best a sphinx, at worst a dry-as-dust pedant. Doi had also compiled a textbook of basic Japanese, but was never able to teach Barker more than a few mispronounced phrases. Every evening the kindly dean came across from his home in Kita Gabon-cho and stared at the curtain rail for what seemed like an eternity, while George racked his brains for something to say. Doi's English, though far in advance of Barker's Japanese, was markedly stilted. The result was conversational stalemate. Barker's notion of discussion was a verbal skirmish in which he possessed the advantage, but here he was a non-starter. In later life Barker would absorb much about oriental culture through his reading. The evidence suggests that, in the early months of 1940, the Japanese simply exasperated him. As the weeks drifted by, he ceased to care very much. Disastrously, he fell back on that refuge of the linguistically isolated: derision.

On 6 February Barker was scheduled to deliver his inaugural lecture. By the evening before he had only managed to prepare three pages. The following morning at ten-thirty he rose to his feet and slowly read them out before two rows of seated staff and students. After thanking the university for inviting him to Japan, and paying a courteous acknowledgement to Hodgson, he announced his theme: the rational incomprehensibility of poetry. He had decided to illustrate this thesis with reference to Christopher Smart and, possibly in deference to Doi, William Blake. 'Both in the Prophetic Books and in *Rejoice in the Lamb*', he declared, 'what the poet is attempting to deliver is an imaginative approximation rather than an intellectual statement.' But distinctions between rational and impressionistic writing should not be drawn too sharply. Blake's verse was most imaginative when it paid close attention to reality. Barker then recalled his own extra-mural lectures of 1938, and amplified: 'It is when he reverts to the exercise of the characteristic of keeping his eye on the object that Blake writes such tremendous poems as "London" or "The Tyger" in which, looking at the object with the intense joy of the poet, he makes it a crystal and sees a moral in it.'[2]

Barker's notes then ran out and his mind went blank. According to the clock at the back of the hall, there was almost an hour still to run. He started improvising with little sense of direction. After a few minutes, he took a sip of water, and examined his audience critically through his spectacles. Their expressions were unchanging. 'So I began to improvise a speech on the inveterate incomprehensibility of poetry – this is true anyhow – until, in the middle, my mind fused and I went blank and knew that I would just walk out if nothing happened to stop me – so I held my heart, apologized for palpitation, drank some more water and saw the double line of absolutely negative faces and went on talking nonsense for an hour.'[3]

That evening he restored his mental composure by taking Jessica to see the film *Maiden in Uniform*. But he still had lectures to write. Deciding that his first subject had been too broad, he chose to devote his next talk to a single poem: Wordsworth's 'Resolution and Independence'. At one o'clock the following Friday he read out the first line – 'There was a roaring in the wind all night . . .' He was beginning the second, when there was a lurch in his stomach, and the desk before him appeared to subside.[4] Back at the house Jessica noticed the ginkgo tree out in the garden mop, mow and stand upright again.[5] In the lecture hall George continued reading almost immediately. Earthquakes, he noted in his diary that evening, were not as bad as he and Jessica had feared. The sensation was certainly not as violent as witnessing an express train hurtling through a station, an experience which invariably terrified and exhilarated him. In the afternoon Doi came round to make sure that the Barkers had survived. More or less, they said. But two German seismologists who lived down the road informed them that, unlike the passing of express trains, earthquakes were liable to grow more terrifying with each recurrence. Be that as it may, one year later, an earthquake image was to steal into Barker's sonnet to his mother, who is described fondly there as 'seismic with laughter'.

For company Barker was driven back on the resident German academics, many of whom taught in Sendai on exchange programmes. At least, he felt, these men did not possess the English failings of self-consciousness and narrowness. On 14 February Professor Schmidt, a Rockefeller Fellow in Philosophy, brought round a copy of Rilke's *Letters to a Young Poet*. He and Barker spent the evening translating, drafting about five pages before midnight. But all the European expatriates, Barker later wrote, had a dead look behind the eyes, as if shell-shocked. The secret of survival in a place like Sendai was clearly self-effacement, an attitude for which Barker knew himself to be ill-equipped. Jessica was beginning to find the isolation unbearable. She took the train back to Tokyo to stay for a few days with the Gilboys, a couple whom they had met shortly after landing.

With Jessica's temporary departure, loneliness loomed. Fortunately Doi had appointed the likeable English-speaking student Hiraku as Barker's 'assistant', responsible for his well being and cultural education. Shortly after breakfast on Thursday, 15 February Hiraku arrived to take him on a tour of the Shinto and Buddhist shrines. It was about midday before they reached a clearing in the woods. There stood several protuberances which, when the snow had been brushed off them, turned out to be stone lanterns decorated with dragons and birds. Containing invocations to the ancestors, these were the Shinto shrines. A further climb would bring them to the Buddhist pagodas. They set out up a mountain path, past souvenir sellers hawking paper fishes and cranes which swayed in the breeze. Eventually they came in sight of a gilded wooden tiara-shaped structure, on the roof of which twin dolphins cavorted. Barker was about to remark that the shrine appeared to be in a state of constant movement, when a monk emerged from its entrance and began sweeping away the snow. Hiraku gave Barker his camera and asked him to take a photograph. While Barker was staring through the viewfinder, the monk stopped sweeping, and advanced, shouting abuse. He was, Hiraku said, yelling that Barker was a foreigner and should leave the shrine at once. They left. Consulting the map, Hiraku proposed a visit to a nearby 'Shrine of the Heavenly Horse'; Barker interrupted him to say that for the last hour they had been followed by a little man wearing a blue uniform with white gloves. 'It is the policeman,' replied Hiraku. He explained that there were military barracks close by.

The Heavenly Horse was an army horse that had taken part in the Russo-Japanese War. They found it in a rickety corral which also enclosed an altar. It was pathetically thin and its stomach sagged like a hammock. Just beyond the palings squatted a middle-aged man in full-length underwear with old newspapers tied round his body and a battered derby down over his eyes: he was feeding the horse with sugar lumps. As Barker and Hiraku turned back, they met the policeman slogging uphill towards the shrine. 'He is going to pay his respects to the horse,' observed Hiraku. 'Then he will follow us home.'[6]

For all its menace and absurdity, Sendai could also be picturesque. After

Hiraku had left that evening, young flautists sat among the ginkgo trees outside the house, filling the darkness with their music. They seemed undeterred by the student athletes practising their javelin throwing, or by the cadets, who could be heard in the distance cheering one another on with shouts of '*Banzai! Banzai!*' (Hurrah! Hurrah!) In his restlessness Barker was drawn out of doors. 'I walked down a side street of licensed brothels,' he noted in his diary that evening, 'and here the pretty whores sat at their windows like dolls . . . Mostly they seemed girls of beauty; their costumes are particularly splendid – and one stood at the door stretching her arms.' As she gestured, the girl repeatedly cooed a dove-like enticement. To Barker, used to seductive Italian, her invitation sounded like the endearment *caro, caro*, 'darling, darling'. She was almost certainly calling *ka eru, ka eru*: 'Come back! Come back!' Alone in bed, he was woken at dawn the next day by the tinkling of bells. Looking out, he saw a hooded figure going from house to house in the pearly light. Barker took him for a beggar. He asked Akeko-san about him over breakfast, but 'elicited only bird-like arpeggios of Japanese and a performance of mime'. It was not until Hiraku appeared a few hours later that he learned the truth. The figure had been the night watchman ringing his tiny bells to discourage burglars.

Hiraku then explained his mission. He had been sent by Dean Doi to congratulate Barker on his inaugural lecture, which the university would like to translate into Japanese. Could the professor spare a copy? Also, the undertakers would soon be here. Yes, the undertakers: those who undertake redecoration. After a few seconds of bewilderment, Barker remembered that a few days before he had applied for the garden to be tidied, his study to be wallpapered, and bells to be installed in several of the rooms. A single file of unshaven and shoeless workmen appeared in the garden, walked around the house three times and entered the kitchen, where Akeko-san presented them with carpet slippers and served them green tea.

Barker sent Hiraku away, promising a copy of his lecture, and withdrew to his study. Looking out of the window, he caught sight of one of the workmen hacking at the roots of the ginkgo tree in the garden of which, in his solitude, he had grown fond. He was about to open the window to order him to stop, when the man's colleagues entered the room and starting drilling a hole in the wall. They asked Barker where he wished the bell-pushes to be placed.

Gestures were adequate for certain things, but Barker's linguistic shortcomings now defeated him. Instead of papering the study, the workmen opened a paint pot and started to daub the walls blue. He hurriedly consulted the dictionary and bawled out the phrase *ka begami*, or 'wallpaper'. Abandoning the study as lost, he decided to make one further effort to save the ginkgo but, as he opened the window to intervene, he saw the tree lying on the ground, with its destroyer squatting among its roots, smoking contentedly. When at last the workmen had left, Barker sat disconsolately in the dining room. To test the new bell-push, he rang for Akeko-san and asked her to bring him a glass of milk. The milk arrived, tasting of fish. Afterwards Barker slumped on the recumbent ginkgo, feeling tired, defeated and not a little ridiculous. It was he who was uprooted.[7]

On Jessica's return Barker began to pull himself together. Term ended on 24 February and he was free to devote himself to his writing. The following Monday his twenty-seventh birthday passed pleasantly. The most welcome present was from home: his first big batch of mail. He started to answer it, mindful all the while of possible intervention by censors. To Upper Addison Gardens he sent back reassuring noises. Sendai was 'like a cathedral town without a cathedral' and Jessica was blossoming. Then he drafted a careful letter to Eliot. What he missed in Japan, he told him, was not pleasure but, oddly enough, personal suffering. Life was bearable on the practical level, though the severe winter had not agreed with Jessica, who was also suffering from a recent smallpox vaccination. Yet something essential was missing: a tormented legacy that he and Eliot shared: what he called 'the primogeniture of tragedy'. 'This', he wrote, 'is the place that Ariadne's thread did not cross, the place without either an axis or an Ixion or a crucifixion, the place where confession is unnecessary.' He now realised that personal suffering for the poet, as for the Christian, was not so much an inconvenience as a source of nourishment:

> When I was wriggling on my hooks in the south of England, sometimes I speculated on what life would be like without the horses of torsions and the torture of the limbs, and now I am beginning to understand that the sensation of suffering is not, or at any rate not wholly, due to one's private exigencies or the individual privations of existence, but is just the local storm of the nexus inherited by the whole nation.[8]

The problem was one, not so much of geographical, as of spiritual, disorientation. Suddenly, he was plunged into a shame culture rather than a guilt culture. Without the stimulus of guilt he felt lost, like a man who finds that, unaccountably, he no longer casts a shadow. What defined Barker as a man and a poet was precisely that sacrificial and liturgical consciousness which, eight years before, he had attempted to offload. Evidently the teachings of Newman and Dale-Roberts had affected him at a deeper level than any such willed rejection could reach.

On 29 February, a belated faculty dinner was held to celebrate Barker's arrival. Ninety professors gathered in the second-floor banqueting hall of Sendai's principal hotel to pay their respects.[9] The hall had not been heated all day. The meal consisted of a small bowl of vegetables and endless supplies of green tea. Barker was distressed by the fact that his hosts' noses ran unchecked as they ate. He was placed next to a Japanese seismologist, who claimed to be 'the best Hodgson friend', and with whom he talked desultorily for about half an hour, before rising to deliver a panegyric to the spirit of English poetry. The tradition of Coleridge, Blake and Tennyson, he announced, had transported itself from Nether Stowey and Felpham and Aldworth. It had settled in Sendai with the purpose of declaring its intentions. Now in wartime, if ever, should poets have the courage to speak out:

> For this reason I can make the personal confession that I am more concerned about the poems I am going to write than I am concerned about other matters with apparently greater claim. The times we are experiencing are so extraordinarily fluctuating that when the opportunity presents itself for a poet to write he must seize it without hesitation, for tomorrow it may not be a pen he holds in his hand. And if the collocation of circumstances is adverse, he must consult his morality as to what to do. For the poet silence is the cardinal sin, for silence in suffering is the prerogative of saints and martyrs. So that, in altogether a greater sense, for the poet that line of Richard's is true:
> Under which king, Bezonian? speak, or die.[10]

There was a violent crash. The green tea skidded across the table top. Looking up from his script, Barker noticed that the walls had developed a kind of 'veiled waver'. The ninety professors were leaving rapidly. He attempted to continue, but Dean Doi grabbed him by the arm and propelled him towards the staircase.

The section of the speech above comes word for word from Barker's manuscript; the Shakespearean line with which it concludes, however, was delivered, not by King Richard, but by Pistol.[11] The aftermath is drawn from a cock-and-bull version of the incident, which Barker published two years later in the *New Yorker*. Admittedly, north-eastern Japan is prone to earthquakes. If Barker's later elaborations are to be believed, however, a remarkably large number of them occurred during his short stay and all during lectures. The reality, as Barker's journal entry for that day confirms, was more prosaic, if upsetting in another way. Barker carried on to the end of his speech, while the audience applauded mechanically in the middle of sentences. Afterwards, the whole assembly sat and smoked, ignoring him until, to his great relief, it was time to leave. Outside the hotel, as he stood tongue-tied with Doi, there was a light dribble of rain.[12]

Back at the house Barker put away his script. It had been intended, he wrote in the margin, as a 'valediction pro patria mea'. On the evidence of his journal entries, however, the country for which he was actively pining was 'The Big One', America. 'O charity,' he pleaded, 'loosen the hands of E. Smart!' Barker was now corresponding with John Fitch to see if he too could help them out of their predicament. In a letter to Edwin Muir he was guarded, contenting himself with a graphic description of the sea voyage: there was, he said, an 'authoritarian gag in my mouth' which he could not remove. But, whatever damage the censor's scissors might inflict on his letters, in his verse Barker was free to speak. All at once poetry became, not merely a preoccupying obsession but a lifeline to himself. He planned a sequence of twenty sonnets to be called 'Pacific' in deference to his location as well as in defiance of the war. On 16 March, in his newly painted study, he began:

> Between the wall of China and my heart
> O exile is . . .

He sent off this first sonnet to Smart, reiterating his appeal. The next day he wrote a second deploring the war – 'O how the eighteen-year-olds in stupefaction/ Go stepping pretty into an imperial monument'. Then on Monday, 18 March, recalling his 'Holy Poems' of the previous year, he compared himself to St John stranded, not on Patmos but on Honshu. On Tuesday he evoked the apparent nullity of Japan:

> And in these islands hung in the fringe of Asia,
> The herbaceous border of the Siberian waste,
> Where I move giddily in disgust or aphasia
> Straddling the huts of paper and paste,
> Here in this vacuum where the goldfish float
> Between transparent planes of mental negation
> But look like thoughts, here on this glass
> I see reflected the mechanism of fate
> Evolving the instruments of destruction
> For all that I have left, the Europe that was,
> Whose historical frieze, in its seizure,
> Shrieks with the voice of Sibelius, crying
> Like a violin in the middle of the sea,
> 'I am dying!'[13]

That evening he sent Smart a cable 'Oh begging rescue'. His own feeling of desertion was reflected in the memorial sonnets for the two sailors lost overboard from the *Fushimi Maru*, composed on Wednesday. The next day was Maundy Thursday, a date in the ecclesiastical calendar which meant much to Jessica. But here the rituals of Europe seemed an irrelevance. In Sonnet XI Barker portrayed himself as looking 'to find a place / Where among the amazing masks and the ginko, / The seismics, the diseases, the natural disasters, / I can clear a place for my own past'. And on the morning of Good Friday, quoting his own letter to Smart of 3 February, he began Sonnet XIII with the line 'It's flowers and curtains for my Chrysostoms', before noting in his journal that, on this day, his new volume of verse was published in London.[14]

Dedicated to Jessica, it bore the title *Lament and Triumph*, reminiscent of Rilke's *Klage und Ruhmung*. In it were the 'Vision of England', the epistles to Thomas and Coleman, the better encounter poems, a series of elegies and two sequences – 'Holy Poems' and 'O Who will speak from a Womb or a Cloud?' which alluded, whether in overt dedication or implied obsequy, to the daughter he and Jessica had given up. The result is a book of unusual coherence or purpose and there is no slackness to be found in it. But it was frustrating to know that the work of the previous two years was now seeing the light of day half a world away, whilst he himself was among people who would almost certainly never read the book and, should they do so, would probably regard it with indifference. Barker had not yet received a copy and his sense of frustration was exacerbated by the realisation that, even in Britain, few would now be attending to poetry. This shift of attention had occurred just as he felt confident of saying something worthwhile:

> I hardly expect the effect of publication to be anything sensational, even in the local sense for now the young writers who would lap it up with love are all in french trenches or english barracks thinking of the terrible promiscuity of god almighty [sic] and adolph hitler [sic]. I call down the curse of the seven snotty orphans and the eight itching niggers on the political panjandrums who have done this disruption upon our lives – upon all of our lives.[15]

Barker's pessimism was ungrounded since, despite – or perhaps because of – war conditions, the response to the book in London was immediate. The very next day the *Times Literary Supplement* paid the handsomest of tributes, not this time to his youth, but to his maturing voice. Here, its anonymous reviewer declared, were all the signs of a new confidence: 'In their increased order and coherence, these new poems reveal a further advance in the control of a remarkable poetic impulse.' Barker's voice was now utterly distinctive, with its use of internal rhyming and its unusual technique of placing rhymes at the beginnings of lines. Above all, this was poetry for the time: 'The sense of an ultimate, underlying and illuminating all the fog of human failure and distress, yet never dimming his sharp awareness of the appalling consequences in human suffering, of that failure, is what gives to this poetry its imaginative breadth and more than modern meaning.'

Without doubt his work was growing in control. In 'Pacific Sonnets', too, sheer profusion gives the lie to the desolation expressed in his journal and letters. Though Barker complained of 'aphasia', Japan was not inhibiting him from writing. Moreover, there was a new tautness in these sonnets, a new intensity and lack of excess, which carried them beyond the already published poems. He was producing the sequence at the rate of two or three sonnets a day. Never before had he written work with such concentration, such a sense of purpose. The very vulnerability of which he complained in his letter to Eliot had in effect become his theme. So, on Saturday, he wrote that there was nowhere now to hide, no beautiful Jerusalem, 'not the small monument / To dogs and poets and homosexual love / Lying embalmed in the sea off a dangerous continent'. And on Easter Sunday, while Jessica found a church to attend, he summed up the end-of-the-world feeling that had actually been, for him, a new beginning:

> And now there is nothing left to celebrate
> But the individual death in a ditch or a plane
> Like a cock o' north in a hurricane.[16]

He spoke too soon. On 25 March there was a cable from Smart, reading 'Come to the California shore' and promising to send $300 as soon as she could manage it. Let him rest assured: she would do everything that she could to help him. That afternoon he rounded off 'Pacific Sonnets' with one beginning 'Goodbye then the island colonized by ideograms, / Of poverty and moongazing, hate and gardens.' He expressed his keenest feelings in his journal. Remembering the indebtedness of writers to patrons, remembering more particularly Sir Philip Sidney, he let out an exclamation of praise and relief: 'Angel Empress. Duchess of Pembroke!'[17]

CHAPTER 15

'ANGEL EMPRESS'

In making arrangements to leave Japan so soon after they had arrived, Barker was reacting to a general sense of threat, but there was much in the political climate to justify his mood. The Japanese navy was already active in the Indo-Japanese Sea and seemed likely, sooner or later, to invade Singapore or Hong Kong. The situation would soon escalate. In January 1941 the Japanese would negotiate a treaty between Vichy France and Siam; by July they would occupy Indo-China. American sanctions would follow, after which it would not take a great deal of prescience to foretell Japan's eventual entry into the war. Had the Barkers stayed until December the following year, they would, on the bombing of Pearl Harbor and the subsequent American declaration of hostilities, have been interned, and in very brutal conditions.

In March 1940 Barker could not have predicted Pearl Harbor, of course, but his disquiet was increasing. He was determined to leave, but absconding would not be easy. He was still a foreign alien in an increasingly hostile environment, pledged to stay, and with limited resources if he did not. The Imperial University had paid his passage, but would not fund his return. His lectureship was not especially remunerative, and the Barkers had no financial reserves to buy a ticket. 'Took 20 yen from the 180 yen left after paying the 18 yen for milk bill,' a typical journal entry reads. Nobody was offering to buy them a ticket back to England, where, in any case, George feared conscription. He does not seem to have considered returning to London at all. As Smart was eager to evacuate them to America (or rather *him*; he spoke little about Jessica in his correspondence) it seemed only sensible to accept her readily offered assistance.

Entry into the United States, however, was far from a foregone conclusion. There were papers to complete, sponsors to find, financial arrangements to make. Most of the necessary certificates were in England. He wrote to Kit asking for manuscripts of existing poems that he could send to Smart in payment for her efforts. He urged Fitch to investigate the question of American citizenship. Fitch was now with Telte aboard the *Banshee*, cruising off the west Florida Coast, but he promised to send the required information as soon as he reached Sarasota.[1]

It was on Smart, however, that the main burden of assistance fell. Having abandoned Mexico and Sapphism, she was now living in Los Angeles with the Smyrna-born painter Jean Varda, and writing letters to all and sundry in her attempt to rescue Barker. 'If George Barker should appear now,' she wrote in her journal, 'I would eat him up with eagerness.'[2] From her parents in Ottawa she had received short shrift. Not unreasonably her mother Louie reacted by asking Elizabeth what right she had to interfere, since Barker was married and had chosen to work in Japan. Her father Russel, a businessman of considerable means, was at first unyielding. He remarked astutely that, the last time his daughter had mentioned Barker he had seemed to need rescuing from England. Rebuffed by her family, Smart then turned to friends and acquaintances. She found a job as a skivvy with a Mrs Russell, but was promptly fired on requesting that her wages be sent to Japan.[3]

From Sendai George continued to exert pressure and, more powerfully, eloquence. On 28 March he wrote acknowledging her telegram and portraying his predicament as dire: 'I have to keep my nose to the outer cosmic grindstone in order to ignore the wretchedness of my immediate conditions.'[4] Since obtaining citizenship seemed complicated, he had decided to apply for visas in the first instance. To acquire them, he would still need sponsors to sign an affidavit of support, for presentation at the American consulate in Tokyo. From Los Angeles, on 6 April, Smart cabled, 'Negotiating. Have patience.' She appealed to her father, who relented and signed. She then set about the more serious business of begging or earning money to buy two sea passages from Yokohama.

From London too there was encouraging news, though the time lag caused by distance had some odd effects. On 27 March, five days after the publication of *Lament and Triumph*, Barker received a letter from Anne Ridler, full of bonhomie, informing him that the proofs had just been sent. George had asked her to pick a poem to be dedicated to her: she had chosen 'Battersea Park'. But all of them were splendid and, like 'Vision of England '38' cried out to be read aloud. 'I do hope with all my heart that they will get some chattering reviews to sell the book and make you known to the dull ass's hoof, and that they will come out before any bombs have upset things.'[5] Mr Eliot was in good health: he was writing verse in the *New English Weekly*, and his Conservatism was upsetting the socialistic H.G. Wells. But there had been no water in his house for weeks and he was having to submit to the attentions of a Portuguese sculptor. The sculptor, who specialised in sharks, much admired Eliot's profile.

Eliot himself wrote. He too was complimentary about the book, which he reported 'has even commanded the approval of the austere Geoffrey Grigson'. He should, Eliot admitted, have replied a lot earlier to Barker's complaining missive. He then attributed Barker's troubles to settling pains. 'It must all seem very remote at first, but I feel that you would do more good in the world teaching English poetry at Sendai than by returning to England to become a conscript. I hope that you will be able to see it that way, too.' He was sorry to hear that Jessica's health was poor but, if the Japanese winters proved severe, might it not be possible for her to return to England without him? 'I suppose that your income would not permit of her spending some of the more inclement months of the year in some more southerly Pacific island?' Apart from that, the gist of his message was that the Barkers should stay put.[6]

Eliot was not to know that his well-meant advice was misjudged. By now, Barker's embarrassments were evident even to his students. The poetry class, for example, had recently swelled to three. The new recruit was called Cho San, had a mouth full of gold teeth, and was ferociously interested in politics. The politics constantly waylaid the group's discussions. One afternoon Barker had been explaining that, despite their earlier problems with the word 'flambeaux', Housman was not really a difficult poet. They should consider the lines:

> The sigh that heaves the grasses
>   Whence thou wilt never rise
> Is of the air that passes
>   And knows not if it sighs.

As Barker finished reading the stanza, Cho San looked searchingly up at him and asked, 'Mr Barker, you are a communist?'[7] It was not the first time that Cho San had put this question. He was wont to ask it two or three times a session. It was also Cho San who encouraged Barker to revive a lapsed tradition whereby literature students took tea with their lecturer every Wednesday afternoon. Two years later Barker was to offer an abbreviated account of some of these teatime chats in the *New Yorker*. Given the latitude required for comic exaggeration, much of the detail rings true. The students told Barker that they liked recent developments in Japan no more than he, but felt powerless to protest. They were doomed for the Chinese bloodbath, and when their turn came it would be a relief. But resistance was pointless. They all hated fascism, which was no more characteristic of Japan than it was of any other nation: 'We Japanese are Romantics; we hate war.' But the choice lay between being killed in China or dying at home as martyrs. They were not prepared to do the second. Surely, countered Barker, protest is never wasted. There had been, for instance, the much-publicised case of Baroness Ishimoto, who had raised her voice against the growing militarisation of Japan, and gone to prison for her pains. If more people did the same, resistance might inaugurate a period of *Showa*, of tranquillity and enlightenment. The students sat there, smoking, unconvinced. They had already seen too much. Arguments of the kind Barker had just advanced showed scant knowledge of the mutations of Japanese history: 'It has all happened too quickly. Japan is suffering from historical indigestion. This gives us bad dreams: aggression, imperialism, violence.'

Such confidences, and the fatalism that went with them, were not heartening. Barker was already booked to deliver a lecture at the Tokyo Imperial University on Saturday, 20 April. He decided that he and Jessica should both spend a week in the capital, using the opportunity to hurry matters along at the American consulate. Hiraku came to see them off. Waiting at the station, they watched as a detachment of soldiers presented a small silver urn to a grey-haired man and woman, dressed in sober clothes. The elderly pair, Hiraku informed Barker, were parents of a victim of the Manchurian War: the urn contained their son. Throughout the ten-and-a-half-hour journey, the couple sat opposite the Barkers. They dozed alternately over the ashes, showing no evident sign of grief. When the train drew in to Ueno Station in Tokyo, a military band was playing on the platform. The bereaved parents walked stiffly towards one of the officers, and silently surrendered the urn. The band blared heartlessly on.[8]

The American consulate shared a building with the embassy at 1 Enokizakamachi. Barker went there on Wednesday, and saw an official who himself appeared to be on the edge of a nervous breakdown. He told Barker that birth certificates for both Jessica and himself would be needed. Barker cabled to Kit asking him to dispatch them, together with their marriage certificate. To Smart he wrote that she should try if possible to let the consulate have documentation establishing his financial bona fides in case they were required for the naturalisation process. The 'Pacific Sonnets' were ready and dedicated to her, as the one who 'sent me ships back to my own nature'.[9] The compliment conveyed no more than the truth. In Japan he felt stifled, condemned to act at variance with himself. The perfect resignation of the bereaved couple in the train had epitomised a stoicism, or an apathy, that lay beyond his comprehension. Significantly, his talk at the university that Saturday was a plea for the poet's privacy, his freedom to attend to his own unique vision. If necessary the writer should be prepared to act in the world's eyes as what the Athenians called an *idiotes*, a purely private man. With a slight shift of logic, Barker then went on to talk about the way that language operates within verse. His argument was that the poet can distil more meanings and ambiguities within a sentence than are available in everyday speech. We know what Blake's statement 'The cut worm forgives the plough' means, although we may be at a loss to explain it. Because the poet can use language in this way, his work represents a form of enlightenment. In times of difficulty, he points in directions which the average citizen may have had difficulty in discerning. 'For what a poet is truly if he is anything is a man crucified not only by his own sensibility but also on his vision of human life in general.' The more tormented he was, the better the poet. Captain Ahab in *Moby Dick* was such a man, and for that reason Melville's novel is as great a work of poetry as any self-declared poem. It is the duty of the poet to follow a path which will lead him, with St John of Patmos, to 'The Poetic Apocalyptic'.[10]

The lecture contradicted itself, since it ended by committing the poet to a prophetic role at odds with the passivity and privacy it had started by defending. It was perhaps symptomatic of Barker's confusion that he had expressed himself in such terms. Somehow or other, Japan had confounded him. All his statements started to bristle with much the same perplexity of attitude. The Barkers returned to Sendai on the following Thursday. On the slow-moving train, he noted, 'the Third Class carriages are crowded to overflow; women squat with their knees up on the seats and their faces turned to the back of the seat. The floors become littered with orange peel, paper stickers, discarded ice-cartons, cigarette packets, almost ankle deep.' For better or for worse, his responses to rural Japan had been as much olfactory as social. Whenever he walked down the street in Sendai called Ichibancho he felt like Sextus Propertius as translated by Ezra Pound: 'And a minute crowd of small boys came from opposite, I do not know what boys, and I am afraid of numerical estimate.' It was a highly subjective, arguably a limited reaction, but Barker had not, in the short time of his stay, acquired the ability to view Japan objectively. 'Sometimes', he wrote of the Japanese, 'they panic,' but it was Barker who was panicking. Reluctantly he returned to his duties. His thrice-weekly lectures – Wednesdays, Thursdays and Fridays – were again attended, he noted, by three whole students. The Wednesday class was devoted to modern English literature, Thursday to unseens. Just before the second of these, he learned 'that in this whole university of 3,000 students [there were 1,052] there was no paper for my students to write their translations'.[11]

On 8 May Barker saw the laudatory review of *Lament and Triumph* which had appeared in the *Times Literary Supplement*. The very same day, in Los Angeles, Elizabeth Smart received from Christopher Isherwood, who was scriptwriting in Hollywood, a promise of money to cover the Barkers' fares. When the money itself failed to arrive, Isherwood sent the equivalent amount again.[12] By the 16th Smart had gathered the necessary affidavits, and so she cabled, 'Better. Indisputable American documents posted today.' On the 20th the same mail brought not only fares, enclosed with an additional $250, but a letter from Fitch pledging support, and the certificates from Kit. Barker dispatched a cable back to Los Angeles which read, 'You're all angels: fares received.'

Suddenly, much too late, Japan seemed beautiful. The Barkers journeyed down to Tokyo on Friday, 24 May through a landscape transformed by spring. Through the window of the train they caught glimpses of 'the miniature Japanese Alps' of the Abukuma mountains as they revolved in the background. The fields were criss-crossed with irrigation channels which from the train had the delicacy of lacework. Figures in the fields, bent over their work, had the poise and poignancy of an artistic composition. Even the rain seemed to have elicited from the foliage a luxuriance that was pretty rather than oppressive. George and Jessica were reminded of the pictures of the eighteenth-century artist Hiroshige. This time, when the train drew into Tokyo station, there was no brass band, only the beaming countenance of Temp Feaver, a friend of Elizabeth's currently working in the Canadian legation. He took them to the Canadian consulate and showed them a photograph of Smart which, George wrote to her in gathering excitement, was as radiant as sunrise over the Rockies.[13]

At the end of May, Smart and Varda left Los Angeles for Anderson Creek, further north along the Californian coast by the broad beaches of Big Sur. They stayed at Saddlebrook Ranch, an artists' commune. Already she was finding Varda cold and remote, and tensions were growing. One day in June Smart began a draft of a work set in California: a prose-poem in which her narrator-self encounters a young poet from across the sea. From Big Sur she continued to write to Barker about times and means of transport. The Barkers should, she told them, meet her in Big Sur. Would it be more expedient to travel directly to Los Angeles or was there a cheaper deal through Vancouver? Within a few days the arrangements were made. George and Jessica would sail from Yokohama to Vancouver and from there down the west coast to California.

Once their plans had been made, the Barkers could relax and enjoy Tokyo. There was no mention now of beggars, of defecation or muck carts. 'Towards the end of my stay in Japan,' George wrote later, 'I found that almost all of those curious things that had formerly alienated or disgusted me, took on a lighter note and became merely ridiculous.'[14] So, in the May sunshine he strolled out to visit the palace of the Emperor Hirohito with an Australian journalist, who advised him to refer to His Highness as 'Charlie'. The palace was so remote from the road that little could be seen through its railings except the trees in the garden. In an attempt see more, Barker stepped on a coping stone that abutted upon the pavement. His shoulder was grabbed from behind by a police officer who berated him in Japanese, incensed at this act of sacrilege against the emperor's divine person. After the journalist had placated him, the officer let go Barker's shoulder and stomped angrily away. Not even such brushes with authority could disconcert Barker now.

The news from Europe was more worrying. On 25 May, the day after the Barkers arrived in Tokyo, 5,000 British and French troops were captured by the Germans at Boulogne. 'European holocaust', George noted tersely in his diary. On the 30th, once the Barkers were back in Sendai, George offered his resignation to the university. The announcement would have been a bitter blow. Hodgson had stayed for fourteen years and the faculty, isolated in the north-east of the country, had prided itself on its resident poet. If poor, long-suffering Kochi Doi felt disappointed, he must also have recognised the pressures under which the Barkers had been labouring. So far as the political situation was concerned, a showdown between Japan and the liberal West was now a near certainty. Japanese anglophiles like Doi and Saito were in a difficult position: valuing their fragile contact with the cultural traditions of Europe, dreading and knowing the worst. Whatever Doi thought, there were no recriminations. Instead he pleaded Barker's case with the authorities and, two days later, called to say that the university had agreed to pay his salary until August and a further 1000 yen for preparing a bibliography of modern poetry. Since Barker had no degree, the faculty would also arrange for an honorary doctorate of letters to be conferred on him after his departure. Under the circumstances, these provisions were outstandingly generous. Term ended on Monday, 10 June. Two days later, as a gesture of good will, Barker gave one extra class on modern poetry. He needed to say farewell to his three loyal students, all of whom, he felt certain, were doomed soon to die. On the 14th George and Jessica packed. The following day they left Sendai.

They spent a last week in Tokyo seeing friends: the Gilboys, Saito, colleagues at the universities of Bunrika and Waseda. Then, at six in the evening on 21 June they embarked on the liner the *Empress of Russia*, bound for Vancouver. Barker had spent four years looking for a job and now he had relinquished it. Japan had not been comfortable and the trappings of academic authority, so dearly gained, had also proved irksome. He was a free agent again and, once more, poor. In the official journal of the English Literary Society of Japan, Professor Rintaro Fukuhara summed up the position with epic tact: 'In 1939, Mr Ralph Hodgson, Professor of Tohoku University for several years, left Japan and this Spring another poet, Mr George Barker, came in his place, but to our disappointment left Japan abruptly after a very short stay.'[15] The Japanese government did not award him the Order of the Rising Sun customary on the resignation of a distinguished expatriate.

In years to come Barker loved to elaborate on his Japanese adventure. He had, he would sometimes claim, spent eleven months in the East, or he had spent two years. He had worked as a British spy. Then, most preposterously, towards the end of his well-travelled life, with glass in hand and daring his fellow carousers to defy him: '*We* in *Japan* . . .' Before the *Empress of Russia* took the Barkers back across the Pacific towards his El Dorado, they had been in Japan for exactly four months and three weeks.

CHAPTER 16

'THE LIPS OF THE POSSIBLE'

America meant more to Barker than luxury and a safe haven. True, in a letter to Kit that spring he had enthused over the possibilities: 'be confident be sanguine be positively sure that this utopia and this el dorado can be and will be mine and yrs within the year and less than the year'.[1] Writing to Smart, he had offered deeper, more revealing hints. Europe is finished, he had told her. He amplified this political jeremiad by breaking with apparent inconsequentiality into an anecdote concerning his Japanese appointment:

> I am definitely proposing to adopt citizenship of the states because when I met a prosperous & aristocratic lawyer in england who had been informed that without receivin [sic] an education let alone a degree at either of the universities I was nevertheless invited to this appointment then he said My good man, is this true, is this really true? And I said No it is not true. And he said, it must be true. I was told so. All right, I said, it is true. So what? Most remarkable, he said, most remarkable, for all the world as if I were factory chimneys capable of whistling a tune. You see what I mean I hope.[2]

The grammar is strangely fractured, as so often when Barker speaks his true mind. This 'prosperous & aristocratic lawyer' recalls Coleridge's 'Man from Porlock', or the interlocutor from one of Barker's own encounter poems. Or perhaps he may be seen as Barker's alter ego, distrustful of his own achievements. In essence, however, he was a personification of British snobbery. Indubitably, the spinner of this yarn, authentic or not, still regarded himself as a rude urchin from the back streets of Fulham who, against all the odds, had broken the closed circle of the class system. In Britain, as Spender was later to admit, Barker's boots had threatened to dirty the carpet. In the United States, people might be less fussy about the marks.

The *Empress of Russia* docked on Monday, 1 July and the Barkers rested for three days in Vancouver with Ira Dilworth, a friend of Smart's. Awaiting them was a letter from Elizabeth, who suggested they journey down to Hollywood, since 'Christopher Isherwood is there and wants to meet you, and I have prepared a little book of information about 20 other people you might possibly like'. If, alternatively, they wished to travel straight to Anderson Creek, they would be very welcome. Having heard of George's abilities as a mechanic, Elizabeth admitted that she would particularly value his assistance with her old Ford, which 'breaks down every few miles, knocks, and has parts that only work fitfully'.[3] Opting for the second of these plans, George cabled to Anderson Creek on the 4th, asking her to meet them at Monterey on the 6th. The night after she received his telegram, Elizabeth had a dream in which she took Jessica for a walk on a cliff near the ranch: 'She said, "This way down?" and I said, "Yes, but be careful," and she smiled and leaped down. How could she? She didn't seem to know she would be killed. At the bottom she was bloody and smashed. George was on a camp bed bent over. I tried to take his hand. He said "Leave me alone." I wept.'[4]

The following morning, the Barkers set out by steamship for the American border, where they were to catch a Greyhound bus that would take them down to San Francisco. But they missed their connection and George wired again to say they would now not reach Monterey until the morning of Sunday the 7th. Would she please meet them off the 10.30 bus at Monterey? After further delays, they arrived early that afternoon. When their bus swept into the bus station, she was waiting for them, her hair loose and glistening in bright sunshine. Barker was later to convey the moment of meeting almost as a rebirth, in imagery connecting Smart with Big Mumma:

> When I reached America again it was July and I had your signature in my breast pocket and the image of the photograph that remains in Tokyo, it remains in my penetralia, and I was truly awaiting the doors of the bridge to be opened; I was truly hung on the lips of the possible. And I saw you standing in a sideways stance of anticipation, in the Spanish sunshine, at the Greyhound bus stop in your green dress, with your hair like an apotheosis when I alighted from the door: and I stepped down into your lap, just as truly as I stepped down from my mother, and I have loved you completely and perfectly from that moment.[5]

Smart's description of the moment is better known, since it constitutes the opening of *By Grand Central Station I Sat Down and Wept*, her fictional re-creation of her relationship with Barker, published in 1945. Jessica came down the steps first. George followed, humping their luggage, awkward and solicitous in his spectacles, blinking into the unfamiliar light. Smart was to write that he did not fit her image of a poet in the least. Despite this carefully observed discrepancy, it is the memory of Jessica at the moment of meeting which lingers:

> I am standing on a corner in Monterey, waiting for the bus to come in, and all the muscles of my will are holding my terror to face the moment I most desire. Apprehension and the summer afternoon keep drying my lips, prepared at ten-minute intervals all through the five-hour wait.
> But then it is her eyes that come forward out of the vulgar disembarkers to reassure me that the bus has not disgorged disaster: her madonna eyes, soft as the newly-born, trusting the untempted. And, for a moment, at that gaze, I am happy to forgo my future, and postpone indefinitely the miracle hanging fire. Her eyes shower me with their innocence and surprise.[6]

The three of them sat in the café opposite the bus station while the Barkers told her of their journey, he uxorious at Jessica's elbow, dancing uneasy attendance with every word. As Elizabeth drove them down above the dramatic, roller-fringed coastline towards Anderson Creek, George crooned his Irish songs; Jessica sat by his side, wordless and impressed, gazing at the redwoods and the curling breakers.

Jessica's slightly overawed silence in Smart's presence is unsurprising, since the two women could scarcely have been more different. Eleven months younger than Barker, Elizabeth was of mixed Irish, Scottish, Huguenot French, Pennsylvania Dutch and New England Puritan ancestry; through her mother's side of the family, she later told him, she also had Sioux blood in her veins. Her father Russel was a self-made, taciturn Canadian lawyer, her mother Louie a capable Ottawa hostess, whose insistence on decorum and unimpeachable moral principles provoked lifelong conflicts in Elizabeth. The Smarts were affluent, well connected and widely travelled. In 1933 Louie had taken nineteen-year-old Elizabeth and her younger sister Jane to England, so that Elizabeth could study piano with Katharine Goodson. Elizabeth had called alone on the dramatist Sir James Barrie at his house in Adelphi Terrace. She had noted on his chin a patch of iodine, which, Barrie protested, would have been neater had *he* had a daughter to look after him.[7] Four years later, in 1937, the Smart family had stayed in Gloucestershire at the home of the lawyer and MP – later, chancellor of the exchequer in the post-war Labour government – Sir Stafford Cripps. She had played Monopoly with Sir Stafford, who, she observed shrewdly, always kept the bank.[8] Elizabeth had entered these observations, and others like them, in her diary. She possessed a talent for garnering significant detail (such as Jessica's madonna-like eyes), as well as a lyrical prose style, and she wished passionately to be a published writer. Her finest gift was a sensitivity to nuances of feeling, both in herself and in others. In life, as in her journals, she had a habit of making candid remarks and promptly correcting herself ('Now you're being mean, Elizabeth'); her candour usually rang truer than her regret. By her early twenties she had become skilful in several capacities: as an accomplished pianist who had mastered Brahms and Scarlatti; as an apprentice poet; as an adept horticulturalist with a neatly ordered knowledge of plants; and as a perceptive reader of literature. Undeniably, she was a very beautiful young woman: beautiful in a haunted, hesitatingly bold, fugitive-insolent way which was reflected in her prose style.

At twenty-seven, she had clearly reached a turning point in her emotional life. She had succumbed to the blandishments of Varda, less out of devotion than awe at his imperious and moody good looks. Long before their relationship had begun, her mind had been on Barker. One day the previous summer, she had gone for a walk with Varda's then mistress Simonette, to whom she had confided her determination to bear Barker's children, since 'no matter what Barker was like, the children would all be wonderful poets'.[9] Her remark had implied an implicit faith both in the transmissibility of talent and in the equivalence of artistic and personal worth. At the time she made it, she had been quite unaware that Barker was married. Only gradually, since corresponding with him in Japan, had the truth of his wedded state impressed itself upon her. Her dream of Jessica 'bloody and smashed' had betrayed the anticipatory guilt into which her knowledge of George's circumstances now plunged her. Faced with the physical presence of her rival, the enormity of her dilemma struck her with added force.

Her predicament was exacerbated by the fact that she immediately liked and respected Jessica, sensing not only the reality of her goodness, but the depth of her trust in her husband. In *By Grand Central Station*, written only a year after these events, she speaks of Jessica looking at George with 'a confidence that appals'. She goes on to portray Jessica, in imagery distilled from George's poetry, as one who has stepped out of a suburban sylvan idyll:

> How can she walk through the streets, so vulnerable, so unknowing, and not have people and dogs and perpetual calamity following her? But overhung with her vines of faith, she is protected from their gaze like the pools in Epping Forest. I see she can walk across the leering world and suffer injury only from the ones she loves. But I love her and her silence is propaganda for sainthood.[10]

Smart was clearly both impressed and disconcerted by Jessica's highmindedness, since she invariably associated strict virtue with the dominating personality of Louie. An uneasiness with unyielding probity emerges in Elizabeth's journals time after time. In 1937, staying with the Crippses, she had soliloquised, 'I feel they think I am a deceiving, gay capitalist, pleasure loving, pretending to be more serious than I am. Yet, of course, I know they don't think that.'[11] On meeting the Barkers, she seems to have discerned in both of them a reserve she found difficult to place or to accept. Like Louie and the Crippses, Jessica had offputting moments of disapprobation. In her presence, Barker could also assume a mask of British correctness. At one and the same time, Smart wished to rip off this mask, and distrusted her own inclinations. Resolution – her undoubted gift – was balanced by self knowledge.

Barker's reactions are more difficult to gauge. It is clear from his diaries that, journeying across the Pacific towards this moment of meeting, he had not quite known what to expect. Elizabeth's photograph had shown him that she was beautiful. The lavish language in which he had replied to her letters, however, stemmed partly from courtesy and partly from gratitude for the energetic steps that she was taking on his behalf. Even after his arrival, his attitude to Elizabeth is very difficult to separate from his rapturous reaction to the freedom of California, which, contrasted with the restrictions he had experienced in Japan, seemed so absolute. The West Coast of America provoked in Barker a strong but mixed response, since he found its overt hedonism both attractive and shallow. Forty years later he expressed this double view pithily: 'I had the impression that in California we had succeeded in being happy by the simple process of removing from our minds any thoughts whatsoever that might turn on any serious subject. This is one of the marvellously accessible ways of being happy. It seemed to me to be, it always seems to me to be, silly.'[12] Whatever may have been his misgivings, the new environment evidently relaxed him. Photographs taken of him at the time show a man transformed: open-shirted, confident, direct of gaze. His eyesight seems temporarily to have improved, enabling him to dispense with spectacles. As the summer advanced, he came to resemble less a pale London scribbler than a tanned matinée idol.

The community of artists and bohemians at Anderson Creek epitomised everything that Barker admired and distrusted in California. In the previous few years it had grown around the imperious, pioneering figure of Jaime de Angulo, a complicated and cantankerous man, who both fascinated Barker and daunted him. The son of a rich Castilian family, de Angulo had spent his boyhood in Paris and his youth in Colorado and Wyoming, where he had fled to escape parental authority, only to find himself isolated by language and reduced to manual work. He had moved on to San Francisco just in time for the 1906 earthquake, during the aftermath of which he had worked as a fire fighter. Encouraged by the Jesuits, he had then studied medicine at Johns Hopkins University. After graduating, he had attended Jung's lectures in Vienna. Jaime had come to Big Sur for the first time in 1915, driving a herd of horses down from Alturas to establish his homestead claim. His neighbours then had been the linguist Alfred Kroeber and the anthropologist Paul Radin, author of *Primitive Religion*. From these two scholars he had acquired an interest in local Indian cultures, aided by his natural flair for languages. In time he had come to speak Achumawi, Tequislatec and Zapotec more fluently than the qualified ethnographers, who made use of his expertise without giving him the job at Berkeley he coveted.[13] Now Jaime kept himself in his ranch perched above the coastal redwoods, drank and thought about D.H. Lawrence, whom he had visited several times in Taos. He spoke Spanish with an incongruous French accent, broke in wild ponies and dared the world to defy him. Henry Miller, who was to know him well after the war, would catch him to a T:

> A lone wolf, divorced from all that he held most dear, waging a perpetual feud with his neighbour Baroda, another Spaniard, poring over his books, his dictionaries (Chinese; Sanskrit; Hebrew; Arabic; Persian to mention but a few), raising a little fruit and vegetables, killing deer in season and out, forever exercising his horses; getting drunk; quarrelling with everyone, even his bosom pals, driving visitors away with a lash, studying in the dead of night, coming back to his book on language, *the* book on language he hoped it would be – and finishing it just before his death . . .[14]

In the meantime, Smart felt that Jaime and Barker were made for one another. One evening in July she took George up to Jaime's homestead, away from both Jessica and Varda. The two men drank far into the the night, swapping stories, boasts and songs. The following morning they rode around the ranch on mustang ponies. When they reached a low outcrop of rock, Jaime spurred his mustang off the ridge into the shallow ravine below, and dared Barker, who had never before ridden a horse, to follow him. He could not do it.[15]

Below Jaime's ranch lay a scattering of log cabins left behind by the convicts who had completed the highway along the coast a mere three years before. The Barkers settled into one of them, with a balcony overlooking the sea. On their balcony, in the balmy evenings of late July, their neighbours gathered to sing. But the nights were cold and they huddled around a rough wood-burning stove fed by windfalls from the forest above. As Jessica endeavoured to make a home, George devoted his mornings to recording his impressions in a series of 'American Odes', initially intended for the Connecticut poetry publisher James Laughlin, whom Smart had already contacted for him. In the afternoons he and

Elizabeth roamed the steep sidetracks in her unreliable Ford. They made trips into Monterey on the pretext of shopping for food. Their actual destination was more usually a record shop in the main street, where they bought 78s of Scarlatti and packets of needles with which to play them.

In mid-July George and Elizabeth's diaries fall silent. Only later, in separate fictional re-creations, were they able to testify to the erotic tension between them. It is clear from these accounts that, from the very beginning, there was some scope for misunderstanding. Each of them, for example, was obsessed with a very different ideal. Smart, for her part, was taken with a romantic notion of the poet as lover. In her novel her way of viewing Barker is derived less from his physical presence – since throughout he is faceless – than from his work. When, in an attempt to repel or else to lure her, he flaunts his bisexual past, he merges with the loved one from 'The Documents of a Death', 'the hermaphrodite whose love looks up through the appletree with a golden indeterminate face'.[16] As he drives her along the coast road, talking wildly, his profile caught in the windscreen resembles that in his poem 'Narcissus'.

Barker's feelings for Elizabeth seem to have blended with his delighted discovery of a new continent, a fresh and heedless mode of life. It must be remembered that, during these fleeting summer weeks, he was viewing Smart not against her native, Puritan Ottawa background, but within the playground context of California in high summer. Since, in this new environment, he was able, as perhaps never before, to give his nature full rein, his growing infatuation became a means of self-discovery. On 22 July his diary breaks silence in a panegyric, the language of which draws heavily on the Catholicism of his youth:

> The grammar of glorification is demonstrated at the flick of her head in the candlelight and at her smile the foundation of vocal admiration collapses in the magnificat. Mythology, in a poverty of raiment, cannot clothe her and god almighty on his throne of grace serves only to adorn the ring on her little finger. O my Canadian![17]

The last phrase alludes obliquely to lines from Donne's Elegy 'On Going to Bed': 'O my America! my new-found-land, / My kingdom, safest when with one man man'd / My Myn of precious stone, My Empire, / How blest am I in discovering thee!' The slight echo tells that for Barker, as for Donne, geographical and sexual discovery were closely allied.

As their mutual attraction grew, moral responsibility weighed on them both. If Jessica was the issue, nobody was more aware of it than Elizabeth, soon to agonise in her diary over the difficulty of allaying either compassion or remorse: 'But who could be proof against the future ghost holding pity like a time bomb in its look of agony? What gangsters of forgetfulness of justification can nature find, or you, god, engage, to quiet these thieves of endurance?'[18] Barker, moreover, found it impossible to square his emotions, either with the Catholic teaching on marriage, or with his very real affection for his wife. After one tense outing on Wednesday, 17th, he wrote in his diary, 'Virtual assassination of J[essica]. The terrible hell; poor chick!'

Yet Elizabeth too felt a victim. At moments the 'corrupt language' of her journal puns on 'traps' and 'spring(e)ing' so as to cause her and Jessica to change places: 'My room echoes with the screams she never uttered and under my floor the vines of remorse get ready to push up through the trap. The cricket drips remembrance into my ear lest I mislay any item of cruelty's fiendish itinerary. The trap is springing and I am in the trap.'[19] Even in *Grand Central Station* she lapses into an almost obsessive plural, as if the disaster looming over the three of them were the product of some indeterminate collective will. The language in which she evokes their situation is less lyrical than tragic. She writes of herself as Macbeth (strange transposition this); the sword of Damocles hangs over them; she envies Syrinx her fate. Towards her rival, her responses are almost hypersensitively acute. She speaks of the child whom she knows Jessica to have given up, of its mother as the madonna of some despoiled Latin shrine.

On 20 July Barker recorded in his diary his growing self-distaste: 'I regard myself as that lowest and least principled of people and the simplest of p(o)ets: a dog.' Still they dallied. Reverting at moments to her strait-laced upbringing, Elizabeth succumbed to coyness. They spent one whole morning on a clifftop overlooking the sea, with her too frightened to be held. A moral paralysis prevailed.

Three whole weeks elapse before the next, stark sentence in his journal: 'X'd first under the redwoods with the coast of California.' This entry is for Monday, 12 August. Later, he would recall Elizabeth shedding her blue dungarees; above them the leaves were already starting to turn. The following day in the log cabin, he awoke to find one of her hairs held by the sweat of his shoulder. He took it in his palms and, walking out into the morning light, laid it softly beneath the trees. Returning to the cabin, he set up his typewriter beside the Oxford *Poems of Gerard Manley Hopkins*. Feeding in a sheet of blue paper, he typed Elizabeth a letter in which, cradling her with epithets, he reached back to childhood for Grandma Taaffe's fondest Gaelic endearments:

Acushla acushla this morning this morning I found the symbol of love on my shoulder curled in the shape of a single length of all glory which I recognized instantly and o with an abelards smile as fallen from your heloise and heliol crown. And what did I do no not enclose it in the leaves of the oxford hopkins or even in my own poems but I took it out into the garden and gave it back whence it originally came so that now there is a species of floral hitherto beyond the experiments of the most gifted horticulturalists: the headless elizabeth lily I made with my own hands here.[20]

He was just summoning on the typewriter keys the memory of yesterday's redwood canopy over their heads, when Jessica walked into the room.

CHAPTER 17

AN AMERICAN ODE

For Dylan Thomas, footloose in wartime Britain, the favourable review accorded to *Lament and Triumph* in the *Times Literary Supplement* had not been welcome. Having been rejected for military service because of his weak lungs, Thomas spent August 1940 in Gloucestershire, where he and Caitlin had been invited to put up for several weeks at the Maltings House, Marsfield with John Davenport, incisive critic, would-be-poet, and soon-to-be schoolmaster. With Davenport, he revived a project first mooted with Desmond Hawkins in 1935, and since worked at with a succession of collaborators: a spoof whodunnit entitled *The Death of the King's Canary*. This projected *roman à clef* was to describe the murder of the imaginary poet Hilary Byrd, newly appointed Poet Laureate, in a country house called Dymock Hall in Suffolk. It was to involve flagrant parodies of various contemporaries. Stung by Barker's growing reputation, Thomas and Davenport now decided to place him first in the firing line.

The story opens at 10 Downing Street where, following the death of the former Laureate, the prime minister (a Stanley Baldwin or Chamberlain figure; certainly not Churchill) is dithering over the choice of a successor. Specimens of work by various contenders have been placed at his elbow by his sycophantic secretary, Faraday. On top of the pile lies *Claustrophosexannal*, a slender volume by a young, polytechnic-educated poet called Albert Ponting. The author's identity is simple to decode. Albert was the Christian name by which George VI was known to his immediate family. Pontings and Barkers were adjacent stores along Kensington High Street. In the following passage the satire may be Davenport's but the skit, with its punning on his collaborator's name, is decidedly Dylan Thomas's:

On top of the books lay a page in Faraday's neat script.

Albert Ponting, born Balham, 1910. Ed. privately. Did Chemistry course at Polytechnic. *Must read*, but I suggest unsuitable.

The Prime Minister picked up a volume called *Claustrophosexannual*. The title was puzzling. He opened the book and began to read:

LAMENTABLE ODE
BY ALBERT PONTING

I, I, my own gauze phantom am,
My head frothing under my arm,
The buttocks of Venus for my huge davenport.
I orgillous turn, burn, churn,
As his rubbery bosom curds my perspiring arm –
The gust of my ghost, I mean –
And he wears no woman-sick, puce, and oriflammed a brow
That, yes, yes, my hair screamed aloud
Louder than death's orchestra or sirocco.
The urge of the purge of the womb of the worm
I renege in the flail-like failing of
The detumescent sun.
This my crepuscular palimpsest is:
I am so greatly him that lazarhouses and such
Lascivious lodges of the unloved
Peel like pomegranates at my nasal touch
And Balham faints in the scalecophidian void.
To him who broods in the nests of my arches,
Fallen or Charing Cross's, like a big bumbling bird,
Before the metropolitan horde
Funicling darkly lairward
I lay the most holy gifts of my spilt flesh:
Far beyond comprehension of golden asinine error
I raise to the mirror the maggots and the lumps of my terror.

He glanced again at his secretary's notes, and raised his eyebrows. He had once been Minister of Education, and he was still keenly interested in all educational questions. 'Privately' sounded fishy, but the Polytechnic, with its reputation for accuracy – empirical tests were a favourite with the Prime Minister – might have spared him this shock. What on earth was a davenport? He walked over to the shelves; and discovered that in English it was an escritoire and in American a settee. It did not seem to clear up the line. He had never been to Balham, and the poem was not enlightening. He glanced through the rest of the book, his eye sliding distastefully from adjective to adjective; but the humourless self-absorption and the faulty syntax of the writer soon defeated him. He drank, poured again, and reached for another book.[1]

Claustrophosexannual was the first of many attempts by Thomas to mock Barker's titles, in this case evidently *Calamiterror*. His parody successfully reduces Barker's innovative syntax to a polysyllabic soup, but it also captures the confluence of the homoerotic with the topographical in *Poems*. When Ponting puts in an appearance, he is 'tall and thin and distinguished and young'. Invited to Dymock Hall, he preens himself before the mirror. He writes constantly. 'He was feeling creative and knew he could do nothing about it; images came with such ease to him as he carefully disarranged his hair and loosened his wool tie that he knew he ought to suspect them ... Against his own criticism he wrote the three images down with an eyebrow pencil.'[2] Throughout the remainder of the novella Ponting assiduously chases serving wenches beneath stairs. He is not, of course, appointed Laureate.

On 20 November 1941, fifteen months after completing *The Death of the King's Canary*, Thomas was invited to address the English Club at the University of Oxford. He read the verse parodies aloud, including the parody of Barker, in his rolling, subtly nuanced voice. Among the impressionable undergraduates in the audience were a 23-year-old John Heath-Stubbs and a nineteen-year-old Philip Larkin.[3]

Meanwhile in London Big Mumma had been battling with the Blitz. While Pa performed Home Guard duties at the Middle Temple, and Kit, despite his glass right eye, awaited entry into the Air Force to check aeroplane parts, she did what she could to maintain the family home in Upper Addison Gardens. One Saturday evening Pa sat in the front room writing a belated letter to George, in the company of Sirrah, who was chasing mice driven out of neighbouring houses by the Luftwaffe. Kit was relaxing at the cinema watching *Tom Brown's Schooldays*; Grandma Taaffe was in Bournemouth.[4] Big Mumma stood in the kitchen preparing supper: roast leg of lamb, baked potatoes and a soothing pudding. Around them, bombs fell among the back streets of west London. 'When a particularly nasty one falls,' wrote Pa, 'she comes out here and lets off steam, about anything and everything and two minutes later she is perfectly calm.' Big Mumma refused to take cover in the public air-raid shelters: 'There's nowhere absolutely safe except the deep underground stations and we do not wish to go there ... And having seen what happens, when a bomb hits these houses, there is no point sitting up in the passages and basements, as many do, so we just go to bed in the normal way.'

As she watched Barker during the weeks in Big Sur, Smart was aware of his anxiety about his family. 'His brother and his mother and his grand-mother', she wrote, drawing on his frightened fantasies, 'lie abandoned in death on the stones of the London underground.' Barker's absorption in their affair had not taken his mind off the situation in England. When he received Pa's letter, he had a vision of the moral stability of home, a world away from the ethical turmoil of his life in California. Taking out the typescript of 'Pacific Sonnets', he decided to supplement them with another, in a more personal vein. He wrote:

> Most near, most dear, most loved and most far,
> Under the window where I often found her
> Sitting as huge as Asia, seismic with laughter,
> Gin and chicken helpless in her Irish hand,
> Irresistible as Rabelais, but most tender for
> The lame dogs and hurt birds that surround her, –
> She is a procession no one can follow after
> But be like a little dog following a brass band.[5]

The memory of Big Mumma's hilarity remained a stabilising factor in her son's fluctuating existence. In the sonnet her mirth seems every bit as convulsive as the earthquakes which had shaken the campus at Sendai. Unlike these, however, her laughter is reassuring and rooted in the familiar. Though the glass of gin and chicken sandwich she clasps heave in response, the general effect is one of rollicking steadiness. Among the 'lame dogs' of the sixth line, none is more indebted to her than the 'little dog' mentioned at the close, who is like George as a toddler, caught up in his mother's wake. When Jessica read this sonnet, as she wrote to Monica, she could not help crying. It was as if she and George were once more safe in their marriage, with Big Mumma close at hand. Two years later Barker showed the poem to Eliot, who congratulated him on writing 'that rare thing, the perfect anthology piece'. It remains his most popular poem.

Such reliability, such death-defying gladness, were now tantalising memories. On that August afternoon in Big Sur when the truth about his relationship with Elizabeth came to light, George and Jessica came as close to a row as Jessica, with her habitual reserve, could manage. Barker had assured his wife that his affections for Elizabeth were negligible. Jessica accused him of lying. According to Elizabeth, who later heard of the exchange from George, 'the first thing she wailed out' was 'Oh why didn't you let me keep the child?'[6] The cry haunted Smart. 'In the night', she wrote in *By Grand Central Station*, 'she moans with the voice of the stream below my window, searching for the child whose touch she once felt and can never forget . . .'[7]

The Barkers and Smart remained uncomfortably in Big Sur for another six weeks, but the tension between them was growing. Barker had fallen into a habit that was soon to become second nature to him of tailoring his promises to the two women in order to fit their very different expectations. On 27 September, with autumn reddening the leaves, all three drove down the coast to Los Angeles in Elizabeth's Ford. In Jessica's mind, as her letters to Monica show, the purpose of this move was to find a secure niche for the winter; in Elizabeth's, as her account in *By Grand Central Station* implies, it was so that she and George could settle Jessica, and then abscond. The Barkers found a room with a Mr and Mrs Bedell at 1635 North Ogden Drive, Hollywood. Elizabeth stayed down the road at 10610 Foothill Drive with a family friend called Mrs Witchner and her lawyer son, Milton. For several days the three of them struggled to maintain an appearance of normality. Jessica wrote home that they were happy and George was applying himself to his Odes. Elizabeth sat listening to the banter of the Witchners and wondered what would happen next.

For some time, little happened. Jessica, however, was not at all happy with the living arrangements, which seemed to her to resemble a *ménage à trois*. She watched over George anxiously minute by minute, convinced that every visit to the shops was an assignation. For Jessica, California had turned into a prison: she had, she soon wrote, learned to hate 'every leaf, person and ray of sunshine in it'.[8]

On 2 October George could bear the tension no longer. Though Smart was living a few blocks down the road, he posted her a letter which ran, 'I insist on coming up – if its domestically impolitic I can arrive incognito & anonymously – and wait a week before my debut but at least at last I shall see you.'[9] Five days later he materialised. Elizabeth and he took her Ford out to San Bernardino on the hills above Los Angeles, where they made love under a waterfall. In *By Grand Central Station* the occasion becomes the consummation of the relationship; ever afterwards, George would refer to it as their nuptials. Unforeseen consequences ensued. Descending the mountain, instead of turning back to Los Angeles, Barker turned the Ford east. After all the nagging and the nerves both of them were, suddenly, tipsy with irresponsible relief. Since they had acted on the spur of the moment, neither knew where they were going, but Jaime had talked enthusiastically of Taos, where he had seen the shrine to Lawrence, and so a vague plan was formed to drive to New Mexico. The couple spent three days on the road. At night they put up at motels, signing guest books 'Mr and Mrs Henrick Van Loon', after the Canadian loon bird.[10] On the fourth morning the Ford drew up at the California–Arizona border and Barker opened the nearside door to speak to the guards.

What happened next must have been frightening, and was permanently to colour Barker's attitude to the United States. Although America would not be at war for another fourteen months, the law-enforcing authorities were jittery and willing to misconstrue even the most trivial irregularity. The previous year Smart had travelled directly from Canada to Mexico by ship. On entering the United States in January, she had simply walked across the border without obtaining a stamp in her passport. Now, when the guards examined it, they found no valid American visa. Barker, however, possessed a visa good for several more months. But the couple were clearly not married and they were in a condition of high excitement. The Mann Act of 1910, popularly known as the 'White Slave Act', stated that it was illegal for a man to cross any interstate boundary with an unmarried woman under twenty-eight. Also, though fornication was not a felony in California, it was in Arizona. The couple were therefore taken in for questioning. The guards could find little against Barker, whom they released almost immediately. Since Smart had entered the country illegally, however, she was detained while they questioned her with some brusqueness. For three hours she recited verses from the *Song of Solomon* under her breath to keep herself sane. She was held overnight, and then informed that she would not be released until she could provide a testimonial. Eventually she gave the guards the telephone number of her Hollywood landlord Milton Witchner, who was an attorney. Witchner phoned her father in Ottawa, who then phoned the Canadian ambassador in Washington. A visa was prepared and dispatched. With some reluctance the FBI took Smart to Hollywood, where she was handed into the safekeeping of the Witchners.

On his return Barker explained his absence to Jessica by claiming that he had been driving to New York on business. The pretext was just feasible since he had already been in touch with the poetry editor Oscar Williams, who coveted the American Odes for his anthology *New Poems, 1940*. Evidently George breathed not a word about Smart, since in a letter Jessica wrote to him later the same month she was to narrate the story of Elizabeth's arrest – an edited version of which had by then been conveyed to her by Witchner via the Bedells – as if it had represented a quite unrelated episode. To spare Jessica's feelings, her well-intentioned hosts had clearly informed her that Elizabeth had been detained during a solitary escapade of her own. Even by this time, so unsuspecting of the extent of her husband's involvement does Jessica seem to have been, that in this letter her indignation was reserved for Elizabeth, whom she accuses of having needlessly implicated Witchner to secure her own release. Jessica clearly came to believe that Smart had mentioned Witchner's name to the border guards specifically to protect her lover Varda, who had entered the States illegally with her that January. That Jessica came to entertain this version of events suggests strongly that she believed Smart to be both duplicitous and emotionally unstable, and her attachment to her husband to be a passing fad. This consoling illusion was difficult to square with the facts, but for the next few months Jessica clung to it with something approaching desperation.

The following week George and Elizabeth eloped again. This time, Barker assured Jessica, he was travelling to New York to see Oscar Williams and would travel by rail. Elizabeth cleared her belongings from the Witchners' home. She abandoned her Ford, telling Milton to sell it and donate the proceeds to Jessica. She left for the station with one enormous suitcase, containing all her portable possessions. After a journey of three days, she and Barker arrived in New York, where they stayed briefly with Elizabeth's married sister Helen, who had an apartment in Manhattan. Two days later, they moved to 67 Seventh Avenue, where Oscar Williams lived with his poet-cum-painter wife Gene Derwood.

Williams was the foremost impresario of poetry publishing in America and also, among more than a few of his British protégés, something of a joke. Slender and bird-like, he wore horn-rimmed glasses of the kind favoured by Wall Street bankers, and had at one time been a high-ranking advertising executive. Subsequently, however, he had experienced some kind of visionary seizure while driving through the southern states. According to Auden, whose poems he published, he had 'then sought medical advice, which could diagnose nothing. Suddenly he realized what was the matter: he wanted to write poetry.'[11] Thereafter, he had forsworn commerce and devoted himself to writing verse and, with a peculiar organisational frenzy, to editing anthologies. In the previous few years he had put together an annual collection of the brightest and best verse published in America, including work by expatriate British poets.

Williams was serious and he was resolute. He would never take no for an answer. Among the few who could resist his importunings was Dylan Thomas, who reserved for him a distinctive form of rhetorical deflation. When asked for a thumbnail description of the man, Thomas savoured the pause before declaring, 'Oscar Williams is . . . the greatest anthologist in America.' On another occasion, pestered by Williams to supply a reference for a grant, he demurred as long as he could. When the request was repeated, he sent a sheet of paper to New York bearing the single sentence: 'In my considered opinion, Oscar Williams is the greatest poet the world has ever known. Dylan Thomas.'[12]

Barker came to share Thomas's unflattering opinion of Williams's literary abilities, but was fond of him nonetheless. 'Impossible Oscar' he was wont to call him behind his back, while his wife was referred to as 'Egyptian Gene'. Together they were 'the Abominables'. Gene was tallish and straight, and possessed a deadpan face with wide eye-sockets, above which her hair was cut in ancient Egyptian style, forming a convex peak at mid-forehead. As a result, according to George, she resembled a Ptolemaic Pharaoh. The Williamses existed at the epicentre of the New York poetry scene, and their apartment was a vortex of literary gossip.

Despite the distant threat of war, October 1940 was a promising month in which to seek an introduction to bohemian New York. Auden was staying in Brooklyn, though Barker failed to visit him, dogged still by the old fear of social exclusion. Peggy Guggenheim was about to re-establish her art gallery. Djuna Barnes had just moved into 5 Patchin Place, a handsome apartment block arranged around a courtyard close to Greenwich Avenue and Tenth Street. Three blocks to the north of this, Anaïs Nin had installed herself in a penthouse at 215 West 13th Street. Barnes avoided her, ostentatiously crossing the road whenever she saw her advancing along the sidewalk. Emily Coleman was soon to arrive from Arizona with her son Johnny, now a bookish young man who wanted to write. Fitch still lived at Riverdale. To these established friends Barker added fresh acquaintances. Dunstan Thompson was a thin, pale, somewhat epicene young poet whose irreverent sense of humour he shared. Barker described him as 'very elegant and dipsomaniac, and I think his poems are too'. Sales of poetry books were yet to be affected by war conditions. Thriving poetry lists were maintained by major houses like Macmillan, and smaller concerns like New Directions, run from Connecticut by Barnes's friend James Laughlin. Experimental verse was well represented at the Gotham Book Mart on West 47th Street, where volumes of verse could be purchased, along with small magazines and recordings of poets reading.

Barker was quick to take advantage of these opportunities. Oscar had picked several of his poems for *New Poems, 1940*. Also through Oscar's intervention, he had soon obtained a contract with Macmillan for a *Selected Poems*. His material circumstances, however, were desperate. His Japanese savings having run out, he and Smart were surviving on her allowance from her father and living out of a suitcase. Since none of his Faber poems had been published in the States, Barker was also less well known in America than in London. Williams was generous with bed and copy space, but there was a limit to his patronage. With freelance work slow in coming, Barker set about trading on his fragile status as a former academic, and began angling for jobs in Kansas, Southwestern and Harvard. None of the fish bit his hook, though Professor Theodore Spenser at Harvard, having read some of Barker's verse, was to invite him up to give a single reading in January 1941. But January was four months away. George and Elizabeth were engrossed in one another, poor, glad and desperate by turns.

At the end of October Smart's allowance stopped coming, blocked by currency restrictions. There was nothing she and George could do but part. On Sunday, 27 October Elizabeth set off for Ottawa by bus. She told Barker that she intended to sell a tract of land and a cabin, her share of the family estate near the Gatineau Hills. With the proceeds, she hoped to be able to support both of them.[13] Barker took her to the bus terminal. He kissed her goodbye, promising to come up to Canada as soon as circumstances permitted. As the bus sped northwards, he retraced his footsteps towards the Williamses.

CHAPTER 18

'FIVE JAWS OF LOVE'

In America Barker was seized by an ethical instability, evident both in his correspondence and in his reactions to those around him. Like Jessica, he was used to the outer decorum of the Old World. The conventions of British society had matched certain inner constraints which, for the rebel in him, it had been a delight to rend. In their absence he was at a loss how to act and how authentically to transgress. Humour and rebellion had been ways of tearing the moral fabric. Jest, he had noted in his journal entry of 1937, had been 'the bright flash of narrowmindedness concentrating the combative will'. Here in America, to all appearances, the context was freer. If in Japan he had felt like someone bereft of his cultural shadow, here he gives the impression of a man shouting in the nave of a great cathedral who finds that the walls return no echo. Barker needed that reverberation, that sense of consequences which the religious call sin, to confirm him even in minor acts of sacrilege. Now the buttresses of British life had been replaced by a form of Puritanism which meant as little to him as the Catholic doctrine of original sin did to the almost pagan Smart. Suddenly, disastrously, there was nothing left for Barker to cherish or violate except, of course, his wife. Towards Jessica he retained a strong feeling of loyalty – she represented, amongst other things, his childhood. For the next five years he would endeavour to give expression to this residual bond through remorse, through pity and, more actively, through genuine if ineffectual attempts at reconciliation.

Back in Hollywood, thrown among strangers, Jessica was going out of her mind. She was lonely and in debt, owing several weeks' rent to the Bedells. She had managed for a while to survive on the money that Milton Witchner had realised from the sale of Elizabeth's Ford – a mere thirty dollars, now all spent. She had heard nothing from George since he and Elizabeth had departed on 7 October, like the nymphs of Eliot's *The Waste Land,* 'leaving no addresses'. Her only hope of contact in New York was the publishing company Harcourt Brace, to whom she had dispatched cable after cable, to no avail. Others, comparative strangers, seemed to be better informed about her husband's movements. Where exactly, she now wrote to him, had he acquired this habit of subterfuge?[1] On the evening of Elizabeth's departure George telephoned Los Angeles to reassure her that everything was under control. Elizabeth loved him, but he did not love her. Despite this, he would be going to join her in Canada. The following day, he wrote to Elizabeth in Ottawa, reporting this conversation quite differently. He had, he assured her, told Jessica that the marriage was over and that she must accept this as inevitable. It was just one day since Elizabeth had left and already he missed her terribly:

> Whatever recollection comes to accost me when I go down the street is always the same golden spaniel at my heels tugging at my emotion with all of your five jaws of love. I think of you seated in the coach going northward so that the strollers along the road or passing motorists or cows who have the sense to lift their gaze can see you but I to whom your gaze is the cynosure of all vision what do I have to be happy with but your hypnotic absence. How could you go away? I am all the pariah mongrels of all desolations who go searching among the ruins of their allegiance: for when you go away I am not only lost, not only so lonely that I feel like islands in the middle of the Pacific, but so deprived of reason for being as being at all that I can cease to be anything but one who waits, like a room when no one is at home.[2]

George had agreed to meet Elizabeth in Ottawa in about ten days. In the meantime he attempted to placate Jessica, for whom, however, his two letters were insufficient: 'I am relying on two tomorrow,' she pined, 'and the next day and the next day.' On the evening of his departure for Canada, he wrote a brief letter to Big Mumma, phrased like a note from the gallows. He told his mother that he could supply her with no address for future correspondence. Life had become so complicated that his future movements were uncertain. 'I am at present in the process of registering for the year of military service which Congress recently introduced here.' Without much hope, he was trying to arrange lecturing work for himself. 'You can see that I find it almost beyond me to write you freely about what I am doing when I remember that when you receive this it may be only ruins you can read it among.'[3]

He immediately set off for Ottawa, unaware as yet of the conflicting *frissons* within the Smart household. He called at the Smart family home: Coltrin Lodge, a large detached villa in the affluent suburb of Rockcliffe Park, where

Elizabeth was staying with her parents, her younger sister Jane and her younger brother Russel. Mr and Mrs Smart had been less than impressed by their daughter's devotion to Barker; even her brother, while more understanding, had felt obliged to toe the family line ('I have never met this guy,' he is made to say in *By Grand Central Station*, 'but he sounds to me like a cad.') Meeting Elizabeth's parents, Barker realised instantly that he was not welcome. He found a cheap room in a guesthouse in the insalubrious district of Hull on the north bank of the Ottawa River, where he and Elizabeth contrived furtive meetings in cafés. Their only ally was Jane, who had recently married a journalist called D'Arcy Marsh. As communication between the guesthouse and Coltrin Lodge was difficult, they acted as intermediaries.

After a few days of these frustrating trysts, Barker was invited by Marsh to go with him to Montreal on a journalistic assignment. The trip was beset with problems. Canada being at war, travel was subject to tighter restrictions than in the States. As Barker and Marsh drove across the St Lawrence River, they were stopped by the police. It appeared that Barker's visa was not in order and so he was arrested and held overnight in a Montreal police cell,[4] an experience that was permanently to jaundice his feelings about Canada. Marsh cabled Smart, who rushed down from Ottawa and, after several hours of negotiation with officials, arranged for Barker's release. They stayed for several nights in a Montreal hotel. Then she took him to the family estate at Kingsmere, where she had spent her summers as a child. The hilly estate surrounded a lake, across which fell the shade of autumnal trees. The temperature, however, was low for early November. Chafed by the chill of the mornings, Barker's throat broke out in a quinsy, an abscess of the tonsils all the more painful in those days before antibiotics. In the second week of November he left for New York.

He fudged his reasons for leaving, telling Smart that he must attend to the Macmillan *Selected Poems* and that his tonsils needed treating as well. All of which was perfectly true; a more cogent reason, however, was his susceptibility to Jessica's appeals. Milton Witchner knew of Smart's Ottawa address, and having extracted it from him, Jessica had sent Barker an urgent letter on the 9th, care of Coltrin Lodge. Anger had rendered Jessica articulate. It was, she wrote, 'amazing how fierce I have become'.[5] The Smarts were ruthless people who would ruin both of them. Even in Hollywood Elizabeth had conned people with her lies. 'People gape if I am introduced to them as your wife, since you are Elizabeths' poet and genius from Japan and apparently I rose like Aphrodite but from the Pacific.'[6] Did he not realise that he was being used? Did he not appreciate how little money she now had?

Although Barker had little money himself, apart from his very small advance from Macmillan, and such funds as Elizabeth could afford, he cabled ten dollars to Los Angeles, together with an edited account of his traumatic jaunt to

Montreal. Jessica's resentment instantly turned to relief. 'It's silly,' she wrote, 'but directly I start writing to you I weep. It is distance and not having the right words and everything. But I have been trying to think only of you today, without my emotions sweeping in on everything, and I am dreadfully sorry that you had such a ghastly time and I believe in you and love you and all the nice things I thank you for a thousand times. But will you shelter me and keep me safe in future, Gran dear. I want to be covered and protected so that I can get resistance and some sort of capability back.'[7] On 15 November, stung by a bitter conscience, Barker sent a telegram requesting Jessica to come east by train. 'I did not know,' she wrote back, 'that one wire could please me so much.'[8]

But he had already arranged for Elizabeth to spend part of the pre-Christmas period with him. With his plans in disarray, Barker found a room at 147 East 33rd Street. In anticipation of their reunion, Jessica had started to darn a threadbare pair of his socks, which previously she had not even been able to look at. On Thanksgiving Day, the Barkers' first in America, she boarded the train for New York, along with what seemed like the entire US navy.

Meanwhile in East 33rd Street Barker awaited the arrival of both women. He had arranged to meet Smart off the night train at Grand Central Station on 24 November, but was in such a state of consternation at these conflicting arrangements that he failed to appear. Elizabeth spent some hours in a bleak overnight café before making her way to 33rd Street, where she and George spent a couple of days. George attempted to reconcile her to Jessica's imminent appearance. Two days later he saw her off on the train to Ottawa, telling her that, come what might, they would meet again at Christmas. Almost immediately, he welcomed Jessica off her train from Los Angeles and settled her into the very same room.[9]

Throughout Advent the Barkers relaxed in Manhattan. They renewed their friendship with Fitch, who was still engaged to Telte, and about to join the Air Corps in Florida. They wandered through the freezing but festive streets admiring the illuminated Christmas trees along Fifth Avenue and the open-air ice rink at the Rockefeller Plaza. When Jessica went to bed, George took the opportunity to write to Smart, breaking off now and then to work on a poem. Circumstances rendered a Christmas visit impracticable. In any case, their snatched meetings and intemperate scurryings across the border were wearing both of them down. By some means or other, they must come up with a permanent solution to their predicament. Any such plan would need to include Jessica. Barker suggested that he and his wife both now move to Canada, where Jessica might perhaps find herself a job.

On Christmas Eve Elizabeth replied. She could think of no job in Ottawa that would suit Jessica, although Canada was, she added, full of the sort of genteel behaviour that Mrs Barker might appreciate.[10] Unable to propose a satisfactory compromise, Elizabeth indulged in fantasies of eloping with George to Bermuda, where they would both become beachcombers, or else to a farm on the New Brunswick Coast. In cold reality, she was sitting in Rockliffe Park with tears dropping off the end of her nose: 'As for me I'm dying, I'm dead. There's only one remedy for me and now it seems as impossible and unattainable as distant as a weekend in Mars. I'm the madman batting his head in every direction, and not even finding a place to begin filing for liberty. O well, I'm only getting back what I gave to Jessica only hers was 1000 times worse. But there are no wells of anything in me not even pity. I'm not even sorry for myself.'[11]

On Boxing Day George wrote back. He was now, he told Elizabeth, praying for ruthlessness. He had even contemplated a Christmas dash up to see her, but Jessica continued to tug at his heart strings:

> Jessica herself sees the axe in the air everywhere and I have no power of tongue to dismiss it: she is as conscious of the tendencies of things as I am conscious of their inevitably being accomplished. I only dread that moment when the mermaid looks up in your eyes before you murder it with disbelief. But you are worth more than murders to me and I would not hesitate had the season been otherwise; but christmas is so full of reminiscences that I could not thrust them back into her face by leaving then. I am so overcome with pity that it is almost paralysis.[12]

Christmas over, Barker began a period of frantic commuting, vainly attempting to placate Jessica whilst hurrying across the border to spend a few days with Elizabeth, who was now pregnant. The lovers spent New Year 1941 together in Montreal as compensation for Christmas. No sooner had George arrived, however, than his quinsy struck again: he was forced to spend two days in the Royal Victoria Hospital. In mid-January he managed another visit, most of which he devoted to making love to Elizabeth between bouts of reading Herodotus in bed. Both had bad colds. George took his back to East 33rd Street, where he lay dreaming of Montreal, with only the copy of Herodotus to remind him of his ecstasy. It was, he now asserted to Smart in a letter, imperative that he should emigrate to Canada, whatever the consequences. He was in such a state of euphoria that even his illness had come to seem erotic:

> Oh, when I think of you I cough poppies and sneeze diamonds and sweat amber: have I endowed you with all those diadems of intellectual

brilliance and kisses and fingernail polish and sensual ecstasy which adorn you whom I never cease thinking of? No, it wasn't from me that you received them, it was our connubial regalia bestowed by episcopal circumstance in honour of our nuptials. How could circumstances ever be praised more than by our act of union? And in return it makes us mythical, so that the slightest of your gestures remains in my mind better than the Elgins or the Russian dance.[13]

Elizabeth, meanwhile, had taken her own cold back to Coltrin Lodge, where she lay in bed concocting hypothetical futures. She had imagined escaping with George to Apple River in Nova Scotia, only to abandon the scheme when Jane warned her that a couple moving to a remote area for no apparent reason would be taken for spies. Barker was due to read at Harvard on 22 January. If he could persuade Jessica to let him leave for Cambridge alone, Elizabeth planned to join him there. The poet and lawyer Frank Scott, whom she had met in Montreal, was currently on attachment at Harvard. She wrote asking if they might stay with him. For the sake of appearances, it would also help if he posed as her paternal uncle. With some misgiving, Scott agreed on both counts.

When Barker arrived at Scott's house in Harvard in the New Year of 1941, he was jumpy and ill at ease and his throat was still inflamed. To cover his nervousness, he started behaving even more outrageously than he normally did with strangers. He earned Scott's bemused admiration by telling him that Britain had a duty to capitulate to Germany in order to supply her poets with a new theme for elegies. This was almost certainly not what Barker believed, but he talked in this fashion well into the small hours. Feeling excluded from the conversation, Smart eventually retired to bed. Once the talk had exhausted itself, Barker and his host fumbled upstairs towards their respective bedrooms. On the stairway they met the French Canadian maid, carrying the tray for Scott's breakfast. Parched by alcohol, and to ease his swollen throat, Barker leaned over. To the maid's evident dismay he removed the jug of fresh orange juice from the tray and emptied it in one long, juddering gulp.[14]

After the reading Elizabeth returned to Ottawa, while George went back to New York. He had agreed to join her again in Montreal on Sunday, 9 February, and would send a cable to confirm. When Barker reached East 33rd Street, however, he was too ill even to wire. Frantically Smart cabled to him: 'Why the silence please. Why the silence?' There was a simple explanation. On 7 February he entered a clinic on East 75th Street, where his tonsils were removed by Dr Fred J. Hunter Jr for $50. The expense was ruinous but, as he wrote to Elizabeth, this was not the worst of it. He wished all of him to be hers and now there was simply less of him for her to have. His letter, though, had failed to reached Ottawa by the 9th, the day on which he was due to set out. In desperation, Smart phoned East 33rd Street. The receiver was picked up by Jessica, who informed her crisply that George was unwell. If it was true that he had arranged to meet Elizabeth in Montreal that weekend, Jessica could only suppose that he would reschedule the visit for a later date and in Ottawa. Jessica then put down the phone.

For Jessica, this telephone conversation set the limit to her endurance. She packed her clothes and fled northwards to Valhalla in White Plains, where she temporarily moved in with Telte. When George returned from the clinic he found an angry note requesting him not to contact her. She was, her note told him, pleased that he was recovering after his operation. For all that, 'You really are a louse. It's staggering what your "great love" has done to you.'[15]

His 'great love' and Jessica's reaction to it intensified Barker's vulnerability. He spent the morning of Friday, 21 February in the now empty room before Smart's picture as if before an icon. In an emotional state between erotic reverie and childish bewilderment, he wrote to Ottawa:

> This is to tell you more than I can ever tell you O far more than colours love one another in poems or rooms love one another in houses or the masculine of Italy loves the mediterranean or than anything and if you do not love me I shall go straight back to england and I mean if you do not love me more than all the world. Now I know quite clearly and quite overpoweringly that it is to no one else of the five hundred million that I belong but to you and if you will not have me I am finished for the species homonculus, for all truly. I want absolutely nothing from anything but you from it all and you only and you are totally and you alone and when I think of our maternal urns hanging into my hand or at my lip then I feel the bitter diamond at the corner of my eye because you are far away.[16]

The following day Elizabeth's sister Jane arrived in New York to stay with Helen. She called round at East 33rd Street, where she found Barker in a high state of tension and excitement. Taking pity, she volunteered to accompany him to Ottawa. Barker agreed, but insisted that they first fetch a suitcase Elizabeth had left at Oscar Williams's apartment. That night he did not go to bed. At five-thirty in the morning he wired Elizabeth, announcing that he and Jane were on their way. The following afternoon Elizabeth confirmed receipt. No sooner had she sent the cable, however, than she was deluged with doubts. She looked at herself in the mirror, and decided that 'I am not the right shape to remain in Ottawa.' She dashed a letter off to Barker, informing him that she was going to the far west of Canada, to find a cottage on one of the islands in Vancouver Sound, where she might plant potatoes in peace and await the birth of their child: 'It's spring there now and the climate is mild like England all year with no snow to speak of, and fertile soil.'[17]

Elizabeth told George that she would leave on 5 March. On the 2nd, abandoning the suitcase, he and Jane caught the night train to Ottawa. Two days later, he and Elizabeth began a journey across Canada to Vancouver. On the way he wrote the latest in his interrupted series of verse epistles, this time to Stephen Spender amid the London bombs:

> I send these lines to speak
> As much to me on this mountain peak
> As to you in the bomb-bright
> Darkness of life and death.
> Where am I, and Love answered
> Wherever the heart truly is:
> Both here in the tall peace
> Of the Rockies, and hawsered
> Heartstrung, to the abyss
> Where, in a plush chair
> You sit reading this
> As the siren, O sweet bitch,
> Mourns in anticipation
> Over the next batch.[18]

As the train was crossing the Rocky Mountains, it suddenly emerged from a tunnel and Elizabeth's face was flooded with light. It reminded Barker of the photograph he had first seen of her in Tokyo.

George and Elizabeth were in no hurry. For ten days they stayed in the Almer Hotel in Vancouver City. Beyond the windowpane, spring was sluggishly arriving. The lovers doodled and swapped insults in a shared journal; they performed a lascivious masquerade of genders. Barker paraded in front of the mirror dressed in oriental drag. In *By Grand Central Station* he poses as an 'Assyrian maid', a phrase suggesting the 'Abyssinian maid' in Coleridge's 'Kubla Khan'. Then they pretended to be two sisters, with George as the younger. 'He had no breasts', Elizabeth wrote, 'and this was nostalgic. O the glittering incest bird.'[19]

Their manic and inventive happiness was far too enjoyable to last. After a few days, they took the ferry across Vancouver Sound to Pender Harbor, where Elizabeth planned to stay for the duration of her pregnancy. Here she rented the disused schoolhouse at Irving's Landing, a convenient ferry ride from the mainland, yet remote from inquisitive eyes: her only close neighbour being Maximiliane Von Upani Southwell, a Viennese woman in her later forties, married to a fisherman with whom she had a ten-year-old son. The schoolhouse was an austere building which Elizabeth cheered up with colour reproductions of the Madonna, painting the door a bright shade of yellow, and hanging on it a quotation from Blake which Barker had used in his Tokyo lecture the previous April: 'The cut worm forgives the plough.' The police arrived to investigate Smart's circumstances. Concluding that she was harmless if eccentric, they left her to her own devices.

The games of cross-dressing in the darkened hotel bedroom had, however, touched off an uneasy sexual nerve in Smart. Late in March her concern intensified when George sent an urgent cable to Fitch. Having joined the US Air Corps, Fitch was at this moment on leave with Telte in Valhalla, where Jessica was still staying. Barker asked Fitch to drive up to meet them in Vancouver City – bringing Jessica with him, if she could be persuaded. Fitch arrived alone, in a large red Buick. Taking the ferry from Pender Harbor, Barker and Elizabeth joined him on the mainland, where the three of them spent several days together in the Almer Hotel.

Bisexual herself, Elizabeth already suspected an equivalent tendency in George. In Big Sur, she remembered, Barker had boasted to her of having made love to a boy in a print shop in Japan 'with arm pits like chalices'. The *Selected Poems* were now complete, and had been dedicated to Elizabeth. On 3 April George and Fitch climbed into the Buick, telling Smart that they were driving up the road to post the typescript to Macmillan.[20] Several hours later they still had not reappeared. She sat on the hotel bed, watching out of the window for the Buick, starting to her feet every time the elevator jangled into action. 'I know', she wrote 'that perhaps his mouth like the centre of a rose closes over John's mouth burning with apologies of love like a baby at the breast.'[21]

By Grand Central Station re-creates her claustrophobia and fear: 'The wallpaper drips gloom, and the walls press in like dread. The dark hotel room is the centre of the whirlpool where no one can any longer rest.' After several days of futile waiting, she crossed alone to Pender Harbor, where in mind-numbing agony she wrote a letter to the only address she had – Fitch's brother in Indianapolis – her handwriting grotesquely scrawling across the page: 'George, I am going crazy. My brain rattles around like a dried pea. I can't sleep and if I do I dream of corpses hidden in ice. I didn't think you could really leave me like that how could you. I could have gone with you at least come back and get me. O COME BACK. I cannot endure this.'[22]

In the meantime, Barker and Fitch had set off on a motoring spree down the West Coast. When they reached California, Fitch cabled to White Plains to inform Telte and Jessica that they were on their circuitous way to New York. The cable did nothing to allay Jessica's disquiet, now on her last dime.

She cabled Vancouver in the vain hope that George was still there. She had gathered that he was on his way, but it was cash that she needed rather than her husband: 'Why leave? I resign. I definitely resign.'

The cable was opened by Elizabeth, who, recognising Jessica's financial predicament, appealed to Jane to see if she could help. Meanwhile, the two men had reached Big Sur. Nostalgically, now that Elizabeth was at a distance, Barker revisited the music shop in Monterey where they had bought their records of Scarlatti. By Saturday, 5 April they had reached San Luis Obispo, from where Barker wrote calmingly to Smart explaining that, come hell or high water, he would return once he had sorted out his marriage. His primary motive for leaving Vancouver, he insisted, had been pity for Jessica, whom he was determined to confront in New York. He could not behave as if his wife did not exist: 'Either I must receive a divorce or never forgive her: and she must acknowledge the process of the personal inevitable: but I shall not desert her; least of all when all the cards are stacked against her, and the wolf screaming at the window. But never will I let you, whose umbilical I also hang upon, live at a remove from me.'[23]

When this letter reached Irving's Landing, Elizabeth found herself in two minds. She acknowledged the force of Barker's marital concern. His pity, however, was too much like Macbeth's 'striding the blast', and had about as much effect on his actual conduct. In *By Grand Central Station* she remarks, 'He did sin against love, and, though he says that it was in Pity's name, and that Pity was only fighting a losing battle with Love, he was useless to Pity, and, in wavering, injured Love, which was, after all, what he had staked all for, all he had, ungamblable.'[24]

Jessica was equally sceptical about Barker's motives. When Fitch next phoned Telte in White Plains to announce their imminent arrival, he learned that Jessica had left. Fitch and Barker sped down to San Bernardino, where Barker revisited the scene of his 'nuptials' with Elizabeth the previous October. Reassuringly he wired to Pender Harbor: 'I send this from a coast indescribably haunted by you. Prepare a corner for me and read Solomon.' Then Fitch and he drove west, towards the Arizona border. Barker was covering the same ground as he had done eight months ago with Smart, as if to exorcise the memory. This time the authorities left him alone. The Buick thundered across the desert, sending trails of sand and dust in its wake. They slept in the car at night. When they arrived in New York on 15 April Barker sent Smart successive telegrams from Fitch's apartment in Riverdale, signing himself 'Abelard', and promising instant return 'with a dove and a gas mask'. His return would have to wait a little while, however, since he could not raise his fare to Vancouver. He was, he cabled on the 28th, marooned in Manhattan with three dollars.

However, it was Smart who was marooned. By 27 April she had been alone for twenty-four days, her only consolations being her copies of *The Art of Egypt* and *Othello* ('O Iago, the pity of it, Iago!'), volumes by Auden, Spender and MacNeice and the quickening baby she carried, whom she was convinced was a boy, 'nor could Nature give me a slap of revival even though I found dogwood bigger than my baby's head and my whole room smelled of Lilac and Appleblossom and the wind rioted my skirt'.[25] On 2 May she dispatched a plaintive wire reading 'Long lost in Babylon. Catch Pender Boat Saturday or sooner and bear me the sun. Andromeda.' Though Barker was in no position to catch the Pender ferry, the text of this cablegram was to re-emerge ten years later as a love lyric, with Andromeda changed to Elizabeth's heroine, Undine.[26] Her next wire pleaded with him to come quickly, but at all costs to avoid cabling Jane, lest parental hands intervene. Instead Barker should write her another airmail letter. On 5 May he did so, informing her that he was mooching around New York trying to ignore the 'tarts with keyrings under their eye-lids and boys with hourglass waists' and to think only of Elizabeth Smart, 'my saffron, my brindle, my Bromdinagian-breasted; my uraeus urethraed, my sweet (christ, I'm out of breath)'.[27]

CHAPTER 19

'DYING FOR YOU, CANADA'

Jessica's predominant mood had long since changed from longing to wrath. Having departed hurriedly from Telte's house in White Plains to avoid Barker, she had made her way to Long Island Sound, where she had taken a job for the summer as general factotum to an Ulsterman running a country and swimming club at Rye. Here, as she later informed Monica, she lived in and her meals were found. In exchange she had to put up with the tantrums of the richer patrons, which grew more demanding as the season advanced. She shepherded them when they were lost, fetched them their bathing things, ordered their meals, did all the typing and was ever so English and polite. She worked like a Trojan until seven in the evening, though she was able to snatch a moment at midday for a dip in the pool. After a couple of weeks, this routine proved something of a strain even for the stoical Jessica. She took to spending long periods of time over a book in the bathroom, where her imperious Ulsterman would not follow her.[1]

She had just one day off a week. On one, 5 May, Barker persuaded her to join him at the university campus at Columbia for a performance at the Brander Matthews Hall of *Paul Bunyan*, the new musical play by Auden and Benjamin Britten. She was cagey about where she was living and, for the time being, so was he. In this way both of them kept their options open. In fact, he and Fitch had taken an apartment, 'charming, large and overfurnished', at 4 Jane Street on the north-eastern fringes of Greenwich Village. The rent was twelve dollars a month, paid initially out of Fitch's air force salary. When John had been recalled to Florida the week before, he had reminded Barker just how generous he had been. The two had had a spectacular tiff. Barker had expected Fitch to leave him his Ford, but, as he angrily reported to Elizabeth, Fitch had other plans: 'He said that he had been compelled to sell the ford to buy the buick. I said of course. He said I have sixty dollars with which to enter the

Air Corpse. Here you have forty of them. And as I know this was untrue (he had, only two or three days previously, announced the windfalling of 220 bucks). I took the forty and parted . . . And now I know how Aristotle felt about that ungracious and ungrateful agrarian alexander. Requiescat in astra Johannes Fitch.'[2]

Barker managed to find the rent for May himself. He spent the month alone in the Jane Street apartment, awaiting the appearance of the Macmillan *Selected*, and watching with some satisfaction as his reputation grew on both sides of the Atlantic. *Harper's* were paying him a dollar a line for his poems. Oscar's annual anthology had appeared with, Barker told Smart, atrocious photographs of everybody, though both his and Auden's had in fact been flattering. From London Tambimuttu reported that Spender had married a superb Russian blonde who gave piano recitals in public (whereas Barker, as he wrote to Smart, had to make do with 'a superb Canadian acrobat who gives exhibitions in private'); John Lehmann had issued the first volume of his Penguin *New Writing in Europe*, encouragingly stating in his preface that, though much of the contents would not survive the years, the best poems of Auden and Spender and Barker most certainly would.[3]

Such fanfares were beginning to draw the attention of the literati to the poet himself. Anaïs Nin, who had elicited Barker's new address from Lawrence Durrell, dropped her card off at Jane Street. Smart had a high opinion of Nin, which Barker did not share, thinking poorly of her intellect. Dreading her visit, he sat banging out a letter to Pender Harbor. Nin, he typed, was to be avoided: 'Any woman who can write fifty volumes of journals is too dangerous and too inhibited and anyhow she suffers from elephantiasis of the cranium.'

His next sentence read, 'O my god my god who was it who entered this room two hours ago with an entourage of three masculines but Anaïs Nin? As I sat typing the word elephantiasis four people descended the steps and started making inquisitive noises . . .'[4] Nin's three male companions were her long-suffering husband Hugo Guiler, banker and engraver, who financed her extravagances while turning a blind eye to her infidelities; her homosexual cousin and one-time lover Eduardo Sanchez; and 'a rather dirty bohemian from Southern California called Sanders Russell'. Barker found Nin affected and flighty, detecting something humourless and insincere behind her wide, kohl-lined eyes. She also appeared to lack subtlety. His impression of her coincided with Peggy Guggenheim's, expressed thirty years later when, entertaining Gore Vidal in Venice, she stared thoughtfully across the twilit Grand Canal and declared, 'She *was* stupid, wasn't she?'[5] Nin and her entourage took George round to West 13th Street, where, amid candle-lit lanterns and Indian serapes, he delivered his opinion of the States. Sanders Russell ogled him, while bearded, check-shirted Sanchez, 'homo but sweet', winked at him over Nin's shoulder. Nin crossed her legs, looked imperious and remarked in her softly gushing, unplaceably accented voice, 'I cannot fit myself into America I am a stranger here.' The statement struck Barker as quaint, both in sentiment and in syntax.

May was drawing to an end and the next month's rent was beyond him. Barker packed all of his 'objects dart' and took the next train to Canada. At Winnipeg he wired to Smart, telling her that he was without a cent, and would have to crawl the rest of the way. Somehow or other he arrived on 28 May to find the British Columbian summer bursting from every branch.

Elizabeth had spent the interval working at her fictionalised account of her relationship with George. It was tentatively entitled *Images of Mica*. The name did not appeal to Barker, who had always prided himself on the resourcefulness of his own titles. He remembered the wording of one of Smart's cablegrams, sent soon after he had failed to meet her train in New York: 'By Grand Central Station I Sat Down and Wept'.[6] So *By Grand Central Station I Sat Down And Wept* the book became, as Elizabeth pulled it into shape during the summer months. In her narrative the principal landmarks of their affair – the furtive early meetings; her arrest in Arizona; the disapproval of her family; Barker's desertion of her in the Almer Hotel – were related in vivid prose. Barker was to have his doubts about its lyricism, finding the metaphors too thickly applied, the passion perhaps too cloying. When the typescript was finished, he typed out his own critique. At its best, he told Smart, her style ravished with its grace; at its worst it reminded him of his own earlier writing. She was 'letting the slip of her soul show'. She would do well to question Edgar Allen Poe's assertion that simplicity is the easiest effect in the world to achieve. 'My god how arrogantly I formerly asserted this in the teeth of Housman – the false teeth as I believed).' He, too, had been drunk with images, but now realised that metaphors offered a region where writers might dwell only so long as they could return to the circumstantial particular. Eliot had remarked about Barker's own too-hurriedly completed verse play *The Johannesburg Mask* that it was 'simply bogged in metaphor'. He could now see that *By Grand Central Station* was written not with the word, the phrase, the sentence, or the mood of the paragraph as unit but with the metaphor as unit. It was true that a writer could ascend to the metaphorical plane and remain there (Matthew Arnold had done that conclusively at the close of 'The Scholar Gypsy'), but ordinary mortals had to climb back down. This, after all, had been the burden of his article 'Poetry and Reality' three years previously. He told Smart that she might well take note of these limitations of the metaphorical mode, as might he.[7]

This is the first example we have of something that Barker was supremely good at and came to specialise in: an exercise in practical criticism serving at the same time as an earnest of friendship, where comment was never patronisingly intended or phrased, but invariably pitched at the most demanding level of sensitivity and intelligence.

Barker stayed in British Columbia for almost exactly a calendar month. With Elizabeth he dawdled in the shade, or wandered hand in hand down the avenue to the house of her neighbour Maximiliane, to whom Elizabeth had decided to dedicate her book. On Maxi's couch they stole moments of concupiscence with mosquitoes biting them inconsiderately, like Donne's famous flea. It was the longest time that they had spent uninterruptedly together. Their relationship deepened to an extent which the hurly-burly of their previous assignations had tended to make impossible.

In Barker's view this marriage of more than minds now required legal, if not sacramental, validation. On 28 June he caught the ferry alone over to the mainland, where he took a room at the Almer Hotel for three days, in order to think over his options. On the morning of 1 July he wrote Elizabeth a letter phrased with a renewed seriousness of intent: 'For six weeks, we must again be parted for a purpose. *I am going to New York to get a divorce.* For fifty hours I have watched my life struggling on the pin of my thinking and from this transfixion which is indeed a minor martyrdom I have received the determination to Alexander these Gordians.'[8] Her response to his proposal is contained in *By Grand Central Station*. 'Why', she now added to its text, 'does he write "minor" martyrdoms? Didn't the crucifixion only last three days? Is it the shortness of the days of torture or the fact that hope still breathes that lets him say minor? How can anything so total not be major?'[9]

The following evening Barker set off by the night train to Ottawa. He travelled third class, and could afford neither a sleeping compartment nor food. He left his suitcases and his typewriter for Smart to redeem at the office of Canadian National in Vancouver City; his books and clothes were still at Irving's Landing. On his way across the Rockies he scribbled Elizabeth a hasty second thought, telling her that, tired and hungry from his journey, he would stop over in Ottawa for a couple of hours and there discuss future arrangements with Jane. Once in New York he would begin divorce proceedings, then purchase the cheapest obtainable vehicle in which to drive back to Vancouver, picking up Jane en route; failing this, they would drive across in Jane's Ford. He did not intend under any circumstances to be absent from the birth of his and Elizabeth's son, whom they were to call Sebastian. 'I love you, Elizabeth my golden bough and this is to implore you to believe what I have written.'[10]

After a hundred stale hours spent mostly in trains, he arrived in Manhattan on Saturday 5 July, determined to make Jessica recognise 'the lineaments of the inevitable'. The city was sweltering. He had intended to stay with the Williamses, but they were out of town on vacation as was, apparently, everybody whom Barker knew. So he took a room in the cheapest place he could find: the Hotel Tudor at 404 East 42nd Street. From there he could just summon the energy to trudge through the humidity of Fifth Avenue as far as Macmillan, where they were having difficulties securing publication rights for the *Selected* from Faber. Macmillan were anticipating a critical *succes d'estime* once rights were secured, and had increased the number of pages to 170.[11] On 11 July, when the Williamses returned from their holiday, Barker begged them for floor space, which was duly granted. In other respects too, his embarrassments were multiplying. He was, he told Elizabeth, being sued for debt by the Bedells. He insisted he had seen Jessica only once, when she had been so visibly depressed he had felt unable to raise the question of a divorce. The *New Republic* had warmly received his contributions to Oscar's anthology, but praise was not food. He was spending his afternoons hanging around the Metropolitan Museum of Art, where 'most of the Madonnas are you'. He had been speaking to 'a dull academician from Kansas' on the remote hunch of a job, but otherwise his prospects were negligible.[12] He spent the next couple of days painting Elizabeth from memory in oils, and reading on Oscar's couch, clad in nothing but a brand-new pair of bathing trunks. He had earned sixty dollars since his return, fifty of which had gone to the Williamses in rent, and the other ten to Jessica. Once more, Macmillan had refused to increase their advance.

When one considers how poor he was, Barker's new bathing trunks are a mystery to which Jessica's letters alone provide the clue. Barker's discussions with his wife, as he now prudently reported to Pender Harbor, had been proceeding sensibly. However, as Elizabeth was inclined to suspect, sense in this instance had entailed reconciliation. In fact, lengthy discussions between husband and wife were now taking place on the ocean shore in Rye, where the Barkers were enjoying pleasant afternoons sunning themselves, two miles to the west of Jessica's beach club. In these conducive surroundings, Jessica had been able to forget the strenuousness of her employer's regime.[13] 'I am dying for you, canada, dying for you' Barker wrote to Irving's Landing. Elizabeth's reception of this eulogy was not improved by a rumour which had reached her from an as yet unspecified source, that Jessica was also pregnant; she therefore now wrote to Barker accusing him of begetting a second Sebastian upon his legally married spouse. On the last day of July he replied, 'You crazy witch. Where did you ever conceive the idea of Jessica and a child? This is the first I have heard of it and I am sure that Jessica is unaware.'[14] By the end of July Barker had discovered the source of the false report in a mutual acquaintance in Manhattan called Horn. On 1 August he walked round to Horn's home and broke two of his teeth: 'My father would have been proud, it was so neat.' Then he went back to 67 Seventh Avenue, and wrote Elizabeth another letter begging for cash.

Barker's ethical confusion was now exacerbated by the anomie of war. Having, as he had informed his mother, registered for the one year's compulsory military service, he was due to be interviewed by the United States Draft Board on 12 August. Another problem was that, with the intensification of the war effort throughout the Commonwealth, it was becoming increasingly difficult for him to enter Canada. Smart was effectively debarred from entering the States, since, still ignorant of her pregnancy, her father withheld the necessary sponsorship. Barker wrote to Smart to tell her that he did not see how he could reach Pender Harbor 'without holding a gun to a guggenheim head'. It was now 8 August, the anniversary of the consummation of their relationship. 'Read Goethe,' he counselled, 'watch over me, pray for my poems, and die every day of love for all things including myself and my son who draws life from your right and left breasts.'[15]

The Draft Board deferred his appointment. In Pender Harbor, where she had put the finishing touches to her novel, Elizabeth moved in to stay with Maxie. She was certain now that George would not arrive in time for the delivery. On 26 August, feeling the stirrings of her labour, she asked a local fisherman, named Reid, to row her across to the Mission Hospital. In Manhattan meanwhile George, ever more conscious of the imminence of the birth, was in an agony of impatience. After a spectacular quarrel with the Williamses, he had been thrown out on to a broiling Seventh Avenue. He had moved across Brooklyn Bridge to stay with a young poet called Francis Lee, married to the daughter of the Italian painter Modigliani. Their flat was at 11 Montague Terrace, just round the corner from two protégés of Oscar's whom he would get to know better: Willard and Marie Maas. But on the evening of his arrival Barker collapsed with a temperature of 102. He was admitted to hospital with suspected pneumonia.[16]

As soon as he was discharged, he set about seriously drumming up the money for his return to Canada. He had borrowed twelve dollars; but would need more, since Jane had wired to inform him that, should he manage to reach Ottawa, it would now be impossible for her to drive him across to Vancouver. 'IS MY SON HERE?' he wrote frantically to Irving's Landing. Elizabeth, however, had long since departed for the mainland. Barker spent the evening with a psychiatrist, who could only prescribe 'suicide'. Though he felt like Samson in bondage, nothing could be done. Negotiating against all the odds for a re-entry permit to Canada, he poured his frustration and longing into a Cycle of Love Poems, addressed to his son Sebastian, who, he was sure, was even now kicking off the bedclothes in Vancouver:

> Let the gentle solstice, like the Fierral Bay,
> Where the Eleven Thousand Virgins keep
> The fishes quiet in their arms, keep him asleep
> All his life long in a long summer day:
> With the empty hour-glass, the four-leaved clover
> The rock for the resurrection, and much love.[17]

On the morning of 6 September he received a telegram from Jane. The infant Sebastian was in fact Georgina Elizabeth, born on 28 August at four-ten in the afternoon.

CHAPTER 20

'YOURS IN PARALLEL'

'He is a love poet of the highest order,' Harold Pinter was to write of Barker forty-one years later; yet, until this crisis in his existence, a reader would scarcely have guessed this. Barker had published no love poems addressed to Jessica; in fact, no poems to her at all until he had betrayed her with Smart. It might reasonably be deduced that his feelings for Smart taught him to express erotic love in verse, even his love for her rival.

The inception of the Cycles of Love Poems of 1941–3 is instructive, since they tell a romantic history in verse. A week after receiving notification of Georgina's birth, Barker left Brooklyn and attempted to re-enter Canada. He was stopped at the border by a 'carroty youth' in uniform. After glancing suspiciously at his Japanese visa, this official informed him that he could proceed no further without the valid re-entry permit which, as on all previous occasions, he had arranged to be posted to Vancouver. From Rouses Point, three miles back from the border, Barker then phoned F.C. Blair, the Advisory Atlantic Superintendent of Immigration, who at first seemed sympathetic, asking for references inside Canada.[1] Unwisely Barker gave him the phone number at Coltrin Lodge, which Blair then dialled. Helen was at home that week: answering the phone, she told the Superintendent that Barker was not a welcome guest in that house 'for reasons', Blair later told him, 'that you know as well or better than we do'. Blair then checked the file, where he found a dossier of documents on Elizabeth and 'her illegitimate child'. On 19 September, Blair wrote to Barker instructing him that, re-entry permit or no re-entry permit, he was not welcome in Canada and might reapply when his divorce from his wife was confirmed.[2]

The same day Barker returned to Brooklyn, from where he dispatched to Elizabeth the First Cycle of Love Poems, typed on a borrowed machine. It consisted of an initial poem to a hypothetical Sebastian, followed by five others in which he adopted Elizabeth's voice and, as in *Alanna Autumnal* eight years before, projected himself into the condition of female desire, with masculine strength as its object:

> Then like a ship at rest in the bay
>   I drop my sails and come home
> To harbour in his arms and stay
>   For ever harboured from harm.
>
> On his foot's beach my combers ride
>   The vaulted corals where he stands,
> And spray against his rock of side
>   Showers that fill his hands.[3]

The context of these verses is Pender Harbor and the speaker Smart. However, when the poems were published, a number of male readers – homosexual or bisexual – were to feel that these lines spoke for them.[4] Such was Barker's fidelity to a woman's responses, the love object might as well have been Fitch as Elizabeth. Effectively, these poems spoke for all.

Subsequent events clarify the Second Cycle. At the end of October Barker was obliged to move out of Montague Terrace. Since Jessica's summer job at Rye was over, the Barkers decided, unbeknown to Elizabeth, to make one last attempt to rebuild their marriage. After several weeks of squatting in a sordid room in the Bowery, Barker was offered for the winter the use of an early American cottage close to the Hudson, five miles north of Nyack.[5] The cottage was on high ground overlooking Rockland Lake, among maple trees burnished by autumn. It was for the most part derelict, the only useable portions being one large living room with a tiny kitchen off it. Even here Barker needed to repair the grate before it could be used, slapping cement on it in a manner of which, Jessica wrote, Pa would not have approved. Then Jessica cooked, read before a wood fire, and caught up with correspondence back home, while George wrote reviews and continued with the love poems. 'The Autumn', he wrote to Smart, who seems by now to have been aware of his cohabitation with Jessica, 'is so excruciatingly reminiscent of Kingsmere (what I saw of it) last autumn, when we made love on top of your sweet mountain.'[6] In this rural calm, which seems to have restored in Jessica the tranquillity she had experienced in Plush, he was at last to voice Jessica's perspective. The Second Cycle begins:

> By the lake where we walked in the summer
>   There where our bed was

> Now the sad cedar sheds our remembered image
>   Like autumn on the grass.
>
> And the rainclouds, giving suck to the mountain
>   Above the lake, foretell
> What in anticipation I recognised
>   Was yours in parallel.[7]

Yet the 'parallel' is also with Elizabeth, with whom Barker had wandered by the lakeside at Kingsmere, and whose baby 'tender under her right breast' is the subject of the next poem. And so the Cycle continued, linking Jessica, Georgina and Elizabeth; their yearning for him, and his for all three. It was a feat of emotional juggling which worked wonderfully well. Having asserted to Elizabeth the falsity of Poe's distrust of simplicity, he was now demonstrating its advantages in verse that was, for him, unprecedentedly limpid and direct.

During this period Barker re-established his pre-war pattern of spending weekdays in the country and weekends in town. Despite occasional reviewing work, money was still very short. So Barker swallowed his pride and went to visit Nin in her penthouse studio at West 13th Street. He adopted a woebegone mask. Sensing in Nin a susceptibility to intensities of mood, he spilled out a confection of pure tragedy. (His embellishments on the truth, however, need to be judged against the fact that Nin's own subterfuges were so ornate that, to keep track of them, she kept a file labelled 'lies'.) He was, he told her, living in the fetid streets of the Bowery (he had, in fact, just left). He was existing amid the poorest of the poor, among alcoholics 'as eroded and distorted as the lepers of Moroccan ghettos'.[8] Jessica was dying of tuberculosis and life was a perpetual crucifixion.

All this was aimed at what Barker, perhaps chauvinistically, took for Nin's gullibility. Nin responded as he had hoped. Barker was, she confided in her diary, 'like a fine trapped animal'; 'his eyes stare like blue porcelain washed by the sea, his words staccato like a typewriter'; 'he is so quick, so sharp, so focused. A taut mind and body, throwing off sparks.'[9] She was inclined to suspect him of posturing until he cried out, 'What can one do when one is removed not once, not twice, but a hundred times from one's true self?'[10] At last she understood; she understood it all.

So convincing were his complaints that Nin invited Barker to join a circle of writers she was organising to provide an unnamed 'collector' with original erotic literature at a dollar a page. 'I supply carbon and paper,' she told him: 'I respect everybody's anonymity.' The anonymity was, in fact, a cloak for an elaborate double-bluff. Barker was led to believe that he would be writing for an impotent potato magnate who was a senator in Washington. In reality, Nin passed the typescripts to the pornographic publisher Gerson Legmann (who later claimed to have 'devoted his life to the clitoris'). Legmann in turn handed the material to someone called 'Slapsie Maxie'. For a 10 per cent commission, Maxie then delivered it to the 'collector' himself, Roy Melisander of Ardmore, Oklahoma. For his part, Melisander was under the impression that every lubricious sentence had been written by Henry Miller.[11]

Nin's invitation provoked in Barker a mixture of reactions. According to her, his sense of humour was tickled by 'the idea of my being the madam of this snobbish literary house of prostitution, from which vulgarity was excluded . . . George Barker felt this was much more humorous and inspiring than begging, borrowing or cajoling meals out of friends.' By contrast, Barker told Smart, 'I declined and declined and declined until I hadn't had anything to eat for nearly two days.'[12] Then, adopting the female voice for a new purpose, he produced a pornographic parody of *By Grand Central Station*. The story was a transposition of Barker's affair with Smart onto his friendship with John Fitch. It concerned a Frenchwoman of twenty-one obsessed with the beauty of an American male hailing, like Fitch, from Indianapolis and, like Fitch again, about to join the Air Corps. As in *By Grand Central Station*, the woman narrates. In dramatic terms, however, the sexual roles are reversed: in the opening scene the woman arrives by ship, as did Barker in 1940, while the man waits for her by the quayside, as Smart waited at Monterey. After dalliance in a hotel, the lovers race southwards through Indianapolis to California, following the exact itinerary of Barker's elopement in Fitch's Buick, six months before.[13]

As Nin reports it, when she handed on these pages, 'the collector thought they were too surrealistic. I loved them. The scenes of lovemaking were disheveled and fantastic.'[14] Barker was paid, but 'he drank away the first money, and I could not lend him anything but more paper and carbons'. So he went on to improvise a couple of tales of gymnastic sexual exhibitionism set in the lobby of the Imperial Hotel, Sendai. Lastly he drafted an imaginary letter written by a woman masturbating with a bunch of geraniums as she awaits her absent lover Pierre ('O darling, come to me with candles and bananas and cucumbers'). In this condition of acute frustration, she is visited by her son Richard, a double-jointed young man with the aspect of a priest:

> I lay awake for what seemed hours, until the heat of my hips was insufferable, when I got up and went to his door and said 'Richard, are you asleep?' Then two arms took me from behind I felt the pressure of an absolutely naked body against my own, and the penetration of an enormous erection of penis entering, even against the resistance of my negligée, entering and breaking through and ramming up between my buttocks.
>
> Then, in an instant, he had torn the garment off me, and forced me to

my knees. And I took the great organ of his sex in my hands and fondled it, inserting my finger nail of my index finger into the orifice, or parting the orifice with my fingers and licking the interior with my tongue. Soon I took the whole length of it into my mouth. His thighs began to quake and move in the action of a piston, till the froth came to my lips, and I took his balls in my hands and tugged and squeezed until, with a gasp, he shot his sperm.

O the thunder and the lightning of that tremendous orgasm! I saw the split dome of the penis come thrusting at me like an express train, all glistening with the sweat of its long journey and the passions of its exertions until, with the great sigh of white steam, it enters its station and comes to rest in my mouth; O, the sweet savour of the juice of my son on my tongue! I caress the great instrument and sooth the big artery that pulses underneath. It trembles and kicks my touch as he gazes down at me. And tenderly, tenderly, draws his index finger over my lips, then gathers me up and carried me to his bed. O, nights of delight no Arabia ever rivalled![15]

The collector preferred this sort of thing and Nin too enjoyed it. Her own erotica, in the meantime, featured a sexual athlete called George, 'badly in need of money', who 'had a weakness in common with many men; when he was in an expansive mood, he loved to recount his exploits'. He sells his sexual services to a veiled woman, much to her satisfaction. Later he discovers that their lovemaking has been watched by a voyeur who has paid to see it from behind a curtain: 'Poor George,' Nin's story concludes. 'For months he was wary of women. He could not believe such perfidy, and such play-acting.'[16]

Barker's months in Sendai were proving useful material and not only in his erotic hackwork. In November, exploiting the growing political tension between Washington and Tokyo, he submitted to the *New Republic* a light-hearted account of his months in Japan. Omitting his own misery there, he concentrated on what he presented as the high comedy of Japanese militarism: soldiers camouflaged with sprigs of foliage jumping out of wayside bushes and surprising innocent pedestrians; the Sendai cadet force with its Lilliputian exercises; the tight-lipped parents with their urn; President Honda with his metallic birds; goggled pilots making repeatedly futile attempts to loop the loop; almond-eyed corporals strutting around like cockerels. The resulting picture was a sort of Gilbert and Sullivan operetta and the intention seems to have been to minimise the Japanese threat.[17]

Calling the article 'Notes from the Largest Imaginary Empire', he posted it in late November. On Sunday, 7 December 214 Japanese aircraft unleashed their attack on Pearl Harbor; 2,403 American servicemen died. The following day the Americans declared war and Barker's article appeared. The Japanese, its author confidently predicted, would never attack America; they had neither the nerve nor the resources. 'Towards the cultivation of the yellow peril so much American sweat has gone', Barker declared, 'that I can only hope that the mistletoe or mud I propose to sling will somehow scotch it.' The piece then rose suavely to its climax: 'I suspect that there is a graver Cochineal Peril than a Yellow.'

The ingenuousness of Barker's dismissal of Japanese militarism here recalls Wyndham Lewis's naïveté over National Socialism in his early study of Hitler, which Barker read as a boy. Barker was never endowed with an acute political sense. From this moment on his witing shows a marked holding back from historical prophecy, or indeed any kind of overt political comment.

Meanwhile Smart, who had left Georgina in Maxie's care, went to stay with her sister Jane in Ottawa where messages began to arrive from Barker, at one moment demanding the overcoat which he had left in Canada, the next promising her loyalty and a secure haven. He was, he told her, recommending *By Grand Central Station* to the Colt Press in San Francisco, publishers of *The Colossus of Maroussi*, Henry Miller's book on Greece, which he had recently reviewed.[18] Whenever possible, he would raise with Jessica the question of a divorce. But there were theological impediments: 'Of course I have spoken. This has devastated her devotion. You know that she is a Roman Catholic and I say this as I would say it of Thomas More or Edmund Campion: it violated her fundamentals to contemplate divorce. I pray for the tongues of angels to persuade. And in the end in the long end I shall. But you must understand that it is like inducing an iconoclasm in her.'[19]

A quarter of a century later, when asked for his impressions of Jessica at that time, Barker compared her to Tonya Zhivago as portrayed by Geraldine Chaplin in *Doctor Zhivago*, David Lean's 1967 film based on Boris Pasternak's novel.[20] Perhaps he meant the Tonya of Robert Bolt's screenplay, the pure-minded and bewildered victim, rather than Pasternak's complicated creation. Yet the analogy conveys something of his feelings for his wife in the autumn of 1941. There are further parallels to be drawn between Smart and Lara Guishar, Zhivago's strong-willed mistress, and between Barker himself and Zhivago, pulled in opposite directions by marital loyalty and a profound, illicit love, his dilemma made still more difficult by the impersonal tides of war.

While striving to hide the extent of his reconciliation with Jessica, Barker now pleaded with Smart to come down and take a furnished room in New York. He was, he said, 'writing erotica like an ecclesiastic' to make this possible.[21] He wrote that he had the remote chance of a job at the University of Michigan, where she might join him. There were also prospects, just as chimerical, of an academic position in Southwestern or Memphis. On 7

December Elizabeth travelled alone to New York. Her plan to spend several weeks with George, however, proved impossible, and she was obliged to spend most of the time staying with her friend Pegi Nicol, snatching a mere two days of misery with the Barkers by the lakeside. The experience was especially tantalising as she and George had neither met nor touched now for six whole months. In the presence of Jessica, who was still apparently ignorant of the existence of Smart's daughter, the subject of Georgina was inevitably taboo. Barker made no mention of divorce proceedings. As soon as Smart returned to Ottawa on Christmas Eve, he started phoning her persistently to protest that it had all been a misunderstanding. He had not been able to talk about divorce in front of his wife. Smart phoned back. Disastrously, as on a previous occasion, the phone was picked up by Jessica, who denied everything that George had said. She and George were, she told Smart, living together quite satisfactorily as man and wife. The sooner Elizabeth accepted this, the better for all concerned. In desperation, Barker then cabled to Ottawa, 'I happen to be very much in love with you and no one else in existence and I am prepared to take all the consequences. But to subject Jessica to the anguish of having this said when you were actually there in the room would have been diabolic.'[22]

As Elizabeth wrote in her journal, 1941 had been a miserable year for all of them. Continuing to entrust Georgina to Maxie, she obtained an American visa with the help of her father, who still knew nothing about his granddaughter. At the end of January 1942, ignoring Barker's importunings, she flew to Washington, where she found herself a clerical position with the British Army Staff. On Rockland Lake, meanwhile, Jessica had succumbed to flu, exacerbated by her growing sense of betrayal. Barker spent the hours collecting wood for the fire, heating milk, nursing his wife and reading. In his frustration and bewilderment, he went for a six-mile walk round the lake and returned determined to confront Jessica. To Smart he wrote, 'I can tell you that I bit my tongue and came home that evening homicidally determined to close my eyes and say that I loved you but when I saw her there with an expression in her face of the tame animal that a word will turn out of the doors to die, and it will go quietly because it is already dead, then I did my Solomon act which was an Alexander act which was also almost a suicide.'[23] Pity still consumed him.

In Washington, Smart moved into 3434 Ashley Terrace with Grisell Hastings, an English acquaintance whose husband was stationed in Washington. She threw herself wholeheartedly into her work. Having quickly mastered office procedures, she soon rose to be personal assistant to the minister in charge of information. One morning in early February Barker travelled down from Penn Station by the Philadelphia Express. En route he read the *Herald Tribune* and scribbed impressions of GIs as they crowded along the seats opposite, or leant against carriage doorways. They reminded him of fallen seraphim from

Paradise Lost; 'Jesus,' a tall infantryman had whispered in maudlin and frustrated longing, 'what I wouldn't give, what I wouldn't give.'[24] In Washington Barker found a new Elizabeth: businesslike, purposeful and discreet. There were to be no afternoons spent caressing on the settee. Barker felt redundant and upstaged, a lover on probation to a busy working woman. Jealousy flared up in him. When he left for New York, she refused to make him a sandwich for the train and, on parting, they did not even embrace. As soon as he reached Nyack, he fulminated in a letter: 'What kills me about you is your selfconsciousness for do you know – naturally you do know – that when we parted I was not permitted to kiss you not even merely kiss you because your "boss" (Love, thou art absolute sole boss of life and death) happened to be hiding in the bushes? *I AM NOT PREPARED TO PLAY 2ND BOSS TO ANYONE INCLUDING CHRIST AND SIR STAFFORD CRIPPS.*'[25]

A new seriousness was showing itself in Barker's writing at the time, in both his published articles and private correspondence. He was existing in a turbulent zone between the gravitational pull of two women, each of whom was in absolute moral earnest. He could not ignore the extremity of Jessica's state. Very much against the grain, he was considering the notion of a divorce; but in so doing she was, he told Elizabeth, walking a tightrope over damnation.[26] His reviews at the time, too, speak eloquently of his mental condition. In a review of Harry Levin's *James Joyce: A Critical Introduction* for the *Nation*, he wrote that the driving force behind Joyce's work was guilt. In *Ulysses* and *Finnegans Wake* Joyce had deliberately violated the thing he had loved: the Church. Barker construed this reflex action with the help of *Portrait of the Artist as a Young Man*, and of Eliot's analysis in his essay 'Baudelaire' of 1930. Only those who believe, Eliot had written, can blaspheme. With this in mind, Barker argued that Joyce's sense of guilt 'arises from the knowledge that blasphemy is possible only to those who venerate the objects of their blasphemy'.[27] Even as he had transfixed the Church with the nail of language, Joyce had 'fought at the end of a religious tether', every word he wrote taking its dynamic from the thing he had sought to escape. Substitute Jessica for the Church, and betrayal for blasphemy, and it was not hard to see how the same reasoning applied to Barker's own condition. Reviewing Jacques Maritain's *Ransoming the Time*, he spoke of an alternative Catholic vision. Maritain 'speaks for the Roman Catholic Church in a voice that the Church itself can never speak in, namely, the secular voice. And this is the voice that, crying in the wilderness of disbelief as passionately as it cries in the chaos of immortality, is only the more clearly heard because it disdains the microphone, the headline and the phoney parable.'[28] In the chaos of his own situation, that voice of traditional Catholic responsibility was proving difficult to ignore.

The chaos continued without abatement. On the expiry of the Nyack lease, he and Jessica moved into cramped quarters at 7 Cranberry Street in Brooklyn. In Washington, meanwhile, Elizabeth arranged for Georgina to join her. On 5 March with Maxie's co-operation, she smuggled her daughter out of Canada and through Washington Airport, having first concocted a story about the baby being the daughter of an absentee British earl. When this lurid fabrication attracted the notice of the press,[29] she took Georgina over the Maryland border to Helen's new home in Baltimore. Here they were visited by Smart's father, who at last learned of the existence of his grandchild but on his return to Ottawa wisely he did not breathe a word to Louie. By now Jessica had also learned of Georgina's birth: in an extraordinary Christian gesture of forgiveness, she sent Smart a telegram of congratulations. At the end of the month George arrived in Washington and finally met his daughter. When he left he arranged for Elizabeth to bring her to New York in April. From Brooklyn he wrote with a heart swelling with pride at this privilege of fatherhood so undeservedly visited upon him, 'For I cannot keep quiet in my recollection or in my pride that I have a daughter of the terrestrial water who lies always in the bend of my arm wherever I am whatever I do or whenever I wish it . . . I had never thought that such a privilege would devolve upon me with so little hesitation.'[30]

Barker strove to muffle all such feelings when with Jessica, but he found his cultivated nonchalance undermined by Elizabeth's letters, which he could not prevent his wife from reading. He felt increasingly isolated. He shared his dilemma with two friends to whom Oscar Williams had recently introduced him: Willard and Marie Maas. The Maases lived in a spacious penthouse flat at 62 Montague Street. Situated on a rise in Brooklyn Heights, their apartment had a roof garden with wide views across the East River towards the skyscrapers of Manhattan. Barker took to spending the evenings there, confiding his predicament to the Maases, and occasionally babysitting for their young son Stephen while they were out. Their intimacy boosted his spirits, but Jessica was wary of it and suspicion merely strengthened her resolve. On Good Friday, 2 April she abruptly left a literary reception which she had been attending in Brooklyn. Entering the lounge of the Hotel St George in Brook Street, she wrote Smart a short letter asserting her confidence in George's love. Whatever Elizabeth thought, their marriage was secure: 'of course he has been living with me all the time and happily and very passionately (this is because from your letters it counts more than anything else with you)'.[31]

On 27 April Barker was to appear before the Draft Board, a procedure all the more serious now that the United States was at war. He arranged that, as soon as the ordeal was over, Elizabeth should travel up from Washington. Jessica was privy to the plan: in her eyes, however, its purpose was for George to announce in the presence of both women that his love for Smart was over. The Draft Board discharged him, but Smart proved less amenable. To make any threatened disowning well nigh impossible, she arrived by air the following week with the important addition of Georgina. It was a way of confronting Jessica with the facts. Elizabeth's confidence is apparent in a series of photographs taken that weekend on the Maases' roof garden. Elizabeth, in a white dress, looks triumphant, well being written on every feature. Barker's face is flooded with slightly cocky relief. The surviving pictures convey a strong sense of family togetherness. The feeling of completeness is less convincing when one recalls the lone figure of Jessica, three blocks away in Cranberry Street.

CHAPTER 21

'THE GEOGRAPHY OF THE BODY'

Jessica found it difficult to reach a conclusive judgement about the Maases, but she knew that she distrusted them. Previously George had managed to keep his more unruly companions clear of his sacrosanct home life. In Brooklyn this proved impossible. Both of the Maases were extroverts: they belonged to a moneyed bohemia she had seldom encountered before and they offended her sensibilities deeply.[1] Marie was seemingly the dominant partner. Born in Brooklyn in 1909, and a graduate of the New York School of Fine and Industrial Art, she had a growing reputation as a maker of avant-garde films characterised by adventurous, slow-moving camera work and an arresting choice of subject-matter and commentary. In later life she was drawn into the Pop Art movement and worked with Andy Warhol, in whose *The Life of Juanita Castro* she was to act, and whose life she was to film. In all of this, she was aided and abetted by her husband Willard, who was said to inaugurate her projects, nominally directing while Marie held the camera. In practice the responsibilities were shared.[2] Self-mocking and slightly camp, smaller than Marie whom he strove to outdo in outrageousness, bisexual and omnivorous in his affections, Willard was a poet whose work had appeared in Oscar's anthologies. Barker was uncertain of the merit of Willard's poems, of which this description of a lizard is characteristic:

> Turquoise somnambulist of June's meridian,
> On his lambent stone of dream, the lizard
> Casts his haloed hymn to the horizon.
> Red-goitred Death, diurnal buzzard
> Perched on the marches of catastrophe
> Eyes the rope hung in the dying sky.

Willard was on leave from the Signal Corps when in the early months of 1942 he and Barker devised a project for an experimental film. Marie was to roll the camera, Willard to direct and Barker to supply the words. All three of them were to appear flagrantly in the flesh. Filmed in black and white, with the cheapest of hand-held 16mm cameras, the scenario consisted of a slow-motion examination of their three naked bodies. Particular attention was paid to the orifices: there was, for example, an exactly focused close-up of Barker's ear, though many of the images were subjected to different kinds of distortion, being shot, for instance, through a dime-store magnifying glass or through the glass top of Marie's coffee table. Barker was asked for a title. He suggested *The Desire and Pursuit of the Hole* (a facetious pun on Baron Corvo's *The Desire and Pursuit of the Whole*, itself an allusion to Plato's *Symposium*). For reasons of taste, this was eventually changed to *The Geography of the Body*. The scenes of nudity and Barker's surreal script had little in common, and, as if to emphasise the disparity, Barker himself delivered the text in the sort of clipped, pukka British accent heard on the soundtracks of 1940s newsreels. Read at breathless speed, it made play with significant events from his own recent life: Smart in Big Sur; the delayed 'nuptials' at Saint Bernardino; the perpetual harassment of his remorse:

> That evening I came to a North African village
> In which the inhabitants were all worshippers of the moon.
> Then Sappho, distraught with the frustration of her passion,
> Gathered up her skirts and, crying in a voice that will be heard forever,
> Threw herself off the cliff of her lover's disdain.
> From waterfalls under which brides practise their long-awaited nuptials,
> Vikings with battles in their hands emerge like murderers.
> O Hawaii, Hawaii, what was the colour of happiness
> When it inhabited your four islands?[3]

After cutting and editing by Marie, *The Geography of the Body* eventually appeared in 1943. A minor cameo of Forties experimentalism, it was later to enjoy a brief vogue in the 1960s, when shown as a short at alternative venues like the Cambridge Film Festival. Prints of it are now very rare.

Not only were the Maases, from Jessica's point of view, intemperate; they were also quite candid in their support of Smart. They provided Elizabeth with a roof whenever she came up from Washington, and encouraged Barker in his affair with ill-disguised relish. To make matters worse, Jessica was continually thrust into their company, where Elizabeth's name was mentioned frequently. There was little that Jessica could do in retaliation. In this unguarded milieu Barker had a hard job denying facts which he had earlier brushed half-effectively under the carpet. On 20 May, he set off from New York once more to see Elizabeth and Georgina. Before leaving, he stood over Jessica in the Maases' apartment, as with self-denying terseness she typed what was virtually a note of capitulation:

Dear Elizabeth,
I'm not going to write a long letter. I think that the important thing is that I grow more and more convinced that Gran will never be able to say that he doesn't love you. I haven't got anything else to say except that I hope he doesn't give you this.[4]

Though Barker did hand Elizabeth the note, resolution was still a long way off. The letter is taken by Elizabeth's biographer as proof of a final parting of the ways. The reality was, however, that since the debacle of the previous December Smart's view of the Barkers' marriage had also changed. Whilst in Pender Harbor, she had been able to convince herself that George and Jessica were living apart. During her visits to Brooklyn she was now forced to acknowledge that, just as long as they inhabited the same continent, Mr and Mrs Barker would continue uneasily as man and wife. Jessica was still at heart clingingly devoted. It had never occurred to her to be unfaithful to Barker in her turn, nor would her religious beliefs have allowed such a course of action. Barker, moreover, despite his wilder protestations, was clearly in two minds. As his writings on theological matters were demonstrating, there was an ancient part of him that still held the Catholic sacraments dear, including – however incomprehensible to the largely agnostic Elizabeth – marriage. He might violate his wedding oath time and time again. He would not, except under the most extreme provocation, unceremoniously ditch it.

To many who knew him at the time, Barker appeared a bizarre mixture of ethical fastidiousness and moral anarchy. This emerges quite clearly in his correspondence with Smart, above all when speaking of her family. While he had every reason to resent Smart's parents, he was more likely to remind Smart of her responsibilities towards them in terms that could sound positively Victorian. When her father fell ill, Barker wrote to Elizabeth in Washington:

Sweet heart I was and am extremely sorry to hear about your father's illness – is it serious or not too serious or just a sick turn of the engines? Anyhow, when you eventually see him you will be considerate and beautiful and clearly an emperor's daughter, so he will look, and be happy. No, never did I or do I desire that you should deliberately or even of necessity bring down distress upon him: I do myself so much respect and weep for the love the father and the mother have for their children – Christ, it is so wholly altruistic and hopeless and a bloody boomerang – that I would wish you to follow your father's proposals and preferences whenever they do not entail a betrayal of him. It is a betrayal of him for you to betray yourself even tho this is a truth that is concealed from him by his love. It is a betrayal of self for you to disremember Love. I see this also with my Buddha's eye that love is what you were born from, for, by, with, to, at, into, and because of. I never visualised before the possibility of a creature occuring who actually inhabited the element of Love like the salamander in fire, or the mermaid in water. Therefore I repeat to you, as I repeated them to our daughter, the best words that the human animal ever said: Ama et fac quod vis, i.e. love, and do what thou wilt.[5]

The final words allude to a popular version of St Augustine's exhortation 'Dilige et quod vis fac', love and do what you wish. It is telling that the Latin verb for 'to love' which Barker employs in his letter is 'amare', with its erotic connotations, rather than the word preferred by the Vulgate, and chosen by St Augustine himself: 'diligere', signifying spiritual esteem or regard. As it is, Barker's version of the axiom represents a palpable relaxation of its teaching. St Augustine means that, if one truly venerates God, one will find oneself obeying his will without effort. The quality which Barker is commending in Elizabeth, by contrast, is the authentic pursuit of her feelings. The idea that one should act at all times freely and in a spirit of love is arguably the key to Barker's character. The problem was that in America in the autumn of 1942 his love, or rather loves, were leading him in two incompatible directions. He still would not disown his marriage. On 19 October Smart's journal read, 'George has hardened his heart.'[6] Although over the previous few months he had come to think of his relationship with Smart as preliminary to marriage, he now went back to regarding it as an affair. Once more it became clandestine. On his visits to Washington, for example, he found that he had nowhere to take Elizabeth. They could scarcely make love in the Hastings' house, nor could they decently impose upon Helen's hospitality. The only solution was to revert to their unsatisfactory practice of stealing hours of passion in cheap hotel bedrooms. On Monday, 9 November, their son Christopher was conceived in one such bedroom in Baltimore. Afterwards, as the air-raid sirens sounded above, Smart lay cradling Barker in her arms, vulnerable as he seemed to her in his penury and general hopelessness. In December she was alone again, crying for him to comfort her. She was now having to face up to the fact that, when not with her, George was solacing Jessica, who had threatened once more to leave him.[7] Yet this rupture, so keenly expected by Elizabeth, still would not take place. Elizabeth came to feel that, without some decisive action by her, in all probability it never would.

Jessica constituted one issue of conscience. Another was the war, which was less and less easy to avoid. Whilst in Japan, and in America before December 1941, Barker had been able to treat the European conflict as something remote. Now the evidence of war was all around him, as one by one even his bohemian acquaintances were drafted into the American armed forces. Barker might convince the Draft Board that he was irrelevant to this global upheaval; he had more difficulty in persuading himself. He considered returning to England, but his unresolved emotional state, combined with an unwillingness to risk either his life or Jessica's on the increasingly perilous waters of the Atlantic stalled him. He also felt a growing responsibility towards Elizabeth and Georgina, all the more so when he reflected on Elizabeth's contribution towards the war effort and his own comparative idleness. Furthermore, there remained the problem, shared by many writers of his generation, of discovering where responsible action lay: in a stand against the palpable evil of fascism, or in a protest, equally resolute, against the conflict itself.

Inevitably Barker's writing was increasingly concerned with these matters. Throughout 1942 the weekly and monthly journals were filled with pieces covering the background to the war. Despite his ludicrously inept prediction the previous December about the intentions of the government in Tokyo, Barker now found himself regarded as something of an expert on Japanese affairs, for, if he knew little enough about the Japanese mind, American readers knew less. Accordingly, he produced a series of articles under the title 'The Improbable Empire', which recycled incidents from his journal for January–June 1940, garnishing them in such a way as to titillate the combined curiosity and xenophobia of urban East Coast America. He took the articles to the *New Yorker*, which, as Jessica reported to Smart, found them delightful. They included everything from Barker's arrival in Yokohama, through his conversations with Saito in Tokyo, his desultory tourism and his abortive teaching of Housman, to the melancholy funeral rites he had witnessed on the train journey. The last of the series described the 'intellectual tea party' at Barker's house in Sendai, at which he had discussed with his students the causes and morality of the Manchurian War:

Hiraku said precipitately, 'Professor Barker, do you like we Japanese?'
    The three of them sat back in their chairs, and I sensed an approaching climax. 'Why, yes, Hiraku,' I said. 'I like you Japanese.' They looked up at me in surprise. 'You three.'
    The discussion became incandescent. They asked why I disliked

the Japanese. I replied because they were subhuman. 'Subhuman?' murmured Hiraku, 'But how?'

It was my opinion, I explained, that any nation which failed to establish in an accepted constitution all the fundamental prerogatives of the human being was subhuman. 'The Japanese nation', I said, 'is suffering at this moment a condition of poverty and privation that only a subhuman people would permit to persist. If the Japanese were human, they would have revolted. They have not revolted. I conclude that they are subhuman.'[8]

It could be that, by this wholesale disparagement of the nation's moral consciousness, Barker hoped privately to discount his entire Japanese experience. At any rate Americans would welcome the suggestion that the Japanese were subhuman; they had, after all, recently endured the humiliating loss of the Philippines, and 12,000 young Americans were languishing in prisoner-of-war camps. Barker's own verdict on the Japanese mind was more problematic.

A more considered response to the war can be found in Barker's *Secular Elegies* and *Sacred Elegies*, begun the same autumn. Like 'Elegy on Spain', these two interlocked sequences meditate on the political manifestation of original sin which leads men to take up arms. Transcending partisanship, they evoke impartially a disaster of spiritual dimensions. Newman's aboriginal calamity is conceived here as a perpetual animus within history: 'Finally we die of pride' is the concluding – and all-inclusive – statement of the second 'Secular Elegy'. Throughout these poems, present emergencies are viewed against the backdrop of a remote European past. *Secular Elegies* opens with an invocation to England ('My pig-faced kingdom with tongues of wrong / And an historical gait of trial and error'). In the following poems, the scenery of the present rolls back to reveal various ancestral figures as prime movers who still inhabit thought and direct action: Cromwell and Milton, rhetorical defenders of freedom; Hood the sailor; Clive the imperialist; Bismarck the creator of modern Germany. The second 'Secular Elegy' refers to the defiant stand against overwhelming odds of the German battleship the *Bismarck*, and to her sinking on 24 May 1941. In it Bismarck is the nineteenth-century politician as well as the ship. HMS *Hood*, the battle-cruiser blown up during an early phase of the action, is also the eighteenth-century admiral:

> Where formerly he saw birds in bushes, now
> The cyclist resting from his uphill labour
> Observes the skull of Cromwell on a bough

> Admonishing his half heart, and he shoulders
> His way upward against the wind to the brow.
>
> The political cartoonist in his bed
> Hears voices break his sleep he does not know:
> The morning papers show what the people said.
> Librarians in their studies, the lights low,
> Sense Milton breathing in his marble head.
>
> The clerk hears Clive cheering in a darkness;
> And from the ponds of commons, in broad day,
> The effigies of great sailors rise in their starkness
> With the *Hood* in their hands, and cry
> 'Nevertheless we mourn also the *Bismark*!'[9]

The lovely image of Milton breathing in his own bust epitomises the world evoked by these poems: the lessons of history and culture inscribed upon its monuments, the shades of the past speaking quietly but insistently to the present. All deeds and gestures are shown to bear patterns of continuity invisible even to those — especially to those — who enact them. The political cartoonist, wrapped up in the immediate hour, is roused by voices from a past of which he may well be ignorant. Seeing beyond the hour to the cause, Barker's verse hovers between the Shelleyan broadsheet manner of 'Vision of England '38' and a fresh gravity:

> Everything that is profound loves the mask,
> Said the Dionysian who never wore one.
> Thus our damnation and condemnation
> Wiser than Nietzsche, never taking a risk,
> Wears the face of a necessary satisfaction.[10]

The 'necessary satisfaction' is another term for St Augustine's doctrine of the just war. The 'mask' recalls both Nietzsche's theories about the theatricality of the personality and the 'mask of burning gold' which Yeats believed all wear in their dealings with the public world. Such forms of expediency are implicitly employed by all who go to war, even by those who do so through an instinctive feeling for justice. As the armies of the Reich and of the Allies launch themselves into the fray, each cheers itself with the seeming unanswerability of its cause. Nonetheless, damnation belongs to them precisely because it is all-inclusive. At this point the *Secular Elegies* link the Battle of the Atlantic with the battle of love:

> Not, Love, when we kiss do the archangels weep
> For we are naked then wherever we are,
> Like tigers in the night, but in our sleep
> The masks go down, and the beast is bare:
> It is not Love but double damnation there.[11]

With *Sacred Elegies*, Barker turns from the public to the private sphere. In his vision of conflict sex is as lethal as war. More dangerous still is the complacent sleep of lovers, coiled in mutual happiness, heedless of the world. *Post coitum omne animal triste est* said Pliny the Elder ('After intercourse every animal is sad'). Barker caps this apothegm, asserting that, because the human animal feels replete after loving, he or she feels him- or herself to be justified, thereby inviting retribution, whether from history or from God. This insight is in effect a theologically orthodox rebuke to Smart's doctrine of emotional fulfilment. In *Sacred Elegies* commentary on sub-lunary affairs slips imperceptibly into theology:

> Lovers for whom the world is always absent
> Move in their lonely union like twin stars
> Twining bright destinies around their cause:
> They dazzle to shadow with the meridian present
> The wallflower world. Redundant it shall resent
> The kiss that annihalates it and the gaze that razes.
> O from their clasp a new astronomy rises
> Where, morning and evening, the dominant Venus
> Dismisses all sad worlds that turn between us,
> And we shall kiss behind our mask of faces.[12]

Seldom since Donne's 'The Sunne Rising' has a poem attempted so frank a portrayal of the mutual sufficiency of sexual love (as Donne has it, 'Nothing else is'). The sensation of the completeness in sex is, however, doubly judged: by the political imperatives of a world at strife ('What knows he of love', Russel Smart had once demanded of his Barker-besotted daughter, 'who lets down his country in her hour of need?') and by a divine love that shames the shivering Eros to nothing. As in Donne, the absorbed gaze of lovers transcends these greater concerns by hubristically annihilating them, eclipsing them with a wink. In the end, the reader is left marvellously uncertain as to who is the more justified: lovers in their myopic privacy or advocates of the greater, public good. Ultimately, even love repudiates its devotees:

> But who at the kiss, who has not seen, over
> The waterfalling hair at the shoulder of Life,
> Death from his own face staring out of a glass?
> Some shall be most alone with a lover, never
> Letting the sweating hand unlock that closet of
> The coffined I.[13]

Towards the conclusion of *Sacred Elegies* the reader is back with Pliny and his spent and melancholy lovers. The failure to escape the trap of our skins is what finally limits all lovers, sacred as well as profane. Both love and praise are an attempt to perform the impossible, whether sweating in intercourse or surpliced in devotion, 'Alone like the statue in an alcove of love'. The last of the *Sacred Elegies* is a hymn to the absent God of agnostic Europe: the first cause towards whom all activity, however seemingly indifferent to Him, aspires. The deity whom it evokes is not, by any means, the orthodox God of Catholic doctrine. Nor does Barker's anti-theology quite coincide with the demonology of, say, Baudelaire, though it steers close to it. Even as he strives to repudiate his God, Barker's anger is checked by an impulse of devotion. Whatever one's religious position – and these poems are very far from being addressed exclusively to believers – one finishes with a sense of the need for a divinity, without whom history has no focus:

> Sergeant with a grudge
> Against the lost lovers in the park of creation,
> Fiend behind the fiend behind the fiend behind the
> Friend. Mastodon with a mystery, monster with an ache
> At the tooth of the ego, the dead drunk judge:
> Wherever Thou art our agony will find Thee
> Enthroned in the darkest altar of our heartbreak
> Perfect. Beast, brute, bastard. O dog my God![14]

Barker clearly felt that in these *Elegies* he had at last achieved a voice that was at once traditional and entirely his own. Dedicated to Willard Maas, they were published the following year by James Laughlin at his New Directions Press at Norfolk, Connecticut. Designed by Carl Purington Rollins of the printing office of the Yale University Press, the first edition was set in linotype Baskerville 'after the edition of the Latin Elegiac Poets printed by John Baskerville of Birmingham in 1772'. The layout emphasised the traditional elements in Barker's own artistic programme. In effect, the *Elegies* fulfilled the objective which, in the year of commencing them, Barker attributed to Jacques Maritain: they spoke for the Roman Catholic Church in a voice that the Church itself could never use: the secular. That such a voice proved both idiosyncratic and, in certain details, heterodox was only to be expected, since Barker was a poet not a theologian. What he produced, nonetheless, was an argument of great subtlety and richness, an expression of his state of mind at the time.

Secular and Sacred Elegies help to explain, for example, his continuing loyalty to Jessica over the winter of 1942–3. Jessica possessed this one great advantage over Elizabeth: however callously Barker might behave, his moral sense coincided with hers. However bitterly Jessica and George might quarrel – and all the signs are that the most they could manage was a low, nerve-racking grumble – they were at least arguing on the same lines and ultimately with the same terms of reference. Barker might be non-communicant but he could still, waking alone in the afternoon in Cranberry Street, find by his bedside a touching note such as this: 'I have gone to St Patricks and should be back again at about 4.45, Gran. Would you meet me and we could go to the Cinema – at any rate I will walk back. It seemed a pity to wake you.'[15]

After all that had happened, George and Jessica were, somewhere deep down, still childhood sweethearts. Undeniably Jessica's superior in wealth, sophistication and literary talent, Smart could not compete against this, though she fought as hard as she could, swinging between resentment and her old habit of self-apology:

> Balls to you, Jessica, with your astute love of the abused. The reason you manage him so cleverly is that you don't love him. He's *your* husband and *your* honour is at stake. You like the pose of the faithful wife. Besides, you anticipate prizes. (Now, you're being vulgar, Elizabeth. O then will the psychoanalyst judge? No, he will say: Tell me what you are afraid to tell me: Well, mother said I must never call anyone common.)[16]

At such moments Louie and Jessica seemed to join forces in branding Elizabeth as delinquent. She reacted to their imagined taunts with fluent, half-convinced answers, the logic of which seemed warped even to herself: if Jessica anticipated 'prizes', it was hard to see what these might be. Where George himself was concerned, there were differences, as the *Elegies* make plain, over the important matter of her gospel of satisfied love. *Secular and Sacred Elegies* at least put paid to that argument. If the elegies expressed the sacred through the secular, Elizabeth was striving to do the opposite: to raise human love to a pitch of sanctity. Where Elizabeth was dogmatic about her Eros, George was erotic about his dogma. Between these two positions, a deep gulf was set.

CHAPTER 22

SINNER AND SAINT

Barker's British reputation was still based on his pre-war poetry. In 1942 the critic Francis Scarfe published his influential study of poetic trends in the interwar period, *Auden and After*. It contained lengthy chapters on both Barker and Thomas, but gave the edge to the former, whom Scarfe characterised as 'a pure poet'. Scarfe began by comparing Barker's work to the paintings of Van Gogh. Like the Dutch master, he argued, Barker in his early days 'had laid on paint in thick, explosive masses', but these apprentice pieces were also distinguished by 'passionate gentleness of image and rhythm'. *Calamiterror*, Scarfe insisted, had drawn on and extended these strengths. While its surrealism recalled Thomas, 'the comparison would be false, because though they are equally "sensational" poets, Barker is more selective and his vocabulary and texture are more refined'. Its sixth section had contained 'the best description of the "Between the wars" period that has been written, showing the individual caught in "a loop of circumstance", and explaining, three years before the invasion of Poland, why poets can no longer exist in Europe.' In sum, *Calamiterror* was 'perhaps the most successful long poem of the thirties'. The verse of *Lament and Triumph* was better still, especially 'Elegy on Spain': 'Of all the poems bearing on the Spanish war, Barker's poem will stand with the highest, next to Auden's "Spain" and not below it.'

Though Barker's reputation was spreading in Britain, he was himself out of touch with developments at home, and his only news came from friends and family who were able to keep him posted intermittently. David Archer had closed his Manchester Contemporary Bookshop and moved to Glasgow, where he continued to siphon off his father's wealth by setting up an arts centre in the rundown city centre. There he had discovered another young poet, W.S. Graham, an engineer from Greenock. In 1942 Archer published Graham's first collection *Cage Without Grievance*[1] reviving The Parton Press to do so. Archer had also diversified into the visual arts, encouraging painters to use his centre as a base. The oldest of these was Jankel Adler, a Polish Jew in his fifties, invalided out of the Polish army in France and now painting stylised pictures of *mutilés de guerre*. Robert Colquhoun and Robert MacBryde were from a younger generation. Rancorously devoted to one another since their days at Glasgow School of Art, they lived in Renfrew Street. Robert Colquhoun was tall, angular and sarcastic; Robert MacBryde, smaller, jocular, fastidious. Together, these two young painters were known as 'the Roberts'. Colquhoun was the more distinguished artist. He had served until recently wth the Royal Army Medical Corps in Edinburgh and Glasgow, where MacBryde, declared unfit for military service, had followed him. Adler introduced him to Picasso's style of the early 1930s, which Colquhoun was soon combining with a Celtic sense of line. When Archer eventually closed the centre in Glasgow, he and the Roberts moved to London.

The continuation of the conflict had also unsettled the Barker family. The bombs had driven George's parents to a flat overlooking Barnes Common, with its genteel dog-walkers. The arrangement lasted until Big Mumma noticed that the Oratory was no longer on a convenient bus route. Cancelling the lease, she forced a reluctant Pa back to a flat in Cornwall Gardens, Earls Court. Monica was driving ambulances through the perilous London streets, returning to tell 'tales of riding craters as though they / were sea surge'.[2] She took a room round the corner from her parents at 7a, Redcliffe Gardens. Kit continued to inspect aeroplane parts through his one good eye,[3] and Eileen had taken her two sons to live in Modbury in Devon, which was convenient for Plymouth where her husband Fletcher Jackson was a naval photographer.[4] Meanwhile Eliot commuted between the Surrey countryside and London, writing *Quartets*.

In Brooklyn wartorn London seemed only faintly imaginable: like a set of sepia prints. To render it more vivid, Barker added several 'Supplementary Personal Sonnets' to his poem for his mother. Each portrayed a friend, the description of whose circumstances amounted necessarily to guesswork. For example, he convinced himself that David Gill had embarked with the Norwegian Expedition and taken part in the attack on Sola Airport at Stavanger on 11 April 1940, where he envisaged him 'hoping for resurrection ... under the stone and the snow'.[5] Gill had in fact been holed up in Hull at the time in question. Perhaps the most successful of these sonnets was the one addressed to Eliot, whom he accurately depicted fire-watching on the roof of Faber's offices in Russell Square 'expecting a bomb or angel through the roof'.[6] The common theme of these sonnets was steadfastness. Barker needed to believe that there was still a part of the world in wartime where the old moral imperatives had force.

By New Year 1943 Barker's dream of becoming an American citizen had faded and he no longer referred to it in his letters to Smart. Nevertheless, he wrote to her insisting that they would be together finally once all this confusion had subsided. To Elizabeth, however, the facts suggested otherwise. As Jessica herself wrote in a callous burst of insight, 'obviously he is not going to live with you, because in that case he would have been living with you all along, wouldn't he?'

Smart had no answer. Her only recourse was to anticipate Barker's return to England, flying before the wind like Cleopatra at the Battle of Actium, in the hope that he, like Mark Antony, would follow her. In February, with the help of her father and a man called Graham Spry, she obtained a job as a 'junior assistant specialist' with the British Information Services in London – much to the delight of Louie, who, still ignorant of Georgina's existence, was convinced that her daughter was now displaying the correct degree of patriotism and moral verve.[7] In early March Smart and Georgina left Washington and spent three chaotic weeks in the Maases' penthouse in Brooklyn. When she booked passages to Liverpool, Barker reassured her that he would follow as quickly as he could. They were to meet in Kew Gardens on 1 July.[8] Jessica, naturally, had no knowledge of this arrangement. On 25 March Smart and Georgina set sail on the liner *Tyndareus*, one of a convoy of ships bound for England. On 4 April, German U-boats attacked and sank three of the ships. The torpedoes grazed the *Tyndareus*, which remained afloat. Smart arrived in Liverpool on Saturday the 10th, and took the train to London. She reported to the Ministry of Information on the Monday morning. Her pregnancy, now seven months advanced, soon attracted attention. On Wednesday morning she was handed her notice.

She took Georgina to Paddington station, where she phoned one of her few close English friends. Didy Asquith, formerly Didy Battye, had met Smart at Government House in Ottawa while she was accompanying Lady Tweedsmuir on a tour of Canada in 1936. Didy was now married to Michael Asquith, the son of Lady Cynthia Asquith and grandson of the Liberal prime minister. Since her husband was away in London, she was living with her five-year-old daughter Annabel in the converted stables of Hinchwick Manor, a large country house at Scarlet Sub-Edge near Stow-on-the-Wold. Didy had two bedrooms, a loft and a large sitting room in a cottage adjoining the stables. In response to her plea, Didy invited Elizabeth and Georgina to share this modest accommodation. When mother and daughter arrived at the tiny station, Didy met them in her MG. As they drove back to Scarlet, Elizabeth turned to her. In explanation for Georgina and her own evident pregnancy, she said, 'You might as well know. These are the poet George Barker's children. We are to meet in Kew Gardens on July 1.'

Barker was later to claim that he had come to England first, a version of history which does his resolution too much credit. There was in fact plenty to detain him in America. Jessica was now three months pregnant with a budding life, whom she and George had provisionally christened 'Thumper'. A child, Barker explained high-handedly to Willard, was the least that he could give his wife. As a result, though, Jessica's moral claim on her husband was stronger than ever. Besides, Barker was far too embroiled in the literary scene in New York to want to depart immediately. He was expanding his circle of friends. Among his new contacts was Ulrica Mayer, to whose mother, Elizabeth, Auden had dedicated his *The Double Man* two years before (issued in England as *New Year Letter*). Barker had also met Richard Eberhardt, Robert Lowell's teacher, who was currently an aerial-gunnery instructor for the US navy. José García Villa, the Filipino poet, was a keen admirer.[9] Through Smart's contacts in Washington, he also met Archibald MacLeish, poetic patriot and Director of the Office of Facts and Figures, and in New York he became acquainted with Kenneth Patchen, a poet whose worst notices, in which he had been called 'Blake-obsessed' and 'careless', tended to resemble Barker's own. To Barker he confessed, 'I'm nothing but a second-rate football player.'[10] It was in the Manhattan apartment of Emily Coleman's son Johnny, however, that Barker ran into a young man who was to affect him most: a pious, bookish, slender, 22-year-old from St Louis, Missouri, currently serving with the Merchant Marine at Sheepshead Bay: John Joseph Farrelly.

Farrelly belonged to a large and devout Roman Catholic family.[11] 'He had already spent two years reading literature at the University of St Louis under the young Marshall McLuhan, who had urged him to go next to Cambridge to study with Leavis.[12] He was fluent, articulate and had begun the long series of prose narratives which, according to his still more pious brother Tom, showed 'a great sense of the disproportion of sin in the world', without pointing to a solution. John had replied that there was no solution except God's redemption 'and I don't know yet how to picture that dramatically'.[13] John Farrelly's charm, at times almost ethereal, impressed everybody. He had also, most touchingly, a protective streak which drew him to Jessica, over whom in the years to come he would keep a watchful and solicitous eye. But Farrelly was a troubled figure. His correspondence revealed a restlessness and lack of contentment that would keep him forever dissatisfied; in the Merchant Marine he felt frustrated and out of place. Embarking for Casablanca with 'five volumes of Anti-Nicene fathers and an armful of Henry James', he reported back to St Louis, 'I am 22 years old and have scarcely laid a brick in the foundation of my full life's work: earning some kind of a living, saving my soul, and forming a prose style. Friday, the day we land, will be a year from the day I arrived at Sheepshead Bay, and I wonder what the year has counted for.'[14] One of his few fixed ambitions was to complete his literary studies at Cambridge. In this aspiration he was encouraged by his closest male friend, also from St Louis: Eugene Augustus Marius Bewley, who in 1943 was a graduate student at Columbia. Marius was four years older than Farrelly, to whom he habitually referred as 'Sergius', and was also from a Catholic family. Where Farrelly was introspective and uncertain, Bewley was larger-than-life and camp. Karl Miller, who later met both men in Cambridge, was to say of Bewley that 'his manner was understood to combine the rhetoric of W.C. Fields and the suavity of the Hollywood-English movie actor George Arliss'.[15] Barker found Farrelly and Bewley entertaining. Characteristically, however, he was more drawn to Farrelly's insecurity.

Such contacts were rewarding, but they could not fill the gap left by Elizabeth. Throughout April and into May George bombarded her with letters and cables, one of which read, 'Everything under control. Kew Gardens postponed one month.'[16] The response was silence. Elizabeth was wise enough to know that to appear not to need him was the better ploy. Barker grew restless and unable to concentrate on his work, drinking more frequently than usual. One evening in May he thrust his fist through a window in the Maases' apartment. Willard found him distressed, over-active, at times manic. In some concern, he wrote to Elizabeth, 'you will learn, my darling, that only firmness and hardness, coupled with your expansive desire and love for him, will save him, and now I know surely that if he is to be saved you must do it'.[17]

In May Barker called at the British consulate in Washington, asking to be repatriated. He was told that a passage would be provided for him on condition that, on arrival in England, he make himself available either for active service or for alternative war work. He explained to friends that it was an issue of conscience: it troubled him increasingly that others were taking the brunt of the conflict while he was continuing his life of, albeit productive, ease in New York. It was less easy to square his decision with his continuing concern for Jessica and their unborn child. Jessica was not disposed to put Thumper at risk by accompanying her husband; she knew enough about Elizabeth's hazardous crossing in April to be convinced of that. Though Barker assured her that he would not be meeting Smart, Jessica knew now how far to trust him. As for the authorities, he had little difficulty persuading them that he was leaving his wife behind for her own sake. Moving Jessica out of Cranberry Street, he settled her into the apartment of a mutual friend, Chloë Hudeburg, at 60 Willow Street in Brooklyn. He asked his new acquaintances Farrelly and Bewley to keep a watchful eye over his wife. Then in June he sailed for England, telling Jessica that he would be back as soon as he conveniently could.

Landing on 15 July he took the train to London and made at once for Cornwall Gardens, where he was reunited with Big Mumma and Pa, Grandma

Taaffe, Monica and Kit. He then cabled Gloucestershire and took the train down to Moreton station, where Didy picked him up in the car.

Tall, gentle and resourceful, Didy was the daughter of a wealthy Greek family of gallery owners.[18] A predominant influence in her childhood years had been her Nanny, Elizabeth Lee, a miner's daughter from North Wales to whom she remained devoted. As a young woman she had attended the London season and had worked briefly as a model. The polite pastimes of London society, however, had soon bored her. She was temperamentally drawn to bohemian life. In July 1943 her husband Michael, a conscientious objector, was away in London performing civilian war work for the Friends' Ambulance Unit. In the meantime, she had found a place for Nanny Lee up at Hinchwick Manor, while she and Annabel occupied the stables. These cramped quarters also accommodated Elizabeth and Georgina, and now George.

What he found was a slightly ramshackle household whose tranquillity was not increased by Barker's announcement, that first weekend, of the existence of Thumper. In Brooklyn, in the early spring of 1943, he had managed to keep Elizabeth and Jessica apart so effectively that neither had suspected the other's condition. The news of Jessica's pregnancy plunged Elizabeth into resentful gloom. Long afterwards Didy would recall her sitting in glum silence deep into the night, hugging herself, unable to accept, or even to understand what she had been told. She reproached Barker with maintaining a double standard: if she, as he insisted, had been faithful to him, why could he not be to her? To this Barker answered that men were simply different from women: polygamy was the nature of the beast. They sat over candles late into the night, sipping whisky while George remained lucid, implacable, determined at all costs to charm.

As the summer wore on, the mood became calmer. Mindful of her position as guest, Elizabeth had gone to some length to make the rooms they were living in tidy and homely. Photographs taken by Didy in July and early August show a harmonious extended family group: Barker suntanned and happy, a newspaper spread out on his knees; Elizabeth heavy with child; baby Georgina with Annabel; and a semi-resident painter called Stovepipe. It seems that the ménage brought out in Barker an appreciation and relish of family life, of which he had been starved in the States. He played with little Annabel in the sandpits. Relaxation stole over him.

To Didy that summer he seemed witty, warm, at his very best. Didy was herself pregnant with her son Kip and in halcyon mood. She and Barker went for walks and bicycle rides in the country, looking for places where he and Elizabeth might settle. On one of these jaunts Didy told George that she had been reading Graham Greene's novel *Brighton Rock*. Barker told her that he identified with Pinkie, the book's delinquent anti-hero. Like Pinkie, he lived a life actively violating the Catholic faith, in which he continued implicitly to believe, without literal observance. Like Pinkie too, he would be saved if at all by a deathbed repentance, a last-minute intervention of divine grace, 'between the stirrup and the ground'.

Such a philosophy, Didy gathered, was a deliberate rejoinder to the prim decencies of British life. In *Brighton Rock* the representative of such decencies is Ira Dankworth, whose common-sense code of right and wrong conflicts with the novelist's, and Pinkie's, belief in absolute good and evil. Right and wrong, in their civic and secular senses, were Barker's guiding lights no more than they were Greene's. His was a riskier policy: passion, damnation, courage. Barker was living in the spirit of the sentence by the French writer Charles Péguy, which serves as an epigraph to a later Greene novel, *The Heart of the Matter*:[19] 'The sinner lies at the very heart of Christianity . . . nobody is more competent than the sinner in matters of Christianity. No one, unless it be the saint.'

CHAPTER 23

'MY TALL DEAD WIVES'

Because the Quakers were Pacifists, the Friends' Ambulance Unit, organised under their auspices, was a rallying point for conscientious objectors during the war. Michael Asquith had been working for the unit for several months; in July 1943 this involved participating in a research programme to test the effectiveness of prophylactics against malaria.[1] After subjecting himself to an intensive course of mosquito bites, Asquith contracted the disease. As a result he was granted sick leave, which he spent with Didy at his brother's flat in Regent's Park. Smart took Barker to meet him there.

The terms of Barker's repatriation entailed some kind of war service and he expressed a strong interest in joining the Ambulance Unit himself. He was still uncertain about his future. His seesawing plans and his increasingly intricate private life bemused many of his friends. In October Anne Ridler wrote to Lawrence Durrell in Cairo, 'I hear that George Barker has one baby being born in the U.S.A. and another one here – or did I tell you – and is thinking of taking refuge in the Church. Having got to England as a volunteer, he now says he is a conscientious objector. The war seems to have been a bad thing for him.'[2]

Barker settled into his old routine of splitting his time between town and country, coming and going more or less as the mood took him. So pervasive was his presence at Scarlet Sub-Edge, however, that Didy had the impression of almost continuous residence. Since Michael was in London, and soon to be posted abroad, Barker was the only adult male in Didy's cramped quarters at Hinchwick Manor. He even performed a very good impersonation of a dedicated pater familias – when he was there. In fact, as the logbook kept by Smart during the last few weeks of her pregnancy shows, his attendance was very spasmodic. Through the summer he fell into the habit of going down to Gloucestershire for two or three days and then disappearing up to London for unpredictable periods.³ Not surprisingly, the subject of pregnancy was very much on his mind. He had been thinking of calling his next volume of verse, which was to include the Elegies and love poems, *The Altars of Dereliction*. Bearing in mind Elizabeth's and Jessica's condition, he now proposed to Faber that the title be changed to *Word in a Bag of Waters*. Philosophically, Eliot replied, 'in the end, a poet must have the title that he wants, and the board are willing, but reluctant . . . I think that the reviewers may have some fun with this obstetrical metaphor'.⁴ To Eliot's relief, Barker substituted *Eros in Dogma*. He could not as yet decide whether to dedicate the book to Eliot or to Jessica's child.

During Barker's absence abroad, much had changed in British poetry. Since Auden's move to America, the fulcrum had shifted. The radical consensus of the 1930s had been replaced by impromptu groupings such as the New Apocalypse, inaugurated in Leeds shortly before the war and in 1943 about to publish its last anthology *The Crown and the Sickle*. The object of the movement, as J.F. Hendry had explained in his introduction to its inaugural anthology, was to explore the myth-making faculty of the poet, though its name also carried a reference to the convulsive events of the time. Barker had a loose connection with the Apocalyse poets through Nicholas Moore, who had published him in the magazine *Seven* in 1939, and through G.S. Fraser, then serving with the army in Cairo, whom he met on leave. However, the New Apocalyse was already dispersing by the time he reached London; nor would he have had much to do with a school which even Fraser finally found perplexing in its aims and mediocre in its performance. Of his old associates, however, Spender was in London, working for the Fire Service and co-editing *Horizon*. John Lehmann, who had already included Barker in *New Writing*, was also there. He was one of very few intellectuals exempted from war service because of his services to literature.

A publication closer to Barker's taste was *Poetry London*, edited by Tambimuttu, with whom he had been corresponding from the States. Barker had already published in Tambi's magazine some of the sexually ambiguous love poems of the 'First Cycle', subtitling them 'From the Montenegran'. He was much attracted by the design on its front cover: a woodcut of a lyre or, as Barker preferred to spell it, 'Liar' Bird.⁵ He found the editor himself irresponsible but irresistible. With his flashing eyes and long, restless fingers, and dressed invariably in a blue melton overcoat done up to the chin, Tambimuttu stalked London, defying its austerity and drabness. He liked to see himself as the epicentre of London literary life and had just brought out *Poetry London*, 9. The original funders having failed, he had signed on with the short-lived publishing firm of Nicholas & Watson ('Nick and Wat'), for whom he worked desultorily in an office in Manchester Square. In reality he spent much of the day dawdling over expense-account lunches in the restaurants of Charlotte Street and every evening in the pubs. He was also attempting to launch a book list entitled Editions Poetry London, the name of which had been suggested by the writer Julian Maclaren-Ross. Editions was supposed to carry an acute accent, a Frenchification which Tambi could not pronounce.[6] He scoured the pubs looking for contributors, but his task was complicated by his reputation for mislaying the manuscripts he acquired. He once lost a study of Buddhist art by William Empson, leaving it in a taxi.

War had introduced a certain ritualism to the literary life of the capital. Since alcohol for domestic consumption was scarce, pubs became the natural and convivial setting for drinking. For the crowd Barker was now mixing with, the evening would habitually start to the north of Oxford Street in the area referred to as 'Fitzrovia' after Fitzroy Square. It northern outpost was the Fitzroy Tavern in Charlotte Street, which, however, the cognoscenti seldom used now. The newly popular pubs were the Black Horse in Rathbone Place, the Burglar's Rest, the Marquess of Granby and the plaid-hung Wheatsheaf, where Nina Hamnet sat next to the bar, rattling a money-box to indicate that she needed a drink. Here the writers, drinkers and aspirants to both roles (of which there were many) lingered, behind great blackout boards in winter. In the warmer months, when double summertime was in force, they drank in daylight until closing. At half-past ten, when they were thrown out, they made their way southwards across Oxford Street to Soho in the borough of Westminster, where the doors stayed open until eleven.

Since England was now cut off from the continent, the area around Old Compton Street had become a substitute Latin Quarter. At its heart was the York Minster towards the lower end of Dean Street. Known as the French House, it was managed by Gaston Berlemont, who was Free French in sympathy and an unmistakable presence with his spreading handlebar moustache. In the Helvetia in Old Compton Street, popularly referred to as the Swiss Pub, Dylan Thomas picked quarrels with soldiers. Striving to disguise his impeccable middle-class origins, the Canadian poet Paul Potts hawked his broadsheet poems among the drinkers. When the pubs closed, people moved on to drinking clubs such as the Gargoyle in Meard Street, where the rules permitted alcohol consumption until early morning, as long as it was accompanied by a nominal, and normally unconsumed, meal.

The streets of Soho had become a cultural oasis, where good conversation blossomed. David Wright, the South African poet, who had graduated from Oriel College, Oxford the previous year, was later to say that on his arrival in Soho he found it the more adequate university: less structured, more stimulating and more rumbustious than any orthodox college (though it had a protocol of its own, and even an unofficial hierarchy of sorts). Barker, now check-shirted and capped to disguise a growing bald patch inherited from Pa, became one of the senior tutors.

His social circle was expanding in interesting ways. Archer, who had migrated back to London, introduced him to W.S. Graham, for whose poetry he felt a strong affinity. Through Graham, Barker met the tragi-comic duo, Robert Colquhoun and Robert MacBryde. Since arriving in London late in 1941, the Roberts had been sharing a studio at 77 Bedford Gardens off Kensington Church Street. The house was a warren of studios accommodating artists of varied talents, most of whom Barker would get to know well. John Minton was a hugely able painter, rich, thinly intense, tousle-haired, promiscuous and, like the Roberts, homosexual. In his cups Minton was a harlequin entertainer; he was prone to manic fits of generosity beneath which Barker sensed an enduring melancholy. Jankel Adler – balding, heron-headed, intense and brooding – had studio space in the building, as did the cartoonist Ronald Searle.[7] Kaye Webb, editor of the cheekily subversive magazine *Lilliput*, lived in the house, commissioning experimental and polemically suggestive artwork. She procured designs from Minton and asked Barker for yet more extracts from his much-used Japanese journal. When the extracts were published in three successive issues of *Lilliput*, Barker embellished his anecdotes with pen-and-wash sketches of his own.[8]

It was the Roberts who set the tone. In 1943 Colquhoun was working part-time as an ambulance driver for Civil Defence, painting in the evenings and angling for commissions from the War Artists' Advisory Committee, helped by occasional handouts from the aristocratic Peter Watson, backer and art editor of *Horizon*. MacBryde – expansive and moody by turns – performed the domestic chores, darned their socks and cooked the meals. Colquhoun was tall and sinewy with a mean, half-shaven look, his cheeks hollow, his gaze direct and challenging. MacBryde was smaller, stockier and chubbier, with thick eyebrows and unkempt hair. He was devoted to the slightly younger and bi-sexual Colquhoun, whom he was rumoured to ration to one woman a month. While these heterosexual encounters were in progress, so legend ran, he would lie beneath the double bed, making sarcastic remarks up through the springs.

During the week the Roberts drank in Soho; at weekends more frequently in the Windsor Castle in Campden Hill Road, or the Old Swan at the top of Kensington Church Street, where they would hold court on Sundays. It was in the Windsor Castle that Barker met them. MacBryde walked up to him and offered his hand. When Barker clasped it he realised too late that it held a broken wineglass. For several seconds, as Barker winced with pain, MacBryde crushed the jagged shards into his palm. When Barker pulled his bleeding hand away, MacBryde said in his thick Ayrshire accent, 'You'll remember this, won't you?' Barker clouted him round the right side of his head, leaving him deaf in one ear for a week.[9]

When he was in London, Barker stayed at Monica's flat in Redcliffe Gardens. He went there on Wednesday, 21 July, promising Elizabeth that he would soon be back. Just before midday on 23 July Smart went into labour. She was admitted into Moreton-in-Marsh hospital, where her son Christopher was born at two-thirty that afternoon. She sent a telegram to Barker, who responded with a two-word cable: 'Forgive me.' Smart remained in hospital until 5 August. On her release, she wrote to Redcliffe Gardens:

> Where are you & what are you doing & are you very unhappy and harassed & if so why don't you write & tell me all about it . . . If it's the bloodhounds or the beautiful pilot or the gay paraders or the tigers of regret or whatever there must be a use for me since my love's not sporadic & periodic but like milk which if not sucked swells up till the breasts are footballs & has to be expressed by force . . .[10]

Her reproach was well worded. By 'beautiful pilot' she meant John Fitch. 'Gay paraders' was a phrase Barker himself had used in all innocence in the introductory stanzas to *Calamiterror*. Smart, however, was fully aware of its homoerotic meaning, employed in streetwise Californian circles since 1930. Though Smart was distrustful of many of Barker's contacts, an oblique and gentle needling was the most extreme tone that she dared use. Eventually Barker returned on the evening of Monday, 9 August. Looking at Christopher as he lay in his mother's arms, he asked, 'Is this your latest production?' He added, 'You really are rather clever.' As ever, the palpable innocence of a sleeping child stirred him. Christopher was his first son. He wrote for him a stanza:

> Sigmund Freud at his bed
> Keep the libidinous beasts at bay;
> And the Assisian at his head
> Teach him the simple games of love
> That the lamb & the lion play.[11]

The next phrase in Smart's letter, 'the tigers of regret', was also well aimed. Guilt, as she well knew, featured strongly in Barker's psyche. Besides, for weeks he had been bombarded by cables from Brooklyn reading, 'Must have cash immediately. Jess.' He had been sending Jessica what little money he could afford, as well as manuscripts for her to sell. On 16 July, and again on the 22nd, he wrote to Willow Street enclosing a pittance. He also protested his love 'from which', replied Jessica, 'I deduct 75 & 3/4 per cent because you are of the chosen few and know words and a little more as men were deceivers ever, but it still doesn't quite work out'. For consolation Jessica had been turning to Barker's American friends. True to their word, Farrelly and Bewley had called to pay their respects. They were, Jessica wrote rapturously to George, 'so young and gay and we all laughed a great deal and I enjoyed having them'. She had already been twice to hospital. What, she wrote to ask, if the baby should be a Thumperess? Her reproaches were all the more stinging for their almost maternal mildness:

> You were in such a habit of lying that you did it when it wasn't even necessary I thought, and that is an impossible way to live. But you are so dreadfully deep in me that whether we can ever get belief and things back I don't know. Don't you think its possible that you have changed so much that we aren't the same kind of people any longer? But I mustn't get churned up Mister Dear or think too deeply now or I don't sleep and that's bad for me. Thumper of course just isn't concerned with things like that and has no consideration of day or night. I know every shade in the sky from dawn to day and sometimes am convinced he is separate from me already. It will be wonderful to hold him and tell him not to be a meanie.[12]

As autumn approached, Smart decided to move her small family up to London. Barker registered Christopher's birth on the morning of 12 August; afterwards Didy took one final family photograph with George in his Burberry and trilby, Elizabeth holding Christopher in the crook of her left arm, Georgina standing by her side. Then the four of them set off by train to Paddington. In Earls Court a lavish welcome awaited them: Big Mumma and Pa; Grandma Taaffe; the three Barker sisters; Eileen's son Young John, now thirteen and not so little, his younger brother Barry and tiny sister Olga; Monica's children Wendy, Pat and Mac. Accepting as ever, knowing moral judgement to be wasted, Big Mumma took one look at Elizabeth, and declared that it was a pity she and George had not met sooner. After a few congested days, Barker found one room at the top of a house in adjacent Coleherne Road, into which he squeezed Smart and her two children. The set-up at Scarlet had been chaotic and happy; Earls Court was cramped and tetchy. During his frequent disagreements with Smart, Barker was apt to take refuge in Monica's room in Redcliffe Gardens, or else he would sweep Georgina to Cornwall Gardens for Big Mumma to dote on. Elizabeth would be left in charge of Christopher, fulminating into her notebook between domestic chores.

On Friday, 27 August, five weeks after the birth of Christopher, Jessica was admitted to hospital in New York, where she gave birth to twins: a girl and a boy. She called the girl Anastasia, adding the second name Clare after the daughter whom they had given up for adoption. The boy became Anthony Sebastian, thus benefiting from the Christian name which Barker had held in reserve for Elizabeth's first child. When Barker broke the news at Coleherne Road, Elizabeth duly noted down these details in a special keepsake book she was compiling to commemorate Christopher's childhood, listing these new half-siblings as her son's kindred. In the wider world, the wonder grew. In New York José García Villa, the Filipino poet, understood that George Barker, his distinguised British colleague, had given birth to two pairs of twins on the same afternoon. And Barker started work on his Third Cycle of Love Poems, alluding to the vexed history of the last four months. The cycle is full of regretful tenderness, and images of remorse:

> My love who sleeps lost in America
> Dreams distance gone, then I am at her side
> Where she lies smiling, because no longer
> Lonely we sleep as the wide seas divide.
>
> Nightly, O nightly, hovering lightly over
> This moment of meeting between chronologies,
> Star in the dark, far in the mid-Atlantic,
> Our two loves, like doves, meet in their kiss.[13]

Though Elizabeth was aware of the existence of the twins, Jessica still knew nothing about Christopher. Her blissful ignorance was short-lived. Barker had been careful to say nothing on the subject in his letters; he could not, however, prevent the Woodward family from finding out the truth. As soon as she elicited the facts, her sister Kit wrote to Jessica. Her interference deepened George's distrust of the Woodwards, whom he was avoiding in any case; it also destroyed the last particle of Jessica's loving trust in George. Her letters had tended to soften towards a cosy, affectionate forgivingness. The tone ceased altogether as soon as she became aware of Elizabeth's second child. To put her mind at rest, Barker wrote to reassure her that Christopher was not his. Elizabeth was, after all, very promiscuous. Jessica knew what to make of this fabrication. 'One day', she wrote, 'I must make out my testimony of the unforgivable and unforgettable things – it would surprise you considerably I think. You were always so sure you were getting away with things and that I was convinced by the most outrageous lies.' Changing tack, Barker then attempted to cast the blame on Kit Woodward, without whom Jessica would have remained serene. The ploy worked no better. 'Re: my vicious sister,'

Jessica retorted, 'I am not concerned with your behaviour now and as she was not the father of Elizabeth's children, mention of her seems superfluous. Will you never learn?'

Feminine anger and resentment closed Barker in on every side. As in the earliest days of his marriage, he seemed hemmed in by Amazons. In the Third Cycle of Love Poems he evoked his guilty dread:

> My tall dead wives with knives in their breasts
> Gaze at me, I am guilty, as they roll
>   Like derelicts in my tempests,
> Baring their innocence to the dirty pole
> Whirled upon which I am a world at rest.
>
> But restless in the bed of the will of things
> I sleep with knives: the wave overhead
>   Shall kiss with fangs
> Red with lipstick of their dead love
> Above me as I lie in the grave of a bed.[14]

The 'beautiful pilot' was also causing concern. Fitch had broken with Telte and, immersed in his air force duties, had stopped writing to Barker. Anxiously George asked Jessica for information, but she had heard nothing. Nor had she time to think about such matters. On her return from the hospital she was without a home, Chloë's apartment being too small for a mother and her newborn twins. Eventually Jessica found a studio apartment on the second floor at 21 Christopher Street, in the heart of Greenwich Village. The accommodation consisted of a single all-purpose room with a curtained recess off it, in which the twins had their bed. The rent was more than she could afford. She took to wearing cast-off dresses begged from Peggy Guggenheim by their mutual friend Emily Coleman. With grim determination, she set about bringing up the twins alone.

Barker's peace of mind was not helped by the physical congestion in Coleherne Road. In the autumn, probably through the offices of David Gascoyne, he met Julian Trevelyan, an illustrator who lived at Durham Wharf in Hammersmith. Trevelyan knew that the basement of A.P. Herbert's nearby house at 9 Hammersmith Terrace was empty. He mentioned Barker's accommodation problems to Herbert, who put the basement at Barker's disposal.[15] Barker, Smart and their two children moved there in October. The flat was so close to the Thames that the washing of the tides against its banks could be heard distinctly, though from basement level the river could not be seen. As the water lapped out of sight, Barker sat in the front room looking up towards the embankment, envisaging the swans. He thought back over the tumult of recent years which had brought him to this insecure pass. These barren, riverine wastes recalled the landscape he had once described in 'Battersea Park', with its 'fog of failure and distress'. He added a seventh lyric to the Third Cycle of Love Poems:

> At this white window by the Thames
> Where swans elide labials of water,
> I sit and I must speak those names
> That, since my tongue is swan on thought,
> Are brought to my mind by these themes.
>
> Here I span stones at twelve, and under
> Bridges rigged by bonfires with ragamuffins
> To warm a wind that chased us. O send a
> Kinder wind to them, the bigger urchins,
> And wherever they are now, Time, be tender.[16]

The Third Cycle was like a journal reflecting his moods. Like the previous cycles, it is predominantly lyrical. Inevitably, however, fits of temper keep breaking through. When they do so, Barker permits himself a colloquial brusqueness. '"Bugger", I hear a whisper, "the door's locked"' begins one stanza, producing a sharp change of tone which was to seem exemplary and daring to some readers, unforgivable to others. The brutally expletive, as George Macbeth remarked long afterwards, was to become a third voice in Barker's poetry of the Forties and Fifties, contrasted with the vatic and the lyrically direct, 'and not always to its detriment, within the same poem'.[17] The disparity seemed at one with his conduct: the warmth, the sudden breaking off, the proud dismissal of too much high-mindedness.

Gascoyne had been spending the war touring as an actor with ENSA. One evening he came to stay at Hammersmith Terrace, where George introduced him to Elizabeth. After Georgina and Christopher were asleep, the three adults talked until the small hours, interrupted only by the sirens. Outside bombers came flying through a searchlit sky which Barker thought resembled a Whistler painting. Elizabeth rushed through to collect her babies, then sat on the stairs cradling them in her arms. As the fire-bombs flickered overhead, David read her Baudelaire's *Les Fleurs du mal* in his passionate, sonorously vowelled French.[18] When the raid was over and Smart was in bed, Barker returned to the sitting room. He found David sitting alone before the fireplace, staring intently at a little dead mouse.[19]

CHAPTER 24

'EQUATING THE PARADOX'

The convulsive changes of the last three years had taken their toll on Barker's physical and mental health. He was increasingly prone to stomach ulcers. Despite the removal of his tonsils, the cold weather badly affected his throat. He had already taken psychiatric advice when in New York; in London he asked literary friends whether they could recommend a doctor. A physician much used by writers, including Cyril Connolly, was Karl Theodor Bluth, a German exile who lived in Kensington; Barker went to see him in the autumn of 1943. When Dr Bluth asked about his state of mind, he replied that he continually heard peacocks screaming.[1] There were peacocks in Holland Park, but none in Hammersmith. Bluth told him that he was a 'religious maniac'. To cure this condition he prescribed Methedrine, a stimulant recently developed to keep pilots awake during long-range bombing raids, but used also in its early days to correct a variety of psychiatric ailments. Barker was soon taking it in increasing doses.

Since he had applied to work for the Friends' Ambulance Unit, the National Service Act required that Barker obtain a certificate of health from the Medical Board. On 11 November he caught a train to Kingston, where an orderly entered his details on his grade card: age 30; height 5ft 9 inches (he was, in fact, somewhat taller); hair 'brown' and eyes 'grey'. He was classified as Grade Four, unfit for any but the lightest forms of war work.[2]

His plans thwarted, Barker brooded in Hammersmith. Every provision he made appeared to be culpable, from one point of view or another. Living in England seemed a betrayal of the near-destitute Jessica. Though little freelance work was available, he sent the proceeds to her. These fitful payments did little to alleviate her poverty, but much to incense Smart, who was struggling to feed her own two children on very slender means. The moment he allowed his thoughts to stray in the direction of Greenwich Village, he attracted Smart's scorn. On 10 January 1944 she wrote in her journal an inventory of grudges, headed 'To George':

> We are obviously supernumerary: You don't need us. Therefore for our own sakes, we must Get Out of it altogether and leave you with what's yours in all senses of the word, what moves you and, what, if anything, you love: I mean Jessie and her wrong-reason twins. Perhaps she loves you enough to carry water and wash dirty nappies and cook and sweep and sit up alone night after night, or perhaps you love her enough to help her when she needs it and to want to be with her occasionally. Anyhow; as you say, the crux of every matter is cash and she has always been able to get cash out of you and always will, even if she has to get the Foreign Office to pursue you: while I have never been able to get a penny, a poem or a word of praise.[3]

When the atmosphere grew intolerable, Barker took sanctuary with his parents. Big Mumma was happy to give him refuge. The presence of an apparently idle son, however, grated on Pa's nerves. George's father was now sixty-three and was still butler at Gray's Inn. He was cherished and feared by his numerous grandchildren, who referred to him as 'Bompa'. To outsiders, however, he seemed formidable. David Wright, who met him two years later, remembered him as 'dark, aquiline, a face reminiscent of Picasso's, baldness augmenting a magnificent forehead, in height between five feet ten and six feet eleven. He was one of those people who, when their wrath is up, do not take thought but add cubits to their stature.'[4] Among the factors contributing to Pa's rages, George's hanging around ranked high.

In the New Year of 1944 Grandma Taaffe died. Since Pa was nearing retiring age, the Barkers decided, for the last time, to move. In the spring they found a spacious flat in a converted house at 23A Stanhope Gardens, off the southern end of Queen's Gate. In later years the flat was to be described by many a visitor who, arriving on the offchance of meeting the poet, encountered the family instead. The entry was from Stanhope Gardens through a stuccoed portico. From a small downstairs lobby two flights of stairs led to the kitchen scullery, the centre of all social activities in the flat. Wright later described it as 'a tall room, not large, where, behind a large all-purpose table, presided Big Mumma with her motley gathering of guests, always provided with drink and, on much rarer occasions, with food ... In this kitchen she reigned throughout the day – a room I cannot remember ever seeing empty ... for besides Big Mumma there were never less than two of her children, or her children's children, her children's friends and her children's children's friends.' One tall sash window looked on to the mews beyond; opposite stood a gas cooker on precarious metal legs. The dining room was next to the kitchen. Seldom used for meals, it was dominated by a vast painting of Kit's entitled *The Conquest of Mexico*, to the left of which George hung a broad-rimmed Spanish hat. Through an arched passage lay a tiled landing, where in one corner Pa kept his wine cabinet, stocked with fine vintages from Gray's Inn, but usually locked. The landing led into a conservatory with Kit's Dulcitone spinet against the far wall. The conservatory, however, was only a mere overture to the living room, called the White Room after the lounge the Barkers had once had in Ladbroke Grove. Here, as Wright recalled, the relatively spartan furniture of the rest of the household was compensated for by 'huge dragon-enfolded jars and vases, chinoiserie lamp-shades, screens, and peacock feathers'. There were 'comfortable plump-cushioned sagging arm-chairs and an engulfing sofa beseiging a marble-browed coal-burning fireplace defended by brass fire irons'. A sideboard held Mumma's collection of Wemyss china pigs. The White Room, however, was Pa's lair, which visitors entered on sufferance. On the wall he hung a portrait of a dark-hued Spanish monk inherited from the American sisters he had once worked for in Paddington: he informed his visitors that this painting was a Rembrandt, though it was almost certainly by a minor Spanish painter of the school of Murillo. From the room three tall French windows overlooking Stanhope Gardens opened on to a balcony which, in the summer months, acted as an overflow for the parties which George and Kit were to hold with increasing frequency, and which sometimes seemed to be attended by half the artists of Soho.

For the next decade George would use this sprawling flat as a second base, sleeping in 'the doll's room', a tiny bedroom on the top floor. The parental home was an ideal bolt-hole when his life elsewhere proved fraught, as it did in the spring of 1944. He had again applied to join the Friends' Ambulance Unit. His medical record, however, counted against him. He reconciled himself to kicking his heels in London for the foreseeable future. In this state of enforced idleness, his loyalties seemed more than ever torn. The Third Cycle of Love Poems, completed in February, harked back to Jessica with an intensity that made Smart feel more than ever redundant. Jealousy stalked him at every turn. The same month, Barker took the train up to Yorkshire to visit the Gills in Hull. On the train he met a middle-aged schoolmistress, who was so impressed by his conversation that she sent him a friendly note afterwards, addressed to Faber & Faber. The secretary at the firm, whose files were not up to date, forwarded this to Jessica in New York, who promptly dispatched a wounding rebuke, care of Monica in Redcliffe Gardens. The tidings of this *mal entendu* eventually reached Elizabeth. When she accused George of yet another betrayal, he took to his bed and had to be nursed by Monica. Shortly before his thirty-first birthday, he wrote to Smart in an attempt to mollify her,

'I spend most of the day in bed doing my best and worst to recuperate from a sort of psychological crack-up. It was like the death by horses of the french I mean being torn in pieces by white mares driven in opposite directions. Who said I had what infatuation with what new woman?'[5]

By March Smart was also seriously in need of a break from emotional and physical pressures. Barker suggested she spend some time alone in Scotland, or even in London while Georgina and Christopher where looked after elsewhere. Instead she decided to retreat to the country with the children. George's sister Eileen, who was still in Modbury in Devon,[6] wanted to take a few weeks' holiday, and asked Elizabeth if she would look after her two younger children while she was away. The cottage was a seventeenth-century building with poor sanitation and no running water; its only claim to distinction was that Oliver Cromwell was believed to have stayed there whilst plotting the relief of Plymouth. Elizabeth now had four young children to look after. Her isolation was broken only by George's intermittent visits. Young John, the Jacksons' oldest child, was now a boarder at Plymouth School. When George took Elizabeth there to see his nephew play cricket, John appeared after the match wearing the uniform of the Officers' Training Corps, to George's visible disquiet. The weeks in Devon did not relieve Elizabeth of her domestic chores, but the separation did something to reconcile her to George. In April, when Eileen returned, the two of them decided to make another attempt to live together in the Cotswolds.

At Scarlet Didy Asquith had recently given birth to a son called Stephen or 'Kip'. As a result, the stables at Hinchwick were now too small to house both families. George and Elizabeth took a largish room in College Farm, Condicote, about a mile distant, with a Mrs Foster and her broad-boned daughter, whom they nicknamed 'Big Girl'. The congestion there defeated Smart's attempts to keep the room tidy and the inevitable squalor irritated George. In the second week of April, warm weather arrived and with it a resurgence in George and Elizabeth's physical passion. In their first week of residence they broke a bedspring, and George began his Fourth Cycle of Love Poems:

> This is the month, Elizabeth,
>   When at the equinox
> Biological life divests its death
>   Equating the paradox
> That crosses its dovetails underneath
>   All internecine sex.
>
> Where silent once, where silent once
>   Bedded in negatives we

> Held hands across the Winter whence
> This April lets us free,
> Now up, now up in the solstice dance
> We join with biology.[7]

In the last week of April Barker went all the way to London to buy a replacement bed spring, arriving back by the midday train on 5 May. The whole family promptly went down with a stomach bug. On their recovery, they explored the countryside, walking the mile journey to Hinchwick Manor to socialise with Didy. Michael Asquith's mother, Lady Cynthia Asquith, secretary to J. M. Barrie, was down from London. Other visitors included Michael himself and another conscientious objector working for the Friends' Ambulance Unit, Donald Horwood. Since Barker had no car, all the errands had to be run by bicycle. Christopher had now acquired the nickname Giffy. When on 8 May he came down with a fever following a vaccination, George pedalled over to Stow-in-the-Wold to fetch glucose. On 14 May preparations were afoot for Kip's christening and Didy arrived from Hinchwick Manor to borrow Mrs Forster's tea urn. In her absence, the tap on a beer barrel was inadvertently opened and five gallons of beer went to waste. Yet, there were compensations. For Kip, at his christening, Barker wrote:

> Long, Seraph with a rabbit's paw
> Lean lightly over him; attend
> His bed with fortune at the four
> Corners where all glories end.[8]

Typing this greeting out, he remembered that Giffy too needed a poem. He substituted 'them' for 'him', and retitled the quatrain 'To Stephen Asquith and Christopher Barker'. There were poems too for Annabel, Didy and Georgina: a 'Scarlet Cycle' to add to the existing Cycles of Love Poems.

On the day after the christening party, George and Elizabeth strolled to the nearby village of Longborough, while Mrs Forster looked after the children. In the village pub Elizabeth drank one and a half pints of cider. *Eros in Dogma* was now in the press: on the return leg to Condicote, she demanded to know to whom it was to be dedicated. When Barker announced that he had dedicated the book to Jessica's twins, Smart lay down in the hedgerow and refused to move. Looking down on her recumbent form, Barker declared that he had not consulted Jessica when he had dedicated his *Selected Poems* to Elizabeth. Why did she now wish to be consulted about the dedication to *Eros in Dogma*? He stalked off, abandoning Elizabeth. Eventually, she came to her senses and walked back to Condicote, where she found George absorbedly reading, whilst wolfing the entire supper which Mrs Forster had prepared for them both. Too stirred up for speech, according to Elizabeth's diary they both got into the bed and made love.[9]

Smart's anxiety about the dedication was a symptom of deeper troubles. Jessica's letters from America were now so harrowing that Barker was taking steps to help her. His current plan was to arrange for Jessica and the children to be repatriated. He had already written to Christopher Street requesting the twins' birth certificates. He even harboured a scheme of returning to New York to fetch Jessica and the children himself. He had not, he assured Jessica in his letters, seen Elizabeth since returning to England; indeed, was not sure where she was. Jessica received these assurances with scarcely veiled impatience. Every flicker of girlishness and flirtatiousness had deserted her. At length, she spelled out her feelings in a letter of wounded recrimination and unblinkered stoicism:

> Since that glorious day in Big Sur I have implored you to stop lying but still you go on and send me farther from you with every lie. I hear from people we know in London that you are seeing Elizabeth – I never thought otherwise – and fighting most of the time. And it is not your 'enemies' that send news but people who like you and are really concerned to see you wreck yourself. I am very sorry for you and think it is a pitiable situation but I know that it will continue as long as Elizabeth lives. You haven't the strength to break with her forever and if you attempt it she will track you down again and as you refuse to tell the truth there is no one that can help you, least of all me. I did everything to help you when you were here and suffered every possible hurt and indignity in consequence but you went to England and left me knowing that she would be there and what would happen. There will be another child and so on and so on. You've just got to realize Gran that one cannot go on having another chance and another indefinitely. You both took the 'gilt off the gingerbread' for me for ever and I am never, never going to entertain it again.[10]

The war in Europe, however, was drawing to a close. On the morning of Friday 19 May, while Barker was in London, Elizabeth was making preparations for a large picnic, when a messenger stopped at College Farm and presented her with a telegram. It informed her that her father had died the previous Thursday morning. She wept into her apron, then continued slicing sandwiches, struggling to hide grief from the children. After the picnic they picked bluebells in the woods as Elizabeth suppressed the taste of death in her mouth. In the evening an envelope arrived by special delivery from the American consulate in London. She opened it, to find it contained a form for Barker to complete to enable him to 'join his wife and children' in New York. All evening, Elizabeth sat over her grief, alone.[11]

Barker returned the following evening. Having lost all patience with him, Smart sent him over to Didy's for supper. And so their lives continued, with happiness caught only intermittently. On 6 June, Mrs Forster knocked on the door of their room at Condicote, and announced the D-Day landings. George and Elizabeth could almost have inferred the news from the sky, across which wave after wave of aircraft had been sweeping on their way towards the Normandy coast from the airbase at Moreton-in-Marsh. Elizabeth went down with a severe chill. To help her over it, George cycled over to Didy's to fetch some Benzedrine, a narcotic that he was now taking with some regularity. Afterwards he fled back to London. For days Elizabeth stayed in bed sniffing and looking up at the sky, thinking of the uncertain outcome of the landings and George's unpredictable return. By 10 June there was still no sign of him. Didy and Elizabeth comforted themselves with the resolution that she should leave George: 'we are, as they say of pilots, finished'.[12]

Pilots were very much on George's and Elizabeth's minds. Not only were the allied planes overhead, 'zooming, banking and circling', as she noted in her diary; in America, they now learned, John Fitch had been reported missing. When Barker appeared from London, he walked immediately to Scarlet Sub-Edge, where he announced to Didy that he had received solemn news. He then locked himself in a side room for two days,[13] finally emerging with an elegy. It was, he told Didy, too private to publish. Six years later the poem was to appear in the volume *News of the World* as 'In Memory of a Friend':

> The salt that at the lashes of
>   All Seven Seas laces the shores
> Grazing my weeping eye of sores,
>   Engenders the more of love.
> Here by the salt tide at the South
>   That washes its coils along
> The coast that lies behind the eyes,
>   His wreck is like a rock in my mouth
> With his body on my tongue.[14]

Despite its intensely private occasion, the elegy entered the Barker canon, being one of the two poems of his which Philip Larkin would include in *The Oxford Book of Twentieth-Century English Verse*.[15] After writing it Barker went back to town and spent several uneasy days in Stanhope Gardens. In mid-June he wrote to Elizabeth asking her to bring the children up to join him. When they arrived his face, wrote Elizabeth, was stiff and ashen. He was taking Benzedrine in increasing doses to stave off the mental and physical pain he felt. As he sat before her, dumb and unreachable, the flying bombs rattled overhead through the night. Elizabeth was at her wits' end: 'Next time,' she wrote, 'if it comes, what will I be asked to do but die?'

They bought Didy a new pair of shoes and returned to the Cotswolds together. On 22 June Didy threw a lively party for Elizabeth Lee's birthday: George inscribed a large birthday card, complete with floral designs.[16] He organised communal games for Nanny Lee and the children and then took the next train for London. Smart expected him to stay there for weeks. On Monday he was back, complaining that the flying bombs had been ruining his sleep.

Doodlebugs were not the only cause of disturbance. Tormented by Jessica's refusal to entertain his entreaties, Barker sat down and wrote her his longest letter yet, imploring, commanding, begging, using every weapon in his rhetorical armoury, repeating himself endlessly in his attempt to justify and persuade:

> I insist that this is the showdown. The war itself would be quite enough for me to contend with but to go on for the next year and more hanging on the responses you may experience to the gutter lies of any tom bitch or harpy – I'm not b. well going to, my dear, I'm not going to. Its about time that you understood that the truth is not a private prerogative of the Woodward family. I'm sick and tired and if you want the children to grow up without me then say so and you can all three spend a long life without me. I've told you I love you till I and the censor have got sick of it. I've sold my soul and my typewriter to keep you at the rate of six or seven £ per week in the States. I've ruined my reputation as a writer &, until this morning, I had nothing in the world to hope for except re-union with you.[17]

He advised Jessica to demand repatriation under the scheme by which he himself had returned. On receiving his exhortation, she wrote him the shortest of notes, outlining her resolution to stay where she was: for her own sake, but mostly for the children's:

> *I will not return* – certainly until after the war. I have nothing to return to and the longer the Atlantic is between us, the happier I

shall be. And that is definitely that. There is no need for us to discuss it again.[18]

'Be happy,' Jessica signed off, 'and for God's sake stop telling such fantastic lies.' She added that she had no knowledge of Fitch's whereabouts. 'Sorry for the smudges. Anastasia again.'

On Sunday, 9 July Elizabeth wrote in her journal that it was exactly four years since she and Barker had met, 'and it is still as messy, if not messier, than ever'. She had now embarked on her third pregnancy, not entirely to George's delight: a new child would be hard to explain to Jessica.[19] Despite these misgivings, the promise of another birth seemed to him to chime with the exuberance of midsummer. For Barker, the miracle of conception had come to stand as a sign of biological grace. Out of his sinning, a new innocence was to be born. Beasts we were, but gods also:

> Shut the Seven Seas against us,
>   Lock the five continents,
> Set sepulchred the North Star
>   In a forsaken tense:
> Lay every Sun and System
>   For ever in a dark bed,
> Nevertheless that day shall dawn
>   That resurrects the dead.
>
> When sleepless the wakes, weeping,
>   Mourn life under every leaf,
> And the Moon covers her eye over
>   Rather than look at our grief,
> When in their dreams the liars and
>   The loveless regret life, –
> Then, then the dove born in every storm
>   Shall arrive bright with an olive.[20]

So, evoking the sweet cocoon of Condicote, that 'village coddled in the valley', the Fourth Cycle draws to its close. That autumn there was no departure. Elizabeth and the children stayed on in the Cotswolds through the winter and into 1945. It was, despite all the disagreements and heartaches, perhaps the most sustained period together that George and Smart were ever to enjoy. In such circumstances Barker discovered in himself a capacity for parenthood, scarcely suspected before. He evinced a new tranquillity, a fresh beneficence, astonished at the

'EQUATING THE PARADOX'

               general care
That Nature, cradling kind in her arm,
Extends to all new things that are:
As, walking clouds, she keeps from harm
The whickering child and weeping lamb.[21]

CHAPTER 25

'A BOHEMIAN MOTORIST'

Eros in Dogma appeared in the November of 1944 on thick, unevenly cut pages, but otherwise none the worse for war shortages. It included the 'Pacific Sonnets', followed by 'Secular and Sacred Elegies', to which Barker had added pseudo-theological titles. The fourth Sacred Elegy, for example, was glossed on the contents page as 'The Actual but Imperfect Union of the Lover and the Poet with the Object of their Love'. The first three cycles of love poems came next, with the 'supplementary personal sonnets' comprising the pieces to his mother, to Kit, Eliot, Spender, Gill and Clare – tucked in at the end. The dedication page bore a five-line poem to the twins, optimistically anticipating their clemency for their father's neglect:

> The two hundred and eighty days that shook
> Your world where it hung in its bag of waters
> Taught me that unworthiness has its daughters
> And tall sons who shall step from shock
> Beautiful with forgiveness in their faces.

The reviews were even-handed. 'Mr George Barker', declared the *Listener*, 'is one of the most easily recognisable of modern poets', and then went on to chart some of his recurrent vices. Barker was too fond of long words and at his worst reminded one of 'a composer indiscriminately overloading the trombones'. For all that, one would put him among the best poets of the day. There was in these poems a voice not heard before, above all in the three memorial sonnets for drowned seamen: 'the dry, allusive, concentrated wit that blows through them with an astonishing effect of pathos is an unusual gift that Mr Barker has not abused'.[1] In the *Times Literary Supplement* the book was compared favourably with Louis MacNeice's *Springboard*, which had also just appeared. 'Mr Barker', wrote the anonymous reviewer, 'is a poet of a profounder and more passionate imagination. He is also more conscious of the darkness of the times.' He was judged to be at his piquant best in the Elegies, which culminated in a powerful picture of the 'Egoists bestriding Europe'. The concluding stanza of the Sacred Elegies, the great antithetical hymn to God, was 'formidably his own'.[2]

When Barker sent a copy to Jessica in New York, even she was touched. Wherever she opened it, she wrote, she came across passages of matchless beauty. She liked the sonnets most and the simplest among them best of all: 'Calling us with a cicadas persistence / To other times and other places' brought back all the restless longing of those months in Japan: 'the lines go singing through my mind and always will'. Everywhere was splendour of a kind, but did it exonerate the mischief? Jessica was not certain if art justified betrayal. 'We must hammer it out together when we are both much older and much wiser,' she wrote. She wished him a pleasant 1945, but had no plans to join him.[3]

In the meantime, while Smart stayed in Gloucestershire with the children, Barker expanded his circle in London, among whom visual artists now outnumbered poets. His own early apprenticeship in drawing had given Barker a natural affinity with painters. He was now growing ever closer to Robert Colquhoun and Robert MacBryde, with whom the wineglass crushing incident in the Windsor Castle had created a fraternal blood bond. In 1944 both the Roberts were working assiduously at painting. (Their reputation as hard drinking wastrels is based on a later period of disappointment and decline.) At work and at play, Barker suspected in them split natures reflective of his own. In their studio at 77 Bedford Gardens Barker would sit as Colquhoun worked on his drawings. It was understood implicitly that neither would discuss his work. However, one does not need to look far into Colquhoun's paintings or Barker's poetry to discern a blend of audacity and finesse, a muscular delicacy common to both. In their austere use of line, their way of seizing upon their subjects by means of the fewest possible brush or pen marks, Colquhoun's compositions even recall Barker's own drawings.

In 1944 Colquhoun was concentrating on figure drawing, in the technique of which he been influenced a little by cubism, a little by Wyndham Lewis, but mostly by Adler. One evening Barker sat watching as Colquhoun worked on his painting *The Fortune Teller*. In it teller and client face each other with much the same shell-shocked blankness as the Polish war veterans in Adler's 'mutilés de guerre'.[4] All Colquhoun's figures had the aspect of victims: even in domestic settings they somehow conveyed the forlorn aftermath of battle. To that extent, Colquhoun's art was a product of the ambience of war. His subjects were often spinsters with their pets, the women's faces angular and blank, their noses aquiline, as if broken and reset. The introspection of these women seemed to reflect a sadness in the artist himself.

Colquhoun was a lively but tragic figure, whose own isolation emerges in a self-portrait of 1940. In it he seems cut off from the world, lugubrious, his eyes nonetheless direct and challenging. He and his paintings of lost souls, caressed into an art in which Barker discerned 'a world fissured, torn apart / Yet reassembled with a stroke of love', brought out in the poet an answering tenderness. Instinctively he understood that the ongoing cabaret of the Roberts' social life was a form of fugue from inner distress. Their personalities were composed of light and shadow; to strangers, however, they were likely to appear merely brash. Dressed in matching red and blue sweaters they would storm the pubs, creating mayhem, almost as a matter of course. Their opening gambit of conversation was commonly insult, an art form of which both were masters. Their favourite objects of scorn were Sassenachs, the War Artists' Committee, and Scotsmen who worked for the English. Like W.S. Graham, they displayed their Scottishness as a badge of honour. To emphasise it, they nursed their accents like well-matured whisky. Paul Potts caught the essence of MacBryde. 'He could', said Potts, 'turn a cup of tea into a feast. He loved children, dancing, singing and giving away money. He'd give you a pound note as simply as most people would give away a cigarette and more quickly than some. He hated bad art, the Hanoverian dynasty and Lyons tea shops; loved Turkish baths, patrons and cooking.'[5]

It took Barker's practised eye to discern that the social performances of the Roberts, like his own, were calculated distractions from artistic solitude and a means of protecting that solitude. The division in Colquhoun's personality was particularly marked. In the pubs virility was of his essence: a controlled, rippling musculature of excess, like taut biceps straining. Beneath the rumbustiousness, the warmth and rancour, lay a melancholy from which his distinctive art emerged. Throughout the late 1940s, hangers-on would travel to the York Minster just to listen to Colquhoun recite Shakespearean soliloquies in his deep, trawling baritone. But his speeches were all taken from the last acts of the tragedies: he performed an especially moving rendition of Macbeth. Colquhoun's voice, a projection *de profundis*, seemed to echo from deep within him. It was to the most elusive depths of the self that it returned, resounding in places where Barker could not, and did not want to, follow him.

Barker needed to be with the Roberts, but he needed just as much to be apart from them. All three were public performers who occasionally retired into their respective privacies. The Roberts appealed to the competitor, the pugilist and social comedian in him. In every sense they were his peers. But his gentler nature led him to seek out less abrasive companions as well. At one of the Roberts' Sunday soirées at the Windsor Castle, he encountered a handsome and vulnerable nineteen-year-old called Bruce Bernard. Bernard was the second of three contrasted and talented brothers. In 1944 he was living at home and experimenting with painting. He had read Barker's verses in *Penguin New Writing*, where they seemed 'bohemian and apocalyptic'. He was something of a loner, with a countervailing need for fraternal male bonding. Despite his youth, Bernard had too secure a sense of his own direction to need to be guided. The introvert in him distrusted the extrovert in Barker. He was independent enough, intelligently scrupulous enough, to stand apart and watch, as Barker spread his charm around him to hypnotic effect.[6]

During one of Smart's rare visits to town, Barker encountered a young man of a different disposition. One evening in December 1944, avoiding the crush of the more fashionable Fitzrovia haunts, he and Elizabeth made their way to an obscure Younger's pub, reached by means of an alley lit by flickering gas lamps. In the bar they met David Wright, a tall, floppy-haired poet from South Africa. Wright had been deaf since contracting scarlet fever at the age of six. With this disadvantage, he was still deeply in love with the English language and with poetry. At the age of eighteen he had come to England to study at the Northampton School for the deaf, where he had cured himself of homesickness by reciting Dryden's 'Ode to St Cecilia' in the dormitory to send himself to sleep. At Oriel College, Oxford he had read English and been Master of the Boats. He had declaimed *Paradise Lost* inwardly until Milton's music had yielded up its melody 'as if the lines had lifted trumpets to their mouths'. Wright had come to London in 1943, attracted by the bohemian life of the Soho pubs, where from his immense height he glared wide-eyed at his drinking companions, lip-reading each *bon mot*. Having written poetry since his school days, he had recently submitted examples of his work to the unreliable Tambimuttu. Wright later described his first meeting with Barker in Fitzrovia that December night as 'stiff and useless'.[7] Barker had not yet learned to articulate so as easily to be lip-read, and Wright had not yet learned to overcome the social awkwardness arising from his handicap. His isolation weighed on Barker. It also impressed him deeply.

By December 1944 Barker's social manner had become a brilliant camouflage, intended to fend the world off by the diversionary method of attracting it on terms set by himself. Clad in American-style check shirts, over which in winter he wore leather jackets, he now invariably sported a cap to cover his baldness. The stoop that Antonia White had noted in 1936 had become second nature to him. In Bruce Bernard's eyes the effect was that of a 'bohemian motorist'. Nonetheless, Barker was beginning to exercise a social and spiritual mesmerism which few who succumbed to it could explain, attracting the young by means of that deep masochism called hero-worship. In the Old Swan, or the Wheatsheaf, or the Duke of Wellington in Wardour Street, he would lean on the bar top, narcissistically composing his features. His face would wear an aloof expression that read 'Come into *my* lair.' Many accepted the invitation: acolytes, moths hovering around his eminent and searing flame. His style of addressing these admirers was half mock-Manhattan ('Get that, *baby*!') and half mock Noël Coward ('silly baby', 'silly child'). The mannerisms provoked both imitation and derision. While such a performance was deeply attractive to those in search of a mentor, it merely amused the painter Lucian Freud. Francis Bacon, who also met Barker at this time, found it infuriating. Not even Barker's closest associates were entirely immune from a temptation to mock. As soon as the saloon doors of the Windsor Castle had swung to behind George's retreating slouch, the Roberts would parrot him mercilessly: 'Silly baby, Colquhoun,' 'Silly child, MacBryde.'[8]

On New Year's Day 1945 Elizabeth was alone in Condicote, making resolutions: 'living (and partly living)'[9] as she put it in her diary, echoing the Chorus of Women from Eliot's *Murder in the Cathedral*. Barker remained at Stanhope Gardens throughout January. By this means, he avoided the chicken pox which Georgina contracted that month; he also missed the later stages of Elizabeth's pregnancy. On the 26th she phoned Stanhope Gardens to suggest coming up to see him. He told her curtly that she was not wanted. Four days later he arrived at College Farm without warning, leaving again in a huff on 4 February. By the end of March Elizabeth was thirteen stone; oppressed by everything and everyone. On 4 April spring arrived abruptly. The pear tree blossomed and so did Smart's hatred of her kind. In her diary she wrote, appropriating Horace this time, 'I HATE the Vulgar Mob and SHUN them.' The mood was a product of pre-natal depression. On 16 April, leaving the children with Didy, she met Barker and Michael Asquith's sister Sue off the train at Moreton. They drove her straight to hospital, where she gave birth to her second son. He was called Sebastian, which was also the second name of Jessica's son Anthony. Two days later Elizabeth received a parcel containing the proofs of *By Grand Central Station I Sat Down and Wept*, which Tambimuttu had accepted for his Editions Poetry London. She sat up in bed correcting its fifty-eight pages.

When the Armistice in Europe was announced on 4 May, George, Elizabeth and the three children went up to town, where they joined the euphoric crowds in Trafalgar Square.[10] The rejoicing, however, was only an interlude in George and Elizabeth's tense relationship. If he was to keep them all, Barker needed to earn money, and London was the one place he could do it. He was still tormented by thoughts of Jessica, in whose recent correspondence he had detected a peevish tone quite unlike that of the girl whom he had married, prompting in him a mixture of pity and dread. On 9 June he received from her the most moving letter yet in which Jessica told him that she was working her fingers to the bone looking after the twins until nine o' clock at night. It was not until she had put them to bed that she could snatch her first meal of the day. Then she would sit and weep from sheer exhaustion. She could not afford the half-dollar needed for a babysitter. Her only relief had been from Emily Coleman's son Johnny, who 'has religion and it makes a deuce of a difference', and had refused an invitation of his own so that she could go out for the evening. Life had turned into unremitting drudgery: 'But you will never understand. One has to care for two babies to understand it. I doubt if I shall ever again have the patience to live with an adult. You say you are shot, but believe me Gran you don't know what it means. And as for love – which I don't believe in any longer anyway – I just would not have the energy. My *ultima thule* is sleep now.'[11]

Barker became obsessed with the image of Jessica as a nappy-washer, exhausted by housework. When in August the atomic bomb was dropped on Hiroshima, he began a sequence of three poems entitled 'News of the World'. In it Jessica's desolation became a symbol for a world languishing under a mushroom cloud of indifference. In the second of the sequence, he adopted her voice:

> 'O washing-board Time, my hands are sore
>   And the backs of the angels ache.
> For the redhanded husband has abandoned me
> To drag his coat in front of his pride,
>   And I know my heart will break.'
>
> In the first year of the last disgrace
>   Peace, turning her face away,
> Coughing in fire and laurels, weeping,
>   Bared again her butchered heart
>   To the sunrise axe of day.[12]

Barker took to phoning 21 Christopher Street from Stanhope Gardens to hear how the twins were faring. The calls continued for several weeks until the quarterly bill arrived and Pa banished the costly appliance from the house. On VJ night, 2 September, Elizabeth was alone in Condicote again, while Barker took to the streets. In the Wheatsheaf, Rathbone Place, he met a tall, lanky, quixotically intelligent poet, half-blind from glaucoma since youth, called John Heath-Stubbs.[13] Heath-Stubbs had studied at Queen's College, Oxford on an exhibition reserved for the partially sighted. He was full of poetic promise, but he considered the history of English literature since *Beowulf* to be one of 'steady decline' and Auden a poet 'of the second rank'.[14] After graduating with a first in English, Heath-Stubbs had worked in teaching and publishing, but had newly set himself adrift on the freelance sea. He had published a long sequence *Wounded Thammuz* and, having taught himself Italian, was preparing a set of translations from Leopardi, whom he encouraged Barker to read. He was also writing a book called *The Darkling Plain*, intended as a study of the brief neoclassical phase in English poetry that immediately preceded Romanticism. In his own work he was attempting to yoke personal confession to an unsentimental and hard-edged classicism. He had already heard Barker give a reading at the United Ethical Church in Bayswater. Barker had declaimed the border ballad 'Tam Lin' with an intensity suggestive of personal identification with its bewitched protagonist. On VJ night in the Wheatsheaf Barker responded to the poet in Heath-Stubbs more warmly than to the scholar. 'A pedantic youth', is how Heath-Stubbs later described himself that evening, 'slashing pomposities' as 'The cloud over Hiroshima / Cast turbid reflections in the beer.'[15]

For all that, Barker and Heath-Stubbs had common concerns. Both strongly resented the label 'neo-Romantic' that was being attached to contemporary poetry and both were prepared to go to some lengths to flout it. One way of doing this was to examine critically the very notion of Romanticism. In August George was once more contacted by the extra-mural department at Cambridge, which hired him for a course of twelve lectures to be delivered between October and December. The resulting course, 'Damn Braces', alluded in its title to Blake's maxim 'Damn Braces, Bless Relaxes'. It was a sustained and informed meditation on the transition from high neoclassicism in the 1740s to high Romanticism in the 1820s. Though biased towards Anglo-Irish writers, it was encyclopaedic in scope and markedly courteous to the students. Barker encouraged questions at the end of each session, then punctiliously drafted replies which he would deliver at the beginning of the next class. The style of interpretation was also refreshingly down to earth. For instance, Barker explained the distinction between classicism and Romanticism by reference to the cash in a poet's pocket:

> Classic writing is not writing executed in a certain style, it is writing executed under certain conditions. If a writer is hungry and poor he tends to see visions of things that he would like to eat and possessions he would like to enjoy. This brings about the individual visions of the Romantic writer. If, conversely, he enjoys a good meal regularly and a number of pleasant possessions he tends to write poems and books in which these things are taken for granted: he writes about impersonal matters. And here, I think, we are reaching a bit nearer to the heart of the matter. The first remark I make about the difference between the Romantic and

the Classic is the remark that Romanticism is mostly a personal concern with things and classicism an impersonal concern with things.

But not all poor writers are romantics and not all rich writers are classics. The reason for this apparent disparity is a trifle more simple than one would expect. Periods of history are poor and hungry as well as poets. So that if a writer is born into one of the poor periods he may sense, quite personally, a sort of impersonal poverty or hunger. He may himself be quite well off, like Shelley, but he will feel the pressure of an impersonal poverty. I conclude, not very originally, that the Classic state is one that happens during a prosperous state of the world, and Romanticism an attitude that happens in a world of unrest or change or mutation.[16]

In August *By Grand Central Station* appeared. With typical inefficiency, *Poetry London* sent Smart the contract for signature when she had already received her complimentary copies. Didy Asquith was now moving from Scarlet Sub-Edge. With Didy absent, there seemed little reason for Elizabeth and the children to stay on. They found a basement flat at 39 Markham Square in Chelsea, conveniently close to Stanhope Gardens, where George could more easily write. The toddlers grew taller, and the babies turned into toddlers. When Sebastian learned to walk, he escaped naked into the night and was rescued by a sailor. He also developed the habit of creeping up behind armchairs and assaulting the back of the sitter's head with the nearest obtainable cosh; so 'Basher' he became, a version of his first name later changed to 'Bashie'. In the cramped basement there were plenty of heads to accost, including George's during his fleeting appearances. Although his visits were far more frequent than they had been to Condicote, in Elizabeth's eyes, however, he was using the flat merely as an annexe to the parental home. They were still not living together as a family and George was planning to return to the States. When spring arrived, Elizabeth was pregnant for the fourth time, to Barker's dismay. He accused her of puncturing her diaphragm in order to conceive. He was affable and angry, hot and cold by turns. His anger emerged in a novella on which he had been intermittently working since Condicote. Intended as a rejoinder to Elizabeth's gospel of libidinous fulfilment, it was provisionally entitled *Of Love*.[17] 'I have a story to relate', it began, 'which proves that Love, with no blood on its knife, does not sleep easily, if it sleeps at all, until every one of its devotees lies dead. The great destroyer. In every bed. In every single bed. In every double bed.'[18]

In May 1946 Barker finally completed the paperwork to enable him to enter the United States. On the last day of the month he embarked on the liner *Kaveena*, bound for Montreal and New York. The liner, he told Smart's children, was 'as big as a house, whiter than a paper boat, with a parson and fifteen babies on board'. He had half-formulated a plan for Elizabeth to join him, with or without the children. The real purpose of the visit, however, was to fetch Jessica. When Jessica realised this, she fled from Christopher Street, taking the twins to stay with Farrelly's parents in Pinook, their large country house on the outskirts of St Louis, Missouri. Meanwhile, Barker was enjoying a few days in Montreal, with Elizabeth's sister Jane. His stay there was probably innocent, though Smart suspected an entanglement between them. When he arrived in New York on 14 June, he found the studio at 21 Christopher Street locked. Jessica had left no note to tell him where she had gone. Once more he turned to Willard and Marie Maas, from where, as a stalling tactic, he wired Smart in London to say that Jessica was obtaining an annulment.

Smart declined to join him in New York. So for the time being he was thrust back on his own devices and began picking up the threads of his friendships. The Maases were as flamboyant as ever. After Willard's release from the Signal Corps, they had set about marketing *The Geography of the Body*, promising George royalties that never seemed to materialise. John Fitch was not dead after all but, having endured a few months in a German prisoner-of-war camp, had resurfaced in Ohio, where he was miserably subsisting and planning to launch an automobile business. He had split up from Telte, who was now engaged to a naval lieutenant whom mutual friends found more suitable because more solid.

John Farrelly had spent the closing months of the war as purser aboard a ship sailing between New York and Murmansk. He had married a woman called Emily Tomkins, with whom he now had a small son named Martin.[19] The marriage had since foundered. He still intended to finish his university studies with Leavis in Cambridge, but in the meantime earned an insecure living reviewing books for Edmund Wilson's *New Republic*. He had become acquainted with Auden's patroness Elizabeth Mayer, who kept open house on Long Island. Benjamin Britten and Peter Pears had lived with Mayer for several months in the early phases of the war; now Farrelly introduced her to Barker. Her daughter Ulrica, who was more interested in painting than in music, escorted Barker around the Museum of Modern Art. Farrelly was soon having an affair with Ulrica, with whom he set up house in an apartment in Rutgers Street. Relieving the pressure on the Maases' hospitality, Barker moved in.[20]

Now that *Eros in Dogma* was out in England, Barker set about consolidating his reputation in the States. He negotiated with Dial Press to publish the three Cycles of Love Poems, with the important addition of the fourth, plus a handful of lyrics he had composed over the last few months. The new volume, called simply *Love Poems*, included one or two pieces in a straightforward ballad metre such as 'O that laddie's a long way from home, and long / long may he rest'. The book also contained a translation from Meleager, and a couple of pieces on the theme of sexual immolation. The imagery of these anticipated his 'Ode against St Cecilia's Day' of four years later:

> Who locked you in the shuddering
>   Rock that will rot and die
> The day that you turn your suffering
>   Face away?
>
> Who fixed you in the form from
>   Which like a ghost in a wall
> You look on the workings of a will that
>   Forgives us all . . .
>
> Who rubs our double death together
>   Save procreative fate
> So that we shed the fire, the child, and each other?
>   Turn, turn away your face![21]

The gaze of the woman addressed in this poem brims with power and sacrificial knowledge. Victim though she seems, her apparent submission is the vehicle of a 'procreative fate' which justifies the violence of their mating. Her eyes accuse him, but they also recognise a power greater than either of them: the workings of a biological, arguably of a theological, destiny.

While in Rutgers Street, Barker kept in touch with Elizabeth's children, promising them presents from the New World on his return. 'I saw yesterday a photograph of us all taken in twenty years' time and Christopher was king in the dominion of candies and Georgina had thirteen thousand party dresses with diamonds and pearls about the hem and basher was heavyweight champion of the world.'

Barker still had not made contact with Jessica, but Farrelly, who was well aware of his frustration, and who of course knew that she was living at his family home, took upon himself the role of intermediary. On 31 August, a cable arrived from Pinook at the Maases' at 62 Montague Street: 'Leaving St Louis 7 p.m. Saturday. Pennsylvania Line. Would love to see. Jessica.'[22] They met, but without resolving anything. As Jessica had predicted, she and George had changed irreversibly since their last meeting. The effect had been to drive them into separate, irreconcilable positions: she into her fugitive and cloistered virtue, he into his confusion. As Jessica's religion was increasingly precious to her, divorce was now and would forever be out of the question.

While Barker was away, Elizabeth reconsidered her future. Her material circumstances were somewhat more favourable. In his will, which had recently passed through probate, her father had left her an annuity of $1,200 a year.[23] Henceforth she would have an income of $100 a month on which to keep herself and the children. The legacy did not make her rich, but it did allow her financial independence, as well as permitting a freedom of movement such as she had not enjoyed in the last three years. She decided to take Georgina, Christopher and Sebastian to live in the west of Ireland. On 3 August, whilst sitting with the children in a windswept Battersea Park, she wrote to Barker informing him that she had found a large house in Roundstone, County Galway, opposite the Aran Islands. Hillcrest House, however, was not available until November. Until then she proposed to stay with a Mrs Jane Evans at Ballyrogan House, Ballymoyle, Arklow, County Wicklow. She invited Barker to join them, if he so wished. In Ireland they would be isolated and both of them might concentrate properly on their work. He was very much missed.[24]

The prospect of Ireland invigorated Barker, brought up on Grandma Taaffe's tales of County Meath. Besides, his American jaunt was beginning to seem an unmitigated catastrophe. All that he had achieved, apart from *Love Poems*, was the revival of his rewarding friendship with Farrelly. Now that Jessica was forever lost to him, he decided to join Smart in Wicklow without delay. For the first time, transatlantic air travel was within his means. In mid-September, he booked a flight to Dublin on one of the 'flying clippers' of the Panamerican fleet. On 21 September, he cabled Elizabeth 'See you for tea tomorrow.' In mid-Atlantic he wrote her a letter calling her his 'adored $100 a weeker' and concluding 'it will *natch* surprise you to learn that I love you'.[25] On the afternoon of 22 September Elizabeth and the children met him at the airport. After a couple of days sightseeing in Dublin, they took him to Wicklow. The following week, Barker and Smart were quarrelling again, just as energetically as ever.

CHAPTER 26

'I WON'T MAKE A FUSS'

One of the few fixed points in Barker's turbulent existence over the previous few years had been his relationship with his younger brother Kit, who was now thirty. Still to make his name as a painter, Kit was beginning to develop a style influenced by the surrealists and by George's verse. *Calamiterror* and George's visionary war poetry had inspired his *Surrealist War Composition, 1942,* in which stark, Daliesque figures confronted one another across a bleak battlescape, a gas mask leering in a mockery of a kiss.[1] Kit's other preoccupation was with the ancient civilisation of the Aztecs. Ever since reading Lawrence's *The Plumed Serpent* in their teens, the Barker brothers had been fascinated by the pre-colonial history of Mexico. Kit's painting *The Conquest of Mexico* now hung in the dining room at Stanhope Gardens. David Wright called to see it that winter: he found 'a huge oil canvas, Aztec in theme, inhabited by angular stylized forms and figures picked out in barbaric colour'.[2] Its subject was a panoramic vision of the humbling of the Emperor Montezuma at the hands of Hernando Cortez.[3] While in the States, George's own interest in Central American history had been revived by reading in *Time* of the discovery of Cortez's jewel-encrusted skull in a remote Mexican monastery. He suggested to Kit that they work together on a drama called *The Degradations of Guatemozin,* to depict the humiliation of Montezuma's successor by the *conquistadors.*

One week after Barker had touched down in Ireland, the project had received a stimulus from an unexpected source. At six o'clock on 29 September the BBC launched a new radio network devoted to cultural affairs. As the Corporation's Director-General William Haley announced that evening, the Third Programme was 'intended to cater for the serious attentive listener of all classes'. It would 'broadcast concerts, operas, plays and other works of art in full'. Under its first controller, George Barnes, its producers were free to commission large-scale writing for the medium, since Haley had insisted that the Third's output should be uninterrupted by fixed points such as news bulletins.[4] By 1946 historical verse drama was an accepted radio genre. It occurred to Barker that *The Degradations of Guatomozin* might make a fine radio play.

Barker could already boast some experience of radio work, having scripted a couple of broadcasts before the war.[5] In the first week of October he travelled to London to oversee a half-hour transmission of his verse.[6] Whilst at Broadcasting House, he discussed *The Degradations of Guatemozin* with E.J. King Bull of the Drama Department. He returned to Arklow the following Wednesday, determined to draft the play over the next six weeks. In between writing he would explore the Wicklow countryside and keep watch over Elizabeth's fourth pregnancy, now well advanced.

Barker had always invested a great deal of emotional capital in Ireland. The reality of it proved troubling. The countryside around Arklow was wild and rugged, the weather was wet, windy and bracing and the natives were less forthcoming than he had hoped. In England he had always cherished the idea of his Irishness. In Ireland the inhabitants regarded him as an Englishman. For the whole of his young manhood he had impressed others with a liquid eloquence, a sublime blarney, apparently Celtic in origin. In Arklow the local vernacular was Gaelic, of which he spoke about five words, and the poverty was on a par with that in rural Japan. Though he himself was as short of money as ever, the sight of utter destitution disturbed Barker deeply. The Irish did not consider Smart and Barker to be poor; nor did they consider him to be a fellow countryman.[7]

In these circumstances George and Elizabeth were driven in on one another; arguing interminably, wearyingly, about their finances. The flight from America had cost Barker £70, emptying his bank account. Apart from the broadcasting work, which he seized on with alacrity, there seemed to be no way of replenishing it. At Ballyrogan House they were guests. When in the first week of November they moved with the children to Hillcrest House in Roundstone on the Galway coast, they had once more to find rent. Elizabeth's legacy took care of their immediate needs, but at the cost of Barker's pride since he could not match her income. The disparity made them no fonder of one another.

For the next ten weeks Hillcrest House was their home. A gaunt edifice with a darkened Regency façade, it stood in the centre of Roundstone, near to the circular cromlech which gave the village its name. From it the mean streets radiated outwards. The house, which was without running water, faced a small bay with a shingly beach. To the back of it lay the Twelve Bens, peaks of the Connemara Hills. In front fishing smacks lay at anchor before the distant, mist-wrapped Aran Isles. Here if anywhere was the legendary Ireland which Synge and Yeats had captured for the metropolitan imagination fifty years before. Barker felt that his heart should have soared, but it could raise itself no higher than Synge's had when confronted with a hardy, embittered, mendacious peasantry. At night the village children pelted the doors of Hillcrest House with stones. Besides, there was the constant din of the Atlantic, so close to Barker's sleeping ears. The Atlantic meant America, whence he had just once more fled, and Jessica, who would not have him. Loafing on the narrow foreshore, he looked across Galway Bay, in the hope of descrying the legendary spirits of Erin. Instead, feminine 'effigies' sashayed towards him across the waves. They resembled the 'Amazons' of one of his early poems, but haggard now, grief-stricken, toughened by resentment. Jessica, Elizabeth and Big Mumma were combined:

> With the gulls' hysteria above me
> I walked near these breakneck seas
> This morning of mists, and saw them,
> Tall the mysterious queens,
> Waltzing in on the broad
> Ballroom of the Atlantic.
>
> All veils and waterfalls and
> Wailings of the distraught,
> These effigies of grief moved
> Like refugees over the water;
> The icy empresses of the Atlantic
> Rising to bring me omen.[8]

Barker was in a stunned, disconnected state of mind, between the blue devils and the deep, grey sea. Methedrine, adopted as a minor medicinal pick-me-up, had now become a habit. He had also become dependent on Benzedrine, hacked from the linings of cigarette lighters with a penknife and then dunked in tea. The combination of either drug with alcohol did little to improve his temper. In England and America he had been able to acquire supplies of Methedrine from the pharmacy. In the Republic of Ireland it could only be obtained on medical prescription. Barker had to persuade some hapless doctor that he was ill.

To overcome this difficulty, and also to apply for a bursary from the Society of Authors, he visited London again in mid-November. From Stanhope Gardens he wrote to Elizabeth with emphatic protestations of love. As a grant of £10 a week seemed to be forthcoming, he promised to return instantly with a pittance and 'an olive branch'.[9] His departure, however was delayed by the prospect of more radio work: a second programme was to be devoted to his poetry on the first Sunday in December, so he would need to stay in London to oversee the transmission. The Mexican play, moreover, meant that he would have to confer constantly with Kit and, to facilitate this, George persuaded him to join them in Roundstone. Because George was detained by the impending broadcast, Kit travelled ahead. On his arrival he told Elizabeth that George would be with them soon. When she went to meet him in Dublin, however, leaving Kit and Mary the maid in charge of the children, all she found was a cable announcing that his bursary was 'in the bag' and promising to join her at once. He himself did not appear.

Furious, Smart returned to Galway. She was immediately suspicious. How did she know that his contacts in London were not other than merely professional? She already had doubts about the few days he had spent with her sister Jane in Montreal; his closeness to Farrelly, whom she considered to be much too deep in his affections, was also worrying. Scarcely was she back in Roundstone before their wrangling recommenced in the form of a letter wafting backwards and forwards to London.[10] Elizabeth entered her complaints on the front of the page; George answered on the verso and sent it back to Ireland. The result was an antiphonal correspondence in the form of a letter shuttling backwards and forwards between Hillcrest House and London, of this sort:

There's Nothing left to a relationship like ours if there's no straightforward trust [there's none] It is obvious that you intended to stay in London for a month or more or why would you have Farrelly write you there and send MSS to 23a? Also, why do you deny us to him?

Answer: I don't discuss you with Farrelly.

You can have Jane and anybody else you want. I won't make a fuss. Why should I? I haven't got you myself so I'm glad she has. If you are waiting in London to have a private word, you are merely going to unnecessary inconvenience. Also you alienate me by the sleight-of-hand and double-dealing.

Answer: You are now making a fuss.

To ensure a calmer ambience on his return to Roundstone, Barker felt that a human buffer was required. Kit's presence had been intended to establish neutral terrain. Kit, however, was used to the relative normality of the Taaffe household in Mornington during his regular visits with Big Mumma; besides, as Elizabeth now wrote to George, 'Kit is not happy here. He is restless and bored and my ill-concealed despair isn't much help to him, no matter how hard I try for him.' Reinforcements were evidently needed. While at Stanhope Gardens, George had taken under his wing Monica's twelve-year-old daughter Veronica. Known as Wendy, she was, in December 1946, a sensitive, convent-educated girl with pale, freckled skin and the broad cheekbones of the Barkers. She had been obsessed with babies ever since Pa had made her a 'Wendy House' at the back of Upper Addison Gardens. Barker told her that Smart's delivery was imminent. Since Wendy was keen to be present at the birth of a new cousin, Monica agreed that she should spend a few weeks in Ireland. On 3 December she and George travelled by train to Holyhead, then took the ferry to Dun Laoghaire. During the long bus ride to Galway, he spread his customary verbal spell, talking to his niece in the inspired, wholly attentive way he so often adopted with the very young. As the bus drew close to Roundstone and the Twelve Bens swam up to meet them, George spun yarns about their origins.[11]

The atmosphere at Hillcrest House was tense, even with Kit and Wendy there to ease matters. Georgina, Christopher and Sebastian were the only ones enjoying themselves. They were, however, set apart from the village children by the hand-made clothes sewn for them by Elizabeth; they were also the only children in Roundstone whose hair was free of lice. Through the short afternoons Georgina and Christopher played on the beach under the watchful eye of Mary.[12] Elizabeth hired the village carpenter to knock up a suite of dining-room furniture scaled down to Georgina's requirements. The miniature table and chairs arrived in plain unvarnished wood, but Elizabeth soon brightened them with red and green gloss paint, lending them the garish attractiveness more usually proper to canal boats.

Meanwhile George worked at *The Degradations of Guatemozin*. He was assisted by Kit, who sketched the Aztec Gods Tezeatlpoca and Quetzalcoatl in pen and researched the historical background. Barker had decided that the play should be in five acts, relating Guatemozin's accession, his attempts to outwit the Spaniards, the siege of his mountain capital, his attempted flight, arrest and death. To broaden the play's appeal, he worked into the text parallels with the humiliation of coloured peoples in other times and places. He anachronistically converted Guatemozin himself into a spokesman for five black youths from Alabama, falsely arrested in 1931 for the rape of two white women in the notorious Scottsboro Case. Knowing that he had precisely fifty minutes of air time, Barker read each page aloud against his wristwatch. Eight minutes twenty-one seconds into Act Five, he declaimed Guatemozin's philippic against racial prejudice before his awe-struck niece:

> They die, they die, over my head they die,
> My forefathers returning to perturb me
> With thunder of my conscience. Return, return
> >   Broken Texcatlipoca
> Return to your mirror! Go home,
> >   Admonitory ghosts,
> Your work of castigation is done on me.
> >   I have learned how to die,
> Perceiving my life this evening in the rain
> >   Approaching me,
> The tears clustering at its eyelashes, the robe
> >   Of shame unfolded,
> I speak now to my peace. When death comes up to me
> >   Whose face shall I see?
> I shall see first my own. But, visited behind mine,
> >   Going down a history
> Of progressive degradation, I shall see
> >   All of your faces
> You coloured races who have sighed and expired
> >   On Asiatic altars
> Erected to the greater glory of white Europe;
> >   Who have sighed and died
> >   On African monuments
> Commemorating the crossed skull of empire.
> I shall find your face there, Lobengula,
> >   And you too, garrotted Ataulpa;
> Untouchable the Mahatma who no prison will watch die,
> >   Here, too, in America, where
> They do not belong, gaoled for what crime at Scottsboro,
> >   The five black boys.[13]

This speech lasted forty-four seconds. Progress on the play had been satisfactory, but Kit was finding his position in the household awkward: part historical adviser; part supervisory uncle; part embarrassed spectator of George and Elizabeth's increasingly acrimonious quarrels. If he and Wendy had been intended to put neutral ground between warring lovers, the plan worked fitfully. The intensity of feeling in the house – George's squall-like, inexplicable rages; Elizabeth's proud phases of withdrawal – were manifest to both of their guests: a source of mortification to Kit, who still idolised his older brother, and of plain puzzlement to Wendy. Wendy, for instance, could not work out why her uncle and his friend were spending so long in the bedroom. Were they, she wondered, praying? As hour after hour elapsed without their re-emergence, it seemed to this convent-bred girl, whom Monica had protected from unworthy influences, as if Elizabeth had kidnapped George. Long evenings were spent like this, with Kit and Veronica kicking their heels around the dark corridors of Hillcrest House, unsure what to do with themselves, or with one another. One evening Wendy decided to take a bath in the cavernous, unheated bathroom upstairs and carried up the heated water from the kitchen range below. She did not think to lock the door. When Kit entered to use the lavatory, both of them froze self-consciously. Kit mumbled civil apologies and backed out into the corridor, closing the door softly behind him. The memory of that moment of embarrassment in the echoing, sex-tormented house remained forever with Wendy, epitomising the emotional unease of those weeks.[14]

Christmas was almost upon them. While George and Kit continued with *Guatemozin*, Elizabeth occupied herself making miniatures of Barker's books and Wendy roamed the chilly foreshore, picking up stones on the beach. One bright morning she encountered a young Franciscan walking in his brown habit. They fell deep into conversation. When she returned to Hillcrest, she spoke of the friar to George, who added him to the text of *Of Love*, where a similarly robed cleric is discovered by the protagonist sauntering along the foreshore in Dorset.

Since there was little money to buy Christmas presents, Smart encouraged everybody, including the children, to produce miniature books inscribed with details of their lives. Wendy made hers diligently, like a diary; Kit's was more impressionistic. Traditional Christmas fare was beyond their means. Elizabeth arranged for a ham to be brought in from Galway town on the cart.

The New Year of 1947 offered no respite from the cold, darkness and depression. It had turned out to be one of the bitterest winters on record. The new Third Programme was forced off the air for two weeks to preserve coal stocks. At Hillcrest House the occupants made do with two buckets of water a day hauled overland and used for all domestic purposes: cooking, drinking and washing. In the evenings they sat by candlelight. The wood-fed fire made so little impression that, as Smart wrote to Marie Maas in New York, 'we shiver hungrily in the dark and think we are going mad, which I daresay we are'.[15] When Barker had finished typing his play, he dispatched it to King Bull at Broadcasting House. No cheque was forthcoming. Barker's principal relief was still Methedrine. One afternoon a doctor arrived at Hillcrest House, his attaché case clasped beneath his arm. Shown into Barker's study, he stayed closeted there for what seemed to Wendy to be several hours. When he emerged, Wendy went into the little room, where she found her uncle beaming with apparent happiness. In answer to her questions, he replied that the doctor had given him 'liquid sunshine'.[16]

When the effects of the drug wore off, the squabbling resumed, as did George and Elizabeth's bickering letter, passed now from hand to hand:

Relationships can't be romantic when there's always another contemporary passion going on. What remains – and it does remain – is a Rock of Gibraltar starkness that stands as anything except the indignity and the degradation of petty deceit.

Answer: I find that I am a little old for 'Romantic attachments'. I know you're not, but I'm prematurely cynical in these affairs – thanks to you. Anyhow it's impossible to go on feeling romantic (that revolting word!) about a woman whose only successful love affair is the one she conducts with herself.

After several days of such sparring, Barker travelled alone by bus to fetch supplies from Galway town. The countryside was dreary under the January sky; the fare was five shillings; he missed the evening bus back. On the locked door of the Skeggington Arms he found a crêpe wreath and the announcement that the proprietor's father had died in the early hours of the morning. When he knocked reverently, the maid showed him to his rookery of a room, dismissing her employer's grief with a flip of the hand. 'It is impossible not to notice that the bar is closed all evening,' Barker wrote in his diary. 'I am broke already, tired, famished and utterly lonely.'[17]

On his return to Hillcrest House, he found the fire lit. The warmth did little to distract him from an overwhelming desire to escape. Kit was missing Stanhope Gardens, and had decided to leave for England. With Wendy's connivance, but scarcely with her full understanding, a plan was hatched. On 4 February Wendy and Kit took the bus back to Dublin, crossed the Irish Sea and boarded a train at Holyhead. Barker had given them clear instructions as to what steps to take on reaching London. From Euston station Kit and Wendy walked straight to the nearest post office. With Catholic guilt heavy on their shoulders, they filled in a telegram form with the following, urgent message:

RE: DEGRADATIONS OF GUATEMOZIN. PRESENCE REQUIRED IMMEDIATELY FOR PRE-REHEARSAL CONSULTATIONS AND SCRIPT CONFERENCE. BROOK NO DELAY. AWAITING PROMPT RESPONSE. KING BULL, BROADCASTING HOUSE.[18]

Hardly daring to look one another in the face, Kit and Wendy counted the words, paid and dispatched the telegram to Galway. As soon as he received it, Barker showed it to Elizabeth. He packed his bags, kissed the children goodbye and set off for the bus station. He reached London the following night. Two weeks later, at 4.03 a.m. on Tuesday, 18 February 1947, his daughter Rose Maximiliane was born at Hillcrest House.

PART THREE

1947–63

O stop the calling killer in the skull
   Like beasts we turn toward!
For was the nightriding siren beautiful
Caterwauling War until her bed was full
   Of the uxorious dead?
Let the great moaners of the seven seas
   Let only the seas mourn,
With the shipwrecked harp of creation on their knees
   Till Cecilia turns to a stone.

        George Barker, 'Ode Against St Cecilia's Day'

CHAPTER 27

CASSIOPEIA

Barker did not return to Roundstone. Instead, he stayed at Stanhope Gardens and took stock. His achievements were undeniably accumulating. He had recently published his seventh book; he had news of the birth of his seventh child. Yet he was sick to death of all the changes in his life. For years he had been moving from pillar to post, with no permanent home of his own. He was tossed between two women, with neither of whom could he live successfully, though neither seemed fully prepared to let him go. In the meantime he was obliged to stay with Big Mumma and an exasperated Pa. In his worst moments it seemed to him as if he and Kit – to whom he remained devoted – were still at the beginning of life's journey, with all still to be done. In Galway that January he had scribbled in his notebook words that spoke shrilly of his mood at the time: 'Heavenly father, this meaningless hegira from dissatisfaction to disappointment and back again. I shall die of exposure soon if my own house evades me much longer.'

Perhaps because his life seemed sometimes so shapeless, he was increasingly drawn towards established poetic structures. He had already cut his teeth on the sonnet and shown his control over the contrapuntal possibilities of free verse. There remained, however, the untried territory of longer traditional forms. The verse of *Eros in Dogma* had attracted widespread praise; the style in which it had been written, however, was coming to appear baroque, convoluted, encrusted like a skin that needed to be shed. Barker longed for tightness and precision. On 26 February 1947 he wrote a poem for his thirty-fourth birthday, part celebration and part resolution. It was in the shape of a sestina, its six rotating line endings chiming through each stanza:

> I am at midday. Bells rage in the stone
> Arch of the chest. The sky wears my handmark

> Where I have held it. Summer the avenue
> Here where Alighieri started a hotter journey,
> Summer more suffering, manhood beating the shoulders,
> Than any winter or April. And on the pavements
>
> Fate, photographer, fixing his handwork;
> Recording, for ever, in image along the avenue
> The lies and the lives we lived. This is a journey
> Dollied by the unsleeping eye. No head and shoulders
> Shunning the sinning loin, but, naked as pavements,
> Every step stopped a monument in stone.[1]

Disruption made him long for peace. One snow-softened evening that February he attended a fund-raising event for *Poetry London*, held by Tambimuttu at the Hog in the Pound pub in South Molton Street in Mayfair. There he met a 22-year-old aspiring writer from Cheshire called Betty Cass. Betty worked as a film cutter at Denham Studios and lived in Belsize Park Gardens. For eighteen months she had been going out with Bruce Bernard, whom she had met in Piccadilly Circus during the festivities for VJ Night. That evening, however, she was alone. At first Barker appeared to mistake her for the American novelist Betty Smith, author of *A Tree Grows in Brooklyn*.[2] She did not know whether this was a hoax; she first played up to her supposed role, then disabused him. When, a few days later, he met her again, she was drinking with Bernard, who reluctantly made a formal introduction. They exchanged phone numbers. Over the following weeks Barker wooed her with words. He spent hours in public houses, relating to her the drama of his love triangle. He was relentlessly harsh towards Elizabeth, with whom he said he had broken up. Jessica he spoke of as a fragile victim on whom he had visited dreadful pain. Since Betty subscribed to a liberal philosophy of personal relations in which children played no part, he made no mention of the existence of his seven offspring. After several days of these *tête a têtes*, they met Dylan Thomas in the Swiss pub, and Barker introduced her to him. 'You're not *another* one of Barker's gorgeous women, are you?' Thomas asked her. 'Where on earth does he *get* you all from?' She felt that she was in thrall to an enchanter: as his spell took hold, it was soon impossible to break loose.

Betty Cass possessed an open-faced, delicate, very English style of beauty. She was chic and articulate, with a flair for brightening second-hand clothes – made necessary by the prevailing climate of austerity – by a single dash of vivid colour. While regarding herself as immature, she appeared self-contained in the eyes of others. Though soft-spoken, she possessed a will almost – but not quite – a match for Barker's own. Jessica had cured him of clinging women.

Betty by contrast had a broadmindedness that suited him, a curiosity about, and openness towards, what in 1947 it was still possible to call 'free love'. Barker immediately noticed in her a fetching mixture of poise and adventurousness: a rare combination in the bohemian London of the late 1940s, where surface brashness was often seen as the hallmark of emancipation. Attracted by excess, he was also drawn towards inhibition: towards Kit in his shyness; Archer hobbled by diffidence; David Wright immured in his deafness; Heath-Stubbs behind the camouflage of his near-blindness. He had striven in vain to protect Jessica. Elizabeth he had now defied. Betty he was both to protect and to defy. She must have seemed, that fraught and confining winter, the ideal solution to his problems. She was the *tabula rasa* upon which he would write what he chose.

He began by re-inventing her in an image of his own devising. She had been christened Betty Pauline Cass. By 1947, however, as Barker was later to confirm, he had known too many Bettys or Elizabeths. He took her surname and lengthened it either to 'Cashenden' or – more orotundly – to 'Cassiopeia', with 'Cass' remaining as a familiar diminutive. By the end of 1947 she would re-emerge as 'Cashenden Cass'.

Barker was rather older than her previous boyfriends and she rather younger than his former women. He placed himself in the role of her tutor, coaching and coaxing her towards his own ways of thinking and acting. He even persuaded her to alter her handwriting, so as to bring it closer to his italic script. Though theoretically emancipated, she was as yet inexperienced in sexual relations – Barker undertook her education. Her landlord in Hampstead, accommodating in all other respects, had his doubts about this aspect of the curriculum so, to complete the seduction, Barker acquired a bedsit in Chelsea.

It turned out, however, that they had different expectations of their roles. As an aspiring writer and consort to a poet, Cass believed that she should preserve their relationship in words, as after all Elizabeth had done. Accordingly she began to keep a journal. But the unblushing exposure of his private life in *By Grand Central Station* which, since its publication in August 1945 had been enjoying something of a *succès d'estime*, had exhausted Barker's patience with this sort of exposure. One evening, when he and Cass were together in her room in Belsize Park, he discovered the notebook and commanded her to stop writing in it forthwith. Cass had not the confidence in her talent that Elizabeth had possessed and so she complied.

Cass had thought that under the new liberal dispensation women were expected to behave with as casual a freedom as their menfolk. Accordingly, after their first session of lovemaking, she swept out of his bedsit with an airy 'See you sometime, then.' Barker, however, considered such offhandedness to be a male prerogative; he was also used to protestations of undying devotion from his women. Affronted by Cass's seeming indifference, he vanished for the next three weeks.[3] When he contacted her again, he was to speak of far-flung places in Cornwall.

In the interval Barker had opted for seclusion and male friendship. For the previous four years W.S. Graham had been living in Mevagissey on the south Cornish coast with his consort Nessie Dunsmuir. Archer had suggested that Barker spend the summer of 1947 in Mevagissey, where he rented a room for him down the road from Graham's tiny fisherman's cottage. Barker had decided to share it with Michael Asquith, who had recently returned from serving with the Friends' Ambulance Unit in Greece. Barker accompanied him down to Cornwall in April.

From London too, with a typewriter and the beginnings of a novel, came a 26-year-old aspiring writer called Ilse Gross, the daughter of a vintner from Bingen in the Rhineland. Ilse had lost her family in Hitler's camps. After secondary education at a school in Geneva, she had come to London, where she had spent the last few years working with various voluntary groups. She was wearied by the war and much in need of simple, unthinking relaxation, as so many Londoners were by then. She took lodgings in the same street as the Grahams, with whom she ate most of her meals. In Mevagissey she found a community of young artists and writers, all endeavouring to wrest some pleasure and purpose from the respite from austerity afforded by this slate-roofed and huddled place, with its lovely stretch of bay.

After the spiritual and physical cramp of the war, Barker revelled in the relief afforded by peacetime Cornwall.[4] David Wright came down for several days and swam in the sea, from which his shaggy, prematurely white head would emerge, flowing with foam. Archer was a frequent visitor, serious and preoccupied, even when pursuing attractive lads through the surf. They lived on monkfish, discarded by the fisherman who had used them as bait to catch pilchards. One evening Barker wrote a wonderful 'Sonnet of Fishes', in which he described himself blundering home at daybreak with cold pilchards in his pocket. He imagined the individual fish at the moment of its capture, unable to comprehend its fate: 'Death, in a dark, in a deep, in a dream, forever.'[5]

In W.S. Graham, Barker had found a spirit and temperament akin to his own. Sydney Graham (or 'Jock', as he was known to his friends) was a lanky and gentle man, with hands like a docker's. He was drawn to inanimate objects and their intricacies – to flutes, watches, fishing nets – references to which studded his poems. He and Barker were both determined outsiders, outlanders, Celtic autodidacts in a literary world dominated by a university-educated Anglo-Saxon intelligentsia, of which they wanted little part. Archer had published both of their initiatory volumes. Both were also writing in an idiom of baroque, muscular grandeur, from which in years to come a leaner and more direct style would emerge. Both were addicted to Benzedrine, and both had women whom they tended to treat as muses. For both poetry was a matter of wilful and sustained control over feelings that, if not expressed in this way, might well destroy the intellect that strove to harness them. The frankness of their conversation – affectionate, brusque, barbed – is caught in a sonnet that Barker wrote to Graham at the time:

> Jock, you with a golden fleece on your sleeve,
> Where's the heart, man, for the egoed sea to shatter
> Sea against rock of heart?[6]

To Ilse, George seemed the wildest creature in this intemperate menagerie. In the Mevagissey pubs, rendering his songs or delivering brilliant one-liners, she thought he resembled a capped Irish labourer; on the beach, torso bared against the sea breezes, a Greek God. When she had finished typing Jock's poems, she would go and see him. He pinned her down with his piercing blue eyes and spoke of his condition of irredeemable dereliction, of his brother Kit whom he had half-blinded, and of the spiritual orthodoxies which he had violated, but which alone enabled him to make sense of his condition. 'I am a religious maniac,' he told her.[7] Ilse was not convinced by the mania, and reserved her judgement about the religion. Between them, as Asquith observed, there was an electric tension of opposites, something rational and clear-headed in Ilse resisting the intrusion of so much narcissistic *angst*. After his many shifts and changes, Barker had, by and large, dispensed with the disguise of mere civility. Or, to put it another way, candour had come to seem to him the final, least penetrable disguise. In Cornwall he let his anguish show with a bravura as candid and urgent as his poems.

The word was now spreading in London that Cornwall was the place to be. Quite independently, late that same spring, Kit was invited by his friend Bill Mackenzie to accompany him to Zennor on the wild north coast. They drove down in an old Ford, which Mackenzie had undertaken to deliver to a mutual acquaintance, the painter Bryan Wynter. Kit and Mackenzie stayed briefly with Wynter at his cottage, the Carn, situated on the rugged escarpment between Zennor and St Ives. Driving onwards through Newlyn on the south coast, they discovered a deserted sail loft above the harbour, which could be theirs for a weekly rent of five shillings. They took it for the summer, agreeing to share it with the painter Graham Court and an absent-minded friend called David Duff. Monica sold a luxurious set of French underwear, a gift from her husband, to enable Kit to move there. He had soon put his mark upon the place, painting a carpet on the bare boards in lieu of a floor covering and draping sails across the beams. In one corner he placed his precious spinet, on which of an evening he would play Elizabethan pavannes and fantasias by Purcell.[8] Kit's painting was now developing out of its pre-war surrealist phase. Up at the Carn Wynter was painting seagulls, dead and alive; Kit too now learned to take his subjects from the natural world around him.

While Kit settled in at Newlyn, George moved backwards and forwards between Mevagissey and London. In London he continued to see Cass; he also saw Robert Colquhoun and MacBryde, who, still enjoying considerable public acclaim, had temporarily moved down to Sussex thanks to Frances Byng Stamper, director of the art-oriented Miller's Press, who had decided that they needed more studio space. Byng had hired a floor for them above an ancient gatehouse at Lewes. One Saturday in May, when George was up from Mevagissey, he and Cass accompanied the Roberts to their new studio by train. On the platform at Victoria Station MacBryde picked up an outrageously camp homosexual by the name of Binkie. He was, as Cass remembers, 'all Max Factor pancake make-up, flouncing hips and vaselined eyelids'. The countryside was a mass of primroses; Binkie created a posy. That evening, Cass remembers, 'there was a dance being held at the town hall and, mostly out of boredom, we went'. She and Binkie took to the floor, where 'he threaded a garland of primroses in my hair, and then tucked what remained behind his ear & thus we danced'.[9] MacBryde was inclined to jealousy, but 'couldn't really manage to work up a scene'.

Back in London George received a set of editorial comments on *The Degradations of Guatemozin* from Eliot, to whom he had submitted the script in advance of transmission. Eliot conceded that the play was well crafted for its intended medium, but his remarks on its diction possessed a characteristic terseness:

Page 14: *I have a kind of replete:* Look up 'replete' in the Dictionary.

page 15: *And let her wear Mexico on her undershirt:* I don't know of any female garment that is ever described as an undershirt.

p. 18. *Whose brew is so lascivious:* I don't think that the adjective lascivious should be applied to a drink. You mean, I assume, arouses lasciviousness.[10]

Eliot strongly advised that the analogy drawn in the play between Spanish colonialism and the Scottsboro Case was misconceived: 'I don't think it would occur to any American negro that his people did not belong in America. The American negro who wants to go back to Central Africa must be a very rare exception indeed.'[11] On Saturday, 10 May, after minor modifications, *The Degradations of Guatemozin* opened the evening's broadcasting on the Third Programme. It was one of the hottest days of an exceptionally fine summer and the temperature outside was Mexican. 'Shutting our eyes against the afternoon glare,' Philip Hope-Wallace wrote afterwards in the *Listener*, 'we tried to visualize Aztecs in decline.' The listening public had not been helped by the fact that, in his anxiety to secure social differentiation, King Bull had encouraged the ranks of the Spanish and Aztec armies to speak in broad cockney accents. Nor, continued Hope-Wallace, had Barker's latinisms, or his habit of inversion, helped. By the time Cortez remarked in Act III, 'Ah, he remembers the dissimulation Montezuma died in a puzzle of', the assiduous listener had forgotten the cause of the original dissimulation, or that Montezuma had ever dissimulated, or to whom. Hope-Wallace's misgivings over the production, and Eliot's strictures on the text, may well have affected Barker: at any rate, he never tried to have the play published.

Barker stayed for some time in London on this occasion, since Cass had announced that she was pregnant. Cass had earlier told him that she was not eager to have babies; childlessness set you free. In view of this reluctance, which she was later to feel less strongly, George was not insistent that she have the child and she, despite inbred misgivings, finally resolved that she should not. They decided on a termination at a clinic in Wigmore Street. 'I was', Cass recalls, 'completely devastated and terrified by the need to do this even though I believed it was right. A Puritan background is just as guilt-inducing as a Catholic one, though George would never acknowledge this.' The operation cost £60 of which he borrowed £30, arriving with the money late in the day. After the operation Cass asked the woman doctor to fit her with a diaphragm, to the relief of Barker, whose reaction was 'Well, now we can fuck a lot without worrying about you getting pregnant.' 'Even now', Cass said fifty years later, 'I feel a kick of anger, yes in the womb or very close to it, and the abortion did come back to haunt us: we were *both* haunted by it.'[12] The incident was to sour their relationship to the end.

Much though Barker attempted to take this episode in his stride, his poetry suggests that he had been troubled by it. Abortion, after all, was a practice to which Roman Catholic teaching was unambiguously opposed. By 1947, however, he seems to have become convinced that each man or woman must make his or her own moral decisions. Taking stock of his solitude while striving to transcend his aloneness through poetry, he wished a heroic stoicism for himself and encouraged this fortitude in others. Such an attitude is evident in his poetry of the time, in which the rhetoric of his pre-war verse hardens into a stony repose, reminiscent of Roman statuary, or of the torsos by Mestrović he had admired as a young man. There is a bitter integrity to much of his writing at this time, such as Heath-Stubbs had taught him to admire in the Italian poet Leopardi, who had battled all his life against sickness and blindness. Suddenly, determinedly, Barker was shearing the excrescences from his verse. In Tambimuttu's *Poetry London* he published a 'Memorial Inscription':

> O Leopardi! O Lion-pawed Seas!
> Give tongue, give tongue against, again
> The mistress of all miseries
> The master of all mysteries.
> O Lion-pawed heart! O voices of stone!
> Shatter the tabernacle in which we grieve,
> Crack the mad jacket in which we rejoice
>   Alive for ever alone.[13]

Barker was determined to break free from or else to redeem his recent history. History, however, had a nasty habit of following him. With her four children, including the still unweaned Rose, Elizabeth had decided to leave Ireland. Through her sister Jane, she learned that the poet and now art critic Ruthven Todd had been in New York since mid-January, completing a catalogue of Blake's drawings and paintings. Tilty Mill, his home near Dunmow in Essex, was unoccupied, his bibliophiliac collection at the mercy of vermin and thieves. Since Todd's research seemed likely to detain him indefinitely in America, Elizabeth undertook to occupy Tilty for a peppercorn rent, paid in dollars by her sister Jane. She arrived in late June with a pile of boxes, the children and a pram, letting George know that they were in Essex if he cared to visit them.[14] The following week George set off by bus for Thaxted. He was going, he told Cass, 'to fetch my boxes'. In Tilty Mill he first set eyes on his baby daughter, Rose. When he returned to London he explained to Cass that he did not think that he would need to visit Tilty Mill again.[15]

Perhaps inevitably under the circumstances, Barker seemed prone to fits of erotic paranoia. On his return to Mevagissey he and Asquith dined with the Grahams one evening. During the meal Nessie related an anecdote with what seemed to Barker unnecessary animation. Misinterpreting her vivacity as a ploy to gain his attention, he turned to Asquith and murmured, 'She's a whore.'[16]

In July Asquith had word that his father was seriously ill in Bath. Since Michael would now have to leave their cottage in Mevagissey, Barker wrote to Cass telling her that he was moving in to the Sail Loft in Newlyn with Kit, and inviting her to join them. Accordingly, Cass gave in her notice at Denham Studios and moved down to Cornwall. The loft, she discovered, had magnificent views over Mount's Bay. Beneath its windows, the harbour hummed. Gulls flapped at the open windows. Universal poverty prevailed. Cass found a haphazard community of residents: Kit played Purcell; Mackenzie tinkered with his motorbike; Duff shared out food packets received from home. In the meantime, Barker continued to make forays to London, on which Cass was not asked to accompany him. One afternoon, without telling his co-tenants, Kit caught the bus to Mevagissey to see Ilse. When Archer visited the loft, he slept on a rough-and-ready hammock made out of a sail. He oozed gently out of it as he slept, waking in a heap on the floor.

Cass, however, soon realised that unpredictable forms of etiquette accompanied the freedom of this strange milieu. Her companions, for example, seemed to possess a limited tolerance for departures from an implied bohemian norm. Cass's parents, who were concerned about her well being now that she had given up her job at the studio, sent her a cheque for ten shillings. Shortly afterwards, during one of George's forays to London, Duff announced that his shoes were stranded at the cobbler's, since he could not afford the bill; Cass spent 7s 6d of her ten shillings redeeming them. She discovered her mistake when Barker returned. Gifts of money were to be spent on beer at the Fisherman's Rest or Tolcarne or else on food rather than on bourgeois accoutrements like footwear. Cass's unthinking act of kindness towards her fellow tenant was immediately interpreted by George as proof of betrayal. She did not possess the experience, or the nerve, to attribute her lover's reaction to mere touchiness. Instead she repented and determined to improve.[17]

In the Newlyn pubs Barker was in his element: playing tunes on an imaginary violin hunched against his shoulder, joining with Kit in rounds of 'The Royal Blackbird'. He was now famous, if rootless. With the members of the Auden set dispersed and Auden himself in America, with the New Apocalypse over and the Dylan Thomas legend still to come, there was a gap in the poetic firmament which Barker could fill. Even his vices were briefly in vogue. That August, Geoffrey Grigson published an incisive pamphlet entitled *Polemic No 7*. In it he attacked Barker, Thomas and Edith Sitwell as loose rhetoricians. To set against them and their work, Grigson proposed an ideal of poetry as 'coherence of rhythm within the variations of a scheme, coherence of form, and poetry as rhyme'. In the next editorial of *Poetry London* Tambimuttu rode to the defence of the assailed poets. He argued for a counter-aesthetic of conscious verbal enjoyment, of hedonistic wordplay, above all of the pun. 'Punning', Tambi declared, 'is the oldest and most pervasive device in poetry from Tamil to Welsh and Anglo-Saxon . . . Punning is the onomatopoeia of meaning.'[18]

Since London was thinking this way, Barker announced his intention to move back there with Cass. Apart from Kit, the other occupants of the Sail

Loft were to move as well. On the evening of their departure from Newlyn, the luckless Duff set his hair alight on the paraffin stove; George extinguished him. The following morning, after the others had left, Ilse moved into the Sail Loft with Kit.

CHAPTER 28

'THIS TEMPERATE OCTOBER'

Barker's sexual attitudes were not untypical of the time. During the war the sexes had enjoyed a measure of equality undreamed of before; by September 1947, however, this egalitarianism was in sharp decline. The weekly magazine *Picture Post* complained that the 'New Look', recently launched by Christian Dior in Paris, was forcing women into restrictive skirts. The war had seen Smart writing fiction and Monica Barker driving ambulances. By 1947 it became possible once more to insist that literature, like industry, was essentially a male preserve. George had been obliged to concede Elizabeth a certain licence in this respect. He preferred to cast the more malleable Cass, chic and *gamine*, in the role of poet's Moll. Cass was not permitted to work or to drive. At first she was not even allowed to write. Before the war Barker had expressed admiration for the work of the American poet Marianne Moore, whom Faber published in London. In defiance of this earlier attitude, he now insisted belatedly that the authorship of verse belonged to men. Poetry should be sinewy and virile, its syntax almost jagged, its sentiments stark. Forgoing the sexually ambiguous voice in which he had written some of his most potent verse, he invented for himself a mask which was exclusively, some thought repugnantly, male.

In October Barker took a bedsit at 3 Clanricarde Mansions in Bayswater, where he introduced Cass to the landlord as 'my wife'. From Bayswater he strolled daily through Kensington Palace Gardens to Stanhope Gardens. He drank with Cass in the Old Swan in Kensington Church Street, where their companions were Heath-Stubbs, Wright, Bruce Bernard and the Roberts when they were in town. On many evenings the South African poet Roy Campbell – Catholic, deeply reactionary, deeply cantankerous – limped in from his lodgings nearby. One day in the saloon bar Bruce Bernard introduced George to his sixteen-year-old brother Jeffrey, who was wearing the officer cadet's uniform of the Naval College, Pangbourne. Already Jeff excelled in the lugubrious comedy of despair: decades later he would exploit this mood in his celebrated 'Low Life' columns in the *Spectator*, in one of which he was to recall, 'George Barker was teasingly and affectionately referred to as "the Master". He liked that . . . He threw me in at the deep end, so to speak, by giving me a volume of poems by Ezra Pound.'[1] At his naval college Jeff had received six of the best for saying 'Fuck'; in the Swan he found a setting where he could swear with impunity and in Barker a friend at whom he could swear with conviction. One morning Barker took him down to his branch of Barclay's Bank in South Kensington. Drawing out three pounds, an average weekly wage at the time, he handed them over without explanation. Jeff found this generosity welcome, but uncharacteristic. It was certainly never repeated. When term resumed, he took a photograph of Cass back to Pangbourne, where he stuck it to the inside lid of his desk.[2]

Barker's swagger in his everyday dealings required a poetic persona to go with it. He had been reading John Heron Lepar's translation of *Le Grand Testament* by François Villon, fifteenth-century miscreant and priest-slayer, whom Eliot considered the supreme medieval French lyricist. Barker was as impressed, even from the evidence of translation, by the figure skating of its rigorous yet subtle stanza as by its tone of moral candour. He had long been prone to conversational confession, but literary confession – a very different matter – necessitated a mask behind which the poet might speak with assumed forthrightness. He was fast losing faith in free verse, which, as Eliot had demonstrated, was a contradiction in terms for the serious poet. Looking for a model of tight stanzaic organisation which would yet leave him free to speak his mind, it occurred to him that Villon's *Testaments* might suit his needs. In October, after a bad cold, and the septicemia of the throat to which this always seemed to lead, he launched on a testament of his own, couched in what he hoped was a fair imitation of Villon's ballade stanza:

> Today, recovering from influenza,
>   I begin, having nothing worse to do,
> This autobiography that ends a
>   Half of my life I'm glad I'm through.
> O Love, what a bloody hullaballoo
>   I look back at, shaken and sober,
> When that intemperate life I view
>   From this temperate October.
>
> To nineteen hundred and forty-seven
>   I pay the deepest of respects,
> For during this year I was given
>   Some insight into the other sex.

> I was the victim, till forty-six,
>   Of the rosy bed with bitches in it;
> But, now in spite of all pretexts,
>   I never sleep a single minute.[3]

Barker knew little modern French, let alone medieval French, and he assumed that the *ballade* was an open-ended form in which one might expand at one's leisure. He was aiming at the colloquial freedom which Auden had allowed himself in his 'Letter to Lord Byron' of 1937, famously written after a similar attack of flu. Auden's stanza had been *rhyme-royal*, a form 'large enough to swim in', chosen because of its relative closeness to the *ottava rima* of Byron's *Don Juan*. Barker had been encouraged by the chattiness and verve, both of Byron's poem and of Auden's. His problem was that the *ballade* is a closed form, whose completion requires an *envoi* to round it off. No such closure was envisaged by Barker, who wanted to extend his verse letter *ad infinitum* if necessary. *The True Confession* was to be posted to the reader in instalments, without even the author knowing at what stage he might wish to sign off. Something of the scurrility of *Don Juan* was also to be incorporated. In Byron's poem, the narrator is all-knowing, while the Don is *naïf*. In *The True Confession*, narrated in the first person, Barker presents himself as corrupt, with occasional visions of innocence. The poem hovers between these two positions, wresting its adopted stanza to the requirements of its volatile speaker, a compound of Byron, Don Juan, Villon, Graham Greene's Pinkie and St Augustine. *The True Confession* was to be a profoundly Catholic poem as well as a brazenly exhibitionist one. Its cynicism was to be the lip-service paid by depravity to holiness. There was to be something at once lacerating and reverent about it.

Barker's detailed confessing went only so far; naïve biographical interpretation of the poem, therefore, misses the point. *The True Confession* is far more concerned with a theology of human sexuality than with any particular relationship. At least two passages – the description of 'the act of human procreation' at the end of the first section, and the evocation in section five of the deity, 'Standing lonely as a mourner / Silent in the bedroom corner' – echo paragraphs in Barker's prose-work-in-progress, still entitled *Of Love*. The most moving sequence of all, a lullaby-lament in section three, alludes to the emotional isolation of Elizabeth. It is also a dirge for Jessica, and for their daughter Clare, metaphorically stillborn:

> I sent a daughter to my love
>   In a painted cradle.
> She took her up at her left breast
> And rocked her to a mothered rest

> Singing a song that what is best
> Loves and loves and forgets the rest.
> I sent a daughter to my love
>   In a painted cradle.
>
> I sent a letter to my love
>   on a sheet of stone.
> She looked down and as she read
> She shook her yellow hair and said
> Now he sleeps alone instead
> Of many a lie in many a bed.
> I sent a letter to my love
>   On a sheet of stone.[4]

Barker found physical movement helped him to compose the poem. His need to see Smart and their children provided a pretext for this. Despite his protestations to Cass, from late autumn 1947 through to early spring 1948 he commuted between London and Tilty on a fairly regular basis. The bus journey to Thaxted took just over an hour: time enough for one carefully turned stanza. Barker adopted a routine of completing one stanza on the way and another on the return journey. By this means the seven sections of the poem were written between October and February. On Thursday, 26 February, 1948, his thirty-fifth birthday, Barker phoned Heath-Stubbs. He summoned him to 3 Clanricarde Mansions, where he read the poem out to him in its entirety.[5]

The garrulous mask of the poem was far from identical with Barker's social persona. As Jeffrey Bernard was quick to note, Barker had moments of reticence, of tact, even of grace. He could also be faultlessly polite. Already his growing fame was causing him to be taken up by high society. The Sitwells, for example, greatly valued his company. At Easter 1946 he had attended one of Edith's celebrated lunches at the Sesame Club in Mayfair, where his fellow guests had been her brother Osbert, Mr and Mrs Louis MacNeice, Mr and Mrs Henry Moore, and the publisher John Lehmann. In December that year the magnanimous Osbert had successfully sponsored him for a two-year bursary of £200 per annum, granted by Hodder & Stoughton. The attack launched by Geoffrey Grigson in *Polemic* 7 on both their reputations had now consolidated his friendship with Edith into an alliance. On 10 December, 1947 she contacted him from Renishaw Hall, her ancestral home near Scarborough, asking him to lunch with her at the Sesame on the 18th. He promptly replied by telegram: 'Eighteenth with pleasure. Letter posted to you this morning.' As Sitwell's biographer Victoria Glendinning remarks, the 'liking for patronage of promising young artists was strong in Edith; she took pleasure in encouraging young (male) poets and fostering young (male) talent'.[6] For Barker, however, the impression of her generosity was eclipsed by her undeniable physical plainness. One evening, many years later, he was to confide in Jeff his personal remedy against premature ejaculation: 'I wait until I become *unbearably* excited. Then, with a *peculiar* mental ferocity, I concentrate upon the visual image of Miss – Edith – *Sitwell*.'[7]

In March 1948 Osbert sponsored Barker again, this time for a Somerset Maugham Award, granted by the Society of Authors to enable young writers to travel abroad. He decided to take Cass to the French village of Collioure, in the Pyrenées Orientales. Collioure was a pretty village, popular with painters since being discovered earlier in the century by André Derain and the Fauvistes. The painter Bryan Wynter, whom he had met in Cornwall, had also spent part of 1947 there. Barker's own motives for choosing this destination were mixed. Roy Campbell, who claimed to have fought for Franco, had revived his interest in bull-fighting, evident since *Elegy on Spain*. Being in a Catalan area, Collioure was one of the few towns in southern France where the authorities permitted the Spanish form of the fight, in which the bull is killed, as opposed to the French variety, in which the animal is merely decorated with rosettes.

In mid-May Barker and Cass travelled down by train. En route they stayed in Paris, where Didy Asquith was then living, following her break-up with Michael. Didy, who had been informed of Barker's itinerary by Elizabeth, went to their hotel, where the concierge phoned up to the bedroom. Tired after the journey, and suspecting a plot by Elizabeth, George sent Cass downstairs in his stead.[8] The two women, strangers to one another, retired to the Café Flore, where Didy told Cass about Elizabeth's children, of whom she had until that moment only a hazy notion. Later in the evening George joined them. After George and Cass had left for the south, Didy wrote to Elizabeth. She reported that the couple seemed devoted; but she doubted that Cass had the stamina to last the course.

In Collioure George and Cass frequented the Café des Sports, presided over by its art-loving patron René Pouce, and his swarthy son Jojo. The walls were hung with minor paintings by Picasso and Matisse, donated by the artists in settlement of their bills. The habitués, who took George and Cass to their hearts, gave them the nickname of 'les beaux sauvages'. For Barker, however, the real attraction of the region was the bull-fight. He had been reading Hemingway's *Death in the Afternoon* and revelled in the lore and history of the sport. He and Cass witnessed a gruelling contest with a stout Muerta bull at nearby Béziers. Afterwards Barker spent many hours illustrating episodes from the history of the matadors in the spilt beer on his tabletop at the café. He rehearsed with obliging Catalan enthusiasts the fate of Manolete, who, three seasons before, had been gored to a lingering death in the ring at Linares.

The subject brought out all of his inbred feeling for ritual, his suspicion that all tragedies are sacrificial and all sacrifices tragic. Long ago he had read in Sir James Frazer's *The Golden Bough* of the cult of the Persian bull-god Mithras, who was regularly depicted sacrificing a bull, or himself being sacrificed in bull form. He knew that man may venerate the beast even as he slays it. He wrote an elegiac sonnet for Manolete, phrased in a new staccato style. Each of its short phrases suggested a stab wound, such as had once despatched the bull-god, or the impalement of Manolete by which the bull had its revenge. The priest turns victim:

> You, king, die. Mithra. Where was death
> Hiding for those ten hours when you lay
> Endowing Linares with that great red legend?
> The Monster. Dead. Drag the bright corpse away.[9]

Barker came to regard bull-fighting and authorship as kindred activities. In any case the writing of verse was a sure test of virility. In April, shortly before his departure from England, Faber had forwarded to him a letter from Anthony Thwaite, a seventeen-year-old pupil at the Kingswood School, Bath. Thwaite enclosed one of his own poems, an improvisation on a single line from *Calamiterror* entitled 'Variation on a Theme by George Barker'. In Collioure, he received another letter from Thwaite, who enquired breathlessly, 'Am I a poet? Do you think I am any good?' When Barker eventually replied, he adopted a man-to-man tone. 'As for the poems themselves,' he wrote, 'nothing more than for gods sake give it up or for gods sake go on. I repeat that I think you should water your muse regularly and since there's more mandrake than man in her, I suggest you use blood.'[10]

The friendship of the drinkers at the Café des Sports was not matched by the co-operation of officialdom. In 1948 Europe was still not free of wartime currency restrictions. Barker had managed to take half the bursary with him. When the remainder arrived without exchange clearance, the village postmaster refused to release it. He also confiscated Barker's passport until the documentation was in order. Eventually all the papers arrived, save one form. Still the money was witheld. A delegation from the Café des Sports set out for the post office. On arriving they protested that this attitude was an insult to a distinguished foreign personage. The money was released and, with it, George's passport.

Barker and Cass arrived back in London on 2 July to find Stanhope Gardens in turmoil. In the midst of it stood Kit, flushed with embarrassment and wearing George's only suit. He explained that he had recently exhibited his first two pictures and was about to get married to Ilse. At the brief ceremony at Holborn Register Office the register was signed by the Labour MP Fenner Brockway, a friend of the bride. Back at Stanhope Gardens the reception heaved with members of the family and friends, who included many of the Cornwall contingent and the Roberts. Late in the afternoon Eileen's husband took a group photograph on the balcony overlooking the gardens. In it are the chief members of this exuberant band: Maurice Carpenter, self-effacing; Monica older now and with her hair up; Cass in her summer sweater and skirt; David Wright loftily trailing a cigarette while towering over Eileen; Kit and Ilse, neither quite daring to look at the camera. George is demonstrating Carpenter's bass flute to nephew John, who stands on a chair behind him. Pa is expansive and commanding, Veronica pre-adolescent and self-conscious. At the very front sits Big Mumma in her gold lamé blouse, broad-shouldered and smiling. Later Barker was photographed alone attempting to play Carpenter's flute, whilst smoking a cigar.

Kit and Ilse had moved from the Sail Loft in Newlyn. They were now living at Noon Veor, a constricted stone-roofed cottage overlooking Zennor church tower and a triangle of sea beyond. David Wright had been staying with them and helping with the £1 a month rent. He would later recall the cottage's location in a slight declivity, 'under a hill / and skyline of a moor'. Young John, who had been footloose in London, had cycled down to join them. Others followed after the wedding: first Heath-Stubbs and then, predictably, George and Cass.

The cottage had one bedroom, which was squeezed into the roof cavity. In the congestion tempers ran short. Money ran even shorter. Soon, to Ilse's undisguised relief, the friends began to disperse to other cottages nearby. Opposite the Tinner's Arms, Zennor's only pub, stood 1 The Row. Since it was unoccupied, George used his charm and tales of homelessness to persuade the landlady to let him rent the tiny house. Below the St Ives Road to the east the ground sloped gradually towards the sea. Halfway down stood the hamlet of Higher Tregerthen, consisting of two cottages separated by a tiny yard. Heath-Stubbs and Wright took the more easterly of the two with Young John and the South African novelist David Lewis. Though the cottage faced south and was topped by a castellated tower, the sea was invisible from it even on the clearest of days. Behind it were gorse and boulders. Entering the low door, Heath-Stubbs would bump his head on the lintel stone. Inside the cottage was quiet and eerie. One night, when a ruminating cow looked in through the candle-lit window, the new tenants thought they had been visited by the devil.[11]

They soon discovered that Higher Tregerthen possessed a dramatic literary history. It was here for seven difficult months from February to September,

1916 that D.H. Lawrence had endeavoured to establish the utopian community he had called 'Rananim'. Lawrence and his wife Frieda had occupied the more westerly of the two cottages. Their companions in the cottage now occupied by Heath-Stubbs and his friends had been John Middleton Murry and Katherine Mansfield. 'Rananim' had broken up amid the quarrels and recriminations described by Murry in *Son of Woman*. The tower of Heath-Stubbs's house overlooked the tiny front door through which Lawrence had once chased Frieda with a frying pan. Later the composer Peter Warlock (Philip Heseltine) had lived higher up the slope in a cottage where he had performed seances. The magus Aleister Crowley had also once lived in the village, where, on a visit to the ancient parish church, he had been doused with holy water by the vicar.[12]

In and around Zennor the Barker brothers and their friends had established a Rananim of their own, or at any rate a dedicated artistic community. The separation between the three households was altogether notional. Using the £25 Pa had given then as a wedding present, Kit bought a 1926 Rover with a canvas body. When the car would not start, it was discovered that the engine had been fitted back to front. The derelict vehicle stayed on blocks in the fields below Noon Veor, where its canvas body was punctured repeatedly by cow's horns. For months, relishing their frustrations, the brothers endeavoured to coax it into something approaching operational life. Whilst George lay on his back fiddling with the axle and Kit read out instructions, Cass chatted to Ilse inside Noon Veor. 'She looked', wrote Ilse later, 'like a young Lauren Bacall and dressed to match. I see her always in a tightly belted trench-coat with her long hair caught in a scarlet knitted cap, the end of which dangled half-way down her back.' Ilse meanwhile had to make do with the clothes she had worn throughout the war. 'Fashion', she noted philosophically, 'was for other people.'

Meanwhile at Higher Tregerthen Heath-Stubbs, Wright and Young John worked on their respective manuscripts. They broke off in the evening to join the others at the Tinner's Arms. In the tiny bar they regularly spent the ten shilling notes kindly enclosed by Big Mumma in her letters to George and Kit. There, over pints of mild and bitter Barker held court in a navy pea-jacket and tartan shirt, his cloth cap askew over his right eye. Even in Zennor he delighted in the role of *poète maudit* – 'half spoiled child', as Wright was later to describe him, 'and half spoiled priest'. In his melancholy and sweet voice, he rendered such songs as 'Green grow the rushes' and ''Twas early'. He particularly relished ballads that spoke of damnation, among them 'Edward, Edward' and 'The Demon Lover', both to tunes supplied by Kit. He also declaimed a poem which Heath-Stubbs had earlier heard him read in London. 'Tam Lin' was a border ballad about a reprobate, snatched away by libidinous fairies. He is redeemed by the love of a young girl, to whom he complains:

> The queen o' Fairies she caught me,
>   In yon green hill to dwell,
> And pleasant is the fairy-land
>   But, an eerie tale to tell!
>
> Ay at the end of seven years
>   We pay a teind to hell;
> I am sae fair and fu' of flesh
>   I'm fear'd it be mysel'.[13]

The collection of misfits at Higher Tregerthen was a focus for local wonder. In any setting Heath-Stubbs and Wright would have been a remarkable pair. In Zennor they seemed outlandish almost to the point of legend, as they steered their way across the St Ives road, one half-sighted, the other unhearing, each complementing the other's disability. In the eyes of the villagers, Heath-Stubbs could be written off as some lopsided Homer. Wright was another matter. Eschewing sign language, he communicated by means of boomed comments, to which the others responded with grotesquely mouthed but voiceless sentences. Barker grew expert at this technique. Foreign words and difficult proper names were gestured. If the conversation took place outside and at night, Wright lit a match to watch his interlocutor's mouth. When performed on the morning bus into St Ives, this pantomime could be alarming. It gradually gave rise to the rumour that Wright was the only member of this coterie organically capable of speech. Barker and the rest came to be thought of as dumb idiots, condemned for ever to the clumsy substitute of semaphore.

For Barker, who had no physical impediment, such blemishes were emblematic gifts of the gods. Wright's deafness enabled him to close himself off from noise and to concentrate upon significant speech. It seemed to Barker that his friend's near isolation resembled the godless void chillingly evoked by the Roman poet Lucretius in his work *De Rerum Natura*. That autumn, shortcutting the lip language, Barker wrote his friend a 'Letter to a Deaf Poet', asserting the need for ordinary human affection to offset the nihilism of a Lucretius, or the ontological scepticism of a Bishop Berkeley. Yet, ultimately, even this consolation proved vain:

> For, finally, it is not the pathos of our essential incommunicability, the silent loneliness of every individual, that seems to me to be total; but

our conviction that this isolation of every creature is really only relative. For, sometimes, we feel, only briefly, that we can speak to each other: this is the pathos. And when George Berkeley proved the totality of this delusion, when he showed each of us that no one else existed, he demonstrated at the same time the suicide of his own proposition. For, although he has persuaded us of the intellectual immaculacy of his conception, he has not brought it home to the human heart. And why? Because the common heart of every single creature (a term I make deliberately paradoxical) is absolutely incommunicable in its loneliness (I think I speak, but whom do I speak to?). The heart of every man is a Coventry and can only be reached by one operation and one only, and this is the working of love. I am so convinced of this truth that I would describe love as the equation, the only equation, which proves that there are other people in the world beside oneself. It was a noble head that defined religion as 'what we do with our solitariness'.[14]

During his own moments of solitude, Barker wandered over the Cornish countryside. Avoiding old mine workings, he discovered abandoned cottages nestling amid yellow-flowering gorse on the hillsides. One afternoon in the late summer he found a solitary house with its slate roof caved in, its walls a riot of hawthorn and holly. When he peered through the unhinged and decaying door, he noticed a scarlet column of fuchsia bleeding from the hearth, as if a stake had been driven through it. It spoke to him of the 'death of a home', of *lacrimae rerum*, the tears at the centre of things: a forlorn and eloquent loneliness that, long afterwards when he wrote of it, no speech – even of the deaf – seemed able to assuage.[15]

1. By the seaside, 1932: *(from left to right)* George Barker, Eileen Jackson (née Barker), Albert Gordon ('Kit') Barker, Marion Frances Barker ('Big Mumma'), John Jackson ('Young John', later John Fairfax), Mr George Barker ('Pa').

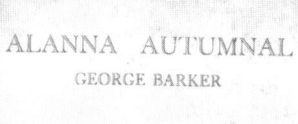

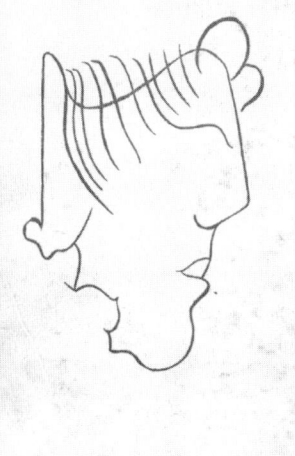

2. George and Monica Barker, 1930.

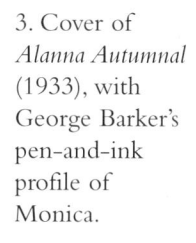

3. Cover of *Alanna Autumnal* (1933), with George Barker's pen-and-ink profile of Monica.

4. Antonia White in 1937.

5. Emily Holmes Coleman at about the same time.

6. Edwin Muir in the 1930s.

7. Jessica Barker in 1937.

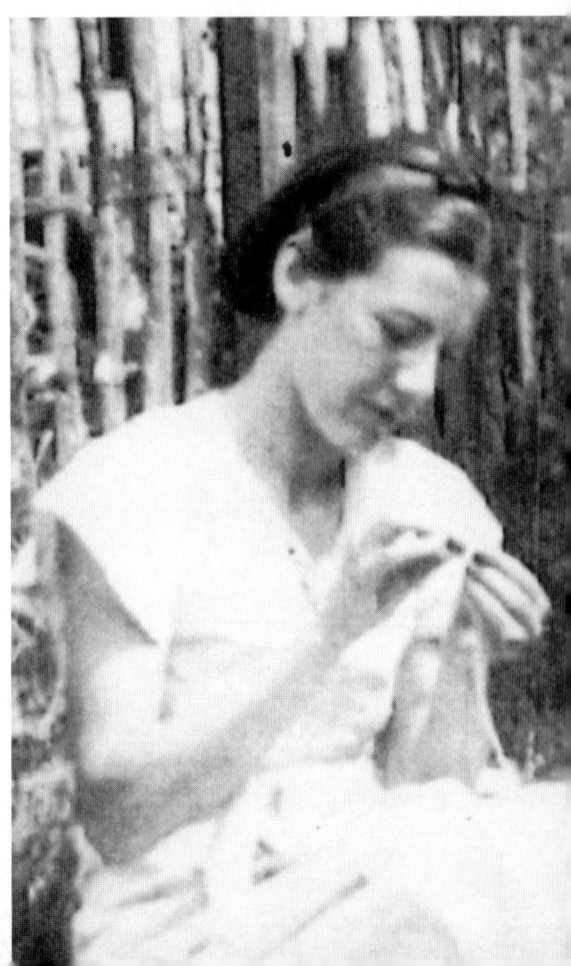

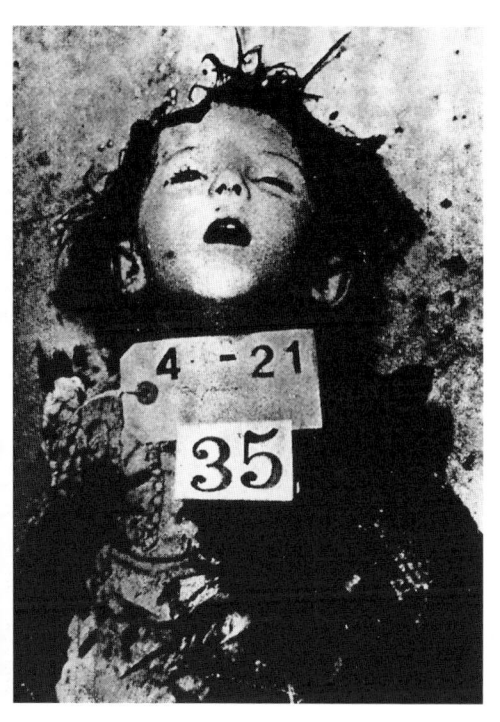

8. Frontispiece to *Elegy on Spain* (1939), showing the five-year-old victim of a Fascist air raid over Barcelona that September: 'O ecstatic is this head of five-year joy . . .'

9. George Barker and Elizabeth Smart in Manhattan, December 1940.

10. George Barker by Gene Derwood, New York, 1943.

11. Oscar Williams in 1940.

12. George Barker and Elizabeth Smart at Scarlet Sub-Edge, Gloucestershire, Easter Monday, 10 April 1944.

13. Pen-and-ink drawing by Kit Barker of the Aztec deity Quetzalcoatl on the typescript of George's radio play *The Degradations of Guatemozin*, written in Galway in December 1946. Note gouging of the sacrificial victim's eye.

14. Reception after Kit and Ilse Barker's wedding, 23a Stanhope Gardens, 2 July 1948: (*from left to right*) Maurice Carpenter ('Carp'), Monica Humble (née Barker), Betty ('Cashenden') Cass, David Wright, Eileen Jackson (née Barker), Kit Barker, Ilse Barker, 'Big Mumma', George Barker, John Fairfax, 'Pa', Veronica ('Wendy') Humble.

15. George smoking a cigar whilst playing Maurice Carpenter's flute.

16. W.S. Graham by John Deakin, July 1952.

17. 'The Roberts': MacBryde (*left*) and Colquhoun (*right*) in their studio.

18. George in Soho, 1951.

19. Cashenden Cass outside Hearne Cottage, mid-1950s.

20. Patrick Swift, *Portrait of Patrick Kavanagh*, crayon on paper, 1956.

21. Dede Farrelly with baby Francis, Rome, July 1963.

22. Robin Prising (*left*) and Willie Coakley (*right*) with Eddie Linden.

23. George with David Gascoyne, October 1981.

24. Elizabeth Smart in Olympia, Greece, 1986.

25. Second wedding reception, Bintry, 29 July 1989, chatting to John Heath-Stubbs.

26. Elspeth Barker at the time of the publication of O Caledonia.

27. 'Venerable and happy . . .': Hampstead, summer 1991.

28. The poet's gravestone in Itteringham churchyard, with sprig of honesty planted in front, and the biographer's son standing behind.

CHAPTER 29

A SCHOOL FOR POETS

Wright's deafness gave him one artistic advantage. It enabled him to concentrate on a problem common to all poets: the seeming inaccessibility of inspiration when first received. In Barker's words this was like 'listening to a long-distance telephone call on a rather bad line'.[1] Since Wright was undistracted by extraneous noise, he could receive the signal more acutely than most. Every evening, in his candlelit bedroom at Higher Tregerthen, he sat drumming on the tabletop in an attempt, first to hear the rhythms in his head, then to fit words to them. One of his problems was that, since he had never 'heard' many of the words he wanted to use, he had great difficulty in establishing their stress pattern.

Despite these obstacles, Wright possessed an instinctive musicality which Barker was quick to detect. One afternoon the two men rambled eastwards around the long headland towards St Ives. On a seaweed-strewn stretch, they discovered a seal resting majestically on its flippers. Seals, declared the deaf man, like to be sung to. He squatted down beside the creature and began in a voice high and wavering. The seal gave him a puzzled stare before rising with infinite dignity, lolloping down the beach and taking to the water.[2]

For twenty-one years Wright had felt thwarted by his deafness. Until 1948 all his poems had been wrapped in a misty romanticism. Stylistically and thematically his work seemed to flinch from the subject of his disability, escaping into a domain of evanescent sensation. Barker helped him to confront himself. He chose the direct method. He faced him straight on, mouthing his advice and exhortations, since he knew by now that Wright understood virtually everything said to him, provided he had a full view of the speaker's mouth and lips and the muscles in the throat. In a metaphorical sense, too, Barker encouraged Wright to 'face' his predicament, teaching him to interpret his disability as a challenge and to employ it as a theme. As the weeks in Zennor rolled by, Wright came to feel like a caged bird fluttering on the threshold of freedom. Not surprisingly, on the brink of flight he experienced a sense of vertigo:

> When the door was opened, the bird
>   Advanced upon the sky,
>   Into the disclosures
> Of liberty, but I heard
> The cage-born one complain
> With losing wing and voice
>   That without a frame
> The sky is hunger and loss.[3]

The 'frame' which Wright required was as much a question of artistic procedure as of spiritual security. He eventually found a satisfactory poetic structure by specialising on 'lip-reading rhymes', where words perceived as identical on a speaker's lips were counted as rhyming. He started to use syllabic metres in which prosodic stress is irrelevant and to locate his poems in recognisable social reality and in his own condition.

At thirty-five Barker had become an unofficial teacher, whose advice was much valued by younger poets. The community at Zennor operated like an extended summer school, all the better for its informality. There were no classes as such, but Barker in effect ran a tutorial system tailor-made to the requirements of each student. Arguably it was Barker's nephew John who posed the greatest challenge. John had recently left Plymouth College without going on to university. He had sloughed off his father's sporting and nouveau-riche affiliations, re-inventing himself as 'John Fairfax', a name which George had proposed as redolent of insurrection and regicide.[4] Ever since visiting his uncle at Boxholme in 1938, he had been used to placing George *in loco parentis*. Now he desired passionately to be a poet. George had overseen his homework when he was still a schoolboy and was aware of his enthusiasm, his loyalty and his indolence. He decided to adopt much the same approach towards his poetic training as he had earlier applied to his academic work. John was to write often, every day if possible. The results were to be shown promptly and mercilessly criticised. When the two men were out walking one afternoon, Barker asked his nephew what he was working on. When John replied, 'Nothing in particular,' Barker plucked a blade of grass from the verge. 'Here', he said, 'lies your subject.' John was to write a poem about the blade of grass, and to deliver it the following evening. He was to continue writing on everyday subjects for as long as it took him to learn that poetry was not so much the product of unpredictable inspiration, as a force to be harnessed through systematic application and hard graft.

These were not the qualities that the world attributed to Barker, whom critics had come to associate with spontaneity rather than discipline. However, as long ago as 1936, Antonia White had remarked on his addiction to routine, his diligent sharpening of pencils and filling of pens each morning, his keeping of regular morning hours at his desk.[5] In Cornwall in 1948 Heath-Stubbs also noted his application and scrupulous attention to detail, and later was to remember him as 'a most rigid and ruthless critic of the work of myself and of others'.[6] Barker subjected Heath-Stubbs to a period of initiation quite as gruelling as Fairfax's or Wright's. He believed him to be excessively the product of a university training and too heavily reliant on a resourceful but limiting talent for imitation. For as long as they were in Zennor Heath-Stubbs had to submit everything that he wrote for comment on subject-matter and style. Barker ruthlessly eliminated everything that was even in the slightest derivative. Clichés and tried formulae were to be abhorred. Allusions, for the time being, were the devil. Every time Heath-Stubbs found himself staring at a conventional word, he was told to think again. 'Make it new!' Barker told him, echoing Ezra Pound, 'Make it new!'

Paradoxically, among these young poets it was Wright who lacked a visual sense. In an attempt to encourage it, Barker compared poems to paintings. In every pictorial masterpiece, he told him – illustrating the analogy with gestures – some correspondence would be discovered between the complete composition and each individual part of it. The same should be true of a poem. Each line should be as sharp as the whole work, and every word as sharp as the line. Wright slowly absorbed this lesson. He retained, however, a sententiousness that Barker was determined to root out. One day, feeling nostalgic for South Africa, Wright showed Barker a short piece about his mother's Christmas cooking. Barker asked him if he intended to publish it. Wright said that he did. Barker replied that, in such an eventuality, he would deliver his judgement in person. 'Sir,' he mouthed with accompanying gestures, 'I shall cut off your balls.'[7]

So Barker the protégé grew into Barker the mentor. The transition enabled him to look his old mentors squarely in the face. On 26 September Eliot turned sixty. At Editions Poetry London, Tambimuttu, who was celebrating the event with a festschrift entitled *T.S. Eliot: A Symposium*, solicited a poem from Barker. The result was 'Verses on the 60th Birthday of Thomas Stearns Eliot', an accolade which, although never falling short of respectful affection, possessed the quiet authority of distance. In its first stanza, Barker described Eliot standing as he had glimpsed him at the outbreak of war: bleakly surveying from his office window the drabness of central London in the dusk. The unimpressionable editor, the splenetic scourge of *After Strange Gods*, the disenchanted moralist, the Anglo-Catholic High Tory, all contribute to this austere portrait. Each of these facets of Eliot's personality seems pitiless; it is through language alone that the poet in Barker tempers justice with clemency, and softens disillusionment into love:

> Outside the huge negations pass
> Like whirlwinds writing on the grass
> Inscriptions teaching us that all
> The lessons are ephemeral;
> But as the huge negations ride
> And deprecate all things outside
> His window, he puts out his hand
> And writes with whirlwinds on the ground
> Asseverations that tame
> The great negations with his name.[8]

The Eliot depicted here is the poet of *The Hollow Men*, of *Sweeney Agonistes* and of the gloomier passages in *East Coker*, a man gripped by a subdued terror similar to that which Barker had himself experienced in his own blank moments. Barker retained a strong sense of spiritual kinship with his mentor, though he knew Eliot's devils to be different from his own. Drink and excess had laid waste Barker's life, as well as drugs such as methedrine and benzedrine, on which he was increasingly reliant; celibacy and asceticism had seemingly laid waste Eliot's. Eliot's achievement, the poem argues, had been to make his demons sing. Barker reiterated this view in March 1949, when he published in the *New English Weekly* a prose tribute entitled 'A Note for T.S. Eliot'. Eliot's power, this essay asserted, stemmed from a scepticism so extreme as to doubt its own judiciousness, combined with the wisdom of an assured faith. Eliot was like his cats, except that his claws reached inwards. There were emotional depths to the man into which even his most sombre poetry could not reach: 'At the dead centre of Eliot is a dark confessional into which none of his poems has ever entered and from which none of his poems has ever emerged.'[9] As in the 'Birthday Verses', a vision of Eliot's essential isolation emerges in this essay: an isolation which Barker was coming to feel must be the lot of all poets. In Wright he had been faced with an aural incommunicability; in Eliot with a spiritual one. The outer impression of desolation, however, had been much the same.

That autumn Barker's sense of the poet's isolated predicament was increasingly drawing him towards the arch-poet of solitude, Coleridge. A hundred and fifty years earlier, in 1798, Coleridge had lived at Nether Stowey in Somerset in a not dissimilar poetic coterie with William and Dorothy Wordsworth and Charles Lamb. Similarity of circumstance took Barker back to the convention of the conversation poem, such as he had attempted before the war. One afternoon in November Cass had gone out walking with the others. Alone in the front parlour of 1 The Row, George sat writing the first of his Zennor Idylls. The confident intimacy of its tone recalled 'This Lime Tree Bower My Prison' written by Coleridge when his own companions went out walking:

> Let me establish in the bitter line
> The empire of that affection every creature
> Keeps as its only kingdom in the winter
> Of the world as it is. Lonely by water
> I bear your faces corniced at my shoulder
> When I look down, dogged and raggedly by disgraces
> I cannot contend with alone. This afternoon
> You, my sweet friends, are gone, and I sit now
> Watching the vacant day pursue its ends
> To bright rage twisting in the quiet sky.[10]

The approaching 'winter of the world' was one for which Barker and his companions were physically ill prepared. 'That Autumn', wrote Ilse many years later, 'the Cornish idyll began to fray at the edges . . . Looking back, we seemed to be always walking somewhere, not somewhere ten minutes away, but for miles and miles, and keeping the cottage supplied with paraffin and coal, keeping lamps clean and trimmed, filling stoves, washing, shopping, just ordinary "living" seemed to take all of one's time and one's strength. Perhaps our energy was sapped by not enough, or not the right, food.' In November Kit enjoyed his first minor professional success when his work was mounted in a two-man exhibition at St Ives. Afterwards he received a visit from George Dix, a director of the Durlacher Gallery in Manhattan, who asked him if he would like to exhibit in New York. The prospect attracted Kit and Ilse, who had been inspired by George's tales of America to think that they might try their luck there.

At Noon Veor the brothers redoubled their efforts with the Rover. The car's canvas sides were patched. Its crankshaft was removed, reground, then reassembled on the kitchen table; its carburettor boiled in Ilse's best saucepan.[11] At Higher Tregerthen the occupants were already dispersing. As November drew to a close, Wright and John Fairfax moved westwards to the still more remote Cove Cottage beneath Gurnard's Head, buffeted by the full force of the Atlantic storms. In the first week of December the Rover stammered into life. One morning George nursed it along the narrow roads with Kit beside him; Cass and Ilse sat behind, each with a cat on her knee. At Salisbury Barker stopped to ask a policeman the way, and was reprimanded for driving with an out-of-date licence. He purchased petrol with the last five-shilling coupon in Ilse's ration book. To buy the last tankful, he traded in his watch. They arrived in London the next day to find that the welcome feast prepared by Big Mumma the evening before had been eaten. They made do with kippers and champagne. The Rover was parked in the mews, lifeless as before.[12]

But for Barker the tutor of young poets there was to be no respite. Awaiting him was more poetry from Anthony Thwaite, to whom he replied,

> I think that you have received the gift of the gab from the Muse and there is nothing more for you to do except keep your lamp burning and your nose clean and to honour the dictionary. Do not worry overmuch about *being* a poet because whenever a building collapses it will fall on you and whenever a rowboat goes down you will be in it, and whenever an international conference fails you will be responsible and whenever a whore has a baby it will be yours. The poet is the scapegoat who disguises himself as a scapegrace. See to it that you acquire the grace to escape from.[13]

Barker then invited Thwaite to meet him at Stanhope Gardens. The youth arrived from his parents' home in Muswell Hill to find his idol's legs sticking out from under the chassis of the Rover. When he timidly announced his presence, George exclaimed, 'At last!' He took the afternoon off to show Thwaite round the Victoria and Albert Museum, looking and talking all the while 'exactly as a poet should'.[14]

Other young men felt the power of Barker's magnetism. In January 1949, in the Wheatsheaf in Rathbone Place, he met Oliver, the oldest and proudest of the Bernard brothers, who had recently returned from serving with the air force in Canada. Barker instinctively sensed in him an unfulfilled ambition to write. When he broached this touchy subject, Oliver snarled back with precocious hauteur, 'I think that you are barking up the wrong creek.' The angry response only made Barker more interested, and he took him for a walk by the Round Pond in Kensington Gardens, talking like a latterday Lord Byron. He was, Oliver felt, 'mad, bad and dangerous to know' and for that reason irresistible, the more alluring because so elusive.[15]

In Pa's eyes, however, too many would-be poets and artists were hanging round his son. Stanhope Gardens was now home to George, Cass, Kit and Ilse, who alone had a job. Ilse's presence barely insulated George from his father's anger. When in late January she and Kit departed for America, confrontation seemed inevitable. That month Wright returned from Gurnard's Head, where his residence had not been a success. Tolerated in Zennor, his bizarre and, to those who did not know of his condition, loutish behaviour had aroused the pettiness of the locals. One evening he had left his flickering lantern outside the Gurnard's Head Hotel while he went inside for a drink. He had returned to find it floating in the water butt. With no help at hand, he had blundered homewards through the pitch dark.[16] One morning he had awoken to find an untidy parcel on his doorstep. It contained six complimentary copies of his first book, *Poems*, which Tambimuttu had finally managed to publish. Wright sat down to read the contents, which to his horror were stuffed with the soft-edged romanticism that George had since taught him to forgo. He had not known whether to throw the books into the sea, or himself, or both together.

For consolation, on his return to London, Wright came round to Stanhope Gardens, where he and George resumed their nocturnal conversations, alternately mouthed and bawled. They drank at the Queen's Elm in the Fulham Road and the public bar of the nearby Denmark Arms, then returned to talk until early morning. In the bedrooms upstairs the only voice that could be heard was Wright's, oblivious of his *fortissimo*. Roused from sleep, Pa refused to endure it. At that moment his frustrations at the ungovernable behaviour of his famous but feckless son found a focus. He came down the stairwell and asked when the conversation would end. George replied that his guests were his own and that he would talk to them as long as he wished. Father and son fell upon one another. They swayed backwards and forwards in the confined space of the kitchen as David and Cass held back, too awed by the violence to intervene. The gas stove rocked on its legs. When the mutual spasm of anger had exhausted itself, the two men stood gasping in the lamplight. George fetched his coat and told Cass to follow him.[17]

CHAPTER 30

'HAPPY, SILLY, A BIT MELLOW'

From Queen's Gate they walked through the night, unable at first to think of anywhere they could stay.[1] As dawn broke they headed for one of the few addresses where they might be more or less welcome. Colquhoun and MacBryde had retained a *pied-à-terre* at 77 Bedford Gardens. There was only one bedroom and one bed. Since much of the time the Roberts were in Lewes, space was available while they were away. It was not an ideal arrangement. Barker frequently seemed most at peace with his temperamental opposites and in their different ways the Roberts were too much like him.

The Roberts were an odd-matched couple: acrimonious, devoted, touchy, hilarious. What they liked was extravagance, truthfulness and aggression. One evening Barker accompanied them to a reading by Hugh MacDiarmid at the Institute of Contemporary Arts, then in Dover Street. Disappointed by MacDiarmid's timid reading manner, which contrasted so markedly with the assertiveness of his verse, Colquhoun sat patiently through the first few lines. He then stood up and demanded in his deep Ayrshire tones, 'Why don't you r-r-read it?' MacDiarmid stammered, 'Why, I'm attempting to read it.' Colquhoun boomed back, 'Well then, r-r-read it. Give us the Grand – Old – Mad – Thing!' 'Be quiet, Robert,' MacBryde clucked, as if to an embarrassingly extrovert husband. 'Be quiet.'[2]

Dover Street was the scene of another encounter when Oliver accompanied Barker to hear Dylan Thomas read. Thomas recited, 'Do not go gentle into that good night' to hushed appreciation. Afterwards Oliver told Barker how moved he had been. Barker responded gravely, 'He's destroying the English language.'

Barker's domestic frustrations were exacerbated by professional uncertainty. Eliot had agreed to issue his recent verse in a volume called *News of the World*. However, he rejected *The True Confession*, which Barker had been sure he would like. The typescript of the prose work *Of Love* had been gathering dust for three years. Now George changed its title, borrowing *The Smile on the Face of the Tiger* from his abortive burlesque travelogue of the late 1930s. For the first time in his life, he decided to use an agent: David Higham of Pearne, Pollinger & Co in Clerkenwell, who also acted for Edith Sitwell. Higham submitted the novella to John Lehmann, who had now launched his own publishing firm. Lehmann accepted the work on condition Barker changed the culminating birth scene, which Rosamond Lehmann, his sister and co-director, thought 'obstetrically impossible'.[3]

Lehmann proved helpful in another respect. In the early months of 1949 the favourite reading matter of both Roberts was Giorgio Vasari's *Lives of the Painters*, which they were soon discussing with Barker at Bedford Gardens and in the pubs. They were particularly drawn to the 'Life of Michelangelo' with its suggestions of homoeroticism and the heroism of struggle. The Roberts had travelled briefly in Italy before the war and they now decided to return there with Barker and Cass. Colquhoun wanted to draw the Siena *palio* and the puppet plays at Modena. Barker knew that Lehmann was enthusiastic to publish an illustrated book about Italy, a country that was just opening up to travellers after the war. Together they proposed to him a volume entitled *At the Tomb of Julius II*, to be written by Barker, and illustrated by Colquhoun. The subject was to be the tomb which Pope Julius II had once commissioned from Michelangelo and which, as Vasari carefully stresses, it took the sculptor forty years to complete. Lehmann undertook to finance the trip, which was to take the form of a pilgrimage in the steps of Michelangelo. Had Lehmann been more familiar with his clients, he would have realised that the book was likely to be about as laggardly of execution as the tomb.[4]

In the second week of May 1949 George, Cass and the Roberts took the Orient Express as far as Brescia. They arrived weary and travel-stained in the late evening to see the town heave into sight 'like a suntanned houri without a yashmak'.[5] Overburdened with luggage, they trudged down the streets without a hope, apparently, of finding a hotel. Barker's notebook captures their disorientation and exhaustion. As they passed, a baroque church 'with a façade like a huge Spanish cowl' leant surreally over the street; a labourer ran across with a wooden stanchion and propped it up. 'In a dream of fatigue' they came across a little inn looking sideways on to a *vialle*. After some haggling over prices, they booked rooms. Barker and Cass were given a double room in which 'the blinds seemed permanently to have been drawn'. After a hasty snack of 'chocolate and mineral water', they fell on to a gargantuan, rococo bed. While MacBryde unpacked, Colquhoun stayed downstairs sketching the kitchen boy.

Barker's notebooks suggest that, after postwar London, Italy seemed to both him and the Roberts to be vast, ornate and forbidding. For the first time in thirteen years he was confronted with the cultural might of Italy. Like the Roberts, he had grown used to operating in a professional environment where the resonance of tradition was less overwhelming; if art was a whispering gallery, here they felt drowned out. 'The tragedy of the artist in Italy', he wrote in his notebook, 'is the tragedy of the latest arrival in Hell or the new boy at school. He is dumbfounded by what has already occurred. Every conceivable and inconceivable variety of the human spirit welcomes him with gestures of dignity and elation – with the consequence that, like the new boy at school, the artist is driven back into sulking vanity, without dignity, without joy, conscious only of the impersonal masonry of the past: "I had not dreamed that life had undone so many."'[6]

From Brescia the travellers made a short trip to Lago d'Iseo, where George turned silent and broody, haunted, Cass thought, by a ghost. The ghost, though he did not admit it, must have been Jessica, with whom he had visited the lake in 1936. The group continued as far as Verona, where Colquhoun drew a sleeping figure. In Venice the undertow of sadness and decadence called to them dangerously. Colquhoun found time to sketch several masked carnival figures, but there were too many distractions. In the evenings along the canal, wrote Barker, 'the voices of singers rise confidently in the cafés' and there were 'urchins with begging hands carrying green birds in boxes'. The Roberts strutted along 'with erections like Guinness bottles', while 'an air of faint anticipation kindled in the eyes of young men at street corners and the sun, rather than preside over the sequel, retired modestly towards America'.[7] At Modena Colquhoun painted the puppet plays and a portrait of a man selling marmot skins. Outside the town, at a resettlement camp run by the Italian government, they met up with Nessie Graham, engaged in volunteer work with refugees. In the camp the continuing frictions of war-ravaged Italy were still apparent, as was the tension between different nationalities: Greek, Albanian, Russian. They decided to move on rapidly. A few days later Nessie called an official 'stupido' and was deported. In Siena George, Cass and the Roberts attended the *palio* horse race in the Piazza del Campo. While the others cheered on the competing teams, Colquhoun peered through the crowd and sketched the horses' heads.

Pursuing their Michelangelo pilgrimage, they continued to Florence, where the streets were glad with bunting for the quincentenary of Lorenzo de' Medici. They left Cass's luggage at a travel agent's office, from where it disappeared never to be seen again. They made for the Accademia to see Michelangelo's unfinished sculpture *The Prisoners*. When an American tourist announced to the gallery that 'The trouble with Michelangelo was that he could never finish anything', Cass recollects Barker creeping up to the four figures, cupping his hands and calling, 'Sweet prisoners, the secret of your beauty lies in the uncompletedness of your creation.' The travellers settled for three weeks in a villa three miles out of the city at Settignano, the village where Michelangelo had grown up, 'a place abundant in blue-grey sandstone', according to Vasari, 'where most of the sculptors are born'. There Colquhoun drew figures from the *festa*.[8] MacBryde donned his apron and prepared lavish meals. They took trams down to the city to visit the churches and the Uffizi. At a bar in the Piazza della Signoria, Barker and MacBryde, 'happy, silly, a bit mellow', stood drinking wine next to a cyclist. His name, he told them, was Donatello.[9]

Barker had with him a letter of introduction to Madame Nostra Giacomo Dussaux, an elderly but voluble aristocrat who lived in a fifth-floor apartment at the top of a medieval building opposite the Bargello. George and Cass called to see her in her 'pearled room' above the city. Madame Dussaux was lame in one leg and dependent, as Cass remembered, 'on an eighteenth-century ebony cane crowned in silver'. As she took her guests around the city, she used the cane to 'cut swathes through the undisciplined Florentine crowds'. Afterwards she walked her guests back up the several flights of stairs to her flat. Outside her front door she paused to regain her breath, before letting them in and holding forth all evening on her two great loves: 'the English poets and the gorgeous and brutal history of Tuscany'.[10]

Madame Dussaux owned an estate half an hour's bus ride from Florence near the supposed birthplace of both Dante and Beatrice. She took George and Cass to stay there for several days. On the second morning she announced a pilgrimage to the birthplace itself, with the parish priest acting as their guide. She planned a banquet, to be enjoyed by all four pilgrims before they set out. The previous evening George had caught the bus back to Florence to drink with the Roberts. At lunchtime the following day the Contessa, Cass and the priest were still waiting for him to return. They ate the banquet, but the pilgrimage was ditched.

Barker had been detained by Colquhoun, who had been sketching alone for hours during their absence. He found his friend sitting on a boulder on the banks of the Arno, chin in hand, regarding the stagnant expanses of the river with great, troubled eyes. George knew this mood of old; yet Colquhoun's dejection seemed to reflect the decay of Florence itself. Together they visited Lorenzo's tomb in the centre of the city, where the fate of the Medici family seemed to blend with Colquhoun's:

> The anarchist stalks across the sky,
> The double cross divides and shines;
> The rat and ass cohabit: the whores

>   Of economics kiss and kill.
>   The greatest and the best, those powers
>   Of Justice and of Truth, now lie
>   Under this stone, under this empty stone
>   By which I sorrow over a living man.[11]

When September arrived the travellers still had not reached their destination, Rome. Nor had they done any work on the book. Tempers were fraying and their lire were much depleted. Following the curve of the Arno, they dragged themselves to the bus station. MacBryde was humping Colqhoun's suitcase as well as his own; in a fit of pique, he turfed it into the river. They boarded a bus so congested that MacBryde was forced to squat on a dicky seat between the rows. He nagged at Colquhoun all the way to Perugia, where the passengers were let out for a few hours. Cass's cool beauty and Colquhoun's tall, moody good looks drew the admiring attention of the Perugians, convinced that they were the leading man and lady of a film. Barker and MacBryde were taken for the crew. A youth rushed up and presented Cass with a bouquet. Exasperated with what he took to be her blatant exhibitionism, MacBryde berated her in the open street.[12]

In Rome the four of them booked into a hotel which turned out to be a brothel. The great effigies of the city's past seemed to mock their unproductiveness. George visited the domed Pantheon, the Roman temple of the time of Hadrian later converted into a church. In the pronaos outside the west door stood a set of sixteen Corinthian columns upon which a family of cats was curled.[13] He was inclined to regard these animals with respect 'since they seem perfectly aware of the imperial inheritance' over which they were sentinels. In the Forum too the scavenger cats appeared to maintain an unspoken kinship with the dead. Barker wrote that he had the impression he was 'looking at feline Cleopatra at last in total possession of ruined Caesar'. In Trastevere he visited the Basilica of Santa Cecilia to see the sculpture by Stefano Maderna, reputedly sculpted from the saint's disinterred body. He had known a reproduction of it in the Brompton Oratory since he was a child. He found the church locked.[14] In the church of S. Pietro in Vincoli, the tomb of Julius was magnificent but, as it proved, inimitable. At any rate, Barker seems to have written nothing about it.

To pacify Lehmann Barker began drafting a novella entitled 'Events of Venetian Evenings'.[15] It featured Madame Dussaux, now promoted to the rank of contessa, who in the story introduces the young male narrator to her niece. It went on to describe a pilgrimage to Dante and Beatrice's birthplace, as Barker and Cass might have experienced it, had their own trip taken place. The climax was a murder, but obstinately the novella refused to come to life. Barker's frustration was as nothing compared to that of Colquhoun who since arriving in the Italian capital had only managed to draw one Roman head. Within a few days he retreated into a depression where Barker could not reach him:

> I thought as I stood by this tomb
> That the cold dead quiet there
> Were no more isolated from
> Each other than the living here:
> I lift a hand of paper to
> You in your exercise of dust,
> And if a little love gets through
> Then we are luckier than most.
> The incommunicable unicorn
> Never to be seen or known
> Lifts its glass horn to everyone
> Until, so fabulously alone,
> We wish we had never been born.
> And thus I write these lines, Colquhoun,
> To wave a word to you across
> That desert deader than the moon
> Separating each one of us.[16]

The travellers now had no money. Unwisely, George wrote a haughty letter of rebuke to Lehmann, as if to a particularly stingy pope. Lehmann replied, 'I am sorry you are in a huff, but I do not feel very wicked.' He had already paid the pilgrims a considerable amount for the yet-to-be-started book on the papal tomb, as well as allowing Barker an advance of £50 against the royalties for *The Smile on the Face of the Tiger*. Under duress, he had even put some extra unearned money on top. He did not see how he could have been more helpful: 'Write to me please,' he concluded, 'and don't lecture me.'[17]

Then the sirocco blew, cold and dry. Both of the Roberts had withdrawn into surly drunkenness and Colquhoun into disaffection. Like latterday Michelangelos the group abandoned Rome, and the project, and fled northwards. They arrived in London at the end of October with nothing to show for themselves but four hangovers, a few sketches, and a great sense of having achieved very little.[18] So, said Cass, the 'splendid fiasco' of the Italian expedition came to an end.

Except that, in November, baulked of his ambition to see the effigy of Cecilia in Rome, Barker paid a return visit to St Wilfrid's side chapel at the Oratory. It was 22 November, Cecilia's feast day, and he had hoped to attend a Mass in her honour.[19] There was none. Instead he wrote his 'Anthem Against St Cecilia's Day', a poem in the long tradition of odes for the saint's festival: Dryden's, Pope's and, more recently, Auden's. In it he recalls the legend that the third-century martyr Cecilia was partially decapitated by intruders in her own house and then left to die, just as Maderna's statue depicts her. In Barker's poem she represents the cost of principles too tenaciously held; she is thus the cause of war as well as its victim. It is because of her supposed obduracy that this anthem for the patron saint of music is directed 'against' her feast day, though the preposition 'against' combines the archaic senses of 'in the presence of' and 'in preparation for' with the modern meaning of 'in opposition to'. It begins by imagining the fallen of the recent war rising from their graves to witness the blasted hopes of the Cold War and ends by fending off the postwar threat of violence which, from a Catholic perspective, is best viewed as a legacy of original sin:

> O stop the calling killer in the skull
>   Like beasts we turn toward!
> For was the nightriding siren beautiful
> Caterwauling War until her bed was full
>   Of the uxorious dead?
> Let the great moaners of the seven seas
>   Let only the seas mourn,
> With the shipwrecked harp of creation on their knees
>   Till Cecilia turns to a stone.[20]

In the chapel, above Maderna's statue, all was hushed. 'Tender Cecilia silence' Barker wrote in his poem, thus earning a correction from Wright, who visited the saint's basicila in Trastevere the following year and later wrote his own ode for the saint, declaring, 'Cecilia there is none: No silence anywhere'.[21]

But Barker's book for Lehmann would not come. With this failure added to his existing load of guilt, and with a cloud of professional frustration hanging over his head, he set about looking for a house. He dispatched a *cri de coeur* to David Gill, now settled once more near Petworth, to see if there was a cottage available in the area. 'A commission to discover the Holy Grail, to find the keys to the Kingdom of Heaven and to solve the dollar gap', replied Gill, would have been simple compared to this. But, as it happened there was on the Petworth estate a deserted and derelict woodman's dwelling 'called Herons or Hearn's Cottage'. It had no running water, but tobacco flowers, and, according to Gill's postcard, wild grapes were growing in the garden. It was folded into the woods of Blackdown, where, 'if you could spit upwards a matter of five hundred feet, you could land your gob neatly through the front door' of Aldworth, once Tennyson's house. The cottage possessed 'a general air of wanting to get its own back on someone', and was 'uninhabitable, except by poets'.[22] George and Cass went down immediately by train. Gill took them to the cottage, which was situated off the road, down a track and across a muddy meadow. At the head of the track was a stud farm and, just up the hill, Parkhurst House, where Gill was planting apple trees.

In April 1950 George and Cass moved in. The core of Hearne Cottage, as they always subsequently called the house, turned out to be a medieval woodcutter's hut. This they made their bedroom. It contained a closet, the door of which had been scored with axe marks, then at some later period decorated with *fleurs de lys*. At night, the spirit of Hearne the Hunter, a legendary figure after whom the building was named, would, so it seemed to Cass, disturb her sleep by bodilessly sidling past the foot of the bed. There was also an Elizabethan extension with beams, tall chimneys and leaded windows. George made his study there. He would sit at his desk and gaze across the cow pasture, carpeted with wild flowers. Strolling up the track of an evening, he would nod to a rustic gentleman who appeared to be the hunter's modern reincarnation as he stalked across the long grass. The reincarnation was in fact the tenant of the Olivera stud farm at the end of the lane. George wrote to Kit in New York that the spirit of Tennyson also seemed to walk the grounds. Each time the two poets met, the late laureate would mutter his verses to distract Barker from his own.[23]

Newly settled in the house, it came to seem to Barker as if, after so many misdemeanours, life had absolved him. In *Poetry London* he published a poem called 'On First Settling into the Country', later retitled 'The Mnemonic Demi-god'. It breathed physical and spiritual relief:

> Here by a wood
> With Aldworth over my head
> I have laid down my board
> And made a bed. The wind
> Hums silently among
> The ash and the sadder alder
> Till I can hear again
> Those heart-breaking voices
> Rise like swans out of every
> Harp of the summer wood
> And every organ and leaf
> Of body and mind. Cease,
> Victims, victors of love,
> And leave in the evening
> The unlonely I alone.[24]

In May came the publication of *News of the World* and the reviews, the best Barker had ever received. In the *Observer* Patric Dickinson spoke of his pity and tenderness, his tragic vision of humanity. Barker had always possessed a lyrical fecundity: 'Now, in this new book, intellect and emotion have been naturally mated at last, to produce poetry of compassion and power. The style is simpler and more sensuous: the verbal extravagances are gone, without loss of vitality. This is his first really mature work, the beginning of a new stage of development.'[25] The *Times Literary Supplement* also noted new departures; *Poetry London* was full of praise. Even in *Greya*, the house journal of Gray's Inn, he was described as 'this distinguished son of a distinguished father'. Soon Pa was recommending the book to the more literary Benchers. He had even, George claimed, set up a stall.

Professional vindication served powerfully to support his new sense of private fulfilment. In an access of energy, he painted the interior of Hearne Cottage from top to bottom in white and cream paint. According to Cass, it now resembled the gate porter's lodge to Paradise. There was something deliberate and triumphant in such nest-building. Barker had never lavished this much care on any of his previous rented houses. After so many years of drifting, of compromise and conflict, he seemed at long last to have established himself as master of his own domain. The word soon spread: to Kit and Ilse, now working at Yaddo, the writers' and artists' retreat to the north of New York; to John Fairfax, paying the penalty of conscientious objection to National Service in Lewes Prison. Wright, who had recently moved into a cubbyhole of a flat above a bombed-out electric appliance shop in Great Ormond Street, visited John in prison to ease his isolation. He was, however, more cheered by the news of his Uncle George, who, as he wrote in a letter to Hearne Cottage, appeared to have been 'infected by a virus of contentment'.[26]

So sanguine had Barker become that he decided he could dispense with convention. In the *New Statesman and Nation* he published a coat-trailing article under the title 'Poet as Pariah'. Its theme was that poets should not be required to take jobs. The article was his most emphatic rebuttal yet of Eliot's belief that poets should earn their keep through a non-literary occupation. Barker now argued that Eliot was the exception who proved an overwhelming rule. There had always been a few poets who had accepted paid employment, 'but between these men and their everyday work a curious affinity must have existed. The proprieties of a bank are remarkably like the proprieties of Eliot's critical writings: each conceals a ruthlessness and a hardheartedness I cannot think that the author of "After Strange Gods" would find uncongenial.' For the most part, however, poets were anarchists:

The poet is an enemy. I take this as axiomatic. Why, therefore, should the poet expect anything from society but discouragement? It is the old Platonic chestnut, and the answer to it is infinitely simpler than the apparent paradox implies. Just as society encourages the scientist to set about the business of destroying everything in the disguise of intellectual curiosity, so society should, properly speaking, be prepared to encourage the poet in his business of showing society why it is not fit to survive, or alternatively, why it is. But society does not want to hear the truth about itself; and demonstrably prefers the flattery of the film director to the few home truths of the poet. It is absolutely hopeless to talk about whether poetry is wanted by society; just as it is perfectly hopeless to talk about whether sex is wanted by society. Poetry is one of a number of things that happen to people no matter whether they like it or not: it resembles boils in adolescence or flirtation between the sexes. It is here, like the far side of the moon, to stay, even though, in disappointment and indignation, it has turned its face away.[27]

A few weeks later, a Bloomsbury bookseller replied in a letter to the *New Statesman*. Since Barker was so indifferent to public opinion, he commented, he for one was anxious to grant him his freedom. Books of verse were seldom commercially viable. Despite the considerable critical success granted to *News of the World*, his shop would not therefore be stocking the volume, since its author evidently no longer had need of his benevolence. The scoffers of Soho, George wrote to Kit, had succumbed to *delirium tremens* of mirth over that particular barb.

With those same scoffers, on 27 May 1950, George and Cass helped to celebrate Jeffrey Bernard's eighteenth birthday at the Swan in Kensington Church Street. Mrs Bernard sent £3 across to the pub to fund the whole Saturday evening. When Roy Campbell called Jeff 'young man', Jeff hit him.[28] Afterwards George, Cass and Jeff travelled down to Lewes and spent Sunday walking the South Downs with the Roberts. Jeff later recalled that Barker 'kindly made me feel accepted and for a moment I felt quite grown-up'.[29]

Lehmann had rejected *Events of Venetian Evenings*[30] on 21 February. He also considered *The Smile on the Face of the Tiger* too long a title for the novella, suggesting instead the Chekhovian resonance of *The Dead Seagull*. Barker found the title bland; he accepted it because it was, Archer claimed, such a perfect description of Lehmann.[31] Even so, decency required last-minute textual changes. Barker had described a Greek character called Theokopolos, indirectly based on Elizabeth's one-time boyfriend Varda, removing his pants in order to have sexual intercourse. Lehmann drew the line at this: 'Theokopolov's trousers simply will not do!'

The True Confession had still not found a publisher. After several disappointments Barker submitted it to Fore Publications, a company established by Randall Swingler and his brother Humphrey shortly before the war as an outlet for radical literature. Swingler had recently joined forces with the Australian Marxist and poet Jack Lindsay, with whom he was co-editing a series of booklets by so-called 'Key Poets'. Their plan was to breathe life into a moribund poetry scene by issuing pamphlet-sized editions of poets not directly associated with the establishment. For communists, their choice was markedly accommodating. First had come Edith Sitwell's *Poor Men's Music*, followed by Maurice Carpenter's *Gentle Exercise* and Norman Cameron's *Forgive Me, Sire*. The inclusion of decadents such as Sitwell incited the anger of the *Daily Worker*, which instantly accused Swingler and Lindsay of revisionism.[32] The paper was not mollified by the addition of Barker's *Confession*, denounced by one of its Marxist contributors for 'unsavoury scratching-the-itch' self-indulgence.

The proofs arrived at Hearne Cottage in August. It had been the dullest summer since the war, the sun having, George wrote to Kit, confined its appearance to three brilliant days in June. The garden was bogged and waterlogged. The harvest seemed likely to be washed away at any moment by a cloudburst. George purchased an ornamental sword in a junk shop and bore it proudly back to the cottage. Cass acquired a kitten called Chi-Chi, dove grey and shell pink, 'with a decided taste for toads'. On 10 August George killed a snake with the sword. The following day he awoke to find a young bat clinging to the door knocker. Visitors were scarce. David Wright, who, as George impishly reported to Kit and Ilse in New York, considered the continuing austerity measures of the Labour government to be detrimental to his career, had decamped to France and Rome. He left his Great Ormond Street flat to Fairfax, now released from prison. George wrote to Kit that Archer had taken to dancing barefoot in public places. 'He says it is a delightful experience if only people would refrain from sprinkling broken glasses on the floor.'[33]

Then, in late August, Barker accompanied Elizabeth, who was up in town on one of her regular sorties from Tilty Mill, to a reception given by the black American actress Hilda Simms at her house near Regent's Park.[34] He fell into conversation with John Malcolm Brinnin, the American academic and poet, fresh from his triumph of introducing Dylan Thomas to America. Brinnin was clearly impressed by Barker and anxious to use him. With good reason: *The Dead Seagull* and *The True Confession* were about to appear within a week of one another. Despite the sense of inadequacy which had been dogging him since the Italian project, he had now published three titles in a year: very different in kind but arguably equal in quality. 1950, he wrote jubilantly to Kit in New York, has after all been a fruitful year.

Not everybody endorsed Barker's satisfaction. That autumn John Davenport brought out an issue of his short-lived periodical *Circus*. It carried a verdict by Dylan Thomas on the verse-making of the expiring decade, called 'How to be a Poet'. The typical poet of the Forties, Thomas declared, had called his books *Heliogarbus in Pentecost*. This poetaster could 'mix his metaphor, bog his cliché, and soak his stolen symbols in stale ass's milk as glibly and glueily as the best of them'.

Thomas's indictment was in reality a verdict, now out of date, on the work of the period up to and including *Eros in Dogma*. As Patric Dickinson had noted, Barker had definitely outgrown that polysyllabic manner. Not that Thomas had noticed. One afternoon that October, just after opening time, the door of the Stag's Head swung open. There in the doorway stood Thomas, rotund, chest heaving. Beneath one mackintoshed arm he carried a copy of *The Dead Seagull*. Its dust jacket displayed a white seagull pierced with an arrow; a figure of St Sebastian embellished its spine. Thomas made his way over to the Yorkshire-born writer and radio producer Rayner Heppenstall, who was standing at the bar, and bought him a drink. 'Do you want to hear something?' he asked. When the two men were settled at their table, Thomas proceeded to read out sentences and whole paragraphs from Barker's novel, amid whoops of mutual laughter.[35]

In November Thomas was asked by Patrick Harvey of the Talks Department of the BBC to chair a programme for the series 'Poetic Licence', to be broadcast on the Third Programme. He agreed on two conditions. He was to choose the subject and Barker was to take part. The programme was to be transmitted on 13 December. Its format was to be 'an unscripted conversational discussion about bad verse'.[36]

CHAPTER 31

'BEAR THE DAY TO ME'

When *The Dead Seagull* appeared in October 1950, it was perhaps inevitable that Smart should interpret it as a riposte to *By Grand Central Station*. Despite his enthusiastic reception of the typescript in 1943, she had good reason to suspect that Barker had since changed his opinion; already by 1947 he was describing her work to Michael Asquith as 'a scream from the ovaries', implying that it was urgent, passionately realised, but lacked artistic restraint. In fact, the two novels address themselves to quite distinct ends and they differ completely in their circumstances. *By Grand Central Station* is set in California, Canada and New York in 1940–41 and follows, with a fair degree of fidelity, its author's affair with Barker, who is, however, not named. *The Dead Seagull* is set in 1934–5, in Worth Matravers. Much local detail is there to identify the village, where Barker had already set 'The Bacchant': the small and unfashionable cottage facing the sea, the Goat and Compass pub 'small as a tea-cosy', like the Square and Compass in Worth; the strip lynchets, across which the newly married couple stroll towards the distant and furious cove; the tiny dining room in which they spend their mornings and from which 'we could look out and watch ships crawl across the horizon, taking a whole afternoon for a voyage that, with our eyes, we could cover in an instant'.

The wife is called Theresa, one of Jessica's baptismal names. A child waits to be born, much as Clare had done in the spring of 1934. Like Jessica, Theresa possesses long dark hair and eyes like cathedral windows. Like Jessica, too, she is much inclined to prayer. She patiently awaits her delivery, while her young poet-husband journeys up to London to secure a grant from a literary society. Into this paradise walks Marsden Forsden, a schoolfriend of Theresa's. She is a tornado of a girl: long-legged, rapacious, tactless, demanding. She arrives with her diminutive, grey-haired, Greek lover, Theokopolos. Marsden lures the narrator away from the marital home and up to London, where they spend several happy, hoggish weeks making love, quarrelling and strolling by the river. Eventually, in disgust with the squalor of Marsden's life and living conditions, the narrator returns to Dorset, where he finds his wife close to childbirth. Jealousy brings her contractions on, but the trauma of their separation and desertion have taken too great a toll and mother and child – a son – soon die, she with a curse upon her lips. The story ends with a long open letter from the protagonist to his deceased wife and his stillborn son, Sebastian, expounding Newman's version of the doctrine of original sin. The letter is supposedly written by the father at a time when the child would have been entering adolescence.

Theokopolos may well have been based on Jean Varda, Elizabeth's lover when Barker met her: in that case he has shrunk, aged and lost his Latin hauteur. Marsden, however, is too storm-tossed, gauche and indiscreet to represent Elizabeth. Her stridency, her coarse good looks, her lack of moderation instead recall Emily Coleman, with whom Barker was intermittently involved at the time when the novel is set. Marsden's Circe-like den by the river is based on 7 Oakley Street, where Barker stayed during his weekly sorties from Plush. The child born at the end is Clare, with her gender altered and her adoption transformed into a death. Both these changes had occurred in poems written by Barker immediately after his daughter's adoption. The name given to the child in the novel is common property, since by 1950 Barker had two sons called Sebastian, one in America and another in England, about both of whom he had reason to feel guilty.

Other details are borrowings from other persons, times and places. It was with Elizabeth, not Jessica, that George was wont to play Scarlatti on the gramophone, as the narrator does with Theresa in the novel (in the first draft, the composer had been Kit's favourite, Purcell). The tipsy squalor in which Marsden lives in Chelsea is Elizabeth's at Condicote. The lake by which the narrator walks racked by contrition is the Lago d'Iseo, which George visited with Jessica in 1937 and which he revisited with Cass in 1949. The vision towards the end of the book of the narrator's child as a living ten-year-old urchin takes place on Sunday, 27 August 1944, one month after Clare's tenth birthday.

The book is almost equally divided between passages of narrative and theological interpretation. The first are perhaps more successful than the second. Certain editorial cuts enforced by John Lehmann led to an occasional abruptness and, as a result, the novel's logic is not entirely convincing. The protagonist is pleased with his perfidies, although he pretends to be disgusted by them. A kind of double vision is caused throughout by the fact that, though the setting is English, the images are often rococo and Italianate, as is the style. Of Marsden's lechery, the narrator declares:

I see in her ... the state of grace worn naturally by us all before the Fall, when the nude mother, with a puzzle of children about her, walked over the fields, unaware that she was again pregnant, unable to recall any events that might have given origin to her babies, conscious only of the sun, the earth, the satisfaction of the body, and an incomprehensible tenderness towards her children. Unable to recall any events that might have given rise to her babies for the ineffable reason that sexual love, to the truly innocent, to the truly innocent in a state of grace, must be as naturally virtuous as any of the bodily obligations, and therefore indistinguishable from them. Without the inherent and inherited magnification of original sin, we live in a world where a sneeze and an orgasm hold a candle to one another, and illuminate nothing.[1]

The theology is peculiar and as personal as it is patristic. Like 'Sacred Elegies', *The Dead Seagull* is concerned with the self-absorbed nature of sexual loving, which excludes the outside world as surely as it excludes God. The book's thesis is easily stated. When in love, we all assume sexual desire and spiritual love to be guided by the same nurturing purpose. Experience, however, suggests that Eros is destructive. Barker derives this view partly from St Augustine's doctrine of sex as the definitive form of original sin, but he adds an individual twist to this orthodox theology. Reproduction relies upon desire. Since desire sometimes renders us callous towards others, it also depends on cruelty. The victims seem implicity aware of this fact: 'The cut worm forgives the plough.' Moreover, cruelty serves as raw material for the operations of divine grace, which requires objects for its eventual clemency. To qualify for forgiveness we must deserve damnation; to earn damnation we must sin. In the sexual sphere sinning is achieved through the act of procreation – 'in sin hath my mother conceived me'. This act itself gives rise to new innocences, who will in turn be corrupted and in turn beg to be forgiven. Good flows from evil. In the concluding words of the novel, 'For freedom is the knowledge of necessity, and the necessity of the human is love, and the necessity of love is existence, and the necessity of existence is two sinning in a bed, and the necessity of two sinning in a bed is to be forgiven. It is thus that our only freedom is to be damned.'[2]

The book has two flaws. First, it cannot quite believe in the mercy that it proposes. In this parable of judgement the sins of the fathers are too literally visited upon the children. The fact that Theresa and Sebastian die, whereas their real-life originals did not, suggests that the author is far more convinced of the reality of nemesis than of divine mercy. The second fault is that the indulgently rueful male voice we hear most of the time traps the book in a perpetual cycle of self-accusation and self-justification. Marsden never speaks at any length and Theresa's only vocal contribution is her dying curse. In this the novella contrasts vividly with *Alanna Autumnal* in which the most effective voice, and the most effectively judgemental, is the sister's. Even in *Janus* the feminine within the male personality is given its say. *The Dead Seagull* possesses neither of these enriching dimensions.

The book's publication caused a chill between George and Elizabeth in the closing months of 1950. For many weeks he avoided Tilty Mill. When in London, he slept in the 'Doll's House' at Stanhope Gardens.

On 4 February 1951 Eileen's husband Philip died unexpectedly. The Barker family gathered for the wake, which Oliver Bernard recorded in his diary. Oliver was torn between anxiety about Jeff, on the run from National Service and a dawning desire for George's niece Veronica. He arrived at Queen's Gate to find Eileen in shock, with Young John, Olga and their younger brother Barry attempting to comfort her. David Wright hung around, ineffectually pressing his attentions on Veronica. Archer came late and then departed abruptly; George drove up from from Hearne. Late in the evening Veronica disappeared upstairs, expecting Oliver to follow her. Instead he stayed in the kitchen, where George, Eileen and David repeated the song 'Irish Eyes' far into the night, until Eileen's eyes filled with tears.

Throughout the earlier part of 1951 Elizabeth kept her distance from George. To make ends meet, she took a job as sub-editor on the magazine *House and Garden*. Since this necessitated her spending the weekdays in London, she persuaded Caspar John, whose father the painter Augustus she had met briefly at Scarlett, to sublet his flat in Flood Street just off Chelsea Embankment. She moved the children there from Essex and sent them to the Froebel school round the corner.[3] John Davenport rented a flat upstairs. Sydney Graham, who had been commuting between lodgings in Norfolk and the Roberts' place in Lewes, moved into Smart's flat at weekends. The two had known one another for months around the circuit of Soho pubs; now they grew closer. Elizabeth had intended the flat to be a metropolitan base where she might write in relative peace. In the upshot it was principally her children who wrote, on the walls. The Roberts themselves were now down on their luck. In December Colquhoun had exhibited his Italian drawings at the Lefevre Gallery, but it was to be his last show there. He had also recently failed to secure a commission from the Festival of Britain. Since the Roberts had by this time lost their studio in Lewes, they camped at Flood Street. By the late spring Archer, Graham and Bill Mackenzie, George's former co-tenant at Newlyn, were all more or less living in the flat, having, as Cass pointedly informed Kit and Ilse in America, 'recently discovered what a wonderful [person] E. Smart is (Are my nails showing?)'.[4]

Meanwhile, now that Barker had lifted his embargo on her writing, Cass began to contribute reviews for *Books of Today*. He reported to Kit that her style was 'very filigree'; he added that she waxed more and more beautiful, as did Chi-Chi, 'the other cat'. Against Smart, however, his anger seethed. By June she and the essentially monogamous Graham were in the throes of an affair. Smart told Barker that the relationship was 'a detour of no real significance', but he was still sufficiently wounded to upbraid her in his journal: 'it really is quite simple: the trust is entirely gone between us'.[5] The affair also complicated his relationship with Graham, of whom he was genuinely fond. Besides, they possessed a common muse in Smart, as Barker had implied in a sonnet:

> Break
> Her sleeping heart with an Ajax fist
> And she, my lifelong love, dovetongued and bright,
> Will sleep with me, for I can patch her pitcher
> Enfountain it, fold, hold, and befriend it.[6]

Barker was caught in a dilemma: implicitly punishing Elizabeth by keeping his distance, he was still prepared to mythologise her in verse as 'the mermaid with immortality in her hair'. In his private myth she consorted with sea images, became Undine the unreachable, the doomed. He remembered a telegram that she had sent him once from Pender Harbor – 'bear the day to me' – and wrote his finest yet love lyric, to which he would always subsequently refer as 'my Undine poem':

> Turn on your side and bear the day to me
> Beloved, sceptre struck, immured
> In the glass walls of sleep. Slowly
> Uncloud the borealis of your eye
> And show your iceberg secrets, your midnight prizes
> To the green-eyed world and to me.[7]

The poem was about making love in the morning, or rather the moment before that occurs. No more exclusively addressed to Elizabeth than the Cycles of Love Lyrics had been, it was a universal erotic aubade and could have been applied just as credibly to Cass as to Elizabeth, or to both women at once in relation to the reverential male psyche. This sort of ambiguity could render him callous. One evening Cass accompanied him on one of his jaunts to Soho. In the pub he grew irritated with her. Departing hastily, he walked down the pavement towards the Underground while she dragged along behind. At the foot of the escalator, he rounded on her with searing eyes, shouting, 'You think that the Undine poem is yours don't you? Well, it's not; it is Elizabeth's.' He then boarded the train with Cassiopeia, destroyed, following after.[8]

In July Oliver married Veronica. For the reception at Stanhope Gardens, Pa provided champagne for everyone at 3s 6d a bottle.[9] Meanwhile, Caspar John had noticed the graffiti on the wall at Flood Street, and ordered Elizabeth to quit his flat. She moved back to Tilty Mill with her children and the Roberts. Barker was expected to turn up to welcome them, but declined. As soon as they had settled the Roberts in as childminders, Elizabeth and Graham set out for Rome. On Sunday, 12 August they reached Spoleto, where Elizabeth's heart softened. Remembering the nuptials at San Bernardino exactly eleven years before, she dashed off a letter to Hearne:

It is 12th August which means eleven years and what is all this foolishness I don't know. It is a waste. How long can anger last? Is it forever? I can see you perfectly vividly counting up these cobbled streets for a thousand and one nights without me. Why are your sins forgivable and not mine? When I smell life then I remember it is such a short time to be alive. When are you going to forgive me?[10]

But Barker sat in Sussex and refused to be drawn. He had learnt to use Hearne Cottage as a refuge, from where he viewed the problems of the wider world with apparent detachment. When the sun was shining the cottage and the pasture behind it appeared so exquisite that he would sit for hours merely gazing. He wrote to Kit that the view induced a state of mind similar to amnesia. It became rather laborious to remember who one was.

In August David Wright announced his engagement to a young actress from New Zealand called Philippa Reid. Late in the month George and Cass went to drink with them in the saloon bar of the Old Duke of Wellington in Wardour Street. There they met the young Anthony Cronin, over from Dublin, who was writing poetry while earning his living as a journalist. Halfway through the evening Barker spotted Dylan Thomas entering the public bar and pushed through the throng to speak to him. Before long Cronin became aware of voices being raised. Thomas was shouting over the hubbub that Barker was an 'Irish shyster', who should leave him in peace.[11] The relationship between the two poets was evidently as touchy as ever. Now it was Barker who made the overtures, aware of Thomas's celebrity, but also genuinely wishing to be friendly. He was often rebuffed.

When Wright married Philippa on 6 October, he invited Barker to be best man. Barker took Cass up to London for the ceremony. After drinks in the Lamb in Lamb's Conduit Street, the wedding party moved on to the

Register Office in Russell Square. They returned to the Lamb, then went on to Wright's flat in Great Ormond Street, where Barker handed David an elegantly wrapped parcel. It contained his wedding present: a small silver ring. He told Wright that he ordered similar ones from a silversmith in London for his own use. When one of them was placed on his penis, it heightened the pleasure of his women. Wright asked him what explanation he gave to the silversmith. Barker answered that the receipts specified 'serviette rings'.[12] Later he wrote David and Philippa an Epithalamium:

> Sweat, wicked kissers, in your stark
> Hate of the whitewashed day;
> By the queen-swarm of your breast
> Where lolls a honeycombing hand
> No peeping constellations may
> Eavesdrop upon you as you clip
> Each other in the old Adam's nest,
> And in an evening silvered cup
> Love's upspringing sunrise catch
> Till the winged bloodhorses of sex
> Dead heat, and meet their match.[13]

In December a new poetry magazine was launched, edited by the poet Tristram Hull with Wright's assistance. *Nimbus* carried contributions from Heath-Stubbs, Wright and John Fairfax. Since Barker now tolerated Cass's journals, she polished up an entry written in Settignano, which went in the first issue. Barker himself wrote a hymn to Methedrine. Calling it 'Dionysian Stanzas', he dedicated it to the doctor who had first prescribed the drug for him: Karl Theodor Bluth:

> Always, behind the grinning glass and the ape
>   I see them stare
> The lipsticked grinning women and the butchered goblets
>   Of Apollo there
> Crying up from the alcohol and the leary dream
> 'It is better to die after all the same'.[14]

The tranquillity of Hearne Cottage had quite reconciled Barker to England. When John Malcolm Brinnin arrived from the States, flushed with the success of his second Dylan Thomas tour and proposing to promote one with Barker, he was met with less enthusiasm than he had hoped. Barker realised that he had not the slightest desire ever to cross the Atlantic again.[15] So he accepted Brinnin's invitation on two conditions. The first was that Cass should accompany him, with all expenses paid. The second was that the readings should be transferred to Madrid.

CHAPTER 32

'RIGOR LEAVIS'

By now Barker had very mixed feelings about the United States. Though he knew many of the country's leading poets personally, his reading of American verse had in fact been fairly sporadic, and he regarded much of what he had seen as lax and ill focused. Since 1946 he had gone to some pains to set a distance between himself and American culture. In the summer of 1948 he had reviewed for *Poetry London* new volumes by Conrad Aiken, Karl Shapiro and his old friend Dunstan Thompson. The title of his review, 'The Fat Lady at the Circus',[1] had implied that American verse was a grotesquely inflated freak. 'Contemporary American poetry', he had concluded, 'is vulgar only because, like the nouveau riche, it is imitative, and not because it is plebeian: and only vigorous – e.g. Kenneth Patchen – when it is so abominably bad that the badness has to be responsible for the vigour. Most of the best American poetry is anaemic, anglo-philian and academic; and when it is not these things it is bombastic, incompetent and bloody.' The academicism particularly dismayed him since he was growing increasingly convinced that the universities now held modern poetry by the throat. Ever since Japan he had come to regard university teachers of literature as people who had never grown up. As poetry grew more school-bound, it relapsed in his eyes into patent immaturity. But the world seemed to be going into short trousers and there was not much that he could do about it. By the early 1950s he felt himself to be besieged by Americans and scholars or, as he preferred to call them, by 'schoolboys'.

The Americans arrived in waves. The harbinger had been Marius Bewley, who reached England in 1949 having completed his studies at Columbia and resolved to write a doctoral thesis under the acerbic F.R. Leavis in Cambridge. Bewley had immediately reported to Barker on the 'Athenian' or homoerotic potential of Cambridge students: 'I just can't decide who belongs to that blessed race, and who doesn't. Your finer British types, I can't take my eyes off them, they're so lovely. I prefer the flow and ripple of manners here, but I can never judge the nature of the moral reality under such frills and ruffles. I'm afraid that I shall always be confused – but, ah, delightfully so.'[2]

In Bewley's wake came John Farrelly, who was at last to read for the English Tripos at Downing College, again under Leavis. In September 1951 he arrived with his sister Doodles, his second wife Lavinia, known as Dede, and their two-year-old daughter Elizabeth. The Farrellys settled themselves into the University Arms Hotel, while John walked to Downing to meet Leavis. Then he wrote to Barker asking if he might see him. The following week he and Dede journeyed to London, where they met George at the Café Royal. Dede found him charming but moody: not, she thought, quite her type.[3]

Two months later, a less welcome transatlantic visitor arrived: Willard Maas. Marie Maas had been lavish with her promises of royalties for *The Geography of the Body*, but no payments had been paid for some years. Eventually Marie had enclosed ten dollars in a letter informing Barker that he was owed thirty. Meanwhile Willard had been writing letters of sentimental lubriciousness to 'George Barker Esq., Stanhope Gardens'. These notes were opened by Pa, who was not pleased to find himself addressed thus: 'And, pretty companion of my middle years, if I get to London there ain't going to be a red redder than the paint we'll pour over that wretched city.'[4] In November 1951 Marie sent Barker a cable informing him that Willard was about to put his plan into effect; the result was an instant defensive reconciliation with Elizabeth, to whom he wrote, 'I suppose you've had one too. I mean the cable that Marie has just sent me from New York informing me about Willard having left for England. In the circumstances, I suggest that we all ought immediately to embark for California.'[5]

When Willard arrived, he was fat, run to seed and had, as Barker told Heath-Stubbs in Noël Cowardian tones, totally lost his '*beaut-ay*'. He steeped himself in the Soho pubs, claiming to anybody who would listen that he was not only the dedicatee of 'Secular and Sacred Elegies', but the subject of the Cycles of Love Poems as well. Small chance, commented George, who could not recall what he had ever seen in him. In their impromptu alliance against this intruder from the past Elizabeth and George began to recapture some of their old fondness for one another. They finished 1951 on the best of possible terms, with George paying almost weekly visits to Tilty. There he fell under the spells of his cherubic five-year-old daughter Rose and Christopher, who at eight had developed an absolute mania for cycling.

Barker celebrated the New Year of 1952 by carousing with Eliot at Hennekey's in the Strand, where his mentor surprised him by alternately drinking single and double gins. Then he disappeared into a fug of cigarette smoke at Hearne to finish a play about Chatterton in Hell, promised to

Desmond Hawkins, now a producer with the BBC in Bristol. Chatterton was an old love, whose canonical sin of suicide he now punished by the interrogation of a celestial policeman. The result, however, was rather more like Barker facing the heeby-jeebies of his conscience:

> *Voice of Chatterton echoing remotely in a great space, like that of a choir-boy*: What do you want of me? What do you want?
> *Interrogator*: If you can bear me I would like to ask of you some questions.
> *Chatterton*: For God's sake, leave me alone. Leave me alone. Let me at least retain the dignity of my condemnation. Have you got nothing better to do than to ask impertinent questions of dead men? Leave me alone. All of your questions could have only one answer. I suffer forever in that garish corner of Hell devised for those who have taken their own lives by violence. Leave me alone.[6]

He delivered the script to Hawkins at the Old Swan, where they were joined by Wright and Roy Campbell. Hawkins, who had not met Barker since the war, was taken aback by the change in him. The shy, self-protective carapace of the early 1930s had been replaced by something loud, gravelly and, from Hawkins's point of view, 'oafish'.[7] Hawkins also had misgivings about the practicability of recreating in a tiny studio in Broadcasting House an aural inferno consisting of 'a susurrus of an infinite number of voices calling one another sweet names'. 'My only weapons, my dear George, will be a studio and microphone and perhaps half a dozen actors, plus some gramophone turntables.'[8]

Barker was quite capable of arranging his own shindy. He had decided that relations with Pa were now sufficiently amicable for him to be able to hold his thirty-ninth birthday at Stanhope Gardens. The celebrations were seemingly invaded by half of Soho. The party went well until, at one in the morning, a message arrived that 'Colonel Barker' was descending the stairs with a horsewhip. The room emptied, apart from some two dozen bodies, whom Eileen's eleven-year-old daughter Olga discovered littered in postures of fervent slumber when she came downstairs for her morning tap-dancing practice.[9] She put on her tap shoes and clattered across the white room, picking her way daintily among the poets and painters. When Big Mumma arrived to cook breakfast, she found that the larder was empty. Among the sleeping guests, Olga darted, performing her steps.

While in America, Kit had exhibited his paintings in New York, San Francisco and St Louis. Ilse meanwhile had published a novel with Putnams, *Fire in the Sun* set in Cornwall and London, in which Kit's loyalty to George is transposed on to the devotion felt by its heroine Veronica Demeade for her poet brother Everett. Early in 1952 Kit and Ilse moved back to England. They toured the Sussex countryside, looking for a house to buy. Nothing was available for under £1,000 and their total means were £200. One Sunday morning George drove them in his Talbot up Bexley Hill to a ridge overlooking Blackdown, not ten miles from Hearne. Just back from the road they found the Old Cottage, Lodsworth, Elizabethan and empty. On the Monday morning Kit went into Haslemere and phoned the agents from the post office. He was told that the Old Cottage belonged to the Provost of Portsmouth, who with a little persuasion from Kit's solicitor, eventually agreed to sell. On 27 March 1952 Kit and Ilse moved in.[10] The brothers spent their spare hours tinkering with the Talbot; at weekends they drank together in the local pubs. Once more the fraternal bond steadied them both.

To George, however, the scholars were beginning to be a worry. The problem was that, in his heart of hearts, Barker believed criticism and creativity to be incompatible. The Mecca of academic criticism in the early 1950s was decidedly Cambridge. Barker was conscious that the 'practical criticism' which had been introduced into the English School there by I.A. Richards shed little light upon his own incantatory verse, on top of which the bracing moral absolutes epitomised by F.R. Leavis were at odds with his whole way of life. Leavis was as powerful an influence in the academic culture of England in the 1950s as Barker was amongst the London bohemians. For young men caught between the ends of criticism and creativity, Leavis and Barker were the North and South Poles of literary life.

At Cambridge Farrelly was now firmly ensconced as Leavis's favourite student. He still harboured ambitions to write, but Leavis had convinced him that the only respectable fiction belonged to a 'Great Tradition', and that novels of lesser stature than Tolstoy's *Anna Karenina* were otiose. Farrelly had attempted to write a work as ambitious in scale as *Anna Karenina*, but had failed. Moreover, as his journals show, he was not sure whether he wished more passionately to be a bohemian artist or a draconian critic. As Heath-Stubbs and Wright had already discovered, it was difficult to be both. Sometimes Farrelly seemed like a moth drawn towards Barker's brilliant blue flame; he also needed, temperamentally, to dance attendance upon the severe doctor. The choice was cruel: to be either saint or sinner. To his right loured the puritanical and hortatory features of Leavis; to his left grinned the subversive gargoyle of Barker. By the summer of 1952 the need to decide between these two presiding geniuses, to reconcile their influences within him, was tearing Farrelly apart. Though he did not know it, he was in this respect acting out one of the principal cultural dilemmas of the decade.

To begin with, he tried dodging in between. Leavis had started to entrust him with minor reviewing commissions for *Scrutiny*, handing him Scott Fitzgerald with the tart instruction, 'Annihilate him!'[11] Farrelly asked Leavis and his wife Queenie to his house in Barton Road. Though both were virtual teetotallers, they soon became – within the limits of their temperance – frequent and enthusiastic visitors. At the beginning of the Lent Term Farrelly invited Barker to Cambridge to give a reading, before which he snapped the photogenic Cass on the Backs. Subsequently Barker too started to call at Barton Road, after first making sure that there would be no danger of bumping into Leavis. Once, when Barker turned up unexpectedly, Farrelly had to postpone his weekly supervision with Leavis. He gave an inflamed appendix as an excuse. Dede conveyed this white lie in person to Leavis, who replied through his nose, and in his voice infamously narrowed by First World War mustard gas: 'Remarkable, Mrs Farrelly. I didn't know a man could come equipped with two appendices. I understood that Mr Farrelly's had been removed already.'

After they were reconciled, Leavis took to walking his supervisee up and down the Barton Road, complaining about Queenie. Once again Farrelly was like Marlowe's Dr Faustus, caught between a Good Angel and a Bad. When Barker announced his next visit, Farrelly walked anxiously to Newnham Village to acquire a bagful of gin bottles. He walked back to Barton Road, clinking as he went. As he fumbled with his door key, he heard his guest crunching on the gravel behind him. He turned to greet him. It was not Barker, but Leavis. Farrelly adjusted his expression, pitched the gin bottles into the hedge and advanced with sycophantic hand extended.[12]

In 1952 Karl Miller was another of Leavis's students at Downing, though of a more robustly independent cast of mind than the impressionable Farrelly, whose tormented fluttering he noted. He was also aware that Marius Bewley, now acting as Leavis's assistant, was strongly drawn to Barker. In Barker's opinion, however, Bewley, who had a genuine talent for criticism, had already strayed too far into the Leavisite camp. He had once been a young man of promise; now, Barker told Miller, 'rigor Leavis' had got him. Bewley for his part confided his suspicions that Leavis too was an 'Athenian'.[13] Neither Miller nor Farrelly believed this piece of scurrility, nor did anybody else.

When Farrelly rented a villa at Dinard on the north Britanny coast for the long vacation, he proposed to invite George and Cass to share it. Before he could, Dede mentioned the holiday casually to the Leavises. Leavis phoned back: 'I'm not going to ask if it's any inconvenience. We're coming.' His acceptance put Barker joining them out of the question. The Leavises stayed for two weeks. After their departure, Dede found a message on the kitchen table: 'Weather variable. Accommodation adequate.'

Meanwhile Barker and Cass were in the south of France. Barker had recently developed an enthusiasm for the works of the Marquis de Sade, whose château

'RIGOR LEAVIS'

at La Coste he was investigating with Cass. In the town they found an inn so picturesquely primitive that its upper storey consisted of a more or less unconverted *grenier*, with bales of straw for furniture and a straw-stuffed mattress for a bed. Barker sat at the window surveying the wide expanses of the plain beyond. In the evenings he recounted the exploits of the marquis with much relish and, Cass thought, embellishment. They consummated their pilgrimage by rummaging for Sadean works in the bookshops.[14]

After this, Barker kept his distance from Cambridge. Ten years later he had his last word on the subject in a satirical ode entitled 'On a Distant Prospect of English Poetry and Downing College'. Frowning in Downing, Bewley, Farrelly and Miller had, it implied, lost more than they had gained:

> What can we learn
> from a loss so grievous?
> Now we shall feel the
> *rigor leavis*.
> Abandoned? No,
> the homonym
> offends the lucid
> mind of him
> whom even the gods –
> reduced to grammar
> as inconclusive
> as a stammer –
> address in an
> uncertain manner.
> Farewell great doctor
> of minor clauses
> parentheses and
> victorious causes
> winged witticisms and
> wingless horses.
> How can we ever
> really thank
> a doctor for being
> so very frank
> that every time
> the queen sickens
> he simply mutters
> What the Dickens
> and to our

> extreme abhorrence
> reveals to us
> King Charles' Head
> belongs in fact to
> D. H. Lawrence.[15]

At Oxford, too, a new generation of students reading English – Geoffrey Hill at Keble, George Macbeth at New College, Anthony Thwaite at Christchurch – was taking stock of Barker's position in the scheme of things. He was invited to read at the university several times. Each visit seemed to him like a sortie into enemy territory and an opportunity to display his difference. On 6 May 1952 he was asked by Thwaite to read to the University Poetry Society. Macbeth procured a crate of sherry for the committee, some of which was sampled in Thwaite's rooms. When the undergraduates and their guest were on their way to the room booked for the reading, Barker clattered down the staircase, shouting out behind him, 'My dear Thwaite, you cost too much.'[16] Throughout the evening Barker made his detachment from the proceedings very clear. Years later Edward Lucie-Smith, then a scholar at Merton, recalled:

> he left us impressed, frightened, and puzzled. Barker's refusal to recognize hierarchical decencies, or the merits of reason or order, and his failure to be impressed by the university itself, all upset us. We failed to recognize in him both a survivor of pre-war Bohemia, and a precursor, in attitudes if not in speech and dress, of the flower-power hippies who were later to show such contempt for our generation of, as they thought, smug conformists. I cannot remember anything that Barker said to us, either at the reading or at the various pubs to which we took him afterwards, but I can still recall the amused, ironic glances he darted at us from time to time from under the heavy lids of his eyes.[17]

Before boarding the train to Paddington, Barker promised to compensate Macbeth for the sherry with 'an apostolic dozen of the very best amontillado'. Thirty years later Macbeth was still waiting.[18]

Behind the posturing, though, lay a considered intellectual position. Barker's belief that academic criticism *per se* was deeply destructive of the creative urge had hardened into dogma. Oliver Bernard was now reading for a degree at Goldsmith's College in London, hoping eventually to subsidise his writing by the financial security of teaching. He showed his work to Barker, who reacted by coaxing him away from too much reliance on influences culled from his studies. Like Farrelly, Bernard was torn between gods. He needed,

Barker thought, to decide between them. When Oliver sent him a poem with Tennysonian echoes, Barker replied:

> I do think that you are permitting your great predecessors to sit rather heavily on your shoulder. One thing, surely, that justifies a new poet is that what he writes is new poetry. To an always reasonable (by this I mean of course to a never reasonable) degree, your poems should, I think, be the declared enemies of your studies, because you ought to enjoy your poems and only scholars enjoy their studies. The scholastic poet is a contradiction in terms. He happens, but like the mule or the tiglon, it would be better if he didn't.[19]

Once, as a very young man, Barker had felt envious of writers with university educations. By 1952 he had long since grown out of this feeling. Universities now appeared to him to be alien territory where he ventured for financial reward and to strengthen his hold over the young. He was, for example, open to the plan of taking an academic residency which might enable him to nurture students' creative work, without involving him in formal instruction. When the biennial Gregory Fellowship in Poetry at Leeds fell vacant that summer, he wrote to Eliot soliciting his aid in bending the ear of Bonamy Dobrée, the incumbent Professor of English. In August, after John Heath-Stubbs had been offered the position, Eliot wrote to say that there was nothing else that he could now do.[20] In 1954, when Heath-Stubbs's tenure was over, Barker applied for the fellowship again. This time the appointment went to Thomas Blackburn, Durham graduate and former schoolmaster, another young poet whom Barker had encouraged in his resolve to concentrate on writing rather than teaching. Increasingly Barker's protegés would obtain the positions he himself coveted. He used these frustrations and privations to intensify his status as a pariah. In the later 1950s, as a quieter, more academically responsible poetry drifted into vogue, the predicament isolated him. It also made him more resolutely defiant with every passing year.

CHAPTER 33

'ART CRAP! POETRY CRAP!'

By the New Year of 1953 Smart's brief affair with Graham was over. Barker could now regard his *entente cordiale* with Tilty Mill as firmly established. There then ensued a period of precarious compatibility between the various components of Barker's life. He settled into a pattern whereby he spent the greater part of the week writing at Hearne, and periods of two of three days staying either at Stanhope Gardens or at Tilty. Each re-emergence from rural seclusion featured, in the eyes of friends, as a catalytic event. Twenty years afterwards Wright would recall the contagious effect:

> On those nights when George was 'up', the pubs in the environs of Old Compton Street would crowd with friends and disciples, mysteriously assembled by some form of ESP or telepathic tocsin. It was a phenomenon I often experienced. About six or seven on any given evening one 'knew', felt in one's bones as it were, that he would be around that night. Sure enough, by nine o'clock in the Pillars of Hercules, the French, or the public bar of the Duke of Wellington, whichever was the establishment in favour at the period, one would find George Barker, tartan-shirted, slightly hunched, standing at the mahogany counter in the middle of a mob of poets and painters, similarly summoned, who would come, as I did, to listen and participate in some of the best talk in London, comic and profound, passionate and humorous.[1]

Another favoured venue was the Colony Room club, founded in 1948 by Muriel Belcher in an upstairs room in Dean Street. Barker drank there with Johnny Minton, exchanging scabrous jokes and improvising odes and elegies, as Minton once put it 'by the dozen. They sweep them up after closing time.' Since the Colony was strictly for members only, Barker had always to be 'signed in' by Elizabeth, who belonged. His authority and independence were more firmly asserted on Sunday nights, when his devotees clustered round him in the Queen's Elm in the Fulham Road. In later years it would come to seem to a crony like Bruce Bernard that every weekend of his youth had culminated thus, with George presiding over a rubgy scrum of admirers, cajoling, punning, needling.

For the occasional weekend Barker chose not to spend in London, there was a bed permanently at his disposal at Tilty Mill, among the company of rogues and rascals to whom Elizabeth played host. Often without warning, he would arrive on Friday evening, clad in black leather gloves and as intent over the wheel as a Grand Prix ace. The unpredictability of these visits puzzled and excited the children. The Roberts were now fixtures at Tilty, where they acted as nannies during Smart's busy office hours in London. Colquhoun was working on the set designs for a production of *King Lear* at Stratford; in the evenings he caroused with MacBryde at the Rising Sun in the village, purchasing drinks on Smart's credit and running up a huge bill. Graham was often down at weekends; in the holidays Eileen's younger children joined the rabble, little Olga finding her feet amongst Elizabeth's growing brood. John Deakin, artist and reluctant photographer of genius, with whom Elizabeth had worked on *Vogue*, hung about. A picture taken on his Rolleiflex in May 1952, captures the carnival atmosphere of those weekends, creating in the process a slightly false sense of family togetherness: spindly legged Georgina tossing a ball; Christopher on his bike; Sebastian hiding behind a car tyre; five-year-old Rose in bare feet, cuddling up to Elizabeth for comfort, and behind them Graham uncharacteristically shy-looking in his jeans; Colquhoun haunted; MacBryde swaggering with dark glasses and a cigarette; George looking proudly down at the children; Young John bashful; Paul Potts noble and sad. Deakin was a perceptive, but slightly detached observer of this coterie. One Sunday evening in 1953, after the children had gone to bed, Barker ensconsed himself in a corner with Colquhoun. When Deakin attempted to split up their *tete à tete*, George remarked, 'My dear Deakin, life is a sea of boiling blood. If I on my island and Colquhuon on his island may not be permitted to wave to one another across the ensanguined flood, it is a pretty sorry state of affairs.' Full of philistine fury, Deakin spat back, 'Art crap! Poetry crap!'[2]

Deakin was the Grand Inquisitor amongst the photographers of the 1950s, using his skill to unmask cultural pretence. But he was just as likely to connive with his subjects in projecting their sense of themselves as rugged or streetwise. One night he told Oliver Bernard that he was going to take his photograph in the morning, dismissing him with a brusque 'Don't shave!' The resulting mugshot was stubbly, hungry, mean-looking. Deakin's portraits of George brought out the proud integrity beneath the mercurial surface, while in Smart's case they exposed the strong facial structure underlying her glamour. Then there was Barker as bruiser, a cut on his left cheek jauntily displayed, chin pugnaciously flaunted, or eyes crossed in mock dementia. The intimacies of this artistic cabal are also to be seen. Deakin portrayed Smart looking girlish, her locks combed out, tucked up in bed with an improving book; or else tarty, with her hair up, offsetting the pallor of one cheek. The Roberts were arranged for the camera as a couple: MacBryde dapper in a bow tie, Colquhoun dark and feral, the two of them facing in complementary and opposed directions. His most abiding images, however, were those that revealed delinquency beneath an aesthetic pose: Lucian Freud long-boned and narcissistic; Francis Bacon, torso bared between two sides of meat, the ribs of all three visible in a spirit of macho camp; Barker again, like a criminal boxer, his hair slicked back with water or Brylcreem, exaggerating the baldness. One night, in the gentlemen's toilet at Piccadilly Circus Deakin caught Barker against the white tiles after a bout of drinking, his cap askew in pseudo-proletarian style, eyes insolently swimming, tie carelessly knotted, heavy-lidded, louche.

The tender harshness of these portraits is true to one aspect of Barker's social life at the time. Elsewhere, in the gilded cage of Hearne, a bucolic softness and ease prevailed. There in the summertime the Bernards and David Wright came and played cricket in the meadow. Kit and Ilse drove across frequently from the Old Cottage at Lodsworth. One February morning, Veronica, her marriage to Oliver now over, celebrated her twenty-first birthday in the cottage. Over the breakfast table George handed her a posy of verses: 'Come home, come home, daughter of grief and war / Come home to the veritable world.'

To preserve this cosy ambience, it was essential to Barker that some of his associates should meet rarely, if ever. At all costs Elizabeth must be kept from Hearne and Cass from Tilty. By 1953 Barker had begun to assume that it was Cass's duty to remain feminine in Sussex, while he enjoyed the masculine pleasures of London. He invented a new persona for her as bucolic nymph or superior milkmaid, and gave her the pet name 'Biddy' to match. The role was anomalous, not least because, as Bruce Bernard recalls, she looked at this period like Christian Dior's delegate to the Communist Party. Barker's expectations were all the more unreasonable since Cass was as drawn to London as he was. Robin Prising, an American poet who visited London then, met them together in Soho. He thought that Cass possessed 'a way of sitting on a stool as if inviting you to knock her off it'. Yet, if she invited missiles, she also gave the distinct impression that, if thrown, 'she would not dodge them'.[3]

And missiles and blows were thrown. Benzedrine had taken an inevitable toll, exacerbating Barker's fits of temper, which he had inherited from his father and paternal grandfather. At Hearne these eruptions would sometimes well up without warning, as if from some deep inner stress. Barker would be amicable for days. Then something would jar and he would flash out with bitter wit, or even with his fists. On one of Cass's eyeballs he raised a blood blister which refused to go away. He was deeply regretful for and humbled by these episodes, so out of keeping with a man who could on other occasions present his niece with affectionate verses over breakfast. The truth was, however, that such rages had now established themselves in the swing of his temperament. They belonged to an aspect of his behaviour that astonished people who, like Young John, had known him in earlier, milder days.

Heath-Stubbs alone recognised that the secret of his friend's mood changes lay in his occasional recitation of the border ballad 'Tam Lin' about a man captured by fairies and transformed into all manner of wild beasts. He will be sacrificed at the seven-year rites unless a girl redeem him and hold him tight. 'Anyone who knew George Barker', in the opinion of Heath-Stubbs, 'would see how close this story was to his own inner experience.'[4] In the ballad a girl called Janet, irresistibly attracted to Tam Lin despite his predicament, cradles him as he is transformed by turns into snake, deer, and then into molten metal:

> 'They'll shape me in your arms, ladye,
>   A hot iron at the fire,
> But hauld me fast, let me nat gae,
>   To be your heart's desire.
>
> 'They'll shape me in your arms, ladye,
>   A mother-naked man;
> Cast your green mantle over me,
>   And sae will I be won.'[5]

Cass was afraid of Barker's outbursts, but ready to accept them as a price she must pay for her chosen way of life. She interpreted them as an inevitable concomitant to an artistic disposition. 'If I belong anywhere at all in this alarming world,' she said later, 'it is with the Romantic movement, and that has to include the gory glory.' In Barker she believed that she had found 'the Holy Grail bogeyman himself'.[6]

The need to keep pace with life in Hearne, Tilty and Stanhope Gardens involved George in numerous rapid exits and entrances. Elizabeth had long grown used to these disruptions. In February 1953, five days before his fortieth birthday, he appeared at Tilty for a weekend *en famille*, and then at noon left abruptly providing no explanation.[7] At times Barker's behaviour was almost pathological. His notebooks – indiscriminately employed as memo pads – were littered with cryptic enquiries such as 'WHERE *ARE* YOU?' With no warning he would descend upon Hearne, expecting Cass to be waiting for him. This inscrutability and unpredictability led him and his partners into curious guessing games. At Hearne he would scribble a note which read, 'Dearest Cass. Meet me at the New Inn 7 p.m. Wednesday not Friday. I have a big surprise for you.' He would then disappear for days, leaving her on tenterhooks, with no company but the cat. On the rare occasions when she was permitted to accompany him to town, he would seldom tell her where they would be spending the night. Often they would find a bed at Stanhope Gardens or else with friends. Barker was, however, quite capable of losing himself in an amicable crowd in the pub, then absconding with them to some unknown address, so that Cass was left to wander the streets of Soho, a ghost lost in the dawn.

With Jeff Bernard, his conversation now was mostly about boxing and athletics. 'We watched the famous race between Christopher Chattaway and Vladimir Kuts one night in the Swiss pub,' Bernard remembered later. 'He lost ten shillings to me on the outcome and paid up saying that I was an "evil boy".'[8] The sheer physicality, the competitive muscularity of sports, still spoke to him, were still in his mind metaphors for art. On Thursday 26 February he awoke on a bright morning at Hearne to find himself forty. That morning, he wrote a poem extolling courage as the definitive poetic and masculine virtue:

> When princes asphyxiate themselves for private reasons
>   What can the rest of us do?
> There is no rest. Such princes in their passions
>   Are dead pilots who
> Teach us what not to do. From their gaudy lessons
>   Retrieve the knowledge
> That tall men walk upright in lightning because
>   It calls for more courage.[9]

Barker's fundamental respect for the integrity of the embattled self comes out in the tributes in prose and poetry which he was to write for Dylan Thomas, following Thomas's death in October that year. Though he and Thomas had always communicated across a distrustful void, readers would never have guessed it from these pieces. 'He goes before me in poems as he goes in dying,' Barker declared in an obituary essay. Thomas's work constituted as he saw it an integrated whole, 'a complete and working body, a natural organism, a shape and a pattern fulfilling and functioning, like a fly's eye or a stellar system'. The *Collected Poems* had been prefaced by a declaration that they had been written 'for the love of man and to praise God': a version, Barker thought, of the first sentence of Ignatius Loyola's *Spiritual Exercises*. With Thomas's death, the fount of praise had dried.[10] Barker later wrote an elegy 'At the Wake of Dylan Thomas', in which he imagined the infant Thomas wandering by the Swansea shore, teasing out torment from seashells:

> This son of pearl was walking beside water
> Taking the pain of sand out of the oyster:
> 'We will make poems,' he said, 'simply from joy.'
>
> And with the same wonder that the first amoeba
> Stepped out of hydrogen and saw God's labour,
> He goggled at glory as though it had just begun.[11]

Unlike Thomas, Barker had done little to encourage a Dionysian myth about himself. He had preferred the privacy of a select group of friends, and the secrecy entailed by his many exits and entrances. In 1953, however, he was driven out of the shadows. During much of that year Barker was obliquely involved in a bitter public controversy concerning the future of British broadcasting.

The storm brewed up in spring, when a debate between the relative merits of 'high-brow' and 'low-brow' culture ran in the newspapers for several weeks, competing for space alongside the Christie murder trial, the Mau Mau campaign in Kenya, and the preparations for the coronation of Elizabeth II. The bone of contention was the Conservative government's plan to license a second television channel, to be financed through advertisements. This scheme worried the BBC, whose monopoly was at risk. It was, however, very welcome to those who resented that monopoly, above all to certain sections of the popular press. The *Daily Sketch* possessed a deep detestation of the BBC and the Third Programme in particular, which it perceived as remote and patronising. In the newspaper's correspondence column, 'Pungent Post', letters were exchanged about the cultural exclusivity of the Third and its refined pronunciation of English: 'You should listen to the Thaird Progrem occasionally!' ran one headline. 'So euphony-ous.' One correspondent raised the question of the Third's pronunciation of 'Sir Walter Raleigh' in a history play: 'Had you hyard? The Thaird's Rorley is really Raleigh? Oh, *rarely?*' The *Sketch* was eager to catch out the Corporation as falling below the high standards set by its first director, Lord Reith.

It found an ideal opportunity. On 13 April at nine-forty in the evening, between a performance of Nielsen's First Symphony and a recital of piano music by Peter Katin, Barker read passages from *The True Confession* live on the Third. The editor of the *Sketch* had been listening in. The following day he sent two reporters to interview the poet at Hearne. They arrived during an April shower. As George and Cass returned from the cinema in Haslemere, they found the car carrying the unfortunate journalists stuck in the meadow, its back wheels churning futilely in the mud. Cass took the men inside the cottage, wrapped them in towels, and heated some soup for them. She asked them if they enjoyed poetry. No, they replied. The following Monday, the extracts from *The True Confession* were repeated in the interval of a serialisation of *A Tale of Two Cities*. The next morning the *Sketch*'s leader read:

WHAT WE THINK:
GILDED FILTH

From the Third Programme of the BBC last night came a tumbling stream of words. It was the repeat performance of George Barker's *True Confession* – extracts from a poem.

Had any newspaper dared to print such gilded filth a storm of protest would have followed. The Lord Chamberlain would never have permitted this on the stage of a public theatre or the Board of Film Censors on a screen.

Dirty thoughts are presented under the guise of culture. It is a challenge to basic dignities, a sexual meandering. It commits blasphemy in a condescending prayer. It covers up a fundamental cynicism with a dazzle of modern poetry.

The Third Programme is a public voice and a public entertainment. Where are its censors? The man responsible for approving this degrading half hour should be sacked.[12]

But the producer survived and for the time being the Corporation rode out the storm. Barker lay low at Tilty for a few days and then emerged as if nothing had happened.

For several months nothing else occurred. But on 13 November the government issued a White Paper called *A Memorandum on Television Policy*, outlining its detailed plans for the new commercial channel. There was an immediate revolt among the Tory peers, some of whom formed a National Television Council to resist the published proposals. The three members of the council were Lord Halifax, Viscount Hailsham and the Archbishop of Canterbury, the Right Reverend Geoffrey Fisher, former headmaster of Repton and a stickler for public probity. Early in the new parliamentary session Halifax tabled a motion in the Lords reading, 'While recognizing the desirability of an alternative programme, this House regrets that it cannot approve of the proposals of H.M. Government as outlined in the Memorandum on Television Policy.'

On the 25th an emergency debate was called in the Lords. Since Halifax had succumbed to flu, the motion was proposed by Lord Hailsham. His speech proved so successful that the following afternoon, when the debate resumed, every seat in the upper house was taken; several peers had to sit on the steps to the throne. So many MPs were watching from the gallery that the House of Commons was inquorate and the Speaker threatened to adjourn. At four forty-five the curmudgeonly Lord Balfour of Inchyre rose to address a packed chamber:

My noble friend Lord Hailsham, when he was speaking of intellectual and ethical standards paid tribute to what happens in children's television. He said that *Andy Pandy* was a family favourite of the Hailshams, and it is of my family as well. But we are rather more liberal. We also have *Muffin the Mule* and *Mr Turnip*. But there are certain features of the children's programmes which should never have been shown. The other day I turned on to a performance featuring Billy Bunter, and the first thing I saw was that somebody was shot in the stomach – not a very pretty sight for one's children.

Viscount Hailsham: Stick to *Listen with Mother*!

Lord Balfour of Inchyre: There is also a concentration upon gangsterism. The children's *Teleclub* concentrates on what is known as jive, dancing and all the superficialities of life. The worst example that I must submit to your Lordships is something that happened in the Third Programme – a piece of pornography which, I believe, should never have been printed, and certainly ought not to have been radioed [sic]. It was on Monday, April 13 last. I will not weary and disgust my Lords with too much of these passages from *The True Confession*: but when we think of the powerful peroration of Lord Samuel, in which he painted the picture of the Latin motto in Broadcasting House signifying the purity and moral integrity of the BBC ['quaecunque pulchra sunt et sincera quaecunque bonae famae'; 'whatsoever is lovely and of good report'], I do not see how the noble Viscount or the most reverend Primate could possibly agree with the last verse of this particularly offensive document that was recently broadcast. I must read eight lines to your Lordships. They are:

> Good God, let me recollect
>   Your many mercies, tall and short,
> The blousy blondes, the often necked,
>   And those whom I should not have thought

> Given wisely to me; nor let forget
>   My grateful memory the odd
> Consolers, too frequently brunette,
>   Who charged me for your mercies, God.

> That is the least offensive part of this particular document. I give your Lordships these examples just to try to debunk some part of the assumption that everything is so perfect with the BBC, and that the standards of commercialism will be so much lower.[13]

With that, the motion collapsed. Bunter and Barker between them had so compromised the integrity of public service broadcasting that the motion in favour of monopoly was rejected by 157 votes to 87. The result brought the Corporation to its knees. The Director-General Sir Alexander Cadogan himself begged their lordships' forgiveness, and promised that the producer concerned would be severely reprimanded. Writing in the *New Statesman* under the pseudonymn Flavius, the editor Kingsley Martin, whom Barker had recently described as 'a de-natured liberal old tom cat', wondered why the apology had been necessary. Admittedly, he commented in his leader, *The True Confession* was a very bad poem, but surely it was not quite *that* awful.[14]

At Gray's Inn the Law Lords had taken to heart Lord Balfour's comments in the upper chamber. They knew that the author of the offending poem was the son of the Inn's Butler (had not the *Greya* described him as 'the distinguished son of an equally distinguished father'?). They remembered the butler pressing upon them copies of his son's last book of poems *News of the World,* and wondered whether copies of this latest effusion might not be obtained for them. Pa attempted to pass off *The True Confession* as an an ephemeral piece, of minor significance in George's *oeuvre*. Finally, however, he was obliged to acknowledge that this time their lordships' interest in poetry stemmed from more than mere politeness. Reluctantly, he complied.

CHAPTER 34

'THAT BOY HAS A TIGER IN HIS LOINS'

In Barker's dealings with young protégés at this period, it is sometimes difficult to discern a demarcation between the nurturing aspect of the relationship and the dangerous or mischievous. Towards his more sensitive disciples, Barker often seems to have acted like a sort of compassionate Svengali.

One weekend in the early summer of 1954 Oliver Bernard arrived late for a house party at Hearne to find that the rest of the company had already departed for the New Inn. Bernard's marriage to Veronica was over: 'I was feeling touchy and insecure and was, I suppose, terrified of being patronised.' When the others returned, Cass offered him a beer in one of the few presentable glasses they had in the house; everybody else was using jam jars. It was of wafer-thin crystal, with three red lines running round the rim. The utensil was, as Cass remembers it,

> a brave attempt to be modern or moderne in a cheapish kind of way. The conversation between Oliver and George had not been flowing easily. There was silence. Oliver began to stare meaningfully at the glass. More silence. Then suddenly Oliver exploded into abusive rage at the glass, that it was the most vulgar pretentious glass that he had ever seen. I was astonished. He had always been charming and pleasant in our meetings at Soho. The evening was now quite late (but not unduly alcoholic) and I was further astonished when George exploded in rage at Oliver, then simultaneously George was ordering Oliver out of the house and Oliver was refusing to stay in it. It seemed to me weird. It was not an instance of George suspecting me of sexual enticement and there was not even an undercurrent of that – Oliver was much too overly handsome for my taste in that direction, though I liked him.[1]

Oliver remembers the contretemps somewhat differently: 'I upbraided George with failing to be in when I had arrived. He responded by saying that, if I wished to scold him, would I kindly not do so whilst sitting in his favourite chair.' With that, a nerve in Oliver gave. He felt sullen and bruised and announced that he was leaving. Barker told him that he was welcome to. Oliver then stalked off down the lane, walking in his distress northwards as far as Godalming, where he came to his senses, and sought shelter in the police station.[2] Later he wrote apologising for his behaviour and received from Barker a letter, the last paragraph of which ran:

> I ask you only to recall very occasionally, that if I speak of personal things, I do so out of a conviction that people who like each other are morally obliged to express their concern: more especially when such people are trying to do the things that you and I are trying to do. But you know this. What you do *not* know should properly be the subject of most of our conversations and because you are a passionate twenty five you are not very anxious to acknowledge the fact that there are such things and this again is right. A poet of my age speaks to a poet of your age in the conscious knowledge that if anything gets through it gets through against the grain. But it gets through for good. What on earth would be the purpose of your being younger than I am if this were not so? I think it fortunate that, at long last, we can speak and I most hope that we shall continue being able to do so. Your personal affairs as I see them are in no real way distinguished from your poetic affairs for the personal affairs of the poet (in the smallest as well as the largest sense) are the poetry. What the hell else could it possibly be? It is why poets have such very STRANGE personal affairs. You know – you should know and you do know – that there exists a co-fraternity of what can only be called spirit among Poets which entitles them to speak of absolutely All things amongst themselves, for if *they* cannot forgive one another, who can? I am concerned for thee, brother Jonathon, and you can't help me shewing it.[3]

The dividing line between affectionate concern and invitation to anarchy ('such *strange* personal affairs') in a communication like this was difficult to locate. Difficult for others, but impossible for Barker himself. When the God in him remembered the Beast in him, he was torn by dreadful remorse. His very poverty sometimes seemed a judgement. When he searched his tattered pockets, what did he discover but the simple rebuke of economics? At night in the low bedroom at Hearne, he would wake in a lather of sweat as a witches' sabbath of self-recrimination passed before his eyes. He began work on a poetic sequence called 'Justice at Midnight', a fantasia on the creative possibilities of guilt. It is set in the bedroom of the cottage, outside which, up and down the moonlit corridor, race the 'wild children / My heart disowns'. They presumably include the twins in America, the neglected ones at Tilty, lost Clare and the potential offspring debarred from the relationship with Cass. They turn and turn:

>   howling out loud
>   For Justice and Vengeance,
>   While, overhead, smiling, blood drips from the jaws
>   Of the heavenly engines.

In this turmoil the poet sees a figure, clearly to be identified with Jessica, approaching him:

>   Towering the far side of the table
>   Tall as the pregnant midnight she
>   Crossed the floor, stepped from a symbol
>   To bring judgement home on me.

He prays desperately to fugitive mercy, that 'dove whom I never knew and shall never know'. He tries self-justification, but the excuses falter on his lips. At the last moment, he discovers what consolation there is lurking inside him in the shape of a surprising and sombre traditionalism:

>   Only the orthodox and huge dead
>   To pluck up by the hair
>   The falling mortal can show
>   Angels ascending there.[4]

Since two halves of him were at loggerheads, dialogue suggested itself to Barker as an appropriate mode. He had always been interested in medieval examples of the genre. Now he sketched out 'Goodman Jacksin and the Angel'. 'This poem', he later explained, 'was originally entitled "a theological eclogue", but this was scrapped because it's pretty obvious.' The setting was the track or right of way from the main road up to the cottage, halfway up which 'stands the five-barred gate at which this dialogue between a farmer and an angel is supposed to happen'. In reality the first speaker was not based on a farmer as such, but on the robust and resourceful manager of the Olivera Stud Farm: 'I think he is remarkable because I have never met a man who, if he set his mind to it, could breed a horse with wings and a unicorn.' The idea of the poem was systematically to dismantle the opposition between the two speakers established at the outset. Superficially 'Goodman Jacksin and the Angel' consists of a conversation between two aspects of the poet himself: Barker the careless sensualist and Barker the would-be traditional Catholic. The Angel, for example, believes that all flesh is evil, a doctrine that Jacksin valiantly contests by claiming that all evil is only 'a good not understood'. Very soon, however, the roles are reversed: the Angel proves himself to be something of a maverick, while the farmer nurses aspirations to divinity. Even in these compromised positions neither can act without the other. In the sphere of sex, supremely, either they must co-operate or die. Indeed, since all begetting is the result of carnal appetite and all babies possess at least a potential for innocence, how can the libido possibly be in error? When it comes to the evocation of childhood, an intensely physical condition which epitomises nonetheless Wordsworthian intimations of immortality, farmer and angel find themselves singing very much the same tune:

JACKSIN:

I watch the boys chasing summer butterflies
Among the summer hedges:
I hear the high and hunting cries
As the sky-blown flier dodges
Between their hands, till, in disguise
Against the dog-rose lodges.
Then they stand silent by the rose
To see a rainbow close its wings.

ANGEL:

And out of the horned and rumpled sheet
Where nightlong in their forking lock
The hissing kissers slew and mock
That image from which they were cast –
Out of that fouled and rocking nest
In which those justly outcast meet
And mount like stray dogs in the street, –
Out, out the innocent image steps.[5]

Biographically considered the poem is an attempt by a rogue Catholic poet to legitimise the anomolous facts of his existence by the construction of a meaningful if heterodox theology. By 1953, let it be remembered, Barker had seven children, but had only had direct dealings with the four who were technically illegitimate. 'Goodman Jacksin and the Angel' represents an attempt by a philoprogenitive philanderer to bring his activities into line with the papal injunction to multiply.[6]

'Goodman Jacksin' was to be the centrepiece of Barker's new collection, *A Vision of Beasts and Gods*, which was to be published on 2 July 1954, after Eliot had had his schoolmasterly way with the proofs ('*ravished bull*: violent and inaccurate. I assume you mean "ravaged bull"'). By the time the book appeared George and Cass were on holiday. In Cambridge that June John Farrelly paid the penalty for his allegiance to the exam-hating Leavis by taking an Upper Second in Part Two of the English Tripos, while Karl Miller reaped the reward of his independence by taking a First. The Farrellys celebrated by renting the Villa Parenti, Via Nizza at Forte dei Marmi on the Italian Riviera. Miller was invited with his fiancée Jane, as were George and Cass. In Paris Farrelly purchased a new Ford V-8, which Barker drove southwards, to be greeted in Italy by cries of 'Che macchina!' At first the weather was sullen, the atmosphere electric, a sort of subdued menace prevailing. Barker wrote back to Kit that everybody in the household was permanently intoxicated on Methedrine, the daily communal intake being about half a bottle.[7] The conversation took on a surreal quality. There was much talk of sex, even of sex toys. Sex was declared by Barker to be synonymous with poetry; both were dangerous and to be pursued assiduously.[8] Sensing in Miller a degree of self-discipline which would equip him well for conventional employment, Barker told Jane that he should be kept in an attic, fed buns and made to avoid any kind of job. Only thus might he be rescued for sex and for poetry: 'That boy has a tiger in his loins.'[9]

On the terrace, where at six the Farrellys served fiery cocktails, Barker was in his element, by turns boastful and self-mocking. When dinner was served, John Farrelly remembered that he still had not written anything to rival *Anna Karenina*, and for shame laid his face in the soup. But the northern Italian sun appeared so sluggish that George, Cass and Farrelly before long determined to drive south until they found it. Barker donned goggles and gloves and took the wheel of the Ford. They covered the sixty-five miles to Florence in an hour and a quarter. The Italians, he wrote to Kit, had perfected the art of motoring, which consisted of screaming from one place to another at the fastest feasible speed, 'since it is suicidal to be on the road in the first place'. They drove as far as Rome before they felt the true Mediterranean warmth on their faces.

When they were back in Forte, there were expeditions to the medieval fishing village of Porto Venere, where Shelley had once lived. It stood at the head of a long causeway leading into the dark blue sea. Landwards it was surrounded by a curtain wall with a gate so narrow that the Ford could not get through. Within, a grotto of rocks encircled a pool where Byron had reputedly once bathed. There was a tiny piazza around a garden where a

Corinthian column supported a moustachioed bust that should have been, but was not, of Garibaldi. By late August the sun had caught up with the party and shone to the point of tedium. Every afternoon George collapsed into a heap in the bedroom, where to relieve his solar malaise he locked the window shutters and turned on the electric light. By early September he and Cass had had enough. They packed and announced their departure for Milan. On the terrace cocktails were advanced by one hour. Then Farrelly drove them through the outskirts of Spezia to take the evening train.[10]

They returned to Hearne to receive the news that *A Vision of Beasts and Gods* had been made the Summer Choice of the newly formed Poetry Book Society and had already received a favourable review in the *Times Literary Supplement*. 'In this book Mr Barker's best poems are occasional,' declared the reviewer. 'He seems to need a death or a marriage or an escape from drowning to focus his imagination.' 'The Death of Manolete' was much liked. Encouraged, Barker wrote to Eliot to ask if he merited a *Collected Poems*. A *Collected*, Eliot replied, would have to wait a little but, yes, by all means he must have one along the lines of those already planned for Auden and Spender.[11]

Back at Stanhope Gardens, the days were passing 'like whirlwind', as Big Mumma characteristically put it. Jeff Bernard had fallen into the habit of sipping whiskies in her company. Oliver too called to pay his respects, finding in her an 'almost childish mischievousness'. One November day Oliver sat with her in the kitchen, watching the smog seethe and swirl in the mews outside. There was silence for several seconds, broken only by the ticking of the clock. Big Mumma rose slowly and announced in her gentle lilt, 'I think I'll be going to church now.' She paused, and then added, 'Where the prayer books have handles.' It was some time before Oliver realised that she was referring to the pub.[12] In February 1955 she experienced a 'slight indisposition', and one of the Fathers of the Oratory made a pastoral visit. He took her hands between his own and murmured, 'You should be thankful to God, Mrs Barker, for he has been very good to you.' 'I should think so,' Big Mumma replied, 'for I have been very good to him.'[13]

Pa had begun to suffer from a gammy leg, but was reassured by the fact that so many of the Benchers at Gray's Inn were called 'Doctor'. The Inn's butler was, said the *Greya*, 'a figure, distinguished and commanding, standing against splendid figures and draperies which open to recall a battlefield in the remote distance: cavalry charging, cannon firing, bayonets bristling, the smoke drifting indistinctly over the scene'.[14] Late one afternoon, while Oliver sat drinking tea with Mumma in the kitchen, George put his head round the door and called, 'Has anyone seen God the Father?'[15]

By early 1955 Monica's children were semi-residents in Stanhope Gardens. Following her divorce from Oliver, Veronica had taken up with an American called Calvin Kentfield, whose novel *The Alchemist's Voyage* was due from Harcourt Brace that autumn. Veronica's brother Patrick, who was hoping to be a painter, was also spending much of his time at Queen's Gate. For several months George too continued to use the flat as his London base, moving between it, Hearne and Tilty. In January 1955, however, Elizabeth's tenancy at Tilty expired when Todd sold the mill. She took a nine-year lease on a large, two-floor flat at 9 Westbourne Terrace in Paddington. From here the children attended their respective boarding schools: Georgina and Rose the Legat Ballet School in Tunbridge Wells, Christopher and Sebastian their prep school in Seaford.

The same spring Anthony Cronin introduced Barker to the Irish painter Patrick Swift, who had moved from Dublin with his wife Oonagh the previous year. In Dublin, Swift had already mounted his only one-man exhibition at the Victor Waddington Gallery. A perfectionist belonging to no definable school, he was never to be popular or successful. He nurtured a deep distrust of abstract avant-garde painting, against which he was to wage a bitter campaign in a series of discursive articles. Instead, he chose to concentrate on, first, trees and plants, to the observation of which he brought some of the geometrical precision of an early Mondrian and, second, on the human figure, in the depiction of which he combined the candour of Kokoschka with the linear directness of Giacometti. The vulnerability and studied seriousness of his many portraits, including those of his friends, also owed something to the influence of Lucian Freud, whom he had met in Dublin, and with whom he now drank in the Colony Room. Despite, or because of, these varied affinities, Swift was as difficult to pigeon-hole as a painter, as Barker was as a poet.

Though remotely related to Dean Swift, like Barker Patrick was a Catholic recusant. Possessed of an acute intelligence that was catholic in both senses of the word, he was caustic, witty and frequently dismissive of what others wrote or painted. But he thought highly of Barker, with whose religious and artistic ideas he felt a strong affinity. Both men were a strange mixture of theological orthodoxy and apostasy.[16] Both also lived in the spirit of Eliot's remark about Baudelaire: 'Genuine blasphemy, genuine in spirit and not purely verbal, is the product of partial belief.' A common respect for Baudelaire was perhaps their most obvious meeting point. Barker had already written a sonnet addressed to Baudelaire, published in *News of the World*; it had declared, 'I serve / Much the same master. Was your good a god?/ I hate my ruler because he will not break me / Under the overloving justice of his rod, Thus but for love I hate him.'[17] Though Swift was perhaps more taken with Baudelaire as art critic than as poet, he also identified with the Frenchman, whom he was to paint, grey and austere, standing amid the clutter of brushes in the corner of his own studio. In time he would come to regard Baudelaire and Barker as spiritual brothers, possessing 'the same view of sin, and this is related to a view of the sexes as divided by their ethical position, man in relation to an absolute, cursed by a sense of the ideal, woman living entirely in her relationships'.[18]

Barker's own relationships with women had recently shifted as a result of Elizabeth's move to Westbourne Terrace, where he was spending more and more of his time. The rapprochement disconcerted Cass, ever wary of Elizabeth's continuing hold over George. He was now in the habit when in London of dropping round to Westbourne Terrace for tea, after which he and Smart would walk to the Lamb and Flag in Covent Garden to drink with Patrick and Oonagh Swift. From there they would go on to the Mandrake Club, which was open after hours. Another consequence of these increasingly frequent visits was that Barker was able to see more of the children. On 23 April he drove Georgina and Rose in their brown school capes back to the Legat School, then returned to Westbourne Terrace in time for drinks and stayed all night. And so it continued with bibulous sedateness until on Saturday 21 May Elizabeth answered the phone to hear Archer's dry and deferential tones, etched with an unaccustomed sadness. The previous day, Ascensiontide, Big Mumma had died in her sleep. Her 'slight indisposition' had been cancer.[19]

The Oratory arranged for the funeral Mass to be said on Monday, 30 May before the burial at Kensal Green Cemetery. The date was highly inconvenient, for on that day Veronica was due to marry Calvin at Kensington Register Office. The family was obliged to split into two groups. Kit and Ilse attended the wedding and signed the register, while George and Cass went to the Oratory. It was a day of unseasonal warmth. The Mass was celebrated in the familiar Latin. Afterwards, as Cass and George walked down the steps onto the Brompton Road, she turned and looked up. Tears were coursing down George's face.[20] Leaving Pa and the main party to follow the hearse to Kensal Green, the two of them walked down the Fulham Road to the Queen's Elm, where the wedding breakfast was in full swing. Elizabeth was there with her sister Jane, who was visiting with her husband D'Arcy. As the drink and the song took hold, the celebration acquired the aspects of both wedding feast and wake. Long afterwards Veronica could recall George wailing into his drink, 'How could the bitch go and leave me?'[21]

Once the mourners and wedding guests had dispersed, Barker and Cass walked back to Stanhope Gardens to find the door locked. After the burial Pa had gone to stay with his sister Grace in Sussex. The word went around that he had forever barred his door against his sons. This was an exaggeration: what the poets and the bums associated with them had to understand was that henceforth the door was barred against *them*. From that time on George avoided the house. Never again would the prodigal go home.

The following month, from the prep school in Seaford, there arrived a letter of condolence from ten-year-old Sebastian:

Dear George,
I hope that you are well.
I am sorry that Big Mumma has died. I'm in the First game for cricket. Weren't Georgina and Rosie lucky to go to school so late. I was sixth in form this fortnight, and my place in class is 13. I was the first to swim in the school swimming bath. I am so sorry that this letter is so short, but I can't think of anything to say. So lots of love, Bashie.[22]

CHAPTER 35

'SO YOU WRITE VERSE TOO, BABY?'

There was something of a watershed in British verse in 1955. This was the year of *The Nightfishing*, W.S. Graham's fifth volume of poems, in which he had achieved a fresh clarity and directness. But it was also the year in which critics began to notice a countervailing shift in the relationship between poetry and the academic world. This was to change the social position of poets; it also introduced a tone of voice not heard before: a revulsion against rhetorical excess and the inception of a new, ironic coolness. In June Anthony Cronin published in *Nimbus* an article called 'Some Old Notes on a New School'.[1] Reviewing two recent novels – Kingsley Amis's *Lucky Jim* and John Wain's *Hurry on Down* – he prefaced his comments by writing of the rise of the provincial don as the arbiter of literary taste. This was another, and sociologically more astute, way of typifying that drift in British letters to which the *Spectator* had more cryptically, the previous October, given the name 'The Movement'. Among the signs of change were a preference on the part of the poets in question for modesty of tone and expression, their deliberate stance of personal detachment and their tendency in personal and practical matters to go for secure, often academic, jobs. Such priorities were no closer to Barker's chosen way of life than they were to Graham's.

The notion of poet as pariah was gradually giving way to that of poet as junior lecturer. Many of the younger writers were working in universities. Geoffrey Hill, whose work had begun appearing in *Nimbus,* was an assistant lecturer at Leeds. Amis, an adept writer of verse as well as a novelist, taught at Swansea. Philip Larkin had just taken up the post of university librarian at Hull. That same year Larkin published *The Less Deceived*, the very title of which sounded like a corrective to the exhibitionist and rhetorical tendencies associated with Barker by his detractors. Literary revolutions breed anthologies. Auden's in the late 1930s had produced Michael Roberts's *New Signatures*. The revolution of the 1950s gave rise to Robert Conquest's *New Lines*. Its preface declared, 'if one had briefly to distinguish between the poetry of the fifties and its predecessors, I believe that the most important general point would be that it submits to no great theoretical constructs nor agglomerations of unconscious commands. It is free from mystical and logical compulsions.'[2] This was hardly an invitation to write sonnets to Baudelaire.

The revolution was unsympathetic to Barker in several respects. His verse had always been singing or incantatory; the new school, by contrast, insisted on the unassuming ordinariness of the speaking voice. He was mystical and mythical; the new mood stressed common sense. Barker inflated reality; the movement deflated it. His *forte* was hyperbole: an inspired, Celtic overstatement; the poets of the younger generation preferred *mezzo piano*, and their favourite figure of speech was understatement. It was as if Grigson, Leavis and Cambridge had won the cultural battle after all.

In August 1955 a couple walked down the rutted track behind Hearne Cottage. They were Anthony Thwaite and his wife Ann, honeymooning in Midhurst before their departure for Japan, where Thwaite had a contract at the University of Tokyo.[3] Thwaite was a maturing poet whose successive affinities were to reflect fairly accurately the artistic evolution of his particular generation. Though he had hero-worshipped Barker in his youth, he was soon to be swept up in the new enthusiasm for Larkin, whose friend and editor he would eventually become. Nonetheless, when he reached Japan in October, he attempted to teach his students Barker's already famous sonnet to his mother. He asked them to identify the addressee and the meaning of the closing lines 'And so I send /O all my faith, and all my love to tell her / That she will move from mourning into morning.' Half of them answered that the sonnet was addressed to the earth, which the closing lines wished might be 'untorn and happy'. This interpretation, thought Thwaite, was fair enough, though hardly accounting for the gin and the chicken. The remaining students said that the poem was addressed to 'the politicans of the U.S.A' and that the end expressed a hope 'that America will strive for world peace'.[4]

The new mood affected many of Barker's friends. In October Farrelly, who had spent the previous academic year in Italy, took up a temporary appointment teaching American literature at Trinity College, Dublin. His closest colleague there was Donald Davie, author of *Purity of Diction in English Verse* and identified by Conquest as one of the key representatives of the emerging school. Davie, for one, could reconcile the writing of poetry with the teaching of it. Farrelly, however, found that teaching did nothing to alleviate his creative aridity, or *rigor Leavis*. He had been writing stories, but soon their slender trickle had dried up, much to Barker's disappointment.

In Dublin Farrelly met Patrick Swift, who was on a return visit to Ireland.

Swift in his turn introduced him to the poet Patrick Kavanagh, author of *The Great Hunger* (1942), an account in verse of poverty and sexual frustration in rural Ireland. Kavanagh was a determined opponent of academic English, with whom nonetheless Farrelly discovered a shared love of *Moby Dick*. Their difference was that, whereas Farrelly took Melville to be a Leavisite novelist of conscience, Kavanagh thought that he resembled Kavanagh: 'We are both originals; Melville has the true Parnassian note. Godlike. Both passionate and uncaring at the same time.'[5] Swift reported back to Barker that Farrelly was adjusting to such talk, once he was outside the confines of Trinity College. The relaxation of attitude was welcome since the rest of Farrelly's existence was spent with what Swift styled 'much less healthy contacts', in other words academic ones.

The tentacles of academe reached into the Barker family itself. Veronica's husband Calvin Kentfield had obtained a one-year appointment teaching creative writing at the University of Iowa, where he took Veronica in September. Thereafter, Monica's children went their separate ways. Twenty-two-year-old Patrick came down to stay near George and Cass in Sussex. He lived in a gypsy caravan parked at Slong Farm, a property owned by Kit's neighbours, the Salamans. For the next few months Patrick breezed in and out of Hearne Cottage in between helping David Gill with his apple-growing business up at Parkhurst Place. Cass was receiving novels for review from *Time and Tide*, whose literary editor, Cronin, regarded this as a way of helping with the household's finances.[6] Patrick, eight years her junior, kept her company while Barker was away in London.

George was aware of the increasing intimacy between Cass and his nephew. He reacted to it with sarcastic taunts and by ostentatiously spending more time with Elizabeth at Westbourne Terrace. Here he continued to follow the development of his children with undisguised pride. At the Legat School Georgina was concentrating on ballet. Christopher was about to enter the King's School, Canterbury. Sebastian had become serious about carpentry and Rose – to whom George still fondly referred as 'Roses' – was now nine.

Michael Asquith, now remarried, was a frequent visitor to Westbourne Terrace. He noticed how much Barker had mellowed since his mother's death, which seemed to have brought out a fresh tenderness in him, especially towards women. Early in 1956 Elizabeth caught hepatitis and was unable to drink alcohol for a year. During her illness and the exhaustion that followed it, Barker took to spending much of the week in her flat. One evening after her recovery, Asquith and his second wife Hase invited them to dinner at Lady Cynthia Asquith's home at Queen's Gate Gardens. After the meal Elizabeth suggested a walk in the garden. Hase Asquith, who suffered from rheumatoid arthritis, found the going excruciating and burst into tears. As soon as her pain became evident, Barker rushed over and put his arms around her. The walk was abandoned.[7]

The sensitivity apparent in such gestures contrasted starkly with his occasional bouts of cruelty. For Hase such touches of sympathetic understanding were a key to his charm. He possessed to an unusual degree the ability to focus exclusively on the needs of another person. This gift was enchanting; it was also, Hase thought, disquieting.

In the closing months of 1955 Barker spent as much time in London as in Hearne. One reason for this was that David Archer had opened another bookshop. His new premises were at 34 Greek Street, opposite the Palace Theatre and diametrically across from the Coach and Horses pub. The shop had a saleroom for new books on the first floor and a lending library at the back. As he accumulated stock, Archer dashed to and fro exclaiming, 'Silly me' with every mishap. When he was out, Barker, Colquhoun or Tristram Hull, former editor of *Nimbus*, stood in for him at the counter. One afternoon, Oliver Bernard turned up in the company of Dom Moraes, a nineteen-year-old poet from Bombay. Moraes's family were originally from Goa and his father was one of the most celebrated journalists in India. Dom had been writing poetry since he was twelve, emulating his gods: Auden, Eliot and Barker. Archer told him that the third of these deities was in town. He phoned Westbourne Terrace, where Barker promised to join them in the Coach and Horses.

When Archer and Moraes walked across to the pub, Barker was already sitting by the door, cowled like a monk in his duffel coat. He fixed Moraes with his hypnotic blue eyes and said, 'So you write verse, too, baby? We are honoured. There are few Hindu princes among us versifiers.' Though his family was Catholic by religion, the agnostic Moraes took this as a compliment. The immense, lumbering form of David Wright appeared. When Dom began a staccato resumé of his career for the sake of the newcomer, Wright turned to Barker for an explanation. 'No offence,' Barker remarked to Moraes. 'No offence. Our South African friend is as deaf as the womb.' Then he turned to Wright and enunciated voicelessly, 'Ain't you baby?' while Wright stared fixedly at his lips.[8]

Barker was spending so much time in London now that he was coming to seem a metropolitan figure, an identification which late that year was to be given literary form. Under its editor John Lehmann, the previous few issues of the *London Magazine* had carried a series of reminiscences about literary life in the city. William Plomer had started the series; Leonard Woolf and V.S. Pritchett followed. Barker was invited to appear next. He wrote at a single sitting one of his most effective prose pieces yet, a memoir beginning with his arrival by pram from Essex at the age of three months and ending with his departure for Plush. In the surviving manuscript he has scarcely altered a line, except for the last. After finishing, he had added, 'I should acknowledge that all my efforts at independence would have failed, had I not been so often encouraged and forgiven again by Marion Frances Taaffe, my mother.' He then crossed the sentence out. It was, of course, the key to the whole essay.[9]

From late 1955 through to the summer of 1956 Barker was often detained in London by radio work. He had met Douglas Cleverdon, one-time bookseller, now a producer in the BBC's Features Department. Cleverdon had been responsible for Dylan Thomas's *Under Milk Wood* the previous year and now wanted Barker to turn his hand to more radio verse drama. Barker had lunch at his flat in Albany Street, where they discussed projects. Knowing Barker's Catholic proclivities, Cleverdon suggested a play about Gerard Manley Hopkins, which, as Barker worked at it during the autumn, became a dialogue between Baudelaire and Hopkins. *News of the World* had included sonnets to both poets, each of whom reflected a different side of Barker's own, Manichean nature: one the guilty voluptuary, the other the self-tormented believer. His plan now, he told Cleverdon, was to examine the double nature of Hopkins as poet and priest, by confronting him with his polar opposite. He intended to employ Baudelaire as a symbol of spiritual pride and its despair, and Hopkins as a symbol of a new humility. *The Gardens of Altering Eros* was to be an exploration of the tension between them, or rather of the inner tensions afflicting each: the Baudelaire within the Hopkins; the Hopkins inside the Baudelaire. The eponymous gardens, representing the libido which each in his own manner wrestled to subsume, were presided over by a third speaking voice: 'Genius Loci'.

> *Baudelaire*: Illusions. Ah, yes, the illusions. The enchanting illusions of the gardens of Eros.
>
> *Genius Loci*: Shall we go down?
>
> *Baudelaire*: And of all the illusions of these gardens, the worst and the best is the illusion, here, of the absence of God. Worst, because most frightful, best because we believe it to be an illusion. For surely, Gerard my friend, it is when we are deprived of his presence that we most fiercely perceive the necessity of his existence? And see then, truly, that if God did not exist, it would be necessary to invent him?
>
> *Hopkins*: Because this is the impossible negative – the abhorrent shuddering chloroform of the absence of God – in which, as most of us know, we could never exist any more than the Christian fish out of the water. We are wound with him round us, like the air we breathe.

How could we breathe and be, without the air of heaven? But we are. So I say we discover God, we do not invent him.[10]

The Gardens of Altering Eros was broadcast on the Third Programme on 9 April 1956. Hugh Burden played Hopkins and Anthony Jacobs Baudelaire. Marjorie Westbury delivered The Voice of the Unknown Eros in a subdued *sprechgesang*. After attending rehearsals, Barker listened at Westbourne Gardens. He realised that Hopkins had got the better of the argument.

Nonetheless his own way of being a Catholic continued to be closer to the deliberate violations practised by Baudelaire. He had been following with some amusement the spiritual growth of Edith Sitwell, who was being lured into Mother Church by Father Martin D'Arcy, the darling of the Catholic rich. On 4 August 1955, Edith had 'done a D'Arcy'; in other words she had been received into the Catholic Church, with Evelyn Waugh and Roy Campbell standing as her godfathers. On 4 October Edith had been confirmed, amid 'the cream of Catholic London'. Thereafter she had confined her *tête à tête* lunches at the Sesame Club to members of her family and fellow Catholics. One day in March 1956, she invited Barker; the only other guest was Osbert. It was a fast day in Lent. When the menu came round, the agnostic Osbert ordered a steak. Edith handed the menu to Barker with the injunction, 'I expect that you would like some of this nice pasta.' Barker growled back, 'I want steak. I am not going to heaven for eating pasta. In any case I don't want to go to heaven; I want to go to hell.'[11]

Barker's next project for Cleverdon was an allegory for speakers and singers called *The Seraphina*. Cleverdon, who was enthusiastic to fix up working relationships between composers and writers, arranged for Barker to collaborate with Lennox Berkeley. The play described a marine odyssey, with musical and acoustic effects. The seafarers were a pair of twins, Josephus and Peter Amadeus, and a middle-aged Irishman called Jimmy Hill. They are on a voyage to the Hesperides, the islands of the western sea which in dramatic terms represent their true selves. They come across Mater Virginia, an island somewhat like Ireland. Instead of pining bachelors, however, it is populated by bashful women who are visited once a year by the male inhabitants of a neighbouring island for the sake of procreation. After nursing, the male children are sent to the island of men; the daughters remain on Mater Virginia. When one of the women swims towards the *Seraphina* Josephus takes a pot-shot at her, only to be condemned by Peter: 'Put up that gun, Josephus, you fool. What harm could she ever do to us?' Next they encounter the head of Orpheus drifting over the waves, luring them to destruction. Resisting its fatal music, they reach their destination; the Hesperides are inhabited by their doubles, whom they promptly slay.

The writing brought out many of Barker's strengths: his strong sense of place, his love of moral paradox, his feeling for the inflections of Irish English, and his spontaneous way with folk forms such as the sea shanty. He explained to Cleverdon that *The Seraphina* was a morality play. The successive episodes were intended to represent the evolution or growth of the human heart. Peter, he wrote in his notebook, stood for its spiritual aspirations, Josephus for its natural or human aspirations, and Jimmy for its innocence. In that case it is innocence who steers them, as Jimmy croons a shanty to his tiller:

> What sailors at sea with a fish in their hands
>   Give Biddy a shove me dear
> Will find any love in far-away lands?
>   Give Biddy a shove me dear.
>
> For the heart of a sailor can find no rest
>   Give Biddy a shove me dear
> This side of the arbours of the west.
>   Give Biddy a shove me dear.[12]

The allegory was richer than Barker's synopsis suggested. Peter represents less spiritual aspiration than moral anxiety, while Josephus embodies moral apathy. Josephus's are the demeaning principles of the average sensual man: 'And whom do you love?' asks Jimmy. 'Oh,' he replies, 'any double-breasted long-legged blue-eyed milk-maid from Hairyfordshire.' It is Josephus, moreover, who shoots at the Woman of Mater Virginia because he may not enjoy her. He is locked in conflict with his twin, who reveals himself as the mouthpiece of the Catholic vision of the play and, in so doing, explains both the true point of the voyage and its ultimate futility:

> If it were possible, this act of perfect expiation, then with it we could encompass the world, like the seas that rock that pole-struck head in their arms, and not the error of a sparrow would escape from the all-embracing exoneration of our love. The Seraphina is encrusted with more than the sores of our three-headed guilt. O what seas will wash and what winds will cleanse our eternally recurrent culpability, and its despair? For everyone is like that man who has knifed his god in order to stuff his hand into the wound and pull out a theology. So that the god who is discovered is always a dead god. And the innocence that is re-captured is pregnant.[13]

It is Jimmy with his Irish common sense, however, who earths the play by anchoring it in ordinary things. He distrusts the higher motives of his fellow mariners just as much as the listener: 'Well, I always had a weak head too, not for drinking, but for thinking.' If any of the characters represent Barker, it is not the brothers with their endless internecine torment, but Jimmy with his half-cocked, beneficent attempts to remain, in a rough and ready sense, amply human. It is Barker the social being who says, 'When you're young, why, you love yourself, which is demonstrably daft; but when you're no longer young, well, then you love everyone and no one, which is demonstrably *im*possible.' Then, echoing Tertullian's *credo quia absurdum est*, he adds, 'So you believe. Because it's impossible.'[14]

Barker sent the play to Eliot, who replied that he was less worried about not understanding the allegory than his fellow Faber directors. He suggested putting it in a volume either with some more poems or else with another verse drama of the same length.[15] In the meantime a radio production was scheduled for October.

CHAPTER 36

'GIVE BIDDY A SHOVE, ME DEAR'

If, in *The Seraphina*, Jimmy's voice is that of Irish peasant common sense, it must be closely related to Big Mumma's. Since her death, Barker had heard her voice more and more insistently in the back room of his mind. It reverberated in his writing and lured him like some siren to cross the Irish Sea. He was in close touch with Dublin anyway, from where John Farrelly was sending him affectionate accounts of academic and pub life. On another of his return visits, Swift fulminated against the suspect Irishness of so-called 'Irish art'. Both Swift and Farrelly were about to become fathers and Farrelly had persuaded Oonagh Swift to stay and have her child 'in Gaelic', despite the superior medical facilities in England. In February 1956 Swift reported that Patrick Kavanagh had spoken as a guest lecturer on modern poetry at University College. He had devoted most of the hour to high praise of George Barker.

Barker had not set foot in his mother's native land since his abrupt departure in 1947. In June 1956, after submitting to Faber the text of his *Collected Poems* including *The True Confession*, which he was resolved should go in, he decided to return. Farrelly was now coming to the end of his year's contract at Trinity. He had been unable to find a job back in America, where, Bewley had informed him, quality counted for nothing unless one possessed a doctorate. Farrelly and Dede decided on one final indulgence in Europe. They had rented for the summer a villa in the hilltop village of Bormes-les-Mimosas, halfway between St Tropez and Hyères. Barker and Cass were to join them, but first they took the ferry across to Ireland to stay with the Farrellys at their Dublin home: Glencullen House near Kilternan.

While Dede took Cass along the banks of the Liffey to visit the wool merchants, Barker spent his time drinking with Farrelly and Swift in McDaid's in Grafton Street, and Keogh's in Anne Street. Momentously, he at last met Patrick Kavanagh, the most interesting Irish poet of his day. Kavanagh was fifty-two, pensive, waspish, idiosyncratic and wretchedly impoverished. His apparent social gaucheness had earned him a reputation for naïveté in Dublin, where the more snobbish and credulous intelligentsia even rumoured him to be as virginal as the thwarted bachelors his poems depicted. Like Barker, he was an inveterate autodidact, having left school at twelve. He now occupied, in the eyes of literary Dublin, a position akin to that of Barker's boyhood hero, Francis Ledwidge. Like Ledwidge, Kavanagh was thought of as a peasant genius, a caricature he fiercely resented.

In June 1956 Kavanagh was in great need of moral support. His health had recently been undermined by an operation for cancer, which had left him with only one lung. His financial circumstances, furthermore, were precarious since four years before he and his publisher brother Peter had used Peter's American earnings to bring out three issues of a vituperative periodical entitled *Kavanagh's Weekly*. Its pages had been full of broadsides against the philistinism of the Irish Republic; as a result he had been attacked by the newspaper the *Sentinel*, whose editors he had unsuccessfully sued in court. Like Barker, he felt isolated by the growing power of university English departments. In Dublin, it seemed to Kavanagh, he was stranded between the twin candles of the New Criticism: Donald Davie at Trinity College and Dennis Donoghue at University College. Pedantry and the censorious spirit of Church and republic were, Kavanagh suspected, squeezing Irish poetry dry. Earlier that year he had experienced a moment of illumination or 'rebirth' by Dublin's Grand Canal, as a result of which he had learned to appreciate the virtues of 'simplicity' and 'how not to care'. He had spent the last few weeks consorting with Farrelly and Swift, whose talk had all been of Barker.

Recently Kavanagh had written an article in *Nimbus*, declaring his need for overseas affiliations. He greeted Barker as an ally. George shared his rough-and-ready, abrasive sense of humour, and his belief in the cleansing properties of forthrightness. One evening Kavanagh told him that, whilst starting to write poetry, he had followed his father's profession as a saddler. Showing him his wallet, Barker offered to let him have both it and its contents, if he could tell him from what kind of leather it was made. Kavanagh could. Reluctantly Barker handed over the money.

Whilst in Ireland, Barker at last had an opportunity to visit the Taaffes. As he had complained as long ago as 1937, not once had he made 'the pilgrimage down the Drogheda road'. In the second week of his stay he drove north with Cass to meet Big Mumma's surviving brothers in a little two-up, two-down house in Mornington. They invited them into the tiny front parlour. For the better part of an hour he sat facing the male members of the Taaffe family, who were seated on stiff-backed chairs. Both parties seemed constrained by a sense of the inadequacy of speech as they attempted to make contact across a chasm of grief that seemed to Cass, the onlooker, to be unbridgeable. Symbolically, these people meant more to Barker than any on earth, and yet there was nothing meaningful he could say to them. After some minutes in the silent room, Cass turned to see his face once more running with tears. She made her excuses and left, waiting quietly in the car until he reappeared and wordlessly drove her back to Dublin.[1]

Meanwhile, Dede had gone ahead to Bormes with the children and a nursemaid to get the villa ready for the holiday. Kavanagh was also invited and joined John, George and Cass on the boat across to Liverpool, from where they drove in Farrelly's Ford to the Dover–Calais ferry. In France they made an inspection of the northern cathedrals: Beauvais, Amiens, Le Mans. After staying at Chartres, they cut through the château country to Tours, then crossed the south-west through the towns of Perigeux – where, as Cass remembers, they enjoyed a particularly sumptuous meal of Perigordian specialities – Cahors and Albi. Once installed in bougainvillaea-hung Bormes, they investigated the local villages. David Gascoyne was now living in Aix-en-Provence. With him they attended events at the Aix festival, including a performance of *Don Giovanni* at the opera house, after which they sat outside a café, drinking wine in the balmy summer air.

Though Cass was to remember these places with affection, she was restless. Since Big Mumma's death, she had borne the brunt of Barker's melancholia. Her own unhappiness was intensified by the fact that, while at Hearne during George's absences in town, she had grown increasingly fond of his nephew, still living in his caravan at Slong Farm. 'By this time, 1956,' she later related, 'I was in love with Patrick, and longed to leave George.' Barker for his part seemed to his companions to be divided between a visible fondness for Cass and an equally evident dismissiveness. At times he appeared to take her for granted; at others, he acted as if he wished to be rid of her. Certainly, he was at least half aware of the strength of her feelings for his nephew. He had learnt to use Cass's nickname 'Biddy' sarcastically, as if she were a plaything, like Biddy, Jimmy's tiller from *The Seraphina*. He would taunt her, repeating endlessly, 'Why don't you two young people run off with one another, Biddy? Like babes in the wood. Why don't you?'

The jibes drove Cass further into her shell. She was torn by competing emotions. 'What people did not see was that, although to the outer world he could be dismissive of me, when we were alone, and he knew that he had gone too far in his taunts, he begged me to forgive, never to leave him. Such is the power of the archetypical poet on even a "modern" young woman, I promised him that I would not leave him and felt bound by my promise.' Cass abided by 'duty', but felt obliged to turn down Barker's frequent, half-sincere offers of marriage, which she found 'insulting to Jessica' even as she 'thanked her for still being alive and still married to him'. Cass felt trapped. 'If only', she later regretted, 'he could have said that the time had come for us to part and given me my freedom. He must have felt this, and responded by tightening his security – my prison walls grew more restricted and the conditions harsher. My confidence collapsed, and I saw myself becoming a pathetic little masochist.'[2]

In France Barker soon grew tired of the fashionable beaches and proposed a visit to Spain, where he could renew his acquaintance with the bull-fight. With Farrelly, he and Cass crossed the border at Port Bau on 17 July and then drove to Barcelona, where they visited the cathedral and the bullring. Money was as tight as ever. Because of postwar currency restrictions, Barker had only been able to withdraw £35 in foreign currency from the Provincial Bank of Ireland and this was now gone. They could not meet their hotel bill and were not free to leave until they did.[3] In London Cleverdon was anxiously awaiting a revised script of *The Seraphina,* so that Lennox Berkeley could start work on the score. 'I learn', he wrote from Broadcasting House, 'that you and Cashenden may be incarcerated indefinitely in a Spanish prison if you can't square your (circular?) hotel.'[4] Somehow they extricated themselves and made their escape, crossing the border on 19 August at La Junquera and returning to Bormes.

At Hearne a letter awaited Barker from Charles Monteith, a recently appointed editor at Faber, concerning the planned *Collected Poems*. It enclosed *The True Confession* which, after careful consideration, the firm's directors had decided to reject: 'This may, I do fully realize, seem a rather pusillanimous attitude to take; but all of us have thought about the matter very carefully and discussed it fully and the decision we have come to is that, all things considered, it would be very much wiser not to include this particular poem.'[5]

The decision was a bitter blow. Despite the public outcry three years earlier, Barker held the *Confession* in high regard. He thought of appealing to Eliot, who was, however, away on his own holiday. Instead, on 10 September, he drafted a carefully worded reply to Monteith, setting out his own case. A pause ensued, during which Eliot returned from his holidays and Monteith took off on his. They coincided just long enough at Russell Square to discuss Barker's rejoinder. The result, the following Monday, was a firm but friendly explanation from Eliot:

> As I have been myself very definitely of the opinion that your 'True Confession' should be omitted from your *Collected Poems*, I think that in view of your letter I ought to tell you, as clearly as possible, why we came to this conclusion. You may have formed the impression from Charles Monteith's letter of July 20 that our wish to exclude this poem was due to squeamishness about some of the subject matter. If this had been the simple reason, we should have considered the possibility of omitting

> certain words or phrases, but our opinion – and mine particularly – is based on very much wider grounds than that.
>
> You think, my dear George, that your 'True Confession' is the best of your poems. I can only in reply say frankly that I think it is one of the worst, and that it is likely to diminish rather than to advance your reputation. In the first place it is obviously and overtly a kind of imitation of Villon's *Testament*. I cannot help thinking that if you knew Villon better – and that does not mean knowing contemporary French well and the French language of the seventeeth century, but the French language as it was in Villon's time – you would have recoiled from the attempt, for Villon is one of their very greatest of all poets (and possibly, excluding dramatic verse, the greatest poet in French literature). I assert that there is no living poet – I would even say that there is no poet in the present century – who in an attempt to imitate Villon would not come out looking very much the worse for wear. I am afraid that the effect of your attempt to emulate the frankness of speech of Villon is merely to make you look like a schoolboy pre-occupied with sex. If you are going to attempt Villon's subject matter, you must pack his punch, and there isn't a living poet who has it.[6]

Eliot added that he was prepared to preface the *Collected Poems* with a note to the effect that the poem had been left out at the publisher's request. Apart from that, there was nothing to be done: 'And remember I have always been, and am, one of your admirers.'

There was no way of evading the force of Eliot's argument. Barker drafted a reasoned and humble response, urging that he had felt emboldened to submit the poem by others' admiration of it. *The True Confession* would continue to split poets and critics: Heath-Stubbs, Thwaite and C.H. Sisson considering it among Barker's finest works, others such as David Gascoyne agreeing with Eliot that it was among his least satisfactory. *Bête noire* or favourite, it continues to arouse passions, and to divide opinion.

The incident unsettled Barker. He was already troubled by increasing friction with Cass, whose feelings of exclusion had been exacerbated by the fact that, whenever he took her to London, there was nowhere now for them to stay as a couple. Pa had left Stanhope Gardens for Sussex and Westbourne Terrace was forbidden territory, for obvious reasons. Besides, Soho was Elizabeth's domain: the lines were drawn more sharply now and Cass knew it. An incident in the autumn served to reinforce this point. Barker and Cass had been at the centre of a throng at the French pub, where late in the evening Elizabeth joined them. The two women hovered, keeping a wary distance from one another. At closing time Elizabeth invited everyone back to Westbourne Terrace to sample some malt whisky, which in those times of shortage she had obtained from abroad. It was an open invitation: open, that is, to everyone except Cass: 'I think Elizabeth thought that I would just vanish or something.' For once, she would not be dismissed so easily. She dragged along in the wake of the company, appearing on the doorstep just as the whisky was about to be poured out. When Elizabeth caught sight of her, she announced that she was tired and went to bed with a headache. The other drinkers carried on regardless, but Cass was left in little doubt as to where they, and Barker, placed the blame.[7]

Back at Hearne, in an Indian summer, George and Cass were seeing more and more of Patrick, who was still eking out a frugal existence in his caravan. Cass supplemented the household income by helping Patrick to pick apples at Parkhurst House, where David Gill's orchards were now fully established. When Barker left for town again, Cass and Patrick were thrust more and more into one another's company. Looking out of the broad windows at the front of the house in mid-September, Elizabeth Gill saw the young couple under the laden boughs. They were deep in conversation, their heads bent over the apple basket.[8]

On 4 October, Cass accompanied Barker to London for the rehearsals and recording of *The Seraphina* at Broadcasting House. Since Marjorie Westbury's singing had been particularly effective in *The Gardens of Altering Eros*, Cleverdon had now cast her as the Voice of the Figurehead of the *Seraphina*. The counter-tenor Alfred Deller sang the part of the Head of Orpheus, and Lennox Berkeley conducted the Sinfonia of London. Barker was delighted with the production and with Berkeley's music; he took particular pleasure in the purity of Deller's voice. By happy chance Cyril Cusack, who played Peter Amadeus, had for the two previous evenings been appearing on the Third as James Joyce, whose spiritual predicament his new role seemed to echo. After the recording George and Cass went to the George pub in Great Portland Street. Back in Portland Place, Cleverdon toiled over the tapes, editing thirty passages in time for transmission at 9.15.

The play was listened to by 0.3 per cent of the adult population of the United Kingdom. Eliot, however, sent his apologies to George, explaining that Thursday was his housekeeper's night off and he had been obliged to dine out with friends: 'one can't very well ask one's hosts to stop talking and turn on the wireless'.[9] Among those who did listen, according to the BBC Audience Research Department, was an osteopath, who thought the play 'of great interest and originality'. A kennelmaid declared, 'I liked it very much, but I can't explain why.' Five minutes after the *Seraphina* had left port, the wife of an insurance broker reported herself as having been 'all at sea'. An accounting clerk conceded that he had enjoyed the songs and a schoolmaster stated that

'Allegory is a tricky business.' But the most common reaction of the listeners, the department concluded, was one of complete 'bewilderment'.[10]

Dwelling on themes suggested by David Gill's apple orchard and by the mild autumn weather, Barker now proposed to Cleverdon a third radio play to deal with the biblical paradise, sex and original sin. Cleverdon expressed qualms – the combination of Barker, sex and religion had, after all, already caused trouble at the BBC – but the project was accepted on the condition that Barker refrained from blasphemy: 'You will', wrote Cleverdon, 'no doubt exercise your well-known moderation.'[11] The play was to deal with the Fall in both its seasonal and theological senses. It was called *Oriel O'Hanlon* after its protagonist Rory, a middle-aged Dubliner living with his sweet biddy wife Roses in unsuspicious harmony. It is autumn, and the trees are heavy with fruit. For their wedding anniversary Rory has just bought his darling a copy of Coventry Patmore's *The Angel in the House* at a second-hand bookshop by the Liffey. Rory is happy and knows that he is. He has the priceless gift of love of whose possession circumstances are about to deprive him. In the park we meet the prostitute Esmerelda, who wonders at their mutual absorption and their innocence. They also run into the organ-grinder Joe, the one love of whose life is Monk, his monkey, who has just unaccountably made his escape. On this perfect day Rory wonders at the absence of evil:

> Where is the shelter in this holy garden?
> Where is the Upas tree of knowledge
> We lay down under? When does the angel
> Reject us and the archangel eject us?[12]

Just then two shots ring out: the park keeper has executed Monk as a public nuisance. Upstairs at the O'Hanlon home Roses is visited by a mysterious Armenian, posing as a dark-cassocked priest. As Rory and Esmerelda sit downstairs, Rory is consumed with jealousy. The seed of suspicion is planted in his mind and, with it, the incursion of the evil he dreads. 'O Rory, O Rory,' Roses cries when he voices his suspicions. 'Orare, orare,' echoes Rory, adding, like some unreasoning Othello: 'Pray, Rose, pray.' When Joe calls at the door for his monkey, he has to be told that the one creature in the world whom he loved is sprawled lifeless beneath the old apple tree. Here Esmerelda finds the animal cradled in the arms of the spurned Roses, who croons:

> O my little monkey, little monkey, little monkey,
>   O my little monkey, what did you do?
> No one can run away from his love on Friday,
>   Or on any other day, too.[13]

At Hearne Barker worked on the play; in London he socialised at Archer's bookshop, where David had decided to revive the Parton Press. One lunchtime in January 1957 Barker was drinking with Moraes in the Coach and Horses, when the thin form of Archer appeared, gesticulating in the doorway. 'Would you mind if I published your poems?' he said to Moraes. 'As a book, I mean.' Once Archer was out of earshot, Barker turned to Moraes and advised him on matters of presentation: 'You choose the paper and font, and mind that David allows you wide margins.'[14] In his typically haphazard way, Archer was making a go of the bookshop. Its ground floor, where Lascelles Abercrombie's son Ralph had been installed as manager, was devoted to literature. Another floor functioned as a gallery, mounting small exhibitions of the work of Colquhoun amongst others. In the basement was a coffee bar run by Moraes's friend Henrietta Abbott, whom the Bernard brothers called 'Piss off darling'. However, Archer's stock-keeping and accounting methods were no more efficient than they had been in Holborn. When customers asked for a book that he had in stock, he would direct them round the corner to Foyle's. His personal generosity and patronage of young writers continued on much the same scale as in the 1930s. Every so often he would approach Moraes and present him with a matchbox. Moraes threw several boxes away before opening one to find a five pound note neatly folded inside.

Barker had now persuaded Archer to bring out a second edition of *The True Confession*, which had been out of print for some time. It was to be hard backed, and printed, at George's insistence, in Bodoni. But the revived press required funding. David sent Moraes down to Castle Eaton to ask for money from General Archer. 'Do you see those three hills over there?' the general asked Moraes, pointing wearily out of the window. 'Used to be in the family, you know. Not any more. That hill paid for Barker's *Thirty Preliminary Poems*. That hill paid for Thomas's *Eighteen Poems*. That hill paid for Gascoyne's *Man's Life Is This Meat*. No more hills left. I do not read poetry myself.'[15]

July seemed set fair to be a fruitful month for Barker. The Parton Press's *True Confession* came out early in the month, three months ahead of Moraes's *Poems*. *Collected Poems, 1930–1955* was promised for Monday the 29th. On the 7th *Oriel O'Hanlon* was broadcast on the Third. Rory was played by Dennis Quilley, Rose by Sheila Manahan, Esmerelda by Mary O'Farrell, and Joe the organ-grinder by Jack MacGowran. The song 'On Top of Old Smokey' was played on a barrel organ, using a barrel specially prepared for the purpose by Richard Pasquale, in his workshop in Highgate.

The play was an augury. 'The trouble with two in a room', says Esmerelda after the seduction scene, 'Is this: / No witness can ever prove / They just played Patience. And not Love.' Barker spent the third week of July at Westbourne Terrace, occupying himself with BBC business and new poetry projects.

August dragged its feet, since there was no money for a holiday. Barker was feeling ill and out of sorts. Disconsolately he returned to Hearne. One Friday night he drove with Cass to Soho. He had one ten shilling note in his pocket. In the French pub they met Elizabeth, who invited Barker to follow her up Dean Street to the Colony Room at Number 41. She did not invite Cass. George and Cass finished their halves, and drifted northways up Dean Street. When they arrived at the entrance of the Colony, Barker shrugged, murmured something about not having the price of a drink and fled up the steep stairs.

There was a beautiful sunset at the end of the street. 'I stood there a while looking at it,' Cass recalls, 'thinking I would not be seeing a sunset in Soho for a long, long time.' Oliver Bernard passed along the pavement; noticing her distress, he stopped to chat. She told him that George and Elizabeth were in the Colony. When Oliver disappeared upstairs to join them, Cass stuck a brief note under the windscreen wiper of Barker's car, explaining that she was returning to the country. She walked back to the French, where she had one last half pint. Alone, she caught a late train down to Hearne.[16]

The following morning Patrick arrived at the cottage. Cass wrote Barker a final note of farewell, which she left on the desk in his study. She took Chi-Chi, now a fully grown warrior cat, in her arms and left with Patrick through the back door. They walked across the cow meadow, along the footpath through the wood to the main road where, in the bright summer sunshine, they waited for the bus to Haslemere. After catching the train to Waterloo, they made their way via Paddington to Oxfordshire, where Cass's mother lived in Chinnor. Cass handed the cat over to her for safekeeping. She told her that she was going to Amsterdam with Patrick to look at paintings. She would never return to Hearne.

Cass had asserted her independence. Hitherto, she had done as she had been told, not once but a hundred times, unaware that she possessed the courage that some day would enable her to break free. Years later she summed up her feelings in these words: 'Two images of it will continue to haunt me: one is of a physically strong man beating up a not physically strong woman. The other is of Shelley's first wife, Harriet (a beautiful simple soul, perhaps a Jessica?) some few years after his abandonment of her and their young children, wandering in unravelled despair through Kensington Gardens and jumping into the Serpentine to drown herself.'[17]

A few days after these events Barker arrived back at the empty cottage and discovered her note. He drove in a fury up Bexley Hill to the Old Cottage, where he harangued Kit and Ilse for an entire afternoon. He was convinced that they knew where she had gone. They did not; nor would they be bludgeoned.[18] Bruce Bernard was staying with them, on holiday from his part-time job sweeping up at Archer's shop. He was bemused by the spectacle of Barker cuckolded by his own nephew. However, Bruce, who remained fond of Cass, had his own reasons for resenting George's hold over her. If she had wished for freedom, it seemed to him entirely reasonable that she should take it. George would not be satisfied. He grew morbid, blaming first himself for Cass's perfidy, then others. He raked over the miseries of the past, including the tragedy of Kit's lost eye. Then he drove to Chinnor; he confronted Mrs Cass, who outstared him for twenty long minutes. Young John was now married and happily settled in the village of Hermitage near Newbury; George phoned him and spoke rantingly of contacting Interpol and the FBI. He then changed tack, growing obsessed with the idea that Cass had sought happiness in North Wales in one of the holiday havens of her childhood. He insisted that John accompany him in search of her. For a week they drove around every seaside resort on the North Wales coast, enquiring after her and drawing nothing but blanks. Returning to Hearne, Barker made a bonfire in which he burned half of Cass's belongings; the rest he incinerated in the fireplace.

After a brief holiday in Amsterdam, the runaway lovers had in fact taken shelter in the very last place where they believed Barker, in his gaudy imaginings, would search for them: in Birmingham. Here they set up a modest home at 6 Wake Green Road, Morely, where they enjoyed uncluttered tranquillity, spoilt only by intermittent dread of the threats that were even now, they were certain, being issued against them.

Meanwhile, shunning the empty cottage, George went to stay with his sister Eileen, who had a house in Kew.[19] He sat alone writing, 'True Love, True Love, what have I done?'[20] Patrick and Cass were not alone in believing that, should word of their address ever get back to him, a double murder would ensue.

CHAPTER 37

'A HORSE STRUCK BY LIGHTNING'

Without Cass, Hearne seemed uninhabitable. Barker took the only course available to him; his wrath and pride teetering, he moved in temporarily with Elizabeth at Westbourne Terrace, where he remained like a caged animal licking its wounds.[1] On 7 September, deciding he was in need of emotional convalescence, Elizabeth took him to Paris, where he embarrassed and inconvenienced her all week by persistently proposing marriage. She told him not to be silly: such aspirations to uxoriousness came far too late in their lives. In any case, he was still married to Jessica.

Back in London he spent all day and much of the night drinking with Elizabeth in the pubs around Paddington. They went to the Colony Room, where they met Minton and his minions, and Francis Bacon who, in George's presence anyway, managed to muffle his dislike. It was 4 October before George had the courage to drive down to Hearne. For comfort he took along Elizabeth and Archer, who helped him to sort out his belongings.[2] The sky glowered; the cottage seemed a husk. They moved out Barker's clothes, his essential books and his radio, but left a trunk beneath his desk containing his precious archive of letters. Still, the spectre of his love would not be laid to rest. He was haunted by the memory of Cass as he had last seen her there, trudging down the lane in her wellington boots with a milk pail. He remembered his rages which, at least in part, had driven her away:

> Into that empty house, whence you have so
> Improvidently taken a last leave
> I again turn in the evening, but find no
> Echo of your possession or your love.
> What walls could ever imitate your dove

> Calling in silence from its amorous cage?
> What eavesdropping shadow ever shift or move
> So near as the whispering icon of your face?
>
> Was it the unicorn of my long horned pride
> Crushed your lost milkmaid underneath that hill?
> I had not thought that any beast could kill
> Such innocence of spirit, but would ride
> Roughshod as through a morning of blue May
> And not leave a hoofmark on the day.
> Now I have seen a butchered dawn lie still
> Where it was broken by the brute I ride.[3]

The brute was his own self. There was a tendency towards anger in him that even now, faced with its consequences, he was unable properly to subdue. He would bridle it in the presence of strangers, but amongst his closer associates it would keep breaking out, lashing at everything in its path. Elizabeth, who was genuinely concerned, tolerated the eruptions for old time's sake. Secretly she knew what his next move would be: he would return to America. In the meantime she put up with his tantrums, his despair, his grief for Big Mumma, his heart-searching over Cass's departure, the endless question, now doubly significant: 'Why did the bitch have to go and leave me?' All the same, Elizabeth took to wearing a crash helmet around the flat. The helmet drew George's derision and then his fury. On 7 December, forgetting that he had nowhere to go, he cleared out clutching his radio.

The next day he was back and so was the wireless. Eventually, even Elizabeth's patience snapped. The following Saturday evening, 15 December, Barker appeared at eleven o'clock with a posse of rowdies from the Swiss. They sprawled on her sofas, rifled her cupboards, helping themselves to her hard-earned whisky. With infinite dignity, Elizabeth stood up. She glared at George straight between the eyes. Then, with a great rush like a bird, she flew at him. Barker grasped her arms, attempting to restrain her. The result was a wrestling match in which neither contestant was quite certain of the holds. Since her limbs were pinioned, Elizabeth used the one weapon she had left. Making to kiss him, she clamped her teeth round his upper lip and bit hard. She felt his flesh yield; his arms went limp. Elizabeth hung on.

By the time the others had forced the wrestlers apart, Barker's lip was hanging by a thread. He was taken to the Casualty Department of Paddington General Hospital, where he received forty stitches. When Jeff Bernard next met him, he had a grotesque scar running obliquely beneath his nose. Then he grew a moustache, which came out red. In her diary, against 15 December,

Elizabeth wrote, 'Bit George's lip.' Barker explained to Heath-Stubbs that she was a Sioux Indian, of whom such behaviour was only to be expected. In due course the wound and the cosmetic moustache became badges of pride. 'Alcibiades', he drawled beneath them, 'had nineteen love bites.'[4]

Elizabeth had intended her attack as an act of catastrophic and final farewell. By Christmas Day, however, the two of them were together again. They ate lunch with the children, then at teatime Archer showed up and all three went to call on Henrietta Abbott. Afterwards, arm in arm like a disreputable Darby and Joan, Barker and Elizabeth walked back through the deserted streets to Bayswater.

Two days later Elizabeth was forty-four. They partied until dawn with Colquhoun and MacBryde. The Roberts had now sunk to a low ebb. They were so poor that Colquhoun could hardly afford the materials to paint with. Deprived of Tilty's safe harbour, they had been staying with Anthony Cronin and his wife in Wembley, where one night MacBryde had chased Colquhoun round the garden in a thunderstorm, brandishing a knife, to the amusement of the Cronins and the terror of the neighbours.[5]

Homelessness was something the Roberts and Barker now had in common. In the New Year of 1958, Barker went down to Hermitage in Berkshire to stay with Young John and his wife. Fairfax sensed his regret, his envy of simple domestic pleasures. In February, on his forty-fifth birthday, he was due in Oxford to lecture to the Literary Society. He met Elizabeth at Paddington and they travelled up together, staying at the King's Head.[6] For his theme Barker chose the symbolic significance of homelessness. Calling his talk 'How to Refuse a Heavenly House', he insisted on the importance of Yeats's statement that the intellect of man is forced to choose between perfection of the life or of the work. The insistence was a rejoinder to Robert Graves's recently published Clark lectures *The Crowning Privilege*, in which Graves had explained that he chose to write fiction in order to fund his poetry. Such a compromise, Barker implied, was Graves's individual choice. For Barker poetry always would be a full-time occupation. Poetry provided a unique slant on the world: 'The poem is a violation of reality in the sense that a lie is a violation of reality: it turns things upside down so that the engines of existence can be seen in operation.'[7] By this means, the poet projected an alternative physics. He was to be distinguished from the madman by one consideration: where the madman made a virtue out of disconnection, the poet devoted himself to the pursuit of connection.

On 8 March 1958, unbeknown to George, Patrick and Cass were married quietly at Birmingham Register Office. On 5 June, as Elizabeth had predicted, Barker left for New York.[8] He sublet Hearne Cottage to Anthony Cronin and his wife Theresa; they could not believe their luck. Roses twined around the front door and the meadow resounded with nightingales. Some of Cass's half-burnt clothing still remained in the grate.[9]

In Manhattan George stayed with Oscar Williams, who had now moved downtown to 35 Water Street. On his arrival he discovered Farrelly comatose on a table. Williams sought to rouse him. 'Don't worry,' Barker said, 'he prefers it like that.'[10] Oscar was delighted to see Barker, for whom he was soon acting again as unofficial agent, organising readings, selling poems at $10 a time, then paying him $20. Barker discovered the world of American verse burgeoning but depressing; it consisted, he complained to Kit, 'of the publication of hundreds of tiny little books of first poems, and none of them worth shaking a stick at'.[11] But at least he could make a living in America, a feat he had never quite managed in what he now called 'the sad isle'.

Oscar helped Barker to broaden his contacts in New York. Wherever the fray was thickest and the talk wildest, Oscar was to be found. Since 1946 he had, however, grown sensitive to the quips of his overseas protégés. Thomas's sardonic debunking had not passed Oscar by; he looked to Barker, if not for moral support, at least for less sarcasm. 'Don't betray me, George,' he pleaded one day. He also said he considered George a conduit of pure inspiration: 'You are a horse struck by lightning.'[12]

Oscar was now mixing with the poets of the Beat generation, particularly with Allen Ginsberg, whose *Howl and Other Poems* had appeared the previous year. Ginsberg and his fellow Beat Gregory Corso, author of *Gasolene*, had recently returned to New York from England. Moraes, now an undergraduate at Jesus College, had invited them to read at Oxford during the Trinity Term. The incumbent Professor of Poetry, W.H. Auden, had conducted them around Christ Church cathedral, where Corso had attempted to kiss his left shoe. On leaving, they had trailed a wake of broken furniture and promises. Now Ginsberg was longing to meet Barker, whom he considered one of his artistic progenitors. Besides, both of them had enjoyed visitations from Blake. Barker's, described in *Calamiterror*, had taken place on the Thames near Sonning; Ginsberg's had materialised on East 57th Street. In Oxford Moraes had asked Ginsberg what Blake had been wearing at the time. 'Oh,' he had replied, 'like a toga, man, the kind of clothes all the people wore in those days.'[13]

In the summer of 1958 Ginsberg was writing light satirical yet visionary screeds such as 'Laughing Gas' and 'Ignu'. Barker's early work seemed to him to share qualities with his own: being at once ambitious, whimsical, acidulous and profound. He especially admired *Calamiterror*, which he regarded as a model for longer poems. Despite this emulation, Barker could not quite return the compliment. After his recent trauma he welcomed the exuberant frivolity of the Beats; all the same, their tendency was towards formal laxity, while his nowadays was away from it. Soon after reaching New York, he read Jack Kerouac's novel *On the Road*, the manuscript of which had originally been written on a cash register roll. He had been unimpressed either by the banality of its opening sentences, or by the intellectual pretensions of its author. He soon expressed his misgivings in a rainbow satire entitled 'Circular from America'. The squib was all the more effective, since the subjects of its good-hearted scorn were invited to share in the joke. When he dispatched this poem to Faber, Eliot clearly relished its zest:

> I hear the Beat
> No not of the heart
> But the dull palpitation
> Of the New Art
> As, on the dead tread
> Mill of no mind,
> It follows its leaders
> Unbeaten behind.
> O Kerouac Kerouac
> What on earth shall we do
> If a single Idea
> Ever gets through?
> The English have seventy
> Gods and no sauce
> (The French have Voltaire
> And Two Maggots of course)
> But ½ an idea
> To a hundred pages
> Now Jack, dear Jack,
> That ain't fair wages
> For labouring through
> prose that takes ages
> Just to announce
> That Gods and Men
> Ought all to study
> The Book of Zen.
> If you really think
> So low of the soul
> Why don't you write
> On a toilet roll?[14]

On 1 August, Elizabeth's children arrived from London to stay with her sister

Jane at Newport, Rhode Island. A few days afterwards George joined them unexpectedly. Christopher did not know whether to be more astonished by his father's inexplicable re-emergence, or by his apparent intimacy with their aunt.[15] Fifteen-year-old Georgina confided to her diary, 'Poets are terrifying people to live with. They rush off at odd moments, and are neither seen nor heard of for months. Then, low [sic] and behold, they suddenly appear on the threshold as if nothing had ever happened. They treat everyone else as though they hardly existed, but are merely there to help their inspirations. They are erratic, mad and so emotional. I adore one special poet.'[16]

Altogether America seemed to Barker endowed with too thin a cultural crust. Beneath its surface, however, lay hedonistic plums. In New York he met friends, new and old. The Farrellys' marriage had by now broken down irretrievably. By August John had decamped to St Louis, leaving Dede in their rambling brownstone at 21 East 72nd Street with their two children: eight-year-old Elizabeth and five-year-old George. Barker called to pay his respects, while living at Oscar's. East 72nd Street offered a comfortable domestic setting if he wanted one; he was not, however, quite in the mood for family life. He called round at Christopher Street, where he had half a dozen tense meetings with Jessica, with whom he had been intermittently in touch. She pressed his responsibilities on him, with limited success. To the twins, understandably, he was a distant figure. 'They will not domesticate me,' he told Dede on his return from these encounters: 'I am reliably unreliable.'[17]

For the last two weeks of August Dede rented a house in Irwina, Pennsylvania, with the children. Barker was invited to join them. He and Dede enjoyed long, luxurious bathes in a dam near the house. The holiday provided him with a respite from the emotional turmoil he had suffered over the previous few months. 'We decided,' recounts Dede, 'if it was feasible, to marry.'

Dede was from a large family in St Louis, Missouri, whose ample fortune had been made in the chemicals business. She possessed a gentle manner and a softly spoken, melodious voice with just a suggestion of a southern lilt. Barker discovered in her an unostentatious generosity, a welcome repose, while his humour brought out in her a submerged and highly appealing *joie de vivre*. Dede clearly felt drawn to bohemian circles, to which she did not, however, belong by temperament. She had no illusions about Barker, whose peccadilloes she had observed in Cambridge, France and Ireland. But she loved his wit, his haphazard largesse, his odd mixture of reverence and irreverence.

There were, of course, impediments to marriage. Jessica was still insistent about the Church's teaching on divorce. John Farrelly was as yet unreconciled to his separation and possessive of the children. For all that, in a moment of decisiveness, George and Dede made for the city where American divorces were reputed to be easiest to obtain: Las Vegas.

They set off in September, explaining to the children that the jaunt was an extension to their holiday.[18] They put up at Frank Sinatra's hotel, the Sands. There were fruit machines in the lobby; at night scantily clad girls pirouetted on nearby balconies. Barker and Dede found the tawdriness intolerable. While their attorneys investigated the legal position, they drove across Yucca Flats and into California, where they visited Death Valley. The very name of this desolate region seemed redolent of an American dream turned to dust. It reminded Barker of *The Four Horsemen of the Apocalypse*, the silent Western of 1921 starring Rudolph Valentino. He began work on an allegory, in which four horsemen ride across from Nevada in the aftermath of an atom bomb. One by one, they yield up the ghost:

> Still the Angel of Death, that fourth horseman,
> Glared from his dead eye:
> 'Jack,' says he, 'so now you know
> It ain't so hard to die.
>
> 'It aint so hard to die, Jack,
> And every mother's son
> One day will sleep beside you there
> When all is said and done.'
>
> 'So haunt the westering desert, Jack,
> Haunt it like mirages,
> And whisper to Los Alamos
> I pay the wages.'
>
> Then that immortal horseman
> Smiled and rode away.
> 'There's never a day', quoth he, 'but dawns
> Redder in Nevada'.[19]

After a few weeks the heat and the garishness became wearying. George and Dede moved out of the brash Sands Hotel into the quieter Twin Lakes Lodge. On 16 September George's visa was extended until January 1959. The divorce proceedings had quickly run aground, since Dede discovered that the necessary preconditions involved either relinquishing custody of her children, or alternatively settling for a prolonged period in Nevada. Since neither option was acceptable, they returned to Manhattan.

While Dede looked after the children at East 72nd Street, Barker rented a large room a block away at 124 East 71st Street. Here he could write in peace and entertain friends in ones and twos. Larger gatherings were held at Dede's brownstone. In October Ginsberg and Corso squatted at Barker's feet on the spacious floor of Dede's upstairs room with their fellow Beat, Peter Orlovsky. Ginsberg was later to recall how rapturously they all responded to Barker's 'Urizonic mentality': 'he kissed Peter Orlovsky, and bit his tongue, by heaven!'

Barker was experiencing one of his rare writer's blocks. For Christmas he was given a German tape recorder. Instead of writing poetry he devoted hours to reading *Winnie the Pooh* into its microphone in a weird collection of accents. He also played back recordings he had surreptitiously made of his continuing sessions with the Beats.[20] The reprise was, he wrote to Oliver, the nearest that he had yet attained to the act of spiritual penance. He felt an occasional spasm of nostalgia for the topers of Soho. Such consolations as New York provided all wore 'pygmy tails and no underpants'. He told Oliver that this state of semi-undress at least facilitated 'the initiatory rites of acquaintance'.[21]

Dede now possessed legal custody of her two children Elizabeth and George. In Missouri, however, Farrelly was far from reconciled to this state of affairs. In January 1959 he drove up from St Louis. Arriving while Dede was out, he bundled the children into the car and took them to his brother Jack's house in St Louis. Dede's only recourse was to kidnap them again. She descended on Missouri and hurried Elizabeth and George into a waiting taxi, across the state line and then to New York by plane.[22]

She was now carrying Barker's child. Amongst other factors, this served temporarily to focus Barker's mind on the possibility of settling in America. There was little to tempt him back to England. Besides, one by one, members of the Barker family seemed to be descending on the United States. Veronica and her husband Calvin were now living in California as, he now discovered, were Patrick and Cass. As two of her children were in the States, Monica had also crossed the Atlantic and settled contentedly in San Francisco. Encouraged by these developments, George applied through the Institute of Contemporary Arts for an extension of his visa. While waiting for it, he supported himself with reading tours arranged for him by Oscar. In Arizona he stayed on a university campus so bleakly utilitarian as to be almost otherworldly: such institutions were, he later reported, 'as far as the first person singular could reach'. One Saturday night he looked in the distance, where he perceived an enormous erection that he took for 'a sexual mirage'. It was the university's central tower, illuminated by pink floodlights in celebration of a football victory against a neighbouring college; 'sublimated extroverts conducted a Saturnalia at its base'. He was swept up in the celebration and ended the night swallowing wine out of a teacup in a lavatory.[23] In the early summer Dede took a house at

Southampton, Long Island where Jessica's twins – both now tall, good-looking and attending Greenwich Village high schools – came briefly to stay. After they had left, Barker and his adoptive brood returned to the city in time for Dede's delivery: a boy, Jimmy, born on Sunday, 8 August 1959.

Soon after the birth George received an urgent message from Oscar. Theodore Roethke had been engaged to teach for the last two weeks of August at an annual writers' conference on Bread Loaf Mountain above Middlebury College, Vermont. Roethke was ill and a replacement was needed. The following Sunday Barker drove up to the hilltop campus, where he settled into a timber-frame hut with spectacular views across the state. The conference had been founded by Robert Frost, who still attended and who outraged Barker by claiming to be a better poet than Yeats. Barker had not had much time to prepare. His behaviour at the first session made an indelible impression on Ron Schuchard, a young writer and scholar who had registered for the course. As soon as he stood up to read, Barker looked across at his audience to find the whole front row occupied by nuns in their black habits. They had come to hear a recital of Roethke's delicately observed, symbolic pieces like 'Words for the Wind', featured in his recent *Selected Poems*. Barker surprised Schuchard by preceding his reading with a volley of obscenities. The nuns fled.[24]

Barker had more luck with the teaching assistants and students, two of whom were to become friends. Among the Writing Fellows was Willie Coakley, a recent graduate of Harvard, where he had come across Barker's work in Oscar's anthologies of the 1940s. Among the students was Carol Weston, a 24-year-old Bostonian with a romantic and impressionable temperament who had left Boston University that June with a degree in comparative literature and remedial reading ('I have a reading problem,' she told him). At Bread Loaf Barker struck alternating poses: with Coakley exhibitionist and encouraging; with Weston tormented and tragic. 'When you go home,' he told her, 'take hold of a copy of *Othello*, and peruse the speech the Moor makes before he takes his own life. *There* you have my condition.' He gave Weston the impression that like Othello he had 'loved not wisely, but too well'. Like the base Indian, he had thrown a pearl away 'richer than all his tribe'; the pearl being Cass. He would drive down to Middlebury at high speed, arriving back with a screech of brakes. Such was his apparent despair, Weston feared he was contemplating Othello's death.[25]

Weston had a job for the summer handing out books in a mental hospital on Long Island. When the fortnight at Bread Loaf was over, Barker drove her down there. On the way he took her to his room at 71st Street, where he typed out a satirical sequence called 'Eight Beatitudes to Denver', an attempt to outdo the Beats at their own stylistic game. When he had finished, he handed her the typescript with a flourish:[26]

> This is not, I know, the place for private revelations.
> Few things are harder than to make love on paper.
> And yet, Sophonisba, when I mislaid my female in Memphis
> How could I ever have known such a Thais would succeed her?
>
> No man could ever resist your collection of long playing records
> And the knot you tie in your hair, why, even a horse would envy it.
> The alacrity with which you leap between sheets, buttocks akimbo,
> What ballerina could equal? I kiss your mouth like a gas ring.[27]

Weston did not appreciate the Beatitudes. When she told him so, he tore the typescript to shreds in front of her. It was, fortunately, the carbon. After he had dropped her at Long Island, he returned to Manhattan and walked with Willie Coakley to the Minetta Tavern on McDougal Street in Greenwich Village, where he introduced him to Oscar. When Oscar left, Barker stayed behind. He whispered into Willie's eager ear, 'Thou art *uno poeta*.'[28] Then he grew expansive: 'Go and do it, baby! Do it better than we did!' Afterwards, he walked with Willie back through Washington Square, arm in arm.

He was clearly enjoying himself. For all that, there seems to have been an undertone of desperation to much of his hectic socialising. With American friends he seemed light-hearted, warm and generous; in his letters back to England, on the other hand, the cynicism of his tone gives his geniality the lie. On 17 September he snatched a moment to write to Oliver Bernard, to whom he confessed that, when he looked back on the last few months in 'Shamerica' he could discern little but 'a series of erotic phantasmagoria, illuminated intermittently by the light of a black eye'. He concluded his letter by remarking that, having slipped out from beneath his bedsheets, Carol was now tugging at his arm, demanding to be taken to the White Horse tavern.[29]

Three days later he embarked on a gruelling inter-state reading tour, organised by the indefatigable Oscar. The first stage was the University of Texas at Austin, where he read the 'Beatitudes to Denver', now nine in number. Then he flew to Los Angeles, where he was put up at the Faculty Club of Occidental College. On Sunday, 18 October he stepped off United Airways Flight 569 to San Francisco to find that his luggage had gone astray and, with it, his only presentable pair of trousers. He was obliged to borrow a pair from the French poet Saint-John Perse, whose *Anabase* Eliot had once translated.[30] Then he set off to meet Monica in a bar. He had not seen his closest sister for many months; when she told him she considered Cass's elopement had been justified, he knocked her off her stool. She refused to give him Patrick and Cass's address. Nonetheless, he discovered their phone number and rang. Cass picked up the receiver. 'She sounded sad,' he reported to Oliver. 'I do not understand human life.'[31] After reading at San Francisco College and the Museum of Art, he went on to Santa Barbara, where on the 9th Dede joined him for a week. At Seattle he read at the University of Washington; then, for the first time in fifteen years, he crossed over to Canada before doubling back to Detroit. There was a final engagement at Notre Dame, Indiana. He arrived, exhausted, at Newark Airport at eight twenty-five on the evening of 12 December.[32]

The trip had not been entirely pleasant. Staying in hotel rooms, reading to half-appreciative audiences, receiving solemn academic attention: these were aspects of American life which had helped destroy Dylan Thomas and which Barker himself had taken pains to avoid since John Malcom Brinnin's invitation of 1951. Having submitted to the chore of reading to college audiences, he found his indifference to the ways of academe deepening into a wry loathing. As time went by, he came to employ the title 'Professor' – especially when applied to himself – as a carefully weighed insult.

CHAPTER 38

'A DIVINE FIAT'

The hurt of Cass's abrupt departure, of course, still smarted. In the past it had usually been Barker who had left his women; the sensation of having been abandoned himself had brought him closer to poets for whom thwarted passion had been a theme. He had always considered the Orpheus of unrequited love to be A.E. Housman, on whom from the close of 1959 he compiled a series of critical observations which read very much like projections of his own state of mind. The poetical attitude of Housman, he remarked, looks like self-pity. It is in fact 'the lovelessness of a nature that cannot quite believe in the existence of love'. On one level Housman seems to want to persuade his readers of his indifference to pain: 'He wishes to give the effect of not caring and not believing, but this wish, like so many of the operations of the human character, has the opposite tied to its tail.' Housman's true condition, he concluded, is one of 'self-contempt for caring too much'.[1]

Barker's immersion in transient socialising during his months in America had been a deliberate displacement of, or distraction from, his emotional wounds. By the end of 1959, however, the cure had done its work. Besides, George and Dede both felt a need to create a physical and psychological distance from America, where the temptations were too gross and the literature seemed to Barker too coarse-fibred. A further consideration was that Farrelly was still unreconciled both to their union, and to the loss of his children. After much thought, Barker and Dede elected for a future in Europe.

On Boxing Day 1959 they flew with the Farrelly children and baby Jimmy to London. Shortly after New Year they settled in Chelsea, taking a lease on a three-storey Georgian house at 27 Margaretta Terrace, just round the corner from Oakley Street, where Barker had once visited Antonia White and Emily Coleman. The first floor of the house had a wrought-iron balcony overlooking a small front garden. In the early hours of a February morning Dede looked out to see Colquhoun and MacBryde wrestling by moonlight among the wintry shrubs.[2] The Roberts had been camping at Westbourne Terrace, neglectful of their painting, which in any case nobody now wanted. Every morning they sauntered down to the York Minster, carrying just enough money in their pockets to purchase their first half pints. They cadged drinks throughout the remainder of the day. Their afternoons were spent in the Mandrake Club, the evenings in the Soho pubs. At closing time, they would return to Westbourne Terrace, once more to try Elizabeth's patience.

Along with the Roberts, the entire bohemian culture of the 1950s seemed to have been seized by terminal decline. Archer's bookshop had shrunk to its basement, where the stock was temporarily piled, pending inevitable closure. *Nimbus* had long ago folded. In place of it there were fresh ventures. Patrick Swift was back in London, where he and Oonagh had settled into the basement of Westbourne Terrace, beneath Elizabeth's flat. With David Wright as co-editor, Swift decided to start a new quarterly. Dom Moraes was co-opted as an unofficial assistant. The periodical, polemical in its rejection of the passing artistic fads of the time, would cover painting as well as poetry. Its chosen title, *X*, algebraically signified 'the incalculable or mysterious quality and influence' characteristic of the best in contemporary culture.

With hindsight, *X* looks very much like the last gasp of New Romanticism. At the time, however, the magazine represented a double protest: against the narrowing of poetic taste associated with the movement, and against the ineluctable drift amongst painters towards abstraction. Eschewing explicit programmes, Swift and Wright dispensed with a manifesto. All that they required of their contributors was that they stood against the established avant-garde. Eclecticism was all and oppositions flourished. In place of an editorial, the first issue commenced with Barker's 'Circular from America'. It continued with an attack by Anthony Cronin on the notion of political commitment in literature, and this in turn was followed by a highly ideological poem by Hugh MacDiarmid, which contained the lines 'Today we are ripe to put an end / To poverty'. Eclecticism could scarcely have ranged more widely.

Despite this, though, *X* never quite avoided giving the impression of being the mouthpiece of a coterie, edited as it was in the basement beneath Elizabeth's flat by two of Barker's protégés. Barker was the 'eminence grise' of the enterprise; he tripped back and forth from Chelsea, counselled tact when dealing with the magazine's backers, and read such manuscripts as Wright and Swift passed on. Together they unearthed several unexpected talents.

Two newcomers proved especially promising, though as remote from one another in temperament as the south and north poles. The only characteristics shared by Brian Higgins and C.H. Sisson were that both were relatively late starters as poets, wrote closely wrought, spiky verse and belonged to no identifiable cabal. Higgins was thirty years old and from Batley in the West Riding of Yorkshire. Barker likened him to one of Shakespeare's fools with his sharpness, his sadness and cunning. Among his attractive qualities were a clumsy amiability and an intelligence which enabled him to analyse his own insecurities and to write about them in terse, funny, self-deprecating verse. Sceptically inclined, mathematically educated, chronically unloved, he arrived in the Museum Tavern, Great Russell Street in response to Wright's summons.[3] He sat at one of the oblong tables, wolfing his food and burping his appreciation, to the faint horror of Moraes, who nonetheless felt nervously guilty towards this unwanted, oversized prodigy of thwarted manhood, who seemed to him always to smell of a chip pan. These gaucheries endeared him to Barker, so fond of the vulnerable and the flawed. A head taller than Higgins, he stared down at him, heaping insults into his rubicund, appreciative face. In July fifteen-year-old Sebastian Barker came home for the holidays from the King's School, Canterbury. He found Higgins installed in a boxroom on the first floor, where Elizabeth was attempting to mother him. He appeared obsessed with providing for his own creature comforts and was ruthless in securing them. Once he disappeared into the afternoon, bearing away a Virginia ham which Elizabeth had bought for dinner.[4] To the quizzical Cronin it seemed as if 'Brian was his own mother'. In September Elizabeth sent Sebastian, who was preparing to return to school, to Allkit in Cambridge Circus with some money to buy a mackintosh. Higgins accompanied him: 'Fancy', he remarked, 'having a mother that buys you macks.'[5] His poems appeared in the June issue of *X*: they were clever and full of need.

Wright and Swift's other discovery could not have been more different. Charles Sisson was an Assistant Secretary in the Ministry of Labour. He was only a year younger than Barker, whose work he had first come across in 1933 when he was an undergraduate reading English and philosophy at Bristol University.[6] Significantly, his attention had been attracted by the poem 'Coward's Song' from *New Verse* about 'The soul lying on the seashore / Even by the ubiquitous sea unnoticed / And ignored'. These lines had reflected a fondness for privacy that was an important strand in Sisson's own artistic and personal make-up. He had preferred them to Auden's certainties; in any case he had himself been 'unnoticed' before tentatively starting to write his own verse in 1950. To the editors of *X*, everything about him seemed unobtrusive. If Higgins wore a mask of gauche enthusiasm, Sisson's chosen camouflage was the pinstripe of civility. Beneath it, however, lay a deep, unbureaucratic commitment to truth in the sense in which Barker himself once defined it in *X*: 'the word means what he sees, because most of the time most of us are blindfold'.[7] His poems fitted in well with the magazine's anti-modernist bias, exemplifying what Wright and Swift had called 'a sceptical curiosity about the prevailing and fashionable attitudes which dominate the scene'. When his first batch of submissions was accepted for the fourth issue, Sisson accepted the editors' invitation to join them for a celebratory drink in the saloon bar of the Red Lion in Duke of York Street, just across from his ministry's offices in St James's Square, where he was introduced to Barker. As the conversation opened out, he realised that he was 'in the presence of a profound humourist'.[8] For a later issue of the magazine, Swift painted portraits of all the major contributors. He depicted Barker sitting by the fireplace in one of Elizabeth's straight-backed chairs, his hands folded, his eyes mesmeric, the lines on his face and the angular shape of his jaw line making him look serious and austere. He painted Sisson in his suit, looking cryptically through his glasses, as if raising a delicate point in the minutes.

Barker's profundity and fun continued to attract apprentice poets. The previous year Moraes's volume *A Beginning* had won him the newly revived Hawthornden Prize. His success had immediately made him a glamorous and much sought-after figure. In March 1960 Compton Mackenzie invited him to spend Easter at his castle in the Highlands. When the invitation fell through, Barker proposed that they visit Scotland together in any case. He packed Dom, Dede, Elizabeth and George Farrelly, Jimmy and their nanny Miss McKinner into his green-upholstered Austin, and drove north.[9] Moraes recalled that 'George drove with intense fury through the Highlands, his blue eyes shining with a fanatic light. There was a great deal of luggage, and some of it had to be strapped to the back.'[10] At Berwick-upon-Tweed Barker turned left and crossed over the Coldstream, where he gave a hurrah in honour of Pa. As they progressed westwards, Dom and George improvised as many internally rhyming lines as they could manage on the pattern of Byron's 'Ah, to float forever in a gondola'. Dom's most impressive effort was 'Och, to float forever on a loch'.

'At one point', Moraes narrated later, 'a motorcycle policeman overtook and stopped us. "Dear heart," said George, "I was only doing forty." The policeman did not seem to like this form of address. "Look behind you," he advised. We all did. One of the suitcases strapped to the back had burst. For miles behind, the heather was strewn with clothes.' They crossed to and from Skye and then drove eastwards to Edinburgh, via Oban and Loch Ness. Barker discovered a distinct affinity with the Monster, a sensitive creature, like himself wounded in love. In Edinburgh he drank with Moraes in the Abbotsford on Rose Street, where their companions were beetle-browed Norman McCaig and Sydney Goodsir Smith. A quarrel began as to whether Lallans was a fit vehicle for verse.[11] Barker, who was usually open to the aural effect of poetry in any tongue, whether he understood it or not, was moved to defend Lallans. The obligations of friendship, however, led him to support Moraes, who adopted the opposite view. The next morning Moraes woke with a throbbing hangover in Goodsir Smith's flat in Dundas Street. As he lay there, sick and defenceless, Smith tormented him by reciting poem after poem in Lallans.

In fact, Barker possessed very mixed feelings about the cultural chauvinism of the Scots. Using the brisk, sardonic line he had employed in his 'American Circular', he now adapted one of Byron's titles for a lampoon called 'Scottish Bards and an English Reviewer':

> A Grieving Pibroch
> Assails my ear:
> 'I tell you, mon,
> This universe
> Will go on getting
> Worse and worse
> Till they pass a law
> That only [sic] Scotch
> Is allowed to think
> Or wear a watch
> Or take a drink.
> For every other
> Earthly nation
> Can tell the time
> From their subjugation
> And as for ratio
> -cination,
> Why, any fool who's
> Not too cliquey
> Knows that it started
> In Auld Reekie,
> And every other
> Heathen knows
> A thistle (Scottish)
> Outsings a rose.[12]

Dede appreciated the expansiveness of the Scots, which reminded her of the warmth of the Irish. England, however, cramped her. In the late summer, when their short lease at Margaretta Terrace came to an end, the family spent some weeks in a hotel near Kensington Gardens. In August the children departed for a holiday in Norway with the nanny Miss McKinner, while

George and Dede drove to Rome, where the 1960 Olympic Games were already in full swing. They arrived on Wednesday, 24 August to find every acceptable hotel room in the capital booked for the duration of the games. So they headed for the seaside resort of Fregene, where for three weeks they stayed in the Hotel dei Pini, enjoying leisurely drinks in the resin-scented garden overlooking the sea. Each day they drove the twenty-seven kilometres into the city for the track events. There they watched Amin Hary win the final of the hundred metres. Barker was delighted by Hary's subsequent pronouncement that 'I am very tired of being the centre of world attention.' He wrote to Kit that the athlete's suspect modesty sounded affectingly like Sydney Graham's.[13]

At the end of September Barker and Dede reassessed their circumstances. They had little reason to return to rain-soaked London, where they had no permanent base. The children had not yet settled into schools. And, in any case, was not Rome, as Father Dale-Roberts had told Barker long ago, the Eternal City? How could one not feel contented, he confessed to Kit, in a city where every motorist enjoyed 'a divine fiat'? His English past dissolved behind him, as did the erotic phantasmagoria of the States. When he looked back now on the long dream of Hearne, he wrote, it seemed to him sealed off from the world, 'like one of those fluffy snowstorms in glass bottles'. The agony of Cass's abrupt departure had faded. At last, he told his brother, invoking Henry James, he had succumbed to a state of merciful forgetfulness: 'Maisie's Aphasia or How to Live Without a Past'.[14]

Accordingly, Dede wired Miss McKinner to bring the children to Rome. When they arrived, the whole family stayed for several weeks in Fregene, while searching for an apartment. The following month, they moved into 72 Via Nemorense, a two-floor maisonette to the west of the city, built over an ancient subterranean water course. In its garden, in late autumn, Barker built a pseudo-oriental birdcage hung with mobiles and perches.[15] The toy seems to have been intended as a present for eight-year-old George Farrelly, possibly to compensate him for all the disruptions and shifts of place. One morning the children woke to find a sparrow caught in the bars. They brought breadcrumbs and water from the house in a vain attempt to sustain it. After two days, like a soul deprived of its platonic element, it died. George Farrelly blotted out the memory of the sparrow, though not of the cage. For Barker, the episode suggested a poem in homage to Catullus, 'A Sparrow's Feather':

> So there, among its gods
> that moaned and whistled in a little wind,
> flapping their paper anatomies like windmills,

> wheeling and bowing dutifully to the
> divine intervention of a child's forefinger,
> there, at rest and at peace among its monstrous
> idols, the little bird died.[16]

Italy, with its ancient literature, its classical and Catholic history, provided Barker with the specific circumstances which, reviewers believed, inspired his best poetry. In any case, as he wrote to Kit, he had for the time being lost patience with England and America, those twin halves of the sick Protestant conscience. In November he drove back to London to fetch the family's effects. The Austin was piled high on the return trip. In Paris the brakes seized up. Since nineteen-year-old Georgina was attending literature classes at the Sorbonne, Barker used the delay to get to know his daughter better. When the car was ready, he drove her south as far as Aix-en-Provence. On the way he encouraged her to talk about herself, an experience which she found 'unsettling'. She told him that she was an introvert; he replied that introverts were probably superior to extroverts, whom, however, he preferred.[17] Once installed back at the Via Nemorense, he wrote to Elizabeth to inform her that Georgina had been 'seismographic' all the way through France. To Kit he reported that his daughter had been in a state of abstracted delight with the countryside in its autumn tints: 'I had never seen Europe looking so marvellous, like a middle aged beauty Peter Paul Rubens had just made love to.' Then he wrote to Georgina herself, advising her on approaches to the study of Rimbaud. She was to read Edgell Rickword's monograph *Rimbaud* and Helen Rootham's translations of the poet. Their trip, he told her, had been an 'enchanting time' and 'an absolutely marvellous thing to happen'.

By early December Rome was cold and overcast. Barker did not mind because 'the sun will come out tomorrow'. Since he had moved house, he decided to give himself a present. He acquired a large mottled block of black and white marble, the veining in which, he wrote ecstatically to Kit, 'looks like a photograph of the human soul (of my soul, in any case)'. He designed a magnificent pseudo-Renaissance frame for it, with a gilded eagle flying at each corner. Then he commissioned a local carpenter to construct the frame, eagles and all. The result was a writing desk so handsome that, when it was delivered to his study, he was almost frightened to use it. 'Only kings and poets', he wrote to Kit, should be permitted to sit there.

He had reached another point of stability, albeit precarious. On 28 December, the Feast of the Holy Innocents, he was able to open a fresh notebook by recording the birth of a son, Edward, delivered that day at the Salvator Mundi Hospital. At the christening eight-year-old George Farrelly became godfather to his half-brother; the child's godmother was one of the few intimate friends

Barker and Dede had made since their arrival three months before: Raffaella Pellizi, wife of a professor at the university.[18] Soon afterwards a forward spring brought the crowds out into the parks. Barker continued his notebook with accolades to the season and his latest child: 'In the spring, when even statues, if closely observed, can be seen to turn their heads and admire what they know must be happening behind them so, sadly, do we. Who dare pursue the urban child across paradise and drag him down, howling and kicking in the Ospedale Salvator Mundi?' He devoted the afternoon to wandering in the gardens above the Forum. 'The sun was almost too hot, although it has only just entered the spring solstice, and oranges lay in profusion under the little trees, and the fountains seemed to jump with a special delight and, of course, the Roman couples were kissing everywhere. On the tomb of Caesar, a pair of carnations had been laid.'[19]

The omens seemed good, and working conditions were excellent. Barker had been tinkering with impressions of America, planning to put them together as a volume to be called 'The Ballad of Yucca Flats'. Now Italian pieces were coming thick and fast: three Roman poems and descriptions of the countryside. He had also written a dedicatory paeon to some of the women in his life: Monica on the Pacific shore with 'the veronica of her daughter'; Eileen, in her cottage 'pensive by Kew Green'; Dede in the fulfilment of her pregnancy. 'Nearly all of the poems in this book', he wrote in the notebook, 'got themselves written in a period of ten weeks in the spring of 1961'. In stark contrast to the dearth of his trip with the Roberts in 1949, he was now able to record, 'I find Rome an extraordinarily good place for writing poems, just as some spots are good for mushrooms. Here I had simply to get up early in the morning and collect the lines. This was the more peculiar in that I had not found it possible to write anything, including private letters, for some two years previously. Now I wonder if it might not be simply a matter of going where the poems are, for it would be as absurd to seek for a Lyre Bird in a library, or the Muse in a museum.'[20]

In March he sent a new poem to Eliot, requesting that the volume now being assembled be renamed after it: *The View from a Blind I*. Its title may contain a reference to the fencing accident of 1935, and the poem itself suggests an attempt to capture something of the transparency of Kit's work as a landscape painter. He had written it late one spring afternoon whilst sitting among children at play near the fountains in the Tivoli Gardens surrounding Hadrian's villa:

> Where once the Emperor
> Mused in his alabaster
> Court in a pool like a wheel

> Saw he, perhaps, the same
> Void in the psychic water?
> Over the Campagna
> As far as I can see
> The farms flourish like flowers
> And the confident olive
> Whispers how civilized
> Man and landscape can be.
> Little rivers assure
> The farmer of his reward
> And a cynical Horace smiles
> From a neat hillside that looks
> Exactly like one of his odes.[21]

Along with the other Roman poems in the new collection, this piece was the result not so much of composition as of self-discovery. Forswearing rhetorical tricks, Barker for once allowed the lines to follow the contours of his thought and feeling. In 1949 he had attempted to compete with Italy by using a self-defeating baroque rhetoric Now, taking his Englishness for granted, he let his words create spontaneous form, like the Tivoli fountains themselves, cascades sculpting their own shapes whilst falling.

CHAPTER 39

'TRANSFIGURING EVERYWHERE'

A mood of euphoria born of sheer relief entered Barker's correspondence at this time. He had been reading Celano's account of St Francis visiting Pope Ugolino to preach the gospel and 'moving his feet in the manner of one dancing, not for play but being driven thereto by the strength of the divine love within him'. To the balletic Georgina he wrote that the saint's behaviour showed 'how instinctive it was to honour things with the dance'.[1] He was, he told her, sitting in his study waiting for spring to turn up 'in that little pink two-seater she uses in these latitudes'. He had been reading a lot at his new marble desk: Catullus and Propertius, in translation first and then in the Latin for the sake of the sounds. He had also managed three whole volumes of a history of China, in which he had been especially pleased with a story of the general who outfaced an invading army by sitting in a tower playing the harp. The army assumed that it was an ambush and slunk away.

Barker felt a little like this general, since Dede, who had inherited the proceeds of her family's business in St Louis, was meeting all essential expenses; in consequence he had not much to do except sit in his tower at the Via Nemorense reading about this, that and the other. Like the Chinese army, his English and American acquaintances had withdrawn. For society he was dependent on his immediate family circle and, beyond them, the resident population of artists, a small group of Italian anglophiles and the occasional visitor. He was introduced to the sculptor Federico Spadini, son of a celebrated painter, who had a house in Fregene. Professor Camillo Pellizi and his wife Raffaella, who were wealthy and biligual patrons of the arts, were warm and supportive, as was the sociologist Federico Ferrarotti, who also had a house in Fregene.

Barker did not speak or read much Italian and made no concerted effort to learn it. His contacts with Italian poets were therefore confined to those who spoke English. But a focus for international literature was provided by the multilingual journal *Botteghe Oscure*, edited by the Principessa Marguerite Caetani. In addition there was an annual summer Festivale dei Poeti, funded by the city's communist-dominated corporation. By 1961, however, the magazine had reached its last edition and the participants at the 1960 festival had dispersed with the swallows in September.

One of the few English-speaking poets who were semi-resident in Rome was Desmond O'Grady, a Cistercian-educated, 25-year-old from Limerick. O'Grady had been living and teaching in the city since reading for the Festivale in June. He was fast becoming something of a professional expatriate, but one who possessed a facility for languages which Barker lacked: he was later to translate, not only from the Italian, but from the Greek and the Arabic as well. In the early months of 1961 he and Barker were fairly constant companions. In Albrecht's, a beer parlour frequented by artists, they sat reminiscing about Dublin bars while the generously attentive muse of Raffaella Pellizi 'hovered angelically above, beside and about'. Together they devised O'Grady's next project: a long narrative poem entitled *Reilly*. Its eponymous anti-hero, a sozzled Irish poet with something of Patrick Kavanagh about him, pursues his Bloom-like itinerary from one watering hole to the next.[2] But O'Grady was to leave Rome the next year to study at Harvard. After his departure English-speaking poets were few and far between.

'The absolute delight of living in Rome', Barker then wrote to Oliver Bernard, half-mocking his own insular dependence on English-speaking companions, 'is that there is absolutely nobody here.' He appreciated this solitude for much the same reason as he relished Piero della Francesca's 'Ideal City', in which there were 'splendid palaces, civic edifices, enormous squares, and no people at all'.[3] To his son Christopher he wrote that he was following Goethe's advice and cultivating seclusion. In February the landlord of the Queen's Elm, Sean Tracy, arrived in Rome in the company of the actor Stanley Baker. Their presence provided a pretext for a lapse from sober grace: Barker had never met 'a couple of more ill-assorted fish'. Apart from such occasions, he reported to Bernard, he was getting drunk less and less frequently. Instead, he was practising the Puritan virtues of 'optimism, concentration and effectuality'.

Rome, he concluded, provided him with ideal conditions for work. He had even reached the state of mind in which he could look at a blank sheet of paper without experiencing 'the heeby-jeebies of a poisoned conscience'. He decided in retrospect that he had come to Italy precisely to write verse 'with a big old can tied to the tail of the verb and by God I mean to do it'. A stoic tone could now be discerned in his letters. He seemed to be both serene and high-minded.

X remained the vital lifeline to his readers in London. He kept in touch with editorial policy through Swift, who reported from Westbourne Terrace that finances were imperilled by the editors' fraught relationship with their backer, Michael Berry, owner of the *Daily Telegraph*. The editors were launching a paramilitary campaign to save the magazine. 'General Swift' was leading the bombardment, ably assisted by 'Private Moraes and Corporal Higgins'. For the June issue in 1961 they were planning a symposium on 'Art and Morality', for which they requested an article about the responsibilities of the poet. Barker's response was 'The Hippogryph and the Water Pistol', an article which declared that poetry was like an animal dragging a tin around with it. The image came from his earlier letter to Bernard, but in the essay he extended the idea by suggesting that this noisy receptacle corresponded to the moral consciousness of the work, which could not be removed without rendering the poetry inaudible. However, when poets spoke of the morality of verse they needed to be careful about what they meant. Poetic ethics were not of the common-or-garden variety. To illustrate his point, Barker drew on one of Keats's letters. Writing to Richard Woodhouse on 27 October 1818, Keats had stressed the open-mindedness of poets: 'What shocks the virtuous philosop[h]er, delights the camelion poet.'[4] Barker improvised a dialogue between philosopher and poet:

> *Moral Philosopher*: What are you doing out there among so many ferocious temptations?
> *Amoral Poet*: Excuse me, out where? This is the human heart I'm in. What are you doing out there among so many ferocious expedients?
> *Moral Philosopher*: Excuse *me*, this is the human mind I'm in.[5]

Barker's emphasis, however, was very different from that of Keats, who had stressed the 'negative capability' of the poet, his ability to empty himself of conviction, even of identity, in order to absorb the essence of the other. Barker's contention rather was that the poet constantly re-invents himself in acts of kaleidoscopic improvisation. Even more at variance with Keats was Barker's insistence that the amoral poet prefers living in open ground beyond social convention in order to heighten his sense of sin, and in so doing, to enjoy the full imposition of divine justice.[6]

The logic of the article was entirely familiar to those closest to him. Dede for one considered 'amoral' to be an appropriate adjective for George, who seemed to her less at odds with society or the Church than determined to elude orthodox and limiting categories.[7] He was certainly changeable, but he also insisted on a strong element of personal integrity and of loyalty to a chosen vocation. Poets and artists were, in his eyes, permitted to be as mercurial as they liked, provided they maintained faith with their craft.

This balancing act between freedom and responsibility was not managed by all artists. Barker was, for example, increasingly disturbed by what he learned of the gradual disintegration of Colquhoun and MacBryde. In Westbourne Terrace, whilst Wright and Swift were editing *X* in the basement, the Roberts were apparently sinking into inertia upstairs. Instead of using drink as a relief from the pressures of painting, Colquhoun was now making it the principal purpose of his days. When Oliver Bernard reported back on the continuing saga of his non-productivity, Barker replied that Colquhoun was mistaking abjectness for humility. One could be humble without abandoning either willpower or self-belief, virtues that Colquhoun now lacked:

> The Will that monstrous instrument of the Diabolos is doing her best to destroy him by avenging herself upon him for his disrespectful behaviour to her. She avenges herself by doing what he demanded, which is not to exist for him. So he can only wish. And therefore he cannot change things at all. He has destroyed the only witch doctor who could have helped him and I mean Miss Eva Will.
>
> It is not either that one doesn't understand and join him in his insistence upon the supreme pointlessness of all daubing scribbling etc. But NO one supposed their wretched poms or scrawls is going to save the Wide Woild by direct or indirect action: But after all & all at the best and worst we gotta give the crewcut demigods something To destroy. I think that Robert is being proud and putting on his private Day of Wrath a few weeks before the divine Papa has his which is rude and rong of Robert becos hes going to have the other one anyhow.[8]

Barker's own newly discovered sense of direction depended crucially on continuing injections of spiritual uplift, for which there were few places better than Italy. His habit of taking off without warning resumed its usual chronic dimensions, as one by one he explored the country's shrines and holy places. He obtained a Contax camera and went round snapping the Etruscan spoils of the Villa Giulia and *The Dying Gaul* in the Museo Capitoline, the results of which he sent to Christopher in Canterbury, and Carol Weston, his former girlfriend in Long Island. He took to the highways and byways in search of history, above all of Catholic history. The lakes of Latium – Albano, Nemi – were in easy reach. More often, however, he made for Umbria, and in particular Assisi.

Barker had long been attached to the cult and order of St Francis. Ever since he had read the *Fioretti*, the *Life* by St Bonaventura and G.K. Chesterton's *St Francis of Assisi* with Father Dale-Roberts, the saint's way of life had seemed the perfect antidote to decadence. Now, at times of crisis, he liked to visit the home and Shrine of Little St Francis. Assisi, the town, he informed

Georgina, was pervaded by a palpable air of sanctity. When he was with Dede, Barker would stay at the Hotel La Rocca, on the slopes below which grew a miraculous rose tree devoid of thorns. But before long he was visiting Assisi by himself, staying with the Franciscans at their friary on a wooded hillside. The brothers offered him bed and board and asked his occupation. When he told them that he was a poet, they replied that he could stay free of charge for several days, provided that before his departure he gave them one poem, preferably on a Franciscan theme. The poem had, though, at all costs to be simple.[9]

The Franciscans, whose sweetness of temper and lack of pomposity Barker much appreciated, represented the acceptable face of orthodoxy. He was much reassured by the provisions of an ecclesiastic order that confined the property of its *fratelli* to a brown habit, a cord girdle and one pair of sandals. If chastity and obedience were well beyond his reach, he had always made something of a speciality of poverty. The joker in him responded to the humour of the brothers, whom St Francis himself had called *joculatores dei*, God's jesters. There was plenty in received tradition to authenticate this view: St Juniper on his seesaw; Francis himself blessing the flames, preaching to the birds or setting out food for the larks on Christmas Day. For complementary reasons the purity and unpretentiousness of St Francis's surviving poems attracted Barker: especially in the famous 'Canticle of Brother Sun'. 'When the sun rises', St Francis is quoted as saying in *The Mirror of Perfection*, 'every man ought to praise God who created it for our use, because through it our eyes are enlightened by day.' When Barker left the friary, he handed the brothers a handwritten copy of 'A Little Song in Assisi':

> Sprightly the cockcrowing
> sun from that stone bed
> high in the hilly morning
> where a saint lay down his head
> steps gallivanting . . .
>
> Peasant and priest toiling
> over the patched hill side,
> the acolyte at his hoeing,
> see from that iron tressel
> the saint's huge brother rising
>
> until, like a lark, lifting
> the valleyed Umbrian veils,
> the heart of Francis, dazzling

> bird in the air, reveals
> The grace of that ragged man
> transfiguring everywhere.[10]

By November Barker was suffering from a poisoned tooth and had to be admitted to the American Hospital in Rome. After his release the prescribed drugs exacerbated his seasonal melancholia and he experienced one of his periodical collapses of self-confidence. He had been receiving affectionate letters from Carol Weston in Long Island. On Wednesday, 8 November he wrote back requesting that the correspondence between them cease 'because it could only bring unhappiness and distress'. The following Monday he sent a passionate disclaimer: 'I was', he wrote, 'for the moment overcome with the conviction that everyone who was ANYTHING AT ALL to do with me suffers in consequence. But it is not true. I would not wish to hurt a hair of you, but for God's sake write.' He signed off 'from the profundities of despair'.[11]

In early December he was cheered by a *cri de coeur* from his daughter Georgina, pleading with him to return to Westbourne Terrace for Christmas.[12] He arrived by air in the late afternoon of 23 December, to find the flat chock-a-block. Several members of Elizabeth's family were visiting from Canada. Brian Higgins was now almost a fixture. Christopher and Sebastian were home from school and Georgina from the Sorbonne. Rose, who had been spending several months in an American High School, was also back at home. Now fifteen, she had inherited more than her fair share of beauty from both parents, together with a matter-of-fact manner superimposed on a nature of almost superstitious susceptibility and intensity. In George she provoked a somewhat un-Franciscan mixture of irritated affection and a great desire to tease:

> I shall walk into Scotland
> With you at my breast
> And all the Kirk elders,
> Those Knoxical men
> Will throw up their hands
> And lock you in gaol,
> You immodest goddess,
> You unvirginal girl.[13]

When Sebastian and Christopher left for a skiing holiday in France, George flew back to Rome, from where he wrote to Kit apologising for not having visited him, since he had merely returned to London for a few days 'in order to renew my capacity for suffering'. Despite this adverse comment, he was still much preoccupied with developments in England. He was, for example, determined that his children should avoid the pitfalls which had vitiated his own early life. His letters to Christopher now were bracing and instructive. He was resolved that his sons should benefit from the Oxbridge education. With this end in view, he advised Christopher to improve his handwriting by imitating the italic script, which he wrote out carefully for him.[14] In contradiction of the views that he himself had held as a teenager, he told Christopher that formal academic instruction could only enrich the mind, making 'the difference between a man constructed out of nothing much, and a man constructed out of that truly beautiful material, appreciation'.

The past continued to haunt him. When advance copies of *A View from a Blind I* arrived in February, his first act was to send the book to his brother, to whom the title was a coded act of penance.[15] By a diversity of means, he was attempting to make reparation for past excesses, but he was not sure where and to whom. He started work on a second *True Confession*, rising at dawn each day to write one complete stanza at the eagle-crested desk. He dedicated it 'To John David Murray Wright';[16] then changed his mind and inscribed it 'To Elizabeth Smart Barker', using the same dedicatory poem:

> I suppose it's possible that we forget
>   The things we'd rather that we never
> Ever remembered, but, though we're very clever,
>   We're really not all that clever, yet.
> When I call devils from the deep
>   The damned things answer only too pronto,
> Skipping up out of the beds of sleep
>   Not at my call, but because they want to.[17]

The second *True Confession* was, if anything, even less of a record of events than the first. It is divided between psychological history and theological disquisition, with the emphasis very much on the second. It starts with Edward's birth, and refers obliquely to his years at Hearne and to Cass's elopement. Autobiography, however, is in the background. Leaving the model of Villon far behind (had not Eliot told him that emulation was hopeless?) the poem reaches out for new modes of articulation. It parodies *Ash Wednesday*. It lets rip with puns.

Its centre and fulcrum, however, is guilt and the poet's flummoxed attempts to assuage it. Since arriving in Rome, Barker had been giving increasing attention to the classics of Catholic theology. He had been re-reading Newman – *The Grammar of Assent* in particular – Tertullian, and Origen. As a result, the second *True Confession* was his most sustained dissertation yet on the mystery of God, and the peregrinations of the soul. As such, it was the first work in which Barker struggled candidly with philosophical problems which had beset him since adolescence. Refusing facile metaphysical consolation, the poem shows him wrestling with the acute problem of framing an agnostic theology of redemption. The silence of Newman's *Grammar of Assent* echoes everywhere, but its returning echo is the only reply the poet receives. He reaches out for a divine yes; he is answered by a numinous perhaps. In the absence of theological certainty, he is reassured by the voice of his categorical imperatives and by a continual sense of wrongdoing, which speculation only serves to enhance:

> An Augustinian anarchist
>   I sit playing on the psalter
> Hymns about the Antichrist
>   Underneath Bernini's altar.
> Altar? Why, that wretched pun
>   Betrays me like an open letter,
> For everything I've ever done
>   Should have been done a little better.[18]

Contrition continued to trouble him. He kept having dreams of Big Mumma. On Ascension Day 1962, the seventh anniversary of her death, these were still so persistent that he addressed to her a second sonnet – which he refrained from publishing – telling her to go back to her grave in London and stay:

> Not for a moment return. Let rather the rain
> Scour those bones that crossed me to the breast,
> And the gale scatter them, whipped and clean,
> Over that city that loved the best
> Than that you now, recalling what had been
> Should, so remembering, come back from your long rest.[19]

Dede came to recognise remorse as a recurrent phase in George's temperament. Whenever he took a drink now, he would clutch his midriff and declare, 'I've a wound in my side.'[20] The daily routine of work on the *True Confession* steadied him. He was still, however, longing for a personal security, which circumstances seemed determined to deny him. In August 1962 a structural survey of the flat at the Via Nemorense revealed that it was slowly sinking into one of Rome's many subterranean rivers. George and the Farrellys had to be out within three months. They moved to Fregene while searching for alternative accommodation. Barker drove the family to stay with Federico Ferrarotti at his summer house near the beach. Harking back to the Byronic couplets he and Moraes had improvised two years previously, he exclaimed, 'O to take my progeny/Across the sea to Fregene.'[21]

That summer, when Elizabeth planned to holiday with her children on the Greek island of Hydra, Christopher decided to visit his father en route. He hitch-hiked down to Fregene, where he stayed at Ferrarotti's house. At first, he was bemused by the connection between his father and the innumerable residents of the villa, whose relationship to himself he found it difficult to define.[22] Christopher had been brought up to believe that George and his mother were married, but separated. The fiction had proved convenient while Sebastian and he were schoolboys at the reputable King's School, Canterbury. Now, for the first time in his life, Christopher was forced to acknowledge the informal nature of the bond between his parents and the fact of George's other family. Only when George patted Edward on the head, saying, 'What a *brave* little thing you are' did Christopher infer that this toddler must be his half-brother. In mollification, George explained the rift between Elizabeth and himself as a remote consequence of Smart's liaison with Graham. The explanation did little to alleviate Christopher's longing for a more conventional family life.

Nonetheless, father and son achieved a rapport based on their common interest in cars. When Barker's Ford broke down, he and Dede went to Rome to buy a replacement. George Farrelly expected them to return with a glistening new car; they returned in the Ford. The next day Barker took Christopher to view an almost new 1961 dark blue Mercedes Benz with American numberplates. Barker borrowed some money from Dede with which to buy it. Before he could do so, he drove Christopher down in the Ford to catch the ferry at Brindisi. On the way he talked in much the same inspired manner as he had when driving Georgina to the south of France two years earlier. Christopher was struck by how superstitious his father was. At one point, while crossing a mountain range, they reached a dip in the road. As they descended, Christopher looked up and saw a *contre-jour* effect on the roadway ahead; against it, a snake scuttled across the tarmac. 'It is a sign from the Gods,' George told Christopher.[23] Later they stopped and bathed naked in a hollow by the roadside. Thinking that his father might appreciate a classical allusion, Christopher unwisely remarked, 'The plebeians wouldn't do this, would they?' He immediately realised his mistake: the former urchin from Thaxted Place was not to be addressed thus by his public-school-educated son. 'Don't you *ever* use that word again,' Barker replied. Two weeks after he had dropped Christopher off at the harbourside at Brindisi, he sent him a card announcing that he had bought the Mercedes, in which he had already driven at 110 miles per hour.[24] On Christopher's twentieth birthday Barker sent him a poem about the snake.

Barker changed the new car's numberplates in Switzerland and for several months referred to it as 'the Benzedrine'. His stay in Fregene was turning into one prolonged summer holiday. In the late afternoons of September George and Elizabeth Farrelly, Jimmy and Edward played on the shore. 'Long sea-beach at Fregene,' he mused in his journal, 'almost empty in the evening, with your enormous September sun resting on the tip of the sea, and only two big dogs disporting themselves along your shore, will you be haunted for ever by the memory of my little sons?' In circumstances like this life seemed a simple matter. Barker decided that all he needed to be happy were 'a small Palladian palace in Tuscany, five mistresses with velvet dresses and long hair, some hunting dogs and woods, a small but elated circle of friends, a cellar of the choicest vintages, three Ferraris, a vast marbled table top supported by golden eagles to practice his scribbling on and, above all, the surgical excision of my conscience.'[25]

Though a Palladian palace was out of the question, in October George and Dede moved with the children into a spacious flat at 1120, Via Cassia. Barker might have experienced an access of peace had it not been for some news from Westbourne Terrace. At five o'clock in the morning of 20 September, Colquhoun had been preparing a small exhibition of monotypes for the Museum Street Galleries when he had suffered a heart attack. Hearing a noise in the next room, MacBryde found his lover lying amongst his drawings. Two minutes later, Colquhoun had died in his arms. Though there had been times of late when Colquhoun had seemed to long for death, the news shocked his many friends. Barker had for some years regarded him as doomed: removed from the event by distance, however, he could summon no consolation to match his prescience. He cut out the obituary from the *Observer* and pasted it into his notebook over the words 'In Memoriam Robert Colquhoun, 1915–1962. Sic gloria transit amoris.' Throughout October he laboured to produce an elegy equal to its subject. Eventually in November, he composed a threnody almost as ornate as the desk on which it was written. He had been used to seeing Colquhoun's vices as the enemies of his virtues. As he now saw them, they were opposite facets of a bitter Scottish conscience:

> By moonlight I see a stallion of Stubbs-Ucello
> Gaunt, long-barreled, yellow, lifting its head
> Proudly out of a bunch of thistle
>
> Which is the Knoxian conception of Scottish
> Responsibility. And now this proud man is dead.
> This Highlander, this skinny Ayrman, this, yes, British

> Mountaineer of spiritual violence
> This draughtsman who was not so much a painter
> As the graphologist of our dying conscience,
>
> Elected to go home to cold Kilmarnock
> And render those he left behind a mere remainder,
> For what he wanted lay north of Cape Wrath and the rock.[26]

Though neither Barker's best poem nor his most finished elegy, interwoven with puns, it was at least a wreath that he could lay at Colquhoun's Ayrshire grave. After writing it he completed the *True Confession* and wondered what to write next. His only original ideas were occurring to him in the shape of prose essays. He considered cobbling together his recent prose with earlier essays and reviews and sending it all to Eliot, to whom he had been promising a volume of literary criticism since 1937.[27] He was minded to call this collection *How to Refuse a Heavenly House*. Nothing, however, came of it.

Yeats had said the human intellect must decide between perfection of the work or of the life. To Barker at his lowest ebb it could seem as if he had elected for imperfection in both. As usual, he was in dire financial straits. It was difficult for him to pick up freelance work in Italy, where there were no opportunities for him to teach. He found this state of involuntary Franciscan penury irksome. His solution was to write to Higgins and Cronin. The trunk containing his trove of letters and manuscripts had been moved from Hearne and was currently stowed beneath the staircase in Westbourne Terrace. He told Higgins and Cronin to take some less important items from it and sell them to the bookseller Bertram Rota or some other dealer. It was an 'esso-es', he said, an emergency.

It was thus with a sense of relief that he heard that *The View From A Blind I* had won the Guinness Prize for 1962; he was joint winner with Robert Graves. He drove back to London for the presentation on Wednesday, 31 October. He was unsure whether to turn up for the ceremony dressed as a bohemian or as a senior man of letters. Opting for bohemianism, he wore a tartan shirt. On arriving at the hall, he experienced a fit of sartorial panic and accused Elizabeth of not forcing him into a suit. Graves read first, *sotto voce* and, Georgina thought, somewhat feebly. Then Barker gave a theatrical rendition of 'A Sparrow's Feather', savouring each word before delivering it: 'he knew the words were perfect, and he seemed to *love* their perfection'.[28]

The audience's reception emphasised his lowly status in the world of British poetry. Graves and Barker were both senior and much published expatriate poets. Yet, whereas Graves was lauded as a celebrity, it seemed to Georgina that Barker was treated with no more than courtesy. It was almost as if her father had won the second prize. Despite this condescending treatment, George went to the pub with Elizabeth and Georgina afterwards and got gloriously drunk on champagne.[29]

He stayed in England for two weeks. He had brought with him the typescript of the second *True Confession;* after a few days he contacted Heath-Stubbs, who came round and listened to him read out sections of the new poem. Then, after calling on Kit and Ilse, Barker drove back to Rome, where he settled in for what he hoped would be an uneventful winter.

CHAPTER 40

'LOVE IS WHAT YOU DO'

A light flurry of snow, the first that many children in Rome had seen, heralded 1963. Barker looked out of his window at the Via Cassia and saw a young Italian kneeling in it with an expression on his face like that of the Madonna at the Annunciation. All traffic had come to a stop in the half-inch-thick drifts. As Barker informed Kit, the Romans were devout people who knew perfectly well that snow was white and descended from Heaven and had therefore to be holy; one did not drive on holy things, except on Sundays.[1] They were perhaps reminded of the time when St Francis rushed out in the snow, rolling in it to quench the fires of carnal lust; or of another occasion when Francis made himself a wife and family out of snowmen, reassuring the Lord that they were quite enough for him.

Barker continued to find the atmosphere of Rome congenial and calming, though London remained very much on his mind. The death of Colquhoun, his elegy for whom had appeared in the *Listener* in January, had reminded him forcefully of his roots and obligations. By February Dede was again pregnant. There was still time for one more visit to England before his new child was born and so he set out in March, determined to be back in time for the delivery.

As ever, the flat in Westbourne Terrace was full. Since Colquhoun's death the shoe-room had been occupied by MacBryde, so immobilised by grief that he was in the habit of storing his urine in bottles beneath his bed: as the other residents tiptoed past the door at night, they would hear him sobbing, singing and crying out. Moraes breezed in and out; Higgins was still around. Sebastian and Rose were both at home, though Christopher had left to study at Princeton and Georgina had joined a dance troupe touring Canadian nightclubs with a female impersonator. *X* having ground to a halt after seven issues, Swift had moved to the Algarve in search of a southern setting similar to Cézanne's.

Elizabeth, however, was still collecting waifs and strays. Recently she had befriended a young painter called Tony Kingsmill, son of Hugh Kingsmill, the Methodist intellectual and literary editor of the *New English Review*. She had also taken under her wing Jill Neville, a young mother from Australia who was living round the corner in Cleveland Square.

Neville was a guest at a gathering in Westbourne Terrace a few days after Barker's arrival. For the occasion she was wearing a new red dress that she had recently bought at Whitely's. George was complimenting her on it when into the room walked a young man whom he had previously met as a graduate student at the British School in Rome: Donald Gardner, nephew of the literary critic and Oxford don, Helen Gardner. Gardner was accompanied that evening by his former fiancée, Elspeth Langlands. Elspeth was a 22-year-old from the Scottish Highlands. She was tall and had striking colouring, her pale skin contrasting with her black hair, which she wore that evening in plaits.[2] Jill noted how their arrival altered the emotional temperature of the room. Somewhat to her relief, Barker's attention drifted away from her and towards the newcomers.

As she entered, Elspeth became aware of Barker at the end of the room: 'leaning against the mantelpiece, snarling at people'. She began talking to Smart, who was warm and welcoming. 'She and I had an instant rapport', Elspeth observed later, 'because she was missing Georgina, and she thought that Georgina and I looked like one another.' After a while, 'the drink got drinkier, and I went to meet the great man'. Handing Elspeth a copy of *The View from a Blind I*, Barker indicated his satirical pieces on the Beats and the Scots, and remarked, 'I suppose you don't like *funny* poems, do you?' 'At that time, of course, I was very serious-minded, and I did not; I was, however, well-mannered enough to be non-committal.' Barker snatched the book and threw it on the floor. 'I was very astonished by his demeanour. I had never met anybody of his age who was so consistently rude and outrageous.'[3] A row ensued and they were separated.

By two in the morning Elspeth had had an argument with Gardner 'who went stomping off, shouting into the night'. Determined not to accompany him, she accepted an offer from Sebastian to sleep on the carpet in his bedroom. They were mounting the stairs when George, now somewhat sobered, came up behind them, and enquired where they were going. When Sebastian answered that he was putting Elspeth up on his floor, George shouted, 'Oh no, you're not!' Waking up Rose, he insisted that a camp bed be made up in her room. 'He actually made the bed up', Elspeth remembered, adding that this was 'unrepeated behaviour, and uncharacteristic'. She left early the following morning. She next saw Barker in the Queen's Elm, where 'I went up and apologised for my rudeness, expecting a much more profuse apology to come from him.' Saying, 'I forgive you, my dear,' he bestowed on her a kiss of benediction.

Elspeth Langlands had grown up in Kincardineshire in the eastern Highlands. Two years after the war, which he spent working with the French Resistance, her father had purchased from the king of Norway a large, windswept, unheated Gothic revival castle called Drumtochty, which he had converted into a preparatory school. Here, at six, Elspeth had become a pupil alongside forty boys, one of whom was the future novelist Allan Massie. 'My parents were very strong on learning things by heart. Poetry immediately. French too. Then Latin at seven, and Greek at nine or ten.[4] This traditional and farsighted provision had been a mixed blessing. It had produced an acutely shy, precociously verbal child, not quite at ease either with herself or her surroundings. At thirteen she had moved on to a girls' public school in Fife, where she had been less happy since her eyes had already been opened to 'language and literature and ideas'. She was homesick, out of place, and considered her fellow pupils to be philistine bores. As a pupil in the lower sixth form, she had been asked to read out loud a passage in Propertius's Elegies describing white oxen wading through the springs of Clitumnus. She had wept tears that were inexplicable to her, apart from being profoundly moved by Propertius's words.[5] Elspeth's reaction had caused embarrassment and amusement to the other girls, who considered the translation a chore. She had decided that she would like to meet a poet and to marry him.

At the age of seventeen she had won a place to read modern languages at Somerville College, Oxford, where she had hoped to study nineteenth-century French literature with the distinguished Baudelaire scholar, Enid Starkie. When it turned out that Dr Starkie was otherwise engaged, she had combined reading French of a different period with the study of modern Greek under the poet C.F. (Constantine) Trypanis. In her third year she had come across Barker's *Collected Poems, 1930–55* on the poetry shelves at Blackwell's. Opening it at the first poem 'Daedalus', she had stood entranced, as had Elizabeth Smart thirty years before.

After leaving Oxford, Elspeth 'worked at loads of trashy jobs in London, constantly being sacked. I went back to Scotland because I was being terrorised and stalked by a madman who claimed to have married me by proxy at the Nigerian embassy.'[6] At the time of meeting Barker, she was in London during the Easter holiday from Drumtochty School, where she had taken temporary employment as a teacher to pay off debts to her father and to be safe from her stalker. She was unconfident, alert and gifted with an eloquence that was a match even for Barker's own. Widely and deeply read in English verse, she could cap Barker's quotations, even of poetry well beyond the common classics. She and Barker shared a penchant for what are often termed 'minor poets'; neither, in any case, thought the customary academic distinction between 'major' and 'minor' to be of more than theoretical significance. At this stage in her life Elspeth had seldom watched television, since 'the television didn't work at Drumtochty; fantail pigeons roosted on the aerial, and the aerial was on top of the central tower in the howling storm'.[7] Her delight, and her skill, lay in the glitter and skirmish of words.

At the end of the Easter holidays she returned to Drumtochty, where she soon received a letter from Barker, informing her of his imminent arrival with Moraes and Kingsmill. When they arrived late one afternoon her father came to her room and announced, 'Your friend Mr Barker has arrived. I have instructed his Indian manservant to put his bags in his room.' Moraes had apparently complied, even while snarling over his shoulder, 'George, I'll get you for this!' Afterwards Mrs Langlands entertained the guests back to afternoon tea, during which Barker stubbed out his cigarette on his shoe before placing the stub in his trouser turn-ups, and stuck chewing gum in his pockets.

Despite this behaviour, as Elspeth recalled, 'my mother was much taken by George; my father had other views'. Sensing this paternal disapproval, the guests decided to move to the Thistle Inn at Auchenblae. A few hours later Elspeth arrived at the head of a column of male colleagues. To Barker her behaviour seemed mysterious and Elspeth herself a puzzling mixture of traits. Like Colquhoun, she was a Calvinist bohemian, but where Colquhoun had been a bohemian in reaction to his Calvinism, Elspeth was a bohemian *and* a Calvinist: precise in her manner and at the same time uninhibited by middle-class conventions. Moreover, Barker was awed by Drumtochty and its austere academic regime: teaching little boys Greek was clearly admirable, but the place savoured too much of 'the moral powers'. Elspeth took her guests back to the room of Allan Massie, now also teaching at the school, where they talked and drank whisky until the small hours. When they returned to the Thistle Inn, they were ejected for their lateness and drunkenness and so took refuge in a nearby market town for the rest of their stay.

Barker went back to Rome, but he saw no point in pretending that his circle of acquaintance there was as wide, or as interesting, as in England. There were compensations: Monica's son Christopher, known to the family as Mack, arrived from California and stayed for several months. Malcolm Winton, a journalist whom Barker had known in London, turned up with his wife and provided another opportunity for drinking. With these notable exceptions, however, Barker was forced to make do with companions who, as Dede complained, made the Roberts appear like angels dropped from Heaven.

On 6 July 1963 George and Dede's third son, Francis, was born. The family took their usual holiday in Fregene, where Dede pushed the pram to and fro under the fascinated gaze of a summer resident, the film director Federico

Fellini. As she walked down the street, Fellini stared at her fixedly; the reason was not apparent until the film *8½* appeared later in the year, featuring a pram-pushing mother.[8]

In reality, Dede's calm maternal front disguised considerable soul-searching. The irregularity of her union with Barker was a source of increasing anxiety to her. Brought up an Episcopalian, she had remained a nominal Anglican during her marriage to Farrelly, who was Catholic, though their two children had been baptised as Catholics in deference to his wishes. Since moving to Rome, however, she had gradually been drawn into the Catholic fold. Partly as a result of Barker's influence, she had taken to visiting Santa Susanna, the American Roman Catholic Church, where she now asked to be received. The priests had told her that, though her domestic situation constituted a barrier, the Church would do everything in its power to secure annulments, so that Barker and she could marry.

By October Barker was instructing the solicitor's firm of Cartwright Cunningham in London with a view to obtaining a divorce from Jessica. He applied for legal aid to pursue the case.[9] It was, however, difficult to fight a legal battle across the Atlantic and Jessica's resistance had hardened with the years. What Dede craved above all was peace, a remote possibility in the present state of uncertainty, and with Barker's behaviour remaining so undisciplined. Besides, she was not at all sure of the durability of Barker's commitment to her. He did not seem cut out for a position in any well-ordered, still less religiously governed, household. She had taken to locking him out on the occasions when he arrived back too late or drunk, so that he would have to spend the night in the Mercedes. Though the couple remained good friends, her patience was sometimes severely tried. By July Barker was employing Post Restante, San Silvestro and the American Express, Piazza di Spagna as his mailing addresses. He was also writing to friends about returning to England, where he had his eye on a very pretty cottage in Norfolk. When this plan fell through, he was left, as he had so often been before, effectively homeless.

So he resumed the harum-scarum bachelor existence of the months following his arrival in the States six years before; he drank in the city bars until late at night and kept what company he could. On occasions his spirits had sunk so low, he now wrote to friends, that he was forced to overcome his disinclination for solitary drinking. There was an Austrian beerhouse in the same street from which Principessa Caetani's now lapsed *Botteghe Oscure* had once appeared. Here he sat alone downing pints of Löwenbräu, transfixed by the blue lion rampant upon the bottle and waiting for the appearance of some non-existent companion. He tried one or two inconclusive romances, none of which amounted to anything. Effectively, he was once more adrift.

In these circumstances, and in this mood of intensified self-distrust, he drove

'LOVE IS WHAT YOU DO'

to Assisi again in September. He arrived in tipping rain, 'where so many have stood with their suitcases full of hope'. In the doorway of a deserted café he watched sheets of water veer towards him across the empty piazza.[10] He was tired, out of sorts and badly in need of solace. He stayed with the brothers for several days, longing against the odds for some kind of resolution to his difficulties.

Raffaella Pellizi was aware of his plight. She put him in touch with a Dutch woman called Contessa Henrietta Antonini, 'a retired coloratura soprano of some seventy summers', who lived on a small estate called Villa del Sole in Ariccia. The villa was near to the shores of Lake Nemi, where the opening and closing chapters of Sir James Frazer's panoptic survey of myth and custom, *The Golden Bough*, one of Barker's favourite books, was set. The Contessa had a small cottage at the bottom of the garden, which she was prepared to let Barker rent for a few thousand lire a week. He immediately wrote to Sebastian exulting that the cottage resembled the gates to Paradise, like Hearne but much hotter. It had 'grapevines outside the door, doves, enough oranges and lemons to exhaust the bells of St Clement's, and a view of the Mediterranean from one window'.[11] The estate was a short stroll from the lake, which the ancients had called *Speculum Dianae*, the hand mirror of Diana.

Barker moved to Ariccia in early October. He left his writing desk in Via Cassia, but compensated by setting up his table close to a window in the front room of his small cottage, from which he could observe the hills falling away towards the distant sea. He paid his respects daily to the contessa up at the big house, striving to hide from her his more irregular habits. One evening he roared off to Rome in the Mercedes and returned in the early morning under cover of darkness. The telephone rang. It was the contessa, inviting him up to the villa to admire the sunrise. Much later, in the twilight, she played to him on her Steinway grand. They walked through a bower above the arbutus-entwined garden and watched the dying embers of the day.[12]

The contessa's musical activities were now confined to regular concert parties, which she hosted up at the big house. She also held poetry and music salons there on Sunday evenings, when tea was served from a samovar with almond biscuits. The verse to be heard was, at best, indifferent, though Barker tolerated it for the contessa's sake. Mellow and candid, she gained his affection with her intimate reminiscences. In exchange for the privilege of staying at her cottage she asked him for one little poem, something like the hymn that he had once given to the brothers of St Francis. It should be about love, but should contain neither regret nor self-pity. The poem should be that Franciscan phenomenon: a piece about love with no guilt attached, a rose bush without thorns. She told him of a passion of hers fifty years previously in Ancona: 'Love', she said to Barker, 'is what you do.'[13]

In early October Barker wrote to Tony Kingsmill in London and invited him to Ariccia. Kingsmill, in the meantime, had been energetically courting Elspeth, whom he had been trying to persuade to go with him to Portugal to visit Patrick Swift. He now worked on persuading her to go with him to Italy instead, with the incentive of a possible journey on to Greece afterwards. 'I did not want to come,' Elspeth now insists. 'Kingsmill persuaded me by reading *The Golden Bough* aloud and also I had just had flu and was working at more boring girl jobs in London.'[14] On the 17th, nonetheless, Kingsmill wrote accepting Barker's suggestion; he added that 'Elspeth of Drumtochty wants to come as well, and I know you'll not be surprised dear George I find it hard to disagree in this with her. Can the Immortal groves of Lake Nemesis [sic] accommodate us both? If not we'll build a nest in a Golden Bough near by and chirrup to you across the vineyards at the libating hour when the sun goes down.'[15] Barker cabled back, 'Thank you for bringing me the most marvellous present!'

At Westbourne Terrace Elizabeth prepared Elspeth for her departure. She brought out 'a black cocktail dress and other joys', including Georgina's brown Legat School cloak, all of which she presented to Elspeth, joking with her that this was a trousseau for her 'nuptials'.[16] Kingsmill and Elspeth set out on 26 October. They spent two days in Paris, where the Legat School cloak got caught in the Metro doors. By prior arrangement, they drank in Les Deux Magots in St Germain, where they found a message from Barker awaiting them. Kingsmill's suspicions were aroused: he spent the train journey to Rome warning Elspeth of Barker's concupiscence.

When their train drew in to Rome station on 29 October, Barker was waiting on the platform. Elspeth stepped down from the high-set carriage wearing Georgina's school cloak; behind her came the shorter Kingsmill, carrying a bottle of Martell brandy which they had picked up in Paris. Barker drove them to Ariccia. As the shadows lengthened, they sat drinking the brandy by the open fireplace in the front room. There was an arbutus spray hanging above the fireplace, which the last rays of the sun turned golden. They talked intently through the night, then watched the sunrise. They did not go to bed until eleven o'clock the next morning.[17]

Slowly the chestnut trees turned golden around the lake. On the frequent sunny days Kingsmill would go out to paint, strapping his easel on his shoulder. One morning, as he got ready to leave, the rain descended; Barker observed Kingsmill lean frustratedly against the window frame, his easel lashed to his shoulder with a coil of rope as if he were carrying his own cross.[18] At length Kingsmill decided the landscape of Latium was more interesting in the drizzle. Barker accompanied him outside and stood watching him paint the misty lake beneath its Roman viaduct. Later the two men walked up a hillside above Lake

Albano to a Renaissance rotunda on its crest. They admired the slopes below, the glimpse of sea at the end of the long, declining valley.

As the downpour persisted, the Contessa Antonini took pity and invited all three of them to the main house, where a young German musician was about to perform a programme of Chopin Preludes on her Steinway. Absorbed in his moody landscapes, Kingsmill declined; Elspeth, however, accepted, pulled on her wellingtons and accompanied Barker along the garden path. In the concert room, as Barker later recounted in a poem, she sat trying to look interested and, having removed one boot, scratched the instep of her right heel while she fumbled for biscuits with her right hand, trying not to make too much noise. At length she whispered to Barker that she was tone-deaf to all forms of music, except that of the bagpipes.[19]

To begin with, Barker's behaviour in Ariccia was more circumspect than it had been in London and Scotland. He was attentive to his guests, frying them bacon and eggs for breakfast as if to persuade them – or at least her – of his domesticity. But as time went on he relaxed into his customary mischievousness, delighting in raising Elspeth's hackles, a provocation to which she found she did not entirely object. She soon discovered they shared a love for Latin poetry, including early medieval devotional texts. Still seeking ways of expressing his grief for his mother, Barker now proposed rendering into English the thirteenth-century hymn *Stabat Mater*, with its vision of the *mater dolorosa* standing at the foot of the cross. After Elspeth had made a literal translation from the Latin of Jacobus de Benedictis, Barker turned it, freely though beautifully, into verse:

> Fountainhead of sorrow
> O mother teach me also
>   to love as I mourn,
> tender me so much of
> your sorrow and your love
>   that my tears burn.
>
> And, mother, grant that I
> may seem also to die
>   on my own cross
> and let me also share
> those words I cannot bear
>   since they are his.[20]

On Christmas Eve Barker, Elspeth and Kingsmill went to Midnight Mass in the tiny parish church of Ariccia. Barker himself spent Christmas Day in Rome with Dede and his sons, while Elspeth and Kingsmill 'went to a Romanian poet in a high rise block' elsewhere in the city. 'We had hard boiled eggs for lunch', she remembers, 'and talked in French; no one understanding any one else's accent.'[21] In the New Year of 1964, Barker took his guests around the Roman art galleries talking absorbedly, fleshing out the bare bones of art history with stories from Vasari's *Lives*. At a certain point Kingsmill found that he was no longer included in the party. He asked Elspeth when the two of them would be journeying onwards, since they had made an ill-defined plan to go to Hydra, about which Elizabeth had enthused in London. Suddenly, however, Greece was on nobody's mind except his own.

Half-consciously, as Barker later conceded, the three of them were implicitly re-enacting the underlying plot of Frazer's *The Golden Bough*. Kingsmill had wandered into the Ariccian grove to find that Barker was the master of it: *Rex Nemorensis*, King of the Wood. According to Frazer's precedent, there was nothing for him but to challenge the king, take the sacred mistletoe and marry the goddess. The parallel, however, was pretty inexact since, at least in Kingsmill's eyes, it was Barker who was stealing Elspeth from him. For days the two men quarrelled intermittently. One evening Elspeth took on a baby-sitting assignment in the city; Barker and Kingsmill drove in to pick her up in the Mercedes. After she had arranged herself in the back, she looked up to see Barker and Kingsmill punching one another in their seats.

Barker's feelings for Elspeth, however, were very far from being simply libidinous. Indeed, he seems already to have decided that the physical body did not hold the answers to life's problems. In February his son Sebastian obtained a place at Corpus Christi College, Oxford to study physiology and he wrote to congratulate him. A few days later he wrote a second letter, warning Sebastian of the limits of the biological:

> I thought that by now you would have resolved that the solution to a happy tenure of this vale of tears cannot be found in the subject of Physiology. For this leads into the bog, into the mire, into the bosom of the hated thing. I suggest that from now on you christen the subject by the name that properly belongs to it: i.e. Love. Where are the physiologies of yesteryear? Where are all the *bella donnas* gone? I could find it in me to approve most heartily of the researches you propose to undertake in this subject so long as your interest remains – what shall I say? – academic.[22]

One morning George and Elspeth awoke to find that Kingsmill had left for Rome by tram. A note of capitulation lay on the kitchen table. (Pursuing his Greek adventure, he was soon to make his own way to Hydra, where

'LOVE IS WHAT YOU DO'

he would eventually settle.) Since Barker was indisputably in possession of the prize, the parting was acrimonious, though the two men were eventually reconciled. Long afterwards Barker would write in his projected autobiography of the humiliation of conquest, the moment of self-knowledge when the victor recognises himself as 'the man whom we always hated, the one who always won, the Victor Vae Ludorum'. Later still, in a poem published in the collection *Villa Stellar*, he would pretend not to know which of them had been victorious:

> When you departed, Kingsmill, why did you leave your
> Humiliation behind like Van Gogh's ear on my kitchen table?
> Was it to teach me again that the victim is always
> The victor, and that the prize cup contains a
> Simply delicious poison? This poison is the knowledge that
> In love as in war we are all defeated anyhow, because
> To win and to love is to die on the vertical points of
> life as death. The opening of the first door
> always, my dear Tony, closes the second for ever.[23]

After Kingsmill's departure. George and Elspeth walked above the lakeside, watching the mimosa trees flaunt their yellow blossoms in the sunshine. They enjoyed lengthy spring siestas at the cottage as the kindling sun trickled through the Venetian blinds. After driving into the city, they sat talking for hour after hour in the Borghese Gardens. At Albano, a few miles from Ariccia, they discovered a perfect niche above the lakeside where, 'with the logic of a poem', nestled a restaurant called Il Paradiso. Here they sat over their aperitifs watching the twilight perform its dance over the water, then returned hand in hand to the cottage as night fell.[24] Later, in Rome, they paid their respects to the shade of the recently deceased Principessa Caetani in the Via Botteghe Oscure, where they sat in the Austrian beerhouse simply looking at one another, Barker not quite believing that she was there.

One evening by the lakeside Barker drafted a couple of poems entitled 'Two Poems Written by Lake Nemi', both full of a sense of calm and mellowness. He seems to have been too happy to have noticed that they had in fact spent the day once more by Lake Albano; in any case, the poetic licence – and the title – remained.[25] Later they paid a visit to the coastal town of Lerici, where white horses chased one another below the fishing smacks in the bay. Florid gentlemen strolled along the promenade, like figures out of Max Beerbohm. Operatic sailors stood upon the quay.

PART FOUR

1964–91

'O I forbid you, maidens a',
   That wear gowd on your hair,
To come or gae by Carterhaugh,
   For the young Tam Lin is there.

'For even about that knight's middle
   O' siller bells are nine;
And nae maid comes to Carterhaugh
   And a maid returns again.'

Fair Janet sat in her bonny bower,
   Sewing her silken seam,
And wish'd to be in Carterhaugh
   Amang the leaves sae green.

She's lat her seam fa' to her feet,
   The needle to her tae,
And she's awa' to Carterhaugh
   As fast as she could gae.

                The Ballad of Tam Lin

CHAPTER 41

'SUCH PEACE UPON THE CONSCIENCE'

By 1964 George Barker was an anomaly. He was a senior poet whose art continued to develop, but whom few of the young knew. He was a religious poet in a secular age, a significant figure in the history of twentieth-century British verse whom academics ignored. Critics like to place their poets tidily in schools. Barker's reputation by contrast was distinctive but dispersed. In the academic year 1960–61 the British poets Geoffrey Hill and John Heath-Stubbs had both been teaching at Ann Arbor University in Michigan. When Geoffrey Hill had advertised a class on 'George Barker and His School', Heath-Stubbs had asked him of whom this grouping consisted. 'Me,' Hill had answered, 'you . . .'[1]

Barker's residence in Italy had complicated this situation. Most of his readers agreed that he was *par excellence* a poet of occasions. He therefore required a setting imbued with ritual, one with its own orchestration of festivals and seasons, to prompt his work. He was also a poet of place, for which he needed a sympathetic landscape. Rome, with its saints' days, monasteries and churches, had supplied both needs. Here his voice had naturally and splendidly flowered. Yet he had now decided to move back to England, where he would be deprived of many of these stimuli, having instead to create occasions in his own mind or else to derive them from the fortunes or misfortunes of friends. The Italian landscape would be a more serious loss. In his better poems of that period his voice had seemed to follow spontaneously the contours of the Campagna or of Tuscany or Umbria; in the finest, the landscape itself had appeared to do the talking. Sometimes this miracle had happened to him in England, but far more rarely.

Return, however, was necessary for all sorts of practical reasons. By March Elspeth knew that she was pregnant. She had not been enthusiastic about the possibilities of bearing and raising children. Barker, however, had encouraged her to view the prospect as one of fulfilment and joy. 'George insisted that we should have a baby together,' she now recalls. '"Babies are *cherubinos*," he would say, "they have wings on." I was easily persuaded. George made me see babies, whom I'd previously ignored and vaguely disliked, in a different way altogether.'² Barker, however, had little means of support in Italy: if born in Rome, the baby would have to be delivered in a private hospital, an expense they could not afford.

But homecoming was not without its own problems. They drove through France with the Mercedes piled high with belongings. After spending a night at Lodsworth, where they found Kit and Ilse entertaining some German art dealers, they arrived at Westbourne Terrace on Monday, 6 April. 'George seemed to think it was perfectly all right to turn up with a concubine,' Elspeth remembers, 'but Elizabeth was not pleased at all. She was very sweet to me – she always was – but I think she found it quite difficult. I thought that her feelings towards George were those of a friend. I was naïve. Now I can understand absolutely, but I couldn't then.'³

As ever, the household was at sixes and sevens. Rose was pregnant by a friend of Willard's called Jeffrey Bolger, to whom Elizabeth was not speaking. Sebastian, now in his first year at Oxford, was spending the Easter vacation at home: he helped unload the car, intrigued by the fact that this consort of his father's was only four years older than he. There was nothing for it but to put the newcomers in the bedroom next to Rose. All of them were conscious of the awkwardness of the situation and understandably edgy. For days they survived in a state of uneasy truce. For Sebastian his father had been little more than an intermittent house guest, wrapped up for the rest of the time in myth. His impression of this elusive parent sharpened during evenings spent together in the first-floor living room, when George talked long and lovingly about the art of poetry.

Elspeth and Rose met up with Fanny, daughter of the Oxford historian Christopher Hill, who was herself pregnant. 'None of us had any idea of what we were supposed to do about being pregnant,' Elspeth recalls. 'I went to see a doctor to confirm, though obviously one knew. So I found out what in fact you were expected to do.' After a couple of uncomfortable weeks she and Barker moved out to a tiny flat in Redcliffe Gardens; the street was up outside and the noise and heat were 'seriously hellish'. In June Barker wrote to Sebastian in Oxford complaining about the road drills, the everlasting babble about Wimbledon tennis in the pubs and the dogs 'micturating' on the lamp posts. Martin Green, former editor of *Nimbus*, had moved on to the publishing firm of MacGibbon & Kee, where he was vigorously promoting Barker's work. He suggested re-issues of the *Confessions* and *The Dead Seagull*. He also commissioned the autobiography that he was convinced Barker should now write. Barker decided to fictionalise his account as *The Memoirs of Lord B*, portraying himself, or his *alter persona*, as a latterday Lord Byron. His working draft started with a swingeing disavowal of the autobiographical art and was never to get much beyond a sketch. But he gritted his teeth and applied himself to the task, in spite of the heat, and the rumpus of the 31 bus forever grinding past the flat, through dust and petrol fumes towards World's End.[4]

By July he was suffering from an additional anxiety, since he was convinced that he had alienated Eliot. Whilst he had been in Rome, the sale of manuscripts from the trunk beneath the stairs at Westbourne Terrace had proceeded apace, but with no very clear sense of direction. George had stipulated to Higgins and Cronin that none of the more significant correspondence should be sold. He now became aware of an uncomfortable fact: in May 1962 fifty-five letters of his from Eliot had featured in the sales catalogue of the House of El Dieff on East 62nd Street, New York. They had since been sold to the Harry Ransom Humanities Research Center at the University of Texas at Austin. Barker grew obsessed with the possibility that Eliot himself might have got wind of this transaction and seen it as an act of betrayal. In August he wrote asking Eliot to act as a character reference in his application for a flat and took the opportunity to explain the inadvertent circumstances behind the sale.[5] Eliot, whose reaction was one of amusement, immediately wrote exonerating him of any blame,[6] but irrationally Barker detected an unspoken rebuke. Again he wrote protesting his innocence. Once more Eliot had to write absolving him of complicity: 'I shall not, of course, have anything more to say to anybody about the matter.'[7] The episode illustrated graphically Barker's insecurity at the time. Eliot was the one person who could still make him feel like a neophyte; the writer for whom his respect was never disguised as contempt and whom he dared not under any circumstances offend. Even now Barker was prone to the unnerving sensation of tumbling back to his beginnings. 'The baby that I threw out with the bath water', he wrote in his notebook that autumn, 'happened, unfortunately, to be me.' To this extent he felt no more securely established than he had as a literary probationer thirty years before.

His inability once more to find a stable home had much to do with these feelings, though this problem proved temporary. By mid-August he and Elspeth had found a basement at 9 Quick Street, a pleasant flat on a quiet residential street in Islington. Moraes, now living in Paddington with a girl called Judy St John, came to help paint it. The flat, which had two bedrooms, the larger of which doubled as a sitting room, was cool and tranquil after Earls Court. The garden was a bombsite, in which grass grew amid the rubble. Barker set up his study in the bedroom-cum-sitting room, where, laying the reluctant autobiography aside, he started on a predominantly free-verse sequence, a summation of the Italian years, called 'Dreams of a Summer Night'.

The sequence was a crazy paving of reminiscence into which were set memories of Assisi, Ariccia and Fregene. It was also an exposition of Barker's theology of natural objects, the transmutation of the ordinary into the divine. Though the style of writing was an extension of his earlier Italian poems, he now went further in allowing the poem to have its say, rather than imposing a form on it. The result was Franciscan in its inspiration and mood: an exercise in the discipline of the everyday. In it even earthenware pots wore haloes. Barker had come to feel that, just as there was 'a dreaming religion that lies sleeping within all things', so poetry was immanent within language and rhythm within syntax. If mysticism could beatify unspectacular objects, poetry could likewise transform non-esoteric words. The secret was to allow poem and subject to express one another in a spirit of unforced appreciation. By seeing precisely and with love, he could achieve a transubstantiation of the real into the marvellous; by writing directly, a metamorphosis of common speech into *cantabile*. The strategic placing of one morpheme could achieve wonders. In lyric ii, for example, multiple discoveries of place and of style are focused on the word and concept 'explain':

> To you, then, still asleep on the holy hill, I send
> Such a word as this to alight at your half-open window
> And awaken you with explanations, as below you, the sunrise
> Explains itself to the Tiber in a series of golden reflections.
> Thus, if I am fortunate, I may find some words prepared to
> bare themselves down to their bones and even to their family secrets:
> For all words, and all objects, particularly the most commonplace, carry
> Invisible robes of theology on their shoulders (and often
> Not invisible) as when the ordinary terracotta flowerpot
> Wears its domestic humility as though it conveyed down the ages
> Some property as sacred as the vessel of Joseph conveyed
> Like a rose perpetually recurring.[8]

After the flat was decorated, George and Elspeth took off in the Mercedes with Dom and Judy to Shropshire on a pilgrimage to Housman country. The fact that Housman had never been closer to Shropshire than the upstairs window of his childhood home in Bromsgrove worried them little. For Barker this was the county of *A Shropshire Lad*, Housman's 'land of lost content', and across it they drove from Wenlock Edge to Bredon Hill and Ludlow church. By the river at Ludlow they found a pub where they stayed for several days. When it rained, Elspeth read aloud the lyric from *Last Poems*, which long ago George had tried on the resistant Japanese:

> We for a certainty are not the first
>   Have sat in taverns while the tempest hurled
> Their hopeful plans to emptiness, and cursed
>   Whatever brute and blackguard made the world.

It was in this way that George and Elspeth were beginning to collect the scraps of shared memory, the makings of a private mythology on which any marriage of minds relies. Housman's *Last Poems*, and the act of reciting them at times of domestic intimacy, became a signal between them, an element in the liturgy of their lives. When they found a large copper bowl in a junk shop, they had handles attached and kept it as a memento of this time. One evening in the hotel bar Elspeth noticed that a drinker who had been sitting in the corner had left abruptly. Barker whispered conspiratorially that he had borne an extraordinary physical resemblance to Oscar Williams. They arrived back in Quick Street to find the hall floor flooded by communications from New York telling of Williams's death.[9] The news distressed George deeply. Oscar had been an enabler, a warm but diffident man with a genius for small mercies. Knowing his penchant for informality, he wrote him his most formal elegy to date, drawing on the imagery of Oscar's book of 1940, *The Man Coming Towards You*:

> There by the stone in the short grass where, resting, you wait
> with your spectacled eye turned on the road up which I approach you,
> yes, I and all of us, sulking or shouting, some without gifts, and none late
> and a few in the knowledge that if they should ever reach you
> you will not, perhaps, be there, sad man of ashes, but gone
> still further on seeking your republic of the elect: . . .[10]

The flat was snug for the winter by the time George and Elspeth's daughter was born at the Princess Beatrice Hospital on 24 November. They named her Raffaella Flora after their Roman friend Raffaella Pellizi and Elspeth's sister Flora, and at two months she was baptised at the Catholic church in Duncan Terrace by Peter Levi, poet and Jesuit, then working as a parish priest at Farm Street. Before the ceremony Barker told Levi that they were about to perform an act of magic.[11] Possibly he had in mind the passages on ceremonial lustration in his old favourite, Frazer's *The Golden Bough*. In any case he seems to have thought of the birth and christening as in some sense purifying him. He wrote his daughter a poem:

> Sacred fountain, let me find
> at the genesis of our kind
> some consolation of the mind.
>
> On this dark November morning
> the aureole of the dawn
> like a golden child is born
>
> so this day takes its origin
> from impulses that begin
> beyond the star we suffer in . . .[12]

Brian Higgins – magnanimous, dishevelled, weakened now by what was soon to reveal itself as heart disease – walked with Elspeth as she pushed the pram through the streets of Islington. On Sundays Barker and his little family took to the streets towards Smithfield. In the quiet afternoons they visited the Church of St Bartholomew the Great where amid the shadows of the retro-choir they came across the sepulchre of Rahere, founder of both church and hospital, and once jester to Henry I. Barker noted that his features resembled Mr Eliot's. Rahere had been an Augustinian monk and prebend of St Paul's. In his mind Barker converted him, 'devout joker, founder and priest', into a proto-Franciscan. Rahere's serious service and professional mirth seemed to make him a forerunner of the *fratelli*, St Francis's 'jongleurs de Dieu', jesters for God. Afterwards, they visited the place of execution of the Scottish martyr William Wallace behind the church. On that and other Sundays they paid their respects to the *Cutty Sark* at Greenwich 'with the winds of the world asleep among her shrouds and the gales / Hushed in her furled sails',[13] and strolled around the derelict warehouses still bordering the Thames: that urban, riverain post-Dickensian wasteland which, as Rosalind Wade noted in the *Poetry Review* that year, the young Barker had once made his own.

On 5 January 1965 Barker opened *The Times* to read of Eliot's death the previous evening. Apart from anything else, the news represented the disquieting removal of the professional support which had steadied him through three decades. But it also meant the lifting of the last constraint upon Barker's personal sense of authority. He wrote at once to Valerie, Eliot's widow:

> He was very kind to me, as he was, I know, to many others. Most of all I think of the constant help he gave to me in matters of circumstance when I was young. If it had not been for him, I could not (to speak too much of myself) have had a chance.[14]

Barker had never quite reconciled himself to the contradictions in Eliot, whose austerity of demeanour had seemed at odds with a deep vein of anarchic humour. As the years passed, he would weave anecdotes portraying his erstwhile mentor as lounge lizard, footpad, Sweeney, nightbird, Mr Hyde. Eliot, he would grow accustomed to relating, had worn green eyeshadow. He had prowled the back streets of London after hours dressed as a policeman. He had kept a secret *pied-à-terre* in the Charing Cross Road, visitors to which were obliged to ask the porter for 'the Captain'.[15] On the evening of Eliot's death, he wrote a set of elegiac stanzas in which Eliot blended with Rahere, jester and saint:

> As to the influence of this Lloyd's Bank clerk
> Upon the state of English poetry, I think
> It was imperious. By this I mean
> He restored to us what had almost gone,
> The moral and intellectual porphyrogenitive.
> And what had been, before his hegemony,
> Expedience and a chaffering of poetic riff-raff
> Underwent, during his magistracy, the
> Imposition of rigorous definitions
> And that sense of spiritual onus
> Inherent in all Pascalian interpretations.
> Also he loved bad jokes.[16]

Barker was consumed with a sense of the luck of the survivor. Others, he knew, had not been so fortunate. David Archer, who had now exhausted his capital, was living on a trust fund organised with some difficulty by Moraes. He called at Quick Street, all customary politeness and diffidence until the moment he rose to leave when, turning in the doorway, he begged for half a crown. In a state of high nervousness, David Gascoyne had returned from France on the advice of his doctors, who had instructed him never again to live alone. The difficulties of these friends exacerbated Barker's own sense of precariousness. He was also far from well. That winter a dormant stomach ulcer suddenly and angrily erupted. 'He was also', as Elspeth recalled, 'being treated for a damaged shoulder, the result of a very silly fight with Allan Massie on the viaduct between Ariccia and Albano following the victory of Cassius Clay over Sonny Liston the previous February, on the eve of his fifty-first birthday, when they were both drunk and had been watching the fight on the bar TV.' As a result of these assorted medical complaints, he was on edge and inclined to take offence, even with those closest to him. David Wright, for instance, retained a strong sentimental attachment to his native South Africa.

In the course of a visit to Quick Street, he insisted that the politics of apartheid should be viewed from two sides. When Barker countered that justice resided uniquely with the African National Congress, the two men quarrelled and Wright did the one thing guaranteed to forestall communication: he stopped watching Barker's mouth. When Barker sensed that his friend was no longer listening to him, he sent Wright flying against the wall with a single blow.[17] Sebastian recollects visiting his father at Christmas, only to find him writhing in agony on the bed.[18] Christopher also remembers calling at Quick Street, where he refused one of his father's cigarettes but later changed his mind and sat smoking one of his own. As he did so, Barker seemed to sense an unspoken accusation hanging in the air. Soon they were brawling.[19] The result, as Elspeth remembered, was 'a horrible drunken adolescent fight' in which the two men broke glasses all over the place, including in the empty baby basket.

If such behaviour suggested a troubled conscience, there was good reason. Barker had already lost his poetic father. Now Pa, who had remarried and lived in Rustington on the Sussex coast, had contracted Hodgkin's disease; in March he was admitted to hospital, where his left leg was amputated. On Good Friday George received from Kit a chilling message: 'it is only proper that you should know, and I feel anyway that you would not want to remain ignorant of his condition. His other leg had become affected making it impossible for him to perform even the most basic physiological tasks for himself. On the advice of the doctor concerned he is now in a nursing home in Littlehampton. He has deteriorated a very great deal, and lapses at times into periods of senility.'[20] Elspeth shamed George into preparing the car for a filial visit. An hour later he reappeared claiming that there was a fault in the engine; a trip to Littlehampton was, he insisted, out of the question. On 21 April Kit saw George in London 'to explain everything'. On the 22nd Pa's other leg was removed, and on 2 May he died. Kit attended the funeral; George did not.

Elspeth was now pregnant again, this time armed with the proper antenatal information. Like Elizabeth before her, she had now decided that the timing of children was a woman's prerogative. 'Both Elizabeth and I', she stressed thirty years later, 'had our children *entirely, deliberately by our own choice*, without consulting George at all.'[21] Late in April, when she and George read in the newspaper of a large farmhouse in the French village Beaufort-sur-Gervanne, they decided to rent it until August. Dom and Judy Moraes drove with them to the south-east of France, where Georgina joined them. Beaufort's lofty walls overlooked a tributary of the Drôme, itself a branch of the river Rhône. The house proved to be huge, but rudimentarily equipped. Into a sink the size of a dinner plate trickled an unreliable water supply, which soon dried up. Elspeth and Judy Moraes, who was also pregnant, washed clothes in the Gervanne, pummelling Raffaella's nappies on the bare stones of the gorge through which the river coursed. Outside the local bistro, Moraes sat entranced by Barker's conversation, his 'face of a pharaoh / Or a dissolute camel, his long hands / Commanding pyramids of words'.[22]

They had brought limited funds with them and what little they had was soon exhausted. To ease their poverty, Moraes undertook to rustle up money from London. His contacts there, however, soon turned out to be unproductive, even, the others came to suspect, imaginary. To impecuniousness and the distrust that it bred, other sources of tension were soon added. The intense mutual involvement of George and Elspeth had the occasional effect of making their companions feel like trespassers on their privacy.[23] Georgina for one, who was much of an age with Elspeth, found that the pervasive amorousness excluded her. One evening she shared a table outside a village bar with her father and Elspeth, who were holding hands; Barker turned apologetically to his daughter and remarked, 'I'm sorry, but we're in love.'[24] France, moreover, meant far less to Barker than Italy, and French culture struck him as a conspiracy. In his notebook he wrote, 'We know nothing of the French. Apart, that is, from what the French have disclosed to us. So our respect and even our affection for them is in direct proportion to what they know about themselves.' In mitigation he added, 'But why should the Italians have remarked of Napoleon, "Not all Frenchmen are thieves, but *buona parte*", when after all that heroic patriot was not, strictly, a Frenchman but an Italian?'[25] Eventually George and Elspeth decided to move on to Rome. They put Raffaella in the car and headed south through the gorge of the Sisteron, past the raging river Durance. Mountains and running streams had always stirred a deep exaltation in Barker. As he drove onwards with his loved ones beside him, 'these two constructed as if it were of flowers / a child and mother who renew / our love like poppies on fire', their surroundings afforded a vision he was to incorporate in the dedicatory poem to Elspeth at the beginning of *Dreams of a Summer Night*:

> Eyes that are kinder far than mine
> have given to me a vision
> of natural absolution
> like dawn unloading roses on
> the mountains of the Sisteron.
>
> High from its gold in the green sky
> the noonday gazes dazzling down
> on ringing meadows where we lie
> hung in their hammocks by the sun,
> the mountains of the Sisteron.

> Or watch the evening flood the peaks
> with shade that never before shone
> such nostrum and such peace
> upon the conscience and upon
> the mountains of the Sisteron.[26]

After a few days in Rome the family returned to London to face the necessity of submitting *Dreams of a Summer Night* to the printers. Barker was also obliged to earn some money by reviewing. When the *Listener* sent him a clutch of travel books about France, he found himself capable of contributing little but unsympathetic impressions of their recent holiday, supplemented by recollections of his time with the Farrellys at Bormes-les-Mimosas. The rest was written by Elspeth, though the piece appeared under his name.[27] Again for the *Listener*, he commented on Constantine Fitzgibbon's *Life of Dylan Thomas*, reiterating Keats on the chameleon poet and the virtuous philosopher, but rebuking Fitzgibbon for having been taken in by Dylan's disguises. Thomas, he insisted, had been a philosopher whom the world had persisted in viewing as a chameleon: 'there were . . . times, as his friends knew, when he retired to a corner of the bar, and imbibed a pint with the unboisterous creature of his own soul'.[28]

In September Brian Higgins was taken ill with severe heart trouble. George and Elspeth visited him in Hammersmith Hospital, where they found him in an oxygen tent. Barker had already agreed to supply a preface to Higgins's first professional volume of verse, aptly entitled *The Northern Fiddler*. As the days passed, it became clear that this notice would have to double as an obituary.

Time was running short since Barker had been appointed to a temporary professorship for the second semester of the American academic year at the State University of New York, Buffalo.[29] The terms of the job made it impracticable for him to do anything but leave Elspeth and Raffaella at Quick Street. He would also of necessity be absent for the birth of their second child.

On their last but one visit to the hospital, Higgins burst into tears and accused himself of selling Eliot's letters to New York. Barker there and then forgave him. On 8 December Higgins died. When asked the cause, the consultant answered that, at the age of thirty-six, Higgins had succumbed to 'premature senility of the heart'.

CHAPTER 42

'UNSCREW ME, MY DEAR'

Barker had put his elegies for Eliot, Oscar Williams and Robert Colquhoun together with memorials to Louis MacNeice and Johnny Minton, who had taken his own life in 1963. Calling the sequence 'Five Memorials for Dead Friends', he recorded it on 7 January 1966 for later transmission on the Third.[1] He completed his tribute to Higgins, whom he envisaged as sitting on some celestial Copacabana Beach with the Great Train Robbers, 'puffing leisurely away at ten-inch cigars'. Higgins had been so dedicated to the muse that he had 'with thanks declined every other job saving that of living' and writing poems.[2] On Friday 14 January, Barker left for Buffalo. For twenty-six years he had also declined all jobs or, which amounted to much the same, failed to obtain them. For the first time since fleeing Japan in 1940, he was now to follow Eliot's advice rather than his own. In the short term he was to earn a monthly pay cheque through teaching.

From the beginning his stay went badly. In the mid-Sixties the University of Buffalo was a thriving academic community whose English department possessed a vital and outward-looking commitment to modern poetry, and whose library contained one of the best collections of twentieth-century verse in North America. The department encouraged British visitors with interests in the field. Grey Gowrie had taught there as a visiting lecturer two years before,[3] and Peter Redgrove was to do so later. A. Alvarez, formerly poetry critic of the *Observer*, whose stock had risen with the publication three years before of his ground-breaking anthology *The New Poetry*, was currently in residence. Buffalo is a meat-packing town and its downtown area seemed unsightly for the most part. It could, nevertheless, lay claim to some arresting architecture, including a number of grain elevators which had once inspired Le Corbusier. It also boasted a worthwhile museum of modern art. Little of this, however, registered with Barker, who was missing

Elspeth and Raffaella too much to notice anything besides his own wretched loneliness.

He arrived to fourteen inches of snow. The campus seemed a labyrinthine monument to concrete. He was allocated Room 382 in the residence block called 'Lisbon', where an internal temperature in the eighties was maintained by central heating. He was given a tiny office in the department of English next to Alvarez. Here he was expected to see students in groups of twenty or more, teaching them modern British poetry and 'Creative Writing', a course whose very title disquieted him, since Dale-Roberts had informed him long ago that God was the only authentic creator. On one occasion he was also required, in the absence of a colleague, to take a class described in the university prospectus as 'Rhetoric', a discipline which, he was amazed to discover, consisted of basic English grammar.[4]

When not engaged in these unarduous activities, Barker sat, sulked and thought of home. Back in Britain Raffaella had been taken by train to the safe haven of Drumtochty. When her labour began, Elspeth went into Queen Mary's Maternity Home, Hampstead, where on Robert Burns Day, Tuesday 25 January, her first son was born. Because he was as unprecedented as Adam, they named him Adam Alexander Rahere George, adding Robert in memory of Elspeth's father, the Roberts and of Burns. Elspeth sat up in bed feeling 'mad with delight' and scolding Sir Maurice Bowra for the ineptness of his *Landmarks in Greek Literature*, which she was reviewing for the *Listener*: 'Blandly, condescendingly, without one word of ancient Greek, he surveys literature up to the 3rd century BC . . . I suppose Sir Maurice has a captive audience, but he should do better by them.'[5]

Elspeth wrote long, fluent letters to Buffalo. At two o'clock every afternoon she could receive visitors. There were none, but she rouged up and mascara'd her eyes nonetheless. She was subject, as people sometimes are in periods of intensity and relative isolation, to flashes of almost telepathic intuition. One afternoon she had just finished applying her make-up when a balding man in a wet rumpled raincoat walked into the room, his hair in disarray. It was Higgins, who announced, 'I've come to see you because you came to see me,' and promptly vanished.[6]

When her Bowra review was published, she spent the fee on a seventeenth-century Chinese carving in amethyst of two tigers twined around a branch amid blossoms, then sent it off to Buffalo for George's fifty-third birthday. He received it in his room and took it across the arctic wastes to his office. He struggled with the packet and his keys, his hands blue and shaking with cold. He opened the door and, leaving it ajar, tore at the wrapping. As he did so, the contents slipped out of the parcel and shattered. This semi-precious wonder which had survived for three hundred years without injury lay in fragments on the hard institutional floor.[7] Half an hour later Alvarez came into the department. Looking through Barker's open door, he saw the poet sitting absorbed, vainly attempting to fit the carving together again. There was a concentration and infinite care about the way in which he did this, qualities so at odds with Barker's boisterous social persona, that Alvarez felt that he had been given an insight into the patient man who put the poems together: the virtuous artist inside the anarchist. Alvarez was moved, but he said nothing. At the end of an hour Barker knocked on his door and announced with touching pride that he had more or less restored the figurine to its proper shape. Alas, it finally proved beyond repair.[8]

Although Alvarez was engaged to be married and understandably preoccupied, he did what he could to alleviate Barker's loneliness. Barker's verse was too highflown for his own taste, but he would have liked to have known the man better. It was the accident with the amethyst carving that had summed up the enigma of his personality. Alvarez had expected a Dionysiac; instead he found a man who was vulnerable and, on occasions, surprisingly shy.

For Barker the smashing of the carving was symbolic of the sheer brutality of Buffalo, destructive alike of amethyst and of people. He was reminded of Wyndham Lewis's novel *Self Condemned*, written ten years before and describing its author's sojourn in Toronto on the opposite shore of Lake Ontario. Like Barker, Lewis's *alter ego* is a visiting professor subject to mild accidents and absurdities epitomising the unsympathetic marginality of the place.

Barker spent his afternoons in a scruffy downtown cinema, where he watched the film *The Singing Nun* eight times. Towards the end of the first month he bought a diary and crossed off each successive day in red. 'One month up,' he noted on Monday, 14 February; and two days later 'four weeks in Buffalo today'.[9] Friday the 18th was 'Pay Day', the only reason apparently for staying, since the rent for Quick Street, Elspeth informed him, had risen by a shilling a week. 'A third of the time up,' he wrote jubilantly on the 22nd. Two days later he squandered some of his dollars on a coat. He was longing for England: the great cathedrals, the ancient university towns, towards which he had always felt ambivalent: at least Oxford and Cambridge were not constructed out of tower blocks. He submitted a long-distance application for a job as a Fellow in Creative Arts at the University of York. Though the title was suspect, the very thought of working in an ancient city, close to a historic abbey church, seems to have revived in him a longing for the old world and for tradition. The post was not to begin until October, yet he rang York to press his claims. He made frantic attempts to get in touch with what he regarded as civilisation. He phoned Drumtochty, but the bell rang futilely in the echoing spaces of the castle. By the time Elspeth's father picked up the receiver, Barker had rung off. 'Where is Dede?' he cabled Raffaella Pellizi on 26 March. To Sebastian at Corpus Christi he wrote of the privilege of studying at Oxford, where 'you can have a helluva better time than here among the wretched eskimoes and bisons'. Oxford provided its students with a proper education, whereas in North America 'the great white elephant of information transforms itself into the poor dead horse that not even you would flog'.[10] He was glad that nobody was sending him gifts of cash, since the only desirable objects of merchandise were bears. 'Buffaloona' he had learnt to call the place, in reference to the loon birds on Lake Ontario, as much as to the self-inflicted madness of his being there at all.

When the baby was strong enough, Elspeth took him to Drumtochty to meet his sister. Raffaella could not twist her tongue around 'Alexander'. She tried 'brother', a form of address that turned into 'Budda' or perhaps 'Buddha', before settling once and for all on 'Bruddy'. While he was sleeping out on the lawn in his frilly robe, the dogs stood guard over him. The family went down to Elie in Fife, where Elspeth's parents had a house near the sea. 'Oh my love,' she wrote to Buffalo, 'I can't *believe* this separation is almost over. I feel as though I've been living in this barren, solitary, cellular state for a millennium. I've even taken to having thoughts about the human condition and being nasty to the dogs. Today I was speaking to Adam Alexander about the folly of thumb sucking when he is supposed to be eating. What I found myself saying was "you mustn't look in the mirror when I'm feeding you."'[11]

Claustrophobia had well and truly overtaken Barker. His diary dragged towards deliverance. 'Five weeks and six days more,' he wrote on 30 March. The following day it was 'five weeks and five days more'. To Georgina, who was suffering from jaundice, he wrote that since the disease was inevitable she should relax and enjoy it. It was much like the 'empty horrors' of Buffalo, where 'I walk up and down these positively Alaskan streets with the air of a promartyr strolling over hot coals: each step is a remission of sin.'[12] Temporary relief was found by forays down to New York City, where he stayed with two former protégés: Robin Prising, whom he had met in Soho in the 1950s, and Willie Coakley, whom he had taken under his wing during the summer school at Breadloaf. They were now happily living together on West 71st Street. They immediately sensed his misery. He had, he told them, attempted to make contact with Jessica and the twins. Jessica, however, had not agreed to meet him. He had become so withdrawn that, when visitors called at their flat, he hid behind a curtain.[13] Back in Buffalo he acquired his longed-for exit permit on the 14th. He set his senior year students their final papers: 'Irony in Twentieth Century Verse', 'The Mystery of Yeats', 'The Atrophy of the Imagination in T.S. Eliot', 'The Spiritual Irresponsibility of Ezra Pound'.[14] It is hard not to discern a certain compensatory levity in these topics. On 7 May he wondered whether madness had overtaken him, since it was still snowing. He planned to leave immediately after collecting his pay cheque on Friday, 13 May. At the last moment he assessed his students' papers, entering the marks wrongly on the grade sheet, so that Alvarez had to sort them out after he had gone.[15] By that time Barker was hovering in mid-Atlantic. He arrived in an early morning mist at Prestwick Airport, with its one runway on the bleak and beautiful estuary of the Clyde. From the tiny observation lounge, Elspeth watched as the stairs were pushed into position. A child in its mother's arms was the first to emerge from the plane, sending her into floods of associative tears. She and George spent hours in Glasgow talking away the last four months of separation, then drove to Drumtochty where were her parents, Raffaella and Bruddy, one parrot, cats, dogs, ferrets and geese.

Barker was so delighted with Scotland that he even had thoughts of buying the kennels of Drumtochty Castle in which to live for ever, but when they returned to Islington the negotiations, to Elspeth's relief, broke down. They spent the summer in London, where George's new agent, John Johnson, sent him a contract with MacGibbon & Kee for the publication of a collected *Essays*, and the autobiography. They renewed contact with Dom and Judy Moraes and with the extended Barker clan. George's eldest sister Olga had inherited Hodgkin's Disease from Pa and like him lost a leg. She drank with George, her zest for life undiminished.

Some months after Colquhoun's death, MacBryde had left London for Spain, where he had briefly stayed with Anthony Cronin. Then he had returned to teach at a summer school in Cork, which he promptly deserted in order to join Kavanagh in Dublin. On the night of 6 May 1966 – according to some reports – he was dancing in the open street outside a pub when a taxi careered round the corner and struck him; other versions say that the door opened straight on to the road so that he walked out under the wheels of an approaching vehicle. When Barker heard of his death, he re-created in his mind those evenings in late wartime London, with the Roberts in their Bedford Gardens studio:

> When that huge room at Notting Hill
> on Sunday nights began to fill
>
> With those whom you loved all too well,
> then I and each one was the most
>
> devoted, O intemperate ghost,
> Of all the lovers you have lost.[16]

After MacBryde's funeral, Kavanagh visited London. He drank with Barker in pubs in Bloomsbury: the Plough in Museum Street, and the Museum Tavern on Great Russell Street. For nights in a row he was seen lurching out of the Museum Tavern at closing time, and relieving himself against a brick in the third row of masonry up from the pavement. (Many years later, after his death, his friends had the brick in question inscribed in Gaelic to this effect, a memorial that remained there until a strait-laced member of the Kavanagh clan demanded its removal.) In the Plough Barker deepened a joking rapport with Kavanagh, which stemmed from their shared love of meticulously phrased insult. Having elicited from mutual acquaintances in Dublin the legend of his friend's perpetual virginity, Barker now exploited it mercilessly. The ultimate vituperative weapon against Paddy, he discovered, consisted of a systematic elimination of the epithet, as follows:

Kavanagh: Barker, you focking cont.
Barker: Kavanagh, you cont.[17]

Barker was suffering some concealed embarrassment because, though he had now contracted to publish his memoirs, he was fundamentally unwilling to write them. The project had formed part of his application for the fellowship at York and the university had appointed him to the position for one year from October, apparently on the understanding that the proposed autobiography would form the basis of his work. Since York was not in convenient commuting distance from London, the family decided to move north for the academic year. They had been led to expect accommodation on campus; instead on arrival they were allocated a furnished 1930s house in suburban Heslington. Raffaella and Bruddy immediately went down with German measles. Every other day George drove to the campus, where he drank instant coffee and discussed the creative efforts of his students in a gazebo allocated to him for the purpose. Since the coffee bore the brandname Maxwell House, he posted a notice on the departmental board inviting students interested in writing to attend consultations with 'Professor Max Welhaus'. But he was not finding relationships with his colleagues in the English department easy. He was not unique among writers-in-residence in discovering that his closest affinities lay less with literary scholars than with practitioners of disciplines like mathematics. The one friendship he managed to establish in the English department was with the lecturer and novelist Tony Ward, who coincidentally had also blinded his brother in one eye. But Ward did not share Kavanagh's appreciation of insult and the relationship came to an abrupt conclusion when they quarrelled at a dinner party.

When the children recovered, Elspeth re-emerged into the world. There was, they discovered, some defensiveness on the score of York being a new and provincial university with a student body as yet totalling only 900. Like many institutions of higher learning established in the early 1960s in the wake of the Robbins Report, it was at one and the same time international in its outlook and regional in its loyalties. This combination of aims could initially work to the disadvantage of outsiders, who had to feel their way gently. After a succession of unrewarding dinner parties, Elspeth was introduced at a departmental party to a second year English student with the words: 'This is Fiona Sinclair. She will cheer you up.' Fiona lived up to her reputation; the two became close friends. After quitting her unsatisfactory lodgings, Fiona was living in a Morris Minor parked off campus. She took to baby-sitting in the Barker household and then moved in, wondering at Barker's absorption in the children as, neglecting the autobiography, he spent his evenings playing games and reading picture books. Among his students, he was attracted less to the academics than to those with strongly individual or esoteric interests, among whom was John Cox, a first year philosophy student much involved with the theory of religion and science. For a time, indeed, York seemed so pleasant that Barker considered buying a house in the West Riding. He wrote a letter to Elizabeth Smart, now living in the Dell, a cottage near Bungay in Suffolk, begging her for a loan for the downpayment. Nothing, however, came of the plan.

He was still stuck with the memoirs. MacGibbon & Kee had requested a straightforward autobiography, but he was quite determined not to submit one. Instead, as in *The True Confession*, Barker chose to adopt a mask, casting his memories in the form of a journal kept by Lord B, a blend of himself and a modern-day Lord Byron. The surviving drafts of the resulting *Life of Lord B* show just how difficult he found the project, how much it ran against the grain of his temperament. He attempted, for example, to rework his relationship with his eldest sister Olga, whom he renamed Ottavia. The purpose seems to have been to convert her into an approximate equivalent of Byron's half-sister, and possible mistress, Augusta. Since Olga's Hodgkin's disease was now well advanced, and the artificial limb with which she had been fitted a talking point between them, the tone achieved was less one of Byronic flippancy than of comic bathos. 'How often this heavenly creature with sapphire eyes had led us into the wilder Bacchanalia,' he wrote, 'more gregarious orgies and remoter pleasures than we know. Such was her sense of the ridiculous that at our last meeting she stood, swaying with whisky, in front of me, insisting that I remove her artificial leg because, like a heron, she could stand better on one.'[18] The mutual feelings of these siblings amount to the literal opposite of incest. 'Unhook the damn thing there,' sighs Ottavia/Olga at one point, indicating her leg. '*Unscrew* me, my dear.'

Barker sketched out sixteen chapters taking him from Chelsea to York, but even these proved troublesome. The only publishable section turned out to be a swashbuckling preface explaining why he could not write the rest. Barker no longer had the heart for prose. Instead he set to work on a sequence of 104 interlocked double quatrains which he initially called *The Golden Epodes*, but then renamed *The Golden Chains* after a Cambridgeshire ballad he had alluded to in one of his poems of the 1930s, 'The Neo-Geordies'. The inception of this sequence owed much to A.E. Housman, whose simplicity he now saw as a challenge: 'I realized', he admitted some years later, 'that I could no longer resist the advances of this wretched old man. The only idea I've ever had of some kind of progression in my own writings is that I sincerely hope that they have advanced out of the Latinate bullshit that I used to love. I used to have to call a poem "Triumphal Ode" or something like that. It was beautiful to me at the time. But then I remember sitting down in York and thinking for Chrissakes I must do something that I want to do. What is it? I wanted to write a hundred little poems of eight lines, rhymed. I did this, and I saw how terribly, terribly hard it is to do.'[19]

Barker had also been spending some time with mini-forms such as the *haiku*. As a result, each section of *The Golden Chains* was to be a rigorous exercise in simplicity. These included apostrophes to doomed or alienated friends: to John Farrelly, called 'Sergius' throughout; to Kingsmill, called 'Artemodorus'. There were poems celebrating sexuality and affection, and meditations on the doomed Eros. The effect was sensuous and somehow oriental, as when recalling his longing for Elspeth in Buffalo:

> I whisper to you, daughter
>   and wife of my desire,
> I drowned in the water
>   I burned in the fire
>
> I hanged in the forked tree
>   and now I am dead.
> Ah, once again, love, come to me,
>   even in this cold bed.[20]

But the real theme of *The Golden Chains* was the futility of words. The book ended with an invocation of the loon bird wailing over the Niagara Falls, its cry as empty as language itself. The sequence therefore concerned itself, turned in and sealed. The purpose was 'to affirm my conviction that this is what all language is about. It is simply the howl of a loon bird, and has no meaning at all'.

In April Barker and Elspeth went to London for a celebration at the Plough in honour of Kathleen Malone, who was about to marry Patrick Kavanagh in Dublin. The gathering was attended by Eddie Linden, one of Sebastian's friends from Oxford who had been invited that night by the art critic Tim Hilton. Linden was an illegitimate Irishman who had grown up in Scotland. Largely self-educated, he had recently come down from Plater College, the Catholic workers' college in Oxford. He was intemperately in love with the whole business of poetry and was soon to make a niche for himself as organiser of readings at the Lamb and Flag in Covent Garden, and as editor of the poetry magazine *Aquarius*. In April 1967 he was finding his way around in literary London.[21] As he entered the pub that evening he noticed an animated couple near the counter. 'I remember seeing this extremely attractive girl standing next to an older man in his fifties,' he wrote later. 'I asked Tim who it was, and he told me that it was Elspeth and George Barker.' A few days later Linden gatecrashed a party at Martin and Fiona Green's flat in Tottenham Street, where he introduced himself to the poet. In later years Linden would sometimes circulate at such gatherings announcing at the top of his voice that he was an Irish Catholic homosexual. 'I ended up getting thrown out, quite rightly so.' But Linden was not just passionate about poets and poetry; he had learnt as much from the Catholic fathers in Scotland as Barker had learned from the Fathers of the Oratory. His was exactly the sort of self-made intelligence to appeal to George.

It was not long before Barker's enthusiasm for Yorkshire collapsed, along with his plan to settle in the county. On 15 June he wrote to Sebastian that there were only two more weeks 'until the end of my tenure at this dump'. Even the West Riding had by now managed to put forth a rose or two, and there were guelder roses at the bottom of his garden 'like packets of Faery Snow'. His application for a lectureship at the University of Lodz in Poland had been rejected, but in September he was due to deliver an address at the international poetry colloquium to be held in Montreal as part of Expo '67.

With these prospects, and with the money from Buffalo and York behind him, he decided to buy a house in London. For the first time in his life, he had some working capital. For the first time he was in a position to do what his parents had never managed: dispense with landlords and rent. They found a pleasant three-storey early Victorian house at 34 Prebend Street, just round the corner from Quick Street, and set about arranging the finances. That summer he had met up with an acquaintance from his days in Rome, the former girlfriend of the journalist Malcolm Winton. She introduced them to her mother Jardine Jackson, who was an estate agent. To her Barker made out a cheque amounting to most of his capital: £510, being the 10 per cent down payment on the purchase price of £5,100.[22] The weeks progressed towards the final exchange of contracts, but Mrs Jackson, a declared bankrupt, was nowhere to be found. 'The next thing that we knew she had vanished, vanished off the face of the earth with all our money.'[23] Barker made frantic enquiries through the city firm of Edgley & Co. in the hope of recovering the deposit. It turned out that for some time Mrs Jackson had been operating under a number different aliases.[24] Because of legal complications, there was no way in which she could be sued for recovery of the debt. In any case, there was no trace of her. It was, the lawyers said, a 'grey area of the law'.

After thirty years of struggle, Barker was once more financially at rock bottom. In early September he flew to the Rencontre Mondiale de Poésie in Montreal, where he delivered his most uncompromising statement yet on the role of the poet. Since he seemed doomed never to own his own home, since ill chance dogged him, he made a virtue out of his need, glorying once again in the position of scapegoat. He reiterated the argument he had expounded in 1950 in 'The Poet as Pariah', decking it in still more lurid colours. The poet was not only a social leper but also a visionary, capable of working wonders of social and spiritual transformation through his power of uniting discrepant perceptions. This point went right the way back to his lecture in Tokyo in April 1940 and as in Japan he gave it a twist of political relevance. 'The anarchy inherent in the whole affair of poetic inspiration lies exactly in the fact of its unpredictability. This is the only quality that the poem shares with the Atom bomb.' The contribution of the poet was indispensable, precisely because society could never tie him down:

> I believe the responsibility or onus of the poet is to assert and affirm the human privilege of perversity. I believe it to be his duty to remind us that even when we are right we are at perfect liberty to change our minds because it is sometimes better to be wrong. I believe the nature of the poet to be at heart anarchic, so that in the inconceivable eventuality of the Ideal Society, a society, that is, possessing no faults to which we could rationally object, it would still be the job of the poet to object. His humanity is Irish, like the Dubliner who, when asked what his politics were, always answered, no matter who held power:
>
> 'I'm again the Government.'[25]

On his return, he rapidly summed up his financial predicament. With two small children, life in Quick Street was already cramped. Elspeth was expecting their third child. Barker's savings were gone. They could now not even rent a place large enough for their needs in London. They scoured the property columns looking for a suitable house in the country. Eventually, in *The Times*, they read a notice from the National Trust advertising a seventeenth-century farmhouse near Aylsham in north Norfolk. As a matter of course, they applied. Barker drove up to see it. It was, he reported on his return, magnificently lovely, yet he had enthused before and Elspeth thought little of it. Through the early autumn he drove round the country looking, but the houses were unsuitable or spoken for. By early October they were despairing. The child was due in a few weeks and they had nowhere to turn. On the offchance Elspeth phoned the National Trust. The Norfolk farmhouse, she was told, had gone.[26] She replaced the receiver and took Bruddy for a walk around the block. When she got back to Quick Street she met a jubilant George. The National Trust had phoned to apologise. The receptionist had heard 'Barker' as 'Parker'. Bintry House was theirs.

CHAPTER 43

BINTRY HOUSE

As they now had no money to make the move, there was little choice but to beg for it. Barker remembered Lawrence Durrell's pre-war offers of help and wrote to him in Provence. Durrell replied that his money was tied up in French land, the value of which had slumped.[1] An anxious few weeks passed. Barker was taking his worries with him to bed, where the answer appeared in a dream. For years Graham Greene, a devoted admirer, had been sending him signed copies of his novels as they came out. Barker should, the dream instructed him, write to Greene in Antibes stating his plight. He did so. A courteous note came back and, with it, the money.[2]

The family drove up on Saturday, 14 October. Bintry House lay just to the north-west of the tiny, ancient village of Itteringham, down a long, curved track. Norfolk, as G.M. Trevelyan writes in *English Social History*, was the first shire in England where brick was extensively used. The whole of Itteringham was built of it: brilliant red-clay brick that powdered between thumb and forefinger when picked up in fragments. Bintry House was no exception. Constructed without foundations, it was a seventeenth-century farmhouse set some twenty yards to the south-east of the site of the house put up in Norman times by the original Bintre. Its porched front façade looked east across aspen trees to the narrow, limpid river Bure. The back commanded uninterrupted views across fields. Outside the kitchen door lay a courtyard, enclosed by flint walls and with a pump in the middle. Beyond were outhouses: a crumbling barn, some stables and a rundown garage. Water was led off from a deep well to the north of the house and gushed fitfully from the taps in the narrow kitchen with its Aga cooker. The rest of the ground floor was a warren of irregularly laid-out rooms: a large playroom where the television eventually went; a lobby with a lavatory off it and telephone; a living room with a cavernous open fireplace. Across the corridor was a third reception room, which was to be given over to ritualistic and raucous re-creations of Fitzrovian evenings. In consequence it was to be dubbed the drinking room, and was otherwise out of bounds. Upstairs, Barker took the attic for his study. (He was later to use a tiny room at the end of the kitchen: later still a large front bedroom overlooking the Bure and the aspens.) The main bedroom was on the first floor. Further along the corridor were sufficient rooms for the adventurous Barker brood, the latest addition to whom, Roderick Joseph Cameron, arrived on 14 November 1967. The Barker children tended to acquire a sonorous rollcall of names, and in practice to be called something quite different. Elspeth had been reading Graham Greene's latest novel *The Comedians*, where she had come across the Caribbean term 'pirogue' for a kind of canoe or dugout. Since this word made Roderick laugh, his siblings promptly distorted it to 'Progue' and then to 'Progles', adopting the latest version as a nickname for their new brother. 'Progles' he remained.[3]

Spacious and full of character, Bintry was the first home in which Barker lived uninterruptedly with his offspring. Gradually a new way of life began to emerge: a reflection of the ambience and setting of the house and of Barker's own personality. It was an intensely family-orientated existence, to which children and animals were central. Ever since Jessica's terrier Sirrah had had to be farmed out to Big Mumma and Pa when she and George had left for Japan, he had been a reluctant animal lover. Chi-Chi had been very much Cass's cat; and in Rome George had defiantly refused to consider the possibility of a domestic pet, citing Sirrah as the reason. But Elspeth had grown up on a Scottish estate where animals were an important part of life; she communicated this priority to the children. In the New Year of 1968 she discovered an advertisement in *Exchange and Mart* for a Dobermann pinscher, whom she purchased with the backlog of the family allowance. The dog was a birthday present for George, who in April went down to Paddington to meet him off the train from Cornwall. Initially he was minded to call him 'Obermann Revisited' in honour of Matthew Arnold. This became 'Matthew Arnold Revisited', subtitled 'Jockey of Norfolk', before settling as 'Dobermann' or 'Dobe'. He was the second item in what was to be a growing menagerie (a black cat called Marmalade had preceded him), and the first animal about whom Barker wrote a poem. Its metre mimicked the dog's movements, its 'feet' finally splaying like Dobermann's own:

> he sprawls and he falls
> over tables and chairs
> and goes over his nose when he
> stalks down stairs.
> He's the colour of seedcake

> mixed with old tar
> and he never knows rightly
> where his feet are . . .[4]

Unexpectedly, this man who had declared, 'Nobody will domesticate me,' and who had resisted so obdurately Jessica's and Dede's need for family stability, lived in the warm embrace of dogs, cats and babies. Though never exactly mellow, Barker was now a representative of the older generation. The urge to kick against authority never disappeared, but Barker's attitude towards life – and certainly the attitude of many of his associates towards him – was henceforth complicated by the fact that, if authority existed, to some extent he embodied it.

A recognition of his enhanced status seems to lie behind his final poem to Eliot, published that year in the *Texas Quarterly*. 'Letter addressed to the Corpse of Eliot' is full of mystical wonderment at the gulf that lies between man and man, between the living and the dead, between artist and mentor – and at the futile straining of language to reach across the void. As the poet leans figuratively over Eliot's grave:

> I hear only the
> hiss of the October
> grass in the small morning
> wind and the idiot
> joy of the
> bird nested at
> twilight, the wild
> fury of a far off
> sea in its orgy of
> anarchy and
> the wide, wide silence of the
> sky. So speechless
> that hollow head lies
> now and cannot hear
> our need or heed our
> fear. Lie still. Lie
> still. Let him sleep.[5]

Norfolk provided Barker with a more consistently rural existence than any he had so far known. Gradually London ceased to be the hub of his existence. In any case, valued friends could always be lured up to Itteringham, where the family came to keep more or less open house at weekends. Weekdays were devoted to work. All morning, sometimes from before dawn, he would write or read steadily at his desk. In the afternoons he might drive the children to the seaside at Cromer or Sheringham, or possibly to one of Norfolk's 659 churches. These extraordinary buildings were the remnants of the wealth created by Norfolk's once-flourishing wool trade. Barker had an especial partiality for Salle, stranded amid fields. On bleak November afternoons, and even at the height of summer, they invariably found that they had these buildings to themselves, as the children ran up and down the flags of the central aisles, inspecting carved figures on pew ends, gargoyles, angels and bosses. Barker's favourite church was the simplest: Thurgarton, 'the barest chapel I know', devoid of transepts or tower, thatched, absurdly far from its village. Thurgarton, however, was a private retreat, which he often visited alone.

On the trips with the children he would spin stories about wild imagined creatures. There were more tales at bedtime. Barker and the children populated the landscape with the products of their collective fancy: Queen La Dancing Umbrella, a swan called Isabella and her spouse Isabeau, who lived in the Bure. In May he fantasised a giant whose den was in the Mercedes' steering wheel. He devised whole sagas about a sailor, an existential wanderer in search of his soul, called Dibby Dubby Dhu.

He wrote poems too for the children, responding to their natural pleasure in word play, extemporising verses that became common property. Many of the resulting pieces, spontaneous and intimate, went into *Runes and Rhymes and Tunes and Chimes* (1969), his first volume of children's verse.

It was not only the Bintry children who knew these verses. In October 1967, just before the move to Norfolk, Barker had received a message from Dede asking him to visit the children in Rome and offering to pay his expenses. He took to spending occasional weeks at the Via Cassia. The visits were to increase with the years. He contrived to sweep Dede's children up in the same imaginative world as their Bintry counterparts, sending specimens of his children's poetry to Rome. He converted 'Dibby Dubby Dhu' into a humorous version of himself in his capacity as chameleon poet. As far as his children in Norfolk were concerned, Dibby Dubby Dhu was an American professor, or a Norfolk farmer, or sometimes a gangster. The children in the Via Cassia knew him as a fisherman at Fregene:

> Dibby Dubby Dhu rose at midnight
>   to sail his boat in the sky.
> He knows that the stars are fishes
>   and he even knows why.

> Ask: 'Why are the stars fishes?'
> Ask Old Dibby Dubby Dhu.
> He'll answer: 'Because they are silver
> and swim about in the blue.'[6]

Over the first few months Barker's life fell into a fresh rhythm. In a letter to Gascoyne he eulogised the 'bare but mysterious landscape' of north Norfolk, and 'the great joy of the children just jumping about in it'.[7] As soon as the family was settled, he invited Kit up with Ilse and their young son, Thomas. Elspeth was struck by the closeness of the brothers: 'Kit got out of the car at the bottom of the garden because he wanted to walk up George's drive to George's house. He was overcome. They retained an intense feeling for one another.'[8] Oliver Bernard, now living near Diss, was a constant visitor. Tristram Hull, who had been editor of the defunct *Nimbus*, was living with his wife Alicia at Thornage near Holt. One evening Raffaella ventured out of the nursery into the moon-blanched corridor. After a few steps she rushed back into the bedroom, announcing that she had met Frankenstein's monster, looming in the dark. The ogre was John Heath-Stubbs, groping towards the bathroom in his underpants.

Maurice Carpenter was between marriages and in effect homeless. In December 1968 he came to stay, earning his keep by helping dig a vegetable patch. On Sunday mornings Raffaella, who was going through a religious phase, would wear her green velvet dress and take 'Carp' up the lane to matins in Itteringham church. He worked and slept in the large front bedroom, where he would sit composing wry sonnets about resisting middle age. In sober fact, Carpenter was decidedly middle-aged. Now he had grown a pointed white beard, which he continually and sagely stroked to the fury of his hosts. He also frequented the Walpole Arms in the village, where he attempted to instil into the farmworkers the radical ideals of Thomas Paine. Even in his own eyes, Carp had become a parody of himself: a cranky, questionable seer who seemed not to resent his own reputation for eccentricity.

One morning in the late summer of 1969 Carpenter had been sitting early over a sonnet. He had placed his coat over the back of the chair, having failed to notice the presence of the one-bar electric fire immediately behind it. Two doors down Bruddy and Progles sat up in bed, enjoying the little white smoke rings as they drifted along the corridor until Raffaella, who was four and responsible, woke up. She rushed out into the passage shouting that the study was on fire. The family doused the flames with wet cloths, but it was the end for Carpenter, who, unaware of this unfolding near disaster, had been enjoying a hearty and solitary breakfast downstairs in the kitchen. Barker drove him and his sagging bags into Aylsham and wordlessly deposited them at the bus stop.[9]

Ever since the year in York Barker had been wrestling with a radio play about the nature of the poetic vocation. It was structured around his tried format of a poetic conscience locked in some afterworld: not Hell this time, but a correctly identified and labelled Limbo. He understood this medieval Catholic location as a condition of suspended animation in which we exist half in and half out of our identities, and in which all action is pointless. 'Limbo', he explained in his notebook, 'is where we know nothing HAPPENS. All decisions are purely aesthetic and meaningless because without consequences. A wilderness of THEORY without action, where there is always a theoretical temptation BECAUSE action is without meaning here.'[10] Into this no-man's-land he cast Yeats, called Mr Sheets-Kelly, and Housman, to whom he gave his own pseudonym from York, Professor Max Welhaus. These protagonists are forced to witness a series of charades in which the pointlessness of all human activity is laid bare. A couple of lovers go through the motions of sexual intercourse, deriving no meaning from the experience except as 'an act of mutual masturbation'. A female muse beckons, but without conviction. The poets hear echoes of their own remorse as a continuous vaporous waterfall which, however, fails to arouse in them the faintest pang of contrition. They meet the shade of Tennyson ('Lord Golfather'), reduced to the merest caricature: he is wearing a specially designed jacket bristling with medals in front but without a back. They encounter the spectre of Rupert Brooke splashing in a well, but he has been reduced to the blond Adonis of legend, and is quite bereft of poems. Soon they are themselves reduced to caricatures, obliged to stand motionless for eternity, as they endlessly parrot their own lines.

Barker had called the play *A Mask of Masks*. The title implied that Limbo is a condition in which the 'mask' Yeats believed all poets should wear absorbs the identity beneath it. By the time it was broadcast on 7 September 1968 the title had been changed to *A Comedy of Masks*.[11] Both titles suggest a secular context, though the play in fact addressed religious questions with which Barker was increasingly preoccupied.

Since arriving back in Britain, Barker had been subtly redefining his sense of Roman Catholicism. Whilst in Rome he had been able to take his religion very much for granted. In nominally Anglican England, by contrast, he had to search for a Catholic subsoil beneath secular ground. He was discussing the problem of faith with Sebastian who, having relinquished his research degree in Science at Oxford, was feeling his way towards a new occupation and a philosophy of life with which to sustain it. Sebastian was deeply interested in religion, to the evident delight of his father, who now hellenised him as 'Sebastos'. He was soon crowing over his son's commerce with the angels and wrote to welcome him into the fold. Though the Church showed plain evidence of corruption, he remarked encouragingly, 'underneath every good and bad circumstance extend the heavenly mosaic floors and pretty damned fouled up with donkey shit and money they are too BUT they are still foundations.'[12] To Eddie Linden, Barker enthused, 'I think, you know, Sebastian's coming over.'

Sebastian did not become a Roman Catholic then, though he was to take this step twenty-eight years later. He was, however, anxious that his father should endorse his plan to be a poet. While still at Oxford he had sent Barker a sheaf of poems, eliciting a warm response:

> Dear Sebastian your verses are very
> Delightful and really rather merry
> For a young man sitting in a college
> Surrounded by all human knowledge.
> The chemistry of love is simply
> What turns adolescents pimply,
> But only god almighty knows
> Why pimples turn into a rose.[13]

Barker cautioned his son against too literal a self-expressive view of verse. Every poet possessed an identity that might be described as 'The First Person Singing'; but this existed at the opposite pole from the ordinary person who walked down the street, being located 'as far from the ego as possible', where it lived 'at the antipodes of the soul' and was 'quite happy simply being'.

Barker had recently received a batch of poetry from Robert Pollet, a friend of Sebastian's from Canterbury and Oxford and now a lecturer at the University of Cameroon in West Africa. He told Sebastian that Pollet's talent laboured under self-consciousness: 'Pollet has, I am sure, the gifts of mind and even of the heart, but the real temptation for a young poet is, ironically enough, having something to say. It is, to use a timely metaphor, as though all the snow that fell had "The Gift of the Heavenly Father" inscribed on each flake. Almost the most serious remark I have ever found about the writing of poems was the title of a Tin Pan Alley song of the fifties: "It ain't what y'do, it's the way that y'do it."' He counselled Sebastian to concentrate less on the matter and more on the manner of his work.

With a relevant twist of thought, he then warned Sebastian off his own earlier artistic vices. An intoxication with words was one symptom of nascent talent; the tendency needed, however, to be curbed.[14] He was clearly aware that, as the child of two writers, Sebastian might succumb to imitation. He quoted Baudelaire at him, 'The first thing that we must do is to murder our fathers.'[15]

By 1968 Barker had had twenty years' experience of advising young poets.

In the summer of 1967 he had discussed the question of poetic training with the poet John Moat at Moat's house in Devon. Moat was anxious to evolve a way of developing the skill of young writers distinct from American methods of teaching 'Creative Writing'. A method which strongly recommended itself was the informal tutorial programme which Barker himself had employed in Zennor in 1948 and which he had continued to practise on and off since.

In Zennor one of the early beneficiaries of this approach had been Barker's nephew John Fairfax. Fairfax was now keen to collaborate with Moat in establishing a writers' summer school. The result of their joint efforts was the Arvon Foundation, which held its first course in 1968. Arvon courses were originally held at Lumb Bank in Yorkshire, a house owned and then donated to the Foundation by Ted Hughes. They were later to spread to other centres at Totleigh Barton in Devon, and Moniack Mhor in Inverness-shire. Whatever the location, however, the atmosphere created was similar to that which had pertained in Zennor, with an experienced writer or writers coaching a small group of neophytes through informal, but uninhibitedly critical, person-to-person sessions. By the year 2000 over a thousand students a year were receiving the benefit of this training.

Barker was convinced that writers could be instructed in learning their craft, provided that they recognised that this was a lifelong process. He continued his own poetic education by reading Thomas Gray and pondering over elegies. To Sebastian he wrote, 'Have been caught up in the irresistible enchantments of Tom Gray, the elegy man. He is to my mind the ONLY poet whose sense of humour never embarrasses and always illuminates.'[16] He was fascinated by the possibility of writing his own country churchyard elegy. In December 1967 his wanderings round the Norfolk countryside took him to Thurgarton Church, stark in winter light. He was later to sketch the church in sepia ink, matching the brown of the ploughed fields around it, capturing the austerity of its architecture in long, thin pen strokes. A poem set in Thurgarton would, he thought, require an equivalent clarity and sobriety. The setting seemed ideal for a modern poem, simple but profound, on the subject of death, belief and non-belief.

Gray's 'Elegy' is one of the great English statements of neo-classical humanism. To write a modern equivalent was to question the validity of such agnostic, humanist verse. Barker's dilemma was that he had never been an agnostic in the strict sense of the word, still less an atheist. The closest he had ever come to either position had been the anti-theism of his early twenties. His solution was to write a poem of apparent doubt. 'At Thurgarton Church' is an exercise in open-ended enquiry. It also excels in that quality which in his 'Letter to the Corpse of Eliot' Barker had called Eliot's 'seeming meaning'. Barker was a master in the art of indicating one progression of meaning to the reader, while surreptitiously travelling in quite a different direction. At first sight 'At Thurgarton Church' resembles a declaration of scepticism; in fact, its credo is merely quizzical. On a first reading, the long 'o' sounds that toll through its seventeen stanzas appear to evoke cosmic and moral hollowness. What the poem says, however, is that meaninglessness is a temptation to which all of us are prone because it seems so comfortable. It is easy to live as if nothing we do ultimately matters; this is the Limbo of *A Comedy of Masks*. Such cultivated inconsequentiality is a characteristic modern desire; but it is also a universal human tendency, since it relieves us of moral responsibility. Ultimately the poem implies that the much-advertised death of God is the result of human indifference. Agnosticism is the apotheosis of human longing:

> As I stand by the porch
> I believe that no-one has heard
> here in Thurgarton Church
> a single veritable word
> save the unspoken No.
>
> The godfathered negative
> that responds to our mistaken
> incredulous and heartbroken
> desire above all to live
> as though things were not so.
>
> Desire to live as though the
> two-footed clay stood up
> proud never to know the
> tempests that rage in a cup
> under a rainbow.
>
> Desire above all to live
> as though the soul was a stone
> believing we cannot give
> or love since we are alone
> and always will be so.[17]

Like a rejected lover, God has simply and obligingly turned away his face. 'At Thurgarton Church' is a poem that re-admits the dialogue of faith by the west door. The masterless dog who howls outside the church porch is as forlorn as post-Christian humanity bereft of God. Despite this, the end of the poem is far from hopeless. The last line depicts the dead lying beneath Thurgarton's churchyard, 'awaiting no judgement day'. The phrase was as ambiguous as a poet could make it, since it suggests either that immortality is an illusion, or that we have nothing to fear from divine wrath. It is surely significant that Barker dedicated the poem to his father.

CHAPTER 44

'THE DAY FORGIVES'

Shortly after moving into Hearne Cottage eighteen years before, Barker had given rein to his sense of gladness in 'Lines on First Moving into the Country'. Later renamed 'The Mnemonic Demigod', the poem had begun with the words 'To fly from the crying ghost / Here have I come to hide / A hope and a heart'. Now, a little over a year after moving into Bintry, he wrote his most accomplished poem yet on the theme of homecoming and expiation. In the earlier poem the emphasis had been on the relief of his own spiritual burdens, now it was far more on the unforced beneficence of the landscape. 'Morning in Norfolk' was an aubade or song to the winter dawn:

> The crimson
> December morning brims over
> Norfolk, turning
> to burning Turner
> this aqueous water colour
> idyll that earlier gleamed
> so green that it seemed
> drowned. What further
> sanction, what blessing
> can the man of heart intend for
> than the supreme remission
> of dawn? For then the mind
> looking backward upon its
> too sullied yesterday,
> that rotting stack of
> resolution and refuse,
> reads in the rainbow sky

> a greater covenant,
> the tremendous pronouncement:
> the day forgives.[1]

It is impossible to read such lines without recognising that Barker appreciated the countryside of north Norfolk with almost a painter's eye. The adjectival phrase 'aqueous water colour' reads at first almost as a tautology, until you discover at the back of it a reference to the Norfolk school of watercolourists whose medium, Barker implies, once served as an almost mimetic equivalent of their subject. Streams water the countryside to the north of Aylsham: the river at the bottom of the poet's garden was the Bure, itself a tributary of the Yare. In Barker's poem the vivid hues of sunrise appear to thicken the watery textures into the opaque brilliance of an oil painting, revealing a fierceness at the heart of the land. Despite this, the final effect is one of softness, almost of mollification. 'Uninsistent' was an epithet that often occurred in the poet's conversation and letters when describing this, his chosen setting. As the years went by its mellowness was a characteristic which he learnt to appreciate, an antidote perhaps to his own temperamental ferocity.

Imperceptibly, old wounds were healing. At the end of 1966, Elizabeth Smart claimed that she had 'fallen out of love with George'. By the following year she was living almost full-time at the Dell, the cottage she had bought a few miles outside Bungay in Suffolk. Smart had initially acquired it as a retreat from the pressures of London: however, she was soon there for most of the week, leaving only for an occasional few days in her rented flat at Peter Street in Soho. The Dell, off the main road and situated next to a gravel pit at the end of a rutted track, was well named for its seclusion and luxuriance amidst unpromising landscape. Here she cultivated a fine garden, drawing on her skills as a horticulturalist, and coaxing from the East Anglian soil an impressive range of trees, flowers, shrubs and herbs. She divided the garden into areas, each named after a distinctive feature: a statuette of a bear, for example, overlooked the 'bear garden'. In July 1967 she wrote in her journal: 'My garden: today two pale spikes of gladioli with a Vogue rose again in bloom and the lobelia looking healthy. Otherwise, the garden is dominated by poppies, marigolds, and nasturtiums. The sweet peas I planted here and there are out and OK but outshone. A late Lupin – pink and yellow – is out. Geraniums. Canary creeper. The bear garden is flowery and wild, dominated by mayweed.' The ground floor of the house was soon book-lined, the shelves of living room and passageway bending beneath her copious library, which included an important collection of the literature of the 1940s. Here with increasing frequency she entertained guests, including the Barkers. Since Elizabeth had renounced her claims over George, her relationship with Elspeth became important and sustaining for both women. Elspeth herself came to regard their rapport as one of 'friendship and love; it brought us to write to one another regularly, and to stay with each other regularly, and to stay with each other independently of George'. Soon Elizabeth was regularly making the forty-mile trip northwards to Bintry, riding over on her moped for Saturday night carousals.[2]

As the Barkers' social life expanded, Bintry became fuller of children and of animals with each successive month. From friends of Ilse's in Sussex, they acquired two donkeys, a mother whom Raffaella christened Flowering Gold and a daughter whom Bruddy baptised Tilda. Raffaella's love of riding was indulged by George until she fell off Flowering Gold and broke her arm, upon which he demanded that both the donkeys be shot; only Raffaella's intercession saved them. The family explored the nearby countryside on foot: Mossy Mere woods for instance, which lay across the cornfield to the north-west of the church, or nearby John's Water, where the children bathed in summer. In the grounds of Mannington Hall, home to a branch of the famous Walpoles, they discovered a ruined chapel with statues: a magic, secret place.

When, in August 1969, Sebastian was married to a strikingly beautiful girl called Julie, he moved to a cottage in the village of Thwaite, south of Norwich, and an hour and a half from Itteringham by car. Sebastian registered for a degree in literature at the new University of East Anglia, thus putting a future in physiological research behind him. It was a decision about which George had mixed feelings: he had been proud of Corpus Christi and his son's dedication to science. When Sebastian and Julie moved to Reepham, a few miles from Itteringham, the feeling of family closeness intensified. In Reepham they lived in the old bakery, which Sebastian restored while supporting his growing family by stripping furniture. At the same time, his apprenticeship as a poet continued under his father's watchful eye.

At Easter 1968 Fiona Sinclair, George's former student from York, drove up from London, bringing with her John Cox, now in his final year. They returned the following autumn, this time accompanied by Fiona's fiancé, a Winchester and Cambridge educated lawyer called Hedley Marten, who was doing his pupillage at Lincoln's Inn. Marten's first meeting with the poet conformed to a pattern that Barker's friendships often assumed. Hedley was intellectual to his fingertips, a classically educated scholar equipped with all the academic advantages that Barker despised, envied and admired. After a raucous, soul-baring Saturday night, he returned to London, from which he wrote, regretting that 'Apollo cannot easily consort with Dionysus'.[3] Nevertheless the two men found that they had much in common. Barker, after all, knew that respect must be paid to the virtuous philosopher as well as the chameleon poet; besides in his opinion Marten had a creative potential that he always seemed to glance at sideways. This askance, self-protective attitude was very attractive to

Barker, who knew only too well the cost of too slavish an adherence to the demands of Dionysus.

In any case, Barker was now disciplining his drinking. Apart from the religiously observed Saturday evening bacchanalia, alcohol was banned from the house. Indeed, during his increasingly frequent visits, John Cox for one was struck by the rigour of the regime at Bintry. From half-past six in the morning, often earlier, the study door was firmly secured from the inside. Nobody – not even the most cherished child – was permitted to enter until lunchtime. When Barker was not writing, he might try out poems on tape; several cassette recorders came to litter his desktop. As well as poetry, he was also bringing together his prose pieces for the volume of *Essays* which he had for some time promised to deliver to Martin Green at MacGibbon & Kee. Green helped him to assemble the journalism of four decades. The result, published in 1970 as *Essays*, was a volume of critical writing that was pungently provocative, entertaining and never academic. It also contained fresh material: a set of philosophical aphorisms called 'Asterisks', culled from earlier notebooks but collated in Quick Street, and 'Maximes', a collection of observations of life in France. If a theory united the volume, it was that poetry was inscrutable, as difficult to analyse or account for as nature itself. In effect, the book represented a reluctant excursion into the alien field of criticism. 'Asterisks' poses the unanswerable question: 'What is the *meaning* of this poem? What is the *meaning* of the sea?'[4]

Literary criticism attracted Barker less and less and science more and more. Sebastian's physical proximity from 1969 helped him to absorb recent scientific theory and he became, for a layman, respectably informed. Such interest was far from irrelevant to his thinking about poetry. In both fields he grew more and more resistant to the naïvely positivist view which insists that all phenomena be explained in quantifiable terms. The collapse of classical mechanistic physics, for example, seemed to him to hold out new hope for art. At any rate, it offered a much wider scope to poetry than that conceded by the bleak and reductionist criticism of I.A. Richards, who had stripped all verse down to a series of 'pseudo-statements'. Increasingly, Barker came to view the function of the poet as analogous to the interactive role ascribed to the observer of subatomic phenomena by Heisenberg's Indeterminacy Principle. Heisenberg had claimed that the scientist transforms the sub-microscopic world while observing it. In Barker's view the poet could achieve an equivalent effect through evocation and description.

For much the same reason he was chary of recent developments in biology and experimental psychology. In rapid succession he read the works of the American behaviourist B.F. Skinner, to which Sebastian had introduced him. Drawing on the earlier research of Pavlov, Skinner had asserted that all human action and thought is reducible to a series of conditioned reflexes. The theory disconcerted Barker for several reasons. Its denial of individual spontaneity seemed to fly in the face of the Christian doctrine of free will. In his book *Verbal Behaviour*, furthermore, Skinner had claimed that everything humans say or write is dictated by patterns of association; the hypothesis appeared to convert the poet into a mere megaphone for the commonplace. Barker sensed behind such theorising the menacing presence of a highly reactionary political programme. His suspicions were confirmed in 1971 when Skinner published a book called *Beyond Freedom and Dignity*, consigning liberty to the status of an illusion. Barker was especially dismayed by Skinner's experimental methods, which involved mistreating rats. Gradually Skinner's vision of human life as a bundle of jerky responses fused with Pascal's dread of the cosmic void to produce a nightmare of impersonality that would recur in Barker's poetry to the end of his life.

A voracious reader, he became an even more ravenous conversationalist, though he preferred individuals to groups, which sometimes made him feel uncomfortable. For Cox, Barker excelled in the creation of a 'magic portable space' where mutual immersion of minds was possible. 'It was almost a sacred space from which the horrors of the everyday were expelled, like the *horkos* of the ancient Greeks, places where lightning had once struck. He had this terrific power of concentrating, an ability to focus enormously upon you when he was with you.'[5] Such *tête à têtes* might occur anywhere: over the long table in the kitchen; in the Mercedes; in a café or a church or, on warm summer evenings, in the arbour that friends had constructed to the west of the house between the playroom window and the barn. In such settings Barker created a ceremony of mutual trust, drawing his interlocutors in, especially the more timid, acting as an open conduit for ideas: enabling them to flow, to clash, to be tested and compared, inducing through these means either active agreement or, more frequently, humorous dissent. By the 1960s conversation in Soho occasionally seemed a parody of itself; it was alive and kicking in Norfolk.

Barker was at this time very much taken with Chinese philosophy, and in particular the schools associated with Confucius and Li Po. John Cox carved him a 'Li Po seat' among the reeds by the river bank and on it, during the warmer months, he would sit for hours contemplating the unruffled progress of the Bure. If others joined him, he would talk of Marshall McLuhan (despite his deleterious influence upon John Farrelly), or of the work of Buckminster Fuller. His increasing preoccupation with connections between poetry and religion had drawn him to Wittgenstein, whose epistemological writings appeared to offer the chance of defining the boundary between that which can be expressed, and that which must forever remain inexpressible. Wittgenstein's *Tractatus* had confined meaningful statements to logical deductions, and object relations: 'everything which is the case'. Beyond, lay the uncharted region of 'that of which we cannot speak'. For Barker this hinterland was the realm of poetry, of the linguistic unknown; in the words of his 'Letter Addressed to the Corpse of Eliot', it was 'the cry of the lonely / bittern at evening by the lake'. In the *Tractatus*, the only feasible reaction to this ineffable sphere is said to be silence, but Barker was also intrigued by fragmentary hints in Wittgenstein's later philosophy as to a possible mystical role for language. He was, Cox discovered, resistant to distinctions between refined and popular literature. When Cox remarked upon what he called the 'wonderful emptiness' of Raymond Chandler's world, Barker agreed strongly. But he also talked to Cox of the persistent appeal of Catholicism, of the 'terrible authority' of the Church and of the exemplary rigour of the saints. He protested himself appalled by the cruelty of St Augustine. He spoke of the chilling severity of the Jesuits, from which the unassuming charity of St Francis had always seemed to him such a blessed relief.[6]

So, even when his personal circumstances were settled, he remained restless and searching. If Carpenter was dying on his feet while proclaiming his agility, Barker was pyrotechnical in his celebration of calm. *Intellectually* indeed, the notion of peace had become suspect to him. To Sebastian, yet to define a religious position, he was to write:

What is it that the acidulous self analysis of your letter seeks to find? It is peace. What is it that compels the intelligence to decline an armistice of the soul? It is a passion for war. Myself I believe that the idea of peace is a delusion ('They created a wilderness and called it peace') . . . I believe the biological definition of life could be expressed in such terms as: 'this creature suffers, thus it is alive'.[7]

Barker's own torment was a constant fear that Bintry might be taken from him, as Hearne had so dramatically been. His mind had been concentrated on the possibility by reading Swinburne's 'Laus Veneris' and the recent unexpurgated re-issue of Aubrey Beardsley's novella *Under the Hill*. Both works portray the vagaries of the legendary German minstrel Tännhauser, whose thraldom to venery roughly parallels Tam Lin's. In the border ballad Tam Lin is trapped by fairies; in the German tale Tännhauser is imprisoned in a mountain called the Venusberg by the goddess of sexual love. He breaks loose and appeals for absolution to the pope, who tells him that he is beyond redeeming. Eventually the dry olive wood of the pope's staff flowers, signalling belated absolution. The redemption comes too late for Tännhauser, who is already back under Venus's orders. In Wagner's opera based on this myth,

Tännhauser is saved by a woman's love; in Barker's reading of the myth there was no expiation. He improvised a set of highly pictorial lyrics under the title 'Venusberg', depicting a frigid universe ice-bound by lechery. The sequence expressed a nightmare less of sexual love, than of copulation as a clockwork reflex, an orgy orchestrated by Skinner. Though the references to the Tännhauser myth were oblique, they were undeniably present: first, in the title of the sequence (which also implies the 'Mons Veneris' or female genitalia), and, second, in the position of the speaker, helplessly enslaved by his own destructive appetites, the voice of which echoes endlessly, 'I cannot / redeem. I redeem / I cannot redeem.' The climax to the sequence was written in Barker's study one daybreak; it consisted of a supplication to the goddess of sex, imploring her to leave this one house of his alone:

> Venus Castratrix, no
> not here. Leave this
> wall of ordered love, these
> cradles of innocence, and
> the domestic day. I
> watch the white-bellied
> saw-toothed Venus slide
> and glide up the
> narrow sun rising reaches
> of the little river in
> Norfolk, leaving, as she passes,
> rolling in dawn
> bright whirls and jets of
> pearl, the heart like a
> bleeding river and crimson
> lake.[8]

Fifteen years later, when his last *Collected Poems* were being compiled, Barker told the editor to cut out 'That "Venusberg" nonsense!' He pretended that his reasons for this exclusion were aesthetic. As art, however, 'Venusberg' is exemplary. The fact is that its vision of corrosive sexuality was just too close to the bone.

The relative tranquillity of Bintry – relative, that is, to Barker's former households – was partly Elspeth's achievement and partly the product of a more-or-less sustained routine. If melancholy recurred, Barker might have occasional recourse either to sedatives or to stimulants. By the late 1960s Benzedrine and Methedrine had become difficult to obtain. He acquired 'purple hearts' and 'speed', from friends such as an obliging and attentive doctor, John MacNeill. His daughter Rose, who was often resident at Bintry or within easy reach at the Dell, was another source.

One by one his children from previous unions were coming back to him. Though Jessica's children were effectively lost to him, he was in constant contact by post and through visits with Dede and her sons. Sebastian he saw several times a week. By 1970 Rose was using Bintry as a refuge from the turbulence of the rest of her life. She had now had a second child, her daughter Jane, by the Ghanaian-born guitarist of the rock group Taj Mahal. At twenty-four she had developed into a vivid, compelling and voluptuous young woman with a temperament summed up by Elspeth as 'exuberant, Irish, given to low life'. It appeared to Oliver Bernard that, of all Barker's children, Rose had most in common with Big Mumma, whose earthiness and wicked sense of humour she shared.[9] She had also inherited Elizabeth's zest for life, a quality which Elspeth's children recognised and admired in her. These strengths co-existed with a disastrous tendency to inflict emotional wounds on herself. Rose was chronically attracted to male losers. Possessing something of Sebastian's seriousness, she had little of his application. Barker was exasperated by the mess she seemed to be making of her life and at the same time admiring of her courage. He had come to revere in others the blend of defiance and vulnerability. Rose had both qualities in abundance. He counselled her:

Dearest of Roses,
You write to me 'I must re-write to you' and I think that you mean you must and will write to me again. I hope this is so, for a reason (and I would continue to hope this is so for a reason) you will not find it hard to forgive, which is the ceremony of mutual love. In the kingdom of the blind the one eyed man may be king, but in the empire of the spirit (I am simply swapping the Germanic imperatives with you) absolutely everyone is dispossessed. We await (it is the destiny of every generation of vipers) the return of the dove with the unbelievable sign in its beak. 'If these islands had not existed they would not have risen out of the sea to crown his passion'. Or, 'Whose is the wisdom we have lost in knowledge, where is the knowledge we have lost in information?' You ask me questions, and you give yourself answers: this, I believe, is as it should be. What should *not* be is the Grammar of Dissent. I think that you castigate your conscience – that is, your spiritual and not your moral conscience – in order to persuade yourself that it exists because it suffers. But the inversion of the proposition is much truer: it suffers simply because it exists. In this sense there is no such luxury as suffering: I myself once had the intellectual temerity to write the line

> The pain is eternal because the cause had died.
>
> I believe (you will forgive the word in your latitudes) that these things are not simply spiritual matters: they are simply religious. I mean by this the seeking for appropriate ceremonies of human (and even, god help us, divine) love. And by love I mean the impulse that draws up out of the sea those islands which exist only in order to crown the love that created them. Enough of this. Ova to you. Kisses.
> Your loving father George.[10]

Barker began to share a quality with Emily Dickinson: his best poems now read like letters, and his best letters like poems. He would answer his children's missives by return of post, often at very great length. This man who had once been so ready to hit out, or to inflict on others acts of casual humiliation, had come to excel above all else in the ceremonial caress of reciprocal affection. 'Ceremony', indeed, was a favourite term of his at the time and the quality informed much of the way he behaved towards his family. The younger children came to recognise and expect certain rituals: the visits to churches; the explanations of place names; the stories; the birthday protocols; the formal and courteous way in which their father would hand them something as simple as a doughnut; the beckoning hand as he called, 'Come to me, child'; the elaborately and affectionately bestowed kiss. Much of this had about it an element of self-mockery, or gestural hyperbole: but the playfulness had a serious depth to it that could be appreciated by anybody with the wit to do so. It buoyed the children up; it supported their world.

In 1970 Barker published his second book of poems for children *To Aylsham Fair*, the 'fair' of the title being the farmers' show held in the nearby town every August. Dedicated to 'Roderick Jo' (Progles), the volume included songs to the seasons, and an address to a domestic tomcat who has forsaken the pleasures of the hearth for nocturnal escapades, 'hunting and stalking et cetera'. There were episodes in the life of the Dibby Dubby Dhu; a dialogue between a heartbroken owl and the moon; and a poem describing the Aylsham show, spoken by a local farmer. Every one of these pieces showed evidence of what, thirty-five years previously, Yeats had called Barker's 'rhythmic invention akin to Gerard Hopkins'. All appealed as much to the ear as to the logical sense. Progles himself, not yet three at the time, remembers sitting mesmerised by the play of cross-rhythms as his father read the poems, but not able to understand a word.[11] About this time Barker told Fiona Sinclair that a child's third birthday – another of the famous 'ceremonies' – should be conducted as a wake for the infantile consciousness, since it marked the end of that complete self-absorption enjoyed by the very young and their departure from the autonomous imaginative world they had occupied until then. It was to this level beneath conscious understanding that these poems, in part at least, were aiming.

While Barker directed the children's artistic development, Elspeth attended to their formal education. She had grown up in a family where reading and a love of the classics were taken for granted. She therefore decided to teach classical Greek to her own brood and to a number of other local children, including Tristram Hull's sons Joshua and Jake. On wintry Sunday afternoons, as the wind wailed outside the kitchen window, and while Elspeth baked buns, cakes, and loaves, she imparted the Greek alphabet, which they all knew by the age of three; then elementary nouns, greetings and grammatical constructions. 'The children wanted to do this; they enjoyed the myths and loved the alphabet; they saw it as a secret code. It was just fun, nothing elaborate.'[12] A little conceited at these attainments, the children would sit apart at birthday parties raising their Corona cherryades with the literary toast 'Ho biblos!'

In the summer of 1970 Elspeth suffered a miscarriage – miserable for her and disconcerting for George, who had come to prize the gift of children above all things. In August, when the film of L.P. Hartley's *The Go Between* was shot in Norfolk, she and the children were taken on as extras. They spent the rest of the summer months cavorting around the pump in the back yard, while their father prepared his latest adult volume, *Poems of Places and People*, for the press. 'The poems of people' included 'Letter Addressed to the Corpse of Eliot' as well as threnodies for MacBryde, for Herbert Read (who had died in 1967) and Vernon Watkins (who had died in 1968). The 'poems of place', notably 'At Thurgarton Church', were celebrations of landscape. All of the pieces were marked by a newfound sense of belonging. Several showed a mastery of conventional form. 'At Thurgarton Church', 'Whipmawhomagate' and two of the 'III Poems Written in Surrey' were stanzaic. Though thematically 'At Thurgarton Church' leant on Gray, its sonorous open vowels also harked back to Tennyson. When Tony Kingsmill received the book on Hydra, he wrote to Barker to say that reading this poem was like listening to a great bell tolling insistently. Barker had also managed a lopsided deployment of the ballad form in 'Drunk Song':

> Johnny are you there, are you there, are you there?
>   Johnny are you there lovely Johnny?
>   I can see the Demon Rum
>   bouncing on its little bum
>   at the bar of Kingdom Come
> and hear the thunder of the Crown and Anchor money.[13]

Other poems explored new techniques. 'Morning in Norfolk', the letter to Eliot, 'Venusberg' and 'Kew Gardens' – which recalls his meeting with David Gascoyne on 1 September 1939 – were written in short lines unfurling in shapes congruent with their meaning. These pieces were to become favourites of Barker's at public readings, where he would declaim them slowly, letting each successive syllable drop into a pool of silence, qualifying through its unique place in the structure the meaning of the words that preceded it.

Since he was working in both stanzaic and free-verse forms, he became increasingly preoccupied with defining the difference between poetry and prose. In April 1971 he gave a fifteen-minute radio talk entitled 'The Jubjub Bird or Some Remarks on the Prose Poem'. A poet, he said, could write something which superficially resembled prose but which possessed the aural density of a poem. Eliot, Blake and Auden had all done this. Between 'Morning in Norfolk' and prose, however, there was a twofold difference. Poetry employed recurrent and hypnotic rhythms, while prose characteristically did not. Poetry also required of the reader a willing suspension of disbelief, where prose by and large did not. To the extent that prose approached a state where both of these conditions were met, it resembled poetry.[14]

At one point, the talk hinted at his own future development. He was speaking of the work of Rimbaud, which 'constituted a deliberate act of violence calculated to blow several large holes in the petrified Versailles of classical French prosody'. Barker had himself, in his more daring moments, performed an equivalent assault on the ossified forms of English metre. He would continue to do so, with results that would soon become clear.

CHAPTER 45

'FRIENDS AND ODDFELLOWS'

As ever, money was in short supply. Barker resuscitated the recently deceased Professor Max Welhaus, and revamped him as an early Viennese exponent of Concrete Poetry, writing out a selection of his 'verses' and ferrying them down to London, where, accompanied by John Cox, he sold them to various book-dealers.[1] Since the pickings from this nefarious trade were minimal, he supplemented them by putting together his third volume of verse for children. *The Alphabetical Zoo* (1972), was a bestiary on the conventional A-to-Z pattern. At the end it featured a mythical fish called the Zong, which swam vertically upon the water, 'condemned to exist in perpetual motion' with a restlessness that seemed to reflect on the author's own spiritual state.

Barker had scarcely enjoyed the experience of Buffalo, but teaching remained another potential source of income. Because creative writing was the one subject he was equipped to teach, and college courses in this discipline were confined to America, America again it would have to be. When an invitation arrived from the University of Wisconsin at Madison to act as visiting professor of creative writing for the academic year 1971–2, he was not in a position to refuse.

As before, the timing was unfortunate. On 8 June 1971 the Barkers' third son Samuel was born. The baby was christened in the chapel of Drumtochty Castle as Samuel Drumtochty Inigo. Allan Massie, who had just finished a stint as a schoolmaster at Drumtochty Castle School and was shortly to embark on a formative period teaching English in Rome, was his godfather.[2] In the absence of an overriding nickname, the baby was henceforth known as Sam. To maintain four children in the depths of the Wisconsin winter would use up most of the funds Barker earned, so there was no choice but for him to leave for Madison alone, leaving Elspeth to manage at Bintry. The envisaged difficulties, however, were less practical than emotional. 'I'd often been on my own with the children,' Elspeth insists. 'Mostly it was much easier than coping with George as well.' Besides, Sebastian and Julie were within easy reach and John Cox was to come up from London to stay in the house. Nonetheless, from his experience in Buffalo, Barker knew that another separation, and period of enforced isolation for him, would be hard. In early September, he reluctantly flew to the States.

It was a gorgeous autumn in Madison. Barker arrived to a temperature of 82°F, and settled into a campus condominium at 10a, University Houses, among a lot of other short-stay academic visitors – Indian philologists, Swiss psychiatrists and professors of geology.[3] The flat was spacious and airy and had a doorknocker that played 'Gaudeamus Igitur'. He reported back that his fifty students were intelligent and had heard of Hopkins, though not of sprung rhythm. Ten days later he had revised his opinion. Writing to Sebastian to commiserate on a miscarriage of Julie's, he conveyed his second impressions. The Hopkins of whom his students had heard was, he now gathered, the founder of Johns Hopkins University. When he had informed them that his Hopkins was a Jesuit priest they had, or so his letters back home claimed, erupted in a chorus of disbelief and protest at this naked papist propaganda.

Realisation of his students' ignorance of British literary tradition seems to have stumped him momentarily. Re-creating these episodes for correspondents back home, he adopted a facetious tone behind which it is not difficult to discern a profound conflict in his own attitudes towards literary creativity. With one part of his mind – the part he usually revealed to students – he genuinely believed that the writing of poetry was an occupation available to everybody. This reassuring egalitarianism, however, was at odds with a rooted conviction akin to Eliot's that the ability to write acceptable verse was a rare gift only worth encouraging in the few. Writing to Sebastian, he resolved this dilemma by recourse to playful mockery: his class, he told him, was divided into two groups: there were the 'Howling Shitters' who believed that spontaneity was everything, and there were the 'Poultry Lovers', who liked what they had read. His adoption of these characteristically hyperbolic descriptions barely disguised the fact that each camp reflected one of his own deeply held beliefs. He too welcomed spontaneity, but he also prized discipline and tradition. His quandary was exacerbated by his discovery that the tradition to which the 'poultry lovers' most easily related was one over which he was also in two minds, consisting as it did of such, to him, comparatively second-rate figures as William Cullen Bryant and Jean Ingelow.

The situation was made no easier by the vogue for 'confessional poetry' then in full flood in American writing programmes. The result was to turn the teacher into a sort of counsellor, therapist or priest. Every morning, George told Sebastian, he sat in his office like a secular confessor making himself available to young people who seemed less interested in poetry than in the state of their souls. His reaction to these passionate diclosures was to direct them towards a place where they could at least confide in an authentic, ordained confessor: he told them all to go and live in Sicily. All seemed to be victims of broken marriages and to possess a hungry nostalgia for some lost Eden of sincerity. To exacerbate matters, the Vietnam War was at its height. Over all the male students there hung the threat of the draft board, an institution much like that before which Barker had been forced to present himself in New York during the autumn of 1941. In this no-man's-land of the Midwest, he wrote, human communication had been consigned to the dustbin of history. In place of ordinary human affection there had emerged something called 'personal relationships', which turned out for the most part to consist of 'passionate acquaintanceships lasting three and a half weeks'.[4] When one morning he described the countryside around Bintry to a young man called Grey Silver, he watched the student's eyes slowly fill with tears.

To begin with Barker felt as lonely as he had at Buffalo. For the first time since those dreadful weeks before the Villa del Sole, he was reduced to sitting alone each evening over his wine, or once over one of the few bottles of Cinzano to be found in the entire city of Madison. In Buffalo he had watched *The Singing Nun* repeatedly to keep himself sane; in Madison he resorted to *One Hundred and One Dalmatians*. His isolation was confounded by the fact that whenever he phoned Bintry, he encountered silence. Fearing the worst, he imagined betrayal, desertion and guilt; he wrote to Sebastian and begged him to intercede.

The reason for the silence soon became apparent. The bill had not been paid, and the phone had been cut off.[5] Two days later, he wrote apologetically to Sebastian: the phone was now working, and he had spoken to his beloved 'Cruella de Ville'. She had agreed to do her utmost to ease the intolerable separation by joining him after Christmas. He would fly back to England on 16 December, and return to America with her early in the New Year. Her presence would make America tolerable to him: 'I cannot', he insisted, 'do it alone.'[6]

In the meantime his solitude intensified the melancholia out of which some of his best work sometimes came. That autumn he had particular cause to grieve. Four years before, on 11 April 1967, Georgina had phoned Elizabeth to tell her that David Archer had died.[7] Georgina's message had expressed a piquant half-truth. For years now Archer's existence had been a living death. Through his own improvidence, the trust fund set up for him by Dom Moraes had long since folded. He had found a job as a sales assistant in the lighting basement at Selfridges, where he had tried to organise a 'cultural group' for the other employees, but being no more efficient at selling anglepoises than he had been at selling books, he had soon been asked to leave.

Archer had sunk to grimmer depths. For months he had survived by cadging pound notes from friends, which he would as often as not spend on a bouquet for the benefactor concerned. He had fallen into the role of full-time scrounger around Soho, bemoaning the dud hand that fate had dealt him: 'I used to sell copies of Dylan's *Eighteen Poems* for 3/6d each. Nowadays they fetch five hundred pounds. It makes me absolutely furious!' At one time Archer had shared a pleasant flat with John Deakin; now he was forced into a Salvation Army hostel in Tower Hamlets. His homosexual activities, never very flourishing, had dwindled to a sorry trawl of rejection and pain. On Saturday, 16 October 1971 he approached Stephen Fothergill, a long-time habitué of the Soho scene, at the entrance to the Swiss Pub in Old Compton Street, clutching a large bottle of aspirins. 'Do you think that these will do the trick?' he asked and fled into the night.[8] Forthergill tried to organise a rescue party, but by now Archer had exhausted both the good will of his friends and his own will to live. That night he went back to the hostel and wrote a few brief letters of explanation to his friends. In the morning the cleaners found him dead. His death certificate recorded the cause as 'acute salicylate poisoning' and listed his occupation as 'shop assistant'. 'His need', wrote Elizabeth in *The Times*, 'was not so much for the money as for the wherewithal to make gestures: grand, courtly, quixotic gestures, like frail representatives of civilisation in our bomb-and-computer age ... He has already merited a rich and civilised footnote in the literary history of our times. He deserves an ode.'[9]

For Barker, Archer's passing was more harrowing than that of Eliot, who at least had died fulfilled. Archer had been his unswerving supporter since that day in September 1932 when, aged nineteen, Barker had first put his head round the door of the Parton Street bookshop. At times Archer had seemed besotted with his protégé: there had doubtless been an element of unrequited homoerotic passion in his loyalty. In Barker he had inspired a mixture of gratitude and guilt, a combination all the more poignant since Archer had epitomised that delicate English self-consciousness towards which he had always felt protectively, if exasperatedly, drawn. Archer's self-consciousness had been intensified, made more eloquent, by his halting courtesy. He was the wounded and flawed being at the implied receiving end of Barker's compassionate aesthetic. Snowbound in Wisconsin, Barker paid tribute:

> To lift a hand
> to those who have gone before us
> those friends and

> oddfellows to whom
> only death can restore us
> (I have heard
> as in day dreams
> them calling sometimes for us
> out of a silence that seems
> like a dead chorus)
> to lift a hand in farewell
> for them at the black bell
> neither you David nor I
> found this a hard thing to do –
> for they, most of them, died
> in a sort of twisted pride
> or as they lifted up
> the whiskey in the cup
> or turning a handsome head
> in honour among the dead
> so that, with the wave
> of a hand toward the grave
> you and I, as they went
> down out of the present,
> could seem to call:
> 'Stand up and speak well
> in the empty hall
> of heaven or empty hell
> for us all.'[10]

This was a magnificently moving piece – arguably the finest elegy for an individual that Barker had so far written. With its gentle and uninsistent rhyme scheme, its sustained rhythm, the piece had the effect of bestowing on the transient bibulous life of pre- and post-war bohemia grace and tragic nobility. Barker could not regret the poem's style, but he deplored the necessity of writing in so sombre a vein. To Sebastian he wrote that he now seemed to sit around like some hideous carrion bird waiting for his friends to drop off 'so that I can start a waking and a flapping and a versifying'.[11] He feared that he was coming a little too close for comfort to his vulture from *The Alphabetical Zoo*: 'I love offal and scrag / or a bit of old rag / and for sweets I eat eyeballs of camels; / the most delicious / of edible dishes / for me is the dead flesh of mammals.'

As the snow of a Madison winter deepened around him, Barker did the work for which he had been hired. Standing out from the anonymous faces in the classroom were those of three students to whom he had very much warmed: Barbara Guenther, Arthur Sacks, and sprightly, humorous Woody Ostrow. Woody had decided that Barker was a great poet whose presence in Madison should be preserved for posterity. He took to hiding with his camera in the shrubbery outside University Houses, hoping to catch a glimpse of The Poet Striding Forth Inspired. Since his subject was fully aware of his presence, what emerged on film was a series of snapshots of the Poet Stalking Forth Enraged. At weekends Barker escaped from the campus. For $15 he purchased a clapped-out Dodge, which he drove up to Illinois. Chicago, he reported, was 'haunted by the ghosts of dead cattle', though the skyscrapers seemed to grow from the lakeside 'like mathematical formulae in crystal'. He flew across to San Francisco to visit his niece Veronica, arriving to her astonishment with a Hungarian princess on each arm. In a fit of despondency he made his way to New York, where Robin Prising and and Willie Coakley at West 71st Street found him deluged by the glooms. Barker was living only for 16 December. His students had caught the mood and had taken to greeting him in the overheated corridors with cries of 'Only nine days to go; only eight days to go.'[12] After the final week of the semester, which passed 'like a slow motion movie of overladen camels crossing snowbound Siberian tundra on Sunday', he flew to Heathrow, where Sebastian had driven the family up to meet him. 'He was obviously', Elspeth commented, 'going out of his mind from loneliness and drink.'

Shortly after Christmas Barker recorded his radio talk 'Homage to Housman' for the Third. In January 1972 he returned to Madison for the second semester with the all-important additions of Elspeth and Sam. The American poet Sebastian Lockwood and his wife Roseanne, then living at Dairy Cottages near Itteringham, volunteered to look after the other children. The Lockwoods moved into Bintry, where they inherited three infants and all the animals.[13] The previous February, for his fifty-eighth birthday, Elspeth had bought Barker a flutter of doves, which had settled in the branches of the large birch tree out on the front lawn. The Lockwoods were to keep the children and the doves under control. In the unimpressed eyes of the children it appeared that, as card-carrying hippies, they had interpreted their duties as serving vegetarian food – including brown rice which they detested – and meditating over rather than feeding, the doves. Elspeth wrote constantly, updating instructions. In the meantime she made a temporary home out of 10a University Houses with its white walls, parquet flooring and french windows. Out in the shrubbery Woody still had not relaxed his vigil, but Barker had learned to appreciate the company of his students as seldom before and Elspeth also took to them. The class of fifty had now split irreparably into factions. The 'Howling Shitters' were no longer even speaking to the 'Poultry Lovers', and each insisted on giving a separate party for George's fifty-ninth birthday. In honour of the celebration the sky was temporarily blue.[14]

Soon George's students prevailed upon Elspeth to read Tennyson and Housman to a select gathering. The result was so gratifying, that a small hall was hired for her to repeat the experiment in front of a larger group of sophomores, juniors and seniors. The group swelled to several hundred students, faculty and townsfolk. 'I probably drank a fair amount before the reading,' Elspeth conceded, 'never having done such a thing in public, and being very nervous.' Barker reported to Sebastian that, 'she read "The Lotos Eaters" like an addict'. Her reading was followed by rapturous applause and by Barker's rendition of 'The Love Song of J. Alfred Prufrock' to the accompaniment of a section from Schubert's Unfinished Symphony booming from loudspeakers.[15]

The winter weather was unrelenting until 21 March, when Barker and Elspeth took the Dodge to Devil's Lake, 'looking for the old demon, but we found nothing but squirrels'. During the Easter break they planned to drive the car to either Texas or New Orleans. But first the exhaust pipe fell off and had to be secured with a coat hanger and then one of Barker's students drove the car headlong into a Porsche. The Barkers made their way to New Orleans in a hired car, watching the climate change with the geographical latitude until they found the full heat of summer along the southern reaches of the Mississippi.[16] By this time in Bintry the Lockwoods were fraught. The doves had flown away and the children had concluded that hippiedom was tyranny in cheesecloth. Elspeth and Sam flew back in April, leaving Barker to his devices for the short remainder of the semester. He consoled himself by smoking marijuana and spending desultory hours observing the yachts scud sideways across Lake Michigan. Having learned that an 'A' grade secured exemption from the Draft, he swallowed his misgivings and submitted a mark sheet consisting exclusively of alphas, before leaving on 14 May.

He was followed to Bintry by a straggle of students. Woody came with his camera and Doug Segal, a creative writing major and enthusiastic amateur musician, arrived with a guitar on which he strummed 'Puff the Magic Dragon' to the children. They feasted on crabs, picnicked at the beach near Holkham Hall and swam in John's Water, soothing after the summer heat. Goldfinches played in the great pine outside the study window, which, as a play on the name of the house, had been christened the Bin Tree. Bruddy, who was now six, was prone to tantrums, during which he lay on the playroom floor and would not be consoled.[17] Barker understood such moodiness, believing it akin to authentic adult melancholy of which he himself had some experience.

On 14 August Barker's radio talk on Housman was broadcast. It defended Housman's poems against the prevailing view of them as 'the lachrymose sentimentalities of a lonely and cynical misanthrope over times and friends gone by'. On the contrary, Barker argued, Housman's work evoked ultimate pathos by reason, paradoxically, of the surface frivolity and acidulous bathos, qualities that might be found in Barker's own work.[18] Pathos, he seemed to imply, was the product less of a conventional or hidebound mind than of a sensibility so deeply stirred as sometimes to reach out for the consolations of the ordinary. Such was the true glory of this poetry, sometimes mistakenly called minor.

In December, again on the Third, he defended the reputation of another reputedly minor poet, Lionel Johnson, whom he called

> one of that small and precious band of poets, the unacknowledged wallflowers. For there are poets who seem to have been constructed of interior illuminations rather than lightning, and therefore do not set the Thames on fire. They are the poets to whose memories few votive offerings are brought by societies of admirers, but whose poems are especially prized, I believe, by other poets ... There is absolutely no danger whatsoever of such poets ever becoming popular: they seem, indeed, to carry a sort of *noli me tangere* written on their faces and their poems. Myself I think it has to do with an innate sense of refinement in the nature both of such men and their work. Neither the poem nor the man has the faculty of inclination to sell itself to anyone at all. Such poets might almost be said to be talking to themselves, and for this reason could be called pure poets in the sense that they do not behave like prostitutes.[19]

Housman and Johnson had not sold out to fashion; nor had Barker. They had not fitted conveniently into a literary movement; neither did he. Forty years before in *Alanna Autumnal* Barker had philosophically referred to himself as 'the minor bird on the bough'. By 1972, he was questioning the whole system of qualitative judgement on which the epithet 'minor' was based.

He was now writing poems of unshowy individuality which took their cue from Archer's death. The poetry of *In Memory of David Archer* meditates on the elusive nature of the deceased; beyond that, it addresses the enigma of human destiny. What force is it, the poems ask, which moulds an individual life into a given shape? What ensures the predominance of one set of consequences over the many hypothetical outcomes attendant upon each person, each poem and each act? It was not Archer's death alone that provoked these thoughts. In January 1972 John Farrelly had died in a distant and solitary bedroom, smothered by his own pillow. It had not been clear whether or not this was an accident. He had been buried in St Louis with the Catholic rites he loved. Barker had also been reassessing his own past, to which several of these pieces allude. In retrospect, such lives seemed flawed but glorious, imperfect yet inevitable. The poems in this book are all responses to Wittgenstein's suggestive hint in the *Tractatus*, 'It is not *the nature* of things that inspires wonder, but their very existence.'[20] That each of us, amid the thicket of hypothetical alternatives, should have led this one life, that each object should have triumphed against the million and one reasons for its not being there, was as much of a mystery to Barker as it had been to Wittgenstein.

The theme of the conquest of the actual over the hypothetical harks back to the opening of Eliot's 'Burnt Norton' ('Footfalls echo in the memory / Down the passage which we did not take / Towards the door we never opened . . .'). But Barker was also aware of its comic potential. One poem describes the poet being stalked along a moonlit Chelsea pavement by a doppelgänger, who turns out to be a dog.[21] The more serious pieces wrestle with symbols for the sublime arbitrariness of existence. That summer Barker went for a walk along the beach at Overstrand, where he discovered driftwood lying on the foreshore. The flotsam became a metaphor:

> The white stones and the old
> odd bits of sea blanched wood,
> Overstrand and the swinging
> lighthouse glimpsed in the mists,
> they flash in the prisms and I
> believe for a moment I see
> the dazzling atoms dancing
> in everything that exists.
>
> The children dance on the shore.
> The waves die on the sand.
> The spray blows to and fro,
> the children dance and die.
> What waves are these that dance
> with the children on the sand?
> I hear them calling, but cannot
> hear what it is that they cry.[22]

Barker had written 'ions' rather than atoms and then thought the word too technical. It was not phosphorescence or electrolysis of which he was speaking, but a way of seeing in multiple dimensions. At one point he had thought the word 'flash' too extreme, since 'even though white stones, and bits of wood, Overstrand, the winged seabirds *do* flash, it is better to underplay it here so that the contrast between physical reality (single vision) and spiritual reality (double vision, triple vision, quadruple vision) is kept clear'.[23] He argued himself into keeping the word, since 'prism' referred to the refractive faculty he was actually addressing. The theme of this poem was what, developing and extending a term from 'Dreams of a Summer Night', Barker called 'the theology of natural objects', the aura worn by every earthly thing as an affirmation of its authenticity, what Hopkins had called its 'inscape' and 'instress'.

Though Barker had been shaken by Archer's death, he was also, as his closest friends sensed, beginning to feel comfortable in the world and to make sense of its processes. Bintry was the context for all this. That summer Sebastian Barker and Sebastian Lockwood converted a piece of Overstrand driftwood into a table. They placed it in the arbour at the back of the house, where George and friends sat drinking on warm Saturday evenings. Like the bee in *The Alphabetical Zoo* he was 'in his own nest' full up with 'exelicious honey'. He was not rich; the metropolitan razzmatazz went on its way regardless, but he inhabited a place where he felt right.

CHAPTER 46

'YOUR POACHER IS A PINCHER'

Martin Green had now left MacGibbon & Kee and co-founded the firm of Martin Brian and O'Keeffe. To mark Barker's sixtieth birthday, which fell in February 1973, he undertook to oversee a *festschrift* under the title *Homage to George Barker on His Sixtieth Birthday*, which he edited with John Heath-Stubbs. The two men solicited tributes from the faithful: encomia from Gascoyne and Ginsberg, from Wright, Thwaite and Sisson. Geoffrey Hill contributed his meticulous, incongruously earnest 'Apology for the Revival of Christian Architecture in England' and G.S. Fraser, now a senior lecturer at the University of Leicester, some fly-by-night quatrains:

> Flash Harry, I used to call you,
> The man for the three-card trick,
> The thimble-rigger, the con man
> With a loverly golden brick,
>
> The cap with perhaps a razor-skip,
> The scarf, the moll called Elsie,
> Holding hunched court in a Fulham pub,
> Not in my snobbish Chelsea . . .[1]

'Elsie', a footnote glossed patiently, was a female Christian name 'adopted for convenience of rhyme only'. In fact, it had long been one of Barker's abbreviations for Elspeth, often yelled down to her from the top of the stairs, or else bawled in the kitchen on smoke-filled Saturday nights. Bound between smart green boards, the book was ready for the birthday junketings at Hedley Marten's flat in Duke Street, just off Manchester Square.

In a shrewd act of legerdemain, the *Listener* invited Barker to review the book. He allowed himself no quarter, mercilessly exposing his own faults, his oversights, his occasional clumsiness of style, the paucity of his education. The problem with the subject of this laudatory compilation, he pronounced, was that, when he should have been studying *The Meaning of Meaning* in Oxford, he had been 'adulterating his adolescence with actresses in the Edgware Road (herein lay the origin of the rather garish bad taste that disfigured so much of his poetry)'; when he should have been practising 'Marxmanship in a Hammersmith cell' he had been 'wasting his days in bed with a girl called snooty-nosed Phlue'; in 1930, when he should have been exercising his wits by animadverting on the death of God, he had been kneeling in the Brompton Oratory 'praying for a shower of pound notes to descend' through its rococo ceiling. In fact, Barker implied, he was a ragamuffin, who had neglected all of his best chances. His harshest judgement, however, was reserved for the poetry itself, whose apparent depth of meaning was a *trompe l'oeil*, an intellectual confidence trick. The poet George Barker, he concluded, was a semantic card-sharper. 'One sincerely suspected that there lay at the heart of the work some philosophical or imaginary judgement about life, death and the great hereafter, but the words did a dance for a moment on the page, the cards and the ideas and the letters changed places and, lo and behold, the philosophical queen had disappeared.'[2] I love the man Barker this side of idolatry, George Barker declared, 'but his poems would have been a lot better if they had been written by John Milton'.

On 2 April he left for a whistle-stop tour of campuses in upper New York State, which had been arranged the previous year. On consecutive days he toured colleges in Utica, Oneanta, Hamilton, Syracuse and Oswego. After a free weekend he went on to Wells College, Aurora and Rochester.[3] He found the trip exhausting and the readings, though lucrative, unstimulating. On his return to Itteringham he walked up the rutted track to the house, a solitary figure clutching a briefcase, relief at his homecoming flooding his face.

He arrived to find the Bin Tree lying across the lawn, felled by a spring gale. The animals were as lively as ever. Dobermann now had a daughter called Miriam, who joined in all the household festivities. On Easter morning, 22 April, she ate every one of the Easter eggs laid out on the window ledge in the main living room for the growing Barker brood.[4] Summer was coming in and, with it, the Bintry idyll. At Blickling fête Bruddy and Progles were enticed into medieval costume, and danced round the village maypole. Bruddy exacted his revenge for this indignity by acquiring a fighting cock called Cedric, who would lie in wait for visitors behind the beech tree at the front of the house, then ambush them, plumage and talons flailing.

Barker's American money lasted until July, when the coffers were empty once more. Turning again to poetry for children, Barker composed a set of verses about two rabbits called Potherskin and Botherskin, whose habits derived from Sam and his best friend 'Widge'.

> They pull up rose trees just because
>   they like to eat the petals
> then secretly they put back in
>   a lot of stinging nettles.
>
> Botherskin and Potherskin
>   like nothing more than taking
> jam tarts that cannot run away
>   because they are still baking.[5]

But, feeling perhaps that Barker's vein of animal poems for children was effectively exhausted, Faber declined immediate publication (a selection from them was published, together with a sampling from the existing three volumes and a few other pieces, in 1997). The standoffishness which characterised the attitude to Barker and his work in English universities continued to exclude him from teaching there. However, that year he did receive an invitation from Nicholas Brooke, Dean of the School of English and American Studies at the University of East Anglia, to consider directing some advanced classes there.[6] After discussing the plans over lunch in the department, Barker returned to Bintry disconsolate and disillusioned, remarking that he found the atmosphere of this forward-looking institution stuffy. He doubted if he would fit in at East Anglia, which in any case showed no further interest in employing him.

In May Fiona Marten received a telegram from Norfolk reading: 'For Chrissakes Help!'[7] She immediately contacted her brother, the inventor Clive Sinclair, who ran a computer business in St Ives. Sinclair, for years a keen reader of modern verse, recognised that Barker was worth supporting and in June 1973 appointed him as cultural adviser to his firm for a period of seven years, at an annual salary of £1,000.[8] As the Barkers' financial woes intensified, more extreme remedies were called for. Tristram Hull had joined with Dennis Savage, a long-term resident of Itteringham, who with his wife Mary lived opposite the church, to set up a design and tailoring business called the Dove Clothing Company, in Dove Street, Norwich. They too were well aware of Barker's predicament. On 9 July they sent him a contract:

> Dear George,
> I am writing to confirm our recent arrangement viz the above.
>   As from September 1973 you will be appointed Cultural Consultant to the Company for a period of twelve months at a salary of sixty pounds per month, the first payment commencing 15 September 1973.

Your knowledge of fabric and costume design in the theatre during the 17th and 18th century will be of particular value to us, but you will be asked to research later periods from time to time.

We expect to discuss our spring collections with you during October.

Would you please let me have the name and address of your bank so that we may institute a monthly standing order.

I hope that you had a pleasant holiday.

Yours sincerely,

SAVAGE AND HULL LIMITED[9]

Barker's 'pleasant holiday' had been a pilgrimage to Italy. Ever since Sebastian had shown a passing interest in religion, Barker had been determined to introduce his son to the cult of St Francis. They decided on a trip to Assisi, hoping to stay en route in France with the parents of Robert Pollet, Sebastian's former classmate at the King's School, Canterbury, who, following his return from teaching in Africa, was now living and writing poetry in Bungay. The Mercedes seemed in fine fettle: when 99,000 miles were on the clock, the car had seized up and Barker and Cox had given it a thorough 100,000 mile service. Now that it was ready, George put Sebastian in the passenger seat and the two of them set off for Italy. The refit had, however, failed to restore the engine to its former vigour. They drove across France at a speed not much exceeding ten miles per hour. In the department of Vosges, the motor foundered. As soon as they arrived at the Pollets' house (which they found locked and empty), Barker read instructions out of the manual, while Sebastian lay beneath the chassis, fitting a timing chain tensioner. After camping for the night nearby, they proceeded at a gentle pace towards Assisi, where they pitched their tent on a rubbish tip at the foot of Rocca Maggiore. Barker took his son to see San Damiano with its minuscule 'Garden of the Canticle of the Sun'. They then visited the saint's own foundation, the Basilica of San Francesco. In the convent of Sacro Covento, Barker pointed out two friars dressed in their traditional black habits, each secured with a white rope girdle, knotted three times. At Il Carcere on a wooded hillside he showed Sebastian the Little Sisters of Saint Clare in their habits of plain grey. In the afternoons they sat in the piazza watching, in the words of a poem written by Sebastian shortly afterwards, the 'copper dome of San Ruffino / Green in the still light'.[10] Barker talked of the little brothers and their humour; he spoke of the saint's limpid poems. He showed Sebastian the olive and mulberry trees associated with episodes in the life of the saint. He explained the significance of that effigy of flawless love: the eternal rose tree without thorns.[11]

Back at Bintry the menagerie grew steadily. Dobe had now turned into a fully operational hunting dog. He rampaged along the banks of the Bure and terrorised the inhabitants. The continuing popularity of *Runes and Rhymes and Tunes and Chimes*, moreover, had made him famous. When Lord Walpole of Mannington Hall tried to remonstrate with Barker about Dobe's churlish and destructive behaviour, he found himself helpless against the intercessions of his young grandson, who romped round him in circles, quoting 'my Octobermann, Obermann, Doberman dog'. The local tenant farmers proved less biddable. When a dead pheasant was discovered and Dobe unfairly suspected of its murder, an outraged landowner raced over to Bintry; he tracked Barker to the outhouse, where he lay beneath the Mercedes. 'Sir,' yelled the splenetic yeoman, 'your Pinscher is a poacher!' 'Sir,' replied Barker without looking up, 'your poacher is a pincher.'[12] The farmer beat an undignified retreat. Later Barker took his mocking revenge in a pasquinade entitled 'Thirteen Farmers'. His efforts with the Mercedes, however, proved fruitless. The car was left in its outhouse, where it rusted into the biosphere and was slowly colonised by spiders.

All this was a welcome distraction from the true business of Barker's life as, morning after mournful morning, he sat in his study upstairs attempting to write. With the Archer poems he had temporarily exhausted the elegiac vein. He searched for a fresh theme but such fallow periods could make him moody. Elspeth was used to the rhythms of his inspiration — he was often buoyant and productive in early autumn and annually experienced a rebirth of inspiration in the spring.[13] Essentially he was an equinoctial poet, but the solstices could leave him floundering. He found deepest winter hopeless for creative work. Instead he would read in the mornings; in the afternoons he might take the younger children for a drive towards the coast in one of the series of second-hand vehicles acquired to replace the defunct Mercedes. There was an old Roman encampment on the road to Cromer; passing it, he would indicate phantom sentries. So vivid were these descriptions that five-year-old Progles believed that he could make out the sheen on their spears.[14] In the winter evenings Barker would sit in the main living room (called by the family the 'rush matting room' with reference to its expensive floor covering) over a fire in the hearth, fed by the supplies of wood that they could ill afford, augmented by wet sticks culled from the grass of Mossy Mere or from the wide fields beyond the barn.

His creative barrenness was at its worst during the weeks immediately following Christmas. When the University of Florida at Miami invited him to teach for the fourteen weeks of the second-semester from January to early April, he accepted, feeling that there was little alternative. Elspeth was expecting her fifth child: once more, he would have to endure a separation during Elspeth's pregnancy. 'Once more', she reminisced, 'it was going to be MUCH easier without him, though of course we all missed him hugely.'

He flew to Florida in mid-January 1974, settling into university housing at 4100, Ventura Avenue, Coconut Grove. Sebastian and his wife Julie now had a young daughter called Chloë: Florida sounded so tempting that they had plans to fly out and join him. Barker discouraged this plan. He told Sebastian that Florida was both expensive and philistine; he was spending his days in a trance of absolute vacancy: eating, swimming, reading such serious books as he could find in a city seemingly without high-class bookshops. Besides, he had no car. Every morning the university authorities arranged for him to be picked up from Ventura Avenue and dropped on campus, where he did his best to appear engrossed in the difficult business of teaching the young to express something – preferably not themselves – on paper.[15]

He flew back to England in early April, cutting short the semester by two weeks and explaining to the department that Elspeth's delivery was imminent.[16] On Good Friday, at two minutes past two in the afternoon, in the Norfolk and Norwich Hospital, a girl was born. She weighed 7 lbs 1 oz, and was named Lily Elizabeth Anna Miranda. She was Barker's fifteenth and last child and was to be the delight of his old age.

While Elspeth was in hospital, Fiona Marten came to look after the other children. A few evenings into her stay, as she reports, she and George were sitting at the long table in the kitchen over their wine, when 'he confided in me that he had fallen in love with this young man called White Knees. He could say that and I could believe him because he had always openly spoken about his bisexuality, so I was very easily duped. Elspeth in the meantime was acutely suspicious that something was going on. When she came out of the hospital after ten days, she said, "Something's been going on hasn't it, in Miami?" I very naïvely – I should have known better really, I was twenty-seven – said, "Oh well, yes, but you know it was only a *man*." Of course, she said, "Absolute nonsense!"; then she hurled her accusation at him, and there was pandemonium.' Elspeth's reaction was straightforward: 'I threw the television and electric kettle at him.' 'It was really absolutely terrible,' Fiona said. 'And then it all emerged that White Knees was really a woman.'[17]

That evening Sebastian drove over to see the new baby. He found the harrying still in progress: 'She kept on rushing up and shaking him, demanding, "What is the colour of her pubic hair? Come on, tell me: what colour is her pubic hair?"' Barker refused to answer. After some hours, the query still unresolved, Sebastian left on tiptoe.[18]

When White Knees took to telephoning long-distance to Bintry, Elspeth wrote her several abusive letters at an address in Miami. Later in the summer White Knees arrived in England: Elspeth 'spoke unpleasantly to her' whenever she phoned. White Knees never braved Bintry: she went to Quidenham and hung around the Carmelite community of nuns. Depression ensued, leading to a half-hearted attempt at suicide. Eventually she was taken into the psychiatric wing of the Norfolk and Norwich. Releasing herself, she took the bus to Bury St Edmunds, where, confiding in the Sisters of the Assumption at the new convent at Hengrave Hall, she requested to be taken in as a postulant.

CHAPTER 47

'DYING UPWARD LIKE HOPE'

'George knew quite well what he had done,' Sebastian declared later. 'The girl had fallen in love with him, but he hadn't with her.' 'I don't think that George had any particular feeling for her,' Elspeth maintained, 'apart from guilt. He hadn't expected her to take his attentions so seriously. He had always had concubines when he was away. I wasn't supposed to know this but of course I did, and really didn't mind as he was so wretched on his own. The White Knees incident was different because of her attachment to him and naïve pursuit.'

In August Barker asked Sebastian to drive him to Bury St Edmunds. He remained silent until they reached Hengrave Hall where he got out, telling his son that he would be no more than half an hour. He did not indicate which of the convent's inmates he was visiting. After about two hours he returned looking wan, eased himself wearily into the passenger seat and told Sebastian to drive off.[1] Sebastian never heard his father mention White Knees again.

Barker was left with a gnawing remorse, and a sense that life had been simpler in Italy, where, as his poem 'The Oak and the Olive', written at this time claims questionably, moral responsibilities had weighed less heavily, so that it was 'perfectly possible to assassinate one's best friend / with a kind of histrionic guiltlessness, because / the sun would continue to shine after the crime'. That September the branches of the oak trees in the surrounding countryside groaned in late summer gales and the roof of the barn behind Bintry threatened to cave in. Barker thought back to Ariccia, where once he had discovered a bright cluster of oranges growing through the skylight of his lavatory: such abundance, he was now prepared to believe, had invariably made him happy. Norfolk presented a very different picture:

> When the chilling
> rain falls upon me in the North I know
> only too well that it does so as
> a moral punitive. I write this in
> a Norfolk August and the rains pour down
> daily upon a landscape that derives
> its masculine nobility from the simple
> fact that it has survived. It has survived
> the flood, the winter, the fall and the black
> nor'-easter. The old oak tree hangs out
> that great twisted bough from which the corpse
> of the criminal cynic has just dropped in decay.
> The clouds do not decorate the sky, they entomb it,
> and the streams have swollen with cataracts. Weeds
> flourish and the summer corn is crushed flat.
> What could ever come from all this hopeless
> melancholy save a knowledge, as by allegory,
> of our culpability? Why, then, should I find
> a child's face bright with tears haunting my mind?[2]

All that lowering, unpromising autumn Barker seems to have been tormented by this contrast between his own guilt and the innocence apparent both in his memories of Italy and in his children as they played around him, at their most ebullient and destructively delightful. One afternoon three-year-old Sam, pedaling from one end of the back yard to the other, collided with the lowered handle of the water pump, which snapped. The pump never worked again.[3] The accident did not appear to worry Sam. In the afternoons, Barker joined in the fun, but his nights were tormented with visions of depravity. He wrote a poem called 'Pascal's nightmare', in which the universe was filled with couples mechanically copulating in obedience to the behaviourist itch, so that 'I see them flickering / in shadows and painted / flames'.[4]

In 'Nietzsche's Dream' he attempted to re-create a vision of an afterlife ruled by the German philosopher's pitiless directives, a domain beyond good and evil; the resulting picture, however, resembled far more closely the Purgatory of medieval Catholic cosmology. In 'The Gardens of the Ravished Psyche' he reached back to a tradition which embraced the Garden of Adonis of Book III, Canto vi of Spenser's *The Faerie Queene*, where 'wont faire Venus often to enjoy / Her deare Adonis joyous company': the prevailing mood of post-coital disillusionment, however, brought Barker's garden closer to the sour mood of Blake's 'The Garden of Love', or the banefulness of Swinburne's 'Garden of Proserpine'.[5] Barker attempted to re-create the state of mind of the American poet John Berryman at the moment when, two years before, he had committed suicide by jumping off a walkway at the University of Minnesota. 'To John Berryman' alludes to the final section of Eliot's *The Waste Land* and seems to assert an even deeper nihilism: 'What was / that word the thunder said? / Nothing. The thunder said / nothing. Nothing.'[6] In 'Azrafel' he reworked the ancient Hebraic legend of the angel of death into a modern tale of retribution visited upon a middle-aged man living contentedly with a much younger woman – a man, in some respects, much like himself.

Guilt and nihilism hounded him, but he was quite aware that these two states of mind contradicted one another. If humans were mere machines, as the behaviourist Skinner contended, moral responsibility was meaningless. Barker devised two talking heads to argue out this paradox, called Gog and Magog. These figures are fleetingly referred to in the books of Genesis, Ezekiel and Revelations. As tutelary deities of the City of London, their statues also preside over Guildhall. Since little else is known about them, Barker felt free to use them for his own purposes. He told listeners to the recently launched Radio Three that, when writing the poems, 'I thought of them as looking rather like walking Henry Moore statues'.[7] He deployed Gog as a mouthpiece for the speculative intelligence with its partiality for totalising explanations; Magog became the inspired dunce at the back of the class forever pointing out inconvenient and invalidating exceptions. Gog was the seeker who asked 'How?', Magog the moralist who countered with 'Why?' Gog was the empiricist who watched life flow past him, the fixed observer of the transient stream, Magog the adventurer who insisted on charting directions. Gog represented the utilitarian or positivist who treated pleasure as the ultimate good; Magog was the arbiter who counted the cost and insisted on remote consequences.

Neither figure was entirely fixed. At times they appeared to shift places. The result was a set of 'Dialogues' between dialectical principles that joined, diverged and rehearsed all sorts of alternative and competing positions. *Dialogues, etc.*, the published volume in which all these poems are collected, is not a polemical work. Barker had come to regard science as a process over which the moral intelligence acted as guardian, exploring its ethical implications. Arguing over Darwin's theory of evolution, for instance, the two talking heads echo one other:

> Said little Magog to Gog
> as they looked down at the sea,
> 'If that's our mother and father
> what kind of Gogs are we?'

And Gog said to little Magog,
'I hear a dove in a tree
burbling like a sermonizer.
But does it hear me?'

Big Gog and little Magog
stared into each other's eyes
and they saw the sun and the moon and the stars
like the diamonds of paradise.

'O Gog,' said little Magog,
'Things all go whence they came.
Let's you and I, my dear friend Gog,
get up and do the same.'

And little Magog and Gog
stepped down into the sea
just as if it was god's blue eye
and they were you and me.[8]

Barker was convinced that games, rituals and sheer nonsense sometimes provided an approach to truth where ratiocination failed. Many of the poems in *Dialogues, etc.* come close, or allude, to nursery rhymes. 'The Ring-a-Roses Tree' is a case in point. Ever since the Great Plague of 1665 British children have transformed death into poety in the dancing game 'Ring a ring a roses', which originated as a ritualistic response to the appearance of the lethal bubonic rash. In this collection of poems Barker understands 'death' as the spiritual paralysis that is brought about by intellectual cynicism. In 'Ring-a-Roses Tree', which, after the dedication page, is the first poem in the book and sets its tone, Barker improvises his own version of an ancient formula to hold mortality, in this sense, at bay:

At the grave of poisoned
intellectual energy
where the intelligence
surrounded with its huge
and hopeless trophies lies,
the cup of suicide still
clutched in a clever hand,
there I have seen the child
step forward, orphaned, and
cast smiling into that grave

> its wretched little ring
> of rose and daisy. Out
> of that overgrown and
> undergrowth grave where now
> belief and faith like maggots
> mock on the rotten bone,
> out of that dirt and out
> of that stone heart I see
> dying upward like hope
> the ring-a-roses tree.[9]

Dialogues, etc. was Barker's darkest collection of poetry. At sixty-two he was holding the idea of the serenity of old age at bay. ('Do not', Eliot had once written, 'speak to me of the wisdom of old men.') That June Barker and Elspeth were invited to Faber & Faber's annual summer party, at which photographs of authors on the list are customarily taken for possible future use. The camera caught him in a benign and affable pose – like that of Yeats's 'sixty year old smiling public man'. He disliked this photograph intensely, which he said reminded him of an unfrocked priest.

In November George flew to Italy again to see Dede and her boys. Dede was now a regular communicant at Santa Susanna, the American Church in Rome; George Farrelly was reading History at Harvard, while Jimmy, Edward and Francis were studying at the American school in Rome. Barker drove his sons to Venice and Assisi, where the contradictory nature of his feelings towards Catholicism emerged. They attended mass at the Basilica of San Francesco, where Barker behaved like a devout *pater familias*, his blue eyes trained soulfully on the distant altar and celebrant. Later, he took Jimmy round the back streets where, as they approached the doors of another church, he whispered, 'Let's go in and *blaspheme*!'[10] The antiphonal ghosts of those fathers of the Oratory, Dale-Roberts and Oddy, were with him still.

On his return from these Italian trips, Barker would be moody and withdrawn. In particular, he was often convinced that Elspeth had been unfaithful while he had been away. The dark and jealous reflex, which would last for days, seemed to her 'an animal reaction' she knew he was powerless to resist.[11] Even in normal times the presence of other men in the house could enrage him: 'He had always been like this. Because of it, one could never have a plumber, carpenter, or electrician in to mend anything. Thus did the house decay.' One Saturday evening, when Bintry was full of guests, he found Elspeth sitting on the knee of Tony Whooley, TEFL teacher and poet of Irish descent, 'because there was nowhere else to sit'. Whooley, who divided his time between Norfolk and London, made no secret of his homosexuality, but this scarcely counted in Elspeth's defence. If she went with female friends for a drink at the Walpole Arms in Itteringham, Barker would often pursue her, suspecting an assignation. Indeed, the real or imagined presence of other men was not even necessary to provoke him. Since Elizabeth and Elspeth had both fallen in love with him through the printed word, he sometimes suspected that other authors might exert the same spell. One evening he caught Elspeth reading Auden in bed and treated this passive condition of appreciation as an act of betrayal. On another occasion he threw a jealous fit as she sat immersed in the travel writings of Patrick Leigh Fermor. A male author did not even have to be living to be a threat; once, Barker flew into a rage on finding his wife alone with Milton.[12]

Such fits of resentment, however, were by and large reserved for the dead or famous; the young, the unestablished, the vulnerable, by contrast, seldom failed to elicit his encouragement. This was especially true of those whom he felt to be outsiders. A characteristic instance was his hospitality towards, and support for, Eddie Linden. Since 1969 Linden had been editing the respected literary magazine *Aquarius* on a shoestring, helped by the occasional meagre grant and the co-operation of a series of unpaid assistants. Every so often he would make the complicated journey up to Itteringham by bus and train from his lonely London bedsit. He recalled these visits in glowing terms: 'Elspeth was a wonderful hostess. She had a sweet and generous nature, and would go out of her way to make you feel at home . . . Being somebody who never had a real home and love myself, I enjoyed this fact; she could be totally unselfish, and put herself out for me.'

The household proved expansive enough to accommodate longer-term visitors, some of whom turned into temporary residents. In 1975 a friend called Ann Nichols came, with her son Danny, to stay, initially to recuperate after a cancer operation; they were welcomed back for several prolonged periods. The three children of Elspeth's maternal uncle, the Brashes, were also put up at Bintry since their mother was dead and their father could not look after them; since they were much of an age with the Barkers' own children, they were easily absorbed into the household. For a while the Brashes, daughter Jane especially, became an integral part of this busy, extended clan. In the mid-1970s the Barkers seriously considered adopting them, but this did not prove possible. Nevertheless, for several years Bintry House contained nine children, for all of whom Barker's slender means had somehow or other to provide.

Barker himself was more mercurial than ever, jousting at his guests with an abusive wit, treating Linden like a lackey. 'Come *hyere*, Linden!' he would shout, expecting him to come running. Such behaviour was a game: 'He could be difficult,' Linden admitted, 'but he could also be extremely loving.

He could pull your leg in an aggressive way, but you were expected to fight back – it was not meant to intimidate you.' The best way of dealing with such treatment, as Fiona Sinclair found, was to stand your ground; if you made your disagreement on a matter of principle clear to him, he respected your independence.[13] But the ploy of stubbornness did not work for everyone. The painter Michael Reynolds, who was temporarily living in Norfolk after some years in Rome, came to draw Barker for a local newspaper. When Reynolds questioned his knowledge of Italian history, their relationship grew so acrimonious that the portrait had to be abandoned.[14] In stark contrast Clive Sinclair warmed to Barker immediately. 'You couldn't help but love him,' he later confessed, 'he made you feel more alive.'[15] When the Warwick Gallery, founded in that city by Danila Pampanini in 1972, started to host readings, Barker was the first poet to be invited. The reading was organised by Anthony Astbury, an English teacher from a nearby prep school, to whom Barker took instantly. When in 1979 Astbury and Geoffrey Godbert founded the Greville Press (named after the Warwick-born poet, Fulke Greville) with financial assistance from Harold Pinter, Barker was among the first authors whom they published. With Astbury, the asperity was seldom in evidence. 'Why,' he asked Astbury, 'why can I never insult you?'[16]

Increasingly, his erudite and quirky friendship with Hedley Marten was coming to complement Elspeth's with Fiona. With Hedley he was invariably gentle. As Marten explained, this was 'because I didn't have a father, for my own father was killed during the Normandy campaign in 1944, when I was one. He perceived that I had this vulnerability, and he never never hurt me. In fact, he was incredibly tender, and the best friend in times of trouble, I mean *the best*.' It could be argued that Barker became a surrogate parent to Hedley, whose emotional need grew even stronger in 1975 when his only sister suffered a severe nervous breakdown.[17] When she was referred for treatment to R.D. Laing, the libertarian psychiatrist at the Tavistock Institute, Barker had as little faith in the outcome as Hedley. Ever since his days with the Freud-obsessed Promethean Society, he had nursed a distrust of psychoanalysis. The poem on the dedicatory page to *Dialogues, etc.*, submitted to Faber that year, ran:

> What we are dying of, dear Doctor,
>   is not the disease:
> What we are dying of, dear Doctor,
>   is the remedies.[18]

Hedley was an intellectual by training and temperament and used to the strict academic discipline which Barker admired, scorned and envied. He became Barker's courier to the London Library, ferrying up to Norfolk tomes on

Italian history and the annals of the more obscure Italian popes. He seemed to Barker to hold the entire cavalcade of European culture in his head and knew in the original Latin poets like Catullus and Propertius, whom Barker could only enjoy in translation. The two men shared a love for Virgil and Ovid, and for Horace, whose euphony was evident to Barker when his poems were read aloud. Marten also guided Barker towards classical music, educating his ear, introducing him in turn to the Schubert symphonies and to the repertoire of Bach keyboard works. When in London, Barker visited the barrister's flat in Duke Street near Manchester Square, and Marten took him across the road to the Catholic church in Spanish Place, where he lurked in the darkened nave while Hedley clambered up to the organ loft and let rip with Bach toccatas.

Their friendship became a dialogue with its distinctive idioms, its codes and jokes. They were themselves like Gog and Magog, with a similar capacity to confuse their respective roles. Marten's gifts were supposedly academic and Barker's more practical; much mirth resulted when either man proved himself superior in the other's province. Together they invented a central European intellectual called Henry Van Loon with a complex and ramifying curriculum vitae which they updated in memoranda, postcards, letters and cartoons. The omnipresence of this figure was, in fact, an old Barker joke, originating in that 'Hendrick Van Loon' whose signature George had improvised in hotel registers when fleeing California with Smart in the winter of 1940. Drawn by Barker in silhouette, Loon bore a passing resemblance to himself. Through the elaboration of his creators, he became a strutting parody of their own shared, antiquarian interests in philology, the classics and Renaissance history.[19]

The conversations they enjoyed took place either in the quiet of Marten's flat or at Bintry during sober hours when Dionysian devils could be kept at a relatively safe distance. They served as pools of quiet, urbane fun and reflection in an existence that had become, in other respects, overrun by children and animals: horses, ponies, hens, 'all', as Elspeth recalls, 'acquired in the same sideways manner'. Raffaella had borrowed and almost broken in, a white stallion called Lightning. She also had a rabbit called Vodka, after the one drink seldom found in the house. Other dependent creatures included several cats of whom, despite his well-attested loathing of all things feline, George was obliged to approve, and a pheasant called Wilberforce, rescued from Dobe's jowls and carefully nurtured by Bruddy until Miriam ate him. Bruddy had acquired an azure-spotted slow-worm called Gloria or Montgomery according to whim as well as a goat called Billy the Kid, the first in caprine history to nibble a privet hedge and live.

At Bintry the children were all precocious, noisy and glad. So full had the house become by 1976 that it was difficult to account for the movements of individuals. Lily was now pale, with long straight, fair hair and blue eyes so enormous as to convey the impression of being bigger than her face. Seemingly constructed of bone china, she looked like an orphaned waif and, when addressed, would raise her right hand in the air, shouting 'Charge!' and promptly do so. One early spring morning Doberman padded out of the house and along the track and to the main road. Lily was awake and followed him through the village and out towards the long hill on the far side. It was some time before she was missed, but after a hectic search they were found, a contented, thumb-sucking two-year-old, following the dog into deeper country.

CHAPTER 48

'THE POEM AND THE FOUNTAIN'

On 23 March 1976, Doberman died and was buried in the wilderness beyond the garden. For some time there would be no substitute for him.[1] Eventually the family acquired a golden Labrador called Honey, who was soon joined by her black and white puppy T-Shirt Smith. At Bintry animals were given as much respect as people, although they sometimes inflicted their own kind of damage. In the month of Doberman's death Raffaella won a scholarship to Norwich Girls' High School. A few days later she was out riding on one of Lady Walpole's horses when it bolted and turfed her into a chestnut tree on the Wolterton estate, shattering her jaw.[2] She spent three weeks in the Norwich and Norfolk Hospital wired up so that she could not talk.

The house had always been a haven for wounded or nesting birds, including George's own children by previous liaisons. Rose now had two children by different fathers. For several years after 1964 she had been hooked on heroin. Still dependent on a range of softer substitutes – Methodone, brandy, wine and Special Brew – she had managed to buy a house in Cambridge with £18,000 inherited from Donald Buchanan, a friend of Elizabeth Smart's from Ottawa; as a result of her improvidence, she lost it within eighteen months. She and the children moved in with Elizabeth at the Dell, but there was a ready refuge for her, too, at Bintry. Here, by the warmth of the Aga, with the cats purring on the hearth and a cup of tea always to hand, she found comfort, consolation and understanding. Elspeth noted how alike Rose and George were. Both possessed an Irish winsomeness and a quick temper. In their cups he would get angry with her and she with him. Rose had looked to George's Catholicism as something that might help sustain her, not realising how heterodox was his way of believing/not believing. One day she returned from the Dell in great distress. Though not a baptised Catholic, still less a confirmed one, she had made her way to St Edmund's Church in St Mary's Street, Bungay and attempted to make her confession. The confession had been garbled and the priests had not understood her. She had then attended Mass in the brick gothic revival chancel. On receiving the host, she had gagged on it, spitting it out on to the red tiled floor. Barker could understand such gestures, which reflected the iconoclast in him. For all that, there was a rage and bewilderment in such behaviour that were distinctive of Rose.[3]

When religion failed her, Rose turned to writing. Her mother's literary style, on which she began modelling her own, was autobiographical and confessional. Accordingly, Rose believed writing to be a means of expressing one's inner self, but the self she had to express was as confused as her attempts to give voice to it. She showed one or two pieces to George, but he had seen too much late adolescent self-evisceration in America to be encouraging.

By the summer of 1976 emotional devastation lay to right and left. Sebastian had moved from Reepham and bought a small house in Newnham Village near Cambridge, which he was working to restore. To others, Sebastian had seemed to lead an enchanted existence with Julie, whom George called 'your wild Hungarian', and their two daughters: three-year-old Chloë, whom George called his 'little Greek', and one-year-old Miranda. Yet, partly as a result of financial strain, the marriage was on the rocks, and divorce proceedings were eventually set in motion. Sebastian wrote his father a screed of howling pain and incoherent reproach, accusing him of not seeing that divorce was the answer to an unhappily married man's ills. Sebastian had not yet followed his father into the Roman fold, but he shared his delight in extreme, almost perverse, paradox. Single-handedly he now undertook to revise the Church's teaching on the sacrament of matrimony to bring it in line with his own conduct – a form of doctrinal opportunism he seems also to have inherited from George. His letter ran, 'Your only fault was that you didn't know how to get divorced. It is a fearful discipline, but it is accomplished by mutual forgiveness. Only when you have got divorced can you get married. This is why the Church is there.'[4]

Barker's religious understanding of suffering co-existed with a strong sense of life's absurdities. He wrote Sebastian a deeply considered reply that posed, without insisting upon, a religious solution to his problems. Avoiding dogmatism or parental knowingness, it outlined an argument which might be summarised as follows. One either possessed a religious understanding of pain – in which case the experience was either tragic or laced with hope, depending on the complexion of one's religion – or one did not possess such an understanding. In the second case, one's suffering was like an inconvenient toothache. Even then, one should, where possible, avoid inflicting pain on others (this was certainly a feat that Barker himself had not always managed).

Beyond that, in an agnostic universe, there was very little that could be done to alleviate personal misery. None of the fashionable panaceas, whether of indulgence or of abstinence, worked. One had just to grin falsely and bear it:

> As for that rather dreadful condition we all operate and delight in, the condition of the animal that seeks its own satisfaction at the expense of others, this is that condition of sublunar injustice which moved Blake to write: 'One law for the lion & the lamb is injustice.' The lambs also exercise their faculty of war: they win when the heroes die in pursuit of the golden fleeces. (Ah, the huge tears of triumph that fall from those flayed and tortured visages.) And as for the Ginsberg version of 'giving up pleasure, lust and its obverse suicidal pain' – I ask you, my dearest Sebastian, how does one 'give up' pain? By 'giving up' the pleasure of lust? These can no more be given up than you can give up the functioning of the five senses. I cannot believe that the answer is to stand on one leg by the River Ganges repeating the word 'No' until one dies. I used to believe that, when I still believed in the river Ganges. The ultimate illusion is to think that the pain really and truly matters. No, I am not subscribing to Dr Pangloss's academy in which all is for the best in the best of all possible worlds. I am proposing that if there is no visionary condition of the spirit, no world of the soul, then the pain does not matter a damn: it is simply ugly. And the ugliness doesn't matter in a world in which there are no aesthetics. But if the spheres of the spiritual do in truth exist then we have to acknowledge that we simply cannot fathom the mystery that envelops human suffering. The suffering is here, and we do not know why.[5]

It was a communication full of nods and winks. After all, when one poet writes to another of 'a world without aesthetics', it is manifestly an invitation to dissent. But if Sebastian did not believe in God (and Barker would almost certainly have added that there was no earthly reason why he should believe in him), his pain, though regrettable, was absurd.

The problem of suffering cropped up again in Barker's conversations with Hedley Marten, whose marriage to Fiona was showing signs of increasing strain. Between Marten and himself, however, there existed a boundary that both men acknowledged and accepted: Marten was a secular liberal humanist whose astringent Wykehamist intellect would not permit him to embrace Barker's religious outlook.[6] So Barker adapted his advice to his friend's agnosticism. As the problems associated with his marriage intensified, Hedley sought relief by sending to Bintry letters that were frank admissions of pain. He knew that he could rely absolutely on Barker's sympathy; he also recognised that there would be no attempt to mollify, or facilely explain away, his wounds. Barker's replies were invariably addressed to Marten's own individual situation, personal and philosophical. He knew that the religious approach here would be a non-starter, so he offered sympathy and understanding, while stressing the fact that there was very little that could be done to stem such emotional agony.

For several months Hedley had been searching Wales for a holiday home that might help to revive Fiona's affections. In the summer of 1976 he found a seventeenth-century longhouse, standing alone at the head of a valley in the Birwin Mountains in Powys. The house, which was without running water, was stone-built with low beams and the date 1625 clearly legible above the lintel. In August 1976, when Fiona was pregnant with their second child, the Martens holidayed there with their three-year-old daughter Laura, George and Elspeth, their five children and the three Brash children. Rose came for a shorter period, as did Sebastian. In the hottest summer for decades they walked through scorching countryside, and splashed in the streams. There were underground fires in the hills, and smoke rose through the heather.

One afternoon George and Hedley took Laura and five-year-old Sam six miles to the waterfall at Vyrnwy. They rested on the rise of a hillock above the cascade, listening to the congregation of waters in the forest below them. As Hedley played with the children in the cool of the shade, Barker sat apart writing lines whose movement mimicked the undulations of the stream:

> What, my dear Hedley, are we doing here at
> the source of water falling from so high that
> it might have found its fount in the clouds in which no
> hand had a hand? And why with two
> small children who do not so much ride on the shoulders
> of stones as flitter round about the fallen boulders
> not seeking, as we do, some sense of origins hidden here
> but having found it? What is this sense of origins they have found
> here among the cascading murmurations of that sound
> you and I know the poem takes its fountaining inception
> from? I think it possible that this perception
> consists of the logos at the heart of all natural facts
> as forgiveness crowns the fulfilment of all human acts
> and as the pathway through the Commission-conifered forest
> began among beds in which the newborn child first
> saw its own death's-head on fire in the air. How
> can I ask why you, Hedley, and I are here now
> when all that I know is, simply, that we are
> here seeking among the fallen gardens and the water falling for

> the knowledge of why we are here? We search among
> the stones and whispering water and the reflections what long
> we shall seek and not find, the impulse of
> that recurring and continual suicide of love
> like the small water that rides to the crest of the mountain
> and casts itself over to create the poem and the fountain.[7]

Barker had gone back to the model of Coleridge's conversation poems with a new confidence and freshness. The example of water had much to do with this, suggesting a shape which the poem followed (Barker was later to make the observation that the word 'poetry' had its root in an Indo-European word implying the sound of water running across stones, though there is in fact little evidence for this).[8] The Vyrnwy poem, which was to serve as the dedicatory piece to his next volume, was a religious statement designed to bridge the gulf between his own position and Hedley's agnosticism, while paying tribute to the lawyer's patience, his 'recurring and continual suicide of love'. During the following months Barker worked on the sequence, which emerged in the winter of the following year as *Villa Stellar*. It was a verse journal of the months between October 1963 and April 1964 when he had courted and won Elspeth. Everything that he now possessed – his special, salvaged domain – stemmed from these months and yet the prevailing tone of the sequence was valedictory, with regret and closure as its dominant notes. *Villa Stellar*, however, ends not with Barker's return to London with Elspeth in the spring of 1964, but with the departure of all those house guests at the end of this crowded holiday in Wales, twelve years later: 'The children are gone. The holiday is over. Outside it is Fall.' As always he was playing with words, since the 'Fall', as well as being a season of the year, alluded once again to Newman's idea of an aboriginal calamity. At this point Barker seems to have remembered the close of Milton's *Paradise Lost* and the lingering, nostalgic look which Adam and Eve, ejected from Paradise as a result of their own fall, cast upon the now unreachable lushness of Eden. We are all of us, the poem implies – lovers, parents, children – continually forfeiting perfection.[9]

That autumn Barker clearly felt that one important phase of the Bintry years was at an end. His view, as he would make it plain to each of his children, had always been that their childhood came to an end at the Jesuitically strategic age of seven.[10] The happy oblivion of their early years, however, closed more emphatically at the academic watershed of eleven. In September Raffaella was to start at Norwich High School for Girls; Barker accompanied her to Norwich to buy the green school uniform.[11] Bruddy and Progles, meanwhile, had abandoned the ways of infancy; they became obsessed with military uniforms and stalked the village in gas masks.[12] On one occasion they placed Lily in an apple barrel and would not let her out.[13] When asked once more to dance round the Maypole at Blickling fête, they frankly and ferociously refused. Never again would Bintry be the glad nursery of memory:

> There, there beyond a
> fall glimmers the long-lost garden.
>
> That garden where we, too, as in a spell
> stared eye into dazed eye and did not see
> that suddenly the holy day was over,
> the flashing lifeguard, the worm in the tree,
> the glittering of the bright sword as it fell,
> and the gate closing for all time be[14]

CHAPTER 49

'WE'LL TO THE WOODS NO MORE'

Nor would Bintry ever again be quite so safe or self-absorbed, even for adults. Hitherto Barker had managed to keep the compartments of his life separate. He would range far afield to perform at public readings: to London for the Poetry Society; to Leicester for the Commonwealth Arts Festival, where he shared a platform with Anne Ridler and Constantine Trypanis. He would visit Dede and the children once or twice a year without any threat to his family life in Norfolk. While in Rome he took the boys round the sights, such as the Villa d'Este or the Villa Giulia.

By 1977 these partitions were coming down. Jimmy was now eighteen and Francis fourteen. Edward, who was sixteen, had decided to prepare for the Oxford University entrance exam. He came to England to attend a crammer in London, making the journey with Dede and George Farrelly. They arranged to meet Barker at the Poetry Society, where he was to give a reading on 21 November. George Farrelly, who was aware that Edward harboured aspirations to be a poet, watched his half-brother's reactions as Barker first turned up late and then promised another meeting at which he never appeared.[1] Dede was used to this sort of boorishness. To see Barker at his inconsiderate worst in the English literary heartland was, however, something of a revelation to their children, used to him minding his p's and q's during his carefully controlled visits to Rome.

After Dede had left for Italy, Edward visited Bintry. Late in the following August he arrived at Itteringham to find the family in the middle of a crisis: Progles, who had been visiting Elspeth's family in Scotland with Bruddy, had been taken ill on the train and rushed to hospital. After an exploratory operation, Progles developed pneumonia through institutional cross-infection; he later inferred, from the seriousness with which this condition was regarded, that he had come close to death. The most remarkable aspect of the episode, however, was that, for the first time, the anxieties of a family emergency were borne by members of two Barker households jointly. Though Elspeth and Dede were yet to meet, Edward continued to visit. He prepared for Oxford while the Bintry children climbed their respective academic ladders. In this they were informally assisted by Barker, who was now resolved that his last family should not suffer from the educational disruptions and privations – the lack of formal guidance – that had dogged the upbringing of their older half-siblings.

Since moving to Bintry Barker was prepared to concede – even occasionally to insist – that the inner decorum of the poem should be matched by an outer decorum of day-to-day existence. Cox noticed that 'he would spend the whole week sober, in the most disciplined fashion'. The exceptions were Saturdays, which followed an unvarying routine. Barker would spend the afternoon in the television room watching the wrestling; during Lily's infancy, cradling her on his knee. At six o'clock he would rise from his armchair and go to have a bath. Visitors arrived in ones and twos. Newcomers would have been instructed to appear at six o'clock precisely 'for a small port and lemon',[2] the terms of the invitation giving the initial impression of a somewhat formal household. Habitués, on the other hand, knew exactly what to expect. Hedley Martin went up for these carousals every few weeks, lured by what he called, 'this exciting prospect. It became an absolute tradition. There was never a dull Saturday night at Bintry. It was always very extreme.'[3]

At six-fifteen, Barker descended the stairs and embraced his guests with warmth. He placed himself at the head of the kitchen table with a packet of menthol cigarettes and the first drink of the night. His acolytes gathered round. Barker started to talk: philosophy, science, history or theology (Bintry was one of the few houses in Britain where in 1977 it was still possible seriously to discuss how many angels danced on the point of a pin). He expatiated on the figures of his own past: 'I hated the boy-scout in Auden and adored the inky-fingered magician.' Or he spoke of the priorities of style: 'A style that is not of its age is to that degree hypocritical historically.' He talked of living poets – 'Have you ever seen Larkin? He's so *ugly*' – and demolished the passing fashion: 'I have always detested formulae, particularly for poems, and particularly French ones.'

At seven Barker withdrew: to the arbour in high summer, at other seasons to the drinking room. The inner circle moved with him, its membership sometimes reshuffled. In the drinking room established cronies settled near the french windows, or beneath the oil painting of Brian Higgins near the bookcase. Newcomers made their way to the hearth, where Barker held court, resting his left elbow on the mantelpiece, scowling at the company, or appraising them with an indulgent, mocking, come-and-get-me smirk. One by one he locked kindred spirits in a fervent *sumo* clasp and subjected them to eyeball-to-eyeball scrutiny. They emerged from this encounter convinced that Barker valued them uniquely. 'Were you aware, young man, that you are that rare and princely thing, a po-et?' he would enquire of a versifier with two printed stanzas to his name. 'For my money, you are the most intelligent member of your generation,' he might remark to some middle-aged intellectual forever slipping off the lower rungs of academic preferment. If any young man who had caught his fancy failed to approach, he would indicate him through the throng with an imperious forefinger: 'Bring me that boy.'

The conversation flowed for a further three hours. Barker spoke of religion: 'I have taken Pascal's wager; who wouldn't?' He dismantled critical categories: 'Whoever called me a New Romantic? I like to think of myself, if at all, as an Old Romantic.' He disparaged his own status in literary history: 'I was once tempted by the elegiac tradition before I realised that, in order to be perfectly eligible, you have to be dead.' He defended his working practice: 'Punning is the ceremonial celebration of the triumphant cerebellum'; 'Style is the *femme fatale* of the Celt'; 'I cannot bear poems that do not have dirty marks on their faces.' He proclaimed his passions, sometimes supporting them with spontaneously improvised proverbs: 'The Romans have a saying: Englishmen who fall in love with Italy become wolves. Where else would a wolf want to go save back to Rome?'

The purpose of his conversation was to speculate and to do so riskily. Barker had no patience with timid opinions and excoriated received attitudes. He turned history on its head: 'I remember at the première of Auden's *The Ascent of F6* saying to Archer, "That is a Fascist play," and him saying to me, "It's not a Fascist play because it's written by Wystan Auden. It can't *be* a Fascist play." Dangerous stuff! Dangerous stuff!' If anybody present mistook his intentions, he would put him right sharply. One evening, knowing Barker's distrust of the then fashionable Larkin, a young poet sought his approval by damning the verse of Larkin's friend Kingsley Amis. He was told firmly that Amis wrote very capable verse.

George's seriousness was shot through with humour. 'The female members of the Promethean Society were all about 102. I don't seduce women of 102. I don't know if *you* do.' Compliments came barbed with correction: 'You read verse very well, young man, you know you do. But don't come fishing for flattery around *here*.' There was, too, a stubborn family pride. 'My wife is a Latin scholar,' he boasted to one guest, 'which is more than *you* are, baby.' 'Tu quoque,' came the reply.

His most cutting anecdotes were often at the expense of those he most liked. Of Thwaite, busy at the BBC, he carped, 'That man sits on so many committees, he must have bench sores.' Impishly – and almost certainly without justice – he cast aspersions on his own early relationship with Maurice Carpenter: 'I know that boy. I know that boy *backwards*.' He fondly mimicked Heath-Stubbs, groping with myopic lechery towards some invisible youth: 'Come *hyere* boy. Are you *seventeen*?'

At around ten o'clock somebody might mention supper. A casserole had often been simmering on the hob all evening; it was served for those who wanted it, though some were past caring. Whatever the hour or mood, there was a customary way of drawing proceedings to a close. One of the lesser acolytes fetched a volume of poetry: Milton, Hopkins, Wordsworth, Coleridge, Tennyson or perhaps the Border Ballads. Very often the volume brought was the *Last Poems* of Housman in the dark blue copy of the Grant Richards 1922 edition from which Barker had taught in Japan. Somebody would volunteer to read: George or one of his guests. Most often, however, it would be Elspeth, whose way of rendering Housman he particularly appreciated: 'Read it, girl,' he would ask with suppressed urgency, 'read it.' As the poet listened with bowed head and closed eyes, Elspeth read the opening lyric ('Beyond the moor and mountain crest') or else the Horatian epigraph:

> We'll to the woods no more,
> The laurels all are cut,
> The bowers are bare of bay
> That once the Muses wore;
> The year draws in the day
> And soon will evening shut:
> The laurels all are cut,
> We'll to the woods no more
> To the leafy woods away,
> To the high wild woods of laurel
> And the bowers of bay no more.[4]

Those round the table listened with an intensity with which they had seldom listened to poetry before. As the verse swelled, Barker sometimes started to weep. Later there might be singing round the fire, as George hunched his shoulder round an imaginary violin, or else one of the more musically adept visitors would perform a solo. Barker was led off towards his bedroom, while the company disappeared into the night or found places to sleep about the house. The privileged guest of the night would subside on the double bed in Barker's study, while from downstairs issued the stertorous snoring of dogs.

Other Saturday evenings ended in discord. For Elspeth, Barker was two men: he was an affectionate husband and father all week; on Saturdays the demon stirred. 'In his cups, he had a genuine fear of damnation and Hell fire, which I should imagine was present to a lesser degree when he was sober.' Terror, or plain anger, could make him explode. 'He would hurl a glass across the room, or throw a plate at the window, or hurl a person across the room,' Elspeth told me. 'Lord Walpole's son-in-law he threw across the room once; Rose's first husband he threw across the room – lots of other people.' On other occasions the recipients of his fury were books. 'He liked chucking things on the fire. He tried to chuck Housman on the fire once, because someone "had not read it correctly". He threw *The Bible Designed to Be Read as a Work of Literature* on the fire; it was still burning the next morning.'[5]

Elspeth coped with these outbreaks as best she could: 'There was no point in trying to soothe him or placate him. The best thing was just to wait until he went to bed really, clear up some of the debris, then creep off to bed yourself. Occasionally I would go off and stay somewhere else for the night. The children were in bed, so they were out of it. Occasionally they were woken up by dreadful screeches; I would simply tell them to go back to bed. The balance of it was that he was a completely different person when sober, and that is what he was all the time for them.'

The remoter consequences could be disastrous. One Saturday evening in the late autumn of 1977, Woody Ostrow, who was over from America, asked Barker what he had been working on. He ordered Elspeth to fetch the final typescript of *Villa Stellar* from where it lay on the study desk, ready to be dispatched to Faber. He asked her to read from it: 'He suddenly accused me of smirking as I read it, which I wasn't. He seized the thing, and chucked it on the fire.' Appalled, Woody made frantic efforts to save the burning pages: 'George smashed him on the head with the coal shovel.' The typescript proved welcome kindling and was soon reduced to cinders. 'I was blamed for it,' Elspeth remembered ruefully.[6] The entire work had to be assembled later from Barker's preliminary notes.

After *Villa Stellar* had been retyped – having survived the immolation, as befitted a sequence whose themes encompass forgiveness and the renunciation of wrath – Barker sent it to Faber with the instruction that it be set in Bodoni, the Italian typeface used by Kit, Carpenter and himself for the Phoenix Press productions of the 1930s. After the prelude evoking the waterfall of Vyrnwy, the first lyric refers to the passage in Propertius describing the white sacrificial cattle wading through the springs of Clitumnus – both poems employ the symbol of water, and both are acts of libation. The allusion to Propertius also represents a private code – since Propertius and Clitumnus were important to both Barker and Elspeth. There follows a sequence of episodes from the history of their courtship in the Villa Sole in Ariccia, the Villa Stellar of the title.

The time lag between event and remembrance is essential to the book's conception. *Villa Stellar* is, among other things, an episodic discourse upon the effects of temporality, and on the distortions brought about by memory and language. The love affair is viewed from the end of a corridor of slanting mirrors, between which words and recollections are deflected, leaving the objectivity of recall in doubt. This was not the first time that Barker had questioned the objective possibilities of truth. In *Villa Stellar*, however, the misgivings are less the result of deliberate casuistry than of a philosophical scepticism as to the ability of language to break free from the prison of the ego. This worry stems partly from what Wittgenstein saw as the limitations of language to convey anything beyond observable fact, and partly from a recognition of the fallibility of memory itself. If the language of love is invalid, and memory itself not to be relied upon, what weight, Barker seems to ask, can be attached to his testimony? Robbed of their referential potency, words are returned endlessly to the sender in a futile parody of truth.

To this subjectivist anxiety is added another prompted by Barker's reading of Skinner, whose experiments seemed to reduce the self to a bundle of conditioned responses. The themes complement one another since, if language and memory are private to the individual, and the individual nothing but such a bundle of reflexes, the result is a nightmare of solipsistic impersonality akin to Pascal's dread of the celestial void. Barker brings this point home by contrasting the birds in the dovecote at the Villa Sole with the pigeons on whom Skinner had performed his experiments. In Catullus doves are symbols of the spirit. As the poet sits in the cage of his personality contemplating his past, what is he: a soul, or a set of reflexes whose selfhood constitutes the fondest of its delusions? Against this nightmare of existential nullity, the poet pits the immediacy of his recollections, re-creating each in descriptive passages, as relaxed as they are sensuous. It is thus with the doves:

> There was this cage of wild doves hung at the wall of the villa
> among occasionally flickering vine-leaves and shadows that never
> seemed, somehow, to move with the sun, for all things were so still in
> the sunlit garden that sometimes I thought it existed
> in a trance of ideal abstraction. The dull hum of the housefly
> hung in the air by a vine-leaf seemed like the far off functioning
> of those heavenly engines we think, sometimes, we overhear.[7]

As the poet and critic Michael Schmidt was to remark, both linguistically and imagistically such writing was extraordinarily direct: 'The long syntactic unfolding of memory, and the literal quality of the perception, the word requiring to be stated as it is, without metaphorical ruffles' were mimetic in complementary ways.[8] There is also an inevitability about the way in which each epiphany is presented, and an unforced pace that was without precedent in Barker's work. Episodes in the Villa Borghese; hours of intimacy with the Contessa; moments of subtle tension with Kingsmill: all evolve with a like naturalness. Lyric XXXI, a dinner scene set in the Alban Hills, confines itself to one metaphor, that of a valley opening its arms towards the sea. The confidence with which the uninsistent eroticism of the sequence is handled is a measure of the distance that Barker had travelled since *Secular and Sacred Elegies*. Throughout *Villa Stellar*, authenticity of feeling is protected against sentimentality or sensationalism by this steady watchfulness, this rhetorical integrity. The tightly wrought sonnet XLIV attracted widespread praise:

> To all appearances the life serene:
> tea in the afternoon with two old ladies; talk
> of this and that, and who and who had been
> seen arm in arm on a Sunday walk;
> how well the new tomato plant; what who said
> when the old cow died; why the milk turned sour.
> He sat and chatted with them by the hour
> until the time came to go in to bed.
>
> The floor boards of the ballroom open up
> The flames. The pillar of. Who are you. Blood.
> Something is burning somewhere. Waltz of Death.
> The fire. I am I am. The flesh. The cup.
> He would start screaming if he only could.
> I feel the fangs and smell the stinking breath.[9]

Here the staccato statements are less stab wounds, as in Barker's poetry of the 1950s, than incisive phrases dropped into a pool of listening silence. The phantasmagoria at the end takes us straight back to Skinner and scientific relativism. The important fact is how controlled and placed the vision is. The lonely visitant in the sonnet's opening octave both is, and is not, the poet, his apparent 'life serene' conducted in the shadow of 'The flesh. The cup'. The observation of his social mask is of a kind accessible to those who know just how perilously thin all such carapaces are, how necessary to all parties. The ensuing scene of disintegration is held rigorously within the metre. There is a discretion about the choice of punctuation: the absence in the sestet of either question or exclamation marks; the suppression of the comma between those two, self-undercutting statements 'I am'. Then the swift reverting to the third-person singular, its grammatical distancing echoing other forms of restraint. Then the catatonic resumption of the first person in the final, clinching line.

CHAPTER 50

'CEREMONIES OF MEMORY'

Barker had kept in touch with Tony Kingsmill since his departure to Hydra in 1964. There is little doubt, however, that he still harboured guilty feelings about his friend, whom, he informed Hedley, he had driven into 'self-exile' by 'stealing Elspeth'.[1] In the mid-1970s Kingsmill had paid the Barkers a visit in Itteringham and afterwards written appreciatively of Barker and Elspeth's 'entwined embrace with destiny'. The writing of *Villa Stellar*, which told their story, had been intended, at least in part, as a gesture of reparation. Once it was in print Barker felt free to reciprocate Tony's visit and in the summer of 1980 accepted an invitation to Hydra. He asked Hedley to go with him, giving him the impression that the trip was to be, at least in part, an act of reconciliation. It would also give Barker an opportunity to see Greece, where Hedley would act as his guide.

That Barker had never before set foot in Greece was remarkable. 'I cannot', he wrote to Jimmy in Rome that year, 'forgive myself for never having visited the Greek islands: I hope to be reborn, some day, as a red-horned goat on the isle of Thera.'[2] In July he flew to Athens and took the ferry across to Hydra, where Hedley joined him after a week. He explained to Hedley that Kingsmill's wife Christina had been suffering from stress through being cooped up on the island; he 'suggested that we took Christina with us'. The three of them crossed to the mainland by ferry, then hired a car in Athens and drove down to the Gulf of Corinth. They travelled across to old Epidaurus, where they walked round the sanctuary of Aesculapius: the great colonnade, the shrine of Aphrodite, the amphitheatre, the rotunda with its once subterranean snakepit. Barker showed only a desultory interest in these relics, seeming to Marten to possess less of an inclination to master the historical and topographical details than he had in Italy. Perhaps he lacked a grasp of the background; perhaps the experience had come a little late in his life. Marten

472

had the impression that what Barker wanted from Greece was not so much specific cultural knowledge as a supply of intimations to feed his poetry.

A minor impediment to Barker's appreciation may well have been that, though he had long immersed himself in classical writers in translation, his deepest exposure had so far been to Latin, rather than Greek, literature. His love of Propertius, Horace and Catullus was not as yet quite matched by an equivalent grasp of the Greek poets nor, though Marten remembers him as 'steeped in Plutarch's *Lives*', had he read the great second-century traveller Pausanias, who would have enabled him to make detailed sense of these ancient sites. The principal impressions of the Greek scene with which his reading had supplied him had been gleaned from Virgil's *Eclogues*, which are set in a fabulous Arcadia: Greece seen through first-century Roman eyes. What happened next, therefore, was the purest fluke: 'We suddenly thought what we were there for was to see Arcadia, because we saw "Arkadia" written on the map.'

Hedley turned the car inland: 'Late one afternoon, when the sun was already in the west, we drove down this valley. Suddenly there was Arcadia: goats, tinkling bells, olive groves, everything golden.' They made for Mount Artemisium, with its shrine to Artemis. Despairing of reaching the mountain before nightfall, they stopped the car in the foothills, where they found a village called Korya, so unspoilt that it seemed to Marten to be drawn from a Virgil Eclogue. They fell into the local taverna; on the terrace they were plied with glass after glass of local honey brandy. They talked of the ancient world, as villagers in black gossiped around them. On the table top the glasses piled up 'like mini swaying towers of Pisa'.[3] That night, and for several days afterwards, they stayed in the loft of a farmhouse overlooking the rolling plain. At daybreak Barker would stand at the open window, staring out at the vista, like an elderly Keats travelling belatedly in the realms of the gold. 'There was a kind of ritual. An old lady would come up the ladder with hot water for George, who would shave in a very grand way, looking out of the window at this magnificent landscape. This is what we felt we had come for. We felt that in a real sense we had arrived.'

Marten was determined that Barker should see Schliemann's excavations: 'One day I said, "Just take the car and go off to Mycenae."' Instead, Barker spent the day driving around the countryside in a dream of appreciation. A few days later they left Korya and drove through Olympia and Pirgos, then cut north-east across the mountains towards Patras. They stayed under Mount Erimanthos, keeping an eye out, as Marten remembers it, for Heracles and the Erimanthine boar.[4] Rejoining the coast at Naupaktos, they drove eastwards to Itea. Barker could just make out Mount Parnassus, its flat top enveloped in cloud. After a rushed visit to Delphi, Barker and Marten made for the airport. Back at Bintry, Barker sent his guide a postcard bearing the one word 'Thankyou'. His deeper sense of indebtedness was expressed by the picture on the other side: a reproduction of Giotto's 'St Martin and the Beggar'.

Throughout the holiday Marten was struck by Barker's feeling for the Apollonian aspects of classical civilisation, epitomised for both of them, as they had been for Winckelmann, Nietzsche and Pater, by certain values: order, restraint, dignity. These were in marked contrast with the behaviour he displayed in public, while drunk; to Marten it now seemed that the Dionysian aspects of his life were, for most of the time, kept in abeyance: 'He was very good at flying some flags while keeping others hidden. He flew the Dionysian flag on Saturdays.'

Slowly, too, what Eliot had once called the 'impersonality' of tradition began to take shape in him. This was most obvious, perhaps, in his austere style of public reading. One evening in August 1979 he was invited to the Orangery in Holland Park to take part in a series of so-called 'Matchlight' readings; the object of the series was to invite two poets an evening to deliver a selection of their own work in the first half and then to sit back during the second half as a group of professional actors recited work by a poet of each writer's choice. Barker arrived in a washed-out pair of jeans, looking, on the face of it, his most casual and contemptuous. The room was candle-lit for the occasion and the audience, by and large, had come to hear the other writer. Barker seemed to dominate the reading. As he set *Poems of Places and People* on the table before him, silence fell. He raised his right hand in a gesture of intensity and clenched command, pursed his lips and announced, 'I will now read to you an elegy I wrote for Eliot.' The reading was slow, hoarse yet incantory, each phrase pitched like a question, urgent, mysterious:

> The catcalls, the wail
> and howlings of the dead
> and gone, these we
> hear but do not know
> they are what
> we hear, for they
> rise in the cry of
> the lonely bittern at
> evening by the lake or
> in the sicken
> -ing sigh of the rose
> as it dies on its
> own thorn or the

>   inconsolable eyes
>   of an eternally
>   lost child. I think
>   that if we hear your
>   posthumous voice
>   it may speak with
>   the torn out tongue
>   of the lark or the
>   shriek of the nailed
>   up rat or the squeak
>   of the blind bat. What
>   is it. What is it. What.
>   I hear you. I hear
>   you. I hear you.

His voice trailed off, and he blinked before turning to 'Morning in Norfolk'. Many in the audience that night were encountering his work for the first time. Some, though honours graduates in English, had never heard of this protégé of Eliot and Yeats. His work was never taught in literature departments (of that, at least, he was glad), and he was seldom mentioned in standard literary histories. He was a living legend yet, as far as the guardians of the canon were concerned, he did not exist. After the interval he sat with lowered head and eyes closed in a corner of the daïs, concentrating intently as the actors read a selection from his chosen poet: naturally, it was Housman. Housman represented another of academia's oversights, for he did not usually feature on courses of Victorian poetry and was invisible to Modernism. Few of those present would have admitted to a partiality for his verses, then thought antiquated and minor (there has been something of a revival since). All in all, the evening provided a lesson in literary values that made the academy, or at least the received and academic view of twentieth-century verse, appear wanting.

In May 1980 Barker read again at the Cambridge Poetry festival. In the audience sat the 34-year-old director of the Carcanet Press, Michael Schmidt. Born in Mexico, educated at Harvard and Oxford, Schmidt had built up in Manchester one of the most distinguished poetry lists in the country. He was also the editor of the literary periodical *Poetry Nation Review*. Like many people, he was used to regarding Barker as a tedious back number. The reading opened his eyes, not to the earlier work, which he still found antipathetic, but to the distinctive manner that had evolved over more recent years. To listen to Barker, he later admitted, was to concede that 'the commonplace wisdom which says that a poet must have a voice, and that voice should be as close as possible to the voice of speech, is an irrelevance'. Barker read in such a way as to lay bare the phrasing, the rhythms and the careful prosody of his poems. 'In his voice, rusted by long exposure to the world, the poems come apart and reconstitute themselves around new phrases and emphases. If you follow the recitation with the text before you, you find that even the most familiar of his poems becomes strange and new.'[5]

Public readings of this sort now constituted one of Barker's few sources of income. Thanks to the kindly intervention of a civil servant in York, and despite his lack of contributions to state benefits, he had managed to qualify for an old-age pension. He also had a Civil List pension of £500 a year, but after tax this amounted to no more than £6 a week. For several years the rent of Bintry House had been paid by the Royal Literary Fund. Barker had nonetheless a family of seven to feed. Even with regular injections of funds by Clive Sinclair, Hedley Marten and others, there was not enough coming in. The family was bailed out of its 'eternal financial despair' by certain pieces of good fortune. In March 1982, for example, Runton Hill Girls' School, a private girls' boarding school on the north Norfolk coast, found itself temporarily in need of a classics teacher. 'The headmistress', Elspeth recounted, 'had heard from someone at a dinner party that I "knew Latin", the current classics teacher being in hospital with kidney disease or similar. I was then invited to stay on. I wasn't qualified for any jobs of any kind, and had always been too busy with offspring and George to take on anything outside the house.'[6] The job entailed a round trip of twenty miles three times a week. Elpseth had failed her driving test many times: 'I never counted. I just did them now and then.' After being caught at the wheel of a car and warned by the Norfolk police, she opted for the subterfuge of an ash blond Doris Day wig and sunspecs. A few weeks later she passed.

In May 1980 Marten took Barker to northern Greece. They hired a car in Athens and drove up to the plain of Thebes and then to Delphi. As they passed Mount Olympus, its summit swathed in swirling black cloud, Barker told Marten that the immortals were sulking. Marten then made a mistake by insisting on taking Barker on a literary pilgrimage to the grave of Rupert Brooke in Skyros. The plan betrayed a misreading of Barker's attitude not simply to Greece, but to English poetry, since Brooke represented precisely those elements in the tradition that Barker had been trying to break from for fifty years. 'Rupert River' he had called him in *A Comedy of Masks*, where he had used him to castigate the myth of doomed, narcissistic loveliness ('People don't want poems,' he had made Brooke say in the play. 'They want poets. Not much but more than the poems. And they've got a lovely one in me.') They rescued the trip from disaster, however, by driving to distant bays with a leaking oil sump, improvising stories about Van Loon's peregrinations in the Sporades. Then they headed back to the mainland. Marten drove Barker to Cape Sounion. As they rounded the bay, they caught sight of the spare but perfect temple to Poseidon out on the headland. 'As we swept round the promontory, he said, "That's just like an immense lion's paw."'[7] They found Byron's initials were carved on the stonework of the temple. After these two journeys, Hedley thought, Barker had got what he wanted out of Greece: 'a sense of the eternal verities is very much what he came back with'.

Slowly, almost unnoticed by himself, Barker's reputation was reviving. One Saturday evening late in 1981 Michael Schmidt pursued his newfound enthusiasm for Barker's verse to Bintry. With him he brought his wife Claire Harman, the editor and biographer of Sylvia Townsend Warner. The Schmidts were not prepared for so abrasive a setting. At first the proceedings went smoothly, with customary greetings and drinks around a damply smouldering fire. Then, braving the lion's wrath, Harman went up to speak to Barker. Barker turned to her and announced to the whole room that she was a lesbian and that there was no point in prolonging the evening's entertainment unless this supposed fact was openly acknowledged. She burst into tears and fled from the room.

Schmidt cannot have felt that such rudeness honoured either himself or his wife, and yet he continued to champion Barker's verse. He began by publishing in *Poetry Nation Review* the long collective elegy that he had heard Barker read in Cambridge. It was a poem of sustained gravity, which wore its stanzaic structure effortlessly. In the taproom of the poet's imagination the great and small of the recent past gather. They are convened less by actual coincidence of place and time – some, like Eliot and the Roberts, can scarcely have been familiars – than by the vigour with which the poet recalls them. 'Elegy' is a poem addressed to the great and not so great, a poem conscious of a public opinion that had already consigned several of these figures unthinkingly to oblivion:

> To you it does not matter who they are
> the tartan shirted daubers and the shrill
> lickspittle poets, always two drinks below par,
> (Or so they said) who swigged and blabbed until
> what with the bleary hubbub, the fag smoke,
> the firework egos and the serpent tongues –
> these ceremonies of memory evoke
> times that resound down twenty years like gongs.[8]

The restoration of Barker's reputation, however, was hindered by the fact that he fitted into no niche in contemporary English poetry, rent by factions that meant little to him. At Faber, Craig Raine, doyen of the 'Martian' school, was in charge of the poetry list. Though there were reasons why the two men should have understood one another – both, for example, had Roman Catholic mothers, and fathers who were boxers – Barker distrusted Raine as heartily as he liked Schmidt. He also suspected that he was being maintained on Faber's list because of institutional loyalty rather than because his verse fitted into any meaningful paradigm of taste. Raine and Schmidt represented the opposite poles of British poetry. They cherished, for example, very different ideals of style and demeanour, Raine valuing the surprising versatility of metaphor, the gymnastics of language, whilst Schmidt seemed to hold fast to an older, steadier view of English verse as a careful, self-effacing craft earthed in certain humane, in essence Christian, values. Though the younger Barker might well have responded to Raine's linguistic programme, by the early 1980s his own poetic aims were far more in step with Schmidt's. The difficulty was that fashion and the media at this time decidedly favoured Raine, some of whose associates appeared to court publicity, whilst Schmidt's by and large shunned it. Though Schmidt was commendably loyal, his new enthusiasm for Barker's work was only partial compensation for a shared sense that the action lay elsewhere. Even if Barker did not feel the consequences of this exclusion, others felt it on his behalf.

In August 1981 Hedley took a farmhouse in the Val d'Este south of Siena. The Marten and Barker families drove down in a Renault and a Dormobile. On the way they camped by Lake Como in an area familiar to Barker since his two visits to the Lago d'Iseo. The house was soon seething with visitors. 'Endless friends just happened to be passing,' Elpseth remembers, 'especially friends of our teen people, and stayed on. At one stage, there were about twenty-eight of us, ranging from seventy years old to two. To feed them all, there were lots of tomatoes to chop every evening. The well ran dry. The Italian owner of the house, which had been let for eight people, came to upbraid us and expel us, but when he heard that George was a poet, all was well, with beaming smiles.'[9] One evening the whole party went to Siena and dined in the piazza near to the cathedral. Amid a clatter of music and a burst of colour, the team from the winning *contrade* in that year's *palio* entered the square, creating a hubbub that held the diners transfixed. One afternoon the farmer below the farmhouse set fire to the stubble, and a great swathe of flame lunged and flickered across the empty maize field beneath the stars. Throughout the holiday Barker was afflicted by intermittent hoarseness and an unrelenting cough. He was weak and returned from the more demanding expeditions exhausted, but he was loath to admit that he was unwell.

Ill health did not prevent him taking pleasure in the success of others. David Gascoyne had spent the previous thirty years in the shadow of mental illness partly caused by his early amphetamine habit. After several years in an institution he had set up home in the Isle of Wight with Judy Tyler Lewis, a volunteer social worker who had taken an interest in his work, and whom he had married in 1975. The publication of his *Collected Verse Translations* by Oxford University Press in 1970 had aroused the interest of scholars, and two volumes of his journals of the 1930s had been issued in 1978 and 1980. On 10 October 1981 Barker drove Elspeth and their two youngest children to celebrate Gascoyne's sixty-fifth birthday at the Arts Centre in Colchester. Those present were struck by the quality of the rapport between the two poets, an understanding composed of tolerance, humour, mockery.

While the Barkers were at the party, a London visitor walked through the twilight up the lane to the house, to which he had been invited. A letter in Elspeth's fluent hand was pinned to the kitchen door, apologising profusely for the family's absence but inviting him to stay the night if he so wished. The visitor entered and found fraying straw hats hung from every object in sight: from shelves and from picture frames and from old table lamps. Around the Aga cooker cats looked up apprehensively. Some of them pawed at the fridge door, which was secured by an elastic strap. Few of the lights worked, and those that did illuminated a decor of light blue walls crowded with shelves around an all-purpose table and bright red chairs. In the rush-matting room the hearth was a mass of grey cinders. The hallway was a dark, cold cavern from beyond which there reverberated an enthusiastic canine mating. The drinking room, abandoned for once of a Saturday, possessed a forlorn look, as if reproving the visitor for coming alone. The bookcases held some volumes borrowed from the municipal library of York in 1966 and never returned. On its canvas square the likeness of balding Higgins stared down, as if looking for something to steal. On a low table in the middle of the room lay the Grant Richards edition of Housman, with Barker's marginalia clearly marked. Other books proclaimed his loves: Francis Thompson, Walter Scott, Tennyson, Hopkins. In the lavatory was evidence of lighter reading: Georgette Heyer and Buckminster Fuller. The study was full of papers, assorted cassette recorders and tapes. Notebooks were piled up on the desk.

The latch clicked and two adolescents entered, dressed in the blazers of the King Edward School, Norwich. In the course of the subsequent conversation, the stranger asked them on what source of income their father relied. 'Dunno,' replied Bruddy. 'Grants and stuff,' offered Progles.

CHAPTER 51

'AT A TIME OF BANKERS'

In conventional terms Barker had not been much of a political animal: he had never once, for example, voted. His opinion of parties and ideologies coincided with Blake's: 'I am really sorry to see my Countrymen trouble themselves about Politics. Princes appear to me to be Fools. Houses of Commons and Houses of Lords appear to me to be fools they seem to be something besides Human Life.'[1] Barker put the point still more bluntly: 'I simply loathe all politicians.'[2] By the early 1980s he felt more alienated from the political process than ever. With the Conservative electoral victory of 1979 and Margaret Thatcher's appointment as prime minister, something narrow and obdurate seemed to have entered the spirit of the nation, a creed alien to Barker's instinctively egalitarian outlook: cupidity disguised as virtue. The Thatcher years – particularly the early years, when her dogma was at its most strident – were unsympathetic times for any who had witnessed the left-wing idealism of the 1930s or who, like Barker, had emerged from a religious background at odds with the prevailing secular Protestantism. The monetarist policies of the Tory government, and their concentration of resources on defence rather than on social welfare, struck him as a betrayal of basic decencies. While the Tory government were proclaiming a revived form of laissez-faire economics, and praising the work ethic described in R.H. Tawney's *Religion and the Rise of Capitalism*, Barker was energetically practising his own brand of anarchic, antinomian Catholicism. He remarked at this time that 'to preserve and to enlarge the rejoicing categories of created things is the duty of the poet'. This preference was not easily reconciled with the government's declared programme of tight control over public spending.

In Barker's view the unacceptable nature of the Tory government was underlined by Mrs Thatcher's renewed emphasis on the special relationship with the United States, and the willingness of the Ministry of Defence to host an armed American presence on British soil. A string of incidents had recently served to underline the political status quo. Itteringham was fifty miles from the American air force base at Bentwaters from which, several afternoons a month, jet fighters raced across the East Anglian skies on training exercises. When they disturbed Barker in his study, he glowered up at them and went on writing. But one morning in November 1980 the aircraft had done much more than interrupt his work. Within sight of Bintry, two planes had performed a series of interweaving aerobatic exercises in the sky. The pilots had lost control, one plane plunging into the sea beyond Sheringham, the other into a watermeadow beyond the Bure. Military police arrived and cordoned off the field, making it inaccessible to all but Bruddy and Progles, who knew their own way through. They collected armfuls of ammunition – lethal missiles for the most part – and bore them back to Bintry, hidden beneath their topcoats. They spent the next few weeks happily lobbing them from one end of the playroom to the other. Less desirable specimens were distributed among friends and acquaintances; one anxious mother eventually informed the police. The next day several constables had arrived and confiscated the weapons, telling Barker's sons that it was through sheer good luck that the house was still standing.[3] In fact, the projectiles, as the boys reassured Elspeth, would have had to travel at a very high speed and then make impact in order to explode.

One of the local protesters against the American military presence in Norfolk was Oliver Bernard, now settled at Kenninghall near Diss. In February 1982 Bernard decided to stage a one-man anti-nuclear demonstration outside the Erpingham Gate of Norwich Cathedral Close. He chained himself to the railings and held up a placard that read BISHOPS AGAINST THE BOMB: 'People were extraordinarily nice, I thought. A waiter from the Maid's Head Hotel would bring me a snack on a tray during the morning. When this failed – perhaps someone complained – the Tatler restaurant sent me endless cups of coffee. I stood there most days from about ten in the morning till five in the afternoon, for more than a year.' The bishop, dean and chapter were not impressed by this gesture. Bernard, however, had a firm ally in Philip Stibbe, headmaster of the cathedral school, who had his own good reasons to distrust nationalistic and imperialistic affiliations. Forty years earlier, whilst serving as an officer during Orde Wingate's first foray into Burma, Stibbe had been left for dead on the field of battle. His life had been saved by a Burmese rifleman, who had stayed with him in the forest and, when captured by the Japanese, had perished under torture rather than reveal the young Englishman's whereabouts. In his book *Return via Rangoon*, Stibbe had written, 'I shall never be worthy of the sacrifice he made. I shall always have the feeling that my life is not my own.' His sense of gratitude and humane tolerance pervaded his teaching of English literature and his work as headmaster. One morning Bruddy and Progles stood amongst the assembled boys in the cathedral nave as Stibbe announced that Mr Bernard's action deserved their support.

Another of Bernard's firm supporters was George. One afternoon in the spring of 1982 Barker drove to Norwich to collect his sons from school. As he got out of the car, he noticed Oliver standing by the gate. He 'stopped in his tracks and then walked towards me with open arms and kissed me'.[4] Bernard's protest – plucky, individualistic, ostensibly absurd – was precisely the sort of political statement to which he could respond: a flicker of defiance in the face of the big battalions.

Barker was looking for ways of incorporating in his work the still, small voice of dissent. The previous winter he had received a round-robin letter from the editor of the Catholic newspaper the *Tablet*, soliciting the opinion of leading poets as to whether it might be possible to write a poem that was at the same time a prayer. He answered that he could not argue the point theoretically; he could, however, attempt the exercise.

Anno Domini, the 1,200-line poem that resulted, was designed from the outset to mark a fresh departure in his work. He later explained the technical processes used whilst writing this work in an interview published in *Poetry Nation Review*, the magazine in which it first appeared:

> I found that I couldn't write it out by hand, but had to speak it into a tape recorder. I was so sick of the sight of my own handwriting: I was sick of the typewriter, and what I was particularly sick of was classical English prosody. What I did was to mouth it into a tape recorder, and try to work out what the dominant rhythm was, in terms of my own voice delivering the lines. That took me two months of analysis. The result is that it's set with an alternating indentation that's nearly as long as the line itself, because it's supposed to be read at one and the same time as one line and two. The break occurs where in the old days you would say that the caesura falls.

By 'classical English prosody' here Barker seems to have meant his old *bête noire*, the iambic pentameter. He evidently adopted the exaggerated indentation as a way of reproducing rhythms as far as possible from the jogtrot associated with this 'classical' line. Faber's designers were to reduce the indentation to fit the poem comfortably on to the printed page; even so, the purpose behind the typographical feature is clear enough and was brought out by Barker when reading the work in public. The effect is of parallel clauses divided by a slight pause. Such a procedure is analogous to the French Alexandrine; in passages such as the opening, though, Barker seems to have intended something closer to the Psalms as intoned to Gregorian chant:

>   at a time of bankers
>   to exercise a little charity;
>   at a time of soldiers
>   to cultivate small gardens;
>   at a time of categorical imperatives
>   to guess about clouds;
>   at a time of politicians
>   to trust only to children and demigods.
>   And from those who occupy the seats of power
>   to turn, today, away . . .

In the same magazine interview Barker spoke of the motivation behind the work. Since he had been consulted by the editor of the *Tablet* about the possibility of combining poetry with prayer, he was asked whether he concurred with Eliot's opinion that writing and praying were two distinct activities which should never be allowed to impinge on one another. His reply endorsed Eliot's dictum, but it also went some distance towards proposing a middle way:

> The fact of the matter is, to put it arrogantly, a poem is a thing communicating between an individual and the world as such; a prayer is an operation of communication between an individual and the divine idea. Those two are completely different itineraries. I think that sometimes you can get a poem, such as the 1,000-line work I've recently done, which operates as if it were a prayer. But if you've got a poem which is at the same time actually a prayer, then you've got a really monstrous and unlikely animal.

Anno Domini goes to some lengths to establish the fact that it is giving this monstrous hybrid no house room. Much of the time, for example, the writing is phrased in the vocative, and yet the object of its supplication is very far from being the God of the Christian church. Barker addresses this presence as 'Jahweh' and 'Paraclete', conventional enough epithets for persons of the Trinity. Within a few lines, however, he is calling the addressee 'Moses', as if speaking to the Old Testament patriarch. He then further confuses matters by employing the name of Leda, who, according to a Greek myth realised in a celebrated sonnet by Yeats, conceived Helen of Troy as a result of being raped by Zeus in the form of a swan. Both Leda and Moses were privy to godly intimacies; neither of them, however, was in any sense divine. The repertoire is further extended as titles applicable to mundane, even petty, human officials are bestowed on this protean being. He is called 'Superior', as if presiding over a monastery, Magister, like a magician, Lord Chief Justice, as if occupying the bench, even – perhaps in deference to the Norfolk meet – 'MFH', that is Master of Fox Hounds.

These accolades are Barker's jokes, but they are also attempts to re-create 'the divine idea' for a secular world by and large indifferent to religious language. Most importantly, they are tactics intended to disturb the trajectory of the poem so that the reader, beguiled by this rollcall of names, will fail at first to register that it is he to whom the poem is being directed. To quote the terms of Barker's interview, *Anno Domini* is 'an operation of communication between an individual and the world as such'. More particularly, it is a statement directed by the individual George Barker – poor, unfashionable, largely unrecognised – to a world seduced by the blandishments of Thatcherism into the worship of money, prestige, and success.

Once the guiding principles behind the poem are recognised, the relevance of the form also becomes apparent. The purpose of the parallel clauses is to lay the monolithic values of Thatcherite capitalism side by side with the fragile aspirations of those whose only wish is to be undemonstratively happy. The public world is outfaced by the private. In persuading us of the superior claims of the second, Barker draws a number of images from his own life: the tears of Lady Banks reputedly once caught in a jordan bottle unearthed by Kit and himself in the grounds of Corfe Castle in the 1930s; the evening spent at Korya with Marten as the villagers gossiped around them; seven-year-old Lily waking in her sun-drenched bedroom at Bintry; Sam bringing flowers.

Ironically perhaps, it is through these personal references that the theology behind the poem emerges into view and, with it, the purpose of all those eccentric invocations. The God whom the poem proclaims and obliquely supplicates is not the God of the powerful – Jehovah, mighty in battle – but the God of the meek, encountered by each of us in his or her moments of self-forgetfulness. It is this God who seems best equipped to tolerate or support those overlooked by the prevailing regime. The poem's wish – a charitable one under the circumstances – is that the leaders of the current administration may be led by this beneficent deity to attend to the needs of those their ideology disregards:

> Accord, then to the stone-dead, somehow,
>   an interpretation of these dialogues
>   with which rocks and stones and trees
>   and particularly water
>   seek continually to answer us.
>   Will your hand hesitate before
>   it unlocks the undertaker's casket

> on the unrepentant old lag, or the couple who,
>   having nicer things, as they feel, to do
> arrive a bit late for their funeral?
>   Extend, that is, if you will, latitude
> to those who steal little things, like, on Sundays,
>   an hour of love. And to Arcadia lead
> those among us who, sleeping alone in suburbia,
>   dream of goatherds and that
> far-off unfabled Korya of honey-tongued brandy
>   and brown bell-hung young goats
> whickering in morning mountains.[5]

Tradition, of course, had always accommodated this vision of the divine: in the Beatitudes of St Matthew's gospel with their pronouncement that the poor are blessed; in Christ's benediction of the crucified thieves; and in the teachings and example of St Francis. Barker's point is that this is precisely the vision of God which the cultural mood of the early 1980s has lost sight of. The government of the day was adept at twisting religion to suit its ends: after all, Margaret Thatcher had arrived at Downing Street in November 1979 to implement her programme of self-help reciting the prayer of St Francis. In reaction against such misapplication, Barker stressed all that confounds the power-mongers and law-makers. The 'little charity' of the poem's opening and closing lines is thus a heretical social virtue; but it is also an aspect of a forgotten teleological design.

Thus construed, Barker's message seems to hark back to certain tenets of English Romanticism. This is hardly surprising since much of Wordsworth's writing, for instance, had been specifically aimed against the free-market economics of his own day. In one respect, however, Barker's poem transcends his nineteenth-century forebears: in his reinterpretation of, and reverence for, science. To Blake, for instance, the physics of his time, with its emphasis on unbreakable laws, had seemed to be in complicity with the unsympathetic policies of the war-waging government of Pitt the Younger. For Barker, by contrast, wise to the theories of Heisenberg and the unaccountable, seemingly delinquent, behaviour of sub-atomic particles – 'the quixotic quanta' or 'the will-o'-the-wisp neutrino' – the anarchic world of contemporary science offered new hope.

The only exception to this welcoming of the scientific is Barker's response to behaviourism, already falling out of favour by the time the poem was written, but still disconcerting to one who, in his youthful 'Octologue of the Emotions', had written enthusiastically about robots. An acclamation of the machine had been an important aspect of the poetic of the 1930s, especially in the work of

Auden and Spender, which Barker himself had sometimes echoed. In Skinner's theories such thinking had, it now seemed to him, borne terrible fruit. In repudiation of this neo-reductionism, Barker produces the most powerful lines of the poem. In the course of *Anno Domini*, his sentence structure journeys well beyond the tentative present infinitives of the opening section to employ a number of verbal moods: the present indicative; the past perfect; even a supplicatory form of the imperative. Nowhere, however, does the writing achieve a more convincing grandeur than when, in ridiculing the mechanisation of the human, Barker uses the authoritative rhetorical question:

> Here is the mad creature
> you have created. Have you built your own
> murder into the marvellous faculties
> we use because we possess?
> What does this shambling machine whisper
> as it crawls and stumbles among rocks and ruins,
> its clockwork eyes clouded with self-hate, its
> terminals cancerous, wetware and wordwrite
> alphanumeric, phonemed,
> automatic forks pick-
> -ing up isotopes, robotics utterly grouched,
> the reproductive generator hanging
> down like an obscene decoration, the
> anthropic spirit skinnered, the
> enigma cybernized,
> the circuit of the nervous system worn
> to a nexus of Freudian wires,
> what does this shambling machine whisper
> when it encounters, down the dark path,
> half way through a Black Forest, of
> a midwinter midnight,
> the huge god riding on a dead white horse?
> What, what does it whisper?
> 'I am a man'?[6]

To readers who knew his earlier poetry, *Anno Domini* seemed to sum up a life's work, and at the same time to chart a completely new course. As Anthony Thwaite wrote in the *Times Literary Supplement* it was 'a beautifully controlled piece of work, allowing all of Barker's sonorities, jokes, puns, proper-name sonorities, coat-trailing dictums, cheeky hyperboles and exaggerated locutions to be accommodated into its movement forward'. Barker's writing had always been energetic but problematical, being occasionally open to the charge of self-repetition, and yet '*Anno Domini* makes one think again.'⁷

The delight attending the poem's appearance in *Poetry Nation Review* was overshadowed by personal tragedy. In March 1982 Rose was preparing for a much-needed holiday in the Balearic islands. She had been living in a cramped council house in Norwich with her two boisterous teenage daughters and two-year-old son James. She had fought free of her heroin addiction but had been taking regular, self-prescribed doses of paracetamol as a mild palliative. Ironing her clothes on the day before her departure, she felt ill; a friend contacted her GP, who diagnosed flu. The following morning, when Rose was due to leave, she felt worse. Another doctor was contacted; he sent her to the Norfolk and Norwich Hospital, where tests disclosed liver failure brought on by paracetamol poisoning. She was sent by ambulance to the liver unit at King's College Hospital in south London, where her condition deteriorated rapidly. The unit had hoped to perform a transplant, but her system was overtaxed, and an operation proved impracticable.

Elizabeth was already in London and Rose's daughter Claudia travelled down from Norwich to be with them. Barker, Georgina, Christopher and Sebastian soon arrived.⁸ That evening they were waiting in the corridor when a doctor emerged from the ward to inform them that Rose had just died. They went back to Georgina's house in Stoke Newington. For Barker, the only way of reconciling himself to Rose's senseless end was to see the event as part of a pattern possessing an almost artistic symmetry. 'The manner of her life and death', he said that evening, 'were perfect.'

When the news reached Bintry Rose's second daughter, Jane, who had not been able to get to London, screamed and screamed while Raffaella held her.⁹ Elizabeth's writer's block lifted just long enough for her to write one lyrical tribute, but for months she went around stunned, blaming herself for the tragedy. She never recovered.

Jane came to live at Bintry. George and Elspeth also looked after little James for several months until Georgina gave him a home. The whole episode had intensified Barker's sense of the mysterious. To view tragedies such as this as the result of accident was simply not his way: always now he looked for a pattern of coincidence. For example, somewhat against the advice of his father, who would have preferred him to adopt a less precarious profession, Christopher had slowly been building up a reputation as a freelance photographer. The following winter he was nearing the crest of a hill in his car when an approaching vehicle overtook and failed to pull over in time. There was an almost head-on collision. When Christopher woke up in hospital, his left eye had been removed. Some days later he looked up to see George standing at the foot of the bed, dressed in an uncharacteristic tweed suit.

He wore an expression of awe and disbelief that caused him, Christopher thought, to resemble doubting Thomas come to thrust his hand in the side of the risen Christ.[10] Forty-eight years before, Barker had sat in a bleak corridor in Hammersmith Hospital waiting as his brother's right eye was taken out. The coincidence was minimal, but George could not but read some meaning into the fact that his brother had once lost his right eye and now his son had lost his left. Stoically, he interpreted the symmetry as the product of some sort of malevolent destiny. At Bintry when he told visitors of Christopher's accident, he added, 'a pair is lost.'

In February 1983 Barker was seventy. For his birthday Schmidt commissioned a *festschrift* to be published in *Poetry Nation Review* and appointed an editor to interview the poet. Wary at first, Barker eventually opened up and spoke at length about his life in the 1930s, medieval verse, Catholic theology and the poetry of Housman. At moments he approached the brink of confession. When asked about the inception of the poem 'Luctus in Morte Infantis' in 1934, he replied, 'That poem was written for a child of mine who was . . .' His voice trailed off and he failed to complete the sentence. For his own contribution to the *festschrift* he proposed a humorous modernisation of Sebastian Brandt's fifteenth-century 'Narrenschiff', 'The Ship of Fools'. Several weeks later the half-complete typescript of this poem was still lying on his desk. The editor asked if the poem was to be completed. The poet yelled, 'Go and finish it your fucking self!' The editor complied, his end-rhymes appearing without change in the magazine, though improved by the author when Faber issued the poem in the volume *Anno Domini*.

Coincidences and flashes of premonition continued to trouble him. Sebastian was now restoring and roofing the shell of a building he had purchased in the Peloponnese. In June he took his father to visit it. They spent a night in a hotel in Kiparissia before visiting Delphi and Olympia. One day Sebastian drove him down to inspect his restoration work. A serpent was lying across the threshold. Barker would not enter the house. When Sebastian asked the reason, he told him about the snake that he and Kit had once drowned in a jam jar behind Ixworth Place.[11]

In all sorts of ways Barker was settling his accounts. He was, for example, worried how much of his work was out of print. He had published ten individual volumes since the *Collected Poems* of 1957, which was now unavailable. Apart from *Anno Domini*, the only volume currently obtainable in book shops was *Villa Stellar*. In spring 1984 Schmidt expressed interest in bringing out an updated *Collected* under the Carcanet imprint. However, Faber were reluctant to release Barker from his contractual obligations, preferring to retain the option to issue a *Collected* volume themselves. It took the intervention of several interested parties, including John Johnson, who had for several years been acting as Barker's agent, to persuade them eventually to do this. Again, the services of an editor were needed as Barker did not have the energy to edit the book himself. Weakened though he was, he was reluctant to seek medical advice until, with the collusion of the doctor, Elspeth tricked him into visiting the surgery in Aylsham, where emphysema was diagnosed and appropriate medication prescribed. After any mental or physical exertion he was now tired and often breathless. However, he managed to rekindle his old energy on Saturday nights, when he treated himself to a large bottle of red Martini.

For all that, Barker's spirit was undimmed and his defiance as bright as ever. By 1984 Sebastian's friend Robert Pollet had settled in a house in Aylsham. Pollet's father was French and a university professor, and his mother English. George had initially met him when visiting the King's School, Canterbury in the early 1960s to give a reading when both Pollet and Sebastian were pupils there. He had retained contact while Pollet had studied first in Oxford, then back in France, subsequently embarking on a short lecturing career in Francophone West Africa. Though unconvinced of Pollet's talent, he had encouraged him in his writing, which was fluent, ornate and scattered with learned references in English and French. Once settled in Aylsham, Pollet became a regular at the Saturday-night celebrations at Bintry House. There he boasted openly of his publications and of his Anglo-French reputation, of which he believed his English acquaintances to be insufficiently aware: 'I have published nineteen whole volumes: *nineteen*! President Léopold Sédar Senghor of Sénégal wrote an introduction to my book, Léopold Sédar Senghor!'

Barker was extremely fond of Pollet, whose pedantic conceit both amused and irritated him. On Saturday, 19 May 1984, the two men commenced a civilised fireside discussion on English versification. The point at issue was whether the metre in English poetry was wholly qualitative (that is, stress-based) as Pollett maintained, or, as Barker contentiously claimed, at least partly quantitative (that is, based on the length of the sounds). In point of fact, Pollet's view was the academically orthodox one, though Barker's was a lot more interesting and illuminating about his own practice. For Barker, accent had always been subordinate to vowel length, and he stuck to this preference even as Pollett insisted on the textbook generalisation that in English, as opposed to Latin verse for example, the stresses in the line are what count. To everybody else in the room the point seemed theoretical and arcane. The issue, however, struck at the heart of the way in which Barker heard, and therefore wrote, verse.

Within minutes, their voices were raised to shouting level: 'quantitative, fuck you', 'qualitative, damn your eyes!' At nine o'clock Barker ordered Pollet out of the house, instructing him never to darken his doorstep again.

The next day Robert wrote apologising, but reiterating his schoolboy point.[12] All reputable authorities were agreed that English verse was qualitative. Because of his advocacy of this truism, Pollet was *persona non grata* at Bintry for several weeks.

CHAPTER 52

'ABSTAIN! ABSTAIN! ABSTAIN!'

Barker's gradually increasing fatigue was not immediately apparent to strangers or to those who only saw him on Saturday nights. On these occasions his fragility was carried off with raffish grace. In reality he was now growing markedly weaker year by year. He did not, for example, have enough energy to seek out the books and magazines where the work of half a century was scattered and bring it together for his new *Collected Poems*. He did not even possess copies of all his nineteen books of verse, still less the periodicals in which his poems had appeared over the years. As a consequence, he asked the editor of his recent birthday *festschrift* to take on the task and invited him down to Bintry to confer. They spent the evening discussing church architecture, St Clement of Alexandria, and the BBC programme *Songs of Praise*, which Barker said 'brings the tears to my eyes'. Little conferring was done. At the very end of the evening he remarked casually, 'Well, I suppose you're getting on with this thing, are you?'

After a night of wine and theology, they retired to their separate rooms at opposite ends of the upstairs landing. At three o'clock in the morning they were both seized with the same physical need. They emerged, stark naked, from their respective doors and stumbled towards the bathroom. Meeting outside the open door, they simultaneously reverted to an inbred politeness. They bowed and scraped in the moonlight as each beckoned the other to precede him. Eventually, out of mere exhaustion, the editor fell into the pitchblack room and fumbled with the light switch.

The following afternoon Barker drove him around the countryside to look at churches. As he opened the throttle along a narrow road between fields the colour of burnt ochre, he quoted de Tocqueville: 'When you go to England, the human intellect is devalued by forty per cent; but the countryside is the most beautiful in the world.' He seemed to his passenger rebellious yet appreciative of tradition, venerable and at the same moment zestfully young.

He would be tamed neither by spurious considerations of respectability, nor by Mrs Thatcher's much-vaunted return to 'Victorian values'. Home-grown hypocrisies had always antagonised him. Soon another moral fashion at variance with all that he stood for arrived from across the Atlantic, in the form of 'political correctness'. Barker could not abide a creed that he felt to be at war with verbal candour; his response to those who espoused such ideas was invariably to deliver the least forgivable sentiment. He had become one of W.B. Yeats's Mad Old Men.

In October 1983 the editors of the *Sunday Times* colour supplement chose Barker and Georgina to feature in the series 'Relative Values', in which well-known people relate to one another were encouraged to reminisce about their shared past. Christopher drove across to Bintry to take the photographs. The interviews were conducted by the paper's staff journalist Georgina Howell. Barker took one look at Howell and concluded that she was a doctrinaire feminist. When she asked about the sources of his poetry, he told her that all of his work was filched from the Kwakiutl Indians. Asked about his attitude to his daughter, he commented, 'Of course it pleases me that she is beautiful. It is a woman's duty to be beautiful. When we have a civilised society, they will put down ugly and stupid women.'[1] Even the palpable affection of Georgina's contribution could not save Barker from the outcry that followed, as the *Sunday Times* readers were no more amused by his remarks than his interviewer had been. There were letters of protest and irate grumblings in the dailies. The response did not disconcert Barker in the least. He had spoken deliberately, in plain defiance of fashion.

To younger friends, used to milder manners and more circumspect speech, such forthrightness seemed exotic, if salutary. Living in Aylsham at this period was the writer Lindsay Clarke, who was beginning work on a novel about the history of alchemy. Entitled *The Chymical Wedding* it was set in Munding, a Norfolk village very like Itteringham. The story takes place partly in the Victorian age and partly in the 1980s. Perhaps its most startling contrast, however, is between the social behaviour of two literary generations: Barker's and Clarke's own. In the first chapter the protagonist, a poet and reluctant lecturer, eavesdrops on a scene of debauchery in a forest clearing. The girl is long-limbed and American, but it is the man who is the object of his fascination: an elderly and lecherous satyr called Edward Nesbit, a poet whose fame dates from the 1930s and whose 'body was scrawny, hollow-chested, the belly rounded like a wineskin over the grizzled cloud of his pubic hair. He must have been over sixty.'[2] Though their first meeting breaks up in disarray, the narrator is irresistibly drawn to this foul-mouthed, sweet-tempered, priapic

Nestor with his elaborate, profane vocabulary and his determination to live on the edge. At one point when they are drinking by a lake, the older man looks up and grants his questioner a glimpse of his chameleon nature: 'I guessed at a lifetime of masks, of protective coloration to keep the world at bay.'[3] Barker was seventy-six when the novel was published, winning the Whitbread Prize for fiction for 1989. Few who knew George doubted that his personality had contributed powerfully to the central figure of Nesbit.[4]

Barker's coughing and shortness of breath continued. He went back to his doctor, who changed his medication. He told Barker that he was not to over-exert himself and should travel to a warm climate if possible during the winter months. The doctor did not know his patient. On his editor's next visit Barker told him, 'The bloody doctor tells me I shouldn't drink, I shouldn't smoke, and I shouldn't fuck. What *else* is there?'

With dreadful accord, his own body and the prevailing cultural climate seemed to be turning against him. Denied the pleasures of the flesh by medical opinion, he was at the same time bombarded with health fads and with all the signs of neo-Puritanism that had swept across the Western world in the wake of the AIDS epidemic. But he had not lived riskily for seventy years to be told towards the close that playing safe would lengthen mere existence. He drafted a *memento mori* in clear italic handwriting, and propped it prominently on the kitchen dresser:

> No smoking
> LUNG KANSER
>
> ★
>
> No Drinking
> Cirrhosis of the Liver
>
> ★
>
> No Loving
> AIDS
>
> ★
>
> ABSTAIN!
>   ABSTAIN!
>   ABSTAIN!
>
>   +
>
>   Live long and then
>   DIE
>   JUST THE SAME[5]

Barker continued to provoke extreme reactions. In 1985 (after previous residences from 1980–2) Sebastian was Writer-in-Residence at the South Park Arts Centre in Bracknell New Town. In May he organised a reading at the centre with the help of Michael Asser, Berkshire's chief librarian and a recent convert to Roman Catholicism. A hundred and forty-five people had turned up to hear three 'Living Masters': Gascoyne, Gavin Ewart and Barker. Before the reading Sebastian asked Asser if he would like to meet his father, who had just arrived at the centre's Terrace Bar. They entered to see a beautiful woman sitting in a far corner next to 'a bundle of rags'. The woman was Elspeth; the rags were Barker, who, inferring Asser's involvement in the organisation of the event even before being introduced, shouted at him in a voice blurred with champagne, 'Are you responsible for all this? I *hate* culture.' But when Sebastian introduced Asser, the mock aggression dissolved to be replaced, as Asser described it, by 'an expressive movement of duffel, revealing a final period Stravinsky face, half masked by a pair of shades. A voice between gold and brillo pad said, "My dear, forgive me."'[6]

The hall was full. Barker had forgotten his copy of *Villa Stellar*, so he borrowed Asser's. After Ewart had amused the audience and Gascoyne had intrigued them, Barker's turn arrived. Slouched in his wooden armchair, he read two lyrics from *Villa Stellar*, and then announced to the audience that he would give them 'something about the death of God'. As his right hand reached out, and the worn voice resumed, they heard words that were both timely and ageless:

> Let who will lay upon the stone
>   of the run-over child a wreath
> inscribed: *Deo Voluntas*. I will not, for there is a mystery here
>   not given to any, yet, to understand.
> The printed shadows of Hiroshima, do they
>   point their evaporated hands at us
> or you? How could it have been you?
>   This is a thing so evil that
> it could have come from nowhere but a mind
>   capable of inventing the idea of evil.[7]

Over drinks afterwards, Barker asked Asser if he was a Roman Catholic. When he replied that he had just been converted by reading Newman, the poet told him a story: 'After his conversion, Newman lived in obscurity in Birmingham. One day he returned to Oxford, the place of his former triumphs and of his greatest influence. He revisited the village outside Oxford where he had built a church. A passer-by saw this old man at the lychgate, crying many tears.' Barker paused before adding, 'I would have given everything to have been one of the tears that fell from Newman's eye.'[8]

Asser was deeply impressed by their *tête à tête*, but Barker's anecdote about a lachrymose Newman gains if one considers its source: Lytton Strachey's biographical essay on Cardinal Manning in *Eminent Victorians*. Strachey has just been telling his readers how in 1860 Manning peevishly interfered with Newman's elevation to cardinal, and cruelly quashed his scheme for an Oratory at Oxford, which would have enabled him to end his days in peace in his beloved university city. Newman returned to Littlemore, the church that he had established in the Oxfordshire countryside shortly before his conversion to Rome, to mourn his lost hopes. The main thrust of Strachey's sardonic narrative is to cast doubts on Manning's impartiality and to mock Newman's grief. The remarkable aspect of Barker's retelling was that it converted this cynicism into compassionate pathos. Of course, Barker had revered Newman since his early adolescence, but the thirteen-year-old who had stared up at the priest's statue outside the Oratory had been daunted as well as stirred. The 72-year-old poet, by contrast, felt sympathetic understanding. It was a measure of the distance that Barker had travelled from the comparatively uncomplicated bohemianism of his early middle age that in 1985 he had come to recognise that an Oriel-educated church dignitary could also feel like an outcast.

Yet, even as his tolerance for authority figures increased, he seemed to become more and more in tune both with his own innate and irrepressible daemon and with the rebelliousness of his children. For Elspeth, the teenage years of her boisterous brood could sometimes be trying. For Barker their behaviour could be irksome also, but his understanding was undeniably enhanced by the fact that he too had been unruly in his time. Raffaella, Bruddy and Progles were now all studying on scholarships at private day schools in Norwich. Both Barker and Elspeth were keen they should eventually go to university. Yet on such matters the children took their cue less from the Oxford-educated Elspeth than from their father, who, while he followed the official line of encouraging scholastic probity, demonstrated in his anarchic and attractive persona the advantages of the opposite. He had dropped out of school at fifteen and now had not only achieved, but also learned, a great deal more than many people who had stayed the course. Which one should his children use as their example?

One by one they abandoned their studies. Raffaella staged a protest against sitting 'A' level papers at school, but agreed to write them at home, refusing thereafter to budge an inch further up the academic ladder. Persecuted by schoolfellows who could not understand the ways of the Barker household,

Bruddy and Progles did not even go that far. To enter the kitchen of Bintry in the late 1980s was like wandering by error, no longer into Neverland, but into the *Rocky Horror Show*. Bruddy's raffish quiff had turned into a Cherokee crest. Progles had shaved all his hair off and wore razor blades in one ear. In time Sam took to wearing black, stuck a pearl in his nose and rambled the countryside by night. Having inherited Barker's adolescent obsession with death, he once bedded down on a grave beneath the stars in Itteringham churchyard. In the behaviour of his sons Barker was confronted with flashbacks to his own younger self: the ruminative, vain, self-doubting adolescent glimpsed in his early journals. 'Have you seen Sam recently?' he asked each visitor to the house. 'He's quite *beau-tiful*, like a young Apollo.'

By imperceptible stages serenity was stealing over Barker as he aged. Ferocity, for one thing, had become exhausting; but Elspeth also recognised a deeper change: 'In the last few years of his life, he had mellowed a great deal, which cannot facilely be put down to his increasing illness. It's just that he was happier in himself. And he began perhaps to look more kindly at people.'[9] Increasingly he used the metaphor of a sea voyage in relation to his advancing age, but it was an odyssey across uncharted seas. Without illusions himself, he could be sharp with those who glibly believed their own sense of navigation to be perfect. From his children's books he revived a pirate called Sanctimonious Bones, eternally in search of land. He took a rhyme scheme based on Edward Lear's and, though his children were no longer small, resumed his habit of nonsense verse in successive 'Voyages of Sanctimonious Bones'. These took the emblematic mariner to a number of unforeseen destinations; all he knew for certain was that, in spite of the compass and sextant of faith, he was well and truly lost:

> As Captain Bones bestrode the deck
>   he felt the timbers shiver:
> 'But why does she quake? Why does she shake?
>   I'm sailing up a river.'
>
> So sweet and smooth the path to truth
>   if you sail up the Tiber
> (unlike the Sutra or the Brahmaputra
>   or rowing over the Khyber).
>
> All rivers come home at last to Rome
>   and all known roads as well:
> For she does not quibble, the Roman Sibyl,
>   she simply contradicts Hell.

'Ah' quoth the Angel, 'This is so,
    but if you sail in reverse
The path's the same but you'll end in the flame
    of Hellfire, only worse.'[10]

Appreciating the precariousness of his dependence on divine mercy, Barker took to quoting with greater frequency a favourite saying of his, the one surviving line of the Greek poet Agathon: 'Not even the gods can undo the past.' He often remarked to visitors that the object of life was to discover 'the meaning of forgiveness', a term which Elspeth knew him to employ in both its theological and its everyday connotation. 'I don't think that he ever looked upon himself with any particular kindness,' she said. 'He hoped for forgiveness, whether we are talking in the sense of absolution or of human forgiveness. And because those who did manage to endure his dreadful behaviour did so because they loved him so much, and what was not dreadful was *so* marvellous, *so* worth having, this was a kind of forgiveness in itself.' He was, he knew, adored by many in this world, and by others resented. For the rest, a hazardous Grace might save him.

CHAPTER 53

'WE'RE LOOKING FOR HENDRICK VAN LOON, MY DEARS'

Throughout these late years Barker was regularly invited to Rome, where Dede was now a permanent resident. He had, he now claimed, 'driven Dede into the church'. Every summer he would wait for her to send his fare, working himself into a state of mild anxiety in case it did not arrive. It always did, since Dede valued the continuity represented by his contact with the boys. Though Edward was in London working as a film-maker and translator, Jimmy and Francis were still Romans. After taking a fine arts degree at Yale, Jimmy had a studio in Rome, and Francis was studying physics at Università La Sapienza. Since Barker's health benefited from a warm climate, his visits increased to one or two a year. Usually he went alone. Elspeth was not invited and was both pleased to see the back of him and happy to welcome him home. The Bintry Barkers became used to the idea that they were members both of a family and of a multinational clan. And then there was Rome's biennial Festivale dei Poeti, to which Barker was invariably invited. The event was organised by the city's communist corporation, which paid the participants a generous fee as well as providing the fare, accommodation, and translators at all of the events. They also met the expenses of a minder, who, in Barker's case, as his emphysema worsened, was increasingly essential. In 1982 he was accompanied by Raffaella. In 1985 he took Oliver Bernard. They arrived in Rome on 24 June to find the temperature in the nineties. Edward picked them up in his Opel at their hotel in the Piazza de Spagna and drove them round the city. The principal readings took place at Ostia on the coast, where David Gascoyne also performed. Afterwards Barker took Bernard to Assisi, where he acted as guide both to the city and to the historic labyrinths of the Roman faith. He had always harboured the hope of converting his familiars to the Church (he still entertained aspirations for Sebastian). To Hedley Marten that June he sent a hospitable postcard showing the Basilica of St Francis and with the simple invitation: 'Come on in!' Marten was a hard case, but Bernard was a different matter. After several days in Assisi, Oliver found himself viewing an entire cultural and religious landscape through Barker's eyes.[1] When the poet returned to Bintry, he announced to all who would listen that Oliver had become a Catholic and was, in consequence – maybe for the first time in the uphill climb of his life – 'luminously happy'. Oliver went further and was received into the tertiary order of St Dominic by Father Bruce Kent in Oxford the following year. When Barker received the news, his expressions of delight were tempered only by his jibes at Bernard's having chosen to become a Dominican rather than a Franciscan. In Soho Jeff was told of his brother's conversion. 'Yes, I've heard,' he scowled. 'He's found God.'

In August 1986 Dede took a villa close to the beach at Sabaudia, eighty miles to the south of Rome. Edward filmed his father there, in a straw hat, expansive, his face tanned and relaxed. A sense of well being seemed to descend with the completion of *Anno Domini* and the prospect of the new *Collected Poems*. Early one evening Edward sensed the condition of silent contemplation out of which his father's poems often seemed to emerge. Barker was standing on the terrace overlooking the sea crowded with bathers, some of whom were waving in the mellow light. 'He said something almost inaudible about tranquillity, about how different his life would have been had it not been lived under the shadow of war. Then he went silent as he stared westwards towards the declining sun.' A few days later he asked Edward to type the manuscript of a new sequence in twelve sections called 'Ikons'. In it, the circumstances of time and place that apparently gave rise to the poem are utterly transformed. All that is left of the seaside setting is a single image of a wave slowly breaking, while the poet's act of staring out to sea is attributed to a monumental face cast in stone.[2] For Edward, however, there was no mistaking the mood of serenity pervading both the moment of origin and the work that it inspired.

The serenity was coloured by a sense of death's proximity. Barker was having to face up to the loss of many within his circle. Hounded by professional disappointments, by drink and by an unaccountable obsession with the muse as Mother Goddess, Robert Pollet had fled to France to die in his mother's arms. Pollet had been a man of considerable latent talent who had somehow never managed, throughout all of the slender volumes he had published, to give full expression to an undeniably distinctive voice. To George, the younger poet seemed to have been the victim of an unreciprocated passion for the muse. In his notebook he sketched out an elegy 'To Robert Pollet':

> I cannot call up the instances that might honour
> Your particular dance with that yellow fanged dame

> Who taught us both to write, because your
> Heart was less in the dance than in the fame
> Of that fashionable whore.
>
> You she had by the short hairs. Ah, Robert, if only
> Your Deux Chevaux had driven to the nearest
> Asylum and not to the Circean disco of the vainly
> Self-crowned where the laureates and their dearest
> And nearest die bitter and lonely.

In July 1985 Patrick Swift died in Portugal, not before seeing the fishing village he had adopted as his home converted into a tourist trap, partly as a result of his passionate description of it in a book about the Algarve which he had co-authored with David Wright. Barker missed his friend's quick wit:

> The brush that he held in his hand
> sign and symbol, instrument and
> artillery of his graphic will
> never, for me, performed as well
> as that bright goldfishing diver
> his tongue: it fished from the river
> secrets only nature seemed
> to know, or the swift mind dreamed.[3]

Elizabeth Smart had been ill for months, suffering from hardening of the arteries. In 1985 she had returned to the Dell after two years as Writer-in-Residence at two Canadian universities – one in Edmonton, the other in Toronto. She had found Canadian academic and social life for the most part dull and inhibited, but had enjoyed the consolation of witnessing a slow revival of interest in her work, especially among feminist scholars. Alice Van Wart, whom she had met in Toronto, was editing her journals, which were eventually to appear in two volumes entitled *Necessary Secrets* and *On the Side of the Angels*. In February 1986 she had attended the wedding of Claudia, Rose's elder daughter, in Norwich and was in exuberant spirits, popping a champagne cork in the car as George drove her from the register office to the reception. Two weeks earlier, she had stayed with Sebastian at his house in Greece; she had insisted that he read her *Anno Domini* in the evenings, but belatedly cautioned him against his father's influence: 'You must understand that there is another side to George that's not very good.' On 4 March she suffered a heart attack when visiting Christopher in his flat in Marshall Street in Soho.[4] Christopher found her dead in an armchair. Sebastian phoned George to break the news, whilst Elspeth was out of the house. When she returned, she found him 'stunned like a winter bird, huddled'. The funeral in South Elmham was magnificently attended, but even more so was the memorial service in St James, Piccadilly. Delayed in a traffic jam, Barker arrived late and breathless to read 'Quia Amore Langueo'. He published no elegy. Instead, on a napkin he inscribed a rebuke in the spirit of her informal nobility:

> O most unreliable of all women of Grace,
> Could you not wait for one last embrace?[5]

In March 1986 Elspeth realised that Barker was hiding a letter from her. Finally, he showed it to her. It came from an address in west London and began:

Dear Mr Barker,
I was born 2 June 1934 at 'Danegelts', Geldeston and registered at Loddon, Norfolk. Apparently I was baptised 'Clare'. Anyway a George Granville Barker and a Winifred Theresa Barker (formerly Woodward) are down as my parents.[6]

So fifty-one year old Clare came to Bintry. She had been raised as Kate, and in ignorance of her parentage. Long before, she had discovered her adoption papers. Determined to seek out her natural parents, she had, however, soon come to a dead end, having been led by near-illegible copperplate on the birth certificate into believing that her father was the deceased playwright and theatre manager, Harley Granville Barker. She had guessed her father's true identity when she read Elizabeth's obituaries. She was nervous of Barker at first but, after an initial awkwardness, the two of them established a warm rapport. She looked, he told her, 'like an oil painting of Jessica', though she also possessed Monica's voice and Rose's wild vivacity. Nature had knocked nurture for six. In his notebook Barker adapted and extended a famous fragment by Sappho:

> After so long, after so long,
>   the lost things come home,
> the crumbs of bread, the marriage bed,
>   the goddess in the foam,
> all that is lost, later or sooner
>   to its home will come.
>
> And I have found, along the shore,
>   where bone and spectre flourish
> a spring of childhood that can heal
>   and with its waters nourish,

> and then by that spring a daughter
> who cannot ever vanish.

Kate remained devoted to Barker for the rest of his life.

Moves towards reconciliation did not always work. Anastasia, the younger of Jessica's twins, came over from America to meet her father. She proved so influenced by Jessica's accumulated resentment as to be resistant to all of his blandishments.[7] 'I was brought up to be judgemental,' she explained to Raffaella. Anastasia found her father, whom she continued to see through Jessica's eyes, frightening. Her evident timidity in his presence, and her equally evident judgement, left him for once at a loss.

As Barker's health declined, he began to use a wheelchair. In it he was pushed around the grounds at Bintry by various members of the family, occasionally proclaiming with grave emphasis, 'We're looking for Hendrick Van Loon, my dears, looking for Van Loon.' The contraption did not limit him; rather, it became a throne. As he reigned from it, it was as if the mantle of public recognition had at last descended upon his shoulders so that the world had enacted Eliot's prognostication, 'You should be prepared to be acclaimed late, if at all.'[8]

The *Collected Poems* appeared in May 1987 and received much public attention. 'To read these poems', said Harold Pinter on Channel Four, 'is like watching somebody walking from line to line effortlessly, as if on water.'[9] In Karl Miller's *London Review of Books* John Bayley, Wharton Professor of English Literature at Oxford, wrote a joint review both of the *Collected Poems* and a reissue of *By Grand Central Station*: it contained some of the most trenchant and constructive comments that Barker had ever received, praising his special feeling for syntax, his facility for linguistic 'glide', 'as if the movement of French or Irish underlaid' his verse.[10] Bayley concluded that Barker had been the only poet of his generation who had chosen to serve the thematic purposes of Modernism through verse that sounded stylistically archaic. The verdict did little to reassure Barker as to the perspicacity of academics. In his eyes it was the edict of an Oxford professor, therefore damnable. To Sebastian he scrawled a limerick:

> There was a Professor called Bayley
> Who criticised Literature daily.
>   He announced 'Every song
>   Is en-tire-ly wrong
> 'Til I play it on *my* ukulele.'[11]

On 7 May 1987 the *Collected* was launched with a reading at the Poetry

Society's headquarters in Earls Court Square. It was so well attended that there was scarcely room to stand in the society's tiny basement bar. At one point, edged by the crush into a corner, the poet was speaking to a middle-aged critic. An elderly female fan forced her way through the throng towards them. Indicating the critic, she enquired, 'I do not know this young gentleman, Mr Barker. Is he by chance one of your sons?' The poet surveyed the sea of heads stretching in every direction. 'I should think so,' he retorted. 'Most people here *are*.'

The book won joint first prize in the British section of the Commonwealth Poetry Prize. Barker turned up for the prizegiving and reading at the Commonwealth Institute, but was too weak to undertake the arduous national tour that followed. Then the *South Bank Show*, London Weekend Television's Sunday evening arts programme, expressed interest. Its editor-in-chief Melvyn Bragg commissioned a film on Barker's life and work, to be written and directed by the Irish novelist and broadcaster Carlo Gebler. Gebler wrote to Barker to explain that he had in mind a scenario based on Rene Clair's 1924 film *Entr'acte*. This was to involve an imaginary funeral, to be filmed in soft focus in Itteringham churchyard, at which the poet's coffin was to run away from its pallbearers, who were to be played by his sons. Magic tricks were to be performed by Barker himself, who was later to ascend to Paradise, led by a female angel in the shape of a ballerina in a tutu.[12] Gebler was minded to call the film *Wothehel Mehitabel* after Don Marquis's book of humorous verse *Archy and Mehitabel* (1927), in which that exclamation is delivered by Archy, a *vers libre* poet who has transmigrated into a cockroach. By the time of the preview in August 1987, which Barker, his friends and family attended, more prosaic counsels had prevailed: the film had been retitled 'George Barker'.

But the funeral sequence survived, as did Barker's assumption into heaven, for which he was filmed sitting in the stable between two immense archangel's wings, wearing a white smock. He was smoking for all he was worth as the ballerina lit his cigarette. Other footage depicted his past life. It included a child's windmill turning outside the rain-splashed window of a flat in the Samuel Lewis Dwellings in Ixworth Place. On the soundtrack, recorded in a hotel in Wells-next-the-Sea, Barker told of an encounter with the muse in the form of a sack of potatoes swinging between the beams of Hearne Cottage. The essence of poetry, he declared, was praise; its purpose was to express 'the joy at the heart of things'. The suspension of disbelief which Coleridge once attributed to poetry was the result of recurrent rhythms, since 'the pulsing of the heart is what suffuses everything including the intelligence'.[13] An off-camera Gebler asked why Barker wrote poetry. He replied, 'because if I did not, like the Mexican Gila monster, I would accumulate my own filth for exactly two years, and then explode'. Curious viewers later scoured the encyclopedia in vain for this attribute of the gila. In a scene shot in the outhouses at Bintry, the poet clambered into the cobwebbed hulk of the Mercedes, and announced that the vehicle was 'so damned old I propose to be buried in it'. In a later sequence he and Elspeth quarrelled openly around the kitchen table. The mustard of his conversation bit through all else. After the film's public screening in January 1988 the Irish novelist Edna O'Brien wrote to him, 'you were stunning, authoritative. Everything you said was fresh from the brain.'[14]

The mustard continued to sting, sometimes unintentionally. One evening Barker and Elspeth had dinner at the Caprice restaurant in Mayfair with Harold Pinter and his wife, the historian Lady Antonia Fraser. 'My dear Harold,' Barker murmured into the playwright's right ear, 'I love you dearly, but why have you married Hayley Mills?' Pinter replied that Lady Antonia bore no resemblance whatsoever to the actress. Later Barker was overcome with guilt. He drafted Pinter a note, protesting that he had harboured 'no intention at all, when we last met, of belittling your beautiful wife. It was – well – Hebraic of you to think so.' Then, troubled by the wording of his own apology, he added a postscript, 'By Hebraic I mean to speak of a nation that has been too much and too often offended.'[15] His reactions smacked of his earlier panic about the selling of Eliot's letters. He would rage and bellow, but when it came down to it there were one or two people he could not bear to think he might have offended, even in jest.

He developed an unobtrusive magnanimity, of which associates who had met him earlier in his life would have believed him incapable. This was nowhere more evident than in his attitude to his children, whom he now watched with affectionate amusement as one by one they found their way into various professions. Raffaella left for London and, with a speed that nobody could quite credit, landed a responsible editorial position on the monthly glossy *Harper's and Queen*, as well as writing spirited articles for the *Evening Standard*. Tired of skulking at home, Bruddy momentarily made his peace with Thatcherism and became 'something in the city' for several months. He then returned to his senses and, after several morose weeks as a roofer, formed the successful rock band Honeychild. After years of wounding the self-esteem of visitors with his sharp-edged cartoons, Progles decided to become a television actor. The progress of all three reminded their father of himself in the 1920s: braggadocio, canniness, personal attractiveness, luck. Lily was manifestly the delight of his old age, though, as Elspeth said, 'she exacerbated his fear of Hell and departure; he couldn't bear the thought of no longer being with her'.[16] He boasted of the achievements of all his children and was there to pick up the pieces when life went wrong.

In London, Raffaella met Hugh St Clair, an old Etonian on the staff of the *Evening Standard* whom she took down to Bintry to meet her father. St Clair had heard rumours of George's sharp tongue and approached their first meeting with apprehension.[17] To his surprise, he met a man who was polite, charming, and highly informative on the subject of churches. He drove Barker around the Norfolk countryside. The poet told him the history of the long-naved parish church at Salle and spoke of his own father with whom, as he conceded, he had not been on the best of terms. St Clair was immediately struck by the singlemindedness with which he had adhered to his craft across half a century of very mixed fortunes. On 25 June 1988, Raffaella and St Clair were married in St Palladius's Episcopalian church in the shadow of Drumtochty Castle. Barker drove up with Elspeth. Despite being in evident physical pain, he insisted on walking his daughter up the aisle to give her away, as tradition, and his own affection and sense of ceremony, demanded.

On 25 August 1988, four months after holding an exhibition at the Newburgh Street Gallery, Kit died. Barker wrote an elegy for him, which harked back to their impecunious beginnings:

> And now, most loved dead,
> we shall not traipse again
> the tenements of Ixworth Place
> Where we trespassed then.
>
> And tattered at the arse
> ransacked the dustbins
> for ragshop junk – jamjars
> and rags and rabbit skins.[18]

On the evening after Kit's death, Sam went down to the Walpole Arms in Itteringham to buy some matches. He was seventeen and had devoted most of his school years to playing football, at which he excelled. He was too young to be riding the motorbike he had borrowed for this particular errand. When he emerged from the pub, he failed to look right and was knocked off the bike by a vehicle. Sam stood up to apologise to the driver, then collapsed in the road. He was rushed into the Norfolk and Norwich Hospital, where it was found that his right leg was so badly smashed that a whole series of operations would be required to restore it. He spent the next five years in and out of hospital, often in great pain as skin, muscles and sinews were systematically grafted on to his leg.[19]

For Barker, Sam's accident recalled his own accident on the Zenith motorbike at the same age in 1929: the bluestone remedy, the months with Big Mumma hovering anxiously at his bedside. It also threatened the loss of a limb such as his father and elder sister Olga had both suffered in their last years. The vast family waited for Sam to experience some kind of extreme emotional reaction. None occurred. He endured it all – the twenty-eight operations, the crutches, the successive bouts of painful hospitalisation – with sublime insouciance and courage. When eventually he was transferred to the Royal Free Hospital in Hampstead, he had a flagrant and mutually rewarding affair with one of his nurses. His leg was saved, but football was an activity of the past.

As Barker weakened physically, he grew in spirit. From early 1988 onwards his health deteriorated markedly. He was several times taken into hospital, either in Aylsham or in Norwich. Little could be done except to stabilise his condition. Increasingly, on the doctor's recommendation, he sought the sun in winter. In January 1989 Edward and Jimmy took him to Egypt. They flew to Cairo and then to Luxor. On their arrival they had to hire him a wheelchair, in which they manoeuvred him around the sites, lifting him bodily into a felucca to be rowed along the Nile. Edward wheeled him around the Valley of the Kings to see the statues. Looking down as he did so, he noticed an expression of awestruck wonder on his father's silent face. Though Barker said nothing, Edward had the impression that, maybe for the first time in his long life, his father had come face to face with something that his imagination needed to scale down in order to assimilate.[20] To Sebastian, Barker wrote, 'I think I'm turning into a God.' The sentence was derived from the dying words of the Emperor Vespasian on 23 June AD 79: 'Vae, puto Deus fio.' It is telling that Barker neglected to render the opening exclamation 'Vae', or 'Alas!' The effect was to convert the Roman's awestruck terror into a mood utterly his own: a blend of wry acceptance and mock-swagger.

On 23 February 1989 Jessica died at a medical centre at Bowling Green, Kentucky. The cause of death was cited as respiratory arrest caused by left-lobe pneumonia. In fact Jessica had been declining, mentally and physically, for years, the first symptoms of Alzheimer's disease having manifested themselves when she was in her late fifties.[21] She had been looked after by Anastasia, whose recent confusion in Barker's presence, and abiding sense of him as a guilty party, had been exacerbated by her knowledge of her mother's condition. The following day Barker's sister Monica died in San Francisco, her address book beside her, the page lying open at George's entry. The news reached Bintry on the 26th, his seventy-sixth birthday; the very same evening Anastasia phoned with the news of Jessica's death.

The coincidence of timing reinforced the valedictory mood in which George had languished since Kit's decease the previous year. When he could, he worked on *Street Ballads*, which was to be his very last collection. All of these poems are suffused with a terminal music. The tone is that of a man who has looked into the seething heart of things and rejoiced. Kit and Monica's deaths in particular had thrown him back to the remote years of their childhood together among the dirty dustbins and the back alleys of Fulham in the years immediately after the First World War. For Barker, however, the privations of those years were still vivid. The experience of childhood poverty had defined his identity.

There is much, thematically, in *Street Ballads* that is reminiscent of earlier collections – the perpetual philosophical might-have-been of the Archer poems; the elegies for Swift and Kit. The volume also included poems and ideas reworked from his children's books. There was an evocation of Auden's melancholy last stay in Oxford, entitled puzzlingly 'Rain at All Souls' (Auden had stayed at Christ Church). Barker also took the opportunity to reprint 'Ben Bulben Revisited', a poem about the legacy of W.B. Yeats commissioned for the academic journal *The Yeats Annual* by its editor Warwick Gould, which had also appeared in Schmidt's *Poetry Nation Review*. 'Ikons', the finest of the poems, draws on his experiences of the Mediterranean world without any specific invocation of geography. What survives of his Egyptian experience, however, is even less than had survived of Greece in *Anno Domini*. There is just a spirit, the gleam of Mediterranean sunlight against ancient monuments, the sense of an aged man listening enraptured to the wash of the sea; beyond that, sculptured blindness, like that of the unseeing statues at the Valley of the Kings, or of a poetical Canute cut into granite: 'you will find a face staring / out of eyes / that cannot see the sea'.[22] In the last stanza the poem breaks into the first person singular, as if the aged mask the poet has already described has become his own face, impassively contemplating a world where all erotic experience and all pain are rendered into art:

> I have not learned the ceremonies of salvation
> if they are not like this. They go,
> the young dog dancing over the old Adam,
> and the flayed babe singing,
> and Aphrodite, her belly full of cupids,
> alighting tiptoe upon rocks,
> all ceaselessly chanting in flames, ceaselessly chanting.[23]

CHAPTER 54

'ENTERING INTO THE KINGDOM'

There was still time for one or two adventures such as getting married, for example. Barker and Elspeth's children had been brought up unaware that their parents were unwedded, though by 1989 this was far from unusual. Over a quarter of a century their relationship had proved itself more enduring than many a conventional marriage. In company Barker consistently referred to Elspeth as his 'wife', even listing her as such in several reference works: his notice in *Who's Who 1989* offered the information that they had been 'married' in 1964. This was less a stretching of the truth than an insistence on the emotional facts of the case.

Jessica's death made the formalisation of their union a possibility at last. Elspeth was naturally aware of the role that Jessica had played in Barker's life; it was written for all to see in *By Grand Central Station* and *The Dead Seagull*. Her name, though, had seldom been mentioned in the house. Raffaella had known of her father's history, but, along with other members of the family, had decided that 'it was important for us all to get on with our lives, rather than raise old ghosts.'[1]

George and Elspeth applied to the United States for the death certificate. While they waited for it to arrive, they arranged a wedding at St Joseph's Roman Catholic Church at Sheringham on Saturday, 29 July. In preparation for the event the parish priest, Father Donnellan, visited the couple at Bintry. Donnellan asked Barker when he had last made his confession. His answer, apparently, was 1932. Donnellan then took him into the playroom, where the two men stayed for over an hour. After the priest had left, the family asked Barker what had been going on. He told them that Donnellan had asked him how many of the ten commandments he had violated in the last fifty-seven years. He had replied that he had broken them all except the sixth: 'Thou shalt not kill.' He had been granted immediate and obliging absolution.[2]

On 29 July the pews of St Joseph's were full. Barker dispensed with the wheelchair, standing throughout the service in a white suit. Afterwards the wedding party returned to Bintry where, on a warm summer's evening, the Barkers entertained their guests in the garden. The Gascoynes journeyed up from the Isle of Wight, and Heath-Stubbs from London. Barker sat in his wheelchair on the front lawn, bearded now and wearing a straw hat. The wedding photographs capture his mood of happiness, roguishness and authority.

For a honeymoon Fiona, George's one-time student from York, and her second husband, the economist Paul Crawford, gave the couple a Tuscan holiday. At the very last moment they took out comprehensive travel insurance with Thomas Cook. Fiona and Paul flew to Italy on 7 August. They were joined by Elspeth, who had made the long journey by train, due to an abiding fear of air travel. Barker and his wheelchair came on a later plane with Lily.[3] Paul met them at Pisa airport and drove them to the ancient towerhouse they had rented for three weeks. It was in the hamlet of Monte in Chianti, overlooking vineyards and forests of scrub oak and pine. Siena lay away to the south. The house was too small for the honeymoon couple, Lily, the Crawfords, their two daughters and Fiona's children by Hedley. After dinner on the terrace, the adults would drink the local wine, listening to dinning cicadas and watching the landscape darken, a belltower in the middle distance providing a solitary light.[4] Barker was exultant, but increasingly unwell. On the second day of their stay the Crawfords took him to consult a local doctor, who erroneously prescribed diuretic drugs to be injected nightly into his backside. Paul Crawford drove him to Siena, where he wheeled him across the campo to the green-and-white marbled front of the cathedral. On entering, Barker dipped his fingers in the stoup and sent the holy water cascading. In the nave he enthused about the influence of African art upon Tuscan, discoursing on the sibyls on the mosaic floor, Hermes Trismegistus and the slaughtered Innocents.

That evening there was an eclipse of the moon. Elspeth and Fiona stayed up to watch while Barker went to bed early. The drugs were dehydrating him. All the next day he stayed in bed. A friend of Fiona's, a homoeopath holidaying in the vicinity, came to visit them. Taken to see the poet, she placed an amethyst crystal beside his bed and crooned New Age incantations over his shivering body while he slept on.

Some days later the Crawfords took him to see a doctor recommended by Cook's. He immediately ordered that the poet be moved to the hospital in Siena. He was placed in a small ward with two other patients, one of them a devoutly Shi'ite Iranian, who each morning thanked Allah out loud for another day's life, once in Parsee and then, for his fellow patients' sake, in English. The

Crawfords took Elspeth out to dinner to keep her spirits up. In the middle of the meal they were approached by anxious waiters who announced that there was an urgent telephone message. Fiona's son Benedict had been left in charge of the younger children in the villa. He had closed all of the shutters against the droning insects, but the girls could not sleep in the glare of the one halogen lamp, so he had leant a foam cushion against it as a shade. The children had woken up to find the whole house filled with dense smoke.

In Siena hospital Barker soon revived, thanks to the medication and the three-course meals, each accompanied by a bottle of Chianti. He had lost interest in sleep. One night he left his bed and, in excited reverie, strode off down the moon-blanched corridors in his nightshirt. He made a complete tour of the adjacent floors, pursued by anxious members of staff. Cornered while entering an empty operating theatre, he was brought back to bed; he lay sedated for three days while Elspeth stayed propped up on cushions on a folding chair, mesmerised by the green cardiac trace on the oscilloscope, and reading accounts of that year's *palio* in the local newspaper.

In *Il Messaggero* she read of the death of the psychiatrist R.D. Laing. She dropped this fact into the intense conversation at the homoeopath's house that night, when invited for supper. The whole company, all of whom were Laing groupies, rose to their feet and hugged one another before casting a half-full bottle of cognac in the open fireplace to speed Laing's shade to its rest.[5] In the quietened hospital room Barker slept on. Four weeks later he was flown back to London, at Cook's expense. He was transported by private ambulance to Bintry, where he emerged in the driveway talking about Sienese mosaics.

In the mid 1960s, after a handful of Elspeth's reviews had appeared in the *Listener*, Barker had bought her a set of black notebooks, hoping that she might fill them. However, she had soon been too busy with childrearing to contemplate sustained writing or reading. As the children grew up she found time to read more. In 1988 she had written a piece about her hens for the *Observer*, who had then asked for a Christmas story. The Barkers had just received news of the arrival of her first grandson, Raffaella's son Roman, on 17 November 1988: 'So I wrote about a journey to see a baby who happened to be my first grandchild.'[6] The Virago Press contacted her a year later and asked her to write a novel. Slowly she had begun one, drawing on some aspects of her Scottish upbringing and also inventing much of it. Though she did not show the result to Barker, his bullying insistence that she persevere conquered her natural self-doubt and diffidence. Knowing his skill with titles, she asked his advice on what to call the book. Barker asked her if she had thought of Scott's lines in 'The Lay of the Last Minstrel': 'O Caledonia! stern and wild / Meet nurse for a poetic child!' When published in 1991 by Hamish Hamilton, to whom her Virago editor had moved, the novel was to be called *O Caledonia*.

'ENTERING INTO THE KINGDOM'

Elizabeth Smart's literary reputation had continued to grow, especially in feminist circles, and was particularly high in her native Canada. Her posthumous recognition caused Barker much pleasure. The feminist cult of St Smart *femme et martyre* by contrast, galled him. Without his permission, his letters to her from 1940 to 1947 had been sold to the National Library of Canada, along with precious early diaries and drafts of his work. This seemed to him regrettable since, though the documents as such were legally part of her estate, the copyright on the text was his; he would have preferred these private communications to be kept, if at all, among his own papers. The publication of Smart's diaries in Canada in 1988 further disturbed him. He wrote to Sebastian, her literary executor: 'I had no knowledge beforehand of either the book *Autobiographies* or the book *Necessary Secrets*.' As biographies of Elizabeth were mooted, he grew restless. When Rosemary Sullivan, who was preparing a biography of Smart eventually to be published under the title *By Heart*, put in an appearance at Bintry, she arrived to find Barker packing for Italy. He was mocking and told her half-truths. She asked permission to quote from his correspondence; he refused to let her use anything except the one resonant phrase 'O my Canadian!'[7] When Sullivan sent him the galleys for his approval, he wrote back to her in Montreal: 'If these proofs are final – that is, if they cannot be corrected – there is no point in this correspondence. I have no wish to make "comments" on your book.' The entire affair caused Barker real pain.

In February 1990 Barker was taken to Carthage by his son Edward and his son-in-law Hugh. They stayed in the Abu Hotel, where Barker sat in his wheelchair in the blue-tiled living room, talking and reading. He was wheeled round the ruins of the ancient city, where he found the Roman remains superior to the Phoenician. It seemed to St Clair that his father-in-law's interest in historical sites had been eclipsed by his delight in the modern. Barker had reverted to the Futurist enthusiasm of his youth. Rather than photograph the ruins, he took repeated snaps of moving cars, factories and industrial installations. His visual observation was, St Clair discovered, as acute as ever, and stimulated by the most unexpected subjects.[8] He had come to abhor sentimentality or fuss. When in difficulty or pain, he declined all help, bawling, 'For God's sake let me die in peace, you bloody nuisance!'

Barker had been advised not to drive by his doctor. Despite this advice, he relieved the tedium of life at Bintry by driving into Aylsham daily to buy a packet of cigarettes. In July he was taken ill in the car. He was rushed to St Michael's Hospital in Aylsham, which he described to Sebastian as 'a charming little cottage hospital full of Hogarthian drunken fishwives disguised as nurses, whose care was nonetheless exemplary'.[9] After a few days he was released. He grew thinner and gaunter in appearance, though also spryer and more jaunty.

From some angles he had come to resemble the elderly Ezra Pound, from others the comedian Spike Milligan. He still smoked far too much: the habit was the nub of his health problems, but it was too late for him to change. In the autumn of 1990, when he sat by the fire with his rug drawn up over his knees, he could have been some decrepit grandee out of Conrad or Kipling, whose stories were a special love in his last few months.

As ever, Arthur C. Clarke, Alexandre Dumas and the academically unrespectable Georgette Heyer featured in his tireless reading. Though science continued to enthral him, including the speculations of Stephen Hawking's *A Brief History of Time*, literary academicism of any kind, together with party politics, continued to be his aversions. Sebastian was researching the background for a long poem about Nietzsche, in the course of which he had read George Steiner's *The Death of Tragedy*. He wrote recommending Steiner's work to his father. Barker replied scathingly about Steiner's idea that the Christian doctrine of redemption made tragedies difficult to write in the post-classical age.[10] Steiner, he thought, suffered from 'that terrible Cambridge disease, intellectual theatricality'. 'Why has he adopted the three Catholic categories of Hell, Purgatory, Heaven', he wanted to know, 'since I understand that he himself does not subscribe to that Communion? What reality do they possess for him? I do not think he really knows what he means when he talks of Hell.' Then he added in wavering handwriting: 'I do not think he has been there.' Though the Christian view of life was not tragic in essence, he argued, a tragedy might well occur 'in Christian terms':

> I think that an air of the heroic – even the morally heroic – can hang around the tragic character, and about the character of tragedy . . . I think furthermore that you yourself may have overlooked one small matter when you insist that the Christian vision has denied itself the tragic outlook for this, I believe is to be found in the great adumbrations of Pascal on the separation of man from God. This is the tragic vision. And it obeys the Aristotelian precept. The tragedy of the separation comes about from a failure in the human character: i.e. it is capable of instituting this separation.[11]

'The separation of man from God' was another way of phrasing Newman's vision of the 'aboriginal calamity' that had engulfed mankind at the Fall. The consequences had necessitated a heroic stoicism which continued to appeal strongly to Barker. In 1939 he had recommended Marlowe's brutal death in a tavern brawl as the pattern for a poet's demise; in 1955 he had told Edith Sitwell that he wanted to go to Hell. In the 'Secular and Sacred Elegies' he had toyed with damnation through blasphemy. In 1990 he was still living in the spirit of Pinkie's remark in *Brighton Rock* that salvation was to be grasped, if at all, 'between the stirrup and the ground'. As he stood facing extinction, clutching to him his misdeeds, his nineteen printed books and his fifteen children, it was indeed possible that Grace might unaccountably swoop down and rescue him. His letter to Sebastian seemed to assert that the definitive tragic moment, and the ultimate possibility of heroism, would consist in the long split second before that intervention improbably occurred.

For visitors he summed up the essence of human life in a quotation from the philosopher Santayana: 'Man is comic in his origin, lyrical in his essence, and tragic in his destiny.' He was less sure than ever about the justification for the intellectual superiority over the other species which human beings arrogated to themselves. He wrote to Sebastian, 'I sometimes dread to think what ideas pass through the intelligence of creatures whom we believe to possess none or, conversely, others who possess too much.' By what right did we ascribe greater complexity of mental organisation to the author of *Thus Spake Zarathrustra* than to, say, a pet cat? It was not entirely certain that even Wittgenstein could match a cur in mental attainment. He had long been fascinated by the concluding aphorism of Ludwig Wittgenstein's *Tractatus Logico-Philosophicus*: 'What we cannot speak about we must pass over in silence.' What Wittgenstein had meant was that there are certain subjects, mystical for the most part, with which philosophy is not competent to deal. For Barker, in his last few months, it came to seem as if a similar limitation embarrassed the poet. He composed a set of meditations, titled 'On Wittgenstein's "That Which cannot be spoken of"' about the impossibility of translating thoughts into speech or verse. Yet the thoughts still kept on coming, too frequently divested of words now, even if words could express that lack:

> A thought, perhaps as of a fading torch
> flickers up in the corridors of the mind
> and I see them, sprawled upon the floor,
> spreadeagled on the wall, piled up like
> dead fish that sliver and flash in the beam
> of dying light, the denizens that expire in the head
> without a word;[12]

By February 1991 *Street Ballads* was at the printer's. Craig Raine at Faber & Faber inconvenienced Barker by requesting an autobiographical blurb 'somewhat less discreet than your *Who's Who* entry – which makes it look as if you've spent your entire life writing poetry'. In reply Barker drafted the briefest of *curricula vitae*, mingling self-deprecation with swagger:

I scrounged around in California, indulged in love affairs with Rooseveltian Psychiatrists in New York, lived on my wits in Italy and at intervals, in order to restore my faculty for suffering, returned to England, always briefly, save for twelve years obscure and therefore idyllic happenings in a woodcutter's cottage in Sussex. I have never had any money. My education was, really, elementary and I remain ill informed upon all serious subjects. I understand the infirm working and the psychology of aspirant poets, but nothing else. It seems that I exercise a peculiar fascination upon Celtic women. I have had several wives of various cheerful dimensions, and my progeny is extended between Kentucky and Fregene.[13]

He sent this note to Raine who, however, was about to leave his post as editor, having been appointed to a fellowship in English at New College, Oxford. In April Raine was replaced by the poet Christopher Reid, who now assumed responsibility for *Street Ballads*. Barker welcomed the handover as a sea change and soon established a warm working relationship with his new editor. In the course of preparing the new volume for publication, Reid sent to Bintry an empty brown envelope without the letter it should have contained. Barker wrote asking if the missing letter could be sent on and added, 'You seem just the sort of man I can do business with.'[14]

Outwardly Barker had become a mercurial, god-fearing, extemporising leprechaun. Through Progles, he had met a remarkable young Glaswegian. Tom was charming and streetwise in a manner which he respected. On the long empty weekday afternoons, when he tired of Georgette Heyer and the thoughts came more naked of words than ever, Tom would keep him company in the Aga-warmed kitchen. They sat swapping tales of devilry (how Eliot, he said, would have loved it). Tom seemed to him to be possessed of a gaiety, a courage, and purity of heart; in sober fact, the young man was a bank robber. 'George', commented Elspeth, 'may or may not have known of Tom's profession. I certainly didn't at the time.'[15] Whether he was aware of his visitor's clashes with the law or not, the dash and vigour of those who took large risks with their lives continued to inspire Barker. Remembering Kavanagh in his cups and the whole procession of rogues and rascals who had passed before his observant eye, he reworked a ballad from the children's books; it was about a local delinquent called red-haired Timothy, whom the vicar of Itteringham had tried in vain to persuade to go back to Borstal:

> The parson does his simple best
> to talk him into going back
> to Borstal but the boy can not
> perceive the need for his arrest.

> I saw him yesterday beside
> the river, stalking with his gun
> a pheasant gaudy as a prince.
> I heard it shriek out as it died.[16]

Barker's sympathy with the lawless had brought him close once more to that pillar of respectability, Housman, with his obsession about felons and their deaths by hanging. To live was a more complex proposition. 'To write simply', George counselled Sebastian at this time, 'is as difficult as to live well.' Most difficult of all was to live consistently which, despite his admiration for disciplined souls like Housman and St Francis, had never been Barker's way. At seventy-eight, he was never more in his element than when speaking to the young men and women whom his children brought home and with whom he spent hour after hour talking and joking, as if he himself were still twenty. Josh, Tristram Hull's son, had turned into a tall, shy, unaffected young man torn between fascination with archaeology and a love of the country pursuits among which he had grown up. He would depart for digs in the Mediterranean and return to tell Barker about them, sharing the excitement of discovery while in the meantime earning his living on the land. Barker did not know whether he felt more affection for him when he was enthusing about the buried legacy of Khania in Crete or stringing up rabbits and 'stalking with his gun'.

The blinking blue light of an ambulance became a familiar sight outside the front porch of Bintry as, through the summer of 1991, Barker was taken to the cottage hospital at Aylsham or else to the Norfolk and Norwich with heart failure. He refused to wear a name tag, protesting, 'I know who I am.' At some level the children were all aware that they would lose him very soon. So was Elspeth, but all of them repressed the thought consciously. Raffaella proceeded with her busy journalistic life in London, while Elspeth kept the house going and fulfilled Hamish Hamilton's schedule for the publicity of her novel.

Those children who were leading metropolitan lives were in constant touch with Norfolk, alert to changes in George's condition. There was an unspoken agreement that, at least at weekends, one or more of them would be there or, failing that, other friends and relatives would step in. Early in October Barker was admitted to hospital again. There was nothing out of the ordinary about this particular seizure, nothing to set it apart from earlier crises. Oliver Bernard went to visit him. Since Oliver had trouble with his eyes, the two poets commiserated with one another about the contrariness the human body in falling ill and the equal cussedness of the government in curtailing medical provision when this occurred. Early the following morning, Barker wrote to Bernard from the ward:

My dear Oliver,
How very pleasant it was to see you, even so briefly, on Saturday evening. But I drop this note to let you know how shocked I am to learn about your defective eyesight. I rather suspect that you will need someone to badger you about the operation – well, anyhow I propose to do so. Not that badgering will produce rabbits from the hat. No, my idea is that the more cases the NHS is seen to be incapable of dealing with, the more shocking the Tory dismantling of the service will appear. (This is the kind of joke one makes at 5.30 a.m., when I write this.) No, this is just an early morning greeting after a night in the dark wood.[17]

Barker was released in a few days. Gathering his remaining strength, he worked through the final proofs of *Street Ballads* and sent them off to London. That month he received a letter from the biographer Miranda Seymour, who was working on her *Ottoline Morrell: Life on the Grand Scale*. She enquired about the Saturday afternoon in May 1936 when the *grande dame* of English literary patronage had called on him in Dorset. Barker replied, re-creating the moment when Lady Ottoline had appeared before his cottage in Plush:

I looked up one morning and saw the longest of Austria's handmade Daimlers draw up at the little white gate. I saw my first historical hallucination step out of the car. This was a very tall figure garbed lavishly in grey silk ... with what I took to be a prizewinning Cowes yacht balanced upon its marvellous auburn head. She wore pearls suspended from her fingers on little golden chains. I realised that I was being visited by a veritable vision ... I think back with admiration and love on the enchanted spheres she inhabited. On her first visit she gave me two cups and saucers.[18]

Elspeth's *O Caledonia* had now appeared. Since Barker seemed a little better, she felt able to leave for three days of public readings in Scotland, returning on Saturday, 26 October. On that day, the last of British summertime, Oliver Bernard came over from Kenninghall for the usual evening carousal. Sam and Edward were up from London and Lily and Cousin Jane completed the party. Barker was too ill to come downstairs. He received his visitors in ones and twos, sitting up in bed. To Oliver he murmured, 'I am entering into the kingdom';[19] to Edward he remarked softly, 'Remember I am a Catholic.'[20]

He awoke to the day of the year that he most hated, the morning when the clocks had gone back. Sam, Edward and Jane left for London. Barker seemed weak. In the early afternoon he rallied and did a little writing in the black notebook that he kept by the bedside. Towards evening he asked Elspeth to read him one of Kipling's stories. He chose a lesser known one, 'The Tomb of His Ancestors', which she read aloud from Somerset Maugham's *A Choice of Kipling's Prose*.[21] As she read, Barker murmured, 'Soften it up, babe, soften it up.' Halfway through, he interrupted to ask, 'Has anyone ever told you that you have the most remarkable eyes?'[22] She finished reading at about a quarter to seven, and went downstairs to cook supper. Lily had walked to the Walpole Arms to fetch some cigarettes. Raffaella, who was on an assignment for *Harper's* in Florence, phoned and arranged to come to Norfolk as soon as she returned. Elspeth replaced the receiver and went back upstairs. As she opened the bedroom door, she saw Barker sitting propped on the pillow with an expression of slight surprise on his face. His heart had stopped.

CHAPTER 55

A SPRIG OF HONESTY

The children gathered at Bintry as arrangements were made for the funeral. Barker had not received the Roman Catholic rite of extreme unction nor, despite his last remark to Edward, had he expressed a specific desire to receive it. It seemed right to the family that he should be buried close to Bintry in the sanctified ground next to Itteringham church, which, as a pre-Reformation structure, had clearly once been Catholic. The vicar of Itteringham, the Reverend Hawkes, was happy to officiate at the funeral. On Saturday, 2 November Lord Walpole tolled the bell in the tower of the tiny parish church. Hedley played Bach's Prelude in B Minor on the organ as the mourners crammed into the pews beneath the whitewashed perpendicular arches. The Catholic priest from Sheringham arrived unexpectedly, causing a flicker of sectarian awkwardness. Earlier, at the house, Progles had placed a drawing that he had made of Sanctimonious Bones in the coffin. The coffin was carried into the church on the shoulders of four of Barker's sons, Edward, Bruddy, Progles and Sam, his son-in-law Hugh, and Tom the bank robber.

As the coffin entered the church, the organ was playing Mozart's 'Ave Verum Corpus'. When Oliver Bernard stepped forward to deliver a reading from the works of St Francis, he looked down the narrow central aisle; Barker progeny stretched the length of the church, as far back as the font. Raffaella read the poem 'The Child's Paradise Lost' from *Runes and Rhymes and Tunes and Chimes*:

> And God Said to the little boy
> as the little boy came out chapel
> 'Little boy, little boy
> did you eat that apple?'
> and the little boy answered 'No Lord.'

The coffin was taken into the churchyard, and laid in a grave in the north-east corner, in a plot bordered by oak, beech and pine. It was the Feast of All Souls.

Barker's obituaries were more plentiful than he would ever have expected. All dwelt on the fraught question of his reputation. *The Times* remarked, quite correctly, that his poetry 'came into fashion, fell out of fashion, and never recovered'. Barker had remained 'a furiously vital, hit-or-miss poet, capable of producing both a disconcerting rhythmic muddle and astonishingly beautiful, pellucid lyrics'. Eliot had been correct to print almost all that he had written. Perceptively, though, the anonymous writer went on to observe that Barker had been a moralist as a result of, rather than despite, his having been a bohemian. Quite erroneously, he or she added that he had not resented his poverty: 'Poverty, which he experienced, did not concern him too much, but women did.'[1] Writing in the *Independent*, Anthony Thwaite evoked Barker's rumbustious social persona, but also his warmth. 'There was something sardonic, faintly menacing and dangerously charismatic about Barker,' who had been 'extreme, excessive, almost idolatrous of his friends'. As a poet and a person he had 'commanded loyalty and sometimes exasperated affection from a large circle that went far beyond the Bohemian'. 'In some way I have never properly faced', Thwaite confessed, 'he was my image of a true poet.'[2] David Gascoyne, who had known Barker longer than anyone living, paid tribute to 'the electric and hilarious nature of our conversations, disputes and gossip, George's inexhaustible flow of verbal felicities and apocryphal anecdotes'. In his last few years 'with white hair and beard, the once dashing and turbulent George' had at long last been 'venerable and happy'.[3]

The most provocative judgement on Barker's life and work, however, was delivered inadvertently. In the last week of October John Carey, Merton Professor of English at Oxford University, had been commissioned to review *By Heart*, Sullivan's life of Elizabeth, in the *Sunday Times*[4]. By pure chance his piece appeared on the day of Barker's death. It bore the headline 'Rebel Without a Clue' and gave no quarter either to Sullivan's biography or to the social and literary world inhabited by Smart and Barker, 'who is, one gathers, still alive'. Since Carey knew little about either writer, his piece necessarily drew all of its facts from the book it castigated, setting them against no independent source of information. For some time Carey had been working on his ambitious study *The Intellectuals and the Masses*, portraying the pride and prejudice of the literary intelligentsia in the early twentieth century. In his review he used Barker implicitly as ammunition for the assault on artistic pretension he was mounting in his work-in-progress. The Barker whom he portrayed was a monster. At the point in Sullivan's book when Smart bit through Barker's upper lip, he declared, 'you feel like cheering'.

The content of the review, and its unfortunate timing, caused anger amongst Barker's family and friends. Allan Massie sprang to Barker's defence in the *Daily Telegraph*. Bruce Bernard sent a personal letter of protest to Professor Carey, who wrote back apologising. In December Carey was invited to the *Sunday Times* Christmas party in London. He was enjoying a quiet glass of wine near a table in the corner, when he looked up to see a 'winged Fury' bearing down on him.[5] It was Raffaella, who delivered a stinging reprimand. She was followed by Elspeth, who rebuked him for having caused offence to her family by his review. Carey attempted to escape across the tabletop. The wall was in the way. 'Be wary, Carey!' Elspeth warned.[6]

In February 1992 *Street Ballads* appeared. The first copies of the book arrived just in time for the memorial requiem mass, which was held at the London Oratory on 26 February, which would have been Barker's seventy-ninth birthday. After the service a reception was held in the Polish Club at 55 Prince's Gate. Heath-Stubbs swayed on stage and talked of how the work of the deceased had been inimical to 'the academic mind'. The academics present looked subdued.

In Italy Dede endowed a mass in perpetuity for Barker's spirit, to be said annually in November in the Basilica of San Francesco in Assisi. At Itteringham churchyard a slate headstone was set up, carved with Barker's name and dates and the words 'BELOVED' and 'Resurgam'. Above these inscriptions was the Lawrentian motif which had appeared on the title pages of the Phoenix Press in the 1930s, depicting the eternal bird arising from the flames. Facing the headstone, among other flowers, a sprig of honesty was planted on the mound.

Among other awards, Elspeth's novel won the prize set up in memory of David Higham, once Barker's agent, and was short-listed for the Whitbread Fiction Prize. Raffaella also wrote a novel, the first of many, called *Come and Tell Me Some Lies*, which drew on memories of her father and of her childhood in Bintry. Its theme was the way in which oral history converts events into legends: 'The myths of my family, favourite fables told again and again, are brought out like battered photographs, nostalgia-scented and made alive by scrambled memory. They are fairy-tales, fantasies grown from a seed of truth into something wild and overblown.'[7]

Lily went off to New York and worked at many jobs, including being a waitress in SoHo.[8] She returned for Christmas and bought Elspeth a pig, which they named Portia. T-Shirt Smith joined Doberman and Honey in the wilderness and was succeeded by a terrier called Jip. At the Old Bailey Progles's friend Tom was found guilty of armed robbery and sent down for eighteen years. After the trial Progles returned to Itteringham and recounted the proceedings to Elspeth and Harold Pinter in the Walpole Arms. Pinter and

Elspeth visited Thurgarton, the church in 'Gaunt Danish stone' which Barker had once compared to 'the Norse longboats that bore / burning the body forth / in honour from the shore / of great fjords long ago'. Later Pinter recorded 'At Thurgarton Church' for the soundtrack of a television film on Elspeth's life and work.

In February 1994 the film was broadcast. The same year from Wormwood Scrubs, Tom sent a request that an open book in granite be set up at the foot of the poet's grave, to be paid for at his expense. On it should be carved two words that he recalled Barker, palm clenched, growling on frostbitten February afternoons at Bintry. In the summertime the stone book was set up on the grave, between the tilting honesty and the phoenix rising. The legend read 'No Compromise'.

Acknowledgements

A chameleon poet sometimes provokes extreme and conflicting reactions; a gregarious and philoprogenitive one often leaves a complex web of human relationships behind him. Under such circumstances a biographer's task is never straightforward. This book would not have appeared without three people whom I cannot thank sufficiently. The first is George Barker himself, who led a colourful life and talked engagingly about it. The second is Will Sulkin, my publisher at Jonathan Cape. The third is Professor John Sutherland, ready with moral support.

Affectionate if belated thanks are due to the late Elizabeth Smart, who received me into her home and garden at the Dell in Suffolk, and shared with me both her table and her reminiscences. I gladly record my gratitude to Elspeth Barker for welcoming both me and my family in her Norfolk home on many occasions, for her fluent store of anecdotes, understanding and good cheer. David and Judy Gascoyne entertained us in the Isle of Wight, where they did much to fill me in on a period of literary history that few can now recall. David and Georgina Buxton ensured that the Frasers were comfortable and well informed in Cornwall. For bed, board and intellectual stimulation in New York, I warmly thank that phenomenal physician and author, Dr Peter Birkett. My stay in Texas was enlivened by the hospitality of Professor Bernth Lindfors. Jonathon Barker, formerly of the Arts Council Poetry Library, now of the British Council, shared with me his enthusiasm for a poet with whom he has much in common including his surname, but not – alas – his DNA.

Among curators and archivists I would like to thank Dr Chris Fletcher and Dr Sally Brown of the British Library, Cathy Henderson and Tara Wenger of the Harry Ransom Humanities Research Center at the University of Texas at Austin, and Frank Mattson of the Henry W. and Albert A. Berg Collection of the New York Public Library. At the National Library of Canada in Ottawa,

Lorna Knight proved an expert and courteous guide to the Elizabeth Smart Papers. In Japan Professor Sadao Koyama, Director of the Library at Sendai University, delved into boxes dating from the 1930s to unearth little-known facts about George Barker's time as a lecturer there. Patrice Donoghue of the Harvard University Archives supplied me with useful information on the Morris Grey Readings in Cambridge, Mass. Robert J. Berholf of the State University of New York assisted me with details of George Barker's semester at Buffalo.

Sincere thanks are extended to the following, all of whom have at one time or other expended time and knowledge to speak, telephone or write to me about Barker or his work, or to supply details of context or background: A(lfred) Alvarez, Hase Asquith, Michael Asquith, Michael Asser, Anthony Astbury, Arthur Barker, Bruddy Barker, Christopher Barker, Ernest Barker, Ilse Barker, Lily Barker, Progles Barker, Raffaella Barker, Sam Barker, Sebastian Barker, Vicky Beatson, the late Bruce Bernard, the late Jeffrey Bernard, Oliver Bernard, Barry Bloomfield, Charles Boyle, Gordon Bowker, David Buxton, Georgina Buxton, Professor John Carey, Veronica Chapin, Eric Church, Alan Clodd, Nest Cleverdon, Willie Coakley, John Cox, Fiona Crawford, Paul Crawford, Father Ronald Creighton-Job, Andy Croft, Anthony Cronin, Therese Cronin, Michael Cullup, Olga Damant, Hilary Davies, Dick Davis, Professor Martin Dodsworth, Kate Ellison, Professor Richard Everhardt, John Fairfax, Dede Farrelly, George Farrelly, Edward Farrelly, Jimmy Farrelly, Cliff Forshaw, Jim Friel, David Gascoyne, Judy Gascoyne, Carlo Gebler, Elizabeth Gill, Geoffrey Godbert, Martin Green, Harriet Griffey, Professor Warwick Gould, the late Peter Levi, Michael Hamburger, Claire Harman, the late Desmond Hawkins OBE, Robin Healey, J.F. Hendry, Professor Geoffrey Hill, Diana ('Didy') Holland-Martin, Warren Hope, Donald Horwood, Rene Horwood, Cass Humble, Patrick Humble, Professor Bruce King, Bobby Hunt, Hugh St Claire, John Heath-Stubbs, Father Martin Jarrett-Kerr CR, Graham Lane, Eddie Linden, Sebastian Lockwood, Christopher Logue, Stephen Maas, Jane March-Beveridge, the late George Macbeth, Professor W.M. Mc Cormack, Heldey Marten, Adele Menken, Professor Karl Miller, Jill Neville, Harold Pinter CBE, Robin Prising, the late Robert Pollett, Anne Ridler, Dr Ron Ramdin, Paul Rassam, Professor Michael Schmidt, Professor Ron Schuhardt, Sir Clive Sinclair, Russel Smart, the late Sir Stephen Spender, Chris Stephens, Deirdre Toomey, Dr Anthony Thwaite, Ann Thwaite, Carol Weston, Tony Whooley, Hermine Williams, Hugo Williams, the late David Wright, Anastasia Clare Barker Wilson and José García Villa.

Michael Asquith, Elspeth, Raffaella and Sebastian Barker and Georgina Buxton read and commented on various drafts, either of the entire book or of sections of it, as did Dede Farrelly, Cass Humble, Christopher Reid and Dr Anthony Thwaite. From all of these I learned much, especially from Christopher Reid at whose suggestion the critical discussion was expanded.

For permission to quote copyright material the author and Jonathan Cape would also like to thank the following: Elspeth Barker for George Barker's published work, correspondence, drafts, notebooks and sketches; Sebastian Barker and the National Library of Canada for the work and correspondence of Elizabeth Smart; the T.S. Eliot estate and Faber & Faber for unpublished quotations from Eliot's letters and other writings; the Harry Ransom Humanities Research Center at the University of Texas at Austin for permission to reproduce manuscript material by Eliot and by John Middleton Murry, Edwin Muir, John Lehmann and Desmond Hawkins; Vicki Beatson for quotations from the work of David Wright; and David Gascoyne for an extract from his poem 'The Sacred Hearth'. For the use of photographs and other graphic material, acknowledgements are due to Ilse Barker (for pictures 1, 13, 14 and 15), Elspeth Barker (for pictures 3 and 8), Sebastian Barker (for pictures 9, 18, 23 and 24), Didy Holland-Martin (for picture 12), Dede Farrelly (for picture 21), Judy Gascoyne (for picture 25), Patrick Humble (for picture 2), Eddie Linden (for picture 22), Oonagh Swift (for picture 20), and Carol Weston (for picture 10). For use of original photographs in their copyright warm thanks to the late Bruce Bernard (for picture 19), Jane Bown (for picture 26) and John Minihan (for picture 27). For permission to reproduce John Deakin photographs acknowledgement is due to James Moores (for the cover) and Condé Nast (for picture 16). Picture 17 is copyright Felix Man. Every effort has been made to contact copyright holders, but if any have inadvertently been overlooked the publishers will be pleased to rectify any omissions brought to their notice at the earliest possible opportunity.

My wife and son witnessed my moods of anguish, elation and despair, of which they were remarkably tolerant. I am grateful to the book's in-house editor Jörg Hensgen, and to its copy-editor Liz Cowen, for their attention to the minutiae of the text, to Xanthi Barker for her picture research, and to Myra Jones and Frank and Philippa Millington for attention to the proofs. If errors of fact or infelicities of tone remain, the responsibility is the author's alone.

References

All references to *Collected Poems* are to the second collected volume, edited by Robert Fraser (London: Faber, 1987). Unclassified manuscripts or typescripts kept at Bintry House, Norfolk, Barker's last home, are cited under 'Bintry'. Some of this material has recently been acquired by the British Library, and is in the process of being catalogued. Material already held and catalogued in the British Library's Department of Manuscripts is cited as BL Add Ms followed by the accession number. Material deposited in the National Library of Canada as part of the Elizabeth Smart archive is cited as 'Canada' followed by the box and, where relevant, the folio number. Material held in the Harry Ransom Humanities Research Center at the University of Texas at Austin is cited as 'Texas'. Material held in the Berg collection of New York Public Library is cited as 'New York'.

Chapter 1   A Street Ballad

1. Journals 1928–32, typescript BL Add Ms 71697; *Alanna Autumnal* (London: Wishart 1933), p.9.
2. John Fairfax, 'Great Grandmother', *100 Poems* (Newbury: Phoenix Press, 1992), p.103.
3. *Collected Poems* (London: Faber, 1987), p.112.
4. George Barker to Jimmy Barker, c. 1976.
5. *Memoirs of the Family of Taaffe*, privately distributed (Vienna, 1856).
6. Thomas Carlyle, *The Life of Oliver Cromwell* (Hutchinson: Home University Library), p.147.
7. *In the Wind's Eye: Byron's Letters and Journals*, ed. Leslie A. Marchant, vol. 9, *1821–2* (London: John Murray, 1979), p.143.
8. John Taaffe, *A Comment on the Divine Comedy of Dante Alighieri* (London: John Murray, 1822).
9. Conversation with Olga Damant, 14 January 1994.
10. Maurice Carpenter, *A Rebel in the Thirties* (Essex: Paperbag Book Shop, 1976), pp.43–4.
11. Charles Barker, handwritten memoirs, in the possession of Ernest Barker.

12 Conversation with Ernest Barker, 16 December 1994. Written recollections of Charles Barker.
13 George Barker to Jimmy Barker, c. 1975.
14 Kit Barker, manuscript recollections and drawings, 1984–8 in the possession of Ilse Barker. Subsequently referred to as 'Kit Barker, Ms recollections, 1984–8'.
15 *Collected Poems*, p.176.
16 'Epistle I', ibid., p.94.
17 'Battersea Park', ibid., p.100.
18 *George Barker*, directed by Carlo Gebler, *South Bank Show*, LWT, 8 January 1988. Subsequently referred to as *South Bank Show*, 1988.
19 Conversation with Ilse Barker, 24 January 1994.
20 Kit Barker, Ms recollections, 1984–8.
21 *South Bank Show*, 1988.
22 *Collected Poems*, p.181.
23 'In Memory of David Archer', xii, *Collected Poems*, p.588.
24 Conversation with Ilse Barker, 24 January 1994.
25 Conversation with Sebastian Barker, 7 July 1995.

Chapter 2   An Aboriginal Calamity

1 Texas. Inscribed in Pa's hand 'Christmas card from my little son, George Barker, aged 5 years'.
2 *Collected Poems*, p.180.
3 *South Bank Show*, 1988.
4 George Sampson, 'A Boy and His Books', *Seven Essays* (Cambridge: Cambridge University Press, 1947), p.5.
5 *South Bank Show*, 1988.
6 'The Imitation of St John', typescript, 1939, Canada, Box 66, f.51.
7 'Coming to London', *Coming to London*, ed. John Lehmann (London: Phoenix House, 1957), p.50.
8 *South Bank Show*, 1988.
9 *Collected Poems*, p.181.
10 'Epistle to Dr Arbuthnot', ll.231–2.
11 George Barker, *Essays* (London: MacGibbon & Kee, 1970), p.67.
12 *South Bank Show*, 1988.
13 *The Complete Poems of Francis Ledwidge*, ed. Lord Dunsany (London: Herbert Jenkins, 1919), p.17.
14 Kit Barker, Ms recollections, 1984–8.
15 BL Add Ms 71698A.
16 Conversations with George Barker, 30 October 1982, National Sound Archive recording, NSA 6537 WR. Edited extracts printed in *Poetry Nation Review*, 31, 9, No.5 1983, p.43. Recording subsequently referred to as National Sound Archive, 1982 and published extracts as *Poetry Nation Review*, 31, 1983.
17 Conversation with George Barker, 30 October 1982.
18 Michael Napier, 'Father Kenneth Dale-Roberts, (1882–1972)', *The Oratory Parish Magazine* (June 1972), pp.3–5.

REFERENCES

19 John Henry Newman, *Apologia pro Vita Sua*, ch. v.
20 National Sound Archive, 1982.
21 *Collected Poems*, p.389.
22 Conversation with Father Creighton Job, 5 October 1994.
23 *Collected Poems*, p.181.
24 Journals, 1928–32.
25 Conversation with George Barker, 20 October 1981.
26 National Sound Archive, 1982.

Chapter 3   'Balthus – Pure Balthus!'

1 Kit Barker, Ms recollections, 1984–8.
2 George Barker, in *Coming to London*, ed. John Lehmann (London: Phoenix House, 1957), pp.50–51. Reprinted in Barker, *Essays*, 67.
3 Kit Barker, 'Remembering'. Manuscript in the possession of Ilse Barker.
4 Journals, 1928–32.
5 Ibid.
6 Ibid.
7 *Tennyson: A Selected Edition*, ed. Christopher Ricks (Harlow: Longman, 1969), p.430.
8 Journals, 1928–32.
9 *Alanna Autumnal*, p.3.
10 Conversation with Anastasia Clare Barker, 28 August 1994.
11 Journals, 1928–32.
12 Ibid.
13 BL Add Ms 71698F.
14 Notebook, 1932–4, BL Add Ms 71698A.
15 Journals, 1928–32.
16 *Alanna Autumnal* p.36.
17 Journals, 1928–32.
18 BL Add Ms 71698A.
19 BL Add Ms 71698F.
20 Journals, 1928–32.
21 Conversation with Ilse Barker, 24 January 1994.
22 *Alanna Autumnal*, p.8.
23 *Essays*, p.70.
24 Notebook, 1932, BL Add Ms 71698A.
25 *South Bank Show*, 1988.
26 Notebook, 1930–1, Canada, Box 62, f.1.
27 Journals, 1928–32.
28 Ibid.
29 BL Add Ms 71698A.
30 Journals, 1928–32; *Alanna Autumnal*, p.3.
31 *Coming to London*, p.56.
32 Journals, 1928–32.
33 Wyndham Lewis, *Hitler* (London: Chatto, 1931), p.85.

34 BL Add Ms 71698F.
35 *Poetry Nation Review*, 31, p.43.
36 *Imitation of St John*, typescript, Canada, Box 66, f.51.
37 *Collected Poems*, p.190.
38 Conversation with Ilse Barker.
39 *Collected Poems*, p.169.
40 *Alanna Autumnal*: pp.83–4.
41 Notebook, 1930–1, Canada, Box 62, f.1, 120.
42 *The Poetry and Prose of William Blake*, ed. Geoffrey Keynes (London: Nonesuch Press, 1927), p.111.
43 Journals, 1928–32.
44 John Middleton Murry, *Son of Woman*, (London: Jonathan Cape, 1931), p.21.
45 *Alanna Autumnal*, pp.30–1.
46 John Middleton Murry to George Barker, 14 March 1932, Texas.
47 Sampson, *Seven Essays*, p.68.
48 *The Adelphi*, New Series, IV (June 1932), pp.641–2.
49 Bodleian Library, Oxford, Arch AA d 151.
50 *Essays*, pp.68–9.
51 Stephen Spender, *Poems* (London: Faber, 1933), pp.19–20.
52 George Barker, *Thirty Preliminary Poems* (London: Parton Press, 1933), p.16. Reprinted in *Collected Poems*, p.827

Chapter 4 'Hand Me That Hammer'

1 *The Twentieth Century*, no.1 (June 1931), p.28.
2 National Sound Archive, 1982.
3 'Coming to London', in *Coming to London* (London: Phoenix House, 1957), pp.53–5. Reprinted also in *Essays*, pp.69–71.
4 Conversations with David Gascoyne, 2–9 April 1994.
5 Rosalind Wade, 'The Parton Street Poets', *Poetry Review*, vol. LIV, no.4 (Winter 1963–4), p.291.
6 *New Verse*, 20 (April–May 1936), p.8.
7 Maurice Carpenter, *A Rebel in the Thirties* (Essex: Paperbag Book Club, 1976), ch.1–3 passim.
8 See Barker's tribute to Randall Swingler, 'that most honest man', in 'Elegy', *Collected Poems*, p.737.
9 Stephen Fothergill, 'David Archer', *SuperReal* 2 (London, 1993).
10 'Coming to London', pp.53–4.
11 Conversation with Desmond Hawkins, 29 November 1995.
12 *Twentieth Century*, 4, no. 24 (February 1933), Verse Supplement, pp.17–18.
13 *New Verse*, 2 (March, 1933), p.2.
14 *Twentieth Century*, 4, no.19 (September 1932), p.10.
15 *The English Auden*, ed. Edward Mendelson (London: Faber, 1977), p.195.
16 Conversation with Sir Stephen Spender, 23 January 1995.
17 *Twentieth Century*, 4, no.24 (February 1933), p.28.
18 *Adelphi*, 5, no. 4 (January 1933), pp.310–11.

19 Wade, 'Parton Street Poets', p.293.
20 Carpenter, *A Rebel in the Thirties*, p.45.
21 *Collected Poems*, p.16.
22 Carpenter, *A Rebel in the Thirties*, p.46.
23 Conversations with David Gascoyne, 5 April 1994.
24 *Alanna Autumnal*, p.67.
25 Ibid., p.64.

Chapter 5   'Mellifluous Smooth Tongue'

1 'Coming to London', p.54.
2 *The Iliad*, I, 34.
3 'Ode', *Thirty Preliminary Poems*, p.1. The writing of it is described in Carpenter, *A Rebel in the Thirties*, p.40.
4 Notebook, 1931, Canada, Box 62, f.1.
5 *Thirty Preliminary Poems*, p.22.
6 *Coming to London*, p.56.
7 Carpenter, *A Rebel in the Thirties*, p.40.
8 *Collected Poems*, p.825.
9 *Thirty Preliminary Poems*, p.21. Appears as 'Narcissus 1' in *Poems* (London: Faber, 1935), p.24, and as 'Narcissus' in *Collected Poems*, p.16.
10 Conversations with David Gascoyne, 5 April 1994.
11 Desmond Hawkins, *When I Was* (London: Macmillan, 1989), p.118.
12 Notebook, 1932–4, BL Add Ms 71696.
13 Edwin Muir to Walter de la Mare, 29 November 1933, Bodleian.
14 Edwin Muir to Walter de la Mare, 7 December 1933, Bodleian.
15 Conversation with Desmond Hawkins, 29 November 1995.
16 Conversation with Elspeth Barker, 1 August 1995.
17 Carpenter, *A Rebel in the Thirties*, p.40.
18 Edwin Muir to Walter de la Mare, 29 November 1933, Bodleian.
19 *Collected Poems*, p.193.
20 Telephone conversation with David Gascoyne, 9 May 1996.

Chapter 6   'Whispering Sibilant Fields'

1 Conversation with Ron Bower, 28 May 1994.
2 Conversation with David Gascoyne, 9 May 1996.
3 *New Verse*, 6 (December 1933), p.20.
4 Carpenter, *A Rebel in the Thirties*, p.46.
5 *Collected Poems*, p.15.
6 *Janus* (London: Faber, 1935), pp.135–6.
7 Journals, 1928–32.
8 *Janus*, p.142.
9 Carpenter, *A Rebel in the Thirties*.
10 *Collected Poems*, p.3.

11 T.S. Eliot to George Barker, 8 March 1934, Texas.
12 T.S. Eliot to George Barker, 12 April 1934, Texas.
13 See especially 'A Note for T.S. Eliot', *New English Weekly*, 11, no.3 (March 1949), pp.188–92.
14 Conversations with George Barker, 26 October 1981. Subsequently referred to as 'Conversations, 1981'.
15 Charles Osborne, *W.H. Auden: The Life of a Poet* (London: Eyre Methuen, 1980), p.61.
16 Anne Ridler to Robert Fraser, 26 May 1983.
17 Eliot to Barker, 29 June 1934.
18 Eliot, testimonial for Barker, 14 May 1936.
19 Carpenter, *A Rebel in the Thirties*, p.48.
20 *Scrutiny*, IV (1935), p.198.
21 Notebook, 1937, BL Add Ms 71697.
22 Notebook, 1934, BL Add Ms 71696.
23 *Collected Poems*, p.8. In *Poems* (London: Faber, 1935) 'Amazons' is the opening poem.
24 Barker to Eliot, 23 May 1934.
25 Eliot to Barker, 1 June 1934.
26 Conversations with Elspeth Barker, 10 November 1993.
27 BL Add Ms 71698C.
28 Letter to George Barker, 20 March 1986.
29 'To C.B', in *Eros in Dogma* (London: Faber, 1944), p.60. Not in *Collected Poems*.
30 *Collected Poems*, p.10.

Chapter 7   Tears in a Bottle

1 BL Add Ms 71698 E.
2 National Sound Archive, 1982.
3 George and Kit Barker, Notebook, 1934, BL Add Ms 71698E.
4 *New Verse*, 11 (October 1934), p.22.
5 BL Add Ms 71697A.
6 *Janus*, p.79.
7 *Listener* (14 November 1934), p.827.
8 T.S. Eliot to George Barker, 15 January 1935, Texas.
9 *Pensées*, III, 206.
10 *Janus*, pp.107–8.
11 T. S. Eliot to George Barker, 4 December 1934, Texas.
12 Valerie Eliot to Robert Fraser, 21 September 1993.
13 Noel Stock, *The Life of Ezra Pound* (London: Routledge & Kegan Paul, 1970), pp.244–9.
14 Carpenter, *A Rebel in the Thirties*, p.47.
15 T.S. Eliot to George Barker, 19 March 1935.
16 George Barker to Michael Roberts, 30 March 1935, New York.
17 *Criterion*, XIV, no. LVII (July 1935), pp.649–51.
18 Carpenter, *A Rebel in the Thirties*, pp.92–3. It is from Carpenter's eyewitness

REFERENCES

account that many of the circumstantial details are derived. But see also *Collected Poems*, pp.611–12.

Chapter 8   Bitter Apples

1   Conversation with Ilse Barker, 24 January 1994.
2   Conversations with George Barker, 19 February 1982.
3   George Barker, *In Memory of David Archer* (London: Faber, 1973), p.49. The version here, though, is heavily fictionalised; there is, for example, no reference to the printing and Carpenter is edited out.
4   *Collected Poems*, p.26.
5   *New Verse*, 15 (June 1935), pp.17–18.
6   Rayner Heppenstall, *Four Absentees* (London: Barrie & Rockliffe, 1960), p.128.
7   W.A. Graham to Jessica Barker, 10 August 1935, Bintry. The house is extensively described.
8   Carpenter, 'Memories of George Barker' in *Homage to George Barker on His Sixtieth Birthday* (London: Martin Brian & O'Keeffe), pp.42–4. But, as W.A. Graham's letter makes clear, Carpenter's date of 'spring 1934' is quite impossible.
9   *Letters on Poetry from W.B. Yeats to Dorothy Wellesley* (London and New York: Oxford University Press, 1964), p.23.
10 *The Oxford Book of Modern Verse, 1892–1935* (Oxford: Clarendon Press, 1936), p.xli.
11 George Barker to Michael Roberts, 11 September 1935, New York.
12 *Times Literary Supplement*, no.1, 754, (12 September 1935), p.563.
13 Notebook, 1936–7, BL Add Ms 71697.
14 Conversation with David Gascoyne, 2–9 April, 1994.
15 Emily Coleman to Djuna Barnes, 27 October 1935. Special Collections Department, University of Delaware Library, Newark, Delaware.
16 Susan Chitty, *Now to My Mother* (London: Weidenfeld & Nicolson, 1985), p.81.
17 Emily Coleman, diaries, 22 March 1936. Special Collections Department, University of Delaware Library, Newark, Delaware.
18 *Antonia White: Diaries 1926–1957*, ed. Susan Chitty (London: Virago, 1992), p.323.
19 Djuna Barnes, *Nightwood* (London: Virago, 1963). Dedicated to Peggy Guggenheim and John Ferrar Holms, p.6. The preface does not appear in the first, 1936, Faber edition, but was commissioned from Eliot for the American edition of the following year. See Eliot's note of 1949 reproduced on p.8.
20 T.S. Eliot to George Barker, 18 January 1935, Texas.
21 George Barker to Phillip Herring, 5 July 1990, quoted in Phillip Herring, *Djuna: The Life and Works of Djuna Barnes* (London: Viking, 1995), p.53.
22 George Barker to Antonia White, 21 May 1936, New York.
23 David Gascoyne, *Collected Journals, 1936–42* (London: Skoob, 1991), pp.22–4.

Chapter 9   'The Mass of Roses Face'

1   Walter de la Mare to George Barker, 18 May 1936, Texas.

2 George Barker to Lady Ottoline Morrell, 26 May 1936, Texas.
3 Edwin Muir to George Barker, 14 February 1936; *Selected Letters of Edwin Muir*, ed. P.H. Butler (London: Hogarth Press, 1974), p.87.
4 'The Sacred Hearth', in *Collected Poems*, ed. Robert Skelton (London: André Deutsch, 1965), pp.101–2.
5 Conversations with David Gascoyne, 5 April 1994.
6 *Collected Poems*, p.48.
7 Gascoyne, *Collected Journals*, p.35.
8 *Authors Take Sides on the Spanish War* (London: Left Review, 1937), p.4.
9 *Collected Poems*, p.60.
10 Notebook, 1937, BL Add Ms 71699A.
11 'Vision at Minterne Magna', *Collected Poems*, pp.804–5.
12 Ibid., p.811.
13 Ibid., p.111.
14 Ibid., pp.90–1.
15 Chitty, *Now to My Mother*, p.86.
16 Dylan Thomas to George Barker in Dylan Thomas, *Collected Letters*, ed. Paul Ferris (London: Dent, 1985). Ferris's date of 4 April 1938, however, is one year too late.
17 *Collected Poems*, pp.93–5.
18 *New Verse*, nos 26–7 (November 1937).
19 Gascoyne, *Collected Journals*, pp.87–91.

Chapter 10   'Sick of Love'

1 *Quia Amore Langueo*, ed. H.S. Bennett (London: Faber, 1937).
2 *Twentieth Century Verse*, 4 (June–July 1937), p.77.
3 Edwin Muir to George Barker, 5 June 1937, *Selected Letters*, pp.48–9.
4 Emily Coleman to George Barker, 5 July 1937, Bintry.
5 Notebook, 1937, BL Add Ms 71697.
6 *Hanlon Omega*, typescript, 1937, Texas.
7 *Collected Poems*, p.806.
8 T.S. Eliot to George Barker, 26 September 1937, Texas.
9 Emily Coleman to George Barker, 22 November 1937, Bintry.

Chapter 11   'The Least Qualified Applicant in England'

1 T.S. Eliot, academic reference for George Barker, TS, Texas.
2 Edwin Muir to George Barker, 31 March 1937; *Selected Letters*, pp.94–5; *Essays on the Theory of Poetry*, typescript, Texas.
3 *Criterion* (October 1937), pp.54–66. Reprinted in *Essays* (London: MacGibbon & Kee, 1970), pp.79–90.
4 T.S. Eliot to George Barker, 24 January 1938, Texas.
5 D.R. Hardman to George Barker, 29 March 1938, Bintry. With Barker's self-memoranda in pen.

6 Antonia White, *Diaries, 1926–1957*, ed. Susan Chitty (London: Virago, 1992), p.127.
7 Ibid., p.126.
8 Conversations with John Fairfax, 16 December 1994.
9 Conversations with Elizabeth Gill, 15 April 1994.
10 Schedule of extra-mural lectures on English poetry, University of Cambridge, 1938–9, Canada, Box 66, f.20.
11 *Collected Poems*, p.807.
12 Ibid., pp.66–7.
13 *Wales*, no.10 (October 1939), p.261.
14 *Seven*, no.8 (Spring 1940), pp.3–6.

Chapter 12   *'There's Someone Here from Japan'*

1 Dylan Thomas to Keidrych Rhys, February 1939, *Collected Letters*, p.358.
2 Dylan Thomas to Vernon Watkins, 29 December 1938, ibid., p.346.
3 Quoted in Martin Seymour-Smith, *Robert Graves: His Life and Works* (London: Hutchinson, 1982), p.373.
4 Vyryan Adams to George Barker, 23 February 1939.
5 *Collected Poems*, p.116.
6 Julian Symons to George Barker, 9 June 1939, New York.
7 George Barker to Julian Symons, 14 June 1939, New York.
8 *New Statesman and Nation* (19 August 1939), pp.19–21.
9 'Therefore All Poems Are Elegies', *New English Weekly*, xv, no.3 (4 May 1939), pp.46–7. Reprinted as foreword to *New Poems 1940*, ed. Oscar Williams (New York: Yardstick Press, 1941). Reprinted in *Essays*, pp.64–6. Reprinted as foreword to *Selected Poems* (London: Faber, 1995).
10 George Barker to Emily Coleman, 18 May 1939, Canada, Box 64, f.2.
11 *Collected Poems*, p.98.
12 *Twentieth Century Literature* (Fall 1987).
13 George Barker to Lawrence Durrell, 22 May 1939. Lawrence Durrell papers, Morris Library of Southern Illinois University, Illinois, misdated 1933.
14 Henry Miller to Anaïs Nin, 6 August 1939 in Henry Miller, *Letters to Anaïs Nin* (New York: Putnam, 1965).
15 Ernest Pickering to George Barker, 12 August 1939, Canada, Box 64, f.84.
16 *Essays*, p.43. First published in *Life and Letters Today* (October 1939).
17 *Collected Poems*, p.120.
18 Conversations with David Gascoyne, 5 April 1994.
19 Conversations with John Fairfax, 16 December 1994.
20 *Collected Poems*, p.199.
21 Stephen Spender, *Journals, 1939–1983* (London: Faber, 1985), p.41.
22 Conversations with Stephen Spender, 9 February 1994.
23 George Barker to Antonia White. Quoted in Chitty, *Now to My Mother*, p.116.
24 George Barker, 'A Note for T.S. Eliot', *New English Weekly*, 11, no.3 (March 1949), pp.188–92.
25 Canada, Box 64, f.15.

26 Walter de la Mare to George Barker, 10 November 1939, Texas.
27 British Council to George Barker, Canada, Box 64, f.53.
28 Conversations with Elizabeth Gill, 15 April 1994.
29 Cable from Tilbury, twelve noon, 18 November 1939, Canada, Box 63.

Chapter 13 'Swept Overboard'

1 'In Memory of a Friend', *Collected Poems*, p.252.
2 Conversation with Dede Farrelly, 13 July 1994.
3 *Selected Poems* (New York: Macmillan, 1941), pp.70–84.
4 Conversation with Elizabeth Gill, 15 April 1994.
5 Elizabeth Smart, *Necessary Secrets* (London: Paladin, 1992), p.222.
6 Ibid., p.227.
7 Ibid., p.240.
8 Rosemary Sullivan, *By Heart: Elizabeth Smart, a Life* (London: Lime Tree, 1991), p.142.
9 Journal entry for 2 January 1940, Black 'Universal Standard' diary, Canada, Box 62, f.2.
10 Journal entry for 1 January 1940.
11 Journal entry for 6 January 1940.
12 *Collected Poems*, p.126.
13 Journal entry for 7 January 1940.
14 *New Yorker* (11 July 1942), p.13.
15 Ibid., pp.13–14.
16 Takeshi Saito, *Keats's View of Poetry*, to which is prefixed an essay on English literature in Japan by Edmund Blunden (London: Cobden-Sanderson, 1929), p.26.
17 *Studies in English Literature*, a quarterly compiled by the English Society of Japan, vol. xx, no.4 (October 1940), 'Members of the Council'.
18 *New Yorker* (11 July 1942), pp.13–14.
19 Takeshi Saito, 'English Literature in Japan: A Brief Sketch', *Studies in English Literature*, vol. VIII, no.3 (July 1928).
20 'Address Delivered at the Bunrika University, Tokyo, Japan, January 27, 1940', Canada, Box 66, f.21.
21 Diary entry for 29 January 1940, *New Yorker* (11 July 1942), p.15.
22 Diary entry for 31 January 1940.
23 *New Yorker* (11 January 1942), p.15.
24 *Lilliput* (January 1944), p.436.
25 Canada, Box 18 f.1 The letter is misdated 2 February, though Barker's diary identifies the date of writing as the following day.
26 Diary entry for 3 February 1940.
27 'Lectures on the English Language and Literature in Colleges and Universities, 1940–1', *Studies in English Literature*, vol. xx, no.4 (October 1940).
28 'St George and the Long-Snouted Allegory', *Essays*, p.178.
29 William Empson, *The Structure of Complex Words* (London: Chatto & Windus, 1951), pp.12–13.
30 Saito, *Keats*, intro. Blunden, pp.13–14.

REFERENCES

31 'English Literature in Japan, *Studies in English Literature*, vol. VIII, no.3.
32 *New Yorker* (11 January 1942), p.16.
33 Kochi Doi, 'The Punctuation of William Blake's Songs', *Studies in English Literature*, vol. XX, no.4 (October 1940).

Chapter 14   'Oh Begging Rescue'

1 *Diaries of Court Ladies of Old Japan*, trans. Amy Lowell and Kochi Doi (London: Constable, 1921).
2 Manuscript and typescript, Canada, Box 66, f.22.
3 Journal entry for 6 February 1940.
4 Journal entry for 9 February 1940.
5 Conversation with Jessica's daughter Anastasia Wyatt-Wilson, 28 August 1994.
6 *New Yorker* (19 September 1942), p.21.
7 Journal entry for 16 February 1940; *New Yorker* (19 September 1942), pp.19–21; *Lilliput* (February 1944), p.70.
8 Canada, Box 66, f.22. The draft letter is inserted between the paragraphs of the manuscript of his inaugural lecture.
9 Journal entry for 29 February 1940.
10 Canada, Box 66, f.21. The script is appended to the manuscript of his talk at Bunrika University, Tokyo, 27 January 1940.
11 *Henry IV, Part II*, v, iii, l.115.
12 *New Yorker* (11 July 1942), p.16.
13 *Collected Poems*, p.123. The original sequence of twenty sonnets appeared in *Eros in Dogma* (London: Faber, 1944), pp.9–18.
14 Journal entry for 22 March 1942. The dates of composition of all of the 'Pacific Sonnets' are noted on the relevant days.
15 Journal, 1940, Canada, Box 62, f.2.
16 *Collected Poems*, p.129.
17 Journal entry for 25 March 1940.

Chapter 15   'Angel Empress'

1 John Fitch to George Barker, 1 April 1940, Canada, Box 64, f.5.
2 Smart, *Necessary Secrets*, p.257.
3 Sullivan, *By Heart*, p.148.
4 George Barker to Elizabeth Smart, 28 April 1940, Canada, Box 18, f.1.
5 Canada, Box 64, f.62.
6 T.S. Eliot to George Barker, Canada, Box 64, f.4.
7 *New Yorker* (8 August 1940), p.16.
8 *New Yorker* (31 October 1942), pp.22–3.
9 George Barker to Elizabeth Smart, 17 April 1940, Canada, Box 18, f.1.
10 *Studies in English Literature*, vol. XX, no.4 (October 1940).
11 Diary entry for 3 May 1940.
12 *By Heart*, pp.148–9.

13 George Barker to Elizabeth Smart, 31 May 1940, Canada, Box 18, f.1.
14 *Lilliput* (March 1944), p.135.
15 *Studies in English Literature*, vol. XX, no.4 (October 1940).

Chapter 16 'The Lips of the Possible'

1 George Barker to Kit Barker, Canada, Box 63, f.10.
2 George Barker to Elizabeth Smart, 28 March 1940, Canada, Box 18, f.1.
3 Elizabeth Smart to George Barker, 28 June 1940.
4 Smart, *Necessary Secrets*, p.263.
5 George Barker to Elizabeth Smart, 4 March 1941, Canada, Box 18, f. 2.
6 Elizabeth Smart, *By Grand Central Station I Sat Down and Wept* (London: Editions Poetry London, 1945), p.2.
7 Smart, *Necessary Secrets*, p.25.
8 Ibid., p.174.
9 Sullivan, *By Heart*, p.112.
10 *By Grand Central Station*, p.20.
11 Smart, *Necessary Secrets*, p.175.
12 *South Bank Show*, January 1988.
13 D.L. Omsted, *Achumawi Dictionary*, University of California Publications in Linguistics, vol. 45 (Berkeley and Los Angeles: University of California Press, 1966), p.3.
14 Henry Miller, *Big Sur and the Oranges of Hieronymus Bosch* (London: Heinemann, 1958), pp.307–8.
15 Conversation with Sebastian Lockwood, 26 August 1993.
16 Smart, *By Grand Central Station*, p.23; *Janus*, p.39.
17 Journal entry for 22 July 1940.
18 Smart, *Necessary Secrets*, p.265.
19 Ibid.
20 George Barker to Elizabeth Smart, 13 August 1940, Canada, Box 18, f.1.

Chapter 17 An American Ode

1 Dylan Thomas and John Davenport, *The Death of the King's Canary* (Harmondsworth: Penguin, 1976), pp.2–4.
2 Ibid., p.21.
3 John Heath-Stubbs, *Hindsights* (London: Hodder & Stoughton, 1993), pp.76–7; Andrew Motion, *Philip Larkin: A Writer's Life* (London: Faber, 1993), p.71.
4 Letter to George Barker from his father, 2 November 1940, Canada, Box 63, f.9.
5 *Collected Poems*, p.167.
6 Smart, *Necessary Secrets*, p.285.
7 Smart, *By Grand Central Station*, p.27.
8 Letter from Jessica Barker to George Barker, 30 October 1940, Canada, Box 63, f.11.
9 George Barker to Elizabeth Smart, 2 October 1940, Canada, Box 18, f.1.

REFERENCES

10 Elizabeth Smart, *Autobiographies* (Vancouver: William Hoffner/Tanks, 1987).
11 'Oscar Williams', *Twentieth Century Authors*, ed. Stanley J. Kunitz and Howard Haycroft (New York: H. W. Wilson, 1942).
12 Conversation with John Heath-Stubbs, 15 November 1994.
13 Sullivan, *By Heart*, p.165.

Chapter 18 'Five Jaws of Love'

1 Letter from Jessica Barker to George Barker, dated 'Thursday evening', Canada, Box 63, f.11.
2 George Barker to Elizabeth Smart, 28 October 1940, Canada, Box 18, f.1.
3 George to Marion Frances Taaffe Barker, October 1940, Canada, Box 63, f.9.
4 Sullivan, *By Heart*, p.166.
5 Jessica Barker to George Barker, Canada, Thursday, Box 63, f.11.
6 Ibid., 'Sunday evening', Canada, Box 63, f.11.
7 Ibid., 'Thursday afternoon'.
8 Ibid., 15 November 1940.
9 Jessica Barker to Monica Humble, 26 November 1941, Canada, Box 63, f.11.
10 Elizabeth Smart to George Barker, 24 December 1940, Canada, Box 18, f.1.
11 Ibid.
12 George Barker to Elizabeth Smart, 26 December 1940, Canada, Box 18, f.1.
13 George Barker to Elizabeth Smart, 'Wednesday', probably 15 January 1941. Postmark 'January 16', Canada, Box 18, f.2.
14 Sandra Djwa, *The Politics of the Imagination: A Life of F.R. Scott* (Toronto: McLelland and Stewart, 1987), p.196.
15 Jessica to George Barker, dated 'Monday', Canada, Box 63, f.11.
16 George Barker to Elizabeth Smart, 21 February 1940, Canada, Box 18, f.2.
17 Elizabeth Smart to George Barker, 24 February 1940, Canada, Box 18, f.2.
18 *Collected Poems*, pp.788-9.
19 Smart, *Necessary Secrets*, p.281.
20 Conversation with Georgina Barker, 15 August 1995.
21 Smart, *Necessary Secrets*, p.281.
22 Elizabeth Smart to George Barker, 4 April 1940, Canada, Box 18, f.2.
23 George Barker to Elizabeth Smart, 5 April 1940, Canada, Box 18, f.2.
24 Smart, *By Grand Central Station*, p.97.
25 Elizabeth Smart to George Barker, 27 April 1940, Canada, Box 18, f.2.
26 *Collected Poems*, p.230.
27 George Barker to Elizabeth Smart, 5 May 1941, Canada, Box 18, f.2.

Chapter 19 'Dying for You, Canada'

1 Jessica Barker to Monica Barker, 26 November 1941, Canada, Box 63, f.11.
2 George Barker to Elizabeth Smart, 5 May 1940, Canada, Box 18, f.1.
3 George Barker to Elizabeth Smart, 5 May 1941, Canada, Box 18, f.2.
4 Ibid.

5 Peggy Guggenheim, *Out of This Century* (London: André Deutsch, 1983), Intro. by Gore Vidal, p. xiii.
6 Conversation with Elizabeth Smart, 31 May 1982.
7 '*By Grand Central Station I Sat Down and Wept* by Elizabeth Smart Here Criticised by George Barker', typescript, Canada, Box 66, f.27.
8 George Barker to Elizabeth Smart, 'Tuesday morning', probably 1 July 1941, Canada, Box 18, f.3.
9 Smart, *By Grand Central Station*, p.100.
10 George Barker to Elizabeth Smart, August 1941, Canada, Box 18, f.3.
11 George Barker to Elizabeth Smart, 6 July 1941, Canada, Box 18, f.3.
12 George Barker to Elizabeth Smart, 11 July, 1941, Canada, Box 18, f.3.
13 Jessica Barker to Monica Barker, 26 November 1941, Canada, papers, Box 63, f.11.
14 George Barker to Elizabeth Smart, 31 July 1941, Canada, Box 18, f.3.
15 George Barker to Elizabeth Smart, 12 August 1941, Canada, Box 18, f.3.
16 George Barker to Elizabeth Smart, 2 September 1941, Canada, Box 18, f.3.
17 'First Cycle of Love Poems', i, *Eros in Dogma* (London: Faber, 1944), p.38. Not in *Collected Poems*.

Chapter 20   '*Yours in Parallel*'

1 George Barker to Elizabeth Smart, 10 September 1941, Canada, Box 18, f.3.
2 F.C. Blair to George Barker, 19 September 1941, Canada, Box 64.
3 *Collected Poems*, p.150.
4 Conversation with Stephen Spender, 23 January 1995.
5 Jessica Barker to Monica Humble, 26 November 1994, Canada, Box 63, f.11.
6 George Barker to Elizabeth Smart, 9 November 1941, Canada, Box 18, f.4.
7 *Collected Poems*, p.152.
8 *The Diary of Anaïs Nin,* vol. 3, *1939–1944*, ed. Gunther Stuhlmann (New York: Harcourt Brace Jovanovitch, 1969), pp.150–1.
9 Ibid., pp.175–7.
10 Ibid., pp.197–8.
11 Noel Riley Fitch, *Anaïs: The Erotic Life of Anaïs Nin* (Boston: Little, Brown, 1993), pp.230–1.
12 George Barker to Elizabeth Smart, 2 November 1941, Canada, Box 18, f.4.
13 Erotica, typescript, Texas.
14 Anaïs Nin, *Delta of Venus* (London: Penguin, 1990), p.xii.
15 Erotica, typescript, Texas.
16 'The Veiled Woman', *Delta of Venus*, pp.65–71.
17 'Notes from the Largest Imaginary Empire', *New Republic* (8 December 1941), p.791.
18 George Barker to Elizabeth Smart, 29 May 1942, Canada, Box 66, f.4.
19 George Barker to Elizabeth Smart, 9 November 1941, Canada, Box 18, f.4.
20 Conversation with Elspeth Barker, 10 November 1993.
21 George Barker to Elizabeth Smart, 3 December 1941, Box 18, f.4.
22 George Barker to Elizabeth Smart, December 1941, Canada, Box 18, f.4.

23 George Barker to Elizabeth Smart, 22 January 1942, Canada, Box 64, f.5.
24 'The Philadelphia Train', in *Essays* (London: MacGibbon & Kee, 1970), p.77.
25 George Barker to Elizabeth Smart, February 1942, Canada, Box 18, f.4.
26 George Barker to Elizabeth Smart, 3 December 1941, Canada, Box 18, f.5.
27 'James Joyce, Heretic', *Nation* (21 February 1942), pp.236–7.
28 'The Dance Before the Altar', *New Republic* (2 March 1942), p.303.
29 Sullivan, *By Heart*, p.190.
30 George Barker to Elizabeth Smart, 'Sunday', Canada, Box 18, f.4.
31 Jessica Barker to Elizabeth Smart, 2 April 1942, Canada, Box 18, f.11.

Chapter 21   'The Geography of the Body'

1 Jessica Barker to George Barker, 10 February 1944, Canada, Box 18.
2 Obituaries for Willard and Marie Maas, *Brooklyn Heights Press* (7 January 1971), pp.3–4.
3 *The Geography of the Body*, dir. Marie and Willard Maas, New York, 1943. Soundtrack 'Contemporary Films', TS, Bintry.
4 Jessica Barker to Elizabeth Smart, 20 May 1942, Smart papers, Canada, Box 18, f.11.
5 George Barker to Elizabeth Smart, 26 November 1941, Canada, Box 18, f.4.
6 Elizabeth Smart, *On the Side of the Angels* (London: Flamingo, 1995), p.15.
7 Jessica Barker to Elizabeth Smart, 2 April 1942, Canada, Box 18, f.11.
8 *New Yorker* (3 August 1942), p.17.
9 *Collected Poems*, p.132. *Sacred and Secular Elegies* in first US edition.
10 Ibid., pp.134–5.
11 Ibid., p.135.
12 Ibid., p.140.
13 Ibid., p.146.
14 Ibid., p.149.
15 Jessica Barker to George Barker, n.d., Canada, Box 63, f.11.
16 Smart, *On the Side of the Angels*, pp.15–16.

Chapter 22   Sinner and Saint

1 W.S. Graham, *Cage Without Grievance* (Glasgow: Parton Press, 1942).
2 Fairfax, *100 Poems*, p.104.
3 Conversation with Ilse Barker, 24 January 1994.
4 Conversation with John Fairfax, 16 December 1993.
5 'To David Gill', *Collected Poems*, p.168.
6 'To T.S. Eliot', *Collected Poems*, p.169.
7 Sullivan, *By Heart*, p.197.
8 Conversation with Didy Holland-Martin, 29 April, 1994.
9 Conversation with José Garcia Villa, 18 August 1993.
10 Conversation with John Heath-Stubbs, 9 March 1995.
11 Conversation with Dede Farrelly, 13 July 1994.

12 Letter from Marius Bewlay to George Barker, 1 November 1949, Bintry.
13 *Letters of John J. Farrelly Jr (1942–5)*, ed. Elizabeth Farrelly Kavanagh (St Louis: Genealogical R & P, 1986), letter of 20 October 1943, p.129.
14 Ibid., letter of 10 October 1943, p.124.
15 Karl Miller, *Doubles: Studies in Literary History* (Oxford: Oxford University Press, 1987), p.382.
16 George Barker to Elizabeth Smart, n.d., Canada, Box 18, f.6.
17 Willard Maas to Elizabeth Smart, 18 March 1943, Canada, Box 35.
18 Conversation with Didy Holland-Martin, 29 April 1994.
19 Graham Greene, *The Heart of the Matter* (London: Heinemann, 1948), epigraph quoting Charles Péguy, 'Pécheurs et saints', *Nouveau Théologien*, XIII, 2 (1911).

Chapter 23 *'My Tall Dead Wives'*

1 Conversation with Michael Asquith, 16 December 1994.
2 Anne Ridler to Lawrence Durrell, 21 October 1943. Lawrence Durrell papers, Morris Library of Southern Illinois University, Illinois.
3 The complete record of his coming and goings is in 'Christopher's Book', Canada, Box 20, f.1.
4 T.S. Eliot to George Barker, 8 June 1944, Texas.
5 Conversation with John Heath-Stubbs, 9 March 1995.
6 J. Maclaren-Ross, *Memoirs of the Forties* (London: Alan Ross, 1965), p.142.
7 Andrew Sinclair, *War Like a Wasp: The Lost Decade of the Forties* (London: Hamish Hamilton, 1989), p.77.
8 'Japanese Journal', *Lilliput* (December 1943; January 1944; February 1944).
9 *South Bank Show*, 1988.
10 Smart, *Autobiographies*, p.79.
11 'Christopher's Book', Canada, Box 20.
12 Jessica Barker to George Barker, 7 August 1943, Canada, Box 63, f.11.
13 *Collected Poems*, p.166.
14 Ibid., p.159.
15 Conversation with David Gascoyne, 5 April 1994.
16 *Collected Poems*, p.164.
17 George Macbeth, 'The Early George Barker', *Poetry Nation Review*, 31 (1983), p.61.
18 Introduction to Elizabeth Smart, *The Collected Poems* (London: Paladin, 1992), p.10.
19 Barker, quoted in 'Fitzrovia and the War', *Listener* (3 October 1974), pp.428–9.

Chapter 24 *'Equating the Paradox'*

1 Conversation with Dede Farrelly, 13 July 1994.
2 Grade card, Kingston Medical Board, Bintry.
3 Smart, *On the Side of the Angels*, p.18.
4 David Wright, 'Memories of 23A', *Homage to George Barker on his Sixtieth Birthday*,

ed. John Heath-Stubbs and Martin Green (London: Martin Brian & O'Keeffe, 1973), p.29.
5 George Barker to Elizabeth Smart, 13 February 1944, Texas.
6 Conversation with John Fairfax, 16 December 1993.
7 *Collected Poems*, p.791.
8 Manuscript and typescript in the possession of Didy Holland-Martin.
9 Smart, *On the Side of the Angels*, p.20.
10 Jessica Barker to George Barker, 4 May 1944, Canada, Box 63, f.11.
11 Smart, *On the Side of the Angels*, p.21.
12 Ibid., p.23.
13 Conversation with Didy Holland-Martin, 29 April 1994.
14 *Collected Poems*, p.252.
15 *The Oxford Book of Twentieth-Century English Verse*, ed. Philip Larkin (Oxford: Oxford University Press, 1976).
16 Conversation with Didy Holland-Martin, 29 April 1994.
17 George Barker to Jessica Barker, n.d., Canada, Box 63, f.11.
18 Jessica Barker to George Barker, 25 July 1944, Canada, Box 63, f.11.
19 Conversation with Cass Humble, 21 May 1994.
20 *Collected Poems*, p.793.
21 Ibid., p.794.

Chapter 25   'A Bohemian Motorist'

1 *Listener* (15 March 1945), p.302.
2 *TLS* (3 February 1945), p.57.
3 Jessica Barker to George Barker, 4 January 1945, Canada, Box 63, f.11.
4 Jankel Adler, *The Mutilated*, 1942–3, Tate Gallery T.372; Robert Colquhoun, *The Fortune Teller*, 1946, Tate Gallery, T.2076.
5 Quoted in Sinclair, *War Like a Wasp* p.79.
6 Conversation with Bruce Bernard, 29 July 1994.
7 'Memories of 23A', *Homage to George Barker*, p.33.
8 Conversation with Bruce Bernard, 29 July 1994.
9 Smart, *On the Side of the Angels*, p.25.
10 Conversation with Michael Asquith, 16 December 1995.
11 Jessica Barker to George Barker, 9 June 1945, Canada, Box 63, f.11.
12 *Collected Poems*, pp.219–20.
13 Conversation with John Heath-Stubbs, 9 March 1995. *Poetry Nation Review*, 31 (1983), p.62.
14 John Heath-Stubbs, *Hindsights: An Autobiography* (London: Hodder & Stoughton, 1993), pp.61, 68.
15 'For George Barker at Seventy', *Poetry Nation Review*, 31, p.62.
16 'Damn Braces', lecture series, 1945, manuscript, New York.
17 Typescript Texas, dated Condicote–London, April–May 1945.
18 *The Dead Seagull* (London: John Lehmann, 1950), p.10.
19 Farrelly, *Letters*, privately printed, unpaginated.
20 Conversation with Karl Miller, 23 March 1995.

21 *Collected Poems*, pp.796–7. In 'The Scarlet Cycle' originally entitled 'To Didy Asquith'. Manuscript and typescript in the possession of Didy Holland-Martin.
22 Cablegram, Bintry.
23 Sullivan, *By Heart*, p.223.
24 Elizabeth Smart to George Barker, 3 August 1946, Bintry.
25 George Barker to Elizabeth Smart, 21 September 1946, Canada, Box 18, f.7.

Chapter 26 'I Won't Make a Fuss'

1 In the possession of Paul Conran.
2 'Memories of 23A', *Homage to George Barker*, p.31.
3 Since destroyed.
4 William Hayley, talking on the origins of the Third Programme on BBC Radio 3, repeated 29 September 1996 as part of Humphrey Carpenter's celebration 'The Envy of the World'.
5 Dylan Thomas, *Collected Letters*, ed. Paul Ferris (London: Dent, 1985), p.605n.
6 *Radio Times* (7 October 1946).
7 Conversation with Elspeth Barker, 10 November 1993.
8 *Collected Poems*, p.237.
9 George Barker to Elizabeth Smart, n.d., Texas.
10 Elizabeth Smart to George Barker, with his replies verso, 4 December 1946, Canada, Box 18, f.7.
11 Conversation with Veronica Chapin, 8 July 1994.
12 Sullivan, *By Heart*, p.236.
13 *The Degradations of Guatemozin*, typescript, Act IV, p.45, Texas.
14 Conversation with Veronica Chapin, 8 July 1994.
15 Elizabeth Smart to Marie Maas, 7 January 1947, Texas.
16 Conversation with Veronica Chapin, 8 July 1994.
17 Notebook, 1946–7, Texas.
18 Conversation with Veronica Chapin, 8, July 1994.

Chapter 27 Cassiopeia

1 *Collected Poems*, p.217.
2 Conversation with Cass Humble, 21 May 1994.
3 Ibid.
4 Kathryn Talbot, *Kit Barker: Cornwall, 1947–1948. Recollections of Painters and Writers* (St Ives: The Book Gallery, 1993), p.1.
5 *Collected Poems*, p.246.
6 Ibid., p.251.
7 Conversation with Ilse Barker, 24 January 1994.
8 Talbot, *Recollections of Painters and Writers*, p.6.
9 Cass Humble to Robert Fraser, 14 November 1995.
10 Eliot to Barker, 27 March 1947, Texas.
11 T.S. Eliot to George Barker, c. May 1947, Texas.

REFERENCES

12 Cass Humble to Robert Fraser, 14 November 1995. Conversation with Cass Humble, 21 May 1994.
13 *Collected Poems*, p.265.
14 Conversation with Elizabeth Smart, 25 July 1982.
15 Conversation with Cass Humble, 21 May 1994.
16 Conversation with Michael Asquith, 16 December 1994.
17 Conversation with Cass Humble, 21 May 1994.
18 *Poetry London*, 11 (September–October, 1947), editorial.

Chapter 28   'This Temperate October'

1 Jeffrey Bernard, *Reach for the Ground: The Downhill Struggle of Jeffrey Bernard* (London: Duckworth, 1996).
2 Interview with Jeff Bernard, 3 August 1994.
3 *Collected Poems*, p.173.
4 Ibid., p.190.
5 Heath-Stubbs, *Hindsights*, p.152.
6 Victoria Glendinning, *Edith Sitwell: A Unicorn Among the Lions* (London: Weidenfeld & Nicolson, 1981), p.55.
7 Conversation with Jeff Bernard, 3 August 1994.
8 Conversation with Cass Humble, 21 May 1994.
9 *Collected Poems*, p.292.
10 Anthony Thwaite, 'A Few Memories: In Homage', *Homage to George Barker on His Sixtieth Birthday* (London: Martin Brian & O'Keeffe, 1973), p.79. Anthony Thwaite to Robert Fraser, 17 May 1995.
11 David Wright, 'Higher Tregerthen', in *Metrical Observations* (Manchester: Carcanet, 1980).
12 Heath-Stubbs, *Hindsights*, p.150.
13 Ibid., p.123.
14 *Essays*, p.51. The 'noble head' was A.N. Whitehead's.
15 *Collected Poems*, p.652, where, however, 'May' is poetic licence.

Chapter 29   A School for Poets

1 David Wright, *Deafness: A Personal Account* (London: Faber, 1990), p.33.
2 Conversation with John Heath-Stubbs, 9 March 1995.
3 David Wright, 'The Cage-Born: to George Barker', *To the Gods and the Shades* (Manchester: Carcanet, 1976), p.25.
4 Conversation with John Fairfax, 16 December 1993.
5 White, *Diaries*, pp.126–7.
6 Heath-Stubbs, *Hindsights*, p.151.
7 Conversation with John Heath-Stubbs, 9 March 1995.
8 *Collected Poems*, p.247.
9 'A Note for T.S. Eliot', *New English Weekly*, 11, no.3 (March 1949), pp.188–91.
10 *Collected Poems*, p.239.

11 Talbot, *Recollections of Painters and Writers*, p.28.
12 Ibid., p.29.
13 George Barker to Anthony Thwaite, 17 February 1949.
14 *Homage to George Barker*, p.80.
15 Conversation with Oliver Bernard, 6 February 1995.
16 Conversation with John Fairfax, 16 December 1993.
17 Conversation with Cass Humble, 21 May 1994.

Chapter 30   'Happy, Silly, a Bit Mellow'

1 Conversation with Cass Humble, 21 May 1994.
2 Conversation with Oliver Bernard, 6 February 1995.
3 John Lehmann to George Barker, 17 February 1949, Texas.
4 Conversation with Cass Humble, 21 May 1994.
5 Notebook, 1949, Texas.
6 Ibid.
7 Ibid.
8 Lefevre Gallery, Exhibition Hand List, December 1950.
9 'In Memory of Robert MacBryde', *Collected Poems*, p.551.
10 Cass Humble to Robert Fraser, 17 June 1995.
11 'At the Tombs of the Medici', *Collected Poems*, p.235.
12 Conversation with Cass Humble, 21 May 1994.
13 Journal, 1949, Texas.
14 Conversation with George Barker, October 1981.
15 Journal, 1949, Texas.
16 *Collected Poems*, pp.298–9.
17 John Lehmann to George Barker, 10 October 1949, Texas.
18 Cass Humble to Robert Fraser, 3 October 1993.
19 Conversation with George Barker, October 1981.
20 'Ode Against St Cecilia's Day', *Collected Poems*, p.215.
21 'Verses to St Cecilia', *To the Gods in the Shades* (Manchester: Carcanet, 1976), p.49.
22 David Gill to George Barker, October 1949, Bintry.
23 George Barker to Kit Barker, n.d. In the possession of Ilse Barker.
24 *Collected Poems*, p.293.
25 *Observer* (14 May 1950), p.7.
26 John Fairfax to George Barker, 20 April 1950.
27 *Essays*, p.122.
28 Conversation with Jeff Bernard, 3 August 1994.
29 Bernard, *Reach for the Ground*, p.71.
30 John Lehmann to George Barker, 21 February 1950, Texas.
31 George Barker to Kit Barker, 12 August 1950. In the possession of Ilse Barker.
32 *Daily Worker* (23 October, 30 October, 2 November, 9 November, 15 November, 28 November 1950).
33 George Barker to Kit Barker, 11 August 1950.

34 John Malcolm Brinnin, *Dylan Thomas in America* (London: Dent, 1956), p.72.
35 Rayner Heppenstall, *Four Absentees* (London: Cardinal, 1988), p.128.
36 Patrick Harvey to George Barker, 17 November 1950, Texas.

Chapter 31   'Bear the Day To Me'

1 *The Dead Seagull* (London: John Lehmann, 1950), p.83.
2 Ibid., p.142.
3 Sullivan, *By Heart*, p.260.
4 Cashenden Cass to Kit and Ilse Barker, 28 August 1951. In possession of Ilse Barker.
5 Notebook, 1951, Texas.
6 *Collected Poems*, p.251.
7 Ibid., p.230.
8 Conversation with Cass Humble, 21 May 1994.
9 Oliver Bernard, *Getting Over It* (London: Peter Owen, 1992), p.129.
10 Elizabeth Smart to George Barker, 12 August 1951, Bintry.
11 Conversation with Tony Cronin, 14 May, 1996.
12 Conversation with John Heath-Stubbs, 9 March, 1995.
13 *Collected Poems*, p.302.
14 *Nimbus*, no.1 (December 1951), p.17.
15 George Barker to Kit Barker, 12 August 1951. In possession of Ilse Barker.

Chapter 32   'Rigor Leavis'

1 'The Fat Lady at the Circus', *Poetry London*, 13 (July–August 1948), pp.38–9.
2 Marius Bewlay to George Barker, 1 November 1949.
3 Conversation with Dede Farrelly, 13 July 1994.
4 Willard Maas to George Barker, dated 'Sunday', Bintry.
5 George Barker to Elizabeth Smart, 13 November 1951, Bintry.
6 Notebook, 1952, Texas.
7 Conversation with Desmond Hawkins, 29 November 1995.
8 Desmond Hawkins to George Barker, 24 January 1952, Texas.
9 Conversation with Olga Damant, 14 January 1994.
10 Conversation with Ilse Barker, 27 October 1995.
11 Conversation with Dede Farrelly, 21 May 1994.
12 Conversation with Karl Miller, 23 March 1995.
13 Karl Miller, *Doubles: Studies in Literary History* (Oxford: Oxford University Press, 1987), p.402.
14 Cass Humble to Robert Fraser, 3 October 1993.
15 *Collected Poems*, pp.816–17.
16 *Homage to George Barker*, p.81.
17 Edward Lucie-Smith, *The Burnt Child: An Autobiography* (London: Gollancz, 1975), pp.126–7.
18 'The Early Barker', *Poetry Nation Review*, 31 (February 1983).

19 George Barker to Oliver Bernard, n.d. In the possession of Oliver Bernard.
20 T.S. Eliot to George Barker, 27 July and 11 August 1952, Texas.

Chapter 33 'Art Crap! Poetry Crap!'

1 *Homage to George Barker*, p.33.
2 Conversation with Oliver Bernard, 12 February, 1995.
3 Conversation with Robin Prising, 16 August 1993.
4 Heath-Stubbs, *Hindsights*, p.123.
5 *The Oxford Book of English Verse, 1250–1918*, ed. Arthur Quiller-Couch, New Edition (London: Clarendon Press, 1939), p.425. The ballad exists in many versions, but it was Quiller-Couch's which Barker favoured and which he invariably recited in company.
6 Cass Humble to Robert Fraser, 2 November 1995.
7 Smart, *On the Side of the Angels*, p.33.
8 Bernard, *Reach for the Ground*, p.72.
9 'Consolatory Verses for the Middle Years', *Collected Poems*, p.304.
10 *Essays*, p.59.
11 *Collected Poems*, p.309.
12 *Daily Sketch* (18 April 1953), p.4.
13 Hansard, Fifth Series, Parliamentary Debates, Lords, vol. 184, cols 712–13.
14 *New Statesman and Nation* (19 December 1953), 'London Diary', pp.786–7.

Chapter 34 'That Boy Has a Tiger in His Loins'

1 Cass Humble to Robert Fraser, 17 June 1995.
2 Conversation with Oliver Bernard, 12 February 1995.
3 George Barker to Oliver Bernard, n.d. In the possession of Oliver Bernard.
4 *Collected Poems*, p.320.
5 Ibid., p.271.
6 Ibid., p.279.
7 George Barker to Kit Barker, August 1944. In the possession of Ilse Barker.
8 Conversation with Karl Miller, 23 May 1995.
9 *Homage to George Barker*, p.53. Conversation with Karl Miller, 23 March 1995.
10 Cashenden Cass, 'The Train to Milan', draft, Bintry.
11 Draft letter, notebook, 1954, Texas.
12 Conversation with Oliver Bernard, 12 February 1995.
13 Ibid.
14 *Greya*, 46 (Michaelmas Term, 1957), p.116.
15 Oliver Bernard to Robert Fraser, 15 February 1995.
16 Conversation with Tony Cronin, 14 May 1996.
17 *Collected Poems*, p.250.
18 *Homage to George Barker*, p.71.
19 Smart, *On the Side of the Angels*, p.34.
20 Conversation with Cass Humble, 25 May 1994.

21 Conversation with Veronica Chapin, 8 July 1994.
22 Sebastian Barker to George Barker, 11 June 1955, Bintry.

Chapter 35 'So You Write Verse Too, Baby?'

1 *Nimbus*, vol. III, no.2 (Summer 1955).
2 *New Lines*, ed. Robert Conquest (London: Macmillan, 1956), pp.xiv–xv.
3 *Homage to George Barker*, p.81.
4 *Nimbus*, vol. III, no.4 (Winter 1956), p.57.
5 Anthony Cronin, *Dead as Doornails* (Dublin: Poolbeg Press, 1980), p.76.
6 Conversation with Tony Cronin, 14 May 1996.
7 Conversation with Michael and Hase Asquith, 16 December 1994.
8 Dom Moraes, *My Son's Father* (London: Penguin, 1991), p.159.
9 Notebook, 1955, Texas.
10 BBC production script. Compare Notebook, 1955, Texas.
11 Heath-Stubbs, *Hindsights*, p.149.
12 George Barker, *Two Plays* (London: Faber, 1958), p.13.
13 Ibid., p.20.
14 Ibid., p.32.
15 T.S. Eliot to George Barker, 13 March 1956, Texas.

Chapter 36 'Give Biddy a Shove, Me Dear'

1 Cass Humble to Robert Fraser, 2 November 1995.
2 Ibid.
3 Conversation with Cass Humble, 12 May 1994.
4 Douglas Cleverdon to George Barker, 10 August 1956, Bintry.
5 Charles Monteith to George Barker, 20 July 1956, Bintry.
6 T.S. Eliot to George Barker, 17 September 1956, Texas.
7 Conversation with Cass Humble, 12 May 1994.
8 Conversation with Elizabeth Gill, 15 April 1994.
9 T.S. Eliot to George Barker, 9 October 1956.
10 Programme report, Audience Research Department, 20 October 1956.
11 Douglas Cleverdon to George Barker, 10 August 1956.
12 *Two Plays*, p.67.
13 Ibid., p.80.
14 Dom Moraes, *My Son's Father* (London: Penguin, 1991), p.167.
15 Dom Moraes, *Never at Home* (London: Penguin, 1992), p.48.
16 Cass Humble to Robert Fraser, 2 November 1995.
17 Ibid.
18 Conversation with Ilse Barker, 24 January 1994.
19 Conversation with John Fairfax, 16 December 1993.
20 *Collected Poems*, p.347.

Chapter 37 'A Horse Struck By Lightning'

1. Smart, *On the Side of the Angels*, p.35.
2. Ibid., p.36.
3. 'The Maidenhair Vessel with the Cradling Chain', *Collected Poems*, p.369.
4. Sullivan, *By Heart*, p.275. Conversation with Elizabeth Smart, July 1982. Conversation with George Barker, October 1981.
5. Anthony Cronin, *Dead As Doornails* (Dublin: Poolbeg Press, 1976), pp.157–61.
6. Smart, *On the Side of the Angels*, p.36.
7. *Collected Essays*, pp.150–8.
8. Smart, *On the Side of the Angels*, p.37.
9. Cronin, *Dead As Doornails*, pp.168–9.
10. Conversation with Robin Prising, 16 August 1993.
11. George Barker to Kit Barker, 7 February 1959.
12. Conversation with Dede Farrelly, 26 May 1995.
13. Moraes, *My Son's Father*, p.202.
14. *Collected Poems*, pp.349–50.
15. Conversation with Christopher Barker, 25 October 1995.
16. Georgina Barker, diary, 14 August 1958.
17. Conversation with Dede Farrelly, 26 May 1995.
18. Conversation with George Farrelly, 27 March 1995.
19. *Collected Poems*, p.361.
20. George Barker to Kit Barker, 7 February 1959.
21. George Barker to Oliver Bernard, 17 September 1959.
22. Conversation with George Farrelly, 27 March 1995; conversation with Dede Farrelly, 26 July 1995.
23. Notebook, 1960, Texas.
24. Conversation with Professor Ron Schuhardt, University College, Oxford, 5 July 1995.
25. Conversation with Carol Weston, 30 August 1993.
26. Ibid.
27. George Barker, *The View from a Blind I* (London: Faber, 1962), p.43.
28. Willie Coakley to George Barker, 9 August 1991.
29. George Barker to Oliver Bernard, 12 September 1959.
30. Conversation with David Gascoyne, 5 April 1994.
31. George Barker to Oliver Bernard, 17 September 1959.
32. Itinerary for George Barker, Poetry Centre, Washington, October–December 1959.

Chapter 38 'A Divine Fiat'

1. 'Some Notes on Housman', *Collected Essays*, p.36.
2. Conversation with Dede Farrelly, 7 May 1995.
3. Moraes, *Never at Home*, pp.98–100.
4. George Barker, 'Brian Higgins', *Collected Essays*, p.190.
5. Conversation with Sebastian Barker, 7 July 1995.

6 'For the Sixtieth Birthday of George Barker', *Homage to George Barker*, pp.84–5.
7 *Collected Essays*, p.113.
8 C.H. Sisson, 'For the Sixtieth Birthday of George Barker', *Homage to George Barker*, p.87.
9 Conversation with Dede Farrelly, 7 May 1995.
10 Moraes, *Never at Home*, p.19.
11 Ibid., pp.52–4.
12 *The View from a Blind I*, pp.56–7.
13 George Barker to Kit Barker, 16 January 1961.
14 Ibid.
15 Conversation with George Farrelly, 27 March 1995.
16 *Collected Poems*, p.343.
17 Conversation with Georgina Barker, 17 July 1995.
18 Conversation with Dede Farrelly, 26 May 1995.
19 Notebook, 1960, Texas.
20 Notebook, 1960–1, Texas.
21 *Collected Poems*, p.372.

Chapter 39 *'Transfiguring Everywhere'*

1 George Barker to Georgina Barker, n.d.
2 Desmond O' Grady to George Barker, 18 April 1988.
3 *Essays*, p.132.
4 'The Hypogryph and the Water Pistol', *X*, vol. 2, no.2 (August 1961); *Essays*, pp.112–19. See Robert Gittings (ed.), *Letters of John Keats* (Oxford: Oxford University Press, 1970), p.157.
5 *Essays*, p.115.
6 Patrick Swift, 'Prolegomenon to George Barker', *Homage to George Barker*, p.58.
7 Conversation with Dede Farrelly, 26 May 1995.
8 George Barker to Oliver Bernard, 1 February 1961.
9 Conversation with George Barker, Bintry, 21 October 1981.
10 *Collected Poems*, p.362.
11 George Barker to Carol Weston, 20 November 1961.
12 Georgina Barker to George Barker, 15 December 1961.
13 Notebook, 1961, Texas.
14 George Barker to Christopher Barker, 15 February 1962.
15 Kit Barker to George Barker, 9 February 1962.
16 Typescript of Dedicatory Poem, in the possession of Vicki Bearton.
17 Ibid. Compare *Collected Poems*, p.378.
18 *Collected Poems*, p.390.
19 'To Marion Taaffe Barker, obiit Ascension Day, 1955'. Manuscript in the possession of Sebastian Barker.
20 Conversation with Dede Farrelly, 26 May 1995.
21 Conversation with Dede Farrelly, 13 July 1994.
22 Conversation with Christopher Barker, 13 October 1995.
23 Ibid.

24 George Barker to Christopher Barker, 17 September 1962.
25 'Asterisks', *Essays*, pp.134-5.
26 *Collected Poems*, p.438.
27 Manuscript letter to Eliot, Notebook, 1962, Texas.
28 Georgina Barker, diary, 31 October 1962.
29 Ibid.

Chapter 40   'Love is What You Do'

1 George Barker to Kit Barker, 13 January 1993.
2 Conversation with Jill Neville, 20 July 1995.
3 Interview with Elspeth Barker, Bintry, 1 August 1996.
4 *The Times Saturday Review* (26 September 1992), p.46.
5 Elspeth Barker, *O Caledonia* (London: Hamish Hamilton, 1991), p.126
6 Elspeth Barker to Robert Fraser, 22 March 1999.
7 Ibid.
8 Conversation with Dede Farrelly, 26 May 1995.
9 Letters from Cartwright Cunningham to George Barker, 9 July 1963 and 31 October 1963, Bintry.
10 'Dreams of a Summer Night', xvi, *Collected Poems*, p.466, where 'November', however, is poetic licence.
11 George Barker to Sebastian Barker, 3 October 1963.
12 *Villa Stellar*, xxi, *Collected Poems*, p.697.
13 *Villa Stellar*, xxxii, *Collected Poems*, p.709.
14 Elspeth Barker to Robert Fraser, 22 March 1999.
15 Tony Kingsmill to George Barker, 17 October 1963, Bintry.
16 Conversation with Elspeth Barker, Bintry, 5 August 1995.
17 *Villa Stellar*, iv, *Collected Poems*, p.681.
18 *Villa Stellar*, xii, *Collected Poems*, p.688.
19 *Villa Stellar*, xvii, *Collected Poems*, p.693.
20 *Collected Poems*, p.449.
21 Elspeth Barker to Robert Fraser, 22 March 1999,
22 George Barker to Sebastian Barker, 17 February 1964.
23 *Villa Stellar*, li, *Collected Poems*, p.726.
24 *Villa Stellar*, xxxi, *Collected Poems*, p.708.
25 George Barker introducing his *Collected Poems*, Poetry Society, 7 May 1987.

Chapter 41   'Such Peace Upon the Conscience'

1 Conversation with John Heath-Stubbs, 9 March 1995.
2 Elspeth Barker to Robert Fraser, 22 March 1999.
3 Conversation with Elspeth Barker, 1 August 1995.
4 George Barker to Sebastian Barker, 30 June 1964.
5 George Barker to T.S. Eliot, 11 August 1964. Cited in letter below.
6 T.S. Eliot to George Barker, 12 August 1964, Bintry.

REFERENCES

7   T.S. Eliot to George Barker, 21 August 1964, citing George Barker to T.S. Eliot, 15 August 1964, Bintry.
8   *Collected Poems*, p.454.
9   Conversation with Elspeth Barker, 1 August 1995.
10 *Collected Poems*, p.428.
11 Conversation with Peter Levi, 20 March 1996.
12 *Collected Poems*, p.441.
13 'The Cutty Sark', *Listener* (18 March 1965), p.425. Appeared as 'Dreams of a Summer Night', vi, *Collected Poems*, p.459.
14 George Barker to Valerie Eliot, 5 January 1965. In the possession of Mrs Eliot.
15 Conversation with George Barker, 10 October 1981.
16 *Collected Poems*, p.436.
17 Conversation with Elspeth Barker, 1 August 1995.
18 Conversation with Sebastian Barker, 7 July 1995.
19 Conversation with Christopher Barker, 25 October 1995.
20 Kit Barker to George Barker, 16 April 1965.
21 Elspeth Barker to Robert Fraser, 20 April 1996.
22 Dom Moraes, *Collected Poems, 1957–1987* (Harmondsworth: Penguin, 1987), p.107.
23 Conversation with Elspeth Barker, 1 August, 1995.
24 Conversation with Georgina Barker, 16 August 1995.
25 'Maximes', *Collected Essays* (London: MacGibbon & Kee, 1970), pp.169, 171.
26 *Collected Poems*, p.426.
27 'La France Perfide', *Listener* (6 January 1966), pp.26–7.
28 'A pond-green corpse', *Listener* (4 November 1965), pp.714–15.
29 Press release, State University of New York, Buffalo, January 1966.

Chapter 42   *'Unscrew Me, My Dear'*

1   BBC transcript, 7 January 1966, Bintry.
2   *Essays*, p.191.
3   Conversation with Xandra Hardy, 9 February 1994.
4   Conversation with George Barker, 24 October 1981.
5   'Tragoedia', *Listener* (10 March 1966), p.358.
6   Conversation with Elspeth Barker, 1 August 1995.
7   Ibid.
8   Telephone conversation with A. Alvarez, 9 September 1995.
9   George Barker, diary for 1966, Bintry.
10 George Barker to Sebastian Barker, 15 March 1966.
11 Elspeth Barker to George Barker, 11 March 1967, Bintry.
12 George Barker to Georgina Barker, n.d.
13 Conversation with Robin Prising and Willie Coakley, 16 August 1993.
14 George Barker, diary for 1966, Bintry.
15 A. Alvarez to Admissions and Records, State University of New York at Buffalo, 10 June 1966.
16 *Collected Poems*, p.549.
17 Conversation with Ron Ramdin, 11 November 1993.

18 Notebook, New York.
19 National Sound Archive, 1982.
20 *Collected Poems*, p.507.
21 Eddie Linden, typed memoirs submitted to Robert Fraser, April 1995.
22 Conversation with Elspeth Barker, 1 August 1995.
23 Ibid.
24 Edgley & Co, solicitors to Elspeth Barker, September 1967, Bintry.
25 *Essays*, p.11.
26 Conversation with Elspeth Barker, 1 August, 1995.

Chapter 43 Bintry House

1 Lawrence Durrell to George Barker, October 1967. Lawrence Durrell papers, Morris Library of Southern Illinois University, Illinois.
2 *South Bank Show*, 1988.
3 Conversation with Elspeth Barker, 1 August 1995.
4 George Barker, *Runes and Rhymes and Tunes and Chimes* (London: Faber, 1969), p.18.
5 *Collected Poems*, pp.556–7.
6 George Barker to Jimmy Barker, 1968, quoting *Runes and Rhymes and Tunes and Chimes*.
7 George Barker to David Gascoyne, 3 November 1969.
8 Conversation with Elspeth Barker, 1 August 1995.
9 Ibid.
10 Draft sketch, 'A Comedy of Masks', New York.
11 BBC script, broadcast 7 September 1969.
12 George Barker to Sebastian Barker, 26 March 1969.
13 George Barker to Sebastian Barker, n.d.
14 Conversation with George Barker, 24 October 1981.
15 George Barker to Sebastian Barker, 12 February 1969.
16 Ibid.
17 *Collected Poems*, pp.534–5.

Chapter 44 'The Day Forgives'

1 *Collected Poems*, pp.538–9.
2 Elspeth Barker to Robert Fraser, 20 April 1996.
3 Conversation with Hedley Marten, 28 September 1995.
4 *Essays*, p.130.
5 Conversation with John Cox, 16 September 1995.
6 Ibid.
7 George Barker to Sebastian Barker, 1976.
8 *Poems of Places and People* (Faber, 1971), pp.60–1. Not in *Collected Poems*.
9 Conversation with Oliver Bernard, 6 July 1995.
10 George Barker to Rose Barker, c. 1970, Canada, Box 25, f.5.

REFERENCES

11 Conversation with Progles Barker, 15 September 1995.
12 Elspeth Barker to Robert Fraser, 22 March 1999.
13 *Collected Poems*, p.552.
14 'The Jubjub Bird or Some Remarks on the Prose Poem', Radio Three, 8 April 1971, typescript, Bintry.

Chapter 45   *'Friends and Oddfellows'*

1   Conversation with John Cox, 16 September, 1995.
2   Conversation with Elspeth Barker, 2 August 1995.
3   George Barker to Sebastian Barker, 15 September 1971.
4   George Barker to Sebastian Barker, 25 September 1971.
5   George Barker to Sebastian Barker, 18 October 1995.
6   George Barker to Sebastian Barker, 20 September 1995.
7   Smart, *On the Side of the Angels*, p.45.
8   Stephen Fothergill, 'David Archer', *SuperReal*, II (1994).
9   Obituary, unsigned, by Elizabeth Smart, *The Times* (21 October 1971), p.19.
10 *Collected Poems*, p.575.
11 George Barker to Sebastian Barker, 3 December 1971.
12 George Barker to Sebastian Barker, 8 December 1971.
13 Conversation with Sebastian Lockwood, 28 August 1993.
14 George Barker to Sebastian Barker, 3 March 1971.
15 George Barker to Sebastian Barker, 23 March 1972.
16 Conversation with Elspeth Barker, 1 August 1995.
17 Conversation with Alexander Barker, 26 September 1995.
18 'Homage to Housman', Radio Three, 14 August 1972.
19 'A Little Honouring of Lionel Johnson', Radio Three, 18 May 1994.
20 Ludwig Wittgenstein, *Tractatus Logico-Philosophicus* (London: Routledge and Kegan Paul, 1971), para. 6.44
21 *In Memory of David Archer* (London: Faber & Faber, 1972), pp.66–7.
22 *Collected Poems*, p.626.
23 Manuscript notes on the Overstrand Poem, 1972, Bintry.

Chapter 46   *'Your Poacher is a Pincher'*

1   *Homage to George Barker*, p.9.
2   *Listener* (8 March 1973), p.315.
3   Itinerary from Robert G. Kosch, University of Rochester, April 1973, Bintry.
4   Conversation with Roderick Barker, 15 September 1995.
5   *Dibby Dubby Dhu: Selected Poems for Children* (London: Faber, 1997), p.63.
6   Nicholas Brooke to George Barker, 19 April 1972.
7   Conversation with Fiona Crawford, 15 September 1995.
8   Clive Sinclair to George Barker, 25 June 1973.
9   Tristram Hull to George Barker, contract of 9 July 1973, Bintry.
10 Sebastian Barker, 'By Rocca Maggiore in Assisi', *Poems* (Reepham: Cygnet Press, 1974).

11 Conversation with Sebastian Barker, 7 July 1995.
12 Conversation with John Cox, 16 September 1995.
13 Conversation with Elspeth Barker, 1 August 1995.
14 Conversation with Progles Barker, 15 September 1995.
15 George Barker to Sebastian Barker, Miami, n.d.
16 Conversation with Elspeth Barker, 1 August 1995.
17 Conversation with Fiona Crawford, 15 September 1995.
18 Conversation with Sebastian Barker, 7 July 1995.

Chapter 47 'Dying Upward Like a Hope'

1 Conversation with Sebastian Barker, 7 July 1995.
2 *Collected Poems*, p.662.
3 Conversation with Elspeth Barker, 1 August 1995.
4 *Collected Poems*, pp.665–6.
5 Ibid., p.663.
6 Ibid., p.641.
7 'The Living Poet', Radio Three, 22 January 1974.
8 *Collected Poems*, pp.639–40.
9 Ibid., p.635.
10 Conversation with Jimmy Farrelly, 13 July 1994.
11 Conversation with Elspeth Barker, 3 August 1995.
12 Conversation with Elspeth Barker, 3 April 1996.
13 Conversation with Fiona Crawford, 15 September 1995.
14 Conversation with Michael Reynolds, 26 June 1995.
15 Conversation with Clive Sinclair, 29 February 1996.
16 Conversation with Anthony Astbury and Geoffrey Godbert, 27 January 1996.
17 Conversation with Hedley Marten, 28 September 1995.
18 *Collected Poems*, p.634.
19 Conversation with Hedley Marten, 28 September 1995.

Chapter 48 'The Poem and the Fountain'

1 Conversation with Elspeth Barker, 1, August 1995.
2 Conversation with Raffaella Barker, 26 September 1995.
3 Conversation with Eddie Linden, 13 October 1995.
4 Sebastian Barker to George Barker, n.d., Bintry.
5 George Barker to Sebastian Barker, 27 August 1976.
6 Conversation with Hedley Marten, 28 September 1995.
7 *Collected Poems*, p.677.
8 *South Bank Show*, 1988.
9 *Collected Poems*, p.731.
10 Conversation with Raffaella Barker, 26 September 1995.
11 Raffaella Barker, *Come and Tell Me Some Lies* (London: Hamish Hamilton, 1994), p.52.
12 Conversation with Bruddy Barker, 26 September 1995.

REFERENCES

13 Conversation with Elspeth Barker, 2 August 1995.
14 *Collected Poems*, p.731.

Chapter 49 'We'll To the Woods No More'

1 Conversation with George Farrelly, 27 March 1995.
2 George Barker to Robert Fraser, 1 October 1981.
3 Conversation with Hedley Marten, 28 September 1995.
4 A.E. Housman, *Last Poems* (London: Grant Richards, 1922), p.10.
5 Conversation with Elspeth Barker, 1 August 1995.
6 Ibid.
7 *Collected Poems*, p.705.
8 Michael Schmidt, 'A Late Conversion', *Poetry Nation Review*, no.31, p.56.
9 *Collected Poems*, p.719.

Chapter 50 'Ceremonies of Memory'

1 Conversation with Hedley Martin, 28 September 1995.
2 George Barker to Jimmy Barker, 1980.
3 Conversation with Hedley Marten, 28 September 1995.
4 Hedley Marten to Robert Fraser, 7 November 1995.
5 Schmidt, 'A Late Conversion', p.56.
6 Elspeth Barker to Robert Fraser, 22 March 1999.
7 Conversation with Hedley Marten, 28 September 1995.
8 *Collected Poems*, p.736.
9 Conversation with Elspeth Barker, 1 August 1995.

Chapter 51 'At a Time of Bankers'

1 William Blake, *The Complete Poetry and Prose*, ed. David W. Erdmann (New York: Doubleday, 1968), p.160.
2 *South Bank Show*, 1988.
3 Conversation with Elspeth Barker, 2 August 1995.
4 Oliver Bernard, *Getting Over It* (London: Peter Owen, 1992), p.151.
5 *Collected Poems*, p.751.
6 Ibid., p.759.
7 *Times Literary Supplement* (29 July 1983), p.813.
8 Conversation with Elspeth Barker, 2 August 1995.
9 Conversation with Georgina Barker, 15 August 1995
10 Conversation with Christopher Barker, 25 October 1995.
11 Conversation with Sebastian Barker, 7 July 1995.
12 Robert Pollet to George Barker, 20 July 1983.

Chapter 52 'Abstain! Abstain! Abstain!'

1 *Sunday Times Magazine* (11 September 1983), p.12.

2   Lindsay Clarke, *The Chymical Wedding* (London: Picador, 1989), p.16.
3   Ibid. p.102.
4   Ibid., p.15.
5   Pen-written note, Bintry.
6   Michael Asser, 'Friday Night and Saturday Morning', typescript, Bintry.
7   *Collected Poems*, p.758.
8   Michael Asser, typescript, p.11, Bintry.
9   Conversation with Elspeth Barker, 2 August 1995.
10 *Street Ballads* (London: Faber, 1992), p.36.

Chapter 53   'We're Looking for Hendrick Van Loon, My Dears'

1   Conversation with Oliver Bernard, 7 February 1995.
2   Telephone conversation with Edward Farrelly, 24 May 1996.
3   *Street Ballads*, pp.6–7.
4   Sullivan, *By Heart*, p.380.
5   Conversation with Georgina Barker, 15 August 1995.
6   Clare Barker to George Barker, 20 March 1986.
7   Conversation with Anastasia Barker, 31 August 1994.
8   T.S. Eliot to George Barker, 26 September 1937, Texas.
9   Harold Pinter reviewing Barker's *Collected Poems*, Channel Four *Book Choice*, 12 June 1987: 'No richer volume of collected poetry has been published in years.'
10 John Bayley, *London Review of Books* (July 1987).
11 George Barker to Sebastian Barker, 10 July 1987.
12 Carlo Gebler to George Barker, 29 November 1986.
13 *South Bank Show*, 1988.
14 Edna O'Brien to George Barker, 19 August 1987, Bintry.
15 George Barker to Harold Pinter, 1 December 1986, draft, Bintry.
16 Elspeth Barker to Robert Fraser, 22 March 1999.
17 Conversation with Hugh St Clair, 1 May 1996.
18 *Street Ballads*, p.54.
19 Conversation with Elspeth Barker, 2 August 1995.
20 Telephone conversation with Edward Farrelly, 24 May 1996.
21 Conversation with Anastasia Barker, 31 August 1994. Death certificate for Jessica Barker, Commonwealth of Kentucky, 8 March 1989.
22 *Street Ballads*, p.25.
23 Ibid., p.28.

Chapter 54   'Entering Into the Kingdom'

1   Conversation with Raffaella Barker, 26 September 1995.
2   Conversation with Edward Farrelly, 13 July 1994.
3   Conversation with Paul and Fiona Crawford, 15 September 1995.
4   Elspeth Barker, 'In Viagliagi', *Aquarius*, 19/20, p.96.
5   Ibid., p.97.
6   Elspeth Barker to Robert Fraser, 22 March 1999.

7 Rosemary Sullivan to George Barker, 1 February 1991, with Barker's draft reply, Bintry.
8 Conversation with Hugh St Clair, 1 May 1996.
9 George Barker to Sebastian Barker, 17 July 1990.
10 George Steiner, *The Death of Tragedy* (London: Faber, 1961), ch. VI.
11 George Barker to Sebastian Barker, 17 July 1990.
12 *Street Ballads*, p.19.
13 Draft biographical blurb for Craig Raine, n.d., Bintry.
14 Conversation with Christopher Reid, 1 December 1994.
15 Elspeth Barker to Robert Fraser, 22 March 1999.
16 *Street Ballads*, pp.8–9.
17 George Barker to Oliver Bernard, October 1991.
18 Miranda Seymour, *Ottoline Morrell: Life on the Grand Scale* (London: Hodder & Stoughton, 1992), p.410.
19 Conversation with Elspeth Barker, 2 August 1995.
20 Elspeth Barker to Robert Fraser, 22 March 1999.
21 *A Choice of Kipling's Prose*, ed. Somerset Maugham (London: Macmillan, 1952), pp.66–7.
22 Raffaella Barker, 'Farewell, my wild gipsy father', *Evening Standard* (13 November 1991), p.20.

Chapter 55   A Sprig of Honesty

1 *The Times* (29 October 1991).
2 *Independent* (29 October 1991).
3 Ibid. *The Tablet* (2 November 1991).
4 John Carey, 'Rebel Without a Clue', *Sunday Times* (27 October 1991), Book Section, p.5.
5 Conversation with John Carey, 29 June 1995.
6 Conversation with Elspeth Barker, 1 August 1995.
7 Raffaella Barker, *Come and Tell Me Some Lies*, p.1.
8 Lily later went to the University of Sussex to read English. Additional information about the later careers of her children has kindly been supplied by Elspeth Barker, who comments: 'Bruddy has become an archaeologist and is currently in Cyprus, then on to Albania. Progles is writing television scripts and has completed a children's book. Sam is a photographer, specialising in portraits.' Elspeth Barker to Robert Fraser, 11 May 2001. Raffaella Barker's fourth novel, *Summertime*, was published in April 2001.

Index

Abbott, Henrietta, 343, 348
Abercrombie, Ralph, 343
Abrahams, Dr, 27
Adler, Jankel, 207, 216, 233
Agathon, 497
Aiken, Conrad, 302
Akeko-san, 130, 136, 137
Alvarez, A., 401, 402, 403, 405
Ames, Delano, 100
Amis, Kingsley, 328, 467
Angulo, Jaime de, 154–5, 163
Antonini, Contessa Henrietta, 383, 385
Aragon, Louis, 42
Archer, David, 39, 41, 42, 43–4, 47, 53, 54, 55, 56, 57, 111, 113, 130, 206–7, 216, 257, 258, 263, 292, 297, 326, 331, 343, 346, 348, 358, 397, 435–7, 442, 467
Archer, General, 343
Archipenko, Alexander, 30, 37, 54
Aristotle, 105
Arnold, Matthew, 181, 413
Asquith, Annabel, 208, 211, 226
Asquith, Lady Cynthia, 208, 226, 330
Asquith, Didy, 208, 211, 212, 213, 218, 225, 226, 228, 229, 236, 239, 269
Asquith, Hase, 330–31
Asquith, Kip (Stephen), 225, 226
Asquith, Michael, 208, 211, 213, 226, 258, 259, 262, 269, 294, 330
Asquith, Sue, 236
Asser, Michael, 494, 495
Astbury, Anthony, 456
Astbury, Benjamin, 75
Auden, W.H., 36, 38, 45, 46, 53, 55, 64, 80, 94, 95, 119, 131, 165, 166, 179, 180, 209, 214, 237–8, 240, 263, 267, 288, 328, 331, 349, 432, 455, 466, 467, 486, 507
Augustine, St, 16, 20, 199, 202, 267, 296, 427

Bacon, Francis, 236, 312, 346
Baker, Stanley, 367

Balfour of Inchyre, Lord, 317–8
Banks, Lady, 484
Banks, Lord, 69
Barker, Adam Alexander Rahere George Robert *see* Barker, Bruddy (Adam Alexander Rahere George Robert; son of George Barker)
Barker, Albert (uncle of George Barker), 9
Barker, Albert Gordon *see* Barker, Kit (Albert Gordon; brother of George Barker)
Barker, Anastasia (daughter of George Barker), 219, 502, 506
Barker, Anthony Sebastian (son of George Barker), 219
Barker, Big Mumma *see* Barker, Marion Frances Taaffe (née Taaffe; 'Big Mumma'; mother of George Barker)
Barker, Bruddy (Adam Alexander Rahere George Robert; son of George Barker), 402, 405, 406, 411, 416, 424, 439, 444, 457, 463–4, 465, 479, 481, 495, 496, 504, 518
Barker, Chloe (grandchild of George Barker), 448, 460
Barker, Christopher (son of George Barker), 199, 217, 218, 219, 221, 225, 226, 241, 242, 247, 303, 311, 325, 330, 351, 367, 369, 371, 372, 374–5, 378, 398, 487–8, 492, 500
Barker, Clare (also known as Kate; daughter of George Barker), 66–7, 267, 295, 501–2
Barker, Claudia (grandchild of George Barker), 487, 500
Barker, Edward (son of George Barker), 363, 372, 374, 375, 454, 465, 466, 498, 499, 506, 511, 516, 518
Barker, Eileen Cecilia *see* Jackson, Eileen Cecilia (née Barker; sister of George Barker)
Barker, Eliza (grandmother of George Barker), 7
Barker, Elspeth (née Langlands; second wife of George Barker), 379–81, 384, 385, 386,

561

387, 391–2, 393, 394, 395, 396, 398, 399, 400, 402, 403, 404, 405, 406, 407, 408, 409, 410, 411, 413, 416, 423–4, 428, 429, 431, 433–4, 438, 439, 443, 447, 448, 450, 454–5, 457, 459, 462, 463, 466, 468–9, 472, 476, 478, 479, 481, 487, 489, 494, 495, 496, 497, 498, 501, 504, 505, 508, 509, 510, 514, 515, 516–7, 520, 521
Barker, Francis (son of George Barker), 381, 454, 465, 498
Barker, George
  family background, 3–10
  education and intellectual influences, 11–21
  teenage years, 22–39
  relationship with Jessica, 24–6, 32–3
  literary contacts and beginning of literary career, 41–8
  publishes *Alanna Autumnal*, 48–50, 51–2
  discussion with the Muirs, 52–3
  developments in poetic style, 53–4
  publishes *Thirty Preliminary Poems*, 54–5
  grows away from literary contacts, 55–6
  marries Jessica, 56–7
  lives in Dorset, 58–65
  writes 'The Bacchant', 60–62
  sends poetry to Eliot, 63
  Eliot's response, 64–6
  moves to Geldeston, 65–6
  birth of Clare, 66–7
  returns to Dorset, 69
  writes 'The Documents of Death', 70–71
  Eliot accepts 'The Bacchant' and 'The Documents of Death' for publication as *Janus*
  receives financial support, 73
  and visitors at Kimmeridge, 73–4
  visits Capri, 75
  moves in with parents, 76
  destroys Kit's eye, 76, 77–8
  lives in Dorset again, 79–82
  widening social circle, 82–7
  visits Walter de la Mare, 88
  visited by Ottoline Morrell, 88
  encouraged by Muir, 88–9
  domestic life, 89, 93
  influenced by Surrealism, 90–91
  and Spanish Civil War, 91
  Eliot accepts *Calamiterror* for publication, 92
  and idea of ghosts of poets, 92–3
  and Dylan Thomas, 93–6
  suggests publication of 'Quia Amore Langueo', 97–8
  publication of *Calamiterror*, 98–9
  writing projects, 99–100
  visits Italy, 100
  Eliot suggests seeking employment, 101–2
  essays, 104–5
  depressed, 105
  obtains extra-mural teaching work, 106
  receives offer of cottage in Sussex, 106
  moves to Sussex, 107
  friendship with the Gills, 107–8
  lectures, 108–9
  developments in poetic writing, 109–10
  Dylan Thomas's opinion of work, 111
  financial problems, 112, 114–5
  writes 'Elegy on Spain', 112–3
  writes essay about elegies, 114
  meets Lawrence Durrell, 115–6
  appointment to lectureship in Japan, 116–7, 118–9
  visits David Gascoyne, 117–8
  leaves England, 120
  journey to Japan, 123, 124–6
  arrival in Japan, 126–8
  at Sendai, 129–32, 133–41
  publication of *Lament and Triumph*, 140–41
  plans to leave Japan, 142–3
  final weeks in Japan, 144–9
  optimistic about prospects in America, 150–51
  meets Elizabeth Smart, 151–2, 154
  impressions of California, 154
  begins relationship with Elizabeth, 156–8
  parodied by Thomas and Davenport, 159–61
  tensions in relationship with Jessica, 162, 163
  increasing involvement with Elizabeth, 163–5, 166–7
  meets the Williamses, 165–6
  relationship with Jessica and Elizabeth, 168–78
  takes apartment in Greenwich Village, 179–80
  growing reputation, 180
  visited by Nin, 180–81
  visits Elizabeth in Canada, 181–2
  decides to ask Jessica for divorce, 182
  spends time with Jessica, 183
  unable to return to Canada, 184, 186
  birth of Elizabeth's child, 184–5
  love poems, 186–8
  attempts reconciliation with Jessica, 187
  erotic writing, 188–90
  writes about Japan, 190–91, 200–201
  continuing conflict between marital loyalty and love affair, 191–5, 197–8, 199–200, 205, 208

INDEX

makes experimental film with the Maases, 197
writes *Secular and Sacred Elegies*, 201–5
and developments in Britain, 206–7
new contacts in America, 209–10
returns to England, 210–11
reunited with Elizabeth, 211
splits time between town and country, 213–4
associates and lifestyle in London, 214–7
and birth of son Christopher, 217
sends money to Jessica, 217–8
lives with Elizabeth and children, 218, 220–21
and birth of Jessica's twins, 219
Jessica's anger, 219–20
physical and mental health problems, 222
difficulties in relationship with Elizabeth, 222–3, 224–5
lives with Elizabeth in Condicote, 225–30
wishes for repatriation of Jessica and twins, 227
publication of *Eros in Dogma*, 232–3
expanding social circle in London, 233–6
concerned about Jessica, 236–7
meets Heath-Stubbs, 237–8
and Elizabeth's move to London, 239
visits America, 239–42
travels to join Elizabeth in Ireland, 242
and joint project for radio with Kit, 243–4, 247–8
in Ireland, 244–5, 247–51
wrangling with Elizabeth, 246, 250
leaves for London, 251
developments in poetic style, 255–6
begins relationship with Cass, 256–8, 261, 262–3
in Cornwall, 258–60, 262–3
broadcast of *The Degradations of Guatemozin*, 261
attitude to women's writing, 265
companions in London, 265–6
begins to write *The True Confession*, 266–8
and the Sitwells, 268–9
in Collioure, 269–70
in Cornwall again, 271–4, 275–7, 279
advice to poets, 275–7, 280
contributes to *T.S. Eliot: A Symposium*, 277–8
returns to London, 280
and Pa, 280–81
stays with the Roberts, 282
work accepted by Lehmann, 283
in Italy, 283–7
moves to Hearne Cottage with Cass, 288–9

writing success, 289–93
work disliked by Thomas, 293
publication of *The Dead Seagull*, 294–7
and Elizabeth's affair with Graham, 298
and Wright's wedding, 299–300
and Americans, 302–3
writes play about Chatterton, 303–4
celebrates thirty-ninth birthday, 304
and academics, 305, 306, 307–9
visits south of France, 306–7
various aspects of social and domestic life, 310–14
mood changes, 312–3
pays tribute to work of Thomas, 314–5
involved in controversy about British broadcasting, 315–8
and Oliver Bernard, 319–20
writes 'Justice at Midnight', 320–21
writes 'Goodman Jacksin and the Angel', 321–3
publication of *A Vision of Beasts and Gods*, 323
meets Swift, 325–6
visits Elizabeth more frequently, 326
death of mother, 326
and revolution in British poetry, 329
and nephew's relationship with Cass, 330
proud of children, 330
sensitivity, 330–31
spends time in London, 331–2
radio plays, 332–5, 341–2, 343
returns to Ireland, 336–8
in France, 338–9
deteriorating relationship with Cass, 338–9, 340–41
in Spain, 339
upset by omission of *The True Confession* from *Collected Poems*, 339–40
second edition of *The True Confession* published, 343
and departure of Cass, 344–5
moves in with Elizabeth temporarily, 346
lip bitten by Elizabeth, 347–8
gives talk at Oxford, 348
returns to America, 348–56
begins relationship with Dede Farrelly, 351–2
returns to London with Dede, 357–8
and X, 358, 367–8
visits Scotland, 360–61
lives in Italy, 362–5, 366–78, 381–7
relationship with his children, 363, 371–2, 374–5
starts work on second *True Confession*, 372–3

writes poem in memory of Colquhoun,
    375–6
joint winner of the Guinness Prize, 376–7
visits London, 378
meets Elspeth Langlands, 379–80
visits Elspeth, 381
difficulties in relationship with Dede, 382
beginning of relationship with Elspeth,
    384–7
returns to England, 391–2
anxieties about Eliot, 393
finds flat with Elspeth, 393–4
visits Shropshire, 394–5
and birth of Raffaella, 395–6
and death of Eliot, 396–7
aggressive behaviour, 397–8
death of father, 398
rents house in France, 398–9
travels to Rome, 399–400
returns to London, 400
works at Buffalo, 401–5
returns from America, 405
and death of MacBryde, 405
works at York university, 406–9
writes *The Golden Chains*, 408
tries to purchase house in London, 409–10
gives an address in Montreal, 410
moves to Bintry House, 412–3
lifestyle, 413–6
writes poems for children, 415–6
publication of *Runes and Rhymes and Tunes
    and Chimes*, 415, 447
writes radio play (*The Comedy of
    Masks*), 417
discusses religion with Sebastian, 417–8
advises Sebastian about poetry, 418
and poetic training, 419
writes 'At Thurgarton Church', 419–21
writes 'Morning in Norfolk', 422–3
and Sebastian's move to Norfolk, 424
meets Marten, 424–5
publication of *Essays*, 425
intellectual interests, 425–7
writes 'Venusberg', 428
good relationship with children, 429–31
publication of *To Aylsham Fair*, 430
prepares *Poems of Places and People* for
    publication, 431–2
publication of *The Alphabetical Zoo*, 433
at University of Wisconsin, 433–9
and death of Archer, 436–7
radio talks, 439–40
themes in *In Memory of David Archer*,
    440–42
Homage to George Barker published as
    tribute for sixtieth birthday, 443–4

tours America, 444
receives financial help, 445–6
visits Italy with Sebastian, 446
difficulty in creative writing, 447
at University of Florida, 447–8
and White Knees, 448–9, 450
writes 'The Oak and the Olive, 450–51
writes 'Nietzsche's Dream', 451–2
writes *Dialogues, etc*, 452–4
visits Dede and family, 454
jealousy, 454–5
hospitality, 455
mercurial behaviour, 455–6
friendship with Marten, 456–7
family life, 457–8
and his children's difficulties, 459–60
writes to Sebastian about problem of
    suffering, 460–61
offers emotional support to Marten, 461–2
in Wales, 462–3
writes *Villa Stellar*, 463
visited by Dede's children, 465–6
Saturday evenings, 466–9
sends *Villa Stellar* for publication, 469–71
visits Greece, 472–4, 476–7
public readings, 474–6
financial problems, 476
revival of reputation, 477
holiday in Italy, 478
and politics, 480–82
writes *Anno Domini*, 482–6
death of daughter Rose, 487
and son Christopher's accident, 487–8
festschrift for seventieth birthday, 488
argues with Pollet, 489–90
old age, 491–517
visits Ialy, 498–9
deaths within his circle, 499–501, 505, 506
reunited with first daughter, 501–2
publication of new *Collected Poems*, 502–3
film on life and work, 503–4
and his adult children, 504–6
works on *Street Ballads*, 506–7
marries Elspeth, 508–9
holidays abroad, 509–10, 511
illness, 509–10, 511–2, 515–6
intellectual ideas, 512–3
autobiographical note, 513–4
sympathy with the lawless, 514–5
final illness and death, 516–7
funeral, 518–9
obituaries, 519
and review by Carey, 519–20
memorial requiem mass, 520
grave, 520, 521
Books:

INDEX

Alanna Autumnal, 3, 24, 27, 29, 33–4, 36, 48–50, 51–2, 59, 60, 86, 97, 297, 440
Alphabetical Zoo, The, 433, 437, 442
Anno Domini, 482–7, 488, 499, 500
Calamiterror, 92, 98–9, 109, 161, 206, 217, 243, 270, 349
Collected Poems, 324, 336, 339–40, 380, 488
Collected Poems (second), xi, 428, 488–9, 491, 499, 502–3
Dead Seagull, The (formerly *Of Love*, then the *Smile on the Face of the Tiger*), 50, 58, 283, 287, 291–2, 293, 294–7, 392, 508
Dialogues, etc, 452–4, 456
Dreams of a Summer Night, 394, 399, 400
Eros in Dogma, 214, 226, 232–3, 240, 255, 293
Essays, 405, 425
Essays on the Theory of Poetry, 88, 104–5
Golden Chains, The, 408
In Memory of David Archer, 440–42
Janus, 50, 60, 72, 79, 81, 84, 86, 124, 297
Lament and Triumph, 140–41, 143, 146, 159, 206
Love Poems, 240–41
News of the World, 282, 290, 291, 318, 325, 332
Poems, 60, 71, 78–9, 80, 100–101, 124, 161
Poems of Places and People, 431–2, 474–5
Runes and Rhymes and Tunes and Chimes, 415, 447, 518
Secular and Sacred Elegies, 201–5, 232, 303, 471, 512
Selected Poems, 166, 170, 176, 183, 226
Selected Poems (1995), xi
Street Ballads, 506–7, 513, 514, 516, 520
Thirty Preliminary Poems, 39, 54–5, 57, 59, 62, 343
To Aylsham Fair, 430
True Confession of George Barker, The, 1, 8–9, 57, 118, 266–8, 282–3, 292, 315–6, 317, 318, 336, 339–40, 343, 392; second part, 18, 20, 372–3, 376, 377
View from a Blind I, The, 364–5, 372, 376, 379
Villa Stellar, 463, 469–71, 472, 488, 494
Vision of Beasts and Gods, A, 323, 324
Barker, George (Pa; father of George Barker), 3, 6–8, 9–10, 11, 13, 22, 27, 28, 31, 33, 47, 74–5, 76, 93, 161, 162, 207, 210, 218, 223, 224, 237, 255, 271, 280–81, 290, 299, 303, 304, 318, 324, 326, 340, 398
Barker, Georgina Elizabeth (daughter of George Barker), 185, 188, 191, 192, 194, 195, 198, 200, 208, 211, 218, 221, 225, 226, 236, 241, 242, 247, 311, 325, 326, 330, 351, 363, 366, 370, 371, 376, 377, 378, 379, 398, 399, 404, 435, 487, 492
Barker, Ilse (née Gross; sister-in-law of George Barker), 258, 259, 263, 264, 271, 272, 279, 280, 281, 290, 292, 297, 304–5, 312, 326, 344, 377, 392, 416, 424
Barker, James (grandchild of George Barker), 487
Barker, Jane (grandchild of George Barker), 429, 487
Barker, Jessica (Jessie) Winifred Theresa (née Woodward; first wife of George Barker), 24–6, 32–3, 37, 56–7, 59, 66–7, 73, 74, 75, 76, 79, 81, 83, 89, 92, 93, 100, 101, 106, 107, 108, 112, 116, 118, 119, 120, 124, 125, 126, 128, 129, 130, 131, 134, 135, 137, 139, 140, 141, 142, 144, 145, 147, 148, 151, 152, 153–4, 155, 156–7, 158, 162, 163, 164–5, 168–9, 170, 171, 172, 174, 176–7, 179, 182, 183, 186, 187, 188, 191, 192, 193, 194, 195, 196, 197, 198, 199–200, 205, 208, 209, 210, 211, 214, 217–8, 218–9, 220, 222, 223, 224, 226, 227, 229–30, 233, 236–7, 240, 241, 242, 245, 256, 257, 267, 284, 294, 295, 338–9, 346, 351, 354, 382, 404, 414, 429, 502, 506, 508
Barker, Jimmy (son of George Barker), 354, 357, 360, 375, 454, 465, 472, 498, 506
Barker, Julie (daughter-in-law of George Barker), 424, 434, 448, 460
Barker, Kit (Albert Gordon; brother of George Barker), 4, 9, 10, 14, 15, 22–3, 25, 26, 27, 28–9, 30, 33, 34, 35, 37, 48, 57, 59–60, 69, 70, 74, 76, 77–8, 79, 81, 89, 90, 93, 97, 99, 107, 118, 119, 123, 142–3, 145, 147, 150, 161, 207, 211, 224, 243, 246–7, 248, 249, 250, 255, 257, 259–60, 262, 263, 264, 270–71, 272, 279, 280, 281, 289, 290, 291, 292, 293, 297, 298, 299, 304–5, 312, 323, 326, 344, 349, 362, 363, 371, 377, 378, 392, 398, 416, 469, 484, 505
Barker, Lily Elizabeth Anna Miranda (daughter of George Barker), 448, 457–8, 464, 466, 484, 504, 509, 516, 517, 520
Barker, Marion Frances Taaffe (née Taaffe; 'Big Mumma'; mother of George Barker), 3–4, 5, 6–7, 7–8, 9, 10, 11, 13, 14, 15, 27, 28, 31, 47, 74, 76, 77, 93, 119, 123, 151, 161, 162, 169, 207, 210, 218, 223, 224, 245, 247, 255, 271, 272, 280, 304, 324, 326, 332, 336, 337, 373, 429, 505
Barker, Miranda (grandchild of George Barker), 460
Barker, Monica Adelaide Ursula *see* Humble, Monica Adelaide Ursula (Mo; née Barker; sister of George Barker)

565

Barker, Olga Annette (sister of George Barker), 8, 25, 27, 405, 407, 505–6

Barker, Progles (Roderick Joseph Cameron; son of George Barker), 413, 416, 430, 444, 447, 463–4, 465, 479, 481, 495, 496, 504, 514, 518, 520

Barker, Raffaella Flora (later Raffaella St Clair; daughter of George Barker), 395, 399, 400, 402, 404, 405, 406, 416, 424, 457, 459, 463, 487, 495, 498, 502, 504, 505, 508, 510, 515, 517, 518, 520

Barker, Roderick Joseph Cameron *see* Barker, Progles (Roderick Joseph Cameron; son of George Barker)

Barker, Rose Maximiliane (daughter of George Barker), 251, 262, 303, 325, 326, 330, 371, 378, 379, 392, 429–30, 459–60, 462, 487

Barker, Samuel Drumtochty Inigo (son of George Barker), 433, 438, 439, 451, 462, 484, 496, 505–6, 516, 518

Barker, Sebastian (son of George Barker), 236, 239, 242, 247, 311, 325, 327, 330, 359, 371, 374, 378, 379, 383, 386, 392, 398, 404, 409, 417–8, 419, 424, 425, 427, 429, 434, 435, 437, 438, 442, 446, 448, 450, 460–61, 462, 487, 489, 494, 498, 500–501, 502, 506, 511, 512, 513, 515

Barker, Thomas (nephew of George Barker), 416

Barker, Walter (grandfather of George Barker), 7

Barnes, Djuna, 83, 85, 114–5, 166

Barnes, George, 243

Barrie, Sir James, 152

Barry, Kevin, 54

Baudelaire, Charles, 20, 204, 221, 325–6, 332, 333, 418

Bayley, John, 502

Beach, Sylvia, 41

Beardsley, Aubrey, 427

Bedell, Mr and Mrs 163, 168, 183

Beethoven, Ludwig van, 38, 39

Belcher, Muriel, 310

Bennett, H.S., 97

Berkeley, Bishop George, 273, 274

Berkeley, Lennox, 333, 339, 341

Berlemont, Gaston, 215

Bernard, Bruce, 235, 256, 265, 311, 312, 344–5, 520

Bernard, Jeffrey, 265–6, 268, 269, 291, 297, 314, 324, 347, 499

Bernard, Oliver, 280, 282, 297, 299, 308–9, 311, 312, 319–20, 324, 331, 344, 353, 355, 356, 367, 369, 416, 429, 481, 482, 498, 499, 515–6, 518

Bernard, Veronica/Wendy *see* Humble, Veronica/Wendy (later Veronica Bernard, then Veronica Kentfield; niece of George Barker)

Bernard, Mrs, 291

Berry, Michael, 368

Berryman, John, 452

Bewley, Eugene Augustus Marius, 210, 218, 302–3, 306, 307, 336

Binkie, 260

Bismarck, Otto von, 201

Blackburn, Thomas, 309

Blair, F.C., 186

Blake, William, 34–5, 37, 91, 110, 132, 134, 176, 238, 262, 349, 432, 451, 461, 480, 485

Blunden, Edmund, 127, 132

Bluth, Karl Theodor, 222, 300

Bolger, Jeffrey, 392

Bolt, Robert, 191

Bonaventura, St, 369

Bossis, Lauro da, 55

Botting, Cecil, 86

Bowra, Sir Maurice, 402

Bragg, Melvyn, 503

Brandt, Sebastian, 488

Brashes, the, 455, 462

Breton, André, 89–90

Brinnin, John Malcolm, 292, 300–301, 356

Britten, Benjamin, 179, 240

Brockway, Fenner, 271

Brooke, Nicholas, 445

Brooke, Rupert, 65, 417, 476

Bryant, William Cullen, 434

Buchanan, Donald, 459

Buñuel, Luis, 90

Burden, Hugh, 333

Burton, Sir Henry, 26

Byron, Lord, 6, 117, 267, 323, 360, 361, 393, 407, 477

Cadogan, Sir Alexander, 318

Caetani, Principesse Marguerite, 367, 382, 387

Cameron, Norman, 79, 292

Campbell, Roy, 265, 269, 291, 304, 333

Campion, Thomas, 74

Carey, John, 519, 520

Carlyle, Thomas, 5

Carpenter, Maurice, 6, 43, 48, 53, 54, 55, 57, 59–60, 62, 65, 73, 74, 76, 77, 78, 79, 80, 81, 271, 292, 416, 468, 469

Carroll, Lewis, 19

Cass, Betty (known as Cass, later Humble, Cass), 256–8, 260, 261, 262, 263, 265, 266, 268, 269, 270, 271, 272, 279, 280, 281, 283, 284, 285, 286, 287, 289, 290, 291, 292,

INDEX

295, 297–8, 298–9, 300, 301, 306, 307, 312, 313, 314, 316, 319, 323, 324, 326, 330, 336, 338–9, 340–41, 344–5, 346, 347, 348, 353, 356, 357, 372
Cass, Mrs, 345
Catullus, 366, 457, 470, 473
Cecilia, Saint, 15, 288
Celano, Thomas of, 366
Chamberlain, Neville, 118
Chambers, E.K., 69
Chandler, Raymond, 427
Chaplin, Geraldine, 191
Chattaway, Christopher, 314
Chatterton, Thomas, 56, 303–4
Chesterton, G.K., 369
Chiron, Louis, 26
Cho San, 144
Christie, Miss, 11
Clair, Rene, 503
Clark, Sir Kenneth, 112
Clarke, Arthur C., 512
Clarke, Lindsay, 492–3
Clay, Cassius, 397
Cleverdon, Douglas, 332, 333, 334, 339, 341, 342
Clive, Robert, 201
Coakley, Willie, 354, 355, 404, 438
Coleman, Emily Holmes, 82–4, 85, 86, 87, 94, 95, 98–9, 102–3, 104, 106, 112, 115, 166, 220, 295, 357
Coleman, Johnny, 82, 166, 209, 237
Coleridge, S.T., 87, 93, 127, 150, 278–9, 463
Colquhoun, Robert, 207, 216, 233–4, 260, 282, 283, 284, 285, 287, 297, 311, 312, 331, 343, 348, 358, 369, 375–6, 378, 381, 401 *see also* Roberts, the
Confucius, 426
Connolly, Cyril, 222
Conquest, Robert, 329
Cornford, John, 42
Corso, Gregory, 349, 353
Cortez, Hernando, 243
Court, Graham, 259
Cox, John, 407, 424, 425, 426, 427, 433, 434, 446, 466
Crawford, Fiona *see* Sinclair, Fiona (later Fiona Marten, then Fiona Crawford)
Crawford, Paul, 509, 510
Cripps, Sir Stafford, 152–3 *see also* Crippses, the
Crippses, the, 154 *see also* Cripps, Sir Stafford
Crivelli, Carlo, 29–30, 34, 67
Cromwell, Oliver, 5, 69, 201, 225
Cronin, Anthony, 299, 325, 328, 330, 348, 358, 359, 376, 393, 405
Cronin, Theresa, 348

Crowley, Aleister, 272
Cunard, Nancy, 40
Cusack, Cyril, 341

D'Arcy, Father Martin, 333
Dale-Roberts, Father Kenneth, 15–16, 19, 20, 27, 39, 72, 137, 362, 369, 402, 454
Dalí, Salvador, 90
Davenport, John, 159, 293, 297
Davie, Donald, 329, 337
Dawson, Peter, 115
Day-Lewis, C., 80
De la Mare, Richard, 63
De la Mare, Walter, 56, 57, 63, 74, 88, 119
De la Motte, Baron, 124
Deakin, John, 311–2, 436
Deller, Alfred, 341
Derain, André, 269
Derwood *see* Williams, Gene (Gene Derwood)
Dickinson, Patric, 290, 293
Dilworth, Ira, 151
Dior, Christian, 265
Dix, George, 279
Dobrée, Bonamy, 309
Doi, Kochi, 129, 132, 133, 134, 135, 136, 138, 148
Doi, Mrs, 129
Donaghue, Dennis, 337
Donne, John, 156, 203
Donnellan, Father, 508
Dryden, John, 235, 288
Duff, David, 259, 263, 264
Dumas, Alexandre, 74, 512
Dunsany, Joseph Plunkett, Lord, 14, 23
Dunsmuir, Nessie *see* Graham, Nessie (Nessie Dunsmuir)
Durrell, Lawrence, 50, 115–6, 124, 180, 213, 412
Durrell, Nancy, 115
Dussaux, Madame Nostra Giacomo, 285

Eberhardt, Richard, 209
Eliot, T.S., xi, xiv, 20, 24, 34, 36, 37, 45, 47, 52, 63, 64–5, 66, 67, 71, 72, 73, 75, 76, 78, 81, 82, 83–5, 91, 92, 97, 98, 99, 101–2, 103, 104, 105, 106, 111, 112, 116, 119, 137, 143–4, 162, 181, 193, 207, 214, 236, 260, 261, 266, 277–8, 282–3, 290–91, 303, 309, 323, 324, 325, 331, 335, 339–40, 341, 350, 355, 364, 376, 393, 396–7, 401, 414, 419, 432, 434, 441, 452, 454, 474, 483, 502, 519
Eliot, Valerie, 396
Eluard, Paul, 42
Empson, William, 36, 37, 132, 215
Evans, Jane, 242

Evans, Jon Randell, 40
Ewart, Gavin, 494

Faber, Father Frederick William, 15, 64
Faber, Geoffrey, 64
Fairfax, John (formerly 'Young John' Jackson; nephew of George Barker), 4, 31, 108, 118, 218, 225, 271, 272, 276–7, 279, 290, 292, 297, 300, 311, 313, 345, 348, 419
Farrelly, Dede (Lavinia), 303, 306, 336, 338, 351, 352, 353, 354, 356, 357–8, 360, 361, 362, 364, 366, 368, 370, 373, 374, 375, 378, 381–2, 386, 414, 415, 429, 454, 465, 466, 498, 499, 520
Farrelly, Doodles, 303
Farrelly, Elizabeth, 303, 351, 353, 360, 375
Farrelly, Emily (née Tomkins), 240
Farrelly, George, 351, 353, 360, 363, 374, 375, 454, 465
Farrelly, John Joseph, 209–10, 218, 240, 241, 242, 246, 303, 305–6, 307, 323, 324, 329–30, 336, 337, 338, 339, 349, 351, 353, 357, 382, 408, 426, 440
Farrelly, Martin, 240
Farrelly, Tom, 209
Feaver, Temp, 147
Fellini, Federico, 381–2
Fermor, Patrick Leigh, 455
Ferrarotti, Federico, 366, 374
Fisher, Geoffrey, Archbishop of Canterbury, 316
Fitch, John Cooper, 123, 124, 139, 143, 147, 166, 171, 176, 177, 179–80, 189, 217, 220, 228, 230, 240
Fitzgerald, Scott, 306
Fitzgibbon, Constantine, 400
Forster, Mrs, 225, 226, 227, 228
Fothergill, Stephen, 436
Francis, St, 16, 366, 369–70, 378, 427, 446, 485, 515, 518
Francis de Sales, St, 16
Franco, Francisco, 91
Fraser, Lady Antonia, 504
Fraser, G.S., 214, 443
Frazer, Sir James, 270, 383, 386, 395
Freud, Lucian, 236, 312, 325
Frost, Robert, 354
Fukuhara, Professor, 128, 148
Fuller, Buckminster, 426, 479

Gardner, Donald, 379
Garman, Douglas, 47, 48
Gascoyne, David, 41–2, 44, 48, 55, 73–4, 83, 86, 87, 89, 90, 91, 95, 108, 117–8, 220, 221, 338, 340, 343, 397, 416, 432, 443, 478–9, 494, 498, 509, 519

Gatenby, Edward, 132
Gebler, Carlo, 503
Gilboys, the, 135, 148
Gill, David, 107, 108, 288, 289, 330, 341, 342
Gill, Elizabeth, 107, 108, 207
Gill, Eric, 97, 107
Ginsberg, Allen, 349, 353, 443, 461
Glendinning, Victoria, 268
Godbert, Geoffrey, 456
Goodson, Katharine, 100, 152
Gould, Warwick, 507
Gowrie, Grey, 401
Graham, Nessie (Nessie Dunsmuir), 258, 262, 284
Graham, W. S. ('Sydney' or 'Jock'), 206–7, 216, 234, 258–9, 297, 298, 299, 310, 311, 328, 374
Grant, Duncan, 112
Granville-Barker, Harley, 9
Graves, Robert, 24, 30, 111–2, 348, 376
Gray, Thomas, 419
Green, Fiona, 409
Green, Martin, 392–3, 409, 425, 443
Greene, Graham, 211, 212, 267, 412, 413
Grigson, Geoffrey, 42, 44–5, 70, 78–9, 81, 111, 144, 263, 268, 329
Gross, Ilse *see* Barker, Ilse (née Gross; sister-in-law of George Barker)
Guatemozin, 247
Guenther, Barbara, 438
Guggenheim, Peggy, 85, 103, 106, 112, 114, 115, 166, 180, 220
Guiler, Hugo, 180
Guinness, Alec, 42
Guinness, Bryan, 73

Hailsham, Viscount, 316, 317
Haley, William, 243, 244
Halifax, Lord, 316–7
Hallam, Arthur Henry, 24
Hamnet, Nina, 96, 215
Hardman, Mr, 106
Harman, Claire, 477
Harmsworth, Desmond, 29
Hartley, L.P., 431
Harvey, Patrick, 293
Hary, Amin, 362
Hastings, Grisell, 192
Hawkes, Reverend, 518
Hawking, Stephen, 512
Hawkins, Desmond, 43, 44, 55, 56, 98, 114, 159, 304
Hayward, John, 119
Hearn, Lafcadio, 127, 128
Heath-Stubbs, John, 161, 237–8, 257, 262, 265, 268, 271, 272, 273, 277, 300, 303, 305,

309, 313, 340, 348, 377, 391, 416, 443, 468, 509, 520
Heisenberg, W.K., 425, 485
Hemingway, Ernest, 269
Hendry, J.F., 214
Heppenstall, Rayner, 79, 293
Herbert, A.P., 220
Heyer, Georgette, 479, 512
Hidaka, Professor, 128
Higgins, Brian, 358–9, 368, 371, 376, 378, 393, 396, 400, 401, 402, 466, 479
Higham, David, 283, 520
Hill, Fanny, 392
Hill, Geoffrey, 308, 328, 391, 443
Hilton, Tim, 409
Hinton, Arthur, 100
Hiraku, 131, 135, 136, 145, 200, 201
Hirohito, Emperor, 147
Hitler, Adolf, 32, 191
Hoare, Sir Alexander, 82, 83
Hodgson, Ralph, 116, 119, 128, 133, 148
Hogg, Quintin, 23
Holbein, Hans, 29
Homer, 52–3
Honda, Kotaro, 130
Hood, Admiral, 201
Hope-Wallace, Philip, 261
Hopkins, Gerard Manley, 104, 332, 333, 434, 442, 479
Hopkinson, Tom, 86
Horace, 457, 473
Hori, Professor, 128
Horwood, Donald, 226
Housman, A.E., 131, 132, 144, 200, 357, 394, 395, 408, 417, 439–40, 468, 469, 475, 479, 488, 515
Howell, Georgina, 492
Hudeburg, Chloë, 210
Hughes, Ted, 419
Hull, Alicia, 416
Hull, Jake, 431
Hull, Joshua, 431, 515
Hull, Tristram, 300, 331, 416, 431, 445, 515
Humble, Cass see Cass, Betty
Humble, Christopher ('Mack'; nephew of George Barker), 218, 381
Humble, Monica Adelaide Ursula (Mo; née Barker; sister of George Barker), 3, 8, 13, 24, 25, 27, 28, 29, 31, 33, 36, 37, 48, 162, 163, 179, 207, 211, 217, 218, 224, 247, 249, 259, 265, 271, 324, 330, 353, 355–6, 364, 506
Humble, Patrick (nephew of George Barker), 218, 325, 330, 338, 341, 344, 345, 348, 353, 356
Humble, Veronica/Wendy (later Veronica Bernard, then Veronica Kentfield; niece of George Barker), 218, 247, 248–9, 250, 271, 297, 299, 312, 319, 324–5, 326, 330, 353, 438
Humble, William Henry (brother-in-law of George Barker), 33
Hunter, Dr Fred J., Jr, 173

Ichikawa, Professor, 128
Ingelow, Jean, 434
Isherwood, Christopher, 119, 131, 146, 151
Ishida, Professor, 128
Ishihata, Professor, 128
Ishimoto, Baroness, 145

Jackson, Barry (nephew of George Barker), 108, 218, 297
Jackson, Eileen Cecilia (née Barker; sister of George Barker), 8, 25, 27, 31, 48, 108, 207, 225, 297, 311, 345, 364
Jackson, Jardine, 409–10
Jackson, John see Fairfax, John (formerly 'Young John' Jackson; nephew of George Barker)
Jackson, Olga (niece of George Barker), 218, 297, 304, 311
Jackson, Phillip Fletcher (brother-in-law of George Barker), 31, 207, 297
Jacobs, Anthony, 333
James, Henry, 362
Jennings, Humphrey, 87
Jodai, Professor, 128
John, Caspar, 297, 299
John of the Cross, St, 85
Johnson, Jack, 75
Johnson, John, 405, 488–9
Johnson, Lionel, 440
Jones, Phyllis, 115
Joyce, James, 193
Julius II, Pope, 283

Kata, Professor, 128
Kavanagh, Kathleen (née Malone), 408–9
Kavanagh, Patrick, 330, 336–7, 338, 405–6, 408–9, 514
Kavanagh, Peter, 337
Keats, John, xiii, xv, 127, 128, 368, 400
Kempis, Thomas à, 16
Kent, Father Bruce, 499
Kentfield, Calvin, 325, 326, 330, 353
Kentfield, Veronica see Humble, Veronica/Wendy (later Veronica Bernard, then Veronica Kentfield; niece of George Barker)
Kerouac, Jack, 350

Keynes, Geoffrey, 34
King Bull, E. J., 244, 249, 261
Kingsmill, Christina, 472
Kingsmill, Tony, 379, 381, 384–5, 386–7, 408, 431, 471, 472
Kipling, Rudyard, 517
Koizumi, Setsuko, 127
Kroeber, Alfred, 155
Kuts, Vladimir, 314

Laing, R.D., 510
Lamb, Charles, 93, 279
Langlands, Elspeth *see* Barker, Elspeth (née Langlands; second wife of George Barker)
Langlands, Mr, 381
Langlands, Mrs, 381
Larkin, Philip, 161, 228, 328, 329, 466, 467
Laughlin, James, 155, 166, 204
Lawrence, D.H., 28, 35, 36, 40, 45, 155, 243, 272
Lawrence, Frieda, 35, 272
Lawrence, T.E., 43
Lean, David, 191
Leavis, F.R., 36, 51, 209, 240, 302, 303, 305–6, 323, 329
Leavis, Queenie, 306
Ledwidge, Francis, 14, 337
Lee, Elizabeth, 211, 229
Lee, Francis, 184
Legmann, Gerson, 188–9
Lehmann, John, 41, 94, 180, 214, 268, 283, 286, 287, 288, 291, 292, 295, 331
Lehmann, Rosamond, 283
Leishman, J.B., 113
Leopardi, Giacomo, 262
Lepar, John Heron, 266
Levi, Peter, 395
Levin, Harry, 193
Lewis, David, 271
Lewis, Judy Tyler, 478–9
Lewis, (Percy) Wyndham, 29, 30, 32, 191, 233, 403
Lewis, Samuel, 10
Li Po, 426
Linden, Eddie, 409, 418, 455–6
Lindsay, Jack, 292
Liston, Sonny, 397
Lloyd, Albert Lancaster, 43
Lockwood, Roseanne, 438, 439
Lockwood, Sebastian, 438, 439, 442
Longspée, William, 110
Lorca, Federico García, 113, 117
Lowell, Amy, 133
Lowell, Robert, 209
Lucie-Smith, Edward, 308
Lucretius, 273

Maas, Marie, 184, 194, 196, 197, 240, 249, 303 *see also* Maases, the
Maas, Willard, 184, 194, 196, 197, 204, 209, 210, 240, 303 *see also* Maases, the
Maases, the, 208, 210 *see also* Maas, Marie; Maas, Willard
Macbeth, George, 221, 308
MacBryde, Robert, 207, 216–7, 233, 234, 260, 282, 283, 285, 286, 311, 312, 348, 358, 369, 375, 378, 405, 431 *see also* Roberts, the
McCaig, Norman, 360
MacDiarmid, Hugh, 73–4, 282, 358
MacGowran, Jack, 343
Mackenzie, Bill, 259, 263, 297
Mackenzie, Compton, 360
McKinner, Miss, 360, 361, 362
Maclaren-Ross, Julian, 215
MacLeish, Archibald, 209
McLuhan, Marshall, 209, 426
MacNeice, Louis, 45, 80, 128, 232–3, 268, 401
MacNeice, Mrs, 268
MacNeill, John, 429
Maderna, Stefano, 15 286, 288
Madge, Charles, 42, 44
Malone, Kathleen, 408–9
Manahan, Sheila, 343
Manning, Cardinal, 495
Manolete, 269, 270
Mansfield, Katherine, 35, 272
Maritain, Jacques, 193, 204
Markiewicz, Countess Constance, 14
Marlowe, Christopher, 117, 512
Marquis, Don, 503
Marsh, D'Arcy, 170, 326
Marsh, Jane (née Smart), 152, 170, 173, 174, 175, 177, 182, 184, 191, 240, 246, 262, 326, 351
Marten, Fiona *see* Sinclair, Fiona (later Fiona Marten, then Fiona Crawford)
Marten, Hedley, 424–5, 456–7, 461–2, 463, 466, 472–3, 474, 476, 477, 478, 484, 498–9, 518
Marten, Laura, 462
Martin, Kingsley, 318
Masefield, John 119
Massie, Allan, 380, 381, 397, 433, 520
Mayer, Elizabeth, 240
Mayer, Ulrica, 209, 240
Mazzuoli, Giuseppe, 15
Medici, Lorenzo de', 284, 285
Melisander, Roy, 189
Melville, Herman, 146, 330
Mestrović, Ivan, 30, 54
Michelangelo, 24, 283, 284, 285

INDEX

Mikai, 125
Miller, Henry, 116, 155, 189, 191
Miller, Karl, 210, 306, 307, 323, 502
Milton, John, 201, 202, 235, 455, 463
Minton, John, 216, 310, 346, 401
Moat, John, 419
Monkhouse, Cosmo, 121
Monro, Alaida, 116
Monro, Harold, 45
Monteith, Charles, 339
Montezuma, Emperor, 243
Moore, Mr and Mrs Henry, 268
Moore, Marianne, 265
Moore, Nicholas, 214
Moraes, Dom, 331, 343, 349, 358, 359, 360, 361, 368, 374, 378, 381, 393, 394, 397, 398, 399, 405, 435
Moraes, Judy (née St John), 393, 394, 398, 405
Morier, Sir James, 13
Morrell, Lady Ottoline, 73, 88, 516
Muir, Edwin, 51–2, 56, 57, 63, 74, 78, 88–9, 98, 102, 104, 105, 114, 119, 139
Muir, Willa, 51–2, 88, 98
Murry, John Middleton, 3, 35–7, 38, 47, 48, 272

Neville, Jill, 379
Newman, Cardinal John Henry, 15, 16–17, 18, 54, 72, 137, 201, 295, 372, 373, 463, 494–5, 512
Nichols, Ann, 455
Nichols, Denny, 455
Nicol, Pegi, 192
Nietzsche, Friedrich, 202, 512
Nin, Anaïs, 116, 166, 180–81, 188, 189, 190
Nuvolari, Tazio, 30

O'Brien, Edna, 504
Oddy, Father Philip Francis, 19, 20, 454
O'Farrell, Mary, 343
O'Grady, Desmond, 367
O'Hanlon, James, 5, 99
Orage, Alfred Richard, 84
Origen, 372
Orlovsky, Peter, 353
Ostrow, Woody, 438, 439, 469
Ovid, 457
Owen, Father John, 67
Owen, Robert, 110

Paalen, Alice, 124
Paalen, Wolfgang, 124
Pampanini, Danila, 456
Pascal, Blaise, 72, 426, 512
Pasquale, Richard, 343
Pasternak, Boris, 191

Patchen, Kenneth, 209, 302
Pausanias, 473
Pears, Peter, 240
Pearse, Patrick, 14
Pickering, Ernest, 116, 117, 118, 128
Péguy, Charles, 212
Pellizi, Professor Camillo, 366
Pellizi, Raffaella, 364, 366, 367, 383, 395, 404
Perse, Saint-John, 355
Piero della Francesca, 367
Pinter, Harold, 186, 456, 502, 504, 520–21
Pliny the Elder, 203, 204
Plomer, William, 331
Plunkett, Joseph, Lord Dunsany see Dunsany, Joseph Plunkett, Lord
Plutarch, 473
Poe, Edgar Allen, 181
Pollet, Robert, 418, 446, 489–90, 499–500
Pope, Alexander, 28, 288
Porteous, Hugh Gordon, 40, 44, 51
Potts, Paul, 215, 234, 311
Pouce, Jojo, 269
Pouce, Rene, 269
Pound, Ezra, 45, 73, 76, 80, 266, 277
Prising, Robin, 312, 404, 438
Pritchett, V.S., 331
Propertius, 366, 380, 457, 469, 473
Pudney, John, 79

Quiller-Couch, Arthur, 70, 97
Quilley, Dennis, 343

Radin, Paul, 155
Rahere, 396
Raine, Craig, 477–8, 513, 514
Read, Herbert, 431
Redgrove, Peter, 401
Rees, Sir Richard, 36
Reid, Christopher, 514
Reid, Philippa (later Philippa Wright), 299, 300
Reith, Lord, 315
Reynold, Michael, 456
Rhys, Keidrych, 110, 111
Richards, I.A., 42, 104–5, 305, 425
Rickword, Edgell, 40, 47, 48, 91, 363
Riding, Laura, 30
Ridler, Anne, 64, 115, 143, 213
Rilke, Rainer Maria, 113–4, 117, 135
Rimbaud, Arthur, 363, 432
Roberts, Michael, 36, 37, 38–9, 45, 51, 56, 75–6, 81, 94, 102, 106, 328
Roberts, the (Robert Colquhoun and Robert MacBryde), 207, 236, 265, 284, 287, 291, 297, 299 see also Colquhoun, Robert; MacBryde, Robert

Roethke, Theodore, 354
Rollins, Carl Purington, 204
Romilly, Esmond, 41
Rootham, Helen, 363
Rossetti, William, 34
Rothschild, Victor, 73
Roughton, Roger, 89, 90, 111
Russell, Sanders, 180

Sacks, Arthur, 438
Sade, Marquis de, 306-7
St Clair, Hugh (son-in-law of George Barker), 504-5, 511
St Clair, Raffaella Flora *see* Barker, Raffaella Flora (later Raffaella St Clair; daughter of George Barker)
St Clair, Roman (grandchild of George Barker), 510, 518
St John, Judy *see* Moraes, Judy (née St John)
Saito, Professor Takeshi, 126, 127, 128, 129, 132, 148, 200
Salamans, the, 330
Sampson, George, 12
Samuel, Lord, 317
Sanchez, Eduardo, 180
Santayana, George, 513
Sappho, 501
Savage, Dennis, 445
Savage, Mary, 445
Scarfe, Francis, 206
Schmidt, Michael, 470, 475-6, 477, 478, 488, 507
Schmidt, Professor, 135
Schuchard, Ron, 354
Scott, Frank, 173
Scott, Walter, 479
Searle, Ronald, 216
Segal, Doug, 439
Seymour, Miranda, 516
Seymouth-Smith, Martin, 112
Shapiro, Karl, 302
Shelley, Harriet, 344
Shelley, Percy Bysshe, 28, 109, 117, 323, 344
Shikebu, Izumi, 133
Sidgwick, F., 69
Silver, Grey, 435
Simms, Hilda, 292
Sinclair, Clive, 445, 456, 476
Sinclair, Fiona (later Fiona Marten, then Fiona Crawford), 407, 424, 430, 445, 448, 456, 461, 462, 509, 510
Singh, Iqbal, 76
Sisson, C.H., 340, 358-9, 359-60, 443
Sitwell, Edith, xii, 28, 48, 263, 268-9, 283, 292, 333, 512
Sitwell, Osbert, 268, 269, 333

Skinner, B.F., 425-6, 428, 452, 470, 486
Smart, Christopher, 134
Smart, Elizabeth, 100-101, 123-4, 130, 139, 141, 142, 143, 145, 146, 147, 150, 151-4, 155, 156-8, 162, 163-5, 166-7, 168, 169, 170, 171, 172-3, 174-6, 177-8, 179, 180, 181, 182, 183, 184, 186, 187, 188, 189, 191, 192, 193, 194, 195, 197, 198-9, 200, 203, 205, 208, 209, 210, 211, 213, 214, 217, 218, 219, 220, 221, 222-3, 224-5, 226-7, 227-8, 229, 230, 233, 235, 236, 237, 239, 240, 241-2, 244, 245, 246, 247, 248, 249, 250, 251, 256, 257, 262, 265, 267, 268, 269, 292, 294, 295 297, 298, 299, 303, 310, 311, 312, 313, 325, 326, 330, 340-41, 344, 346, 347, 348, 350, 358, 359, 363, 371, 372, 374, 376, 377, 379, 380, 384, 392, 398, 407, 423-4, 429, 435, 436, 455, 459, 487, 500-501, 511, 519
Smart, Jane *see* Marsh, Jane (née Smart)
Smart, Louie, 143, 152, 154, 170, 194, 205, 208
Smart, Russel (brother of Elizabeth Smart), 170
Smart, Russel (father of Elizabeth Smart), 143, 152, 170, 194, 198-9, 203, 227, 242
Smiley, Commander, 22
Smith, Betty, 256
Smith, Janet Adam, 51
Smith, Sydney Goodsir, 360, 361
Southwell, Maximiliane (Maxie) von Upani, 175-6, 182, 184, 191, 192, 194
Spadini, Federico, 366
Spender, Stephen, xii, 39, 45, 46, 55, 59, 91, 112, 113, 116, 118, 128, 150, 175, 180, 214, 486
Spenser, Edmund, 13, 92, 101, 451
Spenser, Professor Theodore, 166
Spry, Graham, 208
Stamper, Frances Byng, 260
Starkie, Enid, 380
Steiner, George, 512
Stibbe, Philip, 481, 482
Stovepipe (George Lanbourne), 211
Strachey, Lytton, 495
Sullivan, Rosemary, 511, 519
Swift, Oonagh, 325, 326, 336, 358
Swift, Patrick, 325-6, 329-30, 336, 337, 358, 359, 360, 368, 369, 378, 384, 500
Swinburne, Algernon, 427, 451
Swingler, Humphrey, 292
Swingler, Randall, 43, 292
Symons, Julian, 98, 111, 113
Synge, J.M., 245

Taaff, Father Peter, 5-6

INDEX

Taaffe, Grandma (grandmother of George Barker), 4, 5, 6, 27, 47, 74, 79, 99, 161, 210–11, 218, 223, 242
Taaffe, John (grandfather of George Barker), 4, 5
Taaffe, John (member of Byron's circle), 6
Taaffe, Margaret (aunt of George Barker), 99
Taaffe, Marion Frances *see* Barker, Marion Frances Taaffe (née Taaffe; 'Big Mumma'; mother of George Barker)
Taaffe family, 5–6, 337–8 *see also* names of individuals
Takiushi, 131
Tambimuttu, James Meary, 111, 180, 214–5, 235, 236, 256, 262, 263, 277, 281
Tawney, R.H., 480
Telte, 124, 171, 174, 176, 177, 220
Tennyson, Alfred, Lord, 24, 105, 107, 289, 417, 439, 479
Tertullian, 372
Thatcher, Margaret, 480, 485, 492
Thomas, Caitlin, 95, 159
Thomas, Dylan, xi, xii, 43, 46, 55, 79, 81, 87, 90, 93–5, 98, 111, 112, 115, 159, 161, 165, 206, 215, 256, 263, 282, 292, 293, 299, 300, 314–5, 332, 343, 349, 356, 400
Thompson, Francis, 65, 127, 479
Thompson, Dunstan, 166, 302
Thwaite, Ann, 329
Thwaite, Anthony, 270, 280, 308, 329, 340, 443, 467, 486, 519
Tintoretto, 29, 67
Tocqueville, Alexis de, 491
Todd, Ruthven, 96, 262, 325
Tom (bank robber), 514, 518, 520, 521
Tomkins, Emily (later Emily Farrelly), 240
Tracy, Sean, 367
Trevelyan, G.M., 412
Trevelyan, Julian, 220
Trypanis, C.F. (Constantine), 380
Tweedsmuir, Lady, 208
Tzara, Tristan, 42

Van Wart, Alice, 500
Varda, Jean, 143, 147, 153, 164, 292, 295
Vasari, Giorgio, 283, 285, 386
Verlaine, Paul, 28
Vespasian, Emperor, 506
Vidal, Gore, 180
Villa, José García, 209, 219
Villon, François, 266, 267, 340
Virgil, 457, 473

Wade, Kathleen, 57, 58, 65
Wade, Rosalind, 57, 396
Wain, John, 328

Walpole, Lord, 447, 518
Ward, Tony, 406
Warhol, Andy, 196
Warlock, Peter (Philip Heseltine), 272
Warner, Sylvia Townsend, 477
Watkins, Vernon, 111, 431
Watson, Peter, 216
Waugh, Evelyn, 333
Webb, Kaye, 216
Wedekind, Frank, 58
Wellesley, Lady Dorothy, 73, 80
Wells, H.G., 143
Westbury, Marjorie, 333, 341
Weston, Carol, 354–5, 369, 371
White, Antonia, 83, 85–6, 87, 95, 103, 106, 107, 118–9, 235, 277, 357
White Knees, 448–9, 450
Whooley, Tony, 454
Williams, Gene (Gene Derwood), 165–6 *see also* Williamses, the
Williams, Oscar, 164, 165, 166, 180, 183, 194, 196, 349, 353, 354, 355, 395, 401 *see also* Williamses, the
Williamses, the, 182, 183, 184 *see also* Williams, Gene (Gene Derwood); Williams, Oscar
Wilson, Edmund, 240
Wingate, Orde, 481
Winton, Malcolm, 381, 409
Witchner, Milton, 163, 164, 165, 168, 170
Witchner, Mrs, 163
Wittgenstein, Ludwig, 426–7, 441, 470, 513
Woodhouse, Richard, xv, 368
Woodward, Catherine (mother-in-law of George Barker), 24
Woodward, Jessie Winifred Theresa *see* Barker, Jessica (Jessie) Winifred Theresa (née Woodward; first wife of George Barker)
Woodward, Kit (sister-in-law of George Barker), 24, 100, 219
Woolf, Leonard, 331
Woolf, Virginia, 65
Wordsworth, Dorothy, 279
Wordsworth, William, 93, 117, 134, 279, 485
Wright, David, 8, 215, 223, 224, 235, 243, 257, 258, 265, 271, 272, 273, 275–6, 277, 278, 280, 281, 288, 289, 292, 297, 299, 300, 304, 305, 310, 312, 331, 358, 359, 360, 369, 397–8, 443, 500
Wright, Philippa (née Reid), 299, 300
Wynter, Bryan, 259, 260, 269

Yeats, W.B., xi, 34, 80–81, 82, 98, 202, 245, 348, 376, 417, 430, 507

RELATED TITLES AVAILABLE FROM PIMLICO

Dannie Abse
Goodbye, Twentieth Century: The Autobiography of Dannie Abse

'I've long thought Dannie Abse one of the most remarkable poets now writing.' Godfrey Smith

'His scalpel turns out to be a magical wand.' Elizabeth Jennings

'There is a persistent note of humanism throughout his poetry which is never wishful thinking or mere scepticism.' Peter Porter

Dannie Abse's *A Poet in the Family* was widely acclaimed as a remarkably vivid and entertaining memoir of a poet's childhood and youth. In *Goodbye, Twentieth Century* he revises and expands this early autobiography and, in the second half, brings his life up to the present and the birth of a new century. *Goodbye, Twentieth Century* is a fully rounded, enormously readable account of a poet's life, lived in the worlds of medicine and literature but informed by the powerful influences of Welshness and his Jewish heritage.

£12.50   0-7126-6829-2

Angelica Garnett
Deceived with Kindness: A Bloomsbury Childhood

WINNER OF THE J.R. ACKERLEY PRIZE FOR AUTOBIOGRAPHY

'Passionate, lucid, risky, rash, hard to put down and impossible to forget.' *Observer*

Virginia Woolf was her aunt; Vanessa Bell was her mother. Brought up as the daughter of Clive Bell, her father was in fact Duncan Grant. Angelica Garnett provides a unique and intimate picture of a richly peopled Bloomsbury.

'Beautifully written and admirably honest...refreshing and surprising.' *The Times*

'Anyone who vowed never to read another word about Bloomsbury should relent over this book.' *Sunday Times*

£9.00   0-7126-6266-9

Victoria Glendinning
Trollope

WINNER OF THE WHITBREAD BIOGRAPHY OF THE YEAR AWARD

'**Majestic, capacious, compelling and clear-sighted.**' Hilary Spurling, *Daily Telegraph*

'Glendinning succeeds, as no biographer has done before, in bringing him to life on the page...Here, at last, is an Anthony Trollope whom one can know as a man...The effect is startlingly impressive.' Jonathan Raban, *Independent on Sunday*

'Enormously enjoyable' John Mortimer, Books of the Year, *Sunday Times*

'Altogether excellent' Anita Brookner, *Spectator*

'The finest of several recent lives of Trollope...smoothly written, splendidly readable.' Julian Symons, Books of the Year, *Sunday Times*

'I came to this biography of Trollope with unreasonably high expectations. They were amply fulfilled...A work as readable, richly shifting and well-shaped as a good novel.' Caroline Moore, *The Times*

'A brilliant and subtle interweaving of the man and the work; wonderful.' Joanna Trollope, Books of the Year, *Daily Telegraph*

£14.00   0-7126-9790-X

Jeremy Lewis
Cyril Connolly: A Life

'**A sparkling biography...stylish and funny...unflaggingly entertaining.**' John Walsh, *Independent*

'One of the funniest literary biographies I have ever read...Excellent, wildly funny and informative.' Auberon Waugh, *Literary Review*

'Lewis has produced a big rag-bag of a biography, brimming with energy and enthusiasm...He is a subtle and intelligent critic of Connolly's work, and his sympathy for his subject is unbounded.' Selina Hastings, *Sunday Telegraph*

'An enthralling biography...a probably definitive account of an enchanting man.' David Leitch, *Guardian*

'An exceptionally delightful – and definitive – biography...Like a good novel, this biography is full of memorable scenes in which the hero's character gradually assumes that of a difficult but cherished friend – one whose company annoys and amuses in almost equal terms.' Michael Shelden, *Daily Telegraph*

£12.50   0-7126-6635-4

Andrew Lownie
John Buchan: The Presbyterian Cavalier

'This exemplary biography, full of new insights and fresh documents unearthed and published for the first time, makes fascinating reading.' Robert Carver, *Scotsman*

'Admirably readable, this book will be invaluable to those who are now encountering Buchan's work for the first time.' John Sutherland, *Sunday Times*

'This formidably detailed study is a labour of love by a devoted Buchanite, a nuanced understanding of a figure who, for too long, has been regarded as an extension of his fictional heroes.' *Guardian*

'The book's strongest asset is its literary criticism. He is meticulous in exploring Buchan's non-fiction and poetry, as well as his novels, and a master at teasing out the themes that make Buchan's work so popular.' *Independent on Sunday*

'Trumpets should now sound for Buchan; and I will sound one of my own for Andrew Lownie, who has brought this most extraordinary man to life in a way no previous writer has.' Patrick Cosgrove, *Independent*

£12.50   0-7126-9735-7

Paul O'Keeffe
Some Sort of Genius: A Life of Wyndham Lewis

'Paul O'Keeffe has written a magnificent biography of Lewis, rich in revealing anecdote, with a dark sense of humour that relishes the many ironies of Lewis's life...This will be the definitive biography of Lewis for decades to come.' Lawrence Rainey, *Independent*

'A man of undoubted genius,' T.S. Eliot said of him, '...but genius for what precisely it would be remarkably difficult to say.' Painter and draughtsman, novelist, satirist, pamphleteer and critic, Wyndham Lewis's multifarious activities defy easy categorisation. *Some Sort of Genius* is the compelling biography of a major but neglected figure of twentieth-century modernism.

'A massive work of scholarship, painstaking detective-work and exhaustive detail – a biography in the mould of Richard Ellmann's *James Joyce*.' Andrew Taylor, *Literary Review*

'Paul O'Keeffe has done brilliantly in pointing up many of the myths and falsifications which Lewis encouraged, and in uncovering many new facts. He had a relish for detail...which he uses to telling, and often darkly comic, effect. He builds up a rich picture of a bitter and frustrated life.' Matthew Sturgis, *Times Literary Supplement*

£16.00   0-7126-7339-3

Jay Parini
Robert Frost: A Life

'This should now become the standard biography. A work of scholarship and love like this is rare and, in Frost's case, long overdue.' Lachlan McKinnon, *Guardian*

In this fascinating new biography of Robert Frost (1874–1963), Jay Parini offers a major reassessment of the life and work of America's premier poet of the twentieth century and the only true 'national poet' America has yet produced. Elegantly yet simply, Parini traces the various stages of Frost's colourful life: from his boyhood in San Francisco to the years of farming in New Hampshire, and the sojourn in England, where he befriended Edward Thomas, Ezra Pound and other major figures of modern poetry. Parini follows the astounding rise of Frost's fame and fortunes in America upon his return in 1915. He shows how Frost gradually evolved from poet to cultural icon, becoming a friend of presidents, and a sage whose announcements attracted the attention of the world's press.

'*Robert Frost: A Life* will surely become the definitive biography…it reveals the hidden Frost, and the fundamental oddity of a shy man who became a national institution … A remarkable biography.' Richard Gray, *Literary Review*

'An excellent biographical study.' John Burnside, *Scotsman*

£15.00   0-7126-6487-4

D.J. Taylor
Thackeray

'An excellent biography…accomplished, responsible, imaginative.' Victoria Glendinning, *Spectator*

'Outstanding…On every page of this book there is evidence of a formidable critical and imaginative intelligence at work…A splendid book.' Frank McLynn, *Evening Standard*

'Brilliant…the most enjoyable and skilful biography I have read this year.' A. N. Wilson, *Literary Review*

'Wonderful…An outstanding biography. It is unlikely there will be a better one for many years to come.' Kathryn Hughes, *Mail on Sunday*

'Admirable, engrossing and very enjoyable.' Allan Massie, *Daily Telegraph*

'A compelling biography…Taylor succeeds always in evoking a rich sense of context…without losing the narrative momentum.' Michael Slater, *New Statesman*

'A richly detailed book…Taylor writes with verve and affection and is shrewdly perceptive.' John Carey, *Sunday Times*

£12.50   0-7126-6246-4

Order more Pimlico titles from your local
bookshop, or have them delivered
direct to your door by
BOOKPOST

Dannie Abse, *Goodbye Twentieth Century*	0712668292	£12.50
Angelica Garnett, *Deceived With Kindness*	0712662669	£9.00
Victoria Glendinning, *Trollope*	071269790X	£10.00
Jeremy Lewis, *Cyril Connolly*	0712666354	£12.50
Andrew Lownie, *John Buchan*	0712697357	£12.50
Paul O'Keeffe, *Some Sort of Genius*	0712673393	£15.00
Jay Parini, *Robert Frost*	0712664874	£12.50
D.J. Taylor, *Thackeray*	0712662464	£12.50

FREE POST AND PACKING
Overseas customers allow £2 per paperback

PHONE: 01624 677237

POST: Random House Books
C/o Bookpost, PO Box 29, Douglas
Isle of Man, IM99 1BQ

FAX: 01624 670923

EMAIL: bookshop@enterprise.net

Cheques and credit cards accepted

Prices and availability subject to change without notice.
Allow 28 days for delivery

www.randomhouse.co.uk/pimlico